E DUE

America's Top-Rated Cities: a Statistical Handbook

Volume II
Western Region

1998
6th Edition

Rhoda Garoogian, *Managing Editor*
Andrew Garoogian, *Research Editor*
Patrice Walsh Weingart, *Assistant Editor*

Universal Reference Publications

America's Top-Rated Cities: A Statistical Handbook 1998
ISBN 1-881220-38-7 (4 volume set)
ISBN 1-881220-40-0 (Vol. 1 - South)
ISBN 1-881220-41-9 (Vol. 2 - West)
ISBN 1-881220-42-7 (Vol. 3 - Central)
ISBN 1-881220-43-5 (Vol. 4 - East)

Printed and bound in the United States of America.

Preface

This revised and expanded 1998 edition of *America's Top-Rated Cities* is intended to provide the user with a current and concise statistical profile of 76 "top" U.S. cities with populations over 100,000, based on latest census data and/or current estimates. These cities, selected on the basis of their rankings in various surveys (*Money, Fortune, Entrepreneur, Home Office Computing, Site Selection* and others) were found to be the "best" for business and/or living, during 1997.

There are now four regional guides in the series: Southern, Western, Central and Eastern. Designed with ease of use in mind, each handbook is arranged alphabetically by city and divided into two sections: the business environment and the living environment. Rankings and evaluative comments follow a brief overview. Information is then presented under such topics as cost of living, finances, taxes, population, employment and earnings, commercial real estate, education, major employers, media, crime, climate and more. Where appropriate, comparisons with Metropolitan Statistical Areas (MSA) and U.S. figures are included.

There is also a section listing Chambers of Commerce, economic development groups, and State Departments of Labor/Employment Security, that the reader may wish to contact for further information.

In addition to material provided by public/private agencies/organizations, numerous library sources were also consulted. Also utilized were various web sites on the Internet. Tables and charts are properly cited with the appropriate reference to the source of the data. Those tables which are based on the 1990 Census of Population & Housing: Summary Tape File 3C contain sample data to represent the total population.

Although every effort has been made to gather the most current and most accurate information, discrepancies may occur due to the changing nature in the way private and governmental agencies compile and interpret statistical data.

Information in previous editions should not be compared with data in this edition since some historical and forecast data have been revised.

The *America's Top-Rated Cities* series has been compiled for individuals considering relocating, business persons, general and market researchers, real estate consultants, human resource personnel, urban planners as well as students and others who use public, school, academic and special libraries.

The editors wish to thank all of those individuals who responded to our requests for information. Especially helpful were the many Chambers of Commerce, economic development organizations, labor market information bureaus and city school districts. Their assistance is greatly appreciated.

The mission of Universal Reference Publications is to develop a series of comprehensive but reasonably priced statistical reference handbooks about America's "best" cities. Towards that end we have also published *America's Top-Rated Smaller Cities, Health & Environment in America's Top-Rated Cities* and *Crime in America's Top-Rated Cities*.

We welcome your comments and suggestions for improving the coverage and presentation of data in future editions of these handbooks.

The Editors

Table of Contents

Colorado Springs, Colorado

Denver, Colorado

Eugene, Oregon

Las Vegas, Nevada

Los Angeles, California

Oakland, California

Phoenix, Arizona

Portland, Oregon

Pueblo, Colorado

Riverside, California

Salem, Oregon

Salt Lake City, Utah

San Diego, California

San Francisco, California

San Jose, California

Santa Rosa, California

Seattle, Washington

Tacoma, Washington

Tucson, Arizona

Comparative Statistics

Colorado Springs, Colorado

Background

At an elevation of nearly 6,200 feet above sea level, Colorado Springs is located in relatively flat semi-arid country on the eastern slopes of the Rocky Mountains.

It was here that General William Jackson Palmer, a Civil War hero, envisioned a fine resort community, where clear, crisp mountain air, clean water, generous parks and wide streets would offer a healthful haven to many. He founded Colorado Springs and the Denver & Rio Grande Railroad, a narrow gauge rail line, in 1871.

Growth of the area followed the Cripple Creek gold strikes in the 1890's and the promotion of the tourist-health-resort trade. The city was incorporated in 1872.

In 1917 Colorado Springs consolidated with Colorado City (founded in 1859 as El Dorado City). The establishment of military installations in the area provided the impetus for additional development.

Colorado Springs still maintains its character as a resort city, but it is also important to the high-tech industry and military communities. The surrounding prairie is most important for cattle raising and a considerable amount of grazing land is used for sheep in the summer months.

As a result of its geographic location, Colorado Springs has a mild and dry climate protected from harsh weather by the Rocky Mountains to the west. It experiences relatively sparse precipitation and extremes of weather are comparatively rare and of short duration. Relative humidity is normally low and wind movement moderately high. The Chinook winds cause rapid rises in winter temperatures. Chinook means "snow eater".

General Rankings and Evaluative Comments

- Colorado Springs was ranked #62 out of 300 cities by *Money's* 1997 "Survey of the Best Places to Live." Criteria used: health services, crime, economy, housing, education, transportation, weather, leisure and the arts. The city was ranked #107 in 1996 and #68 in 1995.
  Money, July 1997; Money, September 1996; Money, September 1995

- *Ladies Home Journal* ranked America's 200 largest cities based on the qualities women care about most. Colorado Springs ranked 41 out of 200. Criteria: low crime rate, good public schools, well-paying jobs, quality health and child care, the presence of women in government, proportion of women-owned businesses, size of the wage gap with men, local economy, divorce rates, the ratio of single men to single women, whether there are laws that require at least the same number of public toilets for women as men, and the probability of good hair days. *Ladies Home Journal, November 1997*

- Colorado Springs was ranked #82 out of 219 cities in terms of children's health, safety, and economic well-being. Criteria: total population, percent population change, birth rate, child immunization rate, infant mortality rate, percent low birth weight infants, percent of births to teens, physician-to-population ratio, student-to-teacher ratio, dropout rate, unemployment rate, median family income, percent of children in poverty, violent and property crime rates, number of juvenile arrests for violent crimes as a percent of the total crime index, number of days with pollution standard index (PSI) over 100, pounds toxic releases per 1,000 people and number of superfund sites. *Zero Population Growth, Children's Environmental Index 1997*

- Colorado Springs was among "The 10 Hotbeds of Entrepreneurial Activity" in 1996 with 1.55 start-ups per 100 people. Rank: 6 out of 200 metro areas. *Inc., The State of Small Business 1997*

- According to *Working Mother*, "State lawmakers developed a new funding source for child care by allowing taxpayers to check off a box on state tax forms, thereby designating part of their tax dollars for child care. The new system routes the money to the Quality Child Care Improvement Fund, which will disburse the funds to centers to buy new equipment, set up training programs for caregivers or take other steps to boost the quality of their programs. Colorado also reinstated a law giving middle-income families a tax break for child care—which could save parents hundreds of dollars a year.

  Governor Roy Romer announced a 12-point plan this year to expand and improve child care across the state. Among the more important aspects of the plan: $2 million is earmarked to help renovate child care facilities in rural areas and to increase money for child care subsides.

  Colorado also overhauled its child care licensing laws to make them more effective. State inspectors will now visit centers that have a history of problems more frequently and inspect those that have achieved accreditation less often. A new law requires all centers to post their latest inspection report so parents can see the results. (Colorado is among the 10 best states for child care.)" *Working Mother, July/August 1997*

Business Environment

STATE ECONOMY

State Economic Profile

"Colorado's economy has decelerated steadily over the past year. ....Personal bankruptcy filings are up 18%, one-half the U.S. rate of growth.

Colorado's expansion is not driven by the fortunes of a few dominant industries, as in the cases of Idaho and Nevada. Rather, a broad range of industries throughout the state are making investments and adding workers. The expansion of Colorado's market in terms of population and income has led numerous national retail chains to enter the Colorado market, providing local retailers with stiff competition and leading to casualties. At least seven retail chains have been forced to close their Colorado stores.

Declining affordability in the larger metro areas is causing growth to be pushed out to neighboring smaller metro areas. The nucleus of Colorado's growth is the Denver and Boulder areas. The current expansion of both metro areas represents moderation when compared to the growth of two years ago. Boulder's residential building restrictions and efforts to contain commercial construction are exporting growth to northern Denver and to Greeley, where housing prices are far lower.

Colorado's geographic position in the Rockies between the Plains states and the West Coast makes it a natural gateway through which the emerging western economies will increasingly channel their trade. Colorado has the population and business base in place to maintain steady long-term growth. Colorado is top-ranked for long-term growth." *National Association of Realtors, Economic Profiles: The Fifty States, July 1997*

IMPORTS/EXPORTS

Total Export Sales

Area	1993 ($000)	1994 ($000)	1995 ($000)	1996 ($000)	% Chg. 1993-96	% Chg. 1995-96
MSA[1]	664,289	900,712	954,692	856,994	29.0	-10.2
U.S.	464,858,354	512,415,609	583,030,524	622,827,063	34.0	6.8

Note: (1) Metropolitan Statistical Area - see Appendix A for areas included
Source: U.S. Department of Commerce, International Trade Association, Metropolitan Area Exports: An Export Performance Report on Over 250 U.S. Cities, October 1997

Imports/Exports by Port

Type	Cargo Value			Share of U.S. Total	
	1995 (US$mil.)	1996 (US$mil.)	% Change 1995-1996	1995 (%)	1996 (%)
Imports	0	0	0	0	0
Exports	0	0	0	0	0

Source: Global Trade Information Services, WaterBorne Trade Atlas 1997

CITY FINANCES

City Government Finances

Component	FY92 ($000)	FY92 (per capita $)
Revenue	545,837	1,830.06
Expenditure	589,821	1,977.53
Debt Outstanding	730,034	2,447.63
Cash & Securities	491,808	1,648.91

Source: U.S. Bureau of the Census, City Government Finances: 1991-92

City Government Revenue by Source

Source	FY92 ($000)	FY92 (per capita $)	FY92 (%)
From Federal Government	12,176	40.82	2.2
From State Governments	7,773	26.06	1.4
From Local Governments	7,103	23.81	1.3
Property Taxes	17,949	60.18	3.3
General Sales Taxes	62,186	208.49	11.4
Selective Sales Taxes	3,703	12.42	0.7
Income Taxes	0	0.00	0.0
Current Charges	141,844	475.57	26.0
Utility/Liquor Store	260,137	872.18	47.7
Employee Retirement[1]	0	0.00	0.0
Other	32,966	110.53	6.0

Note: (1) Excludes "city contributions," classified as "nonrevenue," intragovernmental transfers.
Source: U.S. Bureau of the Census, City Government Finances: 1991-92

City Government Expenditures by Function

Function	FY92 ($000)	FY92 (per capita $)	FY92 (%)
Educational Services	0	0.00	0.0
Employee Retirement[1]	0	0.00	0.0
Environment/Housing	37,130	124.49	6.3
Government Administration	10,460	35.07	1.8
Interest on General Debt	9,687	32.48	1.6
Public Safety	52,933	177.47	9.0
Social Services	108,694	364.42	18.4
Transportation	57,267	192.00	9.7
Utility/Liquor Store	284,188	952.81	48.2
Other	29,462	98.78	5.0

Note: (1) Payments to beneficiaries including withdrawal of contributions.
Source: U.S. Bureau of the Census, City Government Finances: 1991-92

Municipal Bond Ratings

Area	Moody's	S & P
Colorado Springs	Aa3	AA-

Note: n/a not available; n/r not rated
Source: Moody's Bond Record, 2/98; Statistical Abstract of the U.S., 1997;
Governing Magazine, 9/97, 3/98

POPULATION

Population Growth

Area	1980	1990	% Chg. 1980-90	July 1996 Estimate	% Chg. 1990-96
City	215,150	281,140	30.7	345,127	22.8
MSA[1]	309,424	397,014	28.3	472,924	19.1
U.S.	226,545,805	248,765,170	9.8	265,179,411	6.6

Note: (1) Metropolitan Statistical Area - see Appendix A for areas included
Source: 1980/1990 Census of Housing and Population, Summary Tape File 3C;
Census Bureau Population Estimates

Population Characteristics

Race	City 1980 Population	%	City 1990 Population	%	% Chg. 1980-90	MSA[1] 1990 Population	%
White	190,007	88.3	242,123	86.1	27.4	342,101	86.2
Black	11,929	5.5	19,610	7.0	64.4	28,257	7.1
Amer Indian/Esk/Aleut	1,244	0.6	2,472	0.9	98.7	3,594	0.9
Asian/Pacific Islander	3,494	1.6	6,631	2.4	89.8	9,673	2.4
Other	8,476	3.9	10,304	3.7	21.6	13,389	3.4
Hispanic Origin[2]	18,392	8.5	25,021	8.9	36.0	33,432	8.4

Note: (1) Metropolitan Statistical Area - see Appendix A for areas included;
(2) people of Hispanic origin can be of any race
Source: 1980/1990 Census of Housing and Population, Summary Tape File 3C

Ancestry

Area	German	Irish	English	Italian	U.S.	French	Polish	Dutch
City	32.6	17.3	18.0	4.7	3.3	4.8	2.5	3.1
MSA[1]	32.9	17.2	17.3	4.6	3.4	4.9	2.6	3.1
U.S.	23.3	15.6	13.1	5.9	5.3	4.2	3.8	2.5

Note: Figures are percentages and include persons that reported multiple ancestry (eg. if a person reported being Irish and Italian, they were included in both columns); (1) Metropolitan Statistical Area - see Appendix A for areas included
Source: 1990 Census of Population and Housing, Summary Tape File 3C

Age

Area	Median Age (Years)	Under 5	Under 18	18-24	25-44	45-64	65+	80+
City	31.0	8.5	26.7	10.9	36.6	16.7	9.2	1.9
MSA[1]	30.2	8.5	27.5	12.0	35.8	16.7	8.0	1.6
U.S.	32.9	7.3	25.6	10.5	32.6	18.7	12.5	2.8

Note: (1) Metropolitan Statistical Area - see Appendix A for areas included
Source: 1990 Census of Population and Housing, Summary Tape File 3C

Male/Female Ratio

Area	Number of males per 100 females (all ages)	Number of males per 100 females (18 years old+)
City	95.8	92.8
MSA[1]	100.5	99.4
U.S.	95.0	91.9

Note: (1) Metropolitan Statistical Area - see Appendix A for areas included
Source: 1990 Census of Population, General Population Characteristics

INCOME

Per Capita/Median/Average Income

Area	Per Capita ($)	Median Household ($)	Average Household ($)
City	14,243	28,928	35,709
MSA[1]	13,664	29,604	35,989
U.S.	14,420	30,056	38,453

Note: all figures are for 1989; (1) Metropolitan Statistical Area - see Appendix A for areas included
Source: 1990 Census of Population and Housing, Summary Tape File 3C

Household Income Distribution by Race

Income ($)	City (%)					U.S. (%)				
	Total	White	Black	Other	Hisp.[1]	Total	White	Black	Other	Hisp.[1]
Less than 5,000	4.6	4.0	8.7	9.1	8.6	6.2	4.8	15.2	8.6	8.8
5,000 - 9,999	7.7	7.4	9.5	11.5	11.6	9.3	8.6	14.2	9.9	11.1
10,000 - 14,999	9.8	9.3	12.5	14.4	13.9	8.8	8.5	11.0	9.8	11.0
15,000 - 24,999	20.6	20.1	26.9	21.9	24.5	17.5	17.3	18.9	18.5	20.5
25,000 - 34,999	17.7	17.5	17.3	20.2	19.2	15.8	16.1	14.2	15.4	16.4
35,000 - 49,999	18.3	19.0	12.8	13.1	12.1	17.9	18.6	13.3	16.1	16.0
50,000 - 74,999	14.0	14.8	9.2	8.0	7.9	15.0	15.8	9.3	13.4	11.1
75,000 - 99,999	4.1	4.5	1.7	0.9	1.0	5.1	5.5	2.6	4.7	3.1
100,000+	3.0	3.3	1.5	1.0	1.1	4.4	4.8	1.3	3.7	1.9

Note: all figures are for 1989; (1) people of Hispanic origin can be of any race
Source: 1990 Census of Population and Housing, Summary Tape File 3C

Effective Buying Income

Area	Per Capita ($)	Median Household ($)	Average Household ($)
City	14,457	29,398	36,235
MSA[1]	14,302	30,928	38,128
U.S.	15,444	33,201	41,849

Note: data as of 1/1/97; (1) Metropolitan Statistical Area - see Appendix A for areas included
Source: Standard Rate & Data Service, Newspaper Advertising Source, 2/98

Effective Household Buying Income Distribution

Area	% of Households Earning						
	$10,000 -$19,999	$20,000 -$34,999	$35,000 -$49,999	$50,000 -$74,999	$75,000 -$99,000	$100,000 -$124,999	$125,000 and up
City	19.8	27.9	18.7	15.5	4.1	1.3	1.3
MSA[1]	18.4	28.0	19.5	16.4	4.7	1.3	1.4
U.S.	16.5	23.4	18.3	18.2	6.4	2.1	2.4

Note: data as of 1/1/97; (1) Metropolitan Statistical Area - see Appendix A for areas included
Source: Standard Rate & Data Service, Newspaper Advertising Source, 2/98

Poverty Rates by Race and Age

Area	Total (%)	By Race (%)				By Age (%)		
		White	Black	Other	Hisp.[2]	Under 5 years old	Under 18 years old	65 years and over
City	10.9	9.1	22.4	21.0	21.0	19.3	15.3	7.8
MSA[1]	10.4	8.9	19.7	19.6	19.6	18.0	14.4	8.1
U.S.	13.1	9.8	29.5	23.1	25.3	20.1	18.3	12.8

Note: figures show the percent of people living below the poverty line in 1989. The average poverty
threshold was $12,674 for a family of four in 1989; (1) Metropolitan Statistical Area - see Appendix A
for areas included; (2) people of Hispanic origin can be of any race
Source: 1990 Census of Population and Housing, Summary Tape File 3C

EMPLOYMENT

Labor Force and Employment

Area	Civilian Labor Force			Workers Employed		
	Dec. '95	Dec. '96	% Chg.	Dec. '95	Dec. '96	% Chg.
City	176,712	187,138	5.9	169,813	181,864	7.1
MSA[1]	237,860	251,905	5.9	228,612	244,836	7.1
U.S.	134,583,000	136,742,000	1.6	127,903,000	130,785,000	2.3

Note: Data is not seasonally adjusted and covers workers 16 years of age and older;
(1) Metropolitan Statistical Area - see Appendix A for areas included
Source: Bureau of Labor Statistics, http://stats.bls.gov

Unemployment Rate

Area	1997											
	Jan.	Feb.	Mar.	Apr.	May	Jun.	Jul.	Aug.	Sep.	Oct.	Nov.	Dec.
City	4.4	3.9	3.8	3.3	3.8	4.5	3.8	3.6	3.5	3.1	3.3	2.8
MSA[1]	4.4	3.9	3.8	3.3	3.8	4.5	3.8	3.6	3.5	3.1	3.3	2.8
U.S.	5.9	5.7	5.5	4.8	4.7	5.2	5.0	4.8	4.7	4.4	4.3	4.4

Note: Data is not seasonally adjusted and covers workers 16 years of age and older; All figures are percentages; (1) Metropolitan Statistical Area - see Appendix A for areas included
Source: Bureau of Labor Statistics, http://stats.bls.gov

Employment by Industry

Sector	MSA[1]		U.S.
	Number of Employees	Percent of Total	Percent of Total
Services	71,000	32.2	29.0
Retail Trade	44,300	20.1	18.5
Government	35,300	16.0	16.1
Manufacturing	27,500	12.5	15.0
Finance/Insurance/Real Estate	11,600	5.3	5.7
Wholesale Trade	6,000	2.7	5.4
Transportation/Public Utilities	12,100	5.5	5.3
Construction/Mining	12,500	5.7	5.0

Note: Figures cover non-farm employment as of 12/97 and are not seasonally adjusted;
(1) Metropolitan Statistical Area - see Appendix A for areas included
Source: Bureau of Labor Statistics, http://stats.bls.gov

Employment by Occupation

Occupation Category	City (%)	MSA[1] (%)	U.S. (%)
White Collar	65.1	63.7	58.1
Executive/Admin./Management	14.1	13.7	12.3
Professional	17.4	16.7	14.1
Technical & Related Support	4.6	4.4	3.7
Sales	12.7	12.7	11.8
Administrative Support/Clerical	16.3	16.2	16.3
Blue Collar	19.2	20.4	26.2
Precision Production/Craft/Repair	9.3	10.0	11.3
Machine Operators/Assem./Insp.	4.6	4.6	6.8
Transportation/Material Movers	2.6	3.0	4.1
Cleaners/Helpers/Laborers	2.7	2.8	3.9
Services	14.8	14.8	13.2
Farming/Forestry/Fishing	0.9	1.1	2.5

Note: figures cover employed persons 16 years old and over;
(1) Metropolitan Statistical Area - see Appendix A for areas included
Source: 1990 Census of Population and Housing, Summary Tape File 3C

Occupational Employment Projections: 1994 - 2005

Occupations Expected to have the Largest Job Growth (ranked by numerical growth)	Fast-Growing Occupations (ranked by percent growth)
1. Janitors/cleaners/maids, ex. priv. hshld.	1. Computer engineers
2. Salespersons, retail	2. Systems analysts
3. Waiters & waitresses	3. Computer scientists
4. General managers & top executives	4. Amusement and recreation attendants
5. Guards	5. Personal and home care aides
6. Marketing & sales, supervisors	6. Guards
7. Truck drivers, heavy & light	7. Human services workers
8. Cashiers	8. Nursery and greenhouse managers
9. Systems analysts	9. Pruners
10. Clerical supervisors	10. Electronic pagination systems workers

Projections cover Colorado.
Source: U.S. Department of Labor, Employment and Training Administration, America's Labor Market Information System (ALMIS)

Average Wages

Occupation	Wage	Occupation	Wage
Professional/Technical/Clerical	$/Week	**Health/Protective Services**	$/Week
Accountants III	-	Corrections Officers	-
Attorneys III	-	Firefighters	-
Budget Analysts III	-	Nurses, Licensed Practical II	-
Buyers/Contracting Specialists II	-	Nurses, Registered II	-
Clerks, Accounting III	420	Nursing Assistants II	-
Clerks, General III	404	Police Officers I	-
Computer Operators II	-	**Hourly Workers**	$/Hour
Computer Programmers II	657	Forklift Operators	-
Drafters II	526	General Maintenance Workers	8.41
Engineering Technicians III	613	Guards I	6.13
Engineering Technicians, Civil III	-	Janitors	6.54
Engineers III	-	Maintenance Electricians	-
Key Entry Operators I	-	Maintenance Electronics Techs II	16.99
Personnel Assistants III	-	Maintenance Machinists	-
Personnel Specialists III	-	Maintenance Mechanics, Machinery	14.28
Secretaries III	513	Material Handling Laborers	8.19
Switchboard Operator-Receptionist	297	Motor Vehicle Mechanics	15.16
Systems Analysts II	939	Shipping/Receiving Clerks	8.20
Systems Analysts Supervisor/Mgr II	-	Tool and Die Makers	-
Tax Collectors II	-	Truckdrivers, Tractor Trailer	-
Word Processors II	473	Warehouse Specialists	-

Note: Wage data includes full-time workers only for 8/96 and cover the Metropolitan Statistical Area (see Appendix A for areas included). Dashes indicate that data was not available.
Source: Bureau of Labor Statistics, Occupational Compensation Survey, 12/96

TAXES

Major State and Local Tax Rates

State Corp. Income (%)	State Personal Income (%)	Residential Property (effective rate per $100)	Sales & Use		State Gasoline (cents/ gallon)	State Cigarette (cents/ 20-pack)
			State (%)	Local (%)		
5.0	5.0	n/a	3.0	3.0	22	20

Note: Personal/corporate income tax rates as of 1/97. Sales, gasoline and cigarette tax rates as of 1/98.
Source: Federation of Tax Administrators, www.taxadmin.org; Washington D.C. Department of Finance and Revenue, Tax Rates and Tax Burdens in the District of Columbia: A Nationwide Comparison, June 1997; Chamber of Commerce

Total Taxes Per Capita and as a Percent of Income

Area	Per Capita Income ($)	Per Capita Taxes ($)			Taxes as Pct. of Income (%)		
		Total	Federal	State/Local	Total	Federal	State/Local
Colorado	27,624	9,705	6,521	3,184	35.1	23.6	11.5
U.S.	26,187	9,205	6,127	3,078	35.2	23.4	11.8

Note: Figures are for 1997
Source: Tax Foundation, Web Site, www.taxfoundation.org

COMMERCIAL REAL ESTATE

Office Market

Class/Location	Total Space (sq. ft.)	Vacant Space (sq. ft.)	Vac. Rate (%)	Under Constr. (sq. ft.)	Net Absorp. (sq. ft.)	Rental Rates ($/sq.ft./yr.)
Class A						
CBD	1,174,150	74,469	6.3	92,000	5,517	10.00-14.00
Outside CBD	2,416,634	175,496	7.3	235,250	138,693	10.00-14.50
Class B						
CBD	1,816,985	105,412	5.8	n/a	108,889	3.50-12.00
Outside CBD	10,760,628	1,043,209	9.7	333,000	384,787	3.00-14.50

Note: Data as of 10/97 and covers Colorado Springs; CBD = Central Business District; n/a not available;
Source: Society of Industrial and Office Realtors, 1998 Comparative Statistics of Industrial and Office Real Estate Markets

"Approximately 230,000 sq. ft. of speculative space is currently under construction in the Colorado Springs marketplace. In addition to this speculative space, approximately 200,000 sq. ft. of user-driven construction is in process, the largest being California Casualty's 120,000 sq. ft. building. Several mid-sized owner-user buildings are also going up, including ITT's regional headquarters (38,000 sq. ft.) and Spacemark (25,000 sq. ft.). Job growth still exceeds the amount of new product being brought to market. Continued strong demand and limited new development are a powerful combination that will keep rents and investor returns rising in 1998." *Society of Industrial and Office Realtors, 1998 Comparative Statistics of Industrial and Office Real Estate Markets*

Industrial Market

Location	Total Space (sq. ft.)	Vacant Space (sq. ft.)	Vac. Rate (%)	Under Constr. (sq. ft.)	Net Absorp. (sq. ft.)	Lease ($/sq.ft./yr.)
Central City	595,458	16,611	2.8	0	-9,350	3.59
Suburban	27,070,247	1,530,687	5.7	1,106,759	653,579	6.95

Note: Data as of 10/97 and covers Colorado Springs; n/a not available
Source: Society of Industrial and Office Realtors, 1998 Comparative Statistics of Industrial and Office Real Estate Markets

"New projects are underway, including major construction for Quantum Corporation, which recently broke ground on the first phase of its 400,000 sq. ft. campus in Fairlane Technology Park. In addition, two speculative projects are in process: the Garden Gateway Plaza (58,000 sq. ft.) and Centennial Commons, (60,000 sq. ft.) both located in the Garden of the Gods area. The coming year will bring predominantly user-driven development, with only limited speculative construction. This controlled activity will keep occupancies well over the 90 percent mark. Rents will remain at the highest levels in more than a decade." *Society of Industrial and Office Realtors, 1998 Comparative Statistics of Industrial and Office Real Estate Markets*

COMMERCIAL UTILITIES

Typical Monthly Electric Bills

Area	Commercial Service ($/month)		Industrial Service ($/month)	
	12 kW demand 1,500 kWh	100 kW demand 30,000 kWh	1,000 kW demand 400,000 kWh	20,000 kW demand 10,000,000 kWh
City	n/a	n/a	n/a	n/a
U.S.	162	2,360	25,590	545,677

Note: Based on rates in effect July 1, 1997; n/a not available
Source: Edison Electric Institute, Typical Residential, Commercial and Industrial Bills, Summer 1997

TRANSPORTATION

Transportation Statistics

Avg. travel time to work (min.)	18.2
Interstate highways	I-25
Bus lines	
In-city	Colorado Springs TS
Inter-city	1
Passenger air service	
Airport	Colorado Springs Airport
Airlines	10
Aircraft departures	18,848 (1995)
Enplaned passengers	1,403,368 (1995)
Rail service	Amtrak Thruway Motorcoach Connections
Motor freight carriers	25
Major waterways/ports	None

Source: OAG, Business Travel Planner, Summer 1997; Editor & Publisher Market Guide, 1998; FAA Airport Activity Statistics, 1996; Amtrak National Time Table, Northeast Timetable, Fall/Winter 1997-98; 1990 Census of Population and Housing, STF 3C; Chamber of Commerce/Economic Development 1997; Jane's Urban Transport Systems 1997-98; Transit Fact Book 1997

Means of Transportation to Work

Area	Car/Truck/Van		Public Transportation			Bicycle	Walked	Other Means	Worked at Home
	Drove Alone	Car-pooled	Bus	Subway	Railroad				
City	77.9	12.9	1.2	0.0	0.0	0.5	3.2	0.9	3.4
MSA[1]	74.6	13.3	1.0	0.0	0.0	0.4	6.2	1.0	3.5
U.S.	73.2	13.4	3.0	1.5	0.5	0.4	3.9	1.2	3.0

Note: figures shown are percentages and only include workers 16 years old and over;
(1) Metropolitan Statistical Area - see Appendix A for areas included
Source: 1990 Census of Population and Housing, Summary Tape File 3C

BUSINESSES

Major Business Headquarters

Company Name	1997 Rankings	
	Fortune 500	Forbes 500
Phil Long Dealerships	-	422

Note: Companies listed are located in the city; Dashes indicate no ranking
Fortune 500: companies that produce a 10-K are ranked 1 - 500 based on 1996 revenue
Forbes 500: private companies are ranked 1 - 500 based on 1996 revenue
Source: Forbes 12/1/97; Fortune 4/28/97

Minority Business Opportunity

One of the 500 largest Hispanic-owned companies in the U.S. are located in Colorado Springs. *Hispanic Business, June 1997*

Colorado Springs is home to one company which is on the Hispanic Business Fastest-Growing 100 list (greatest sales growth from 1992 to 1996): System Technology Associates Inc. (engineering & software devel.) *Hispanic Business, July/August 1997*

Small Business Opportunity

According to *Forbes*, Colorado Springs is home to one of America's 200 best small companies: Analytical Surveys. Criteria: companies must be publicly traded, U.S.-based corporations with latest 12-month sales of between $5 and $350 million. Earnings must be at least $1 million for the 12-month period. Limited partnerships, REITs and closed-end mutual funds were not considered. Banks, S&Ls and electric utilities were not included. *Forbes, November 3, 1997*

HOTELS & MOTELS

Hotels/Motels

Area	Hotels/ Motels	Rooms	Luxury-Level Hotels/Motels		Average Minimum Rates ($)		
			♦♦♦♦	♦♦♦♦♦	♦♦	♦♦♦	♦♦♦♦
City	30	3,641	0	1	60	98	n/a
Airport	2	188	0	0	n/a	n/a	n/a
Suburbs	9	1,788	0	0	n/a	n/a	n/a
Total	41	5,617	0	1	n/a	n/a	n/a

Note: n/a not available; Classifications range from one diamond (budget properties with basic amenities) to five diamond (luxury properties with the finest service, rooms and facilities). Source: OAG, Business Travel Planner, Summer 1997

CONVENTION CENTERS

Major Convention Centers

Center Name	Meeting Rooms	Exhibit Space (sf)
Antlers Doubletree Hotel	19	14,607
Best Western Palmer House	5	2,000
The Broadmoor Hotel	36	53,000
Cheyenne Mountain Conference Resort	30	31,828
Colorado Springs City Auditorium	3	10,500
Pikes Peak Center	3	13,500

Source: Trade Shows Worldwide 1997

Living Environment

COST OF LIVING

Cost of Living Index

Composite Index	Housing	Utilities	Groceries	Health Care	Trans-portation	Misc. Goods/ Services
102.0	115.8	70.5	98.8	127.4	105.2	94.1

Note: U.S. = 100
Source: ACCRA, Cost of Living Index, 3rd Quarter 1997

HOUSING

Median Home Prices and Housing Affordability

Area	Median Price[2] 3rd Qtr. 1997 ($)	HOI[3] 3rd Qtr. 1997	Afford-ability Rank[4]
MSA[1]	130,000	58.8	154
U.S.	127,000	63.7	--

Note: (1) Metropolitan Statistical Area - see Appendix A for areas included; (2) U.S. figures calculated from the sales of 625,000 new and existing homes in 195 markets; (3) Housing Opportunity Index - percent of homes sold that were within the reach of the median income household at the prevailing mortgage interest rate; (4) Rank is from 1-195 with 1 being most affordable
Source: National Association of Home Builders, Housing Opportunity Index, 3rd Quarter 1997

Average New Home Price

Area	Price ($)
City	154,231
U.S.	135,710

Note: Figures are based on a new home with 1,800 sq. ft. of living area on an 8,000 sq. ft. lot.
Source: ACCRA, Cost of Living Index, 3rd Quarter 1997

Average Apartment Rent

Area	Rent ($/mth)
City	707
U.S.	569

Note: Figures are based on an unfurnished two bedroom, 1-1/2 or 2 bath apartment, approximately 950 sq. ft. in size, excluding all utilities except water
Source: ACCRA, Cost of Living Index, 3rd Quarter 1997

RESIDENTIAL UTILITIES

Average Residential Utility Costs

Area	All Electric ($/mth)	Part Electric ($/mth)	Other Energy ($/mth)	Phone ($/mth)
City	--	35.29	31.49	20.39
U.S.	109.40	55.25	43.64	19.48

Source: ACCRA, Cost of Living Index, 3rd Quarter 1997

HEALTH CARE

Average Health Care Costs

Area	Hospital ($/day)	Doctor ($/visit)	Dentist ($/visit)
City	542.50	65.11	75.40
U.S.	392.91	48.76	60.84

Note: Hospital - based on a semi-private room. Doctor - based on a general practitioner's routine exam of an established patient. Dentist - based on adult teeth cleaning and periodic oral exam.
Source: ACCRA, Cost of Living Index, 3rd Quarter 1997

Distribution of Office-Based Physicians

| Area | Family/Gen. Practitioners | Specialists | | |
		Medical	Surgical	Other
MSA[1]	79	167	183	205

Note: Data as of 12/31/96; (1) Metropolitan Statistical Area - see Appendix A for areas included
Source: American Medical Assn., Physician Characteristics & Distribution in the U.S., 1997-1998

Hospitals

Colorado Springs has 3 general medical and surgical hospitals, 2 psychiatric. *AHA Guide to the Healthcare Field 1997-98*

EDUCATION

Public School District Statistics

District Name	Num. Sch.	Enroll.	Classroom Teachers[1]	Pupils per Teacher	Minority Pupils (%)	Current Exp.[2] ($/pupil)
Academy 20	21	14,049	768	18.3	n/a	n/a
Cheyenne Mountain 12	7	3,301	163	20.3	n/a	n/a
Colorado Springs 11	59	32,960	1,688	19.5	26.5	4,525
Hanover 28	2	149	10	14.9	n/a	n/a
Harrison 2	19	10,686	643	16.6	n/a	n/a
Widefield 3	15	8,353	442	18.9	n/a	n/a

Note: Data covers the 1995-1996 school year unless otherwise noted; (1) Excludes teachers reported as working in school district offices rather than in schools; (2) Based on 1993-94 enrollment collected by the Census Bureau, not the enrollment figure shown in column 3; SD = School District; ISD = Independent School District; n/a not available
Source: National Center for Education Statistics, Common Core of Data Survey; Bureau of the Census

Educational Quality

School District	Education Quotient[1]	Graduate Outcome[2]	Community Index[3]	Resource Index[4]
Academy-Colorado Springs	129.0	147.0	124.0	115.0

Note: Nearly 1,000 secondary school districts were rated in terms of educational quality. The scores range from a low of 50 to a high of 150; (1) Average of the Graduate Outcome, Community and Resource indexes; (2) Based on graduation rates and college board scores (SAT/ACT); (3) Based on the surrounding community's average level of education and the area's average income level; (4) Based on teacher salaries, per-pupil expenditures and student-teacher ratios.
Source: Expansion Management, Ratings Issue 1997

Educational Attainment by Race

| Area | High School Graduate (%) | | | | | Bachelor's Degree (%) | | | | |
	Total	White	Black	Other	Hisp.[2]	Total	White	Black	Other	Hisp.[2]
City	87.8	89.1	86.6	70.7	69.2	27.5	29.3	16.3	13.3	12.1
MSA[1]	88.3	89.5	88.1	71.7	71.3	25.8	27.4	15.7	12.8	11.8
U.S.	75.2	77.9	63.1	60.4	49.8	20.3	21.5	11.4	19.4	9.2

Note: figures shown cover persons 25 years old and over; (1) Metropolitan Statistical Area - see Appendix A for areas included; (2) people of Hispanic origin can be of any race
Source: 1990 Census of Population and Housing, Summary Tape File 3C

School Enrollment by Type

| Area | Preprimary | | | | Elementary/High School | | | |
| | Public | | Private | | Public | | Private | |
	Enrollment	%	Enrollment	%	Enrollment	%	Enrollment	%
City	3,038	55.2	2,466	44.8	43,594	93.6	2,979	6.4
MSA[1]	4,421	57.8	3,225	42.2	64,283	94.1	4,008	5.9
U.S.	2,679,029	59.5	1,824,256	40.5	38,379,689	90.2	4,187,099	9.8

Note: figures shown cover persons 3 years old and over; (1) Metropolitan Statistical Area - see Appendix A for areas included
Source: 1990 Census of Population and Housing, Summary Tape File 3C

School Enrollment by Race

Area	Preprimary (%)				Elementary/High School (%)			
	White	Black	Other	Hisp.[1]	White	Black	Other	Hisp.[1]
City	85.3	8.2	6.5	8.8	82.8	8.9	8.2	11.0
MSA[2]	85.7	7.4	6.8	8.8	83.2	8.8	7.9	10.5
U.S.	80.4	12.5	7.1	7.8	74.1	15.6	10.3	12.5

Note: figures shown cover persons 3 years old and over; (1) people of Hispanic origin can be of any race; (2) Metropolitan Statistical Area - see Appendix A for areas included
Source: 1990 Census of Population and Housing, Summary Tape File 3C

SAT/ACT Scores

Area/District	1997 SAT				1997 ACT	
	Percent of Graduates Tested (%)	Average Math Score	Average Verbal Score	Average Combined Score	Percent of Graduates Tested (%)	Average Composite Score
Colorado Springs SD	33	538	550	1,088	69	21.5
State	30	539	536	1,075	62	21.5
U.S.	42	511	505	1,016	36	21.0

Note: Math and verbal SAT scores are out of a possible 800; ACT scores are out of a possible 36
Caution: Comparing or ranking states/cities on the basis of SAT/ACT scores alone is invalid and strongly discouraged by the The College Board and The American College Testing Program as students who take the tests are self-selected and do not represent the entire student population.
Source: Colorado Springs School District #11, Division of Planning, Research & Evaluation, 1997; American College Testing Program, 1997; College Board, 1997

Classroom Teacher Salaries in Public Schools

District	B.A. Degree		M.A. Degree		Ph.D. Degree	
	Min. ($)	Max. ($)	Min. ($)	Max. ($)	Min. ($)	Max. ($)
Colorado Springs	23,611	32,087	25,730	40,563	32,087	51,158
Average[1]	26,120	39,270	28,175	44,667	31,643	49,825

Note: Salaries are for 1996-1997; (1) Based on all school districts covered; n/a not available
Source: American Federation of Teachers (unpublished data)

Higher Education

Two-Year Colleges		Four-Year Colleges		Medical Schools	Law Schools	Voc/ Tech
Public	Private	Public	Private			
1	2	2	4	0	0	16

Source: College Blue Book, Occupational Education 1997; Medical School Admission Requirements, 1998-99; Peterson's Guide to Two-Year Colleges, 1997; Peterson's Guide to Four-Year Colleges, 1997; Barron's Guide to Law Schools 1997

MAJOR EMPLOYERS

Major Employers

Broadmoor Hotel
Colorado Interstate Gas
Current Inc. (mail order)
Space Mark (management consulting)
Memorial Hospital
Walter Drake & Son (mail order)
Western Pacific Airlines
Rocky Mountain Service Systems (building cleaning)

C. David Cook Publishing
Colorado Springs Utilities
Goodwill Industries of Colorado Springs
Kaman Sciences Corp. (engineering)
Snyder Services (help supply services)
Western Forge Corp. (metal products)
C&D Enterprises (guard services)

Note: companies listed are located in the city
Source: Dun's Business Rankings 1997; Ward's Business Directory, 1997

PUBLIC SAFETY

Crime Rate

Area	All Crimes	Violent Crimes				Property Crimes		
		Murder	Forcible Rape	Robbery	Aggrav. Assault	Burglary	Larceny -Theft	Motor Vehicle Theft
City	6,199.9	3.6	71.9	136.8	269.5	998.1	4,304.3	415.7
Suburbs[1]	2,589.6	5.6	18.3	19.0	205.4	625.4	1,544.2	171.7
MSA[2]	5,115.3	4.2	55.8	101.4	250.2	886.2	3,475.1	342.4
U.S.	5,078.9	7.4	36.1	202.4	388.2	943.0	2,975.9	525.9

Note: Crime rate is the number of crimes per 100,000 pop.; (1) defined as all areas within the MSA but located outside the central city; (2) Metropolitan Statistical Area - see Appendix A for areas incl.
Source: FBI Uniform Crime Reports 1996

RECREATION

Culture and Recreation

Museums	Symphony Orchestras	Opera Companies	Dance Companies	Professional Theatres	Zoos	Pro Sports Teams
10	2	1	2	2	1	0

Source: International Directory of the Performing Arts, 1996; Official Museum Directory, 1998; Chamber of Commerce/Economic Development 1997

Library System

The Pikes Peak Library District has 13 branches, holdings of 1,314,363 volumes and a budget of $11,832,870 (1995). *American Library Directory, 1997-1998*

MEDIA

Newspapers

Name	Type	Freq.	Distribution	Circulation
Black Forest News	n/a	1x/wk	Local	1,000
Colorado Springs Independent	Alternative	1x/wk	Local	27,500
Gazette	General	7x/wk	Local	105,955
Hispania	Hispanic	1x/wk	Local	15,000
Mountaineer	n/a	1x/wk	Local	15,000

Note: Includes newspapers with circulations of 1,000 or more located in the city; n/a not available
Source: Burrelle's Media Directory, 1998 Edition

AM Radio Stations

Call Letters	Freq. (kHz)	Target Audience	Station Format	Music Format
KTWK	740	n/a	M	Oldies
KGLN	980	General	M	Oldies
KCBR	1040	Religious	M/T	Christian
KRDO	1240	General	S/T	n/a
KVOR	1300	General	N/S/T	n/a
KKCS	1460	General	N/T	n/a
KCMN	1530	General	M/N/S	Adult Standards
KWYD	1580	General	M/T	Christian

Note: Stations included broadcast in the Colorado Springs metro area; n/a not available
Station Format: E = Educational; M = Music; N = News; S = Sports; T = Talk
Source: Burrelle's Media Directory, 1998 Edition

FM Radio Stations

Call Letters	Freq. (mHz)	Target Audience	Station Format	Music Format
KCME	88.7	General	E/M	Classical/Jazz
KEPC	89.7	General	M/N/S	Alternative
KTLF	90.5	Religious	M/N/S	Christian/MOR
KRCC	91.5	General	M/N	n/a
KSPZ	92.9	n/a	M	Oldies
KILO	93.9	General	M/N/S	AOR
KRDO	95.1	General	M/N	Adult Contemporary
KKFM	98.1	General	M	Classic Rock
KKMG	98.9	n/a	M	Contemporary Top 40
KVUU	99.9	General	M/N/S	Adult Contemporary
KKCS	101.9	General	M/N/S	Country
KBIQ	102.7	General	M	Adult Contemporary/Christian
KSKX	105.5	General	M/N/S	Country
KKLI	106.3	General	M	Adult Contemporary

Note: Stations included broadcast in the Colorado Springs metro area; n/a not available
Station Format: E = Educational; M = Music; N = News; S = Sports; T = Talk
Music Format: AOR = Album Oriented Rock; MOR = Middle-of-the-Road
Source: Burrelle's Media Directory, 1998 Edition

Television Stations

Name	Ch.	Affiliation	Type	Owner
KOAA	5	NBC	Commercial	Evening Post Publishing Company
KKTV	11	CBS	Commercial	Ackerley Media
KRDO	13	ABC	Commercial	Harry W. Hoth
KXRM	21	Fox	Commercial	KXRM Partnership

Note: Stations included broadcast in the Colorado Springs metro area
Source: Burrelle's Media Directory, 1998 Edition

CLIMATE

Average and Extreme Temperatures

Temperature	Jan	Feb	Mar	Apr	May	Jun	Jul	Aug	Sep	Oct	Nov	Dec	Ann
Extreme High (°F)	71	72	78	87	93	99	98	97	94	86	78	75	99
Average High (°F)	41	44	51	61	68	79	85	81	75	63	49	41	62
Average Temp. (°F)	29	32	39	48	55	66	71	69	61	50	37	30	49
Average Low (°F)	17	20	26	34	42	52	57	55	48	36	24	17	36
Extreme Low (°F)	-20	-19	-3	8	22	36	48	39	22	7	-5	-24	-24

Note: Figures cover the years 1948-1993
Source: National Climatic Data Center, International Station Meteorological Climate Summary, 3/95

Average Precipitation/Snowfall/Humidity

Precip./Humidity	Jan	Feb	Mar	Apr	May	Jun	Jul	Aug	Sep	Oct	Nov	Dec	Ann
Avg. Precip. (in.)	0.3	0.4	1.3	1.3	2.6	2.1	2.6	3.4	1.0	0.9	0.6	0.5	17.0
Avg. Snowfall (in.)	6	6	10	5	2	0	0	0	Tr	3	7	8	48
Avg. Rel. Hum. 5am (%)	57	60	62	62	69	67	66	71	66	59	60	59	63
Avg. Rel. Hum. 5pm (%)	48	43	39	34	39	36	36	43	36	36	45	52	41

Note: Figures cover the years 1948-1993; Tr = Trace amounts (<0.05 in. of rain; <0.5 in. of snow)
Source: National Climatic Data Center, International Station Meteorological Climate Summary, 3/95

Weather Conditions

Temperature			Daytime Sky			Precipitation		
10°F & below	32°F & below	90°F & above	Clear	Partly cloudy	Cloudy	0.01 inch or more precip.	0.1 inch or more snow/ice	Thunder-storms
21	161	18	108	157	100	98	33	49

Note: Figures are average number of days per year and covers the years 1948-1993
Source: National Climatic Data Center, International Station Meteorological Climate Summary, 3/95

AIR & WATER QUALITY

Maximum Pollutant Concentrations

	Particulate Matter (ug/m³)	Carbon Monoxide (ppm)	Sulfur Dioxide (ppm)	Nitrogen Dioxide (ppm)	Ozone (ppm)	Lead (ug/m³)
MSA¹ Level	76	5	n/a	n/a	0.08	0.01
NAAQS²	150	9	0.140	0.053	0.12	1.50
Met NAAQS?	Yes	Yes	n/a	n/a	Yes	Yes

Note: (1) Metropolitan Statistical Area - see Appendix A for areas included; (2) National Ambient Air Quality Standards; ppm = parts per million; ug/m³ = micrograms per cubic meter; n/a not available
Source: EPA, National Air Quality and Emissions Trends Report, 1996

Pollutant Standards Index

Data not available. *EPA, National Air Quality and Emissions Trends Report, 1996*

Drinking Water

Water System Name	Pop. Served	Primary Water Source Type	Number of Violations in Fiscal Year 1997	Type of Violation/ Contaminants
Colorado Springs Utility	320,000	Surface	1	Failure to filter

Note: Data as of January 16, 1998
Source: EPA, Office of Ground Water and Drinking Water, Safe Drinking Water Information System

Colorado Springs tap water is supplied from watersheds on Pikes Peak and Continental Divide. It's pure, filtered and fluoridated.
Editor & Publisher Market Guide, 1998

Denver, Colorado

Background

From almost anywhere in Denver, one can command a breath-taking view of the 14,000 ft. Rocky Mountains. However, the early settlers of Denver were not attracted to the city because of its vistas. They were there in search of gold.

In 1858, rumors were abound that gold had been discovered in Cherry Creek, one of the waterways on which Denver stands. When those prospectors left their pans, and headed back East. Later it was discovered there really was gold; and silver as well. By 1867, Denver had been established, built on the wealth of silver and gold.

Today, Denver bears little resemblance to the dusty frontier village of yesteryear, with its sparkling dramatic skyline of glass and steel towers. With an excellent location, the "Mile High City" has become a manufacturing distribution and transportation center that serves not only the western regions of the United States, but the entire nation. Denver is also home to many companies that are engaged in alternative fuel research and development.

Sitting compatibly with an economic renaissance is a lively cultural, recreational, and educational scene. Throughout the year, one may attend a concert at the Boettcher Concert Hall of the Denver Arts Center; take a drive through the Denver Mountain Park Circle Drive; enjoy the environment that a college campus, such as the University of Colorado, adds to a city; see the Colorado Rockies, one of baseball's new major league teams; or take advantage of skiing and summer mountain activities—just 90 minutes away.

Denver enjoys the invigorating climate that prevails over much of the central Rocky Mountain region, without the extremely cold mornings of the higher elevations during winter, or the hot afternoons of summer at lower altitudes. Extremes of cold or heat are generally of short duration. Low relative humidity, light precipitation and abundant sunshine characterize Denver's weather. Spring is the cloudiest, wettest and windiest season, while autumn is the most pleasant.

General Rankings and Evaluative Comments

- Denver was ranked #46 out of 300 cities by *Money's* 1997 "Survey of the Best Places to Live." Criteria used: health services, crime, economy, housing, education, transportation, weather, leisure and the arts. The city was ranked #85 in 1996 and #37 in 1995. *Money, July 1997; Money, September 1996; Money, September 1995*

- Denver appeared on *Fortune's* list of "North America's Most Improved Cities" Rank: 2 out of 10. The selected cities satisfied basic business-location needs and also demonstrated improvement over a five- to ten-year period in a number of business and quality-of-life measures.

  In response to the days when the energy companies were leaving and taking large numbers of residents with them, Denver has taken steps to reverse this trend. "The first order of business...was to make Denver...an attractive place to stay. Getting a new convention center built in 1990 on time and under budget went a long way toward boosting the city's morale....

  Denver achieved further stability by capitalizing on low costs to attract...back-office and support services....The city is now home to many large financial service companies....Denver's economic rebirth has created other issues for the city. In 1991 immigration surpassed emigration, and the growth has been non-stop ever since. Housing developments are creeping into the foothills of the Rocky Mountains. Modern office parks tower over what was once scrubland....

  This could be a recipe for disastrous urban sprawl, but the city has been vigilant in inventing ways to keep people coming to the city center. Most spectacular, perhaps, has been the conversion of the Lower Downtown area....This once-decaying collection of vacant warehouses is now bustling with packed microbreweries, sleek restaurants, and hip, exposed-brick lofts.

  Perhaps the crowning achievement for the city was the decision to host the 1997 Summit of the Eight world leaders' conference..." It brought numerous journalists who could write about Denver's revival. *Fortune, 11/24/97*

- *Ladies Home Journal* ranked America's 200 largest cities based on the qualities women care about most. Denver ranked 59 out of 200. Criteria: low crime rate, good public schools, well-paying jobs, quality health and child care, the presence of women in government, proportion of women-owned businesses, size of the wage gap with men, local economy, divorce rates, the ratio of single men to single women, whether there are laws that require at least the same number of public toilets for women as men, and the probability of good hair days. *Ladies Home Journal, November 1997*

- Denver is among the 10 healthiest cities for women. Rank: 8 out of 10. Criteria: 1) number of doctors, psychologists and dietitians; 2) quality of hospital gynecology departments; 3) number of working mothers; 4) rate of violent crimes; 5) cleanliness of air and water; 6) number of fitness opportunities; 7) quality of public schools. *American Health, January/February 1997*

- Denver was ranked #146 out of 219 cities in terms of children's health, safety, and economic well-being. Criteria: total population, percent population change, birth rate, child immunization rate, infant mortality rate, percent low birth weight infants, percent of births to teens, physician-to-population ratio, student-to-teacher ratio, dropout rate, unemployment rate, median family income, percent of children in poverty, violent and property crime rates, number of juvenile arrests for violent crimes as a percent of the total crime index, number of days with pollution standard index (PSI) over 100, pounds toxic releases per 1,000 people and number of superfund sites. *Zero Population Growth, Children's Environmental Index 1997*

- Denver appeared on *New Mobility's* list of "10 Disability Friendly Cities". Rank: 1 out of 10. Criteria: affordable and accessible housing, transportation, quality medical care, personal assistance services and strong advocacy.

[Denver] "...offers a multitude of services and conveniences, a fully accessible mainline metro transportation system and exceptionally strong advocacy....Personal assistance programs are available, medical facilities are plentiful, and Craig Hospital has terrific support services for people with head or spinal cord injuries.

Look to Denver also for a wide range of recreational and cultural activities: peerless adaptive sports, both integrated and disability-specific arts programs, active ballet and theater, a symphony orchestra and two opera companies. Coors Stadium—is one of the most accessible in the country and, like the Denver Center for the Performing Arts, features universal seating...." *New Mobility, December 1997*

- Denver is among the 20 most livable cities for gay men and lesbians. The list was divided between 10 cities you might expect and 10 surprises. Denver was on the cities you wouldn't expect list. Rank: 9 out of 10. Criteria: legal protection from antigay discrimination, an annual gay pride celebration, a community center, gay bookstores and publications, and an array of organizations, religious groups, and health care facilities that cater to the needs of the local gay community. *The Advocate, June 1997*

- *Yahoo! Internet Life* selected "America's 100 Most Wired Cities & Towns". 50 cities were large and 50 cities were small. Denver ranked 11 out of 50 large cities. Criteria: Internet users per capita, number of networked computers, number of registered domain names, Internet backbone traffic, and the per-capita number of Web sites devoted to each city. *Yahoo! Internet Life, March 1998*

- Denver was among "The 10 Hotbeds of Entrepreneurial Activity" in 1996 with 1.58 start-ups per 100 people. Rank: 5 out of 200 metro areas. *Inc., The State of Small Business 1997*

- According to *Working Mother,* "State lawmakers developed a new funding source for child care by allowing taxpayers to check off a box on state tax forms, thereby designating part of their tax dollars for child care. The new system routes the money to the Quality Child Care Improvement Fund, which will disburse the funds to centers to buy new equipment, set up training programs for caregivers or take other steps to boost the quality of their programs. Colorado also reinstated a law giving middle-income families a tax break for child care—which could save parents hundreds of dollars a year.

Governor Roy Romer announced a 12-point plan this year to expand and improve child care across the state. Among the more important aspects of the plan: $2 million is earmarked to help renovate child care facilities in rural areas and to increase money for child care subsides.

Colorado also overhauled its child care licensing laws to make them more effective. State inspectors will now visit centers that have a history of problems more frequently and inspect those that have achieved accreditation less often. A new law requires all centers to post their latest inspection report so parents can see the results. (Colorado is among the 10 best states for child care.)" *Working Mother, July/August 1997*

Business Environment

STATE ECONOMY

State Economic Profile

"Colorado's economy has decelerated steadily over the past year. ....Personal bankruptcy filings are up 18%, one-half the U.S. rate of growth.

Colorado's expansion is not driven by the fortunes of a few dominant industries, as in the cases of Idaho and Nevada. Rather, a broad range of industries throughout the state are making investments and adding workers. The expansion of Colorado's market in terms of population and income has led numerous national retail chains to enter the Colorado market, providing local retailers with stiff competition and leading to casualties. At least seven retail chains have been forced to close their Colorado stores.

Declining affordability in the larger metro areas is causing growth to be pushed out to neighboring smaller metro areas. The nucleus of Colorado's growth is the Denver and Boulder areas. The current expansion of both metro areas represents moderation when compared to the growth of two years ago. Boulder's residential building restrictions and efforts to contain commercial construction are exporting growth to northern Denver and to Greeley, where housing prices are far lower.

Colorado's geographic position in the Rockies between the Plains states and the West Coast makes it a natural gateway through which the emerging western economies will increasingly channel their trade. Colorado has the population and business base in place to maintain steady long-term growth. Colorado is top-ranked for long-term growth." *National Association of Realtors, Economic Profiles: The Fifty States, July 1997*

IMPORTS/EXPORTS

Total Export Sales

Area	1993 ($000)	1994 ($000)	1995 ($000)	1996 ($000)	% Chg. 1993-96	% Chg. 1995-96
MSA[1]	930,960	1,089,812	1,385,282	1,502,865	61.4	8.5
U.S.	464,858,354	512,415,609	583,030,524	622,827,063	34.0	6.8

Note: (1) Metropolitan Statistical Area - see Appendix A for areas included
Source: U.S. Department of Commerce, International Trade Association, Metropolitan Area Exports: An Export Performance Report on Over 250 U.S. Cities, October 1997

Imports/Exports by Port

Type	Cargo Value			Share of U.S. Total	
	1995 (US$mil.)	1996 (US$mil.)	% Change 1995-1996	1995 (%)	1996 (%)
Imports	0	0	0	0	0
Exports	0	0	0	0	0

Source: Global Trade Information Services, WaterBorne Trade Atlas 1997

CITY FINANCES

City Government Finances

Component	FY92 ($000)	FY92 (per capita $)
Revenue	1,171,128	2,414.50
Expenditure	1,649,475	3,400.70
Debt Outstanding	3,344,088	6,894.46
Cash & Securities	3,050,975	6,290.15

Source: U.S. Bureau of the Census, City Government Finances: 1991-92

City Government Revenue by Source

Source	FY92 ($000)	FY92 (per capita $)	FY92 (%)
From Federal Government	27,272	56.23	2.3
From State Governments	220,732	455.08	18.8
From Local Governments	585	1.21	0.0
Property Taxes	99,485	205.11	8.5
General Sales Taxes	209,574	432.08	17.9
Selective Sales Taxes	36,912	76.10	3.2
Income Taxes	0	0.00	0.0
Current Charges	271,743	560.25	23.2
Utility/Liquor Store	85,275	175.81	7.3
Employee Retirement[1]	40,161	82.80	3.4
Other	179,389	369.84	15.3

Note: (1) Excludes "city contributions," classified as "nonrevenue," intragovernmental transfers.
Source: U.S. Bureau of the Census, City Government Finances: 1991-92

City Government Expenditures by Function

Function	FY92 ($000)	FY92 (per capita $)	FY92 (%)
Educational Services	21,970	45.30	1.3
Employee Retirement[1]	23,633	48.72	1.4
Environment/Housing	145,678	300.34	8.8
Government Administration	68,531	141.29	4.2
Interest on General Debt	202,929	418.38	12.3
Public Safety	182,870	377.02	11.1
Social Services	267,167	550.81	16.2
Transportation	538,812	1,110.86	32.7
Utility/Liquor Store	112,513	231.97	6.8
Other	85,372	176.01	5.2

Note: (1) Payments to beneficiaries including withdrawal of contributions.
Source: U.S. Bureau of the Census, City Government Finances: 1991-92

Municipal Bond Ratings

Area	Moody's	S & P
Denver	Aa2	AA

Note: n/a not available; n/r not rated
Source: Moody's Bond Record, 2/98; Statistical Abstract of the U.S., 1997;
Governing Magazine, 9/97, 3/98

POPULATION

Population Growth

Area	1980	1990	% Chg. 1980-90	July 1996 Estimate	% Chg. 1990-96
City	492,365	467,610	-5.0	497,840	6.5
MSA[1]	1,428,836	1,622,980	13.6	1,866,978	15.0
U.S.	226,545,805	248,765,170	9.8	265,179,411	6.6

Note: (1) Metropolitan Statistical Area - see Appendix A for areas included
Source: 1980/1990 Census of Housing and Population, Summary Tape File 3C;
Census Bureau Population Estimates

Population Characteristics

Race	City 1980 Population	City 1980 %	City 1990 Population	City 1990 %	% Chg. 1980-90	MSA[1] 1990 Population	MSA[1] 1990 %
White	375,628	76.3	337,623	72.2	-10.1	1,391,592	85.7
Black	59,095	12.0	60,319	12.9	2.1	94,989	5.9
Amer Indian/Esk/Aleut	4,318	0.9	5,314	1.1	23.1	12,216	0.8
Asian/Pacific Islander	8,934	1.8	10,763	2.3	20.5	36,687	2.3
Other	44,390	9.0	53,591	11.5	20.7	87,496	5.4
Hispanic Origin[2]	92,348	18.8	106,554	22.8	15.4	208,264	12.8

Note: (1) Metropolitan Statistical Area - see Appendix A for areas included;
(2) people of Hispanic origin can be of any race
Source: 1980/1990 Census of Housing and Population, Summary Tape File 3C

Ancestry

Area	German	Irish	English	Italian	U.S.	French	Polish	Dutch
City	22.4	13.2	13.2	3.8	2.0	3.7	2.4	2.3
MSA[1]	32.0	16.8	17.2	5.0	2.3	4.6	2.8	2.9
U.S.	23.3	15.6	13.1	5.9	5.3	4.2	3.8	2.5

Note: Figures are percentages and include persons that reported multiple ancestry (eg. if a person reported being Irish and Italian, they were included in both columns); (1) Metropolitan Statistical Area - see Appendix A for areas included
Source: 1990 Census of Population and Housing, Summary Tape File 3C

Age

Area	Median Age (Years)	Age Distribution (%) Under 5	Under 18	18-24	25-44	45-64	65+	80+
City	33.8	7.3	21.8	9.5	37.6	17.4	13.7	3.5
MSA[1]	32.7	7.8	25.9	8.8	37.8	18.2	9.3	2.0
U.S.	32.9	7.3	25.6	10.5	32.6	18.7	12.5	2.8

Note: (1) Metropolitan Statistical Area - see Appendix A for areas included
Source: 1990 Census of Population and Housing, Summary Tape File 3C

Male/Female Ratio

Area	Number of males per 100 females (all ages)	Number of males per 100 females (18 years old+)
City	95.1	92.0
MSA[1]	96.5	93.6
U.S.	95.0	91.9

Note: (1) Metropolitan Statistical Area - see Appendix A for areas included
Source: 1990 Census of Population, General Population Characteristics

INCOME

Per Capita/Median/Average Income

Area	Per Capita ($)	Median Household ($)	Average Household ($)
City	15,590	25,106	33,983
MSA[1]	16,539	32,852	40,841
U.S.	14,420	30,056	38,453

Note: all figures are for 1989; (1) Metropolitan Statistical Area - see Appendix A for areas included
Source: 1990 Census of Population and Housing, Summary Tape File 3C

Household Income Distribution by Race

Income ($)	City (%)					U.S. (%)				
	Total	White	Black	Other	Hisp.[1]	Total	White	Black	Other	Hisp.[1]
Less than 5,000	7.6	5.8	14.4	13.0	11.5	6.2	4.8	15.2	8.6	8.8
5,000 - 9,999	11.3	10.8	13.1	13.2	14.5	9.3	8.6	14.2	9.9	11.1
10,000 - 14,999	10.8	10.0	12.2	15.0	13.7	8.8	8.5	11.0	9.8	11.0
15,000 - 24,999	20.1	19.8	21.0	21.4	22.5	17.5	17.3	18.9	18.5	20.5
25,000 - 34,999	16.0	16.5	12.3	16.3	15.7	15.8	16.1	14.2	15.4	16.4
35,000 - 49,999	15.3	15.8	14.2	13.0	12.6	17.9	18.6	13.3	16.1	16.0
50,000 - 74,999	11.5	12.4	9.2	6.7	7.5	15.0	15.8	9.3	13.4	11.1
75,000 - 99,999	3.5	4.0	2.5	1.0	1.5	5.1	5.5	2.6	4.7	3.1
100,000+	3.9	4.8	1.2	0.5	0.5	4.4	4.8	1.3	3.7	1.9

Note: all figures are for 1989; (1) people of Hispanic origin can be of any race
Source: 1990 Census of Population and Housing, Summary Tape File 3C

Effective Buying Income

Area	Per Capita ($)	Median Household ($)	Average Household ($)
City	16,812	27,453	36,768
MSA[1]	18,348	37,622	45,521
U.S.	15,444	33,201	41,849

Note: data as of 1/1/97; (1) Metropolitan Statistical Area - see Appendix A for areas included
Source: Standard Rate & Data Service, Newspaper Advertising Source, 2/98

Effective Household Buying Income Distribution

Area	% of Households Earning						
	$10,000 -$19,999	$20,000 -$34,999	$35,000 -$49,999	$50,000 -$74,999	$75,000 -$99,000	$100,000 -$124,999	$125,000 and up
City	20.2	25.3	16.3	13.8	4.4	1.8	2.2
MSA[1]	14.2	22.9	19.3	21.1	7.8	2.7	2.7
U.S.	16.5	23.4	18.3	18.2	6.4	2.1	2.4

Note: data as of 1/1/97; (1) Metropolitan Statistical Area - see Appendix A for areas included
Source: Standard Rate & Data Service, Newspaper Advertising Source, 2/98

Poverty Rates by Race and Age

Area	Total (%)	By Race (%)				By Age (%)		
		White	Black	Other	Hisp.[2]	Under 5 years old	Under 18 years old	65 years and over
City	17.1	12.4	27.0	31.3	30.6	29.4	27.4	12.7
MSA[1]	9.7	7.5	24.6	22.6	22.3	15.9	13.5	9.5
U.S.	13.1	9.8	29.5	23.1	25.3	20.1	18.3	12.8

Note: figures show the percent of people living below the poverty line in 1989. The average poverty threshold was $12,674 for a family of four in 1989; (1) Metropolitan Statistical Area - see Appendix A for areas included; (2) people of Hispanic origin can be of any race
Source: 1990 Census of Population and Housing, Summary Tape File 3C

EMPLOYMENT

Labor Force and Employment

Area	Civilian Labor Force			Workers Employed		
	Dec. '95	Dec. '96	% Chg.	Dec. '95	Dec. '96	% Chg.
City	272,124	283,534	4.2	260,366	274,874	5.6
MSA[1]	1,047,752	1,095,077	4.5	1,013,776	1,070,262	5.6
U.S.	134,583,000	136,742,000	1.6	127,903,000	130,785,000	2.3

Note: Data is not seasonally adjusted and covers workers 16 years of age and older; (1) Metropolitan Statistical Area - see Appendix A for areas included
Source: Bureau of Labor Statistics, http://stats.bls.gov

Unemployment Rate

Area	1997											
	Jan.	Feb.	Mar.	Apr.	May	Jun.	Jul.	Aug.	Sep.	Oct.	Nov.	Dec.
City	5.0	4.2	4.1	3.5	3.8	4.4	3.6	3.7	3.5	3.1	3.4	3.1
MSA[1]	3.7	3.1	3.1	2.7	3.0	3.4	2.8	2.8	2.7	2.4	2.6	2.3
U.S.	5.9	5.7	5.5	4.8	4.7	5.2	5.0	4.8	4.7	4.4	4.3	4.4

Note: Data is not seasonally adjusted and covers workers 16 years of age and older; All figures are percentages; (1) Metropolitan Statistical Area - see Appendix A for areas included
Source: Bureau of Labor Statistics, http://stats.bls.gov

Employment by Industry

Sector	MSA[1]		U.S.
	Number of Employees	Percent of Total	Percent of Total
Services	329,800	30.6	29.0
Retail Trade	197,700	18.3	18.5
Government	148,200	13.7	16.1
Manufacturing	94,000	8.7	15.0
Finance/Insurance/Real Estate	85,900	8.0	5.7
Wholesale Trade	69,000	6.4	5.4
Transportation/Public Utilities	85,000	7.9	5.3
Construction	63,000	5.8	4.5
Mining	6,800	0.6	0.5

Note: Figures cover non-farm employment as of 12/97 and are not seasonally adjusted;
(1) Metropolitan Statistical Area - see Appendix A for areas included
Source: Bureau of Labor Statistics, http://stats.bls.gov

Employment by Occupation

Occupation Category	City (%)	MSA[1] (%)	U.S. (%)
White Collar	64.8	67.1	58.1
Executive/Admin./Management	14.1	15.4	12.3
Professional	17.3	16.0	14.1
Technical & Related Support	4.1	4.5	3.7
Sales	11.4	12.9	11.8
Administrative Support/Clerical	18.0	18.3	16.3
Blue Collar	18.6	19.6	26.2
Precision Production/Craft/Repair	7.2	9.0	11.3
Machine Operators/Assem./Insp.	4.5	4.1	6.8
Transportation/Material Movers	3.3	3.4	4.1
Cleaners/Helpers/Laborers	3.5	3.1	3.9
Services	15.6	12.4	13.2
Farming/Forestry/Fishing	1.0	0.9	2.5

Note: figures cover employed persons 16 years old and over;
(1) Metropolitan Statistical Area - see Appendix A for areas included
Source: 1990 Census of Population and Housing, Summary Tape File 3C

Occupational Employment Projections: 1994 - 2005

Occupations Expected to have the Largest Job Growth (ranked by numerical growth)	Fast-Growing Occupations (ranked by percent growth)
1. Janitors/cleaners/maids, ex. priv. hshld.	1. Computer engineers
2. Salespersons, retail	2. Systems analysts
3. Waiters & waitresses	3. Computer scientists
4. General managers & top executives	4. Amusement and recreation attendants
5. Guards	5. Personal and home care aides
6. Marketing & sales, supervisors	6. Guards
7. Truck drivers, heavy & light	7. Human services workers
8. Cashiers	8. Nursery and greenhouse managers
9. Systems analysts	9. Pruners
10. Clerical supervisors	10. Electronic pagination systems workers

Projections cover Colorado.
Source: U.S. Department of Labor, Employment and Training Administration, America's Labor Market Information System (ALMIS)

Average Wages

Occupation	Wage	Occupation	Wage
Professional/Technical/Clerical	$/Week	**Health/Protective Services**	$/Week
Accountants III	808	Corrections Officers	566
Attorneys III	1,322	Firefighters	751
Budget Analysts III	846	Nurses, Licensed Practical II	-
Buyers/Contracting Specialists II	654	Nurses, Registered II	-
Clerks, Accounting III	478	Nursing Assistants II	-
Clerks, General III	396	Police Officers I	733
Computer Operators II	450	**Hourly Workers**	$/Hour
Computer Programmers II	681	Forklift Operators	-
Drafters II	454	General Maintenance Workers	11.20
Engineering Technicians III	616	Guards I	6.49
Engineering Technicians, Civil III	634	Janitors	7.62
Engineers III	956	Maintenance Electricians	18.41
Key Entry Operators I	362	Maintenance Electronics Techs II	16.70
Personnel Assistants III	506	Maintenance Machinists	17.73
Personnel Specialists III	816	Maintenance Mechanics, Machinery	16.16
Secretaries III	553	Material Handling Laborers	7.50
Switchboard Operator-Receptionist	357	Motor Vehicle Mechanics	16.00
Systems Analysts II	958	Shipping/Receiving Clerks	9.30
Systems Analysts Supervisor/Mgr II	1,317	Tool and Die Makers	17.32
Tax Collectors II	717	Truckdrivers, Tractor Trailer	15.98
Word Processors II	-	Warehouse Specialists	-

Note: Wage data includes full-time workers only for 1/96 and cover the Metropolitan Statistical Area (see Appendix A for areas included). Dashes indicate that data was not available.
Source: Bureau of Labor Statistics, Occupational Compensation Survey, 5/96

TAXES

Major State and Local Tax Rates

State Corp. Income (%)	State Personal Income (%)	Residential Property (effective rate per $100)	Sales & Use		State Gasoline (cents/ gallon)	State Cigarette (cents/ 20-pack)
			State (%)	Local (%)		
5.0	5.0	0.84	3.0	4.3	22	20

Note: Personal/corporate income tax rates as of 1/97. Sales, gasoline and cigarette tax rates as of 1/98.
Source: Federation of Tax Administrators, www.taxadmin.org; Washington D.C. Department of Finance and Revenue, Tax Rates and Tax Burdens in the District of Columbia: A Nationwide Comparison, June 1997; Chamber of Commerce

Total Taxes Per Capita and as a Percent of Income

Area	Per Capita Income ($)	Per Capita Taxes ($)			Taxes as Pct. of Income (%)		
		Total	Federal	State/Local	Total	Federal	State/Local
Colorado	27,624	9,705	6,521	3,184	35.1	23.6	11.5
U.S.	26,187	9,205	6,127	3,078	35.2	23.4	11.8

Note: Figures are for 1997
Source: Tax Foundation, Web Site, www.taxfoundation.org

Estimated Tax Burden

Area	State Income	Local Income	Property	Sales	Total
Denver	2,220	0	1,125	621	3,966

Note: The numbers are estimates of taxes paid by a married couple with two kids and annual earnings of $65,000. Sales tax estimates assume they spend average amounts on food, clothing, household goods and gasoline. Property tax estimates assume they live in a $225,000 home.
Source: Kiplinger's Personal Finance Magazine, June 1997

COMMERCIAL REAL ESTATE

Office Market

Class/Location	Total Space (sq. ft.)	Vacant Space (sq. ft.)	Vac. Rate (%)	Under Constr. (sq. ft.)	Net Absorp. (sq. ft.)	Rental Rates ($/sq.ft./yr.)
Class A						
CBD	10,300,400	992,500	9.6	n/a	397,100	14.00-17.51
Outside CBD	10,007,400	1,020,300	10.2	902,000	502,600	15.45-23.00
Class B						
CBD	12,500,000	1,596,900	12.8	n/a	72,200	11.33-14.29
Outside CBD	28,655,600	3,461,200	12.1	1,701,800	-249,800	12.73-18.25

Note: Data as of 10/97 and covers Denver; CBD = Central Business District; n/a not available;
Source: Society of Industrial and Office Realtors, 1998 Comparative Statistics of Industrial and Office Real Estate Markets

"Southeast Denver remains the prime market in the metropolitan area. The Denver Tech Center, in particular, attracts both local expansions and corporate relocations from out of state. Large blocks of space are increasingly difficult to find here, however, which has led some users to reconsider downtown. New sports stadiums and the revived 'Lower Downtown' warehouse district, now successfully turned into an entertainment mecca, add to downtown's renewed attractiveness. Speculative construction is reappearing in hot suburban markets, but is widely characterized as 'demand-driven' and should not appreciably alter the fundamentally positive dynamics of Denver's office market." *Society of Industrial and Office Realtors, 1998 Comparative Statistics of Industrial and Office Real Estate Markets*

Industrial Market

Location	Total Space (sq. ft.)	Vacant Space (sq. ft.)	Vac. Rate (%)	Under Constr. (sq. ft.)	Net Absorp. (sq. ft.)	Net Lease ($/sq.ft./yr.)
Central City	24,926,521	883,124	3.5	300,000	226,371	3.25-5.00
Suburban	108,037,139	5,655,631	5.2	2,352,592	620,927	4.50-8.50

Note: Data as of 10/97 and covers Denver; n/a not available
Source: Society of Industrial and Office Realtors, 1998 Comparative Statistics of Industrial and Office Real Estate Markets

"Proposed 1998 speculative construction in excess of 3.3 million sq. ft. are projected, slightly lower than 1997's total and perhaps a response to a small uptick in the market vacancy rate from 4.7 percent last year to five percent this year. Continued demand should keep vacancy from rising beyond the five percent range, however, Lease prices will rise but at a more modest pace than has been the case over the last several years. Most new construction will be in Denver's northeast market, centered around I-70 and I-225. Developers are eyeing parcels further east around Denver International Airport as well." *Society of Industrial and Office Realtors, 1998 Comparative Statistics of Industrial and Office Real Estate Markets*

Retail Market

Shopping Center Inventory (sq. ft.)	Shopping Center Construction (sq. ft.)	Construction as a Percent of Inventory (%)	Torto Wheaton Rent Index[1] ($/sq. ft.)
43,174,000	678,000	1.6	14.48

Note: Data as of 1997 and covers the Metropolitan Statistical Area - see Appendix A for areas included; (1) Index is based on a model that predicts what the average rent should be for leases with certain characteristics, in certain locations during certain years.
Source: National Association of Realtors, 1997-1998 Market Conditions Report

"Denver's retail rent index rebounded in 1997 after falling slightly in the previous year. Much of the increase resulted from the absorption of a large portion of the nearly 1 million square feet of new product that were added in 1996. All eyes in the area are focused on the $101.5 million Pavilions project in Downtown Denver. Tenants include NikeTown, Virgin Records and Hard Rock Cafe, among others. The project is another example of the entertainment-oriented retail trend found in many places around the nation. Officials are hoping the project will revitalize the 16th Street Mall area. The pace of retail construction in the Denver area will likely slow over the next few years, until demand catches up." *National Association of Realtors, 1997-1998 Market Conditions Report*

COMMERCIAL UTILITIES

Typical Monthly Electric Bills

Area	Commercial Service ($/month)		Industrial Service ($/month)	
	12 kW demand 1,500 kWh	100 kW demand 30,000 kWh	1,000 kW demand 400,000 kWh	20,000 kW demand 10,000,000 kWh
City	104	1,896	20,785	446,844
U.S.	162	2,360	25,590	545,677

Note: Based on rates in effect July 1, 1997
Source: Edison Electric Institute, Typical Residential, Commercial and Industrial Bills, Summer 1997

TRANSPORTATION

Transportation Statistics

Avg. travel time to work (min.)	20.8
Interstate highways	I-25; I-70; I-76
Bus lines	
In-city	Regional Transportation District, 825 vehicles
Inter-city	2
Passenger air service	
Airport	Denver International
Airlines	16
Aircraft departures	178,535 (1995)
Enplaned passengers	14,328,458 (1995)
Rail service	Amtrak; Light Rail
Motor freight carriers	77
Major waterways/ports	None

Source: OAG, Business Travel Planner, Summer 1997; Editor & Publisher Market Guide, 1998; FAA Airport Activity Statistics, 1996; Amtrak National Time Table, Northeast Timetable, Fall/Winter 1997-98; 1990 Census of Population and Housing, STF 3C; Chamber of Commerce/Economic Development 1997; Jane's Urban Transport Systems 1997-98; Transit Fact Book 1997

A survey of 90,000 airline passengers during the first half of 1997 ranked most of the largest airports in the U.S. Denver International ranked number 6 out of 36. Criteria: cleanliness, quality of restaurants, attractiveness, speed of baggage delivery, ease of reaching gates, available ground transportation, ease of following signs and closeness of parking. *Plog Research Inc., First Half 1997*

Means of Transportation to Work

Area	Car/Truck/Van		Public Transportation			Bicycle	Walked	Other Means	Worked at Home
	Drove Alone	Car-pooled	Bus	Subway	Railroad				
City	68.6	13.1	7.8	0.0	0.0	0.9	5.3	1.0	3.4
MSA[1]	75.6	12.6	4.3	0.0	0.0	0.4	3.0	0.8	3.4
U.S.	73.2	13.4	3.0	1.5	0.5	0.4	3.9	1.2	3.0

Note: figures shown are percentages and only include workers 16 years old and over;
(1) Metropolitan Statistical Area - see Appendix A for areas included
Source: 1990 Census of Population and Housing, Summary Tape File 3C

BUSINESSES

Major Business Headquarters

Company Name	1997 Rankings	
	Fortune 500	Forbes 500
Leprino Foods	-	148
MediaNews Group	-	339
NW Transport Service	-	487

Note: Companies listed are located in the city; Dashes indicate no ranking
Fortune 500: companies that produce a 10-K are ranked 1 - 500 based on 1996 revenue
Forbes 500: private companies are ranked 1 - 500 based on 1996 revenue
Source: Forbes 12/1/97; Fortune 4/28/97

Fast-Growing Businesses

Denver was ranked #24 out of 24 (#1 is best) in terms of the best-performing local stocks in 1996 according to the Money/Norby Cities Index. The index measures stocks of companies that have headquarters in 24 metro areas. *Money, 2/7/97*

Women-Owned Businesses: Number, Employment, Sales and Share

Area	Women-Owned Businesses in 1996				Share of Women-Owned Businesses in 1996	
	Number	Employment	Sales ($000)	Rank[2]	Percent (%)	Rank[3]
MSA[1]	77,600	207,900	23,620,700	19	39.8	3

Note: (1) Metropolitan Statistical Area - see Appendix A for areas included; (2) Calculated on an averaging of number of businesses, employment and sales and ranges from 1 to 50 where 1 is best; (3) Ranges from 1 to 50 where 1 is best
Source: The National Foundation for Women Business Owners, 1996 Facts on Women-Owned Businesses: Trends in the Top 50 Metropolitan Areas, March 26, 1997

Women-Owned Businesses: Growth

Area	Growth in Women-Owned Businesses (% change from 1987 to 1996)				Relative Growth in the Number of Women-Owned and All Businesses (% change from 1987 to 1996)			
	Num.	Empl.	Sales	Rank[2]	Women-Owned	All Firms	Absolute Difference	Relative Difference
MSA[1]	56.9	276.5	303.4	24	56.9	38.6	18.3	1.5:1

Note: (1) Metropolitan Statistical Area - see Appendix A for areas included; (2) Calculated on an averaging of the percent growth of number of businesses, employment and sales and ranges from 1 to 50 where 1 is best
Source: The National Foundation for Women Business Owners, 1996 Facts on Women-Owned Businesses: Trends in the Top 50 Metropolitan Areas, March 26, 1997

Minority Business Opportunity

Six of the 500 largest Hispanic-owned companies in the U.S. are located in Denver.
Hispanic Business, June 1997

Denver is home to two companies which are on the Hispanic Business Fastest-Growing 100 list (greatest sales growth from 1992 to 1996): VPM Funding Co. (mortgage banking svcs.) and AGEISS Environmental Inc. (environ. consulting svcs.) *Hispanic Business, July/August 1997*

Denver was listed among the top 25 metropolitan areas in terms of the number of Hispanic-owned companies. The city was ranked number 23 with 11,788 companies. *Hispanic Business, May 1997*

Small Business Opportunity

Denver was included among *Entrepreneur* magazines listing of the "20 Best Cities for Small Business." It was ranked #6 among large metro areas. Criteria: risk of failure, business performance, economic growth, affordability and state attitude towards business. *Entrepreneur, 10/97*

Denver was ranked #7 out of 219 in terms of the best cities to start and grow a home-based business by *Home Office Computing*. Criteria: economic growth, population growth, industrial diversity, business climate, market access systems, work flexibility, lifestyle, education level, intellectual capital, age, and home-based business score (zoning flexibility, community support, regulatory streamlining). "Denver is network central—home-based entrepreneurs needn't look far to find other like-minded folks in this Mile High City. Networking events are publicized in local newspapers almost every day, and the chamber of commerce offers a program called BusinessPlus for the small-business community. The program provides small-business training on everything from dealing with regulations to time management. Additionally just 10 miles east in Aurora is the Rocky Mountain Home-Based Business Association, and 25 miles to the west is the Mount Evans Home-Based Business Association. The state of Colorado also offers a business start-up program called Leading Edge that was customized to meet the specific needs of home-based businesses." *Home Office Computing, December 1997*

According to *Forbes*, Denver is home to two of America's 200 best small companies: Koala, Prima Energy. Criteria: companies must be publicly traded, U.S.-based corporations with latest 12-month sales of between $5 and $350 million. Earnings must be at least $1 million for the 12-month period. Limited partnerships, REITs and closed-end mutual funds were not considered. Banks, S&Ls and electric utilities were not included. *Forbes, November 3, 1997*

HOTELS & MOTELS

Hotels/Motels

Area	Hotels/ Motels	Rooms	Luxury-Level Hotels/Motels		Average Minimum Rates ($)		
			◆◆◆◆	◆◆◆◆◆	◆◆	◆◆◆	◆◆◆◆
City	35	8,650	2	0	60	132	126
Airport	26	6,191	1	0	n/a	n/a	n/a
Suburbs	39	5,048	0	0	n/a	n/a	n/a
Total	100	19,889	3	0	n/a	n/a	n/a

Note: n/a not available; Classifications range from one diamond (budget properties with basic amenities) to five diamond (luxury properties with the finest service, rooms and facilities).
Source: OAG, Business Travel Planner, Summer 1997

CONVENTION CENTERS

Major Convention Centers

Center Name	Meeting Rooms	Exhibit Space (sf)
Colorado Convention Center/Currigan Exhibition Hall	48	408,000
Currigan Exhibition Hall	21	300,000
Denver Coliseum	n/a	65,000
Denver Merchandise Mart	166	162,200
National Western Complex	4	600,000

Note: n/a not available
Source: Trade Shows Worldwide 1997

Living Environment

COST OF LIVING

Cost of Living Index

Composite Index	Housing	Utilities	Groceries	Health Care	Trans-portation	Misc. Goods/ Services
106.4	119.6	82.9	101.4	122.4	112.7	98.6

Note: U.S. = 100; Figures are for the Metropolitan Statistical Area - see Appendix A for areas included
Source: ACCRA, Cost of Living Index, 3rd Quarter 1997

HOUSING

Median Home Prices and Housing Affordability

Area	Median Price[2] 3rd Qtr. 1997 ($)	HOI[3] 3rd Qtr. 1997	Afford-ability Rank[4]
MSA[1]	138,000	68.0	105
U.S.	127,000	63.7	–

Note: (1) Metropolitan Statistical Area - see Appendix A for areas included; (2) U.S. figures calculated from the sales of 625,000 new and existing homes in 195 markets; (3) Housing Opportunity Index - percent of homes sold that were within the reach of the median income household at the prevailing mortgage interest rate; (4) Rank is from 1-195 with 1 being most affordable
Source: National Association of Home Builders, Housing Opportunity Index, 3rd Quarter 1997

It is projected that the median price of existing single-family homes in the metro area will increase by 9.6% in 1998. Nationwide, home prices are projected to increase 6.6%.
Kiplinger's Personal Finance Magazine, January 1998

Average New Home Price

Area	Price ($)
MSA[1]	163,750
U.S.	135,710

Note: Figures are based on a new home with 1,800 sq. ft. of living area on an 8,000 sq. ft. lot; (1) Metropolitan Statistical Area - see Appendix A for areas included
Source: ACCRA, Cost of Living Index, 3rd Quarter 1997

Average Apartment Rent

Area	Rent ($/mth)
MSA[1]	731
U.S.	569

Note: Figures are based on an unfurnished two bedroom, 1-1/2 or 2 bath apartment, approximately 950 sq. ft. in size, excluding all utilities except water; (1) Metropolitan Statistical Area - see Appendix A for areas included
Source: ACCRA, Cost of Living Index, 3rd Quarter 1997

RESIDENTIAL UTILITIES

Average Residential Utility Costs

Area	All Electric ($/mth)	Part Electric ($/mth)	Other Energy ($/mth)	Phone ($/mth)
MSA[1]	–	43.33	37.58	21.07
U.S.	109.40	55.25	43.64	19.48

Note: (1) (1) Metropolitan Statistical Area - see Appendix A for areas included
Source: ACCRA, Cost of Living Index, 3rd Quarter 1997

HEALTH CARE

Average Health Care Costs

Area	Hospital ($/day)	Doctor ($/visit)	Dentist ($/visit)
MSA[1]	498.30	62.71	73.29
U.S.	392.91	48.76	60.84

Note: Hospital - based on a semi-private room. Doctor - based on a general practitioner's routine exam of an established patient. Dentist - based on adult teeth cleaning and periodic oral exam; (1) Metropolitan Statistical Area - see Appendix A for areas included
Source: ACCRA, Cost of Living Index, 3rd Quarter 1997

Distribution of Office-Based Physicians

Area	Family/Gen. Practitioners	Specialists Medical	Specialists Surgical	Specialists Other
MSA[1]	437	1,234	923	1,054

Note: Data as of 12/31/96; (1) Metropolitan Statistical Area - see Appendix A for areas included
Source: American Medical Assn., Physician Characteristics & Distribution in the U.S., 1997-1998

Hospitals

Denver has 9 general medical and surgical hospitals, 2 psychiatric, 1 children's general, 1 children's other specialty. *AHA Guide to the Healthcare Field 1997-98*

According to *U.S. News and World Report,* Denver has 3 of the best hospitals in the U.S.: **University Hospital**, noted for AIDS, endocrinology, geriatrics, neurology, pulmonology, rehabilitation, rheumatology, urology; **Children's Hospital**, noted for pediatrics; **National Jewish Center**, noted for pulmonology;   *U.S. News and World Report, "America's Best Hospitals", 7/28/97*

Saint Joseph Hospital is among the 100 best-run hospitals in the U.S.
Modern Healthcare, January 5, 1998

EDUCATION

Public School District Statistics

District Name	Num. Sch.	Enroll.	Classroom Teachers[1]	Pupils per Teacher	Minority Pupils (%)	Current Exp.[2] ($/pupil)
Denver County 1	112	64,322	3,271	19.7	72.9	5,632
Expeditionary Boces	1	290	13	22.3	n/a	n/a
Mapleton 1	11	4,991	244	20.5	n/a	n/a

Note: Data covers the 1995-1996 school year unless otherwise noted; (1) Excludes teachers reported as working in school district offices rather than in schools; (2) Based on 1993-94 enrollment collected by the Census Bureau, not the enrollment figure shown in column 3; SD = School District; ISD = Independent School District; n/a not available
Source: National Center for Education Statistics, Common Core of Data Survey; Bureau of the Census

Educational Quality

School District	Education Quotient[1]	Graduate Outcome[2]	Community Index[3]	Resource Index[4]
Denver County	93.0	62.0	97.0	121.0

Note: Nearly 1,000 secondary school districts were rated in terms of educational quality. The scores range from a low of 50 to a high of 150; (1) Average of the Graduate Outcome, Community and Resource indexes; (2) Based on graduation rates and college board scores (SAT/ACT); (3) Based on the surrounding community's average level of education and the area's average income level; (4) Based on teacher salaries, per-pupil expenditures and student-teacher ratios.
Source: Expansion Management, Ratings Issue 1997

Educational Attainment by Race

Area	High School Graduate (%)					Bachelor's Degree (%)				
	Total	White	Black	Other	Hisp.[2]	Total	White	Black	Other	Hisp.[2]
City	79.2	83.5	75.0	54.0	50.4	29.0	33.9	14.5	10.3	6.9
MSA[1]	85.5	87.6	79.1	64.2	60.2	28.9	30.8	17.2	14.3	9.6
U.S.	75.2	77.9	63.1	60.4	49.8	20.3	21.5	11.4	19.4	9.2

*Note: figures shown cover persons 25 years old and over; (1) Metropolitan Statistical Area -
see Appendix A for areas included; (2) people of Hispanic origin can be of any race
Source: 1990 Census of Population and Housing, Summary Tape File 3C*

School Enrollment by Type

Area	Preprimary				Elementary/High School			
	Public		Private		Public		Private	
	Enrollment	%	Enrollment	%	Enrollment	%	Enrollment	%
City	4,579	57.3	3,410	42.7	55,388	85.9	9,065	14.1
MSA[1]	19,953	57.9	14,488	42.1	248,623	91.8	22,151	8.2
U.S.	2,679,029	59.5	1,824,256	40.5	38,379,689	90.2	4,187,099	9.8

*Note: figures shown cover persons 3 years old and over;
(1) Metropolitan Statistical Area - see Appendix A for areas included
Source: 1990 Census of Population and Housing, Summary Tape File 3C*

School Enrollment by Race

Area	Preprimary (%)				Elementary/High School (%)			
	White	Black	Other	Hisp.[1]	White	Black	Other	Hisp.[1]
City	70.2	14.0	15.7	27.6	55.5	18.7	25.8	39.3
MSA[2]	87.3	5.1	7.5	12.3	81.1	7.3	11.7	18.2
U.S.	80.4	12.5	7.1	7.8	74.1	15.6	10.3	12.5

*Note: figures shown cover persons 3 years old and over; (1) people of Hispanic origin can be of any
race; (2) Metropolitan Statistical Area - see Appendix A for areas included
Source: 1990 Census of Population and Housing, Summary Tape File 3C*

SAT/ACT Scores

Area/District	1997 SAT				1997 ACT	
	Percent of Graduates Tested (%)	Average Math Score	Average Verbal Score	Average Combined Score	Percent of Graduates Tested (%)	Average Composite Score
Denver PS	n/a	522	526	1,048	n/a	19.4
State	30	539	536	1,075	62	21.5
U.S.	42	511	505	1,016	36	21.0

*Note: Math and verbal SAT scores are out of a possible 800; ACT scores are out of a possible 36
Caution: Comparing or ranking states/cities on the basis of SAT/ACT scores alone is invalid and
strongly discouraged by the The College Board and The American College Testing Program as
students who take the tests are self-selected and do not represent the entire student population.
Source: Denver Public Schools, Department of Planning, Research & Program Evaluation, 1997;
American College Testing Program, 1997; College Board, 1997*

Classroom Teacher Salaries in Public Schools

District	B.A. Degree		M.A. Degree		Ph.D. Degree	
	Min. ($)	Max. ($)	Min. ($)	Max. ($)	Min. ($)	Max. ($)
Denver	23,460	36,853	26,132	43,210	31,692	52,529
Average[1]	26,120	39,270	28,175	44,667	31,643	49,825

*Note: Salaries are for 1996-1997; (1) Based on all school districts covered
Source: American Federation of Teachers (unpublished data)*

Higher Education

Two-Year Colleges		Four-Year Colleges		Medical Schools	Law Schools	Voc/Tech
Public	Private	Public	Private			
1	5	3	6	1	1	37

Source: College Blue Book, Occupational Education 1997; Medical School Admission Requirements, 1998-99; Peterson's Guide to Two-Year Colleges, 1997; Peterson's Guide to Four-Year Colleges, 1997; Barron's Guide to Law Schools 1997

MAJOR EMPLOYERS

Major Employers

Children's Hospital Association
Denver Board of Water Commissioners
Denver Publishing
Lang Management
Provenant Health Partners
Rocky Mountain Hospital & Medical Service
Shareholder Services
Teletech Teleservices

Colorado National Bank
Denver Post
Gates Rubber Co.
Nationsway Transport Service
Public Service Co. of Colorado
Rose Healthcare Systems
St. Joseph Hospital

Note: companies listed are located in the city
Source: Dun's Business Rankings 1997; Ward's Business Directory, 1997

PUBLIC SAFETY

Crime Rate

Area	All Crimes	Violent Crimes				Property Crimes		
		Murder	Forcible Rape	Robbery	Aggrav. Assault	Burglary	Larceny -Theft	Motor Vehicle Theft
City	6,647.1	12.4	69.3	257.1	403.5	1,508.6	3,345.3	1,050.9
Suburbs[1]	4,946.4	3.1	38.0	97.7	214.2	800.0	3,425.5	368.0
MSA[2]	5,415.9	5.7	46.6	141.7	266.4	995.7	3,403.3	556.5
U.S.	5,078.9	7.4	36.1	202.4	388.2	943.0	2,975.9	525.9

Note: Crime rate is the number of crimes per 100,000 pop.; (1) defined as all areas within the MSA but located outside the central city; (2) Metropolitan Statistical Area - see Appendix A for areas incl.
Source: FBI Uniform Crime Reports 1996

RECREATION

Culture and Recreation

Museums	Symphony Orchestras	Opera Companies	Dance Companies	Professional Theatres	Zoos	Pro Sports Teams
18	2	5	2	6	1	4

Source: International Directory of the Performing Arts, 1996; Official Museum Directory, 1998; Chamber of Commerce/Economic Development 1997

Library System

The Denver Public Library has 22 branches, holdings of 1,882,487 volumes and a budget of $n/a (1995-1996). Note: n/a means not available. *American Library Directory, 1997-1998*

MEDIA

Newspapers

Name	Type	Freq.	Distribution	Circulation
Colorado Leader	General	1x/wk	Local	2,200
Colorado Statesman	n/a	1x/wk	Regional	13,000
The Daily Journal	n/a	5x/wk	Area	6,500
Denver Catholic Register	Religious	1x/wk	Local	89,000
Denver Herald Dispatch	General	1x/wk	Local	8,500
The Denver Post	General	7x/wk	State	353,786
Denver Weekly News	Black	1x/wk	Local	10,000
Intermountain Jewish News	Religious	1x/wk	Local	50,000
La Voz Hispana de Colorado	Hispanic	1x/wk	Area	18,250
Rocky Mountain News	n/a	7x/wk	Local	293,449
El Semanario, The Weekly Issue	Hispanic	1x/wk	National	21,500
Washington Park Profile	General	1x/mo	Regional	17,000
Westword	General	1x/wk	Local	110,000

Note: Includes newspapers with circulations of 1,000 or more located in the city; n/a not available
Source: Burrelle's Media Directory, 1998 Edition

AM Radio Stations

Call Letters	Freq. (kHz)	Target Audience	Station Format	Music Format
KLZ	560	Religious	M	Adult Contemporary/Christian
KHOW	630	n/a	T	n/a
KLTT	670	Religious	E/M/T	Christian
KTLK	760	n/a	M/N/S/T	n/a
KOA	850	General	N/S/T	n/a
KPOF	910	General	E/M/N/T	Christian/Classical
KRKS	990	Religious	M	Christian
KMXA	1090	Hispanic	M/N/S	Spanish
KCUV	1150	Hispanic	M/N/S	Contemporary Top 40/Spanish
KVVS	1170	Hispanic	M	n/a
KBCO	1190	General	M/N/S	AOR/Adult Contemporary/Alternative
KBNO	1220	Hispanic	M/N/S/T	Adult Contemporary/Adult Standards
KRRF	1280	n/a	T	n/a
KKYD	1340	n/a	E	n/a
KEZW	1430	n/a	M/N/S	Adult Standards/Big Band
KDKO	1510	n/a	M/N/S	Urban Contemporary
KQXI	1550	Religious	N/T	n/a
KYGO	1600	General	M	Country

Note: Stations included broadcast in the Denver metro area; n/a not available
Station Format: E = Educational; M = Music; N = News; S = Sports; T = Talk
Music Format: AOR = Album Oriented Rock; MOR = Middle-of-the-Road
Source: Burrelle's Media Directory, 1998 Edition

FM Radio Stations

Call Letters	Freq. (mHz)	Target Audience	Station Format	Music Format
KUVO	89.3	Hispanic	M/N/S	Jazz
KCFR	90.1	General	M/N/S	Classical
KWBI	91.1	Religious	M	Christian
KJMN	92.1	Hispanic	M/N/S/T	Spanish
KVOD	92.5	General	M/N/S	Classical
KTCL	93.3	n/a	M/N/S	Alternative
KRKS	94.7	Religious	M/N/S/T	Christian
KHIH	95.7	General	M	Adult Contemporary/Jazz
KXPK	96.5	General	M/N/S	Alternative
KBCO	97.3	General	M	Alternative/Classic Rock
KYGO	98.5	General	M	Country
KIMN	100.3	General	M	Adult Contemporary
KOSI	101.1	General	M	Adult Contemporary
KRFX	103.5	n/a	M/N/S	Classic Rock
KALC	105.9	n/a	M/N/S	Adult Contemporary
KBPI	106.7	n/a	M	AOR/Alternative
KQKS	107.5	General	M/N	Adult Contemporary

Note: Stations included broadcast in the Denver metro area; n/a not available
Station Format: E = Educational; M = Music; N = News; S = Sports; T = Talk
Music Format: AOR = Album Oriented Rock; MOR = Middle-of-the-Road
Source: Burrelle's Media Directory, 1998 Edition

Television Stations

Name	Ch.	Affiliation	Type	Owner
KCNC	4	CBS	Commercial	Westinghouse Broadcasting Company
KRMA	6	PBS	Public	Council for Public Television
KMGH	7	ABC	Commercial	McGraw-Hill
KUSA	9	NBC	Commercial	Gannett Company Inc.
KBDI	12	PBS	Public	Front Range Educational Media Corp.
KTVD	20	UPN	Commercial	Channel 20 TV Company
KDVR	31	Fox	Commercial	Fox Television Stations Inc.
KRMT	41	n/a	Non-Commercial	Faith Bible Chapel
KCEC	50	Univision	Commercial	Golden Hills Broadcasting
KUBD	59	INTV	Commercial	Paxson Communications Corporation

Note: Stations included broadcast in the Denver metro area
Source: Burrelle's Media Directory, 1998 Edition

CLIMATE

Average and Extreme Temperatures

Temperature	Jan	Feb	Mar	Apr	May	Jun	Jul	Aug	Sep	Oct	Nov	Dec	Ann
Extreme High (°F)	73	76	84	90	93	102	103	100	97	89	79	75	103
Average High (°F)	43	47	52	62	71	81	88	86	77	67	52	45	64
Average Temp. (°F)	30	34	39	48	58	67	73	72	63	52	39	32	51
Average Low (°F)	16	20	25	34	44	53	59	57	48	37	25	18	37
Extreme Low (°F)	-25	-25	-10	-2	22	30	43	41	17	3	-8	-25	-25

Note: Figures cover the years 1948-1992
Source: National Climatic Data Center, International Station Meteorological Climate Summary, 3/95

Average Precipitation/Snowfall/Humidity

Precip./Humidity	Jan	Feb	Mar	Apr	May	Jun	Jul	Aug	Sep	Oct	Nov	Dec	Ann
Avg. Precip. (in.)	0.6	0.6	1.3	1.7	2.5	1.7	1.9	1.5	1.1	1.0	0.9	0.6	15.5
Avg. Snowfall (in.)	9	7	14	9	2	Tr	0	0	2	4	9	8	63
Avg. Rel. Hum. 5am (%)	62	65	67	66	70	68	67	68	66	63	66	63	66
Avg. Rel. Hum. 5pm (%)	49	44	40	35	38	34	34	34	32	34	47	50	39

Note: Figures cover the years 1948-1992; Tr = Trace amounts (<0.05 in. of rain; <0.5 in. of snow)
Source: National Climatic Data Center, International Station Meteorological Climate Summary, 3/95

Weather Conditions

Temperature			Daytime Sky			Precipitation		
10°F & below	32°F & below	90°F & above	Clear	Partly cloudy	Cloudy	0.01 inch or more precip.	0.1 inch or more snow/ice	Thunder-storms
24	155	33	99	177	89	90	38	39

Note: Figures are average number of days per year and covers the years 1948-1992
Source: National Climatic Data Center, International Station Meteorological Climate Summary, 3/95

AIR & WATER QUALITY

Maximum Pollutant Concentrations

	Particulate Matter (ug/m³)	Carbon Monoxide (ppm)	Sulfur Dioxide (ppm)	Nitrogen Dioxide (ppm)	Ozone (ppm)	Lead (ug/m³)
MSA[1] Level	96	7	0.024	0.033	0.11	0.05
NAAQS[2]	150	9	0.140	0.053	0.12	1.50
Met NAAQS?	Yes	Yes	Yes	Yes	Yes	Yes

Note: (1) Metropolitan Statistical Area - see Appendix A for areas included; (2) National Ambient Air Quality Standards; ppm = parts per million; ug/m³ = micrograms per cubic meter; n/a not available
Source: EPA, National Air Quality and Emissions Trends Report, 1996

Pollutant Standards Index

In the Denver MSA (see Appendix A for areas included), the Pollutant Standards Index (PSI) exceeded 100 on 1 day in 1996. A PSI value greater than 100 indicates that air quality would be in the unhealthful range on that day. *EPA, National Air Quality and Emissions Trends Report, 1996*

Drinking Water

Water System Name	Pop. Served	Primary Water Source Type	Number of Violations in Fiscal Year 1997	Type of Violation/ Contaminants
Denver Water Board	1,000,000	Surface	None	None

Note: Data as of January 16, 1998
Source: EPA, Office of Ground Water and Drinking Water, Safe Drinking Water Information System

Denver tap water is alkaline, 53% of supply hard, 47% of supply soft; West Slope, fluoridated. East Slope, not fluoridated.
Editor & Publisher Market Guide, 1998

Eugene, Oregon

Background

In 1846 Eugene F. Skinner, for whom the city is named, and his family settled in the lushly green Willamette Valley. In 1853 the town was named the seat of the newly created Lane County. The city was incorporated in 1862 and in 1876 the University of Oregon was established.

Eugene is now Oregon's second largest city and a major processing and shipping center for lumber. Lane County produces a large percentage of America's plywood and is known as the lumber and wood products capital of the world.

Another significant industry in the greater Eugene area is agriculture. The rich fertile soil of the Willamette Valley, together with the mild climate and long growing season create excellent conditions for seed and grain crops.

As Eugene slowly diversifies its economy from dependence on timber, new industry endeavors include food processing, computer software, manufacturing, and biotechnology.

The city will become the site for the new Hyundai Semiconductor computer-chip factory. It will be a $1.3 billion facility. In addition a German manufacturer of silicon wafers is investing over $300 million in the second phase of its facility and LSI Logic is working on a $4 billion research development/manufacturing plant, scheduled to open in early 1998. *World Trade 4/97*

The Coast Range, west of the city, acts as a barrier to coastal fog, but active storms cross with little hindrance. The Cascade Range to the east blocks all but the strongest continental air masses. When eastern air does flow into the valley during dry, hot summer weather an extreme fire hazard can develop. In the winter, however, clear, sunny days and cool, frosty nights result. Temperatures are largely controlled by maritime air from the Pacific Ocean so that long periods of extremely hot or cold weather never occur.

For recreational activities there is always skiing in the Cascade Mountains.

General Rankings and Evaluative Comments

- Eugene was ranked #66 out of 300 cities by *Money's* 1997 "Survey of the Best Places to Live." Criteria used: health services, crime, economy, housing, education, transportation, weather, leisure and the arts. The city was ranked #118 in 1996 and #66 in 1995. *Money, July 1997; Money, September 1996; Money, September 1995*

- *Ladies Home Journal* ranked America's 200 largest cities based on the qualities women care about most. Eugene ranked 109 out of 200. Criteria: low crime rate, good public schools, well-paying jobs, quality health and child care, the presence of women in government, proportion of women-owned businesses, size of the wage gap with men, local economy, divorce rates, the ratio of single men to single women, whether there are laws that require at least the same number of public toilets for women as men, and the probability of good hair days. *Ladies Home Journal, November 1997*

- Eugene was ranked #28 out of 219 cities in terms of children's health, safety, and economic well-being. Criteria: total population, percent population change, birth rate, child immunization rate, infant mortality rate, percent low birth weight infants, percent of births to teens, physician-to-population ratio, student-to-teacher ratio, dropout rate, unemployment rate, median family income, percent of children in poverty, violent and property crime rates, number of juvenile arrests for violent crimes as a percent of the total crime index, number of days with pollution standard index (PSI) over 100, pounds toxic releases per 1,000 people and number of superfund sites. *Zero Population Growth, Children's Environmental Index 1997*

- Eugene was chosen as one of "America's 10 Best Bike Towns". Rank: 3 out of 10.

  "The town has nearly 100 miles of bike routes; bike racks on all city buses; four bike bridges across the Willamette; and a respected city bike coordinator.

  Eugene also has nearly 20 bike shops (10 of them first-class); the Center for Appropriate Transport, a combination workshop, think tank and hang-out spot for bike advocacy; and such bike manufacturers as Green Gear and Co-Motion Cycles." *Bicycling, August 1997*

- According to *Working Mother*, "Oregon has taken a number of small steps to improve child care: A new background check on caregivers has been instituted, which includes an FBI check for criminal offenses. The state has also mandated an orientation session for anyone who wishes to open a family child care business. The two-hour briefing offers an overview of what it takes to make a home-based child care business work, and what training and support is available from the community and the state. The idea is to put the brakes on anyone who might enter the profession thinking it's an easy job and then close up shop and leave parents in the lurch—a fairly common scenario. The innovation seems to be working. Our certifier said she has not yet had to go out on a complaint for anyone who has gone through this overview.' says Janis Sabin Elliot of the state's Child Care Division.—Oregon has also stepped up its efforts to insure children's health and safety. For instance, it now has more power to revoke the licenses of child care providers in serious violation of rules.

  Family child care could be improved in this state if a bill pending before the legislature becomes law. Among other things, it would require providers to have training in CPR and first aid, which should be a basic standard for any good child care program." *Working Mother, July/August 1997*

Business Environment

STATE ECONOMY

State Economic Profile

"Oregon is entering its fourth year of high growth....Income growth continues to outpace the U.S., as it has throughout the decade.

...Oregon's semiconductor industry is now large enough that it is being supplemented by a number of supplier firms moving into the state, further bolstering the economy.

Oregon's lumber and timber industry will benefit from its proximity to expanding housing markets in California and Washington, which are less likely to buckle under rising interest rates than markets elsewhere in the U.S.

Enron's takeover of Portland General Electric may benefit the economy due to the substantial rate cuts being promised by the merged utility. Lower energy costs would help preserve Oregon's competitive edge as deregulation lowers utility rates in higher cost regions of the country.

Strong economies in Washington and California may slow migration into Oregon, stifling demand for new housing. This would cause the construction industry to constrict, and house price appreciation to decelerate from current high rates. A rising dollar/yen ratio also poses a risk to export demand for Oregon's timber products.

Oregon's outlook remains good. The semiconductor industry appears to have weathered recent declines in chip prices, and all plants under construction appear headed for completion. The long-term outlook is for slower expansion, with some uncertainty as to what will replace semiconductors as the main engine of growth. The diversity of Oregon's economy minimizes this risk, however, and Oregon remains top ranked for future growth." *National Association of Realtors, Economic Profiles: The Fifty States, July 1997*

IMPORTS/EXPORTS

Total Export Sales

Area	1993 ($000)	1994 ($000)	1995 ($000)	1996 ($000)	% Chg. 1993-96	% Chg. 1995-96
MSA[1]	157,946	173,094	190,328	168,902	6.9	-11.3
U.S.	464,858,354	512,415,609	583,030,524	622,827,063	34.0	6.8

Note: (1) Metropolitan Statistical Area - see Appendix A for areas included
Source: U.S. Department of Commerce, International Trade Association, Metropolitan Area Exports: An Export Performance Report on Over 250 U.S. Cities, October 1997

Imports/Exports by Port

Type	Cargo Value			Share of U.S. Total	
	1995 (US$mil.)	1996 (US$mil.)	% Change 1995-1996	1995 (%)	1996 (%)
Imports	0	0	0	0	0
Exports	0	0	0	0	0

Source: Global Trade Information Services, WaterBorne Trade Atlas 1997

CITY FINANCES

City Government Finances

Component	FY92 ($000)	FY92 (per capita $)
Revenue	298,657	2,548.16
Expenditure	294,926	2,516.33
Debt Outstanding	218,482	1,864.10
Cash & Securities	75,606	645.07

Source: U.S. Bureau of the Census, City Government Finances: 1991-92

City Government Revenue by Source

Source	FY92 ($000)	FY92 (per capita $)	FY92 (%)
From Federal Government	5,929	50.59	2.0
From State Governments	10,105	86.22	3.4
From Local Governments	3,867	32.99	1.3
Property Taxes	34,661	295.73	11.6
General Sales Taxes	0	0.00	0.0
Selective Sales Taxes	2,556	21.81	0.9
Income Taxes	0	0.00	0.0
Current Charges	25,988	221.73	8.7
Utility/Liquor Store	187,910	1,603.26	62.9
Employee Retirement[1]	0	0.00	0.0
Other	27,641	235.83	9.3

Note: (1) Excludes "city contributions," classified as "nonrevenue," intragovernmental transfers.
Source: U.S. Bureau of the Census, City Government Finances: 1991-92

City Government Expenditures by Function

Function	FY92 ($000)	FY92 (per capita $)	FY92 (%)
Educational Services	3,519	30.02	1.2
Employee Retirement[1]	0	0.00	0.0
Environment/Housing	27,709	236.41	9.4
Government Administration	14,564	124.26	4.9
Interest on General Debt	1,741	14.85	0.6
Public Safety	26,408	225.31	9.0
Social Services	0	0.00	0.0
Transportation	22,036	188.01	7.5
Utility/Liquor Store	188,544	1,608.67	63.9
Other	10,405	88.78	3.5

Note: (1) Payments to beneficiaries including withdrawal of contributions.
Source: U.S. Bureau of the Census, City Government Finances: 1991-92

Municipal Bond Ratings

Area	Moody's	S & P
Eugene	Aa2	n/a

Note: n/a not available; n/r not rated
Source: Moody's Bond Record, 2/98; Statistical Abstract of the U.S., 1997; Governing Magazine, 9/97, 3/98

POPULATION

Population Growth

Area	1980	1990	% Chg. 1980-90	July 1996 Estimate	% Chg. 1990-96
City	105,624	112,669	6.7	123,718	9.8
MSA[1]	275,226	282,912	2.8	306,862	8.5
U.S.	226,545,805	248,765,170	9.8	265,179,411	6.6

Note: (1) Metropolitan Statistical Area - see Appendix A for areas included
Source: 1980/1990 Census of Housing and Population, Summary Tape File 3C; Census Bureau Population Estimates

Population Characteristics

| Race | City | | | | % Chg. 1980-90 | MSA[1] | |
| | 1980 | | 1990 | | | 1990 | |
	Population	%	Population	%		Population	%
White	100,384	95.0	105,137	93.3	4.7	269,668	95.3
Black	927	0.9	1,360	1.2	46.7	2,069	0.7
Amer Indian/Esk/Aleut	977	0.9	1,012	0.9	3.6	3,180	1.1
Asian/Pacific Islander	2,542	2.4	3,935	3.5	54.8	5,552	2.0
Other	794	0.8	1,225	1.1	54.3	2,443	0.9
Hispanic Origin[2]	2,117	2.0	3,214	2.9	51.8	7,010	2.5

Note: (1) Metropolitan Statistical Area - see Appendix A for areas included;
(2) people of Hispanic origin can be of any race
Source: 1980/1990 Census of Housing and Population, Summary Tape File 3C

Ancestry

Area	German	Irish	English	Italian	U.S.	French	Polish	Dutch
City	30.3	16.7	21.5	3.6	3.4	5.6	2.3	3.8
MSA[1]	31.0	17.7	21.4	2.9	4.5	6.0	2.1	4.3
U.S.	23.3	15.6	13.1	5.9	5.3	4.2	3.8	2.5

Note: Figures are percentages and include persons that reported multiple ancestry (eg. if a person reported being Irish and Italian, they were included in both columns); (1) Metropolitan Statistical Area - see Appendix A for areas included
Source: 1990 Census of Population and Housing, Summary Tape File 3C

Age

| Area | Median Age (Years) | Age Distribution (%) | | | | | | |
		Under 5	Under 18	18-24	25-44	45-64	65+	80+
City	32.2	5.9	21.1	16.7	34.1	15.4	12.7	3.4
MSA[1]	33.9	6.6	24.4	11.7	32.7	18.2	13.1	2.8
U.S.	32.9	7.3	25.6	10.5	32.6	18.7	12.5	2.8

Note: (1) Metropolitan Statistical Area - see Appendix A for areas included
Source: 1990 Census of Population and Housing, Summary Tape File 3C

Male/Female Ratio

Area	Number of males per 100 females (all ages)	Number of males per 100 females (18 years old+)
City	92.5	89.7
MSA[1]	95.1	92.0
U.S.	95.0	91.9

Note: (1) Metropolitan Statistical Area - see Appendix A for areas included
Source: 1990 Census of Population, General Population Characteristics

INCOME

Per Capita/Median/Average Income

Area	Per Capita ($)	Median Household ($)	Average Household ($)
City	13,886	25,369	33,056
MSA[1]	12,570	25,268	31,613
U.S.	14,420	30,056	38,453

Note: all figures are for 1989; (1) Metropolitan Statistical Area - see Appendix A for areas included
Source: 1990 Census of Population and Housing, Summary Tape File 3C

Household Income Distribution by Race

Income ($)	City (%)					U.S. (%)				
	Total	White	Black	Other	Hisp.[1]	Total	White	Black	Other	Hisp.[1]
Less than 5,000	8.3	7.3	16.5	27.6	17.0	6.2	4.8	15.2	8.6	8.8
5,000 - 9,999	12.3	12.2	20.3	13.7	12.2	9.3	8.6	14.2	9.9	11.1
10,000 - 14,999	10.2	10.3	14.0	7.8	10.4	8.8	8.5	11.0	9.8	11.0
15,000 - 24,999	18.4	18.6	15.7	15.1	13.4	17.5	17.3	18.9	18.5	20.5
25,000 - 34,999	15.5	15.7	13.8	12.1	16.9	15.8	16.1	14.2	15.4	16.4
35,000 - 49,999	16.3	16.5	11.8	11.7	15.4	17.9	18.6	13.3	16.1	16.0
50,000 - 74,999	12.3	12.5	3.9	9.4	10.2	15.0	15.8	9.3	13.4	11.1
75,000 - 99,999	3.3	3.4	4.1	1.4	3.7	5.1	5.5	2.6	4.7	3.1
100,000+	3.3	3.4	0.0	1.1	0.8	4.4	4.8	1.3	3.7	1.9

Note: all figures are for 1989; (1) people of Hispanic origin can be of any race
Source: 1990 Census of Population and Housing, Summary Tape File 3C

Effective Buying Income

Area	Per Capita ($)	Median Household ($)	Average Household ($)
City	14,879	27,854	36,082
MSA[1]	13,992	28,759	35,559
U.S.	15,444	33,201	41,849

Note: data as of 1/1/97; (1) Metropolitan Statistical Area - see Appendix A for areas included
Source: Standard Rate & Data Service, Newspaper Advertising Source, 2/98

Effective Household Buying Income Distribution

Area	% of Households Earning						
	$10,000 -$19,999	$20,000 -$34,999	$35,000 -$49,999	$50,000 -$74,999	$75,000 -$99,000	$100,000 -$124,999	$125,000 and up
City	19.6	24.0	17.2	14.9	4.1	1.3	1.9
MSA[1]	19.4	27.0	18.2	15.0	3.7	1.1	1.5
U.S.	16.5	23.4	18.3	18.2	6.4	2.1	2.4

Note: data as of 1/1/97; (1) Metropolitan Statistical Area - see Appendix A for areas included
Source: Standard Rate & Data Service, Newspaper Advertising Source, 2/98

Poverty Rates by Race and Age

Area	Total (%)	By Race (%)				By Age (%)		
		White	Black	Other	Hisp.[2]	Under 5 years old	Under 18 years old	65 years and over
City	17.0	15.9	30.5	34.2	26.9	18.3	14.3	8.1
MSA[1]	14.5	13.8	28.4	29.5	24.0	21.4	16.1	9.0
U.S.	13.1	9.8	29.5	23.1	25.3	20.1	18.3	12.8

Note: figures show the percent of people living below the poverty line in 1989. The average poverty threshold was $12,674 for a family of four in 1989; (1) Metropolitan Statistical Area - see Appendix A for areas included; (2) people of Hispanic origin can be of any race
Source: 1990 Census of Population and Housing, Summary Tape File 3C

EMPLOYMENT

Labor Force and Employment

Area	Civilian Labor Force			Workers Employed		
	Dec. '95	Dec. '96	% Chg.	Dec. '95	Dec. '96	% Chg.
City	66,722	68,982	3.4	63,137	65,837	4.3
MSA[1]	159,349	164,589	3.3	149,828	156,237	4.3
U.S.	134,583,000	136,742,000	1.6	127,903,000	130,785,000	2.3

Note: Data is not seasonally adjusted and covers workers 16 years of age and older;
(1) Metropolitan Statistical Area - see Appendix A for areas included
Source: Bureau of Labor Statistics, http://stats.bls.gov

Unemployment Rate

Area	1997											
	Jan.	Feb.	Mar.	Apr.	May	Jun.	Jul.	Aug.	Sep.	Oct.	Nov.	Dec.
City	5.7	5.9	5.8	5.0	4.0	4.4	4.3	4.3	4.2	4.1	4.5	4.6
MSA[1]	6.3	6.6	6.4	5.6	4.4	4.9	4.8	4.8	4.7	4.6	5.0	5.1
U.S.	5.9	5.7	5.5	4.8	4.7	5.2	5.0	4.8	4.7	4.4	4.3	4.4

Note: Data is not seasonally adjusted and covers workers 16 years of age and older; All figures are percentages; (1) Metropolitan Statistical Area - see Appendix A for areas included
Source: Bureau of Labor Statistics, http://stats.bls.gov

Employment by Industry

Sector	MSA[1]		U.S.
	Number of Employees	Percent of Total	Percent of Total
Services	37,300	26.6	29.0
Retail Trade	29,900	21.3	18.5
Government	25,800	18.4	16.1
Manufacturing	21,000	15.0	15.0
Finance/Insurance/Real Estate	7,400	5.3	5.7
Wholesale Trade	6,400	4.6	5.4
Transportation/Public Utilities	4,700	3.4	5.3
Construction	7,400	5.3	4.5
Mining	200	0.1	0.5

Note: Figures cover non-farm employment as of 12/97 and are not seasonally adjusted;
(1) Metropolitan Statistical Area - see Appendix A for areas included
Source: Bureau of Labor Statistics, http://stats.bls.gov

Employment by Occupation

Occupation Category	City (%)	MSA[1] (%)	U.S. (%)
White Collar	66.0	55.6	58.1
Executive/Admin./Management	12.9	11.1	12.3
Professional	20.4	14.2	14.1
Technical & Related Support	3.4	3.0	3.7
Sales	14.0	12.4	11.8
Administrative Support/Clerical	15.3	14.9	16.3
Blue Collar	18.6	26.6	26.2
Precision Production/Craft/Repair	7.4	10.4	11.3
Machine Operators/Assem./Insp.	4.7	6.4	6.8
Transportation/Material Movers	2.9	5.0	4.1
Cleaners/Helpers/Laborers	3.6	4.7	3.9
Services	13.8	14.2	13.2
Farming/Forestry/Fishing	1.6	3.6	2.5

Note: figures cover employed persons 16 years old and over;
(1) Metropolitan Statistical Area - see Appendix A for areas included
Source: 1990 Census of Population and Housing, Summary Tape File 3C

Occupational Employment Projections: 1996 - 2005

Occupations Expected to have the Largest Job Growth (ranked by numerical growth)	Fast-Growing Occupations[1] (ranked by percent growth)
1. Salespersons, retail	1. Semiconductor processors
2. General office clerks	2. Social welfare service aids
3. Food preparation workers	3. Home health aides
4. Cashiers	4. Social service tech.
5. Waiters & waitresses	5. Computer engineers
6. Truck drivers, heavy & tractor trailer	6. Credit analysts
7. Registered nurses	7. Screen printing machine setters
8. Truck drivers, light	8. Other social scientists
9. Janitors/cleaners/maids, ex. priv. hshld.	9. Architects
10. All other profess., paraprofess., tech.	10. Mechanical engineering techs.

Projections cover Lane County.
Note: (1) Excludes occupations with employment in the lowest 20%
Source: Oregon Employment Department, Workforce Analysis Section, Oregon Micro-OIS, 1996-2005

Average Wages

Occupation	Wage	Occupation	Wage
Professional/Technical/Clerical	$/Week	**Health/Protective Services**	$/Week
Accountants III	-	Corrections Officers	-
Attorneys III	-	Firefighters	-
Budget Analysts III	-	Nurses, Licensed Practical II	-
Buyers/Contracting Specialists II	-	Nurses, Registered II	-
Clerks, Accounting III	406	Nursing Assistants II	-
Clerks, General III	351	Police Officers I	-
Computer Operators II	-	**Hourly Workers**	$/Hour
Computer Programmers II	-	Forklift Operators	10.91
Drafters II	-	General Maintenance Workers	9.93
Engineering Technicians III	-	Guards I	5.26
Engineering Technicians, Civil III	-	Janitors	6.76
Engineers III	-	Maintenance Electricians	14.93
Key Entry Operators I	250	Maintenance Electronics Techs II	15.23
Personnel Assistants III	-	Maintenance Machinists	13.93
Personnel Specialists III	-	Maintenance Mechanics, Machinery	13.36
Secretaries III	473	Material Handling Laborers	7.58
Switchboard Operator-Receptionist	327	Motor Vehicle Mechanics	12.91
Systems Analysts II	877	Shipping/Receiving Clerks	10.58
Systems Analysts Supervisor/Mgr II	-	Tool and Die Makers	-
Tax Collectors II	-	Truckdrivers, Tractor Trailer	10.69
Word Processors II	-	Warehouse Specialists	9.54

Note: Wage data includes full-time workers only for 3/95 and cover the Metropolitan Statistical Area (see Appendix A for areas included). Dashes indicate that data was not available.
Source: Bureau of Labor Statistics, Occupational Compensation Survey

TAXES

Major State and Local Tax Rates

State Corp. Income (%)	State Personal Income (%)	Residential Property (effective rate per $100)	Sales & Use		State Gasoline (cents/ gallon)	State Cigarette (cents/ 20-pack)
			State (%)	Local (%)		
6.6[a]	5.0 - 9.0	n/a	None	None	24[b]	68

Note: Personal/corporate income tax rates as of 1/97. Sales, gasoline and cigarette tax rates as of 1/98; (a) Minimum tax $10; (b) Does not include a 1 - 2 cents local option tax
Source: Federation of Tax Administrators, www.taxadmin.org; Washington D.C. Department of Finance and Revenue, Tax Rates and Tax Burdens in the District of Columbia: A Nationwide Comparison, June 1997; Chamber of Commerce

Total Taxes Per Capita and as a Percent of Income

Area	Per Capita Income ($)	Per Capita Taxes ($)			Taxes as Pct. of Income (%)		
		Total	Federal	State/Local	Total	Federal	State/Local
Oregon	24,918	9,062	5,799	3,263	36.4	23.3	13.1
U.S.	26,187	9,205	6,127	3,078	35.2	23.4	11.8

Note: Figures are for 1997
Source: Tax Foundation, Web Site, www.taxfoundation.org

COMMERCIAL REAL ESTATE

Data not available at time of publication.

COMMERCIAL UTILITIES

Typical Monthly Electric Bills

Area	Commercial Service ($/month)		Industrial Service ($/month)	
	12 kW demand 1,500 kWh	100 kW demand 30,000 kWh	1,000 kW demand 400,000 kWh	20,000 kW demand 10,000,000 kWh
City	n/a	n/a	n/a	n/a
U.S.	162	2,360	25,590	545,677

Note: Based on rates in effect July 1, 1997; n/a not available
Source: Edison Electric Institute, Typical Residential, Commercial and Industrial Bills, Summer 1997

TRANSPORTATION

Transportation Statistics

Avg. travel time to work (min.)	15.7
Interstate highways	I-5
Bus lines	
In-city	Lane County TD
Inter-city	1
Passenger air service	
Airport	Mahlon Sweet Field
Airlines	4
Aircraft departures	8,474 (1995)
Enplaned passengers	301,741 (1995)
Rail service	Amtrak
Motor freight carriers	29
Major waterways/ports	None

Source: OAG, Business Travel Planner, Summer 1997; Editor & Publisher Market Guide, 1998; FAA Airport Activity Statistics, 1996; Amtrak National Time Table, Northeast Timetable, Fall/Winter 1997-98; 1990 Census of Population and Housing, STF 3C; Chamber of Commerce/Economic Development 1997; Jane's Urban Transport Systems 1997-98; Transit Fact Book 1997

Means of Transportation to Work

Area	Car/Truck/Van		Public Transportation			Bicycle	Walked	Other Means	Worked at Home
	Drove Alone	Car-pooled	Bus	Subway	Railroad				
City	69.0	9.9	3.3	0.0	0.0	5.8	6.9	1.0	4.0
MSA[1]	73.4	11.4	2.3	0.0	0.0	2.9	4.5	1.1	4.4
U.S.	73.2	13.4	3.0	1.5	0.5	0.4	3.9	1.2	3.0

Note: figures shown are percentages and only include workers 16 years old and over;
(1) Metropolitan Statistical Area - see Appendix A for areas included
Source: 1990 Census of Population and Housing, Summary Tape File 3C

BUSINESSES

Major Business Headquarters

Company Name	1997 Rankings	
	Fortune 500	Forbes 500

No companies listed.

Note: Companies listed are located in the city; Dashes indicate no ranking
Fortune 500: companies that produce a 10-K are ranked 1 - 500 based on 1996 revenue
Forbes 500: private companies are ranked 1 - 500 based on 1996 revenue
Source: Forbes 12/1/97; Fortune 4/28/97

Small Business Opportunity

According to *Forbes*, Eugene is home to one of America's 200 best small companies: Percon. Criteria: companies must be publicly traded, U.S.-based corporations with latest 12-month sales of between $5 and $350 million. Earnings must be at least $1 million for the 12-month period. Limited partnerships, REITs and closed-end mutual funds were not considered. Banks, S&Ls and electric utilities were not included. *Forbes, November 3, 1997*

HOTELS & MOTELS

Hotels/Motels

Area	Hotels/ Motels	Rooms	Luxury-Level Hotels/Motels		Average Minimum Rates ($)		
			♦♦♦♦	♦♦♦♦♦	♦♦	♦♦♦	♦♦♦♦
City	10	1,329	0	0	n/a	n/a	n/a

Note: n/a not available; Classifications range from one diamond (budget properties with basic amenities) to five diamond (luxury properties with the finest service, rooms and facilities).
Source: OAG, Business Travel Planner, Summer 1997

CONVENTION CENTERS

Major Convention Centers

Center Name	Meeting Rooms	Exhibit Space (sf)
Lane County Convention Center & Fairgrounds	8	64,800

Source: Trade Shows Worldwide 1997

Living Environment

COST OF LIVING

Cost of Living Index

Composite Index	Housing	Utilities	Groceries	Health Care	Trans-portation	Misc. Goods/ Services
105.5	122.6	73.6	94.7	120.0	105.7	101.2

Note: U.S. = 100
Source: ACCRA, Cost of Living Index, 3rd Quarter 1997

HOUSING

Median Home Prices and Housing Affordability

Area	Median Price[2] 3rd Qtr. 1997 ($)	HOI[3] 3rd Qtr. 1997	Afford-ability Rank[4]
MSA[1]	n/a	n/a	n/a
U.S.	127,000	63.7	–

Note: (1) Metropolitan Statistical Area - see Appendix A for areas included; (2) U.S. figures calculated from the sales of 625,000 new and existing homes in 195 markets; (3) Housing Opportunity Index - percent of homes sold that were within the reach of the median income household at the prevailing mortgage interest rate; (4) Rank is from 1-195 with 1 being most affordable; n/a not available
Source: National Association of Home Builders, Housing Opportunity Index, 3rd Quarter 1997

Average New Home Price

Area	Price ($)
City	172,267
U.S.	135,710

Note: Figures are based on a new home with 1,800 sq. ft. of living area on an 8,000 sq. ft. lot.
Source: ACCRA, Cost of Living Index, 3rd Quarter 1997

Average Apartment Rent

Area	Rent ($/mth)
City	626
U.S.	569

Note: Figures are based on an unfurnished two bedroom, 1-1/2 or 2 bath apartment, approximately 950 sq. ft. in size, excluding all utilities except water
Source: ACCRA, Cost of Living Index, 3rd Quarter 1997

RESIDENTIAL UTILITIES

Average Residential Utility Costs

Area	All Electric ($/mth)	Part Electric ($/mth)	Other Energy ($/mth)	Phone ($/mth)
City	71.50	–	–	19.18
U.S.	109.40	55.25	43.64	19.48

Source: ACCRA, Cost of Living Index, 3rd Quarter 1997

HEALTH CARE

Average Health Care Costs

Area	Hospital ($/day)	Doctor ($/visit)	Dentist ($/visit)
City	387.50	54.05	89.40
U.S.	392.91	48.76	60.84

Note: Hospital - based on a semi-private room. Doctor - based on a general practitioner's routine exam of an established patient. Dentist - based on adult teeth cleaning and periodic oral exam.
Source: ACCRA, Cost of Living Index, 3rd Quarter 1997

Distribution of Office-Based Physicians

Area	Family/Gen. Practitioners	Specialists		
		Medical	Surgical	Other
MSA[1]	117	157	135	134

Note: Data as of 12/31/96; (1) Metropolitan Statistical Area - see Appendix A for areas included
Source: American Medical Assn., Physician Characteristics & Distribution in the U.S., 1997-1998

Hospitals

Eugene has 1 general medical and surgical hospital, 1 alcoholism and 1 other chemical dependency. *AHA Guide to the Healthcare Field 1997-98*

EDUCATION

Public School District Statistics

District Name	Num. Sch.	Enroll.	Classroom Teachers[1]	Pupils per Teacher	Minority Pupils (%)	Current Exp.[2] ($/pupil)
Bethel Sch Dist 052	8	4,471	211	21.2	n/a	n/a
Crow-Applegate-Lorane SD 66	4	453	28	16.2	n/a	n/a
Eugene Sch Dist 04j	45	18,371	833	22.1	n/a	n/a

Note: Data covers the 1995-1996 school year unless otherwise noted; (1) Excludes teachers reported as working in school district offices rather than in schools; (2) Based on 1993-94 enrollment collected by the Census Bureau, not the enrollment figure shown in column 3; SD = School District; ISD = Independent School District; n/a not available
Source: National Center for Education Statistics, Common Core of Data Survey; Bureau of the Census

Educational Quality

School District	Education Quotient[1]	Graduate Outcome[2]	Community Index[3]	Resource Index[4]
Eugene	117.0	129.0	94.0	129.0

Note: Nearly 1,000 secondary school districts were rated in terms of educational quality. The scores range from a low of 50 to a high of 150; (1) Average of the Graduate Outcome, Community and Resource indexes; (2) Based on graduation rates and college board scores (SAT/ACT); (3) Based on the surrounding community's average level of education and the area's average income level; (4) Based on teacher salaries, per-pupil expenditures and student-teacher ratios.
Source: Expansion Management, Ratings Issue 1997

Educational Attainment by Race

Area	High School Graduate (%)					Bachelor's Degree (%)				
	Total	White	Black	Other	Hisp.[2]	Total	White	Black	Other	Hisp.[2]
City	88.6	88.7	90.0	84.9	80.1	34.9	34.7	42.1	38.6	25.8
MSA[1]	83.0	83.2	86.4	77.7	75.1	22.2	22.0	32.3	25.3	16.4
U.S.	75.2	77.9	63.1	60.4	49.8	20.3	21.5	11.4	19.4	9.2

Note: figures shown cover persons 25 years old and over; (1) Metropolitan Statistical Area - see Appendix A for areas included; (2) people of Hispanic origin can be of any race
Source: 1990 Census of Population and Housing, Summary Tape File 3C

School Enrollment by Type

Area	Preprimary				Elementary/High School			
	Public		Private		Public		Private	
	Enrollment	%	Enrollment	%	Enrollment	%	Enrollment	%
City	1,195	52.5	1,083	47.5	14,203	92.7	1,121	7.3
MSA[1]	3,211	58.8	2,246	41.2	42,499	94.5	2,469	5.5
U.S.	2,679,029	59.5	1,824,256	40.5	38,379,689	90.2	4,187,099	9.8

Note: figures shown cover persons 3 years old and over;
(1) Metropolitan Statistical Area - see Appendix A for areas included
Source: 1990 Census of Population and Housing, Summary Tape File 3C

School Enrollment by Race

Area	Preprimary (%)				Elementary/High School (%)			
	White	Black	Other	Hisp.[1]	White	Black	Other	Hisp.[1]
City	95.4	0.7	3.9	3.5	92.3	1.6	6.2	3.8
MSA[2]	96.3	0.6	3.2	3.1	94.4	1.0	4.6	3.7
U.S.	80.4	12.5	7.1	7.8	74.1	15.6	10.3	12.5

Note: figures shown cover persons 3 years old and over; (1) people of Hispanic origin can be of any race; (2) Metropolitan Statistical Area - see Appendix A for areas included
Source: 1990 Census of Population and Housing, Summary Tape File 3C

SAT/ACT Scores

Area/District	1997 SAT				1997 ACT	
	Percent of Graduates Tested (%)	Average Math Score	Average Verbal Score	Average Combined Score	Percent of Graduates Tested (%)	Average Composite Score
Eugene SD4J	58	566	551	1,117	11	23.7
State	50	524	525	1,049	12	22.3
U.S.	42	511	505	1,016	36	21.0

Note: Math and verbal SAT scores are out of a possible 800; ACT scores are out of a possible 36
Caution: Comparing or ranking states/cities on the basis of SAT/ACT scores alone is invalid and strongly discouraged by the The College Board and The American College Testing Program as students who take the tests are self-selected and do not represent the entire student population.
Source: Eugene School District 4J, Education Center, Instruction Department, 1997; American College Testing Program, 1997; College Board, 1997

Classroom Teacher Salaries in Public Schools

District	B.A. Degree		M.A. Degree		Ph.D. Degree	
	Min. ($)	Max ($)	Min. ($)	Max. ($)	Min. ($)	Max. ($)
Eugene	25,759	37,044	28,726	44,424	32,034	49,540
Average[1]	26,120	39,270	28,175	44,667	31,643	49,825

Note: Salaries are for 1996-1997; (1) Based on all school districts covered
Source: American Federation of Teachers (unpublished data)

Higher Education

Two-Year Colleges		Four-Year Colleges		Medical Schools	Law Schools	Voc/ Tech
Public	Private	Public	Private			
1	0	1	2	0	1	11

Source: College Blue Book, Occupational Education 1997; Medical School Admission Requirements, 1998-99; Peterson's Guide to Two-Year Colleges, 1997; Peterson's Guide to Four-Year Colleges, 1997; Barron's Guide to Law Schools 1997

MAJOR EMPLOYERS

Major Employers

Chambers Communications Corp.
Seneca Sawmill Co.
Western Electronics Corp.
Far West Steel Corp.
Troutman Investment

Eugene Water & Electric Board
Guard Publishing
Lane Transit District (bus line)
States Industries (lumber)
Whittier Wood Products

Note: companies listed are located in the city
Source: Dun's Business Rankings 1997; Ward's Business Directory, 1997

PUBLIC SAFETY

Crime Rate

Area	All Crimes	Violent Crimes				Property Crimes		
		Murder	Forcible Rape	Robbery	Aggrav. Assault	Burglary	Larceny -Theft	Motor Vehicle Theft
City	9,932.6	1.6	40.8	221.0	339.2	1,560.7	7,147.1	622.2
Suburbs[1]	4,916.3	4.8	39.9	74.6	169.3	1,064.5	3,174.4	388.7
MSA[2]	6,898.0	3.5	40.3	132.4	236.5	1,260.5	4,743.9	481.0
U.S.	5,078.9	7.4	36.1	202.4	388.2	943.0	2,975.9	525.9

Note: Crime rate is the number of crimes per 100,000 pop.; (1) defined as all areas within the MSA but located outside the central city; (2) Metropolitan Statistical Area - see Appendix A for areas incl.
Source: FBI Uniform Crime Reports 1996

RECREATION

Culture and Recreation

Museums	Symphony Orchestras	Opera Companies	Dance Companies	Professional Theatres	Zoos	Pro Sports Teams
5	1	1	1	2	0	0

Source: International Directory of the Performing Arts, 1996; Official Museum Directory, 1998; Chamber of Commerce/Economic Development 1997

Library System

The Eugene Public Library has no branches, holdings of 275,779 volumes and a budget of $3,287,202 (1995-1996). Note: n/a means not available. *American Library Directory, 1997-1998*

MEDIA

Newspapers

Name	Type	Freq.	Distribution	Circulation
Oregon Daily Emerald	n/a	5x/wk	Campus & community	10,000
The Register-Guard	General	7x/wk	Local	75,140

Note: Includes newspapers with circulations of 500 or more located in the city; n/a not available
Source: Burrelle's Media Directory, 1998 Edition

AM Radio Stations

Call Letters	Freq. (kHz)	Target Audience	Station Format	Music Format
KUGN	590	General	N/T	n/a
KORE	1050	Religious	M/N/T	Christian
KPNW	1120	General	M/N/S/T	n/a
KDUK	1280	General	M	Contemporary Top 40
KNRQ	1320	General	M	Alternative
KNND	1400	General	M/N/S	Country
KKXO	1450	General	M	Adult Standards

Note: Stations included broadcast in the Eugene metro area; n/a not available
Station Format: E = Educational; M = Music; N = News; S = Sports; T = Talk
Source: Burrelle's Media Directory, 1998 Edition

FM Radio Stations

Call Letters	Freq. (mHz)	Target Audience	Station Format	Music Format
KQFE	88.9	Religious	E/M/N/T	Christian
KLCC	89.7	n/a	M/N	n/a
KLCO	90.5	General	M/N	n/a
KWAX	91.1	n/a	M	Classical
KRVM	91.9	General	M	Alternative
KAVE	92.1	n/a	n/a	n/a
KKNU	93.1	n/a	M	Country
KMGE	94.5	General	M	Adult Contemporary
KNRQ	95.3	General	M	Alternative
KZEL	96.1	General	M	Classic Rock
KUGN	97.9	General	M/N/S	Country
KODZ	99.1	General	M	Oldies
KEHK	102.3	General	M	Adult Contemporary/Alternative/Classic Rock/Jazz/Oldies
KDUK	104.7	n/a	M	Contemporary Top 40

Note: Stations included broadcast in the Eugene metro area; n/a not available
Station Format: E = Educational; M = Music; N = News; S = Sports; T = Talk
Source: Burrelle's Media Directory, 1998 Edition

Television Stations

Name	Ch.	Affiliation	Type	Owner
KEZI	9	ABC	Commercial	KEZI Inc.
KVAL	13	CBS	Commercial	Retlaw Broadcasting Co.
KMTR	16	NBC	Commercial	Wicks Broadcasting Group
KMTZ	23	NBC	Commercial	KMTR Inc.
KLSR	25	Fox	Commercial	California Oregon Broadcasting Inc.
KEVU	34	UPN	Commercial	California/Oregon Broadcasting Inc.
KMTX	46	NBC	Commercial	KMTR-TV

Note: Stations included broadcast in the Eugene metro area
Source: Burrelle's Media Directory, 1998 Edition

CLIMATE

Average and Extreme Temperatures

Temperature	Jan	Feb	Mar	Apr	May	Jun	Jul	Aug	Sep	Oct	Nov	Dec	Ann
Extreme High (°F)	67	69	77	86	93	102	105	108	103	94	76	68	108
Average High (°F)	46	51	55	61	67	74	82	82	76	64	53	47	63
Average Temp. (°F)	40	44	46	50	55	61	67	67	62	53	46	41	53
Average Low (°F)	33	35	37	39	43	48	51	51	48	42	38	35	42
Extreme Low (°F)	-4	-3	20	27	28	32	39	38	32	19	12	-12	-12

Note: Figures cover the years 1948-1992
Source: National Climatic Data Center, International Station Meteorological Climate Summary, 3/95

Average Precipitation/Snowfall/Humidity

Precip./Humidity	Jan	Feb	Mar	Apr	May	Jun	Jul	Aug	Sep	Oct	Nov	Dec	Ann
Avg. Precip. (in.)	7.8	5.6	5.3	3.0	2.2	1.4	0.4	0.8	1.4	3.6	7.6	8.2	47.3
Avg. Snowfall (in.)	4	1	1	Tr	Tr	0	0	0	0	Tr	Tr	1	7
Avg. Rel. Hum. 7am (%)	91	92	91	88	84	81	78	82	88	93	93	92	88
Avg. Rel. Hum. 4pm (%)	79	73	64	57	54	49	38	39	44	61	79	84	60

Note: Figures cover the years 1948-1992; Tr = Trace amounts (<0.05 in. of rain; <0.5 in. of snow)
Source: National Climatic Data Center, International Station Meteorological Climate Summary, 3/95

Weather Conditions

Temperature			Daytime Sky			Precipitation		
32°F & below	45°F & below	90°F & above	Clear	Partly cloudy	Cloudy	0.01 inch or more precip.	0.1 inch or more snow/ice	Thunder-storms
54	233	15	75	115	175	136	4	3

Note: Figures are average number of days per year and covers the years 1948-1992
Source: National Climatic Data Center, International Station Meteorological Climate Summary, 3/95

AIR & WATER QUALITY

Maximum Pollutant Concentrations

	Particulate Matter (ug/m³)	Carbon Monoxide (ppm)	Sulfur Dioxide (ppm)	Nitrogen Dioxide (ppm)	Ozone (ppm)	Lead (ug/m³)
MSA[1] Level	78	6	n/a	n/a	0.11	0.02
NAAQS[2]	150	9	0.140	0.053	0.12	1.50
Met NAAQS?	Yes	Yes	n/a	n/a	Yes	Yes

Note: (1) Metropolitan Statistical Area - see Appendix A for areas included; (2) National Ambient Air Quality Standards; ppm = parts per million; ug/m³ = micrograms per cubic meter; n/a not available
Source: EPA, National Air Quality and Emissions Trends Report, 1996

Pollutant Standards Index

Data not available. *EPA, National Air Quality and Emissions Trends Report, 1996*

Drinking Water

Water System Name	Pop. Served	Primary Water Source Type	Number of Violations in Fiscal Year 1997	Type of Violation/ Contaminants
Eugene Water & Electric Board	135,000	Surface	None	None

Note: Data as of January 16, 1998
Source: EPA, Office of Ground Water and Drinking Water, Safe Drinking Water Information System

Eugene tap water is neutral, very soft.
Editor & Publisher Market Guide, 1998

Las Vegas, Nevada

Background

Upright citizens can accuse Las Vegas of many vices, but not of hypocrisy. Back in 1931, the city officials of this desert town, located 225 miles northeast of Los Angeles, saw gambling to be a growing popular pastime. To capitalize upon that trend, the city simply legalized it. Gambling combined with spectacular, neon-lit entertainment, lures over 28 million visitors a year to this escapist, fantasy playground.

Before Wayne Newton saw his name in lights or Siegfried and Roy made white lions disappear, Las Vegas was a temporary stopping place for a diverse group of people. In the early 1800's, Las Vegas was a watering place for those on the trail to California. In 1855 the area was settled by Mormons, but they left two years later. Finally, in the late 1800's, the land was used for ranching.

In the beginning of the twentieth century, the seeds of the present Las Vegas, began to sprout. In 1905 the arrival of the Union Pacific Railroad sprinkled businesses, saloons, and gambling houses along its tracks. Then, during the great depression, men working on the nearby Hoover Dam, spent their extra money in the establishments. Finally, gambling was legalized, hydro-electric power from the Hoover Dam lit the city in neon, and hotels began to compete for the brightest stars and the plushest surroundings. Like the dreams of many people who come to the city and hope to get rich quick Las Vegas was an overnight success.

Seniors are coming to settle in Las Vegas at the rate of about 11,000 a year increasing the over-65 population in Clark County (which includes Las Vegas) from about 60,000 in 1987 to nearly 104,000 in 1994. The state of Nevada led the nation in growth among these retirees between 1990 and 1994 and there seems to be no let up in sight. The attraction for seniors includes no state income tax, low property taxes, reasonably priced housing, plenty of entertainment, and a dry climate.

Las Vegas is the nation's fastest growing metropolitan area and is thriving because the gambling industry is booming. Four mega hotels have opened in the past year and about $6 billion in hotel and casino construction is planned for the next three years. Some 3,000 move to Las Vegas each month, most of them in construction and casino work related to gambling. However, the growth has brought the usual urban problems of congested traffic and a rise in crime, including gang violence. *New York Times May 4, 1997*

One of the more serious problems facing Las Vegas because of its remarkable population growth is that the city is draining its water supply and is due to run short of water in 2007. Las Vegas uses 325 gallons daily per person, more than any city in the world. The city has now decided to raise water rates and to also encourage conservation by home owners and businesses with the use of desert landscaping which can reduce water use by as much as 80%. Rather reluctantly, Las Vegas is now imitating Tucson (AZ), the model city of water conservation. *USA Today 11/17/97*

Las Vegas is located near the center of a broad desert valley, which is almost surrounded by mountains ranging from 2,000 to 10,000 feet. The four seasons are well defined. Summers display desert conditions, with maximum temperatures usually in the 100 degree range. The nights are relatively cool due to the closeness of the mountains. For about 2 weeks almost every summer warm, moist air predominates causing higher than average humidity and scattered thunderstorms, occasionally quite severe. Winters, on the whole, are mild and pleasant with daytime temperatures averaging near 60 degrees and clear skies prevailing. Strong winds, associated with major storms, usually reach the valley from the southwest or through the pass from the northwest. Winds over 50 miles per hour are infrequent but, when they do occur, are the most troublesome of the elements, because of the blowing dust and sand associated with them.

General Rankings and Evaluative Comments

■ Las Vegas was ranked #86 out of 300 cities by *Money's* 1997 "Survey of the Best Places to Live." Criteria used: health services, crime, economy, housing, education, transportation, weather, leisure and the arts. The city was ranked #114 in 1996 and #9 in 1995. *Money, July 1997; Money, September 1996; Money, September 1995*

■ *Ladies Home Journal* ranked America's 200 largest cities based on the qualities women care about most. Las Vegas ranked 128 out of 200. Criteria: low crime rate, good public schools, well-paying jobs, quality health and child care, the presence of women in government, proportion of women-owned businesses, size of the wage gap with men, local economy, divorce rates, the ratio of single men to single women, whether there are laws that require at least the same number of public toilets for women as men, and the probability of good hair days. *Ladies Home Journal, November 1997*

■ Las Vegas was ranked #81 out of 219 cities in terms of children's health, safety, and economic well-being. Criteria: total population, percent population change, birth rate, child immunization rate, infant mortality rate, percent low birth weight infants, percent of births to teens, physician-to-population ratio, student-to-teacher ratio, dropout rate, unemployment rate, median family income, percent of children in poverty, violent and property crime rates, number of juvenile arrests for violent crimes as a percent of the total crime index, number of days with pollution standard index (PSI) over 100, pounds toxic releases per 1,000 people and number of superfund sites. *Zero Population Growth, Children's Environmental Index 1997*

■ Sun City Summerlin, located 8 miles northwest of Las Vegas, is among America's best retirement communities. Criteria: communities must have state-of-the-art facilities, newly built homes for sale, and give you the most value for your money in every price range. Communities must also welcome newcomers of all races and religions. *New Choices, July/August 1997*

■ *Yahoo! Internet Life* selected "America's 100 Most Wired Cities & Towns". 50 cities were large and 50 cities were small. Las Vegas ranked 22 out of 50 large cities. Criteria: Internet users per capita, number of networked computers, number of registered domain names, Internet backbone traffic, and the per-capita number of Web sites devoted to each city. *Yahoo! Internet Life, March 1998*

■ Las Vegas was among "The 10 Hotbeds of Entrepreneurial Activity" in 1996 with 1.50 start-ups per 100 people. Rank: 7 out of 200 metro areas. *Inc., The State of Small Business 1997*

■ According to *Working Mother,* "Governor Miller is showing new interest in child care: He is now co-chair of the National Governor's Association's Children's Task Force. He has also urged the legislature to increase child care funding which among other benefits would allow the state to apply for federal child care money. To do that, however, state lawmakers must pledge to put up state matching funds, a move which had not yet been approved by the state legislature as we went to press. Advocates in this state describe the legislature as apathetic on child care issues.

Licensing standards here remain inadequate, but there has been an effort to improve them. The state's child care licensing board has proposed new rules, including one that would require more training for directors and teachers at child care centers.

A statewide summit on child care and economic development looked at how high-quality child care helps a community's economy. The meeting was sponsored by a private child care organization in conjunction with the governor's office. Participants vowed to make child care better by improving licensing standards. These plans are still vague, however." *Working Mother, July/August 1997*

Business Environment

STATE ECONOMY

State Economic Profile

"Nevada's economy could decelerate rapidly or keep its expansion intact, depending on developments in its housing market and gaming industry....

Nevada's gaming industry remains healthy. Convention attendance for the year is up 18%. However, gaming revenue in 1996 in Las Vegas was up just 1.2%, the smallest increase since 1991.

Aside from a sharp retreat from current gaming expansion plans, a softer housing market is Nevada's biggest downside risk. From 1990 to 1996, Nevada issued 188,000 building permits, while gaining more than 384,000 new residents. Based on typical household sizes, there appears to be an excess supply of new units. Reflecting the oversupply, price appreciation in the nation's fastest growing state decelerated during 1996 to less than 3% by year end, according to the FHLMC/FNMA repeat-purchase house price index. Permit activity is 18% below year-ago levels in early 1997. Should building activity accelerate later in 1997, or should in-migration decelerate sharply, the downside risks for Nevada increase substantially.

Population growth in Nevada remains strong. Last year, Nevada's population grew by 4.5%, more strongly than every other state. In-migration to Reno actually increased in 1996, taking the MSA's growth rate to 2.6%, while population growth in Las Vegas decelerated to the still strong pace of 5.1%, primarily due to reduced in-migration. Nevada will continue to grow rapidly, driven by growth in the entertainment and gaming industries, and manufacturing and distribution industries.

Nevada is dependent on the California economy. Many of the state's new residents originate in California. As the California economy strengthens, the flow of new households will diminish; however, California tourists will still contribute to the state's positive outlook. Longer term, the outlook carries much more risk. Though it is diversifying, Nevada's future still depends heavily on gaming. Once U.S. growth declines or gaming's growth peaks, Nevada's economy will suffer accordingly." *National Association of Realtors, Economic Profiles: The Fifty States, July 1997*

IMPORTS/EXPORTS

Total Export Sales

Area	1993 ($000)	1994 ($000)	1995 ($000)	1996 ($000)	% Chg. 1993-96	% Chg. 1995-96
MSA[1]	n/a	n/a	n/a	n/a	n/a	n/a
U.S.	464,858,354	512,415,609	583,030,524	622,827,063	34.0	6.8

Note: (1) Metropolitan Statistical Area - see Appendix A for areas included; n/a not available
Source: U.S. Department of Commerce, International Trade Association, Metropolitan Area Exports: An Export Performance Report on Over 250 U.S. Cities, October 1997

Imports/Exports by Port

Type	Cargo Value			Share of U.S. Total	
	1995 (US$mil.)	1996 (US$mil.)	% Change 1995-1996	1995 (%)	1996 (%)
Imports	0	0	0	0	0
Exports	0	0	0	0	0

Source: Global Trade Information Services, WaterBorne Trade Atlas 1997

CITY FINANCES

City Government Finances

Component	FY92 ($000)	FY92 (per capita $)
Revenue	235,480	787.15
Expenditure	245,705	821.33
Debt Outstanding	133,726	447.01
Cash & Securities	179,013	598.40

Source: U.S. Bureau of the Census, City Government Finances: 1991-92

City Government Revenue by Source

Source	FY92 ($000)	FY92 (per capita $)	FY92 (%)
From Federal Government	3,001	10.03	1.3
From State Governments	69,670	232.89	29.6
From Local Governments	28,735	96.05	12.2
Property Taxes	29,868	99.84	12.7
General Sales Taxes	0	0.00	0.0
Selective Sales Taxes	14,122	47.21	6.0
Income Taxes	0	0.00	0.0
Current Charges	48,252	161.29	20.5
Utility/Liquor Store	0	0.00	0.0
Employee Retirement[1]	0	0.00	0.0
Other	41,832	139.83	17.8

Note: (1) Excludes "city contributions," classified as "nonrevenue," intragovernmental transfers.
Source: U.S. Bureau of the Census, City Government Finances: 1991-92

City Government Expenditures by Function

Function	FY92 ($000)	FY92 (per capita $)	FY92 (%)
Educational Services	250	0.84	0.1
Employee Retirement[1]	0	0.00	0.0
Environment/Housing	35,910	120.04	14.6
Government Administration	37,584	125.63	15.3
Interest on General Debt	5,742	19.19	2.3
Public Safety	83,735	279.91	34.1
Social Services	2,393	8.00	1.0
Transportation	55,817	186.58	22.7
Utility/Liquor Store	6	0.02	0.0
Other	24,268	81.12	9.9

Note: (1) Payments to beneficiaries including withdrawal of contributions.
Source: U.S. Bureau of the Census, City Government Finances: 1991-92

Municipal Bond Ratings

Area	Moody's	S & P
Las Vegas	A1	n/a

Note: n/a not available; n/r not rated
Source: Moody's Bond Record, 2/98; Statistical Abstract of the U.S., 1997;
Governing Magazine, 9/97, 3/98

POPULATION

Population Growth

Area	1980	1990	% Chg. 1980-90	July 1996 Estimate	% Chg. 1990-96
City	164,674	258,295	56.9	376,906	45.9
MSA[1]	463,087	741,459	60.1	1,201,073	62.0
U.S.	226,545,805	248,765,170	9.8	265,179,411	6.6

Note: (1) Metropolitan Statistical Area - see Appendix A for areas included
Source: 1980/1990 Census of Housing and Population, Summary Tape File 3C;
Census Bureau Population Estimates

Population Characteristics

Race	City				% Chg. 1980-90	MSA[1]	
	1980		1990			1990	
	Population	%	Population	%		Population	%
White	134,493	81.7	202,604	78.4	50.6	602,818	81.3
Black	21,101	12.8	29,472	11.4	39.7	70,484	9.5
Amer Indian/Esk/Aleut	1,223	0.7	2,415	0.9	97.5	6,939	0.9
Asian/Pacific Islander	3,858	2.3	9,332	3.6	141.9	26,087	3.5
Other	3,999	2.4	14,472	5.6	261.9	35,131	4.7
Hispanic Origin[2]	12,787	7.8	31,249	12.1	144.4	80,704	10.9

Note: (1) Metropolitan Statistical Area - see Appendix A for areas included;
(2) people of Hispanic origin can be of any race
Source: 1980/1990 Census of Housing and Population, Summary Tape File 3C

Ancestry

Area	German	Irish	English	Italian	U.S.	French	Polish	Dutch
City	21.2	15.7	15.0	7.5	3.2	4.9	3.2	2.2
MSA[1]	22.2	15.9	15.7	7.6	3.1	4.8	3.4	2.4
U.S.	23.3	15.6	13.1	5.9	5.3	4.2	3.8	2.5

Note: Figures are percentages and include persons that reported multiple ancestry (eg. if a person reported being Irish and Italian, they were included in both columns); (1) Metropolitan Statistical Area - see Appendix A for areas included
Source: 1990 Census of Population and Housing, Summary Tape File 3C

Age

Area	Median Age (Years)	Age Distribution (%)						
		Under 5	Under 18	18-24	25-44	45-64	65+	80+
City	32.5	8.2	24.8	9.9	35.4	19.7	10.3	1.5
MSA[1]	33.0	7.6	24.4	10.0	34.5	20.7	10.5	1.4
U.S.	32.9	7.3	25.6	10.5	32.6	18.7	12.5	2.8

Note: (1) Metropolitan Statistical Area - see Appendix A for areas included
Source: 1990 Census of Population and Housing, Summary Tape File 3C

Male/Female Ratio

Area	Number of males per 100 females (all ages)	Number of males per 100 females (18 years old+)
City	102.2	102.4
MSA[1]	103.0	102.4
U.S.	95.0	91.9

Note: (1) Metropolitan Statistical Area - see Appendix A for areas included
Source: 1990 Census of Population, General Population Characteristics

INCOME

Per Capita/Median/Average Income

Area	Per Capita ($)	Median Household ($)	Average Household ($)
City	14,737	30,590	37,719
MSA[1]	15,109	30,746	38,595
U.S.	14,420	30,056	38,453

Note: all figures are for 1989; (1) Metropolitan Statistical Area - see Appendix A for areas included
Source: 1990 Census of Population and Housing, Summary Tape File 3C

Household Income Distribution by Race

Income ($)	City (%)					U.S. (%)				
	Total	White	Black	Other	Hisp.[1]	Total	White	Black	Other	Hisp.[1]
Less than 5,000	5.1	3.9	13.7	7.1	7.8	6.2	4.8	15.2	8.6	8.8
5,000 - 9,999	8.0	7.4	13.0	7.2	7.1	9.3	8.6	14.2	9.9	11.1
10,000 - 14,999	8.8	8.3	12.8	9.1	10.5	8.8	8.5	11.0	9.8	11.0
15,000 - 24,999	17.8	17.6	17.4	20.8	20.0	17.5	17.3	18.9	18.5	20.5
25,000 - 34,999	17.8	17.9	15.2	19.7	20.9	15.8	16.1	14.2	15.4	16.4
35,000 - 49,999	19.7	20.4	14.9	19.1	19.9	17.9	18.6	13.3	16.1	16.0
50,000 - 74,999	14.8	15.7	9.5	12.1	10.3	15.0	15.8	9.3	13.4	11.1
75,000 - 99,999	4.4	4.8	2.3	3.4	2.4	5.1	5.5	2.6	4.7	3.1
100,000+	3.5	3.9	1.2	1.4	1.1	4.4	4.8	1.3	3.7	1.9

Note: all figures are for 1989; (1) people of Hispanic origin can be of any race
Source: 1990 Census of Population and Housing, Summary Tape File 3C

Effective Buying Income

Area	Per Capita ($)	Median Household ($)	Average Household ($)
City	16,736	35,593	43,567
MSA[1]	17,275	35,632	44,843
U.S.	15,444	33,201	41,849

Note: data as of 1/1/97; (1) Metropolitan Statistical Area - see Appendix A for areas included
Source: Standard Rate & Data Service, Newspaper Advertising Source, 2/98

Effective Household Buying Income Distribution

Area	% of Households Earning						
	$10,000 -$19,999	$20,000 -$34,999	$35,000 -$49,999	$50,000 -$74,999	$75,000 -$99,000	$100,000 -$124,999	$125,000 and up
City	15.4	23.2	19.9	19.3	7.0	2.1	2.5
MSA[1]	15.3	24.2	19.3	19.1	7.3	2.5	2.7
U.S.	16.5	23.4	18.3	18.2	6.4	2.1	2.4

Note: data as of 1/1/97; (1) Metropolitan Statistical Area - see Appendix A for areas included
Source: Standard Rate & Data Service, Newspaper Advertising Source, 2/98

Poverty Rates by Race and Age

Area	Total (%)	By Race (%)				By Age (%)		
		White	Black	Other	Hisp.[2]	Under 5 years old	Under 18 years old	65 years and over
City	11.5	8.8	25.8	16.7	19.5	17.2	15.9	10.8
MSA[1]	10.5	8.4	23.8	15.7	17.1	16.2	14.4	9.1
U.S.	13.1	9.8	29.5	23.1	25.3	20.1	18.3	12.8

Note: figures show the percent of people living below the poverty line in 1989. The average poverty threshold was $12,674 for a family of four in 1989; (1) Metropolitan Statistical Area - see Appendix A for areas included; (2) people of Hispanic origin can be of any race
Source: 1990 Census of Population and Housing, Summary Tape File 3C

EMPLOYMENT

Labor Force and Employment

Area	Civilian Labor Force			Workers Employed		
	Dec. '95	Dec. '96	% Chg.	Dec. '95	Dec. '96	% Chg.
City	203,293	214,971	5.7	193,076	207,154	7.3
MSA[1]	652,679	686,165	5.1	618,370	660,642	6.8
U.S.	134,583,000	136,742,000	1.6	127,903,000	130,785,000	2.3

Note: Data is not seasonally adjusted and covers workers 16 years of age and older;
(1) Metropolitan Statistical Area - see Appendix A for areas included
Source: Bureau of Labor Statistics, http://stats.bls.gov

Las Vegas was listed among the top 20 metro areas (out of 114 major areas) in terms of projected job growth from 1997 to 2002 with an annual percent change of 3.7%.
Standard & Poor's DRI, July 23, 1997

Unemployment Rate

Area	1997											
	Jan.	Feb.	Mar.	Apr.	May	Jun.	Jul.	Aug.	Sep.	Oct.	Nov.	Dec.
City	4.5	4.2	4.0	4.1	4.0	4.9	4.8	4.5	4.6	4.1	3.8	3.6
MSA[1]	4.8	4.5	4.1	4.1	4.1	4.9	4.9	4.5	4.6	4.2	3.8	3.7
U.S.	5.9	5.7	5.5	4.8	4.7	5.2	5.0	4.8	4.7	4.4	4.3	4.4

Note: Data is not seasonally adjusted and covers workers 16 years of age and older; All figures are percentages; (1) Metropolitan Statistical Area - see Appendix A for areas included
Source: Bureau of Labor Statistics, http://stats.bls.gov

Employment by Industry

Sector	MSA[1]		U.S.
	Number of Employees	Percent of Total	Percent of Total
Services	288,800	44.6	29.0
Retail Trade	112,900	17.4	18.5
Government	69,900	10.8	16.1
Manufacturing	22,200	3.4	15.0
Finance/Insurance/Real Estate	31,200	4.8	5.7
Wholesale Trade	21,100	3.3	5.4
Transportation/Public Utilities	33,300	5.1	5.3
Construction	66,300	10.2	4.5
Mining	2,200	0.3	0.5

Note: Figures cover non-farm employment as of 12/97 and are not seasonally adjusted; (1) Metropolitan Statistical Area - see Appendix A for areas included
Source: Bureau of Labor Statistics, http://stats.bls.gov

Employment by Occupation

Occupation Category	City (%)	MSA[1] (%)	U.S. (%)
White Collar	50.6	51.4	58.1
Executive/Admin./Management	11.1	11.4	12.3
Professional	9.5	9.3	14.1
Technical & Related Support	3.0	3.0	3.7
Sales	12.5	13.2	11.8
Administrative Support/Clerical	14.5	14.5	16.3
Blue Collar	21.9	21.1	26.2
Precision Production/Craft/Repair	11.2	10.9	11.3
Machine Operators/Assem./Insp.	2.7	2.6	6.8
Transportation/Material Movers	4.1	4.0	4.1
Cleaners/Helpers/Laborers	3.9	3.6	3.9
Services	26.4	26.4	13.2
Farming/Forestry/Fishing	1.2	1.1	2.5

Note: figures cover employed persons 16 years old and over; (1) Metropolitan Statistical Area - see Appendix A for areas included
Source: 1990 Census of Population and Housing, Summary Tape File 3C

Occupational Employment Projections: 1994 - 2005

High Demand Occupations (ranked by annual openings)	Fast-Growing Occupations (ranked by percent growth)
1. Waiters & waitresses	1. Detectives/investigators, private
2. Cashiers	2. Systems analysts
3. Salespersons, retail	3. Physical therapists
4. Guards	4. Medical records technicians
5. Blackjack dealers	5. Physical therapy assistants and aides
6. Maids/housekeepers	6. Paving/surfacing/tamping equipment oper.
7. Janitors/cleaners/maids, ex. priv. hshld.	7. Loan officers & counselors
8. General managers & top executives	8. Radiologic technicians
9. General office clerks	9. Paralegals
10. Marketing & sales, supervisors	10. Respiratory therapists

Projections cover Clark County.
Source: Nevada Labor Market Information, Occupational Projections, 1994-2005

Average Wages

Occupation	Wage	Occupation	Wage
Professional/Technical/Clerical	$/Week	**Health/Protective Services**	$/Week
Accountants III	-	Corrections Officers	-
Attorneys III	-	Firefighters	-
Budget Analysts III	-	Nurses, Licensed Practical II	-
Buyers/Contracting Specialists II	-	Nurses, Registered II	-
Clerks, Accounting III	414	Nursing Assistants II	-
Clerks, General III	463	Police Officers I	-
Computer Operators II	444	**Hourly Workers**	$/Hour
Computer Programmers II	612	Forklift Operators	-
Drafters II	543	General Maintenance Workers	9.12
Engineering Technicians III	694	Guards I	6.41
Engineering Technicians, Civil III	-	Janitors	9.29
Engineers III	-	Maintenance Electricians	18.61
Key Entry Operators I	332	Maintenance Electronics Techs II	16.79
Personnel Assistants III	-	Maintenance Machinists	-
Personnel Specialists III	-	Maintenance Mechanics, Machinery	18.87
Secretaries III	519	Material Handling Laborers	9.81
Switchboard Operator-Receptionist	335	Motor Vehicle Mechanics	18.37
Systems Analysts II	912	Shipping/Receiving Clerks	9.40
Systems Analysts Supervisor/Mgr II	-	Tool and Die Makers	-
Tax Collectors II	-	Truckdrivers, Tractor Trailer	16.09
Word Processors II	-	Warehouse Specialists	-

Note: Wage data includes full-time workers only for 12/92 and cover the Metropolitan Statistical Area (see Appendix A for areas included). Dashes indicate that data was not available.
Source: Bureau of Labor Statistics, Occupational Compensation Survey

TAXES

Major State and Local Tax Rates

State Corp. Income (%)	State Personal Income (%)	Residential Property (effective rate per $100)	Sales & Use State (%)	Sales & Use Local (%)	State Gasoline (cents/ gallon)	State Cigarette (cents/ 20-pack)
None	None	1.00	6.5	0.5	23[a]	35

Note: Personal/corporate income tax rates as of 1/97. Sales, gasoline and cigarette tax rates as of 1/98; (a) Does not include a local option tax of 1 - 10 cents
Source: Federation of Tax Administrators, www.taxadmin.org; Washington D.C. Department of Finance and Revenue, Tax Rates and Tax Burdens in the District of Columbia: A Nationwide Comparison, June 1997; Chamber of Commerce

Total Taxes Per Capita and as a Percent of Income

Area	Per Capita Income ($)	Per Capita Taxes ($)			Taxes as Pct. of Income (%)		
		Total	Federal	State/Local	Total	Federal	State/Local
Nevada	29,237	10,440	6,975	3,465	35.7	23.9	11.9
U.S.	26,187	9,205	6,127	3,078	35.2	23.4	11.8

Note: Figures are for 1997
Source: Tax Foundation, Web Site, www.taxfoundation.org

Estimated Tax Burden

Area	State Income	Local Income	Property	Sales	Total
Las Vegas	0	0	1,575	0	1,575

Note: The numbers are estimates of taxes paid by a married couple with two kids and annual earnings of $65,000. Sales tax estimates assume they spend average amounts on food, clothing, household goods and gasoline. Property tax estimates assume they live in a $225,000 home.
Source: Kiplinger's Personal Finance Magazine, June 1997

COMMERCIAL REAL ESTATE

Office Market

Class/Location	Total Space (sq. ft.)	Vacant Space (sq. ft.)	Vac. Rate (%)	Under Constr. (sq. ft.)	Net Absorp. (sq. ft.)	Rental Rates ($/sq.ft./yr.)
Class A						
CBD	627,700	25,000	4.0	0	-5,000	29.04-29.04
Outside CBD	2,466,798	176,319	7.1	532,891	501,585	21.00-30.00
Class B						
CBD	513,390	37,284	7.3	0	-26,817	12.00-21.60
Outside CBD	8,125,197	960,099	11.8	406,718	789,538	15.60-25.80

Note: Data as of 10/97 and covers Las Vegas; CBD = Central Business District; n/a not available;
Source: Society of Industrial and Office Realtors, 1998 Comparative Statistics of Industrial and Office Real Estate Markets

"The Las Vegas Valley has roughly 940,000 sq. ft. of space scheduled to come on line in 1998. Virtually all of it will be built in the northwest, east, and southeast submarkets. Office development is largely controlled by three companies: the Howard Hughes Corporation, American Nevada Corp. and Thomas and Mack Co. All three firms have been prudent about building only to meet demand, which has resulted in keeping the office vacancy fairly low (currently about 9 percent overall and less than 7 percent for Class 'A' space). There is a strong interest in investment purchases, although locating opportunities in such a small (12 million sq. ft.) office market is somewhat difficult." *Society of Industrial and Office Realtors, 1998 Comparative Statistics of Industrial and Office Real Estate Markets*

Industrial Market

Location	Total Space (sq. ft.)	Vacant Space (sq. ft.)	Vac. Rate (%)	Under Constr. (sq. ft.)	Net Absorp. (sq. ft.)	Net Lease ($/sq.ft./yr.)
Central City	31,080,018	2,121,005	6.8	803,952	997,248	4.32-7.80
Suburban	17,803,001	2,560,241	14.4	1,520,834	2,361,572	3.36-7.20

Note: Data as of 10/97 and covers Las Vegas; n/a not available
Source: Society of Industrial and Office Realtors, 1998 Comparative Statistics of Industrial and Office Real Estate Markets

"With overall vacancy now creeping to the 10 percent mark, industrial developers are beginning to scale back their plans. Moreover, the rise in lease and sales prices are expected to slow considerably as tenants now have more locational choice. Build-to-suit activity has slowed as well, owing to the ready inventory of existing space. Still, the Las Vegas market boasts fairly high lease prices, which of course translates to high transactions values. In 1998, Las Vegas' expansion will roll along, and a reduction in new supply at this point in the cycle will keep lease prices high and insure excellent overall returns for investors." *Society of Industrial and Office Realtors, 1998 Comparative Statistics of Industrial and Office Real Estate Markets*

Retail Market

Shopping Center Inventory (sq. ft.)	Shopping Center Construction (sq. ft.)	Construction as a Percent of Inventory (%)	Torto Wheaton Rent Index[1] ($/sq. ft.)
20,854,000	1,786,000	8.6	17.36

Note: Data as of 1997 and covers the Metropolitan Statistical Area - see Appendix A for areas included; (1) Index is based on a model that predicts what the average rent should be for leases with certain characteristics, in certain locations during certain years.
Source: National Association of Realtors, 1997-1998 Market Conditions Report

"The Las Vegas MSA once again led the nation in population and personal income growth. Not surprisingly, the area's booming growth has created one of the nation's most active retail markets. The area's retail rent index fell slightly in 1997—a correction to the massive 31% increase in 1996. New construction has most frequently been tenant-driven, particularly toward big-box retail structures. New casino development continues, including Bally's 2,800-room Paris Casino/Resort due in 1998, and the 3,000-room Gellagio. Las Vegas is expected to lead the nation in employment growth through the turn of the century, particularly in the services and trade sectors. The area's retail market should follow suit, highlighted by rising rents." *National Association of Realtors, 1997-1998 Market Conditions Report*

COMMERCIAL UTILITIES

Typical Monthly Electric Bills

Area	Commercial Service ($/month)		Industrial Service ($/month)	
	12 kW demand 1,500 kWh	100 kW demand 30,000 kWh	1,000 kW demand 400,000 kWh	20,000 kW demand 10,000,000 kWh
City	91	1,744	28,987	666,353
U.S.	162	2,360	25,590	545,677

Note: Based on rates in effect July 1, 1997
Source: Edison Electric Institute, Typical Residential, Commercial and Industrial Bills, Summer 1997

TRANSPORTATION

Transportation Statistics

Avg. travel time to work (min.)	20.6
Interstate highways	I-15
Bus lines	
In-city	Citizens Area Transit (CAT), 190 vehicles
Inter-city	7
Passenger air service	
Airport	McCarren International
Airlines	16
Aircraft departures	130,890 (1995)
Enplaned passengers	12,657,051 (1995)
Rail service	Amtrak
Motor freight carriers	57
Major waterways/ports	None

Source: OAG, Business Travel Planner, Summer 1997; Editor & Publisher Market Guide, 1998; FAA Airport Activity Statistics, 1996; Amtrak National Time Table, Northeast Timetable, Fall/Winter 1997-98; 1990 Census of Population and Housing, STF 3C; Chamber of Commerce/Economic Development 1997; Jane's Urban Transport Systems 1997-98; Transit Fact Book 1997

A survey of 90,000 airline passengers during the first half of 1997 ranked most of the largest airports in the U.S. McCarren International ranked number 7 out of 36. Criteria: cleanliness, quality of restaurants, attractiveness, speed of baggage delivery, ease of reaching gates, available ground transportation, ease of following signs and closeness of parking. *Plog Research Inc., First Half 1997*

Means of Transportation to Work

Area	Car/Truck/Van		Public Transportation			Bicycle	Walked	Other Means	Worked at Home
	Drove Alone	Car-pooled	Bus	Subway	Railroad				
City	74.0	15.8	2.8	0.0	0.0	0.7	3.6	1.7	1.5
MSA[1]	74.8	15.4	1.9	0.0	0.0	0.8	3.7	2.1	1.5
U.S.	73.2	13.4	3.0	1.5	0.5	0.4	3.9	1.2	3.0

Note: figures shown are percentages and only include workers 16 years old and over;
(1) Metropolitan Statistical Area - see Appendix A for areas included
Source: 1990 Census of Population and Housing, Summary Tape File 3C

BUSINESSES

Major Business Headquarters

Company Name	1997 Rankings	
	Fortune 500	Forbes 500
Fletcher Jones Management Group	-	381
Tang Industries	-	165
Tracinda	-	131

Note: Companies listed are located in the city; Dashes indicate no ranking
Fortune 500: companies that produce a 10-K are ranked 1 - 500 based on 1996 revenue
Forbes 500: private companies are ranked 1 - 500 based on 1996 revenue
Source: Forbes 12/1/97; Fortune 4/28/97

Fast-Growing Businesses

Las Vegas is home to one of *Business Week's* "hot growth" companies: Anchor Gaming. Criteria: sales and earnings, return on capital and stock price. *Business Week, 5/26/97*

According to Deloitte & Touche LLP, Las Vegas is home to two of America's 100 fastest-growing high-technology companies: Casino Data Systems and Teletek Inc. Companies are ranked by percentage growth in revenue over a five-year period. Criteria for inclusion: must be a U.S. company developing and/or providing technology products or services; company must have been in business for five years with 1992 revenues of at least $50,000. *Deloitte & Touche LLP, January 7, 1998*

Minority Business Opportunity

One of the 500 largest Hispanic-owned companies in the U.S. are located in Las Vegas. *Hispanic Business, June 1997*

Small Business Opportunity

Las Vegas was included among *Entrepreneur* magazines listing of the "20 Best Cities for Small Business." It was ranked #8 among large metro areas. Criteria: risk of failure, business performance, economic growth, affordability and state attitude towards business. *Entrepreneur, 10/97*

According to *Forbes*, Las Vegas is home to one of America's 200 best small companies: Anchor Gaming. Criteria: companies must be publicly traded, U.S.-based corporations with latest 12-month sales of between $5 and $350 million. Earnings must be at least $1 million for the 12-month period. Limited partnerships, REITs and closed-end mutual funds were not considered. Banks, S&Ls and electric utilities were not included. *Forbes, November 3, 1997*

HOTELS & MOTELS

Hotels/Motels

| Area | Hotels/ Motels | Rooms | Luxury-Level Hotels/Motels | | Average Minimum Rates ($) | | |
			♦♦♦♦	♦♦♦♦♦	♦♦	♦♦♦	♦♦♦♦
City	76	52,246	5	0	49	66	172
Airport	23	19,950	1	0	n/a	n/a	n/a
Suburbs	2	117	0	0	n/a	n/a	n/a
Total	101	72,313	6	0	n/a	n/a	n/a

Note: n/a not available; Classifications range from one diamond (budget properties with basic amenities) to five diamond (luxury properties with the finest service, rooms and facilities).
Source: OAG, Business Travel Planner, Summer 1997

CONVENTION CENTERS

Major Convention Centers

Center Name	Meeting Rooms	Exhibit Space (sf)
Alexis Park Resort and Spa	15	n/a
Caesars Palace	24	90,000
Cashman Field Center	16	98,100
Las Vegas Convention Center	89	1,300,000
Sands Expo and Convention Center	23	1,006,750
Thomas & Mack Center-Univ. of Nevada	5	67,000

Note: n/a not available
Source: Trade Shows Worldwide 1997

Living Environment

COST OF LIVING

Cost of Living Index

Composite Index	Housing	Utilities	Groceries	Health Care	Trans- portation	Misc. Goods/ Services
106.2	110.1	76.1	107.4	124.2	107.5	105.9

Note: U.S. = 100
Source: ACCRA, Cost of Living Index, 3rd Quarter 1997

HOUSING

Median Home Prices and Housing Affordability

Area	Median Price[2] 3rd Qtr. 1997 ($)	HOI[3] 3rd Qtr. 1997	Afford- ability Rank[4]
MSA[1]	125,000	65.6	121
U.S.	127,000	63.7	–

Note: (1) Metropolitan Statistical Area - see Appendix A for areas included; (2) U.S. figures calculated from the sales of 625,000 new and existing homes in 195 markets; (3) Housing Opportunity Index - percent of homes sold that were within the reach of the median income household at the prevailing mortgage interest rate; (4) Rank is from 1-195 with 1 being most affordable
Source: National Association of Home Builders, Housing Opportunity Index, 3rd Quarter 1997

It is projected that the median price of existing single-family homes in the metro area will increase by 5.7% in 1998. Nationwide, home prices are projected to increase 6.6%.
Kiplinger's Personal Finance Magazine, January 1998

Average New Home Price

Area	Price ($)
City	142,667
U.S.	135,710

Note: Figures are based on a new home with 1,800 sq. ft. of living area on an 8,000 sq. ft. lot.
Source: ACCRA, Cost of Living Index, 3rd Quarter 1997

Average Apartment Rent

Area	Rent ($/mth)
City	764
U.S.	569

Note: Figures are based on an unfurnished two bedroom, 1-1/2 or 2 bath apartment, approximately 950 sq. ft. in size, excluding all utilities except water
Source: ACCRA, Cost of Living Index, 3rd Quarter 1997

RESIDENTIAL UTILITIES

Average Residential Utility Costs

Area	All Electric ($/mth)	Part Electric ($/mth)	Other Energy ($/mth)	Phone ($/mth)
City	–	51.89	28.86	11.42
U.S.	109.40	55.25	43.64	19.48

Source: ACCRA, Cost of Living Index, 3rd Quarter 1997

HEALTH CARE

Average Health Care Costs

Area	Hospital ($/day)	Doctor ($/visit)	Dentist ($/visit)
City	351.50	58.75	91.00
U.S.	392.91	48.76	60.84

Note: Hospital - based on a semi-private room. Doctor - based on a general practitioner's routine exam of an established patient. Dentist - based on adult teeth cleaning and periodic oral exam.
Source: ACCRA, Cost of Living Index, 3rd Quarter 1997

Distribution of Office-Based Physicians

| Area | Family/Gen. Practitioners | Specialists | | |
		Medical	Surgical	Other
MSA[1]	200	508	426	427

Note: Data as of 12/31/96; (1) Metropolitan Statistical Area - see Appendix A for areas included
Source: American Medical Assn., Physician Characteristics & Distribution in the U.S., 1997-1998

Hospitals

Las Vegas has 5 general medical and surgical hospitals, 2 psychiatric, 1 other specialty. *AHA Guide to the Healthcare Field 1997-98*

University Medical Center is among the 100 best-run hospitals in the U.S.
Modern Healthcare, January 5, 1998

EDUCATION

Public School District Statistics

District Name	Num. Sch.	Enroll.	Classroom Teachers[1]	Pupils per Teacher	Minority Pupils (%)	Current Exp.[2] ($/pupil)
Clark County School District	198	166,788	8,095	20.6	39.3	4,546

Note: Data covers the 1995-1996 school year unless otherwise noted; (1) Excludes teachers reported as working in school district offices rather than in schools; (2) Based on 1993-94 enrollment collected by the Census Bureau, not the enrollment figure shown in column 3; SD = School District; ISD = Independent School District; n/a not available
Source: National Center for Education Statistics, Common Core of Data Survey; Bureau of the Census

Educational Quality

School District	Education Quotient[1]	Graduate Outcome[2]	Community Index[3]	Resource Index[4]
Las Vegas	87.0	101.0	98.0	61.0

Note: Nearly 1,000 secondary school districts were rated in terms of educational quality. The scores range from a low of 50 to a high of 150; (1) Average of the Graduate Outcome, Community and Resource indexes; (2) Based on graduation rates and college board scores (SAT/ACT); (3) Based on the surrounding community's average level of education and the area's average income level; (4) Based on teacher salaries, per-pupil expenditures and student-teacher ratios.
Source: Expansion Management, Ratings Issue 1997

Educational Attainment by Race

| Area | High School Graduate (%) | | | | | Bachelor's Degree (%) | | | | |
	Total	White	Black	Other	Hisp.[2]	Total	White	Black	Other	Hisp.[2]
City	76.3	79.4	68.1	57.0	49.8	13.4	14.0	9.4	11.5	6.2
MSA[1]	77.3	79.6	70.6	60.0	53.4	13.8	14.4	9.0	12.3	7.0
U.S.	75.2	77.9	63.1	60.4	49.8	20.3	21.5	11.4	19.4	9.2

Note: figures shown cover persons 25 years old and over; (1) Metropolitan Statistical Area - see Appendix A for areas included; (2) people of Hispanic origin can be of any race
Source: 1990 Census of Population and Housing, Summary Tape File 3C

School Enrollment by Type

| Area | Preprimary | | | | Elementary/High School | | | |
| | Public | | Private | | Public | | Private | |
	Enrollment	%	Enrollment	%	Enrollment	%	Enrollment	%
City	2,190	53.4	1,914	46.6	36,848	93.0	2,781	7.0
MSA[1]	6,818	61.6	4,254	38.4	108,051	94.3	6,526	5.7
U.S.	2,679,029	59.5	1,824,256	40.5	38,379,689	90.2	4,187,099	9.8

Note: figures shown cover persons 3 years old and over;
(1) Metropolitan Statistical Area - see Appendix A for areas included
Source: 1990 Census of Population and Housing, Summary Tape File 3C

School Enrollment by Race

Area	Preprimary (%)				Elementary/High School (%)			
	White	Black	Other	Hisp.[1]	White	Black	Other	Hisp.[1]
City	79.8	13.2	6.9	8.7	71.3	15.8	12.9	17.6
MSA[2]	84.1	9.8	6.1	8.2	74.9	13.7	11.4	14.9
U.S.	80.4	12.5	7.1	7.8	74.1	15.6	10.3	12.5

Note: figures shown cover persons 3 years old and over; (1) people of Hispanic origin can be of any race; (2) Metropolitan Statistical Area - see Appendix A for areas included
Source: 1990 Census of Population and Housing, Summary Tape File 3C

SAT/ACT Scores

Area/District	1997 SAT				1997 ACT	
	Percent of Graduates Tested (%)	Average Math Score	Average Verbal Score	Average Combined Score	Percent of Graduates Tested (%)	Average Composite Score
Clark County SD	33	512	502	1,014	36	21.2
State	32	509	508	1,017	39	21.3
U.S.	42	511	505	1,016	36	21.0

Note: Math and verbal SAT scores are out of a possible 800; ACT scores are out of a possible 36
Caution: Comparing or ranking states/cities on the basis of SAT/ACT scores alone is invalid and strongly discouraged by the The College Board and The American College Testing Program as students who take the tests are self-selected and do not represent the entire student population.
Source: Clark County School District, Testing & Evaluation, 1997; American College Testing Program, 1997; College Board, 1997

Classroom Teacher Salaries in Public Schools

District	B.A. Degree		M.A. Degree		Ph.D. Degree	
	Min. ($)	Max ($)	Min. ($)	Max. ($)	Min. ($)	Max. ($)
Las Vegas	24,566	31,297	28,898	40,116	32,278	49,632
Average[1]	26,120	39,270	28,175	44,667	31,643	49,825

Note: Salaries are for 1996-1997; (1) Based on all school districts covered; n/a not available
Source: American Federation of Teachers (unpublished data)

Higher Education

Two-Year Colleges		Four-Year Colleges		Medical Schools	Law Schools	Voc/ Tech
Public	Private	Public	Private			
0	0	1	0	0	0	21

Source: College Blue Book, Occupational Education 1997; Medical School Admission Requirements, 1998-99; Peterson's Guide to Two-Year Colleges, 1997; Peterson's Guide to Four-Year Colleges, 1997; Barron's Guide to Law Schools 1997

MAJOR EMPLOYERS

Major Employers

Bally's Grand	Caesars Palace
Circus Circus Casinos	Desert Palace
Harrah's Las Vegas	Horseshoe Club Operating Co.
Hotel Ramada of Nevada	Imperial Palace
Las Vegas Hilton Corp.	Mirage Casino-Hotel
New Castle Corp.	Rio Resort Properties
Sunrise Hospital	Treasure Island Corp.
University Medical Center of Southern Nevada	Checker Cab Co. of Nevada
Nevada Yellow Cab	

Note: companies listed are located in the city
Source: Dun's Business Rankings 1997; Ward's Business Directory, 1997

PUBLIC SAFETY

Crime Rate

Area	All Crimes	Violent Crimes				Property Crimes		
		Murder	Forcible Rape	Robbery	Aggrav. Assault	Burglary	Larceny -Theft	Motor Vehicle Theft
City	6,849.8	19.4	57.1	439.1	496.0	1,402.1	3,482.7	953.4
Suburbs[1]	6,353.8	13.7	42.4	191.3	478.6	1,501.4	3,488.8	637.5
MSA[2]	6,702.5	17.7	52.8	365.5	490.8	1,431.6	3,484.5	859.6
U.S.	5,078.9	7.4	36.1	202.4	388.2	943.0	2,975.9	525.9

Note: Crime rate is the number of crimes per 100,000 pop.; (1) defined as all areas within the MSA but located outside the central city; (2) Metropolitan Statistical Area - see Appendix A for areas incl.
Source: FBI Uniform Crime Reports 1996

RECREATION

Culture and Recreation

Museums	Symphony Orchestras	Opera Companies	Dance Companies	Professional Theatres	Zoos	Pro Sports Teams
7	2	1	2	1	0	0

Source: International Directory of the Performing Arts, 1996; Official Museum Directory, 1998; Chamber of Commerce/Economic Development 1997

Library System

The Las Vegas-Clark County Library District has 24 branches, holdings of 2,000,000 volumes and a budget of $19,417,208 (1995-1996). *American Library Directory, 1997-1998*

MEDIA

Newspapers

Name	Type	Freq.	Distribution	Circulation
El Mundo	Hispanic	1x/wk	Area	20,000
Las Vegas Israelite	Religious	2x/mo	National	43,000
Las Vegas Review-Journal	n/a	7x/wk	Area	161,000
Las Vegas Sun	General	7x/wk	Area	40,000
Nifty Nickel	General	1x/wk	Local	80,000

Note: Includes newspapers with circulations of 1,000 or more located in the city; n/a not available
Source: Burrelle's Media Directory, 1998 Edition

AM Radio Stations

Call Letters	Freq. (kHz)	Target Audience	Station Format	Music Format
KDWN	720	General	N/S/T	n/a
KXNT	840	General	S/T	n/a
KBAD	920	General	M/S/T	Big Band
KNUU	970	n/a	N	n/a
KXNO	1140	General	E/N	n/a
KLAV	1230	General	T	n/a
KRLV	1340	General	T	n/a
KENO	1460	General	N/S/T	n/a

Note: Stations included broadcast in the Las Vegas metro area; n/a not available
Station Format: E = Educational; M = Music; N = News; S = Sports; T = Talk
Source: Burrelle's Media Directory, 1998 Edition

FM Radio Stations

Call Letters	Freq. (mHz)	Target Audience	Station Format	Music Format
KCEP	88.1	Black	E/M/N/S/T	Christian/Contemporary Top 40/Jazz/Oldies/R&B/Urban Contemporary
KNPR	89.5	n/a	M/N	Classical
KILA	90.5	General	M/N/S	Christian
KUNV	91.5	General	M/N/S/T	Adult Contemporary/Adult Standards/AOR/Alternative/Big Band/Christian/Classic Rock/Classical/Country/Contemporary Top 40/Easy Listening
KOMP	92.3	General	M	AOR
KBGO	93.1	General	M	Oldies
KWNR	95.5	General	M	Country
KKLZ	96.3	General	M/N/S	Classic Rock
KXPT	97.1	General	M	Adult Contemporary/Alternative
KLUC	98.5	General	M	Contemporary Top 40
KMZQ	100.5	General	M	Adult Contemporary
KFMS	101.9	General	M	Country
KEDG	103.5	General	M	Alternative
KQOL	105.5	General	M	Oldies
KRCY	105.9	n/a	M	Oldies
KSNE	106.5	General	M	Adult Contemporary

Note: Stations included broadcast in the Las Vegas metro area; n/a not available
Station Format: E = Educational; M = Music; N = News; S = Sports; T = Talk
Music Format: AOR = Album Oriented Rock; MOR = Middle-of-the-Road
Source: Burrelle's Media Directory, 1998 Edition

Television Stations

Name	Ch.	Affiliation	Type	Owner
KVBC	3	NBC	Commercial	Sunbelt Broadcasting Inc.
KVVU	5	Fox	Commercial	Meredith Corporation
KLAS	8	CBS	Commercial	Landmark Communications Inc.
KLVX	10	PBS	Public	Clark County School District
KTNV	13	ABC	Commercial	WTMJ Inc.
KFBT	33	WB	Commercial	Dan Koker
KBLR	39	n/a	n/a	Summit Media L.L.C.

Note: Stations included broadcast in the Las Vegas metro area
Source: Burrelle's Media Directory, 1998 Edition

CLIMATE

Average and Extreme Temperatures

Temperature	Jan	Feb	Mar	Apr	May	Jun	Jul	Aug	Sep	Oct	Nov	Dec	Ann
Extreme High (°F)	77	87	91	99	109	115	116	116	113	103	87	77	116
Average High (°F)	56	62	69	78	88	99	104	102	94	81	66	57	80
Average Temp. (°F)	45	50	56	65	74	84	90	88	80	68	54	46	67
Average Low (°F)	33	38	43	51	60	69	76	74	66	54	41	34	53
Extreme Low (°F)	8	16	23	31	40	49	60	56	43	26	21	11	8

Note: Figures cover the years 1948-1990
Source: National Climatic Data Center, International Station Meteorological Climate Summary, 3/95

Average Precipitation/Snowfall/Humidity

Precip./Humidity	Jan	Feb	Mar	Apr	May	Jun	Jul	Aug	Sep	Oct	Nov	Dec	Ann
Avg. Precip. (in.)	0.5	0.4	0.4	0.2	0.2	0.1	0.4	0.5	0.3	0.2	0.4	0.3	4.0
Avg. Snowfall (in.)	1	Tr	Tr	Tr	0	0	0	0	0	0	Tr	Tr	1
Avg. Rel. Hum. 7am (%)	59	52	41	31	26	20	26	31	30	36	47	56	38
Avg. Rel. Hum. 4pm (%)	32	25	20	15	13	10	14	16	16	18	26	31	20

Note: Figures cover the years 1948-1990; Tr = Trace amounts (<0.05 in. of rain; <0.5 in. of snow)
Source: National Climatic Data Center, International Station Meteorological Climate Summary, 3/95

Weather Conditions

Temperature			Daytime Sky			Precipitation		
10°F & below	32°F & below	90°F & above	Clear	Partly cloudy	Cloudy	0.01 inch or more precip.	0.1 inch or more snow/ice	Thunder-storms
< 1	37	134	185	132	48	27	2	13

Note: Figures are average number of days per year and covers the years 1948-1990
Source: National Climatic Data Center, International Station Meteorological Climate Summary, 3/95

AIR & WATER QUALITY

Maximum Pollutant Concentrations

	Particulate Matter (ug/m^3)	Carbon Monoxide (ppm)	Sulfur Dioxide (ppm)	Nitrogen Dioxide (ppm)	Ozone (ppm)	Lead (ug/m^3)
MSA[1] Level	328	10	n/a	0.027	0.10	n/a
NAAQS[2]	150	9	0.140	0.053	0.12	1.50
Met NAAQS?	No	No	n/a	Yes	Yes	n/a

Note: (1) Metropolitan Statistical Area - see Appendix A for areas included; (2) National Ambient Air Quality Standards; ppm = parts per million; ug/m^3 = micrograms per cubic meter; n/a not available
Source: EPA, National Air Quality and Emissions Trends Report, 1996

Pollutant Standards Index

In the Las Vegas MSA (see Appendix A for areas included), the Pollutant Standards Index (PSI) exceeded 100 on 13 days in 1996. A PSI value greater than 100 indicates that air quality would be in the unhealthful range on that day. *EPA, National Air Quality and Emissions Trends Report, 1996*

Drinking Water

Water System Name	Pop. Served	Primary Water Source Type	Number of Violations in Fiscal Year 1997	Type of Violation/ Contaminants
Las Vegas Valley Water District	500,000	Purchased surface	None	None
Southern Nevada Water System	500,000	Surface	None	None

Note: Data as of January 16, 1998
Source: EPA, Office of Ground Water and Drinking Water, Safe Drinking Water Information System

Las Vegas tap water is alkaline, hard.
Editor & Publisher Market Guide, 1998

Los Angeles, California

Background

There is as much to say about Los Angeles, as there are unincorporated and incorporated municipalities under its jurisdiction. Simply put, Los Angeles is big; and in the words of one of its residents, "If you want a life, you need a car in LA"

Los Angeles acquired its many neighborhoods and communities like Hollywood, Glendale, Burbank, and Alhambra, when those cities wanted to share in the water piped into Los Angeles from the Owens River. To obtain it, the cities were required to join the Los Angeles municipal system. Due to those annexations, Los Angeles is now one of the largest U.S. cities in both acreage and population. It is one of the most racially diverse as well.

The city tires to connect the communities in its far flung empire through a rather Byzantine system of freeways. This is what gives Los Angeles its reputation as a congested, car-oriented culture, wherein people have to schedule their days around the three hour rush hour.

Despite these nightmares, Los Angeles is a city with a diversified economy and 325 days of sunshine a year. What was formerly a sleepy pueblo of forty-four people founded in 1781, with chickens littering the quasi-footpaths called streets, is now a city leading in commerce, transportation, finance, and entertainment—especially entertainment. With 3/4 of all motion pictures made in the United States still produced in the Los Angeles area and the headquarters of the major studios such as MGM and Universal located in "municipalities" unto themselves in Los Angeles, one can hardly disassociate Los Angeles from entertainment.

According to recent studies by the Carronade Group and Bay Area Economic Forum, Los Angeles has led the nation in multimedia employment since 1994. Exports are also surging with the Port of Los Angeles as the country's second busiest container port.

Downtown Los Angeles is also seeing the construction of its first modern industrial park, The Alameda Trade Center, a 20-acre project that is downtown's only Foreign Trade Zone. *Site Selection Oct/Nov 1997*

The climate of Los Angeles is normally pleasant and mild throughout the year. What is unusual about the climate of the Los Angeles metropolitan area is the pronounced difference in temperature, humidity, cloudiness, fog, rain and sunshine over fairly short distances.

Both high and low temperatures become more extreme, and the average relative humidity drops as one goes inland and up foothill slopes. Relative humidity is frequently high near the coast, but may be quite low along the foothills.

Most rain falls during the months of November through March, while the summers are very dry. Destructive flash floods occasionally develop in and below some mountain canyons. Snow is often visible on nearby mountains in the winter, but is extremely rare in the coastal basin. Thunderstorms are infrequent.

At times, high concentrations of air pollution affect the Los Angeles coastal basin and adjacent areas, when lack of air movement combines with an atmospheric inversion. In the fall and winter the Santa Ana winds pick up considerable amounts of dust and reach speeds of 35 to 50 miles per hour in the northern and eastern sections of the city, with higher speeds in outlying areas in the north and east, but rarely reach coastal sections of the city.

Sunshine, fog, or clouds depend a great deal on topography and distance from the ocean. Low clouds are common at night and in the morning along the coast during spring and summer. Near the foothills, clouds form later in the day and clear earlier. Annual percentage of fog and cloudiness is greatest near the ocean. Sunshine totals are highest on the inland side of the city.

General Rankings and Evaluative Comments

- Los Angeles was ranked #22 out of 300 cities by *Money's* 1997 "Survey of the Best Places to Live." Criteria used: health services, crime, economy, housing, education, transportation, weather, leisure and the arts. The city was ranked #40 in 1996 and #94 in 1995. *Money, July 1997; Money, September 1996; Money, September 1995*

- *Ladies Home Journal* ranked America's 200 largest cities based on the qualities women care about most. Los Angeles ranked 170 out of 200. Criteria: low crime rate, good public schools, well-paying jobs, quality health and child care, the presence of women in government, proportion of women-owned businesses, size of the wage gap with men, local economy, divorce rates, the ratio of single men to single women, whether there are laws that require at least the same number of public toilets for women as men, and the probability of good hair days. *Ladies Home Journal, November 1997*

- Los Angeles was ranked #201 out of 219 cities in terms of children's health, safety, and economic well-being. Criteria: total population, percent population change, birth rate, child immunization rate, infant mortality rate, percent low birth weight infants, percent of births to teens, physician-to-population ratio, student-to-teacher ratio, dropout rate, unemployment rate, median family income, percent of children in poverty, violent and property crime rates, number of juvenile arrests for violent crimes as a percent of the total crime index, number of days with pollution standard index (PSI) over 100, pounds toxic releases per 1,000 people and number of superfund sites. *Zero Population Growth, Children's Environmental Index 1997*

- Los Angeles is among the 20 most livable cities for gay men and lesbians. The list was divided between 10 cities you might expect and 10 surprises. Los Angeles was on the cities you would expect list. Rank: 3 out of 10. Criteria: legal protection from antigay discrimination, an annual gay pride celebration, a community center, gay bookstores and publications, and an array of organizations, religious groups, and health care facilities that cater to the needs of the local gay community. *The Advocate, June 1997*

- Los Angeles was selected by *Swing* magazine as being one of "The 10 Best Places to Live" in the U.S. It was also named the "Best Place for Nightlife" (Silver Lake). The cities were selected based on census data, cost of living, economic growth, and entertainment options. Swing also read local papers, talked to industry insiders, and interviewed young people. *Swing, July/August 1997*

- *Yahoo! Internet Life* selected "America's 100 Most Wired Cities & Towns". 50 cities were large and 50 cities were small. Los Angeles ranked 16 out of 50 large cities. Criteria: Internet users per capita, number of networked computers, number of registered domain names, Internet backbone traffic, and the per-capita number of Web sites devoted to each city. *Yahoo! Internet Life, March 1998*

- *Reader's Digest* non-scientifically ranked the 12 largest U.S. metropolitan areas in terms of having the worst drivers. The Los Angeles metro area ranked number 3. The areas were selected by asking approximately 1,200 readers on the *Reader's Digest* Web site and 200 interstate bus drivers and long-haul truckers which metro areas have the worst drivers. Their responses were factored in with fatality, insurance and rental-car rates to create the rankings. *Reader's Digest, March 1998*

- Los Angeles Dodgers (professional baseball), headquartered in Los Angeles, is among the "100 Best Companies to Work for in America." Criteria: trust in management, pride in work/company, camaraderie, company responses to the Hewitt People Practices Inventory, and employee responses to their Great Place to Work survey. The companies also had to be at least 10 years old and have a minimum of 500 employees. *Fortune, January 12, 1998*

- According to *Working Mother*, "Lawmakers here—on both sides of the aisle—have agreed that the state must kick in more money to help working parents find and pay for child care. To that end, Governor Pete Wilson has proposed a significant expansion of the state's child care budget—an additional $277 million in state and federal funds. The new money would pay for care for about 90,000 more kids a year; and for preschool for another 13,000. In addition, some $45 million will be spent on recruiting and training caregivers for infants and toddlers.

To help parents become more informed consumers, California passed a law that many consider a step backward. It allows family child care providers to care for two more kids, without hiring additional help. This means a family child care provider can now care for up to eight kids, instead of six, without additional help. The new rule also worries child care advocates because it may limit infant care in California. When caregivers take in the two extra older children, they must reduce the number of babies in their care. (California is among the 10 best states for child care.)'' *Working Mother, July/August 1997*

Business Environment

STATE ECONOMY

State Economic Profile

"California's expansion is strong and stable....Entertainment and filmmaking remain steady contributors to the state's improved income growth and labor markets....

California's banking industry is consolidating and shedding workers. Improved credit conditions and healthy balance sheets make many remaining California thrifts likely takeover targets for out-of-state banks.

Delinquency rates on consumer credit have declined for the past two years and are well below the U.S. average. Mortgage foreclosure rates remain high, but they are down from the peak of one year ago when mortgage lenders took advantage of the improved housing market to shed nonperforming loans. California consumers remain cautious, however. Retail sales growth last year of 5% was no better than the national average.

Housing prices are up in northern California, and the number of units sold is rising throughout the state. Multifamily units dominated construction activity last year. With population growth accelerating and income growth outpacing the U.S. for the first time this decade, demand for single-family homes will strengthen.

Housing prices are up in northern California, and the number of units sold is rising throughout the state. Multifamily units dominated construction activity last year. With population growth accelerating the income growth outpacing the U.S. for the first time this decade, demand for single-family homes will strengthen.

Construction will contribute to the near-term expansion as home building accelerates. The greatest risk to the California economy is that the rising dollar could choke off foreign demand for California's export products. Longer term there will be some consolidation among high-tech firms, and high costs will limit the breadth of industrial development. California will remain an average performer over the long term." *National Association of Realtors, Economic Profiles: The Fifty States, July 1997*

IMPORTS/EXPORTS

Total Export Sales

Area	1993 ($000)	1994 ($000)	1995 ($000)	1996 ($000)	% Chg. 1993-96	% Chg. 1995-96
MSA[1]	20,013,560	22,224,815	24,730,952	24,437,945	22.1	-1.2
U.S.	464,858,354	512,415,609	583,030,524	622,827,063	34.0	6.8

Note: (1) Metropolitan Statistical Area - see Appendix A for areas included
Source: U.S. Department of Commerce, International Trade Association, Metropolitan Area Exports: An Export Performance Report on Over 250 U.S. Cities, October 1997

Imports/Exports by Port

Type	Cargo Value			Share of U.S. Total	
	1995 (US$mil.)	1996 (US$mil.)	% Change 1995-1996	1995 (%)	1996 (%)
Imports	57,291	56,324	-1.69	14.63	14.68
Exports	23,197	15,806	-31.86	10.14	6.67

Source: Global Trade Information Services, WaterBorne Trade Atlas 1997

CITY FINANCES

City Government Finances

Component	FY94 ($000)	FY94 (per capita $)
Revenue	7,467,028	2,104.72
Expenditure	6,694,966	1,887.10
Debt Outstanding	8,460,944	2,384.87
Cash & Securities	15,529,657	4,377.32

Source: U.S. Bureau of the Census, City Government Finances: 1993-94

City Government Revenue by Source

Source	FY94 ($000)	FY94 (per capita $)	FY94 (%)
From Federal Government	312,296	88.03	4.2
From State Governments	346,215	97.59	4.6
From Local Governments	78,934	22.25	1.1
Property Taxes	641,813	180.91	8.6
General Sales Taxes	257,686	72.63	3.5
Selective Sales Taxes	521,310	146.94	7.0
Income Taxes	0	0.00	0.0
Current Charges	1,174,874	331.16	15.7
Utility/Liquor Store	2,340,416	659.69	31.3
Employee Retirement[1]	1,049,124	295.71	14.1
Other	744,360	209.81	10.0

Note: (1) Excludes "city contributions," classified as "nonrevenue," intragovernmental transfers.
Source: U.S. Bureau of the Census, City Government Finances: 1993-94

City Government Expenditures by Function

Function	FY94 ($000)	FY94 (per capita $)	FY94 (%)
Educational Services	55,359	15.60	0.8
Employee Retirement[1]	712,170	200.74	10.6
Environment/Housing	855,381	241.10	12.8
Government Administration	294,329	82.96	4.4
Interest on General Debt	322,899	91.02	4.8
Public Safety	1,028,188	289.81	15.4
Social Services	19,092	5.38	0.3
Transportation	609,918	171.92	9.1
Utility/Liquor Store	2,300,962	648.57	34.4
Other	496,668	140.00	7.4

Note: (1) Payments to beneficiaries including withdrawal of contributions.
Source: U.S. Bureau of the Census, City Government Finances: 1993-94

Municipal Bond Ratings

Area	Moody's	S & P
Los Angeles	Aa	AA

Note: n/a not available; n/r not rated
Source: Moody's Bond Record, 2/98; Statistical Abstract of the U.S., 1997; Governing Magazine, 9/97, 3/98

POPULATION

Population Growth

Area	1980	1990	% Chg. 1980-90	July 1996 Estimate	% Chg. 1990-96
City	2,966,850	3,485,398	17.5	3,553,638	2.0
MSA[1]	7,477,503	8,863,164	18.5	9,127,751	3.0
U.S.	226,545,805	248,765,170	9.8	265,179,411	6.6

Note: (1) Metropolitan Statistical Area - see Appendix A for areas included
Source: 1980/1990 Census of Housing and Population, Summary Tape File 3C; Census Bureau Population Estimates

Population Characteristics

Race	City 1980 Population	%	City 1990 Population	%	% Chg. 1980-90	MSA[1] 1990 Population	%
White	1,842,050	62.1	1,845,133	52.9	0.2	5,044,718	56.9
Black	504,301	17.0	485,949	13.9	-3.6	990,406	11.2
Amer Indian/Esk/Aleut	19,296	0.7	14,919	0.4	-22.7	43,689	0.5
Asian/Pacific Islander	206,536	7.0	341,986	9.8	65.6	955,329	10.8
Other	394,667	13.3	797,411	22.9	102.0	1,829,022	20.6
Hispanic Origin[2]	816,076	27.5	1,370,476	39.3	67.9	3,306,116	37.3

Note: (1) Metropolitan Statistical Area - see Appendix A for areas included;
(2) people of Hispanic origin can be of any race
Source: 1980/1990 Census of Housing and Population, Summary Tape File 3C

Ancestry

Area	German	Irish	English	Italian	U.S.	French	Polish	Dutch
City	8.0	5.6	6.2	3.1	1.9	1.9	2.4	0.8
MSA[1]	10.6	7.3	8.0	3.5	1.9	2.3	2.0	1.2
U.S.	23.3	15.6	13.1	5.9	5.3	4.2	3.8	2.5

Note: Figures are percentages and include persons that reported multiple ancestry (eg. if a person reported being Irish and Italian, they were included in both columns); (1) Metropolitan Statistical Area - see Appendix A for areas included
Source: 1990 Census of Population and Housing, Summary Tape File 3C

Age

Area	Median Age (Years)	Age Distribution (%) Under 5	Under 18	18-24	25-44	45-64	65+	80+
City	30.6	8.0	24.7	12.7	36.0	16.6	9.9	2.2
MSA[1]	30.6	8.2	26.2	11.9	35.1	17.1	9.7	2.1
U.S.	32.9	7.3	25.6	10.5	32.6	18.7	12.5	2.8

Note: (1) Metropolitan Statistical Area - see Appendix A for areas included
Source: 1990 Census of Population and Housing, Summary Tape File 3C

Male/Female Ratio

Area	Number of males per 100 females (all ages)	Number of males per 100 females (18 years old+)
City	100.7	99.6
MSA[1]	99.5	97.7
U.S.	95.0	91.9

Note: (1) Metropolitan Statistical Area - see Appendix A for areas included
Source: 1990 Census of Population, General Population Characteristics

INCOME

Per Capita/Median/Average Income

Area	Per Capita ($)	Median Household ($)	Average Household ($)
City	16,188	30,925	45,701
MSA[1]	16,149	34,965	47,252
U.S.	14,420	30,056	38,453

Note: all figures are for 1989; (1) Metropolitan Statistical Area - see Appendix A for areas included
Source: 1990 Census of Population and Housing, Summary Tape File 3C

Household Income Distribution by Race

Income ($)	City (%)					U.S. (%)				
	Total	White	Black	Other	Hisp.[1]	Total	White	Black	Other	Hisp.[1]
Less than 5,000	6.0	4.6	10.2	6.8	6.3	6.2	4.8	15.2	8.6	8.8
5,000 - 9,999	9.6	7.7	16.8	9.9	10.9	9.3	8.6	14.2	9.9	11.1
10,000 - 14,999	8.7	7.3	10.9	11.0	12.3	8.8	8.5	11.0	9.8	11.0
15,000 - 24,999	16.7	14.6	18.1	21.2	23.6	17.5	17.3	18.9	18.5	20.5
25,000 - 34,999	14.5	13.9	14.2	16.2	17.2	15.8	16.1	14.2	15.4	16.4
35,000 - 49,999	15.7	16.3	13.4	15.6	15.2	17.9	18.6	13.3	16.1	16.0
50,000 - 74,999	14.6	16.5	10.6	12.3	10.1	15.0	15.8	9.3	13.4	11.1
75,000 - 99,999	6.3	7.9	3.3	4.1	2.6	5.1	5.5	2.6	4.7	3.1
100,000+	7.9	11.2	2.4	3.0	1.8	4.4	4.8	1.3	3.7	1.9

Note: all figures are for 1989; (1) people of Hispanic origin can be of any race
Source: 1990 Census of Population and Housing, Summary Tape File 3C

Effective Buying Income

Area	Per Capita ($)	Median Household ($)	Average Household ($)
City	14,176	29,515	41,879
MSA[1]	14,521	34,165	44,632
U.S.	15,444	33,201	41,849

Note: data as of 1/1/97; (1) Metropolitan Statistical Area - see Appendix A for areas included
Source: Standard Rate & Data Service, Newspaper Advertising Source, 2/98

Effective Household Buying Income Distribution

Area	% of Households Earning						
	$10,000 -$19,999	$20,000 -$34,999	$35,000 -$49,999	$50,000 -$74,999	$75,000 -$99,000	$100,000 -$124,999	$125,000 and up
City	18.6	23.4	16.2	14.8	5.7	2.1	3.6
MSA[1]	16.0	22.8	17.8	18.3	6.9	2.4	3.4
U.S.	16.5	23.4	18.3	18.2	6.4	2.1	2.4

Note: data as of 1/1/97; (1) Metropolitan Statistical Area - see Appendix A for areas included
Source: Standard Rate & Data Service, Newspaper Advertising Source, 2/98

Poverty Rates by Race and Age

Area	Total (%)	By Race (%)				By Age (%)		
		White	Black	Other	Hisp.[2]	Under 5 years old	Under 18 years old	65 years and over
City	18.9	13.1	25.3	25.4	28.2	27.7	27.8	10.5
MSA[1]	15.1	10.6	21.2	20.9	22.9	22.0	21.9	9.2
U.S.	13.1	9.8	29.5	23.1	25.3	20.1	18.3	12.8

Note: figures show the percent of people living below the poverty line in 1989. The average poverty threshold was $12,674 for a family of four in 1989; (1) Metropolitan Statistical Area - see Appendix A for areas included; (2) people of Hispanic origin can be of any race
Source: 1990 Census of Population and Housing, Summary Tape File 3C

EMPLOYMENT

Labor Force and Employment

Area	Civilian Labor Force			Workers Employed		
	Dec. '95	Dec. '96	% Chg.	Dec. '95	Dec. '96	% Chg.
City	1,768,027	1,823,759	3.2	1,627,652	1,702,838	4.6
MSA[1]	4,413,112	4,557,466	3.3	4,103,659	4,284,946	4.4
U.S.	134,583,000	136,742,000	1.6	127,903,000	130,785,000	2.3

Note: Data is not seasonally adjusted and covers workers 16 years of age and older; (1) Metropolitan Statistical Area - see Appendix A for areas included
Source: Bureau of Labor Statistics, http://stats.bls.gov

Unemployment Rate

Area	1997											
	Jan.	Feb.	Mar.	Apr.	May	Jun.	Jul.	Aug.	Sep.	Oct.	Nov.	Dec.
City	9.0	8.6	8.2	8.1	7.7	8.0	8.6	7.9	7.5	7.1	7.0	6.6
MSA[1]	7.8	7.5	6.9	6.8	6.7	6.8	7.5	7.0	6.6	6.3	6.3	6.0
U.S.	5.9	5.7	5.5	4.8	4.7	5.2	5.0	4.8	4.7	4.4	4.3	4.4

Note: Data is not seasonally adjusted and covers workers 16 years of age and older; All figures are percentages; (1) Metropolitan Statistical Area - see Appendix A for areas included
Source: Bureau of Labor Statistics, http://stats.bls.gov

Employment by Industry

Sector	MSA[1]		U.S.
	Number of Employees	Percent of Total	Percent of Total
Services	1,293,400	32.7	29.0
Retail Trade	622,400	15.7	18.5
Government	545,500	13.8	16.1
Manufacturing	673,600	17.0	15.0
Finance/Insurance/Real Estate	222,100	5.6	5.7
Wholesale Trade	268,200	6.8	5.4
Transportation/Public Utilities	214,900	5.4	5.3
Construction	113,100	2.9	4.5
Mining	5,700	0.1	0.5

Note: Figures cover non-farm employment as of 12/97 and are not seasonally adjusted;
(1) Metropolitan Statistical Area - see Appendix A for areas included
Source: Bureau of Labor Statistics, http://stats.bls.gov

Employment by Occupation

Occupation Category	City (%)	MSA[1] (%)	U.S. (%)
White Collar	58.5	59.9	58.1
Executive/Admin./Management	12.5	13.2	12.3
Professional	14.7	14.4	14.1
Technical & Related Support	3.1	3.4	3.7
Sales	11.3	11.6	11.8
Administrative Support/Clerical	16.8	17.4	16.3
Blue Collar	26.2	26.6	26.2
Precision Production/Craft/Repair	10.3	11.0	11.3
Machine Operators/Assem./Insp.	8.8	8.2	6.8
Transportation/Material Movers	3.0	3.4	4.1
Cleaners/Helpers/Laborers	4.0	4.0	3.9
Services	13.9	12.3	13.2
Farming/Forestry/Fishing	1.4	1.2	2.5

Note: figures cover employed persons 16 years old and over;
(1) Metropolitan Statistical Area - see Appendix A for areas included
Source: 1990 Census of Population and Housing, Summary Tape File 3C

Occupational Employment Projections: 1994 - 2001

Occupations Expected to have the Largest Job Growth (ranked by numerical growth)	Fast-Growing Occupations[1] (ranked by percent growth)
1. Salespersons, retail	1. Home health aides
2. General office clerks	2. Computer engineers
3. Guards	3. Paralegals
4. Waiters & waitresses	4. Personal and home care aides
5. Instructional aides	5. Human services workers
6. Food preparation workers	6. Tax preparers
7. Truck drivers, light	7. Merchandise displayers/window trimmers
8. Accountants & auditors	8. Physical therapy assistants and aides
9. Cashiers	9. Film editors
10. General managers & top executives	10. Systems analysts

Projections cover Los Angeles County.
Note: (1) Excludes occupations with employment of less than 800 in 2001
Source: State of California, Employment Development Department, Labor Market Information Division, Information Services Group

Average Wages

Occupation	Wage	Occupation	Wage
Professional/Technical/Clerical	$/Week	**Health/Protective Services**	$/Week
Accountants III	860	Corrections Officers	746
Attorneys III	-	Firefighters	-
Budget Analysts III	861	Nurses, Licensed Practical II	-
Buyers/Contracting Specialists II	666	Nurses, Registered II	-
Clerks, Accounting III	506	Nursing Assistants II	-
Clerks, General III	482	Police Officers I	928
Computer Operators II	497	**Hourly Workers**	$/Hour
Computer Programmers II	677	Forklift Operators	-
Drafters II	641	General Maintenance Workers	-
Engineering Technicians III	654	Guards I	6.85
Engineering Technicians, Civil III	775	Janitors	7.70
Engineers III	999	Maintenance Electricians	20.30
Key Entry Operators I	-	Maintenance Electronics Techs II	19.22
Personnel Assistants III	-	Maintenance Machinists	-
Personnel Specialists III	829	Maintenance Mechanics, Machinery	18.05
Secretaries III	637	Material Handling Laborers	6.57
Switchboard Operator-Receptionist	371	Motor Vehicle Mechanics	18.70
Systems Analysts II	1,002	Shipping/Receiving Clerks	10.72
Systems Analysts Supervisor/Mgr II	1,575	Tool and Die Makers	19.21
Tax Collectors II	777	Truckdrivers, Tractor Trailer	15.67
Word Processors II	528	Warehouse Specialists	13.47

Note: Wage data includes full-time workers only for 12/95 and cover the Metropolitan Statistical Area (see Appendix A for areas included). Dashes indicate that data was not available.
Source: Bureau of Labor Statistics, Occupational Compensation Survey, 5/96

TAXES

Major State and Local Tax Rates

State Corp. Income (%)	State Personal Income (%)	Residential Property (effective rate per $100)	Sales & Use		State Gasoline (cents/ gallon)	State Cigarette (cents/ 20-pack)
			State (%)	Local (%)		
8.84[a]	1.0 - 9.3	0.74	6.0	2.25	18[b]	37

Note: Personal/corporate income tax rates as of 1/97. Sales, gasoline and cigarette tax rates as of 1/98; (a) Minimum tax is $800. The tax rate on S-Corporations is 1.5%; (b) Does not include 1 cent local option tax
Source: Federation of Tax Administrators, www.taxadmin.org; Washington D.C. Department of Finance and Revenue, Tax Rates and Tax Burdens in the District of Columbia: A Nationwide Comparison, June 1997; Chamber of Commerce

Total Taxes Per Capita and as a Percent of Income

Area	Per Capita Income ($)	Per Capita Taxes ($)			Taxes as Pct. of Income (%)		
		Total	Federal	State/Local	Total	Federal	State/Local
California	27,117	9,321	6,287	3,034	34.4	23.2	11.2
U.S.	26,187	9,205	6,127	3,078	35.2	23.4	11.8

Note: Figures are for 1997
Source: Tax Foundation, Web Site, www.taxfoundation.org

Estimated Tax Burden

Area	State Income	Local Income	Property	Sales	Total
Los Angeles	1,824	0	2,700	701	5,225

Note: The numbers are estimates of taxes paid by a married couple with two kids and annual earnings of $65,000. Sales tax estimates assume they spend average amounts on food, clothing, household goods and gasoline. Property tax estimates assume they live in a $225,000 home.
Source: Kiplinger's Personal Finance Magazine, June 1997

COMMERCIAL REAL ESTATE

Office Market

Class/Location	Total Space (sq. ft.)	Vacant Space (sq. ft.)	Vac. Rate (%)	Under Constr. (sq. ft.)	Net Absorp. (sq. ft.)	Rental Rates ($/sq.ft./yr.)
Class A						
CBD	21,779,000	3,829,845	17.6	0	912,155	16.00-28.00
Outside CBD	n/a	n/a	n/a	n/a	n/a	n/a
Class B						
CBD	7,652,111	2,011,237	26.3	0	67,763	12.00-18.00
Outside CBD	n/a	n/a	n/a	n/a	0	n/a

Note: Data as of 10/97 and covers Los Angeles-Central; CBD = Central Business District; n/a not available;
Source: Society of Industrial and Office Realtors, 1998 Comparative Statistics of Industrial and Office Real Estate Markets

"Vacancy in post-1980 era Class 'A' buildings will be under 10 percent by the end of 1998, according to our SIOR reporter. No new development is planned, although some rehabbing of Class 'B' and 'C' buildings may begin over the next couple of years. With no new competition on the horizon, investors will continue to vigorously pursue properties still priced significantly below replacement cost. More than any other submarket, downtown benefits from the continued improvements to L.A.'s mass transit network, a factor that will work to downtown's favor over the long haul. While it has a long way to go, this market is steadily improving from the disastrous market conditions of the early and mid-1990s. The Los Angeles Lakers and Kings will begin playing 1999 at a new arena to be built downtown, which will improve the area's image and visibility." *Society of Industrial and Office Realtors, 1998 Comparative Statistics of Industrial and Office Real Estate Markets*

Industrial Market

Location	Total Space (sq. ft.)	Vacant Space (sq. ft.)	Vac. Rate (%)	Under Constr. (sq. ft.)	Net Absorp. (sq. ft.)	Net Lease ($/sq.ft./yr.)
Central City	244,527,749	16,756,091	6.9	1,000,000	2,656,047	2.90-5.04
Suburban	n/a	n/a	n/a	n/a	n/a	n/a

Note: Data as of 10/97 and covers Los Angeles; n/a not available
Source: Society of Industrial and Office Realtors, 1998 Comparative Statistics of Industrial and Office Real Estate Markets

"Continued strengthening of the Southern California economy will further tighten the Central Los Angeles market. Vacancies, currently about seven percent, are unlikely to drop much further, as much of the currently available space is functionally obsolete and woefully inadequate for modern warehousing and distribution operations. There are approximately one million sq. ft. of industrial space under construction throughout all of Central Los Angeles, including Catellus Development's 36 acre Pacific Springs Industrial Park. Leasing and sales activity are reportedly very strong. Submarkets which are experiencing the greatest activity include the downtown area, where much of L.A.'s garment and toy manufacturing takes place, and the I-5 Corridor, including the City of Commerce, which has a healthy mix of assembly, manufacturing, food distribution, and trucking activity." *Society of Industrial and Office Realtors, 1998 Comparative Statistics of Industrial and Office Real Estate Markets*

Retail Market

Shopping Center Inventory (sq. ft.)	Shopping Center Construction (sq. ft.)	Construction as a Percent of Inventory (%)	Torto Wheaton Rent Index[1] ($/sq. ft.)
98,960,000	790,000	0.8	11.81

Note: Data as of 1997 and covers the Metropolitan Statistical Area - see Appendix A for areas included; (1) Index is based on a model that predicts what the average rent should be for leases with certain characteristics, in certain locations during certain years.
Source: National Association of Realtors, 1997-1998 Market Conditions Report

"Demographics has worked against Los Angeles' retail sector in recent years as the area has experienced negative net migration. Tepid population growth has come exclusively from increased household size rather than new households. The retail rent index has fallen over the last 7 years; however, a turnaround is expected next year. After bottoming out in 1993, taxable retail sales matched their 1990 level in 1995, and jumped 4.8% in 1996. Another sign of Los Angeles' recovery is the revival of the area's tourism industry, which has been hampered by several years of negative publicity. Very little retail construction is expected in the near future, adding to the overall health of the market." *National Association of Realtors, 1997-1998 Market Conditions Report*

COMMERCIAL UTILITIES

Typical Monthly Electric Bills

Area	Commercial Service ($/month)		Industrial Service ($/month)	
	12 kW demand 1,500 kWh	120 kW demand 30,000 kWh	1,000 kW demand 400,000 kWh	20,000 kW demand 10,000,000 kWh
City[1]	176	3,287	32,764	747,465
U.S.[2]	162	2,360[a]	25,590	545,677

Note: (1) Based on rates in effect January 1, 1997; (2) Based on rates in effect July 1, 1997; (a) Based on 100 kW demand and 30,000 kWh usage.
Source: Memphis Light, Gas and Water, 1997 Utility Bill Comparisons for Selected U.S. Cities; Edison Electric Institute, Typical Residential, Commercial and Industrial Bills, Summer 1997

TRANSPORTATION

Transportation Statistics

Avg. travel time to work (min.)	26.5
Interstate highways	I-10; I-5
Bus lines	
In-city	Los Angeles County MTA, 2,107 vehicles
Inter-city	1
Passenger air service	
Airport	Los Angeles International
Airlines	66
Aircraft departures	234,058 (1995)
Enplaned passengers	21,072,273 (1995)
Rail service	Amtrak; Metrolink
Motor freight carriers	4,415
Major waterways/ports	Port of Los Angeles

Source: OAG, Business Travel Planner, Summer 1997; Editor & Publisher Market Guide, 1998; FAA Airport Activity Statistics, 1996; Amtrak National Time Table, Northeast Timetable, Fall/Winter 1997-98; 1990 Census of Population and Housing, STF 3C; Chamber of Commerce/Economic Development 1997; Jane's Urban Transport Systems 1997-98; Transit Fact Book 1997

A survey of 90,000 airline passengers during the first half of 1997 ranked most of the largest airports in the U.S. Los Angeles International ranked number 30 out of 36. Criteria: cleanliness, quality of restaurants, attractiveness, speed of baggage delivery, ease of reaching gates, available ground transportation, ease of following signs and closeness of parking. *Plog Research Inc., First Half 1997*

Means of Transportation to Work

Area	Car/Truck/Van		Public Transportation			Bicycle	Walked	Other Means	Worked at Home
	Drove Alone	Car-pooled	Bus	Subway	Railroad				
City	65.2	15.4	10.4	0.0	0.0	0.6	3.9	1.4	3.1
MSA[1]	70.1	15.5	6.4	0.0	0.0	0.6	3.3	1.3	2.7
U.S.	73.2	13.4	3.0	1.5	0.5	0.4	3.9	1.2	3.0

Note: figures shown are percentages and only include workers 16 years old and over;
(1) Metropolitan Statistical Area - see Appendix A for areas included
Source: 1990 Census of Population and Housing, Summary Tape File 3C

BUSINESSES

Major Business Headquarters

Company Name	1997 Rankings	
	Fortune 500	Forbes 500
Atlantic Richfield	52	-
Northrop Grumman	185	-
Occidental Petroleum	129	-
Pacific Enterprises	497	-
Pacific Holding	-	423
Roll International	-	261
Times Mirror	400	-
Topa Equities	-	326

Note: Companies listed are located in the city; Dashes indicate no ranking
Fortune 500: companies that produce a 10-K are ranked 1 - 500 based on 1996 revenue
Forbes 500: private companies are ranked 1 - 500 based on 1996 revenue
Source: Forbes 12/1/97; Fortune 4/28/97

Fast-Growing Businesses

According to *Inc.*, Los Angeles is home to one of America's 100 fastest-growing private companies: R.J. Gordon & Co. Criteria for inclusion: must be an independent, privately-held, U.S. corporation, proprietorship or partnership; sales of at least $200,000 in 1993; five-year operating/sales history; increase in 1997 sales over 1996 sales; holding companies, regulated banks, and utilities were excluded. *Inc. 500, 1997*

Los Angeles was ranked #8 out of 24 (#1 is best) in terms of the best-performing local stocks in 1996 according to the Money/Norby Cities Index. The index measures stocks of companies that have headquarters in 24 metro areas. *Money, 2/7/97*

Women-Owned Businesses: Number, Employment, Sales and Share

Area	Women-Owned Businesses in 1996				Share of Women-Owned Businesses in 1996	
	Number	Employment	Sales ($000)	Rank[2]	Percent (%)	Rank[3]
MSA[1]	314,400	681,500	105,334,600	2	37.3	20

Note: (1) Metropolitan Statistical Area - see Appendix A for areas included; (2) Calculated on an averaging of number of businesses, employment and sales and ranges from 1 to 50 where 1 is best; (3) Ranges from 1 to 50 where 1 is best
Source: The National Foundation for Women Business Owners, 1996 Facts on Women-Owned Businesses: Trends in the Top 50 Metropolitan Areas, March 26, 1997

Women-Owned Businesses: Growth

Area	Growth in Women-Owned Businesses (% change from 1987 to 1996)				Relative Growth in the Number of Women-Owned and All Businesses (% change from 1987 to 1996)			
	Num.	Empl.	Sales	Rank[2]	Women-Owned	All Firms	Absolute Difference	Relative Difference
MSA[1]	77.9	213.3	299.0	22	77.9	45.4	32.5	1.7:1

Note: (1) Metropolitan Statistical Area - see Appendix A for areas included; (2) Calculated on an averaging of the percent growth of number of businesses, employment and sales and ranges from 1 to 50 where 1 is best
Source: The National Foundation for Women Business Owners, 1996 Facts on Women-Owned Businesses: Trends in the Top 50 Metropolitan Areas, March 26, 1997

Minority Business Opportunity

Los Angeles is home to three companies which are on the Black Enterprise Industrial/Service 100 list (largest based on gross sales): Karl Kani Infinity Inc. (mens'/boys' wear, footwear, sports apparel, licensing); African Development Public Investment Co. (African commodities and oil trading); Surface Protection Industries Inc. (paint & specialty coatings manufacturer). Criteria: 1) operational in previous calendar year; 2) at least 51% black-owned; 3) manufactures/owns the product it sells or provides industrial or consumer services. Brokerages, real estate firms and firms that provide professional services are not eligible. Black Enterprise, July 1997

Nine of the 500 largest Hispanic-owned companies in the U.S. are located in Los Angeles. *Hispanic Business, June 1997*

Los Angeles is home to one company which is on the Hispanic Business Fastest-Growing 100 list (greatest sales growth from 1992 to 1996): Cisco Bros. Corp. (furniture mfg.) *Hispanic Business, July/August 1997*

Los Angeles was listed among the top 25 metropolitan areas in terms of the number of Hispanic-owned companies. The city was ranked number 1 with 208,129 companies. *Hispanic Business, May 1997*

HOTELS & MOTELS

Hotels/Motels

Area	Hotels/Motels	Rooms	Luxury-Level Hotels/Motels		Average Minimum Rates ($)		
			♦♦♦♦	♦♦♦♦♦	♦♦	♦♦♦	♦♦♦♦
City	55	12,626	5	2	74	139	207
Airport	54	12,488	0	0	n/a	n/a	n/a
Suburbs	205	26,259	6	1	n/a	n/a	n/a
Total	314	51,373	11	3	n/a	n/a	n/a

Note: n/a not available; Classifications range from one diamond (budget properties with basic amenities) to five diamond (luxury properties with the finest service, rooms and facilities).
Source: OAG, Business Travel Planner, Summer 1997

Los Angeles is home to one of the top 100 hotels in the world according to *Travel & Leisure*: Hotel Bel-Air. Criteria: value, rooms/ambience, location, facilities/activities and service. *Travel & Leisure, September 1997*

CONVENTION CENTERS

Major Convention Centers

Center Name	Meeting Rooms	Exhibit Space (sf)
CaliforniaMart	140	35,000
Fairplex	17	240,000
Hollywood Palladium	2	50,000
Universal Amphitheater	1	14,000
Century Plaza Hotel and Tower	34	30,000
Los Angeles Convention and Exhibition Center	65	653,000
Shrine Auditorium & Expo Center	3	54,000
UCLA Conference Services, Univ. of California	228	n/a

Note: n/a not available
Source: Trade Shows Worldwide 1997

Living Environment

COST OF LIVING

Cost of Living Index

Composite Index	Housing	Utilities	Groceries	Health Care	Trans-portation	Misc. Goods/ Services
116.1	131.9	115.5	113.1	111.1	107.4	107.6

Note: U.S. = 100; Figures are for the Metropolitan Statistical Area - see Appendix A for areas included
Source: ACCRA, Cost of Living Index, 3rd Quarter 1997

HOUSING

Median Home Prices and Housing Affordability

Area	Median Price[2] 3rd Qtr. 1997 ($)	HOI[3] 3rd Qtr. 1997	Afford-ability Rank[4]
MSA[1]	165,000	47.2	178
U.S.	127,000	63.7	–

Note: (1) Metropolitan Statistical Area - see Appendix A for areas included; (2) U.S. figures calculated from the sales of 625,000 new and existing homes in 195 markets; (3) Housing Opportunity Index - percent of homes sold that were within the reach of the median income household at the prevailing mortgage interest rate; (4) Rank is from 1-195 with 1 being most affordable
Source: National Association of Home Builders, Housing Opportunity Index, 3rd Quarter 1997

It is projected that the median price of existing single-family homes in the metro area will increase by 6.9% in 1998. Nationwide, home prices are projected to increase 6.6%.
Kiplinger's Personal Finance Magazine, January 1998

Average New Home Price

Area	Price ($)
MSA[1]	172,920
U.S.	135,710

Note: Figures are based on a new home with 1,800 sq. ft. of living area on an 8,000 sq. ft. lot; (1) Metropolitan Statistical Area - see Appendix A for areas included
Source: ACCRA, Cost of Living Index, 3rd Quarter 1997

Average Apartment Rent

Area	Rent ($/mth)
MSA[1]	724
U.S.	569

Note: Figures are based on an unfurnished two bedroom, 1-1/2 or 2 bath apartment, approximately 950 sq. ft. in size, excluding all utilities except water; (1) Metropolitan Statistical Area - see Appendix A for areas included
Source: ACCRA, Cost of Living Index, 3rd Quarter 1997

RESIDENTIAL UTILITIES

Average Residential Utility Costs

Area	All Electric ($/mth)	Part Electric ($/mth)	Other Energy ($/mth)	Phone ($/mth)
MSA[1]	–	90.03	30.33	19.94
U.S.	109.40	55.25	43.64	19.48

Note: (1) (1) Metropolitan Statistical Area - see Appendix A for areas included
Source: ACCRA, Cost of Living Index, 3rd Quarter 1997

HEALTH CARE

Average Health Care Costs

Area	Hospital ($/day)	Doctor ($/visit)	Dentist ($/visit)
MSA[1]	602.80	55.00	54.00
U.S.	392.91	48.76	60.84

Note: Hospital - based on a semi-private room. Doctor - based on a general practitioner's routine exam of an established patient. Dentist - based on adult teeth cleaning and periodic oral exam; (1) Metropolitan Statistical Area - see Appendix A for areas included
Source: ACCRA, Cost of Living Index, 3rd Quarter 1997

Distribution of Office-Based Physicians

Area	Family/Gen. Practitioners	Specialists		
		Medical	Surgical	Other
MSA[1]	2,043	5,992	4,212	4,674

Note: Data as of 12/31/96; (1) Metropolitan Statistical Area - see Appendix A for areas included
Source: American Medical Assn., Physician Characteristics & Distribution in the U.S., 1997-1998

Hospitals

Los Angeles has 40 general medical and surgical hospitals, 5 psychiatric, 1 tuberculosis and other respiratory disease, 1 obstetrics and gynecology, 1 orthopedic, 1 prison hospital, 2 other specialty, 1 children's general, 1 children's other specialty. *AHA Guide to the Healthcare Field 1997-98*

According to *U.S. News and World Report,* Los Angeles has 7 of the best hospitals in the U.S.: **UCLA Medical Center**, noted for AIDS, cancer, cardiology, endocrinology, gastroenterology, geriatrics, gynecology, neurology, orthopedics, otolaryngology, pediatrics, pulmonology, rheumatology, urology; **Cedars-Sinai Medical Center**, noted for AIDS, cardiology, gastroenterology, gynecology, orthopedics, pulmonology, rheumatology; **Los Angeles County-USC Medical Center**, noted for AIDS, pulmonology, rheumatology; **Doheny Eye Institute**, noted for ophthalmology; **Children's Hospital**, noted for pediatrics; **UCLA Neuropsychiatric Hospital**, noted for psychiatry; **UCLA Medical Center (Jules Stein Eye Institute)**, noted for ophthalmology; *U.S. News and World Report, "America's Best Hospitals", 7/28/97*

EDUCATION

Public School District Statistics

District Name	Num. Sch.	Enroll.	Classroom Teachers[1]	Pupils per Teacher	Minority Pupils (%)	Current Exp.[2] ($/pupil)
Los Angeles Unified	642	647,612	25,788	25.1	88.7	4,954

Note: Data covers the 1995-1996 school year unless otherwise noted; (1) Excludes teachers reported as working in school district offices rather than in schools; (2) Based on 1993-94 enrollment collected by the Census Bureau, not the enrollment figure shown in column 3; SD = School District; ISD = Independent School District; n/a not available
Source: National Center for Education Statistics, Common Core of Data Survey; Bureau of the Census

Educational Quality

School District	Education Quotient[1]	Graduate Outcome[2]	Community Index[3]	Resource Index[4]
Los Angeles	82.0	55.0	67.0	123.0

Note: Nearly 1,000 secondary school districts were rated in terms of educational quality. The scores range from a low of 50 to a high of 150; (1) Average of the Graduate Outcome, Community and Resource indexes; (2) Based on graduation rates and college board scores (SAT/ACT); (3) Based on the surrounding community's average level of education and the area's average income level; (4) Based on teacher salaries, per-pupil expenditures and student-teacher ratios.
Source: Expansion Management, Ratings Issue 1997

Educational Attainment by Race

Area	High School Graduate (%)					Bachelor's Degree (%)				
	Total	White	Black	Other	Hisp.[2]	Total	White	Black	Other	Hisp.[2]
City	67.0	75.8	69.9	47.2	33.0	23.0	28.8	13.3	15.5	5.6
MSA[1]	70.0	76.7	73.8	53.2	39.2	22.3	25.6	14.8	17.7	6.0
U.S.	75.2	77.9	63.1	60.4	49.8	20.3	21.5	11.4	19.4	9.2

Note: figures shown cover persons 25 years old and over; (1) Metropolitan Statistical Area - see Appendix A for areas included; (2) people of Hispanic origin can be of any race
Source: 1990 Census of Population and Housing, Summary Tape File 3C

School Enrollment by Type

Area	Preprimary				Elementary/High School			
	Public		Private		Public		Private	
	Enrollment	%	Enrollment	%	Enrollment	%	Enrollment	%
City	25,962	52.4	23,600	47.6	531,302	86.8	80,848	13.2
MSA[1]	74,476	54.3	62,585	45.7	1,430,190	88.5	185,714	11.5
U.S.	2,679,029	59.5	1,824,256	40.5	38,379,689	90.2	4,187,099	9.8

Note: figures shown cover persons 3 years old and over;
(1) Metropolitan Statistical Area - see Appendix A for areas included
Source: 1990 Census of Population and Housing, Summary Tape File 3C

School Enrollment by Race

Area	Preprimary (%)				Elementary/High School (%)			
	White	Black	Other	Hisp.[1]	White	Black	Other	Hisp.[1]
City	55.2	17.0	27.8	34.2	41.3	14.5	44.2	57.5
MSA[2]	58.1	14.5	27.5	32.1	46.5	11.9	41.6	52.3
U.S.	80.4	12.5	7.1	7.8	74.1	15.6	10.3	12.5

Note: figures shown cover persons 3 years old and over; (1) people of Hispanic origin can be of any race; (2) Metropolitan Statistical Area - see Appendix A for areas included
Source: 1990 Census of Population and Housing, Summary Tape File 3C

SAT/ACT Scores

Area/District	1997 SAT				1997 ACT	
	Percent of Graduates Tested (%)	Average Math Score	Average Verbal Score	Average Combined Score	Percent of Graduates Tested (%)	Average Composite Score
Los Angeles USD	40	452	432	884	14	18.1
State	45	514	496	1,010	11	21.0
U.S.	42	511	505	1,016	36	21.0

Note: Math and verbal SAT scores are out of a possible 800; ACT scores are out of a possible 36
Caution: Comparing or ranking states/cities on the basis of SAT/ACT scores alone is invalid and strongly discouraged by the The College Board and The American College Testing Program as students who take the tests are self-selected and do not represent the entire student population.
Source: Los Angeles Unified School District, Information Technology Division, 1997; American College Testing Program, 1997; College Board, 1997

Classroom Teacher Salaries in Public Schools

District	B.A. Degree		M.A. Degree		Ph.D. Degree	
	Min. ($)	Max. ($)	Min. ($)	Max. ($)	Min. ($)	Max. ($)
Los Angeles	29,529	37,159	29,682	40,963	34,721	51,898
Average[1]	26,120	39,270	28,175	44,667	31,643	49,825

Note: Salaries are for 1996-1997; (1) Based on all school districts covered
Source: American Federation of Teachers (unpublished data)

Higher Education

Two-Year Colleges		Four-Year Colleges		Medical Schools	Law Schools	Voc/ Tech
Public	Private	Public	Private			
3	1	2	11	2	6	53

Source: College Blue Book, Occupational Education 1997; Medical School Admission Requirements, 1998-99; Peterson's Guide to Two-Year Colleges, 1997; Peterson's Guide to Four-Year Colleges, 1997; Barron's Guide to Law Schools 1997

MAJOR EMPLOYERS

Major Employers

Associated Students UCLA	Atlantic Richfield
Times Mirror Co.	California Commerce Club
Career Group (employment agencies)	Children's Hospital of Los Angeles
Fire Insurance Exchange	Fox Inc. (motion pictures)
Framers Group	Good Samaritan Hospital
Los Angeles County MTA	Los Angeles Memorial Coliseum Commission
Medical Management Consultants	Southern California Gas
Transamerica Occidental Life Insurance	Garment Technologies (textile products)
Truck Underwriters Association	

Note: companies listed are located in the city
Source: Dun's Business Rankings 1997; Ward's Business Directory, 1997

PUBLIC SAFETY

Crime Rate

Area	All Crimes	Violent Crimes				Property Crimes		
		Murder	Forcible Rape	Robbery	Aggrav. Assault	Burglary	Larceny -Theft	Motor Vehicle Theft
City	6,725.3	20.3	41.8	720.1	1,014.2	1,025.3	2,717.7	1,185.9
Suburbs[1]	4,666.2	11.9	27.2	362.9	562.3	889.8	1,963.6	848.4
MSA[2]	5,442.4	15.1	32.7	497.5	732.7	940.9	2,247.9	975.6
U.S.	5,078.9	7.4	36.1	202.4	388.2	943.0	2,975.9	525.9

Note: Crime rate is the number of crimes per 100,000 pop.; (1) defined as all areas within the MSA but located outside the central city; (2) Metropolitan Statistical Area - see Appendix A for areas incl.
Source: FBI Uniform Crime Reports 1996

RECREATION

Culture and Recreation

Museums	Symphony Orchestras	Opera Companies	Dance Companies	Professional Theatres	Zoos	Pro Sports Teams
29	9	4	12	6	1	4

Source: International Directory of the Performing Arts, 1996; Official Museum Directory, 1998; Chamber of Commerce/Economic Development 1997

Library System

The Los Angeles Public Library System has 65 branches and holdings of 6,064,978 volumes (budget not available). *American Library Directory, 1997-1998*

MEDIA

Newspapers

Name	Type	Freq.	Distribution	Circulation
A.C.C. Newspaper	Religious	1x/wk	Local	40,000
The African Times	Black	2x/mo	National	85,000
The Argonaut	General	1x/wk	Local	60,000
Central News/Journal/Star Wave	Black	1x/wk	Local	635,000
Inglewood Hawthorne Wave	Black	1x/wk	Local	42,400
Investor's Business Daily	n/a	5x/wk	National	235,000
The Jewish Journal	Religious	1x/wk	Local	55,000
Korean Central Daily	Asian	6x/wk	Area	50,000
La Ola	Hispanic	2x/wk	Local	415,102
La Opinion	Hispanic	7x/wk	Local	103,000
La Opinion Para Ti	Hispanic	1x/wk	Area	221,287
Larchmont Chronicle	General	1x/mo	Local	71,217
La Voz Libre	Hispanic	1x/wk	Local	44,500
L.A. Weekly	General	1x/wk	Regional	175,000
Los Angeles Jewish Times	Religious	1x/wk	Local	67,000
Los Angeles Times	n/a	7x/wk	Area	1,021,121
Lynwood Press	Black	1x/wk	Local	42,400
Montebello Comet	General	1x/wk	Local	92,500
New Times, Los Angeles	n/a	1x/wk	Local	100,000
The Nikkei Weekly	Asian	1x/wk	National	40,000
Scoop	General	1x/wk	Local	100,000
The Tidings	Religious	1x/wk	Local	40,000
Vida Nueva	Hispanic	1x/wk	Local	100,000
Wilshire Center, Westlake, Pico-Union & Koreatown Independent	Black	1x/wk	Local	200,000
World Reporter	Asian	1x/wk	Regional	200,000
Wyvernwood Chronicle	Hispanic	1x/wk	Local	92,000

Note: Includes newspapers with circulations of 40,000 or more located in the city; n/a not available
Source: Burrelle's Media Directory, 1998 Edition

Television Stations

Name	Ch.	Affiliation	Type	Owner
KCBS	2	CBS	Commercial	Westinghouse Broadcasting Company
KNBC	4	NBC	Commercial	General Electric Company
KTLA	5	WB	Commercial	Tribune Broadcasting Co.
KABC	7	ABC	Commercial	ABC Inc.
KCAL	9	n/a	Commercial	Fidelity Television
KTTV	11	Fox	Commercial	Fox Television Stations Inc.
KCOP	13	UPN	Commercial	Chris Craft Inc.
KSCI	18	n/a	Commercial	International Media Group
KWHY	22	n/a	Commercial	Harriscope of Los Angeles, Inc.
KCET	28	PBS	Public	Community Television of Southern California
KMEX	34	Univision	Commercial	Perenchio Television Inc.
KNET	38	n/a	Commercial	Venture Technologies Group
KHSC	46	HSN	Commercial	Silver King Broadcasting
KVEA	52	Telemundo	Commercial	Reliance Capital Group
KDOC	56	n/a	Commercial	Golden Orange Broadcasting Company Inc.
KSTV	57	Galavision	Commercial	Costa de Oro Television, Inc.
KLCS	58	PBS	Public	Los Angeles Unified School District
KRCA	62	n/a	Commercial	Fouce Amusements Enterprises

Note: Stations included broadcast in the Los Angeles metro area
Source: Burrelle's Media Directory, 1998 Edition

AM Radio Stations

Call Letters	Freq. (kHz)	Target Audience	Station Format	Music Format
KLAC	570	General	M	Country/Oldies
KAVL	610	General	N/S/T	n/a
KFI	640	n/a	T	n/a
KVCA	670	Hispanic	M/N/S/T	Spanish
KTZN	710	General	T	n/a
KABC	790	General	T	n/a
KIEV	870	General	T	n/a
KRRA	900	General	M	Spanish
KKHJ	930	Hispanic	M/N/S	Adult Contemporary/Spanish
KFWB	980	General	N/S	n/a
KTNQ	1020	Hispanic	M	Spanish
KNX	1070	General	N	n/a
KRLA	1110	General	M/N	Oldies
KXTA	1150	General	M/S	Contemporary Top 40
KORG	1190	General	T	n/a
KBET	1220	n/a	M/N/T	Adult Contemporary
KYPA	1230	General	T	n/a
KGIL	1260	General	M/N	Oldies
KFRN	1280	Religious	M/N	Christian/Classical
KAZN	1300	Asian	E/M/N/S/T	Adult Contemporary/Adults Standards/Contemporary Top 40/Easy Listening
KWKW	1330	Hispanic	M	n/a
KVOY	1340	n/a	M/T	Adult Standards/Big Band
KLTX	1390	General	T	n/a
KALI	1430	Black/Hisp	M/N/S	Spanish
KTYM	1460	Religious	M/T	Christian
KUTY	1470	Hispanic	M	n/a
KNSE	1510	Hispanic	M/N/S	Spanish
KXMG	1540	Hispanic	M	Spanish
KBLA	1580	Asian	M/N/S	n/a
KMNY	1600	General	E/N/T	n/a

Note: Stations included broadcast in the Los Angeles metro area; n/a not available
Station Format: E = Educational; M = Music; N = News; S = Sports; T = Talk
Source: Burrelle's Media Directory, 1998 Edition

FM Radio Stations

Call Letters	Freq. (mHz)	Target Audience	Station Format	Music Format
KLON	88.1	General	E/M/N	Jazz
KCSN	88.5	General	E/M/N/S/T	Alternative/Classic Rock/Classical/Country/Gospel/Jazz/R&B/Spanish
KSPC	88.7	General	M/N/S	n/a
KFAC	88.7	General	M	Classical
KXLU	88.9	General	M/N	n/a
KCRU	89.1	n/a	n/a	n/a
KPCC	89.3	General	M/N/T	Alternative/Big Band
KCRW	89.9	n/a	M/N	Adult Contemporary/AOR/Alternative
KSAK	90.1	General	M/N/S/T	AOR/Adult Contemporary/Alternative/Big Band/Classic Rock/Classical/Country/Contemporary Top 40/Hard Rock/Jazz/Oldies
KPFK	90.7	General	E/M/N/T	Alternative/Christian/Classical/Jazz
KCPB	91.1	General	M	Classical
KUSC	91.5	General	M	Classical
KKBT	92.3	General	M/N/S/T	R&B/Urban Contemporary
KRCI	92.7	n/a	M/N/S	Adult Contemporary
KCBS	93.1	General	M	Classic Rock/Oldies
KFOX	93.5	n/a	M/N/S	n/a
KZLA	93.9	General	M	Country
KTWV	94.7	General	M/N	Easy Listening
KLOS	95.5	General	M	AOR
KFSG	96.3	Religious	M/N/T	Adult Contemporary/Christian
KLSX	97.1	General	M/T	Adult Contemporary/Alternative/Classic Rock
KVAR	97.5	n/a	M	Spanish
KLAX	97.9	Hispanic	M	Contemporary Top 40
KRXV	98.1	General	M	Adult Contemporary
KYSR	98.7	General	M/N/S	Adult Contemporary
KHWY	98.9	General	M	Adult Contemporary
KGGI	99.1	General	M	Adult Contemporary
KHYZ	99.5	General	M/N/S	Adult Contemporary
KKLA	99.5	General	M/T	Christian
KXEZ	100.3	General	M	Adult Contemporary
KRTH	101.1	General	M	Oldies
KSCA	101.9	Hispanic	M	Adult Contemporary/Alternative/Spanish
KJLH	102.3	Black	M	R&B/Urban Contemporary
KIIS	102.7	General	M	Adult Contemporary/Contemporary Top 40
KACD	103.1	General	M/N/S	Adult Contemporary
KTPI	103.1	n/a	M	Country
KBCD	103.1	General	M	Adult Contemporary
KOST	103.5	General	M	Adult Contemporary
KACE	103.9	n/a	M	Oldies/R&B
KBIG	104.3	General	M	Adult Contemporary
KKGO	105.1	General	M	Classical
KBUE	105.5	Hispanic	M/N/S	n/a
KAVC	105.5	Religious	T	n/a
KPWR	105.9	General	M	Urban Contemporary
KGMX	106.3	General	M/N/S	Adult Contemporary
KROQ	106.7	General	M	Alternative
KLVE	107.5	Hispanic	M	n/a

Note: Stations included broadcast in the Los Angeles metro area; n/a not available
Station Format: E = Educational; M = Music; N = News; S = Sports; T = Talk
Music Format: AOR = Album Oriented Rock; MOR = Middle-of-the-Road
Source: Burrelle's Media Directory, 1998 Edition

CLIMATE

Average and Extreme Temperatures

Temperature	Jan	Feb	Mar	Apr	May	Jun	Jul	Aug	Sep	Oct	Nov	Dec	Ann
Extreme High (°F)	88	92	95	102	97	104	97	98	110	106	101	94	110
Average High (°F)	65	66	65	67	69	72	75	76	76	74	71	66	70
Average Temp. (°F)	56	57	58	60	63	66	69	70	70	67	62	57	63
Average Low (°F)	47	49	50	53	56	59	63	64	63	59	52	48	55
Extreme Low (°F)	27	34	37	43	45	48	52	51	47	43	38	32	27

Note: Figures cover the years 1947-1990
Source: National Climatic Data Center, International Station Meteorological Climate Summary, 3/95

Average Precipitation/Snowfall/Humidity

Precip./Humidity	Jan	Feb	Mar	Apr	May	Jun	Jul	Aug	Sep	Oct	Nov	Dec	Ann
Avg. Precip. (in.)	2.6	2.3	1.8	0.8	0.1	Tr	Tr	0.1	0.2	0.3	1.5	1.5	11.3
Avg. Snowfall (in.)	Tr	0	0	0	0	0	0	0	0	0	0	0	Tr
Avg. Rel. Hum. 7am (%)	69	72	76	76	77	80	80	81	80	76	69	67	75
Avg. Rel. Hum. 4pm (%)	60	62	64	64	66	67	67	68	67	66	61	60	64

Note: Figures cover the years 1947-1990; Tr = Trace amounts (<0.05 in. of rain; <0.5 in. of snow)
Source: National Climatic Data Center, International Station Meteorological Climate Summary, 3/95

Weather Conditions

Temperature			Daytime Sky			Precipitation		
10°F & below	32°F & below	90°F & above	Clear	Partly cloudy	Cloudy	0.01 inch or more precip.	0.1 inch or more snow/ice	Thunder-storms
0	< 1	5	131	125	109	34	0	1

Note: Figures are average number of days per year and covers the years 1947-1990
Source: National Climatic Data Center, International Station Meteorological Climate Summary, 3/95

AIR & WATER QUALITY

Maximum Pollutant Concentrations

	Particulate Matter (ug/m^3)	Carbon Monoxide (ppm)	Sulfur Dioxide (ppm)	Nitrogen Dioxide (ppm)	Ozone (ppm)	Lead (ug/m^3)
MSA[1] Level	109	15	0.011	0.045	0.20	0.06
NAAQS[2]	150	9	0.140	0.053	0.12	1.50
Met NAAQS?	Yes	No	Yes	Yes	No	Yes

Note: (1) Metropolitan Statistical Area - see Appendix A for areas included; (2) National Ambient Air Quality Standards; ppm = parts per million; ug/m^3 = micrograms per cubic meter; n/a not available
Source: EPA, National Air Quality and Emissions Trends Report, 1996

Pollutant Standards Index

In the Los Angeles MSA (see Appendix A for areas included), the Pollutant Standards Index (PSI) exceeded 100 on 89 days in 1996. A PSI value greater than 100 indicates that air quality would be in the unhealthful range on that day. *EPA, National Air Quality and Emissions Trends Report, 1996*

Drinking Water

Water System Name	Pop. Served	Primary Water Source Type	Number of Violations in Fiscal Year 1997	Type of Violation/ Contaminants
LA Dept of Water & Power	3,600,000	Surface	None	None

Note: Data as of January 16, 1998
Source: EPA, Office of Ground Water and Drinking Water, Safe Drinking Water Information System

Los Angeles tap water hardness ranges from 4.2-15.1 gpg. The alkalinity also varies, ranging from 5.4-8.6 gpg. The Owens River Aqueduct accounts for approximately 70% of the water supply and is slightly alkaline and moderately soft with 4.2 gpg total hardness.
Editor & Publisher Market Guide, 1998

Oakland, California

Background

Oakland, the birthplace of author Bret Harte, was originally part of the Rancho San Antonio granted to Don Luis Peralta in 1820. As a result of the Gold Rush of 1849 and the influx of Americans, the Peralta family lost control of the area which was then developed by three settlers: Horace Carpentier, Edson Adams, and Andrew Moon. In 1851 ferry service to San Francisco began shortly after in 1852, Oakland was incorporated as a town and then as a city in 1854. It became the western terminus of the now Southern Pacific Railroad.

Annexations of adjacent land and the 1906 earthquake of San Francisco resulted in a rapid rise in population which continued through World War II.

Oakland, located to the east of San Francisco on a hillside, is a major industrial center and port. Its name reflects the numerous oak trees which dot the landscape.

The early settler foresaw an inner harbor at San Antonio Creek, an inlet of San Francisco Bay. As the harbor developed so did the city's commerce and industry. Shipbuilding is a flourishing business. Other major industries include chemicals, glass, electrical equipment, calculating machines, baby food, biological and pharmaceutical products as well as automobiles and trucks. The city is also home to some large Army and Navy supply depots.

Although just across the bay from San Francisco, the Oakland area experiences much more sunshine and temperatures which are usually about five degrees warmer. The city experiences high humidity with little rain.

General Rankings and Evaluative Comments

- Oakland was ranked #24 out of 300 cities by *Money's* 1997 "Survey of the Best Places to Live." Criteria used: health services, crime, economy, housing, education, transportation, weather, leisure and the arts. The city was ranked #75 in 1996 and #135 in 1995. *Money, July 1997; Money, September 1996; Money, September 1995*

- *Ladies Home Journal* ranked America's 200 largest cities based on the qualities women care about most. Oakland ranked 174 out of 200. Criteria: low crime rate, good public schools, well-paying jobs, quality health and child care, the presence of women in government, proportion of women-owned businesses, size of the wage gap with men, local economy, divorce rates, the ratio of single men to single women, whether there are laws that require at least the same number of public toilets for women as men, and the probability of good hair days. *Ladies Home Journal, November 1997*

- Oakland was ranked #178 out of 219 cities in terms of children's health, safety, and economic well-being. Criteria: total population, percent population change, birth rate, child immunization rate, infant mortality rate, percent low birth weight infants, percent of births to teens, physician-to-population ratio, student-to-teacher ratio, dropout rate, unemployment rate, median family income, percent of children in poverty, violent and property crime rates, number of juvenile arrests for violent crimes as a percent of the total crime index, number of days with pollution standard index (PSI) over 100, pounds toxic releases per 1,000 people and number of superfund sites. *Zero Population Growth, Children's Environmental Index 1997*

- *Yahoo! Internet Life* selected "America's 100 Most Wired Cities & Towns". 50 cities were large and 50 cities were small. Oakland ranked 49 out of 50 large cities. Criteria: Internet users per capita, number of networked computers, number of registered domain names, Internet backbone traffic, and the per-capita number of Web sites devoted to each city. *Yahoo! Internet Life, March 1998*

- *Reader's Digest* non-scientifically ranked the 12 largest U.S. metropolitan areas in terms of having the worst drivers. The San Francisco-Oakland metro area ranked number 12. The areas were selected by asking approximately 1,200 readers on the *Reader's Digest* Web site and 200 interstate bus drivers and long-haul truckers which metro areas have the worst drivers. Their responses were factored in with fatality, insurance and rental-car rates to create the rankings. *Reader's Digest, March 1998*

- According to *Working Mother,* "Lawmakers here—on both sides of the aisle—have agreed that the state must kick in more money to help working parents find and pay for child care. To that end, Governor Pete Wilson has proposed a significant expansion of the state's child care budget—an additional $277 million in state and federal funds. The new money would pay for care for about 90,000 more kids a year; and for preschool for another 13,000. In addition, some $45 million will be spent on recruiting and training caregivers for infants and toddlers.

  To help parents become more informed consumers, California passed a law that many consider a step backward. It allows family child care providers to care for two more kids, without hiring additional help. This means a family child care provider can now care for up to eight kids, instead of six, without additional help. The new rule also worries child care advocates because it may limit infant care in California. When caregivers take in the two extra older children, they must reduce the number of babies in their care. (California is among the 10 best states for child care.)" *Working Mother, July/August 1997*

Business Environment

STATE ECONOMY

State Economic Profile

"California's expansion is strong and stable....Entertainment and filmmaking remain steady contributors to the state's improved income growth and labor markets....

California's banking industry is consolidating and shedding workers. Improved credit conditions and healthy balance sheets make many remaining California thrifts likely takeover targets for out-of-state banks.

Delinquency rates on consumer credit have declined for the past two years and are well below the U.S. average. Mortgage foreclosure rates remain high, but they are down from the peak of one year ago when mortgage lenders took advantage of the improved housing market to shed nonperforming loans. California consumers remain cautious, however. Retail sales growth last year of 5% was no better than the national average.

Housing prices are up in northern California, and the number of units sold is rising throughout the state. Multifamily units dominated construction activity last year. With population growth accelerating and income growth outpacing the U.S. for the first time this decade, demand for single-family homes will strengthen.

Housing prices are up in northern California, and the number of units sold is rising throughout the state. Multifamily units dominated construction activity last year. With population growth accelerating the income growth outpacing the U.S. for the first time this decade, demand for single-family homes will strengthen.

Construction will contribute to the near-term expansion as home building accelerates. The greatest risk to the California economy is that the rising dollar could choke off foreign demand for California's export products. Longer term there will be some consolidation among high-tech firms, and high costs will limit the breadth of industrial development. California will remain an average performer over the long term." *National Association of Realtors, Economic Profiles: The Fifty States, July 1997*

IMPORTS/EXPORTS

Total Export Sales

Area	1993 ($000)	1994 ($000)	1995 ($000)	1996 ($000)	% Chg. 1993-96	% Chg. 1995-96
MSA[1]	4,181,478	5,113,244	6,372,463	7,309,195	74.8	14.7
U.S.	464,858,354	512,415,609	583,030,524	622,827,063	34.0	6.8

Note: (1) Metropolitan Statistical Area - see Appendix A for areas included
Source: U.S. Department of Commerce, International Trade Association, Metropolitan Area Exports: An Export Performance Report on Over 250 U.S. Cities, October 1997

Imports/Exports by Port

Type	Cargo Value			Share of U.S. Total	
	1995 (US$mil.)	1996 (US$mil.)	% Change 1995-1996	1995 (%)	1996 (%)
Imports	19,207	15,946	-16.98	4.91	4.16
Exports	11,551	10,944	-5.26	5.05	4.62

Source: Global Trade Information Services, WaterBorne Trade Atlas 1997

CITY FINANCES

City Government Finances

Component	FY92 ($000)	FY92 (per capita $)
Revenue	565,865	1,508.62
Expenditure	553,502	1,475.66
Debt Outstanding	1,144,082	3,050.16
Cash & Securities	1,156,249	3,082.60

Source: U.S. Bureau of the Census, City Government Finances: 1991-92

City Government Revenue by Source

Source	FY92 ($000)	FY92 (per capita $)	FY92 (%)
From Federal Government	29,072	77.51	5.1
From State Governments	67,586	180.19	11.9
From Local Governments	5,202	13.87	0.9
Property Taxes	112,760	300.62	19.9
General Sales Taxes	30,440	81.15	5.4
Selective Sales Taxes	37,347	99.57	6.6
Income Taxes	0	0.00	0.0
Current Charges	148,042	394.68	26.2
Utility/Liquor Store	0	0.00	0.0
Employee Retirement[1]	25,834	68.87	4.6
Other	109,582	292.15	19.4

Note: (1) Excludes "city contributions," classified as "nonrevenue," intragovernmental transfers.
Source: U.S. Bureau of the Census, City Government Finances: 1991-92

City Government Expenditures by Function

Function	FY92 ($000)	FY92 (per capita $)	FY92 (%)
Educational Services	12,395	33.05	2.2
Employee Retirement[1]	45,635	121.66	8.2
Environment/Housing	109,447	291.79	19.8
Government Administration	36,674	97.77	6.6
Interest on General Debt	73,861	196.92	13.3
Public Safety	126,180	336.40	22.8
Social Services	1,033	2.75	0.2
Transportation	72,534	193.38	13.1
Utility/Liquor Store	0	0.00	0.0
Other	75,743	201.93	13.7

Note: (1) Payments to beneficiaries including withdrawal of contributions.
Source: U.S. Bureau of the Census, City Government Finances: 1991-92

Municipal Bond Ratings

Area	Moody's	S & P
Oakland	A1	AA-

Note: n/a not available; n/r not rated
Source: Moody's Bond Record, 2/98; Statistical Abstract of the U.S., 1997;
Governing Magazine, 9/97, 3/98

POPULATION

Population Growth

Area	1980	1990	% Chg. 1980-90	July 1996 Estimate	% Chg. 1990-96
City	339,337	372,242	9.7	367,230	-1.3
MSA[1]	n/a	2,082,914	n/a	2,209,629	6.1
U.S.	226,545,805	248,765,170	9.8	265,179,411	6.6

Note: (1) Metropolitan Statistical Area - see Appendix A for areas included
Source: 1980/1990 Census of Housing and Population, Summary Tape File 3C;
Census Bureau Population Estimates

Population Characteristics

Race	City 1980 Population	%	City 1990 Population	%	% Chg. 1980-90	MSA[1] 1990 Population	%
White	131,127	38.6	120,855	32.5	-7.8	1,374,257	66.0
Black	159,351	47.0	163,526	43.9	2.6	303,632	14.6
Amer Indian/Esk/Aleut	2,753	0.8	2,325	0.6	-15.5	13,784	0.7
Asian/Pacific Islander	28,053	8.3	55,332	14.9	97.2	270,136	13.0
Other	18,053	5.3	30,204	8.1	67.3	121,105	5.8
Hispanic Origin[2]	32,133	9.5	49,267	13.2	53.3	266,283	12.8

Note: (1) Metropolitan Statistical Area - see Appendix A for areas included;
(2) people of Hispanic origin can be of any race
Source: 1980/1990 Census of Housing and Population, Summary Tape File 3C

Ancestry

Area	German	Irish	English	Italian	U.S.	French	Polish	Dutch
City	7.1	5.6	6.1	2.5	1.1	1.6	1.3	0.8
MSA[1]	16.9	12.4	13.0	6.0	1.9	3.5	2.0	1.8
U.S.	23.3	15.6	13.1	5.9	5.3	4.2	3.8	2.5

Note: Figures are percentages and include persons that reported multiple ancestry (eg. if a person reported being Irish and Italian, they were included in both columns); (1) Metropolitan Statistical Area - see Appendix A for areas included
Source: 1990 Census of Population and Housing, Summary Tape File 3C

Age

Area	Median Age (Years)	Age Distribution (%) Under 5	Under 18	18-24	25-44	45-64	65+	80+
City	32.6	8.0	24.8	10.1	36.1	16.8	12.2	3.0
MSA[1]	33.2	7.5	24.2	10.0	36.4	18.7	10.7	2.3
U.S.	32.9	7.3	25.6	10.5	32.6	18.7	12.5	2.8

Note: (1) Metropolitan Statistical Area - see Appendix A for areas included
Source: 1990 Census of Population and Housing, Summary Tape File 3C

Male/Female Ratio

Area	Number of males per 100 females (all ages)	Number of males per 100 females (18 years old+)
City	91.4	89.2
MSA[1]	96.0	94.2
U.S.	95.0	91.9

Note: (1) Metropolitan Statistical Area - see Appendix A for areas included
Source: 1990 Census of Population, General Population Characteristics

INCOME

Per Capita/Median/Average Income

Area	Per Capita ($)	Median Household ($)	Average Household ($)
City	14,676	27,095	37,100
MSA[1]	18,782	40,621	49,478
U.S.	14,420	30,056	38,453

Note: all figures are for 1989; (1) Metropolitan Statistical Area - see Appendix A for areas included
Source: 1990 Census of Population and Housing, Summary Tape File 3C

Household Income Distribution by Race

Income ($)	City (%)					U.S. (%)				
	Total	White	Black	Other	Hisp.[1]	Total	White	Black	Other	Hisp.[1]
Less than 5,000	6.4	3.4	8.8	7.4	5.2	6.2	4.8	15.2	8.6	8.8
5,000 - 9,999	12.8	9.2	16.6	11.5	11.0	9.3	8.6	14.2	9.9	11.1
10,000 - 14,999	9.5	7.3	11.0	10.8	9.0	8.8	8.5	11.0	9.8	11.0
15,000 - 24,999	17.5	15.4	18.9	19.0	23.1	17.5	17.3	18.9	18.5	20.5
25,000 - 34,999	15.1	15.1	15.1	15.3	17.6	15.8	16.1	14.2	15.4	16.4
35,000 - 49,999	15.0	16.2	13.6	15.7	17.8	17.9	18.6	13.3	16.1	16.0
50,000 - 74,999	13.1	15.8	10.7	12.9	10.7	15.0	15.8	9.3	13.4	11.1
75,000 - 99,999	5.6	8.4	3.4	4.6	3.5	5.1	5.5	2.6	4.7	3.1
100,000+	4.9	9.1	1.9	2.8	2.2	4.4	4.8	1.3	3.7	1.9

Note: all figures are for 1989; (1) people of Hispanic origin can be of any race
Source: 1990 Census of Population and Housing, Summary Tape File 3C

Effective Buying Income

Area	Per Capita ($)	Median Household ($)	Average Household ($)
City	14,519	28,788	38,516
MSA[1]	18,754	43,519	51,401
U.S.	15,444	33,201	41,849

Note: data as of 1/1/97; (1) Metropolitan Statistical Area - see Appendix A for areas included
Source: Standard Rate & Data Service, Newspaper Advertising Source, 2/98

Effective Household Buying Income Distribution

Area	% of Households Earning						
	$10,000 -$19,999	$20,000 -$34,999	$35,000 -$49,999	$50,000 -$74,999	$75,000 -$99,000	$100,000 -$124,999	$125,000 and up
City	18.7	23.6	15.4	15.1	6.1	2.2	2.3
MSA[1]	11.9	19.0	17.9	23.6	11.0	4.0	3.8
U.S.	16.5	23.4	18.3	18.2	6.4	2.1	2.4

Note: data as of 1/1/97; (1) Metropolitan Statistical Area - see Appendix A for areas included
Source: Standard Rate & Data Service, Newspaper Advertising Source, 2/98

Poverty Rates by Race and Age

Area	Total (%)	By Race (%)				By Age (%)		
		White	Black	Other	Hisp.[2]	Under 5 years old	Under 18 years old	65 years and over
City	18.8	9.0	23.9	22.6	21.7	32.1	30.3	11.0
MSA[1]	9.3	5.9	21.1	12.4	13.2	14.7	13.7	7.0
U.S.	13.1	9.8	29.5	23.1	25.3	20.1	18.3	12.8

Note: figures show the percent of people living below the poverty line in 1989. The average poverty threshold was $12,674 for a family of four in 1989; (1) Metropolitan Statistical Area - see Appendix A for areas included; (2) people of Hispanic origin can be of any race
Source: 1990 Census of Population and Housing, Summary Tape File 3C

EMPLOYMENT

Labor Force and Employment

Area	Civilian Labor Force			Workers Employed		
	Dec. '95	Dec. '96	% Chg.	Dec. '95	Dec. '96	% Chg.
City	179,282	181,581	1.3	168,157	171,948	2.3
MSA[1]	1,143,540	1,161,695	1.6	1,098,419	1,123,181	2.3
U.S.	134,583,000	136,742,000	1.6	127,903,000	130,785,000	2.3

Note: Data is not seasonally adjusted and covers workers 16 years of age and older;
(1) Metropolitan Statistical Area - see Appendix A for areas included
Source: Bureau of Labor Statistics, http://stats.bls.gov

Unemployment Rate

Area	1997											
	Jan.	Feb.	Mar.	Apr.	May	Jun.	Jul.	Aug.	Sep.	Oct.	Nov.	Dec.
City	7.7	7.3	6.9	6.9	6.9	7.3	7.9	7.5	7.4	6.9	6.0	5.3
MSA[1]	4.9	4.6	4.3	4.3	4.3	4.6	4.9	4.6	4.5	4.2	3.7	3.3
U.S.	5.9	5.7	5.5	4.8	4.7	5.2	5.0	4.8	4.7	4.4	4.3	4.4

Note: Data is not seasonally adjusted and covers workers 16 years of age and older; All figures are percentages; (1) Metropolitan Statistical Area - see Appendix A for areas included
Source: Bureau of Labor Statistics, http://stats.bls.gov

Employment by Industry

Sector	MSA[1]		U.S.
	Number of Employees	Percent of Total	Percent of Total
Services	288,200	29.6	29.0
Retail Trade	161,900	16.6	18.5
Government	172,400	17.7	16.1
Manufacturing	120,700	12.4	15.0
Finance/Insurance/Real Estate	55,900	5.7	5.7
Wholesale Trade	60,900	6.2	5.4
Transportation/Public Utilities	61,800	6.3	5.3
Construction	51,000	5.2	4.5
Mining	2,300	0.2	0.5

Note: Figures cover non-farm employment as of 12/97 and are not seasonally adjusted;
(1) Metropolitan Statistical Area - see Appendix A for areas included
Source: Bureau of Labor Statistics, http://stats.bls.gov

Employment by Occupation

Occupation Category	City (%)	MSA[1] (%)	U.S. (%)
White Collar	63.8	67.4	58.1
Executive/Admin./Management	13.9	16.4	12.3
Professional	18.1	16.7	14.1
Technical & Related Support	4.2	4.7	3.7
Sales	10.1	12.1	11.8
Administrative Support/Clerical	17.6	17.6	16.3
Blue Collar	20.1	20.7	26.2
Precision Production/Craft/Repair	7.9	10.2	11.3
Machine Operators/Assem./Insp.	4.9	4.0	6.8
Transportation/Material Movers	3.5	3.2	4.1
Cleaners/Helpers/Laborers	3.7	3.3	3.9
Services	14.9	10.8	13.2
Farming/Forestry/Fishing	1.2	1.1	2.5

Note: figures cover employed persons 16 years old and over;
(1) Metropolitan Statistical Area - see Appendix A for areas included
Source: 1990 Census of Population and Housing, Summary Tape File 3C

Occupational Employment Projections: 1994 - 2001

Occupations Expected to have the Largest Job Growth (ranked by numerical growth)	Fast-Growing Occupations[1] (ranked by percent growth)
1. General managers & top executives	1. Computer engineers
2. Salespersons, retail	2. Systems analysts
3. Cashiers	3. Technical writers
4. Waiters & waitresses	4. Personal and home care aides
5. Secretaries, except legal & medical	5. Emergency medical technicians
6. Computer engineers	6. Engineers, electrical & electronic
7. General office clerks	7. Electrical equipment assem., precision
8. Sales reps, non-technical, exc retail	8. Solderers/brazers
9. Truck drivers, light	9. Engineers, other
10. Systems analysts	10. Food service and lodging managers

Projections cover Alameda County.
Note: (1) Excludes occupations with employment of less than 400 in 2001
Source: State of California, Employment Development Department, Labor Market Information Division, Information Services Group

Average Wages

Occupation	Wage	Occupation	Wage
Professional/Technical/Clerical	$/Week	**Health/Protective Services**	$/Week
Accountants III	881	Corrections Officers	710
Attorneys III	1,461	Firefighters	905
Budget Analysts III	-	Nurses, Licensed Practical II	653
Buyers/Contracting Specialists II	724	Nurses, Registered II	1,034
Clerks, Accounting III	517	Nursing Assistants II	367
Clerks, General III	490	Police Officers I	938
Computer Operators II	521	**Hourly Workers**	$/Hour
Computer Programmers II	663	Forklift Operators	14.49
Drafters II	644	General Maintenance Workers	11.37
Engineering Technicians III	652	Guards I	7.35
Engineering Technicians, Civil III	791	Janitors	9.79
Engineers III	1,031	Maintenance Electricians	20.43
Key Entry Operators I	363	Maintenance Electronics Techs II	19.90
Personnel Assistants III	-	Maintenance Machinists	19.87
Personnel Specialists III	856	Maintenance Mechanics, Machinery	18.19
Secretaries III	620	Material Handling Laborers	-
Switchboard Operator-Receptionist	407	Motor Vehicle Mechanics	19.98
Systems Analysts II	1,020	Shipping/Receiving Clerks	12.01
Systems Analysts Supervisor/Mgr II	-	Tool and Die Makers	-
Tax Collectors II	610	Truckdrivers, Tractor Trailer	16.31
Word Processors II	524	Warehouse Specialists	11.42

Note: Wage data includes full-time workers only for 1/95 and cover the Metropolitan Statistical Area (see Appendix A for areas included). Dashes indicate that data was not available.
Source: Bureau of Labor Statistics, Occupational Compensation Survey

TAXES

Major State and Local Tax Rates

State Corp. Income (%)	State Personal Income (%)	Residential Property (effective rate per $100)	Sales & Use State (%)	Sales & Use Local (%)	State Gasoline (cents/ gallon)	State Cigarette (cents/ 20-pack)
8.84[a]	1.0 - 9.3	n/a	6.0	2.25	18[b]	37

Note: Personal/corporate income tax rates as of 1/97. Sales, gasoline and cigarette tax rates as of 1/98; (a) Minimum tax is $800. The tax rate on S-Corporations is 1.5%; (b) Does not include 1 cent local option tax
Source: Federation of Tax Administrators, www.taxadmin.org; Washington D.C. Department of Finance and Revenue, Tax Rates and Tax Burdens in the District of Columbia: A Nationwide Comparison, June 1997; Chamber of Commerce

Total Taxes Per Capita and as a Percent of Income

Area	Per Capita Income ($)	Per Capita Taxes ($)			Taxes as Pct. of Income (%)		
		Total	Federal	State/Local	Total	Federal	State/Local
California	27,117	9,321	6,287	3,034	34.4	23.2	11.2
U.S.	26,187	9,205	6,127	3,078	35.2	23.4	11.8

Note: Figures are for 1997
Source: Tax Foundation, Web Site, www.taxfoundation.org

COMMERCIAL REAL ESTATE

Office Market

Class/Location	Total Space (sq. ft.)	Vacant Space (sq. ft.)	Vac. Rate (%)	Under Constr. (sq. ft.)	Net Absorp. (sq. ft.)	Rental Rates ($/sq.ft./yr.)
Class A						
CBD	6,006,182	1,048,047	17.4	0	-397,147	16.20-26.40
Outside CBD	3,750,654	305,036	8.1	0	-78,813	15.60-26.88
Class B						
CBD	7,677,858	1,239,341	16.1	0	n/a	11.88-21.00
Outside CBD	8,786,126	1,134,724	12.9	0	n/a	12.00-24.00

Note: Data as of 10/97 and covers Oakland; CBD = Central Business District; n/a not available;
Source: Society of Industrial and Office Realtors, 1998 Comparative Statistics of Industrial and Office Real Estate Markets

"Despite the dreary 1997, demand should increase in 1998 as adjoining markets—specifically Downtown San Francisco, Silicon Valley and the I-680 Corridor (Contra Costa County) continue to tighten. Increased interest is reported from computer and software firms in Class 'A' properties as rents are very competitive with suburban markets. Downtown Oakland will continue to benefit from the BART rail system which serves the CBD. However, as federal government tenants move into their own new buildings, large vacancies are expected for some time in existing properties. New construction for both the University of California's Berkeley campus and state and city offices could rob any speculative buildings of their tenants as well." *Society of Industrial and Office Realtors, 1998 Comparative Statistics of Industrial and Office Real Estate Markets*

Industrial Market

Location	Total Space (sq. ft.)	Vacant Space (sq. ft.)	Vac. Rate (%)	Under Constr. (sq. ft.)	Net Absorp. (sq. ft.)	Net Lease ($/sq.ft./yr.)
Central City	24,267,338	2,468,803	10.2	250,000	1,317,488	2.88-6.48
Suburban	80,287,801	7,543,129	9.4	662,460	7,598,857	3.36-6.12

Note: Data as of 10/97 and covers Berkeley, Emeryville, Hayward, Oakland, Richmond, San Leandro and Union City; n/a not available
Source: Society of Industrial and Office Realtors, 1998 Comparative Statistics of Industrial and Office Real Estate Markets

"Total speculative development started in 1997 was 500,000 sq. ft. Nearly 2.2 million sq. ft. is anticipated for 1998. This is the first major quantity of new product to be brought to market in many years. This will help satisfy the 'pent-up' demand that has forced vacancies near the 10 percent mark. Most future industrial and warehouse activity will be concentrated in the Hayward/Union City sub-market. This is one of the few sub-markets that has environmentally clean, reasonably priced industrial parcels. Bio-tech and other R&D businesses will gravitate to the Emeryville/Berkeley sub-market. Pension funds and REITs will continue to compete for industrial acquisitions. Nearly all large speculative industrial buildings are institutionally owned." *Society of Industrial and Office Realtors, 1998 Comparative Statistics of Industrial and Office Real Estate Markets*

Retail Market

Shopping Center Inventory (sq. ft.)	Shopping Center Construction (sq. ft.)	Construction as a Percent of Inventory (%)	Torto Wheaton Rent Index[1] ($/sq. ft.)
36,833,000	91,000	0.2	13.69

Note: Data as of 1997 and covers the Metropolitan Statistical Area - see Appendix A for areas included; (1) Index is based on a model that predicts what the average rent should be for leases with certain characteristics, in certain locations during certain years.
Source: National Association of Realtors, 1997-1998 Market Conditions Report

"Oakland's retail sector is beginning to pull out of its recent slump. The area's retail index jumped 6.7% in 1997, after declining four of the five years between 1992 and 1996. Consolidation in the retail trade industry has hurt the East Bay market. Both the general merchandise and food store categories experienced job losses in recent years. Payrolls in general merchandise dropped 2.4% in 1996. Bay Area insiders feel that retailers are lagging behind other sectors of the area's recovering economy, since consumers are buying bigger-ticket items such as homes and cars. Population growth, however, is expected to rise over the next several years, matching the national rise." *National Association of Realtors, 1997-1998 Market Conditions Report*

COMMERCIAL UTILITIES

Typical Monthly Electric Bills

Area	Commercial Service ($/month)		Industrial Service ($/month)	
	12 kW demand 1,500 kWh	100 kW demand 30,000 kWh	1,000 kW demand 400,000 kWh	20,000 kW demand 10,000,000 kWh
City	231	3,420	41,622	565,537
U.S.	162	2,360	25,590	545,677

Note: Based on rates in effect July 1, 1997
Source: Edison Electric Institute, Typical Residential, Commercial and Industrial Bills, Summer 1997

TRANSPORTATION

Transportation Statistics

Avg. travel time to work (min.)	25.8
Interstate highways	I-80
Bus lines	
In-city	AC Transit
Inter-city	4
Passenger air service	
Airport	Oakland International
Airlines	11
Aircraft departures	78,202 (1995)
Enplaned passengers	4,750,857 (1995)
Rail service	Amtrak; Bay Area Rapid Transit
Motor freight carriers	1,318
Major waterways/ports	Port of Oakland; San Francisco Bay

Source: OAG, Business Travel Planner, Summer 1997; Editor & Publisher Market Guide, 1998; FAA Airport Activity Statistics, 1996; Amtrak National Time Table, Northeast Timetable, Fall/Winter 1997-98; 1990 Census of Population and Housing, STF 3C; Chamber of Commerce/Economic Development 1997; Jane's Urban Transport Systems 1997-98; Transit Fact Book 1997

A survey of 90,000 airline passengers during the first half of 1997 ranked most of the largest airports in the U.S. Oakland International ranked number 15 out of 36. Criteria: cleanliness, quality of restaurants, attractiveness, speed of baggage delivery, ease of reaching gates, available ground transportation, ease of following signs and closeness of parking. *Plog Research Inc., First Half 1997*

Means of Transportation to Work

Area	Car/Truck/Van		Public Transportation			Bicycle	Walked	Other Means	Worked at Home
	Drove Alone	Car-pooled	Bus	Subway	Railroad				
City	57.0	14.1	11.5	5.9	0.2	1.1	4.9	1.8	3.6
MSA[1]	68.6	13.2	3.9	4.7	0.4	1.0	3.1	1.4	3.7
U.S.	73.2	13.4	3.0	1.5	0.5	0.4	3.9	1.2	3.0

Note: figures shown are percentages and only include workers 16 years old and over;
(1) Metropolitan Statistical Area - see Appendix A for areas included
Source: 1990 Census of Population and Housing, Summary Tape File 3C

BUSINESSES

Major Business Headquarters

Company Name	1997 Rankings	
	Fortune 500	Forbes 500
APL	480	-
Crowley Maritime	-	166
Golden West Financial	488	-
Safeway	65	-

Note: Companies listed are located in the city; Dashes indicate no ranking
Fortune 500: companies that produce a 10-K are ranked 1 - 500 based on 1996 revenue
Forbes 500: private companies are ranked 1 - 500 based on 1996 revenue
Source: Forbes 12/1/97; Fortune 4/28/97

Women-Owned Businesses: Number, Employment, Sales and Share

Area	Women-Owned Businesses in 1996				Share of Women-Owned Businesses in 1996	
	Number	Employment	Sales ($000)	Rank[2]	Percent (%)	Rank[3]
MSA[1]	81,300	154,100	20,164,300	20	39.8	3

Note: (1) Metropolitan Statistical Area - see Appendix A for areas included; (2) Calculated on an averaging of number of businesses, employment and sales and ranges from 1 to 50 where 1 is best; (3) Ranges from 1 to 50 where 1 is best
Source: The National Foundation for Women Business Owners, 1996 Facts on Women-Owned Businesses: Trends in the Top 50 Metropolitan Areas, March 26, 1997

Women-Owned Businesses: Growth

Area	Growth in Women-Owned Businesses (% change from 1987 to 1996)				Relative Growth in the Number of Women-Owned and All Businesses (% change from 1987 to 1996)			
	Num.	Empl.	Sales	Rank[2]	Women-Owned	All Firms	Absolute Difference	Relative Difference
MSA[1]	63.9	248.2	333.5	21	63.9	41.6	22.3	1.5:1

Note: (1) Metropolitan Statistical Area - see Appendix A for areas included; (2) Calculated on an averaging of the percent growth of number of businesses, employment and sales and ranges from 1 to 50 where 1 is best
Source: The National Foundation for Women Business Owners, 1996 Facts on Women-Owned Businesses: Trends in the Top 50 Metropolitan Areas, March 26, 1997

Minority Business Opportunity

Two of the 500 largest Hispanic-owned companies in the U.S. are located in Oakland.
Hispanic Business, June 1997

Oakland was listed among the top 25 metropolitan areas in terms of the number of Hispanic-owned companies. The city was ranked number 13 with 22,386 companies.
Hispanic Business, May 1997

HOTELS & MOTELS

Hotels/Motels

Area	Hotels/ Motels	Rooms	Luxury-Level Hotels/Motels		Average Minimum Rates ($)		
			◆◆◆◆	◆◆◆◆◆	◆◆	◆◆◆	◆◆◆◆
City	6	1,087	0	0	n/a	n/a	n/a
Airport	9	1,461	0	0	n/a	n/a	n/a
Suburbs	54	6,555	0	0	n/a	n/a	n/a
Total	69	9,103	0	0	n/a	n/a	n/a

Note: n/a not available; Classifications range from one diamond (budget properties with basic amenities) to five diamond (luxury properties with the finest service, rooms and facilities).
Source: OAG, Business Travel Planner, Summer 1997

CONVENTION CENTERS

Major Convention Centers

Center Name	Meeting Rooms	Exhibit Space (sf)
Oakland-Alameda County	5	120,000
Oakland Convention Center	13	48,000
Henry J. Kaiser Auditorium	4	24,900

Source: Trade Shows Worldwide 1997

Living Environment

COST OF LIVING

Cost of Living Index

Composite Index	Housing	Utilities	Groceries	Health Care	Trans-portation	Misc. Goods/ Services
n/a	n/a	n/a	n/a	n/a	n/a	n/a

Note: U.S. = 100; n/a not available
Source: ACCRA, Cost of Living Index, 3rd Quarter 1997

HOUSING

Median Home Prices and Housing Affordability

Area	Median Price[2] 3rd Qtr. 1997 ($)	HOI[3] 3rd Qtr. 1997	Afford-ability Rank[4]
MSA[1]	220,000	41.8	184
U.S.	127,000	63.7	–

Note: (1) Metropolitan Statistical Area - see Appendix A for areas included; (2) U.S. figures calculated from the sales of 625,000 new and existing homes in 195 markets; (3) Housing Opportunity Index - percent of homes sold that were within the reach of the median income household at the prevailing mortgage interest rate; (4) Rank is from 1-195 with 1 being most affordable
Source: National Association of Home Builders, Housing Opportunity Index, 3rd Quarter 1997

It is projected that the median price of existing single-family homes in the metro area will increase by 8.8% in 1998. Nationwide, home prices are projected to increase 6.6%.
Kiplinger's Personal Finance Magazine, January 1998

Average New Home Price

Area	Price ($)
City	n/a
U.S.	135,710

Note: n/a not available
Source: ACCRA, Cost of Living Index, 3rd Quarter 1997

Average Apartment Rent

Area	Rent ($/mth)
City	n/a
U.S.	569

Note: n/a not available
Source: ACCRA, Cost of Living Index, 3rd Quarter 1997

RESIDENTIAL UTILITIES

Average Residential Utility Costs

Area	All Electric ($/mth)	Part Electric ($/mth)	Other Energy ($/mth)	Phone ($/mth)
City	n/a	n/a	n/a	n/a
U.S.	109.40	55.25	43.64	19.48

Note: n/a not available
Source: ACCRA, Cost of Living Index, 3rd Quarter 1997

HEALTH CARE

Average Health Care Costs

Area	Hospital ($/day)	Doctor ($/visit)	Dentist ($/visit)
City	n/a	n/a	n/a
U.S.	392.91	48.76	60.84

Note: n/a not available
Source: ACCRA, Cost of Living Index, 3rd Quarter 1997

Distribution of Office-Based Physicians

Area	Family/Gen. Practitioners	Specialists		
		Medical	Surgical	Other
MSA[1]	474	1,527	945	1,188

Note: Data as of 12/31/96; (1) Metropolitan Statistical Area - see Appendix A for areas included
Source: American Medical Assn., Physician Characteristics & Distribution in the U.S., 1997-1998

Hospitals

Oakland has 3 general medical and surgical hospitals, 1 children's general. *AHA Guide to the Healthcare Field 1997-98*

EDUCATION

Public School District Statistics

District Name	Num. Sch.	Enroll.	Classroom Teachers[1]	Pupils per Teacher	Minority Pupils (%)	Current Exp.[2] ($/pupil)
Oakland Unified	89	52,452	2,211	23.7	93.2	5,387

Note: Data covers the 1995-1996 school year unless otherwise noted; (1) Excludes teachers reported as working in school district offices rather than in schools; (2) Based on 1993-94 enrollment collected by the Census Bureau, not the enrollment figure shown in column 3; SD = School District; ISD = Independent School District; n/a not available
Source: National Center for Education Statistics, Common Core of Data Survey; Bureau of the Census

Educational Quality

School District	Education Quotient[1]	Graduate Outcome[2]	Community Index[3]	Resource Index[4]
Oakland	81.0	53.0	118.0	71.0

Note: Nearly 1,000 secondary school districts were rated in terms of educational quality. The scores range from a low of 50 to a high of 150; (1) Average of the Graduate Outcome, Community and Resource indexes; (2) Based on graduation rates and college board scores (SAT/ACT); (3) Based on the surrounding community's average level of education and the area's average income level; (4) Based on teacher salaries, per-pupil expenditures and student-teacher ratios.
Source: Expansion Management, Ratings Issue 1997

Educational Attainment by Race

Area	High School Graduate (%)					Bachelor's Degree (%)				
	Total	White	Black	Other	Hisp.[2]	Total	White	Black	Other	Hisp.[2]
City	74.4	85.9	73.3	54.6	45.6	27.2	46.0	14.1	17.9	10.8
MSA[1]	83.4	87.1	76.3	73.7	63.3	29.9	32.7	15.6	29.3	12.9
U.S.	75.2	77.9	63.1	60.4	49.8	20.3	21.5	11.4	19.4	9.2

Note: figures shown cover persons 25 years old and over; (1) Metropolitan Statistical Area - see Appendix A for areas included; (2) people of Hispanic origin can be of any race
Source: 1990 Census of Population and Housing, Summary Tape File 3C

School Enrollment by Type

Area	Preprimary				Elementary/High School			
	Public		Private		Public		Private	
	Enrollment	%	Enrollment	%	Enrollment	%	Enrollment	%
City	3,366	60.8	2,169	39.2	53,247	86.7	8,167	13.3
MSA[1]	22,693	54.3	19,124	45.7	293,406	89.3	35,303	10.7
U.S.	2,679,029	59.5	1,824,256	40.5	38,379,689	90.2	4,187,099	9.8

Note: figures shown cover persons 3 years old and over;
(1) Metropolitan Statistical Area - see Appendix A for areas included
Source: 1990 Census of Population and Housing, Summary Tape File 3C

School Enrollment by Race

Area	Preprimary (%)				Elementary/High School (%)			
	White	Black	Other	Hisp.[1]	White	Black	Other	Hisp.[1]
City	27.9	52.3	19.8	11.6	16.1	52.1	31.8	18.0
MSA[2]	68.2	14.7	17.1	13.0	56.9	18.2	24.8	17.5
U.S.	80.4	12.5	7.1	7.8	74.1	15.6	10.3	12.5

Note: figures shown cover persons 3 years old and over; (1) people of Hispanic origin can be of any race; (2) Metropolitan Statistical Area - see Appendix A for areas included
Source: 1990 Census of Population and Housing, Summary Tape File 3C

SAT/ACT Scores

Area/District	1996 SAT				1996 ACT	
	Percent of Graduates Tested (%)	Average Math Score	Average Verbal Score	Average Combined Score	Percent of Graduates Tested (%)	Average Composite Score
Oakland USD	n/a	444	418	862	n/a	n/a
State	45	511	495	1,006	11	21.0
U.S.	41	508	505	1,013	35	20.9

Note: Math and verbal SAT scores are out of a possible 800; ACT scores are out of a possible 36
Caution: Comparing or ranking states/cities on the basis of SAT/ACT scores alone is invalid and strongly discouraged by the The College Board and The American College Testing Program as students who take the tests are self-selected and do not represent the entire student population. 1996 SAT scores cannot be compared to previous years due to recentering.
Source: Oakland Unified School District, 1996; American College Testing Program, 1996; College Board, 1996

Classroom Teacher Salaries in Public Schools

District	B.A. Degree		M.A. Degree		Ph.D. Degree	
	Min. ($)	Max. ($)	Min. ($)	Max. ($)	Min. ($)	Max. ($)
Oakland	27,580	41,320 n/a	n/a	30,332	44,879	
Average[1]	26,120	39,270	28,175	44,667	31,643	49,825

Note: Salaries are for 1996-1997; (1) Based on all school districts covered; n/a not available
Source: American Federation of Teachers (unpublished data)

Higher Education

Two-Year Colleges		Four-Year Colleges		Medical Schools	Law Schools	Voc/ Tech
Public	Private	Public	Private			
2	1	0	5	0	0	15

Source: College Blue Book, Occupational Education 1997; Medical School Admission Requirements, 1998-99; Peterson's Guide to Two-Year Colleges, 1997; Peterson's Guide to Four-Year Colleges, 1997; Barron's Guide to Law Schools 1997

MAJOR EMPLOYERS

Major Employers

American President Lines
Clorox Co.
Mother's Cake & Cookie Co.
San Francisco Bay Area Rapid Transit
TRW Financial Systems
World Savings & Loan Association

Children's Hospital Medical Center
East Bay Municipal Utility District Water System
Permanente Medical Group
Safeway New Canada
Waste Management of Alameda Co.

Note: companies listed are located in the city
Source: Dun's Business Rankings 1997; Ward's Business Directory, 1997

PUBLIC SAFETY

Crime Rate

Area	All Crimes	Violent Crimes				Property Crimes		
		Murder	Forcible Rape	Robbery	Aggrav. Assault	Burglary	Larceny -Theft	Motor Vehicle Theft
City	10,526.5	25.0	86.5	973.3	1,110.1	1,627.9	5,341.5	1,362.4
Suburbs[1]	5,386.0	6.5	26.9	220.3	349.9	900.2	3,274.8	607.4
MSA[2]	6,250.3	9.6	37.0	346.9	477.7	1,022.5	3,622.3	734.3
U.S.	5,078.9	7.4	36.1	202.4	388.2	943.0	2,975.9	525.9

Note: Crime rate is the number of crimes per 100,000 pop.; (1) defined as all areas within the MSA but located outside the central city; (2) Metropolitan Statistical Area - see Appendix A for areas incl.
Source: FBI Uniform Crime Reports 1996

RECREATION

Culture and Recreation

Museums	Symphony Orchestras	Opera Companies	Dance Companies	Professional Theatres	Zoos	Pro Sports Teams
8	1	1	1	1	1	3

Source: International Directory of the Performing Arts, 1996; Official Museum Directory, 1998; Chamber of Commerce/Economic Development 1997

Library System

The Oakland Public Library has 15 branches, holdings of 923,968 volumes and a budget of $13,446,666 (1995-1996). *American Library Directory, 1997-1998*

MEDIA

Newspapers

Name	Type	Freq.	Distribution	Circulation
Bay Area Press	General	1x/mo	Area	81,000
Berkeley Tri-City Post	Black	1x/wk	Area	20,000
Daily Construction Service (Northern California)	n/a	5x/wk	Area	2,200
El Cerrito Journal	n/a	1x/wk	Local	13,800
El Mundo	Hispanic	1x/wk	Local	31,950
The Montclarion	n/a	2x/wk	Local	31,000
Oakland Post	Black	2x/wk	Local	49,500
Oakland Tribune	n/a	7x/wk	Area	79,959
The Piedmonter	General	1x/wk	Local	7,000
Richmond Post	Black	2x/wk	Local	18,000
San Francisco Post	Black	2x/wk	Local	22,000

Note: Includes newspapers with circulations of 1,000 or more located in the city; n/a not available
Source: Burrelle's Media Directory, 1998 Edition

AM Radio Stations

Call Letters	Freq. (kHz)	Target Audience	Station Format	Music Format
KABL	960	n/a	M	Adult Standards
KFAX	1100	Religious	N/T	n/a
KDIA	1310	Black	M	Christian/R&B

Note: Stations included broadcast in the Oakland metro area; n/a not available
Station Format: E = Educational; M = Music; N = News; S = Sports; T = Talk
Source: Burrelle's Media Directory, 1998 Edition

FM Radio Stations

Call Letters	Freq. (mHz)	Target Audience	Station Format	Music Format
KPFB	89.3	General	E/M/N/T	AOR/Adult Contemporary/Adult Standards/Alternative/Big Band/Christian/Classic Rock/Classical/Country/Contemporary Top 40/Easy Listening
KOHL	89.3	General	M	Contemporary Top 40
KCRH	89.9	General	E/M/N/S	n/a
KZSU	90.1	General	E/M/N/S	Alternative/Big Band/Christian/Classic Rock/Classical/Country/Jazz/Oldies/R&B/Urban Contemporary
KFNO	90.3	General	M	Christian
KALX	90.7	General	M/N/S	Alternative
KPFA	94.1	General	E/M/N/T	n/a
KRTY	95.3	General	M/N/S	Country
KKIQ	101.7	General	M/N	Adult Contemporary
KEAR	106.9	General	E/M	Christian

Note: Stations included broadcast in the Oakland metro area; n/a not available
Station Format: E = Educational; M = Music; N = News; S = Sports; T = Talk
Music Format: AOR = Album Oriented Rock; MOR = Middle-of-the-Road
Source: Burrelle's Media Directory, 1998 Edition

Television Stations

Name	Ch.	Affiliation	Type	Owner
KTVU	2	Fox	Commercial	Cox Enterprises Inc.
KFTL	64	n/a	Commercial	Family Stations, Inc.

Note: Stations included broadcast in the Oakland metro area
Source: Burrelle's Media Directory, 1998 Edition

CLIMATE

Average and Extreme Temperatures

Temperature	Jan	Feb	Mar	Apr	May	Jun	Jul	Aug	Sep	Oct	Nov	Dec	Ann
Extreme High (°F)	72	79	86	92	100	101	101	102	106	101	85	75	106
Average High (°F)	56	60	62	66	68	71	71	72	74	71	64	57	66
Average Temp. (°F)	50	54	56	58	60	63	64	65	66	63	57	51	59
Average Low (°F)	44	47	49	51	52	55	56	57	57	55	51	46	52
Extreme Low (°F)	30	32	36	38	42	47	48	40	50	44	38	27	27

Note: Figures cover the years 1945-1993
Source: National Climatic Data Center, International Station Meteorological Climate Summary, 3/95

Average Precipitation/Snowfall/Humidity

Precip./Humidity	Jan	Feb	Mar	Apr	May	Jun	Jul	Aug	Sep	Oct	Nov	Dec	Ann
Avg. Precip. (in.)	3.7	2.7	2.7	1.1	0.4	0.1	0	0	0.3	1.1	2.3	3.1	17.6
Avg. Snowfall (in.)	Tr	Tr	0	0	0	0	0	0	0	0	0	Tr	Tr
Avg. Rel. Hum. 7am (%)	84	83	81	78	77	79	83	85	84	82	81	83	82
Avg. Rel. Hum. 4pm (%)	68	65	62	59	60	60	62	63	60	60	64	69	63

Note: Figures cover the years 1945-1993; Tr = Trace amounts (<0.05 in. of rain; <0.5 in. of snow)
Source: National Climatic Data Center, International Station Meteorological Climate Summary, 3/95

Weather Conditions

Temperature			Daytime Sky			Precipitation		
10°F & below	32°F & below	90°F & above	Clear	Partly cloudy	Cloudy	0.01 inch or more precip.	0.1 inch or more snow/ice	Thunder-storms
0	< 1	3	99	168	98	59	0	6

Note: Figures are average number of days per year and covers the years 1945-1993
Source: National Climatic Data Center, International Station Meteorological Climate Summary, 3/95

AIR & WATER QUALITY

Maximum Pollutant Concentrations

	Particulate Matter (ug/m³)	Carbon Monoxide (ppm)	Sulfur Dioxide (ppm)	Nitrogen Dioxide (ppm)	Ozone (ppm)	Lead (ug/m³)
MSA[1] Level	45	4	0.011	0.022	0.14	0.02
NAAQS[2]	150	9	0.140	0.053	0.12	1.50
Met NAAQS?	Yes	Yes	Yes	Yes	No	Yes

Note: (1) Metropolitan Statistical Area - see Appendix A for areas included; (2) National Ambient Air Quality Standards; ppm = parts per million; ug/m³ = micrograms per cubic meter; n/a not available
Source: EPA, National Air Quality and Emissions Trends Report, 1996

Pollutant Standards Index

In the Oakland MSA (see Appendix A for areas included), the Pollutant Standards Index (PSI) exceeded 100 on 11 days in 1996. A PSI value greater than 100 indicates that air quality would be in the unhealthful range on that day. *EPA, National Air Quality and Emissions Trends Report, 1996*

Drinking Water

Water System Name	Pop. Served	Primary Water Source Type	Number of Violations in Fiscal Year 1997	Type of Violation/ Contaminants
Alameda County Water District	286,400	Surface	None	None

Note: Data as of January 16, 1998
Source: EPA, Office of Ground Water and Drinking Water, Safe Drinking Water Information System

Oakland tap water is alkaline, soft and fluoridated.
Editor & Publisher Market Guide, 1998

Phoenix, Arizona

Background

Phoenix, the arid "Valley of the Sun", and the capital of Arizona, was named by the English soldier/prospector, "Lord Darell" Duppa for the mythical bird of Ancient Greek/Phoenician lore. According to the legend, the Phoenix was an awesomely beautiful bird that destroyed itself with its own flames. When nothing remained but embers it would rise again from the ashes, young and more awesome and beautiful than before. Like the romantic tale Duppa hoped that his city of Phoenix would rise again from the "ashes" of a mysteriously abandoned Hohokam village.

Many might agree that Phoenix fulfilled Duppa's wish. Within fifteen years after its second founding in 1867, Phoenix had grown to be an important supply point for the mining districts of northcentral Arizona, as well as an important trading site for farmers, cattlemen, and prospectors.

At around this time, Phoenix entered a "wild, wild west" phase, wherein stagecoaches, saloons, gambling houses, soldiers, cowboys, and miners all contributed to a pungent air of outlawry. It took two public hangings near the end of the 1800's to set a dramatic example.

Today, Phoenix is just as exciting as ever, but more law-abiding. Many people continue to be attracted to Phoenix's natural beauty, and their comfort here is aided by the invention of air-conditioning. Despite the occasional sprawling suburb and identity-erasing shopping mall, one cannot help noticing the sophisticated blend of Spanish, Indian and cowboy influences that give the city such great architecture and arts and crafts.

In the last five years downtown Phoenix has undergone a major renaissance with the completion of a history museum, an expanded art museum, a new central library and a renovated concert hall. Other projects under way include the $48 million Arizona Science Center and a new baseball stadium Since 1991 nearly $1 billion has been spent on construction in the downtown area, all financing coming from city, county and private sources.

Phoenix is the country's seventh largest city with more than one million people. By the year 2000 the Phoenix MSA is projected to grow to more than 2.7 million persons. This increase in population will help make Phoenix an attractive location for companies that are expanding in the fields of electronics and communications.

The city, also known as the "Silicon Desert", has already attracted a number of high-technology projects, including Sky Broadcasting and SKYMCA. *World Trade 4/97*

Temperatures range from very hot in summer to mild in winter. The normal high temperature is over 90 degrees from early May through early September. Many days each summer will exceed 110 degrees in the afternoon and remain above 85 degrees all night. However, the low humidity of desert air mitigates the discomfort one might expect from such high temperatures.

General Rankings and Evaluative Comments

- Phoenix was ranked #36 out of 300 cities by *Money's* 1997 "Survey of the Best Places to Live." Criteria used: health services, crime, economy, housing, education, transportation, weather, leisure and the arts. The city was ranked #34 in 1996 and #91 in 1995. *Money, July 1997; Money, September 1996; Money, September 1995*

- *Ladies Home Journal* ranked America's 200 largest cities based on the qualities women care about most. Phoenix ranked 76 out of 200. Criteria: low crime rate, good public schools, well-paying jobs, quality health and child care, the presence of women in government, proportion of women-owned businesses, size of the wage gap with men, local economy, divorce rates, the ratio of single men to single women, whether there are laws that require at least the same number of public toilets for women as men, and the probability of good hair days. *Ladies Home Journal, November 1997*

- Phoenix was ranked #137 out of 219 cities in terms of children's health, safety, and economic well-being. Criteria: total population, percent population change, birth rate, child immunization rate, infant mortality rate, percent low birth weight infants, percent of births to teens, physician-to-population ratio, student-to-teacher ratio, dropout rate, unemployment rate, median family income, percent of children in poverty, violent and property crime rates, number of juvenile arrests for violent crimes as a percent of the total crime index, number of days with pollution standard index (PSI) over 100, pounds toxic releases per 1,000 people and number of superfund sites. *Zero Population Growth, Children's Environmental Index 1997*

- Sun City Grand, located 18 miles northwest of Phoenix and Sun Lakes, PebbleCreek and Saddlebrooke, located in greater Phoenix, are among America's best retirement communities. Criteria: communities must have state-of-the-art facilities, newly built homes for sale, and give you the most value for your money in every price range. Communities must also welcome newcomers of all races and religions. *New Choices, July/August 1997*

- *Yahoo! Internet Life* selected "America's 100 Most Wired Cities & Towns". 50 cities were large and 50 cities were small. Phoenix ranked 26 out of 50 large cities. Criteria: Internet users per capita, number of networked computers, number of registered domain names, Internet backbone traffic, and the per-capita number of Web sites devoted to each city. *Yahoo! Internet Life, March 1998*

- Salt River Project, headquartered in Phoenix, is among the "100 Best Companies for Working Mothers." Criteria: pay compared with competition, opportunities for women to advance, support for child care, flexible work schedules and family-friendly benefits. *Working Mother, October 1997*

- According to *Working Mother,* "Arizona has lively advocates who have produced wonderful studies showing how kids benefit from high-quality child care. And these advocates have made some progress. This year, for example, they convinced reluctant lawmakers to pass a bill that requires all school-age programs to be licensed. Yet the legislature still refused to fund additional inspectors to oversee these programs. Without funds for new staff, the average inspector's job caseload jumps by a third—giving them each more than 100 programs to visit." *Working Mother, July/August 1997*

Business Environment

STATE ECONOMY

State Economic Profile

"Arizona's economy is maintaining its strong expansion....Growth in personal bankruptcy filings is 30%, about the U.S. pace of growth....

Arizona communities close to the Mexican border are benefiting from the North American Free Trade Agreement (NAFTA) through increased trade links with Mexico. However, workers imported from other parts of the nation have filled many of the newly created positions. This is because the new jobs being created on the U.S. side require skills that do not match the skills of many of the local residents. In the near term, Southern Arizona communities will benefit since the new job opportunities will attract in-migrants who will support the growth of local services and the housing market. To date there is little evidence of a large outflow of Arizona firms over the border; however, the Arizona Department of Economic Security estimates that sixteen companies have left Arizona for Mexico, representing nearly 1,000 jobs statewide.

Over the last few years, call centers and other back-office operations have fueled expansion. Business services employment in the state is growing at a 12% year-over-year pace currently, and has posted double-digit growth for 32 months. However, business services is cyclical. This development is worrisome for an economy already vulnerable to national business cycles. While enjoying the upside of this dependence during the current expansion, Arizona may suffer inordinately in the next recession.

Arizona is expected to remain one of the nation's fastest-growing states through the remainder of the decade. However, growth is expected to slow from its torrid pace of recent years. Where in the past Arizona's risks were driven by its dependence on natural resource industries (citrus, copper, cattle) and tourism, it is now facing a new pattern of risk due to its concentration in high-tech manufacturing and business services. Migration and business relocations from California will slow as that state's recovery matures. Nonetheless, Arizona is top-ranked for long-term growth." *National Association of Realtors, Economic Profiles: The Fifty States, July 1997*

IMPORTS/EXPORTS

Total Export Sales

Area	1993 ($000)	1994 ($000)	1995 ($000)	1996 ($000)	% Chg. 1993-96	% Chg. 1995-96
MSA[1]	4,498,943	5,561,094	6,780,426	7,912,060	75.9	16.7
U.S.	464,858,354	512,415,609	583,030,524	622,827,063	34.0	6.8

Note: (1) Metropolitan Statistical Area - see Appendix A for areas included
Source: U.S. Department of Commerce, International Trade Association, Metropolitan Area Exports: An Export Performance Report on Over 250 U.S. Cities, October 1997

Imports/Exports by Port

Type	Cargo Value			Share of U.S. Total	
	1995 (US$mil.)	1996 (US$mil.)	% Change 1995-1996	1995 (%)	1996 (%)
Imports	0	0	0	0	0
Exports	0	0	0	0	0

Source: Global Trade Information Services, WaterBorne Trade Atlas 1997

CITY FINANCES

City Government Finances

Component	FY94 ($000)	FY94 (per capita $)
Revenue	1,278,756	1,196.38
Expenditure	1,336,272	1,250.19
Debt Outstanding	2,789,058	2,609.38
Cash & Securities	2,063,016	1,930.11

Source: U.S. Bureau of the Census, City Government Finances: 1993-94

City Government Revenue by Source

Source	FY94 ($000)	FY94 (per capita $)	FY94 (%)
From Federal Government	96,842	90.60	7.6
From State Governments	243,093	227.43	19.0
From Local Governments	31,748	29.70	2.5
Property Taxes	117,431	109.87	9.2
General Sales Taxes	154,701	144.73	12.1
Selective Sales Taxes	77,878	72.86	6.1
Income Taxes	0	0.00	0.0
Current Charges	251,977	235.74	19.7
Utility/Liquor Store	118,803	111.15	9.3
Employee Retirement[1]	53,630	50.18	4.2
Other	132,653	124.11	10.4

Note: (1) Excludes "city contributions," classified as "nonrevenue," intragovernmental transfers.
Source: U.S. Bureau of the Census, City Government Finances: 1993-94

City Government Expenditures by Function

Function	FY94 ($000)	FY94 (per capita $)	FY94 (%)
Educational Services	17,026	15.93	1.3
Employee Retirement[1]	28,082	26.27	2.1
Environment/Housing	307,490	287.68	23.0
Government Administration	97,887	91.58	7.3
Interest on General Debt	137,561	128.70	10.3
Public Safety	273,250	255.65	20.4
Social Services	1,044	0.98	0.1
Transportation	175,196	163.91	13.1
Utility/Liquor Store	220,487	206.28	16.5
Other	78,249	73.21	5.9

Note: (1) Payments to beneficiaries including withdrawal of contributions.
Source: U.S. Bureau of the Census, City Government Finances: 1993-94

Municipal Bond Ratings

Area	Moody's	S & P
Phoenix	Aa1	AA+

Note: n/a not available; n/r not rated
Source: Moody's Bond Record, 2/98; Statistical Abstract of the U.S., 1997;
Governing Magazine, 9/97, 3/98

POPULATION

Population Growth

Area	1980	1990	% Chg. 1980-90	July 1996 Estimate	% Chg. 1990-96
City	789,704	983,403	24.5	1,159,014	17.9
MSA[1]	1,509,052	2,122,101	40.6	2,746,703	29.4
U.S.	226,545,805	248,765,170	9.8	265,179,411	6.6

Note: (1) Metropolitan Statistical Area - see Appendix A for areas included
Source: 1980/1990 Census of Housing and Population, Summary Tape File 3C;
Census Bureau Population Estimates

Population Characteristics

Race	City 1980 Population	%	City 1990 Population	%	% Chg. 1980-90	MSA[1] 1990 Population	%
White	673,488	85.3	803,691	81.7	19.3	1,801,570	84.9
Black	37,747	4.8	51,237	5.2	35.7	74,295	3.5
Amer Indian/Esk/Aleut	11,645	1.5	18,337	1.9	57.5	38,309	1.8
Asian/Pacific Islander	8,429	1.1	15,990	1.6	89.7	35,208	1.7
Other	58,395	7.4	94,148	9.6	61.2	172,719	8.1
Hispanic Origin[2]	116,736	14.8	194,118	19.7	66.3	340,117	16.0

Note: (1) Metropolitan Statistical Area - see Appendix A for areas included;
(2) people of Hispanic origin can be of any race
Source: 1980/1990 Census of Housing and Population, Summary Tape File 3C

Ancestry

Area	German	Irish	English	Italian	U.S.	French	Polish	Dutch
City	24.6	15.0	14.5	5.1	3.0	4.1	3.2	2.3
MSA[1]	26.4	15.5	16.5	5.1	2.9	4.4	3.3	2.7
U.S.	23.3	15.6	13.1	5.9	5.3	4.2	3.8	2.5

Note: Figures are percentages and include persons that reported multiple ancestry (eg. if a person reported being Irish and Italian, they were included in both columns); (1) Metropolitan Statistical Area - see Appendix A for areas included
Source: 1990 Census of Population and Housing, Summary Tape File 3C

Age

Area	Median Age (Years)	Age Distribution (%) Under 5	Under 18	18-24	25-44	45-64	65+	80+
City	31.0	8.5	27.1	10.5	35.2	17.5	9.7	1.8
MSA[1]	32.0	8.0	26.1	10.5	33.5	17.4	12.5	2.6
U.S.	32.9	7.3	25.6	10.5	32.6	18.7	12.5	2.8

Note: (1) Metropolitan Statistical Area - see Appendix A for areas included
Source: 1990 Census of Population and Housing, Summary Tape File 3C

Male/Female Ratio

Area	Number of males per 100 females (all ages)	Number of males per 100 females (18 years old+)
City	98.0	96.0
MSA[1]	96.9	94.6
U.S.	95.0	91.9

Note: (1) Metropolitan Statistical Area - see Appendix A for areas included
Source: 1990 Census of Population, General Population Characteristics

INCOME

Per Capita/Median/Average Income

Area	Per Capita ($)	Median Household ($)	Average Household ($)
City	14,096	29,291	37,159
MSA[1]	14,970	30,797	38,996
U.S.	14,420	30,056	38,453

Note: all figures are for 1989; (1) Metropolitan Statistical Area - see Appendix A for areas included
Source: 1990 Census of Population and Housing, Summary Tape File 3C

Household Income Distribution by Race

Income ($)	City (%)					U.S. (%)				
	Total	White	Black	Other	Hisp.[1]	Total	White	Black	Other	Hisp.[1]
Less than 5,000	5.7	4.8	14.3	9.7	9.9	6.2	4.8	15.2	8.6	8.8
5,000 - 9,999	8.0	7.5	13.5	9.9	10.5	9.3	8.6	14.2	9.9	11.1
10,000 - 14,999	9.1	8.6	11.1	12.6	13.0	8.8	8.5	11.0	9.8	11.0
15,000 - 24,999	19.4	19.0	21.0	23.1	23.1	17.5	17.3	18.9	18.5	20.5
25,000 - 34,999	16.9	16.8	15.6	18.3	17.9	15.8	16.1	14.2	15.4	16.4
35,000 - 49,999	18.2	18.8	13.1	15.2	15.3	17.9	18.6	13.3	16.1	16.0
50,000 - 74,999	14.2	15.3	8.0	8.1	7.6	15.0	15.8	9.3	13.4	11.1
75,000 - 99,999	4.6	5.0	2.1	2.0	1.7	5.1	5.5	2.6	4.7	3.1
100,000+	3.9	4.3	1.2	1.2	1.1	4.4	4.8	1.3	3.7	1.9

Note: all figures are for 1989; (1) people of Hispanic origin can be of any race
Source: 1990 Census of Population and Housing, Summary Tape File 3C

Effective Buying Income

Area	Per Capita ($)	Median Household ($)	Average Household ($)
City	14,294	30,184	38,004
MSA[1]	15,241	32,216	40,254
U.S.	15,444	33,201	41,849

Note: data as of 1/1/97; (1) Metropolitan Statistical Area - see Appendix A for areas included
Source: Standard Rate & Data Service, Newspaper Advertising Source, 2/98

Effective Household Buying Income Distribution

Area	% of Households Earning						
	$10,000 -$19,999	$20,000 -$34,999	$35,000 -$49,999	$50,000 -$74,999	$75,000 -$99,000	$100,000 -$124,999	$125,000 and up
City	18.4	26.4	18.3	16.0	4.9	1.6	1.8
MSA[1]	17.3	25.5	19.0	17.3	5.5	1.9	2.1
U.S.	16.5	23.4	18.3	18.2	6.4	2.1	2.4

Note: data as of 1/1/97; (1) Metropolitan Statistical Area - see Appendix A for areas included
Source: Standard Rate & Data Service, Newspaper Advertising Source, 2/98

Poverty Rates by Race and Age

Area	Total (%)	By Race (%)				By Age (%)		
		White	Black	Other	Hisp.[2]	Under 5 years old	Under 18 years old	65 years and over
City	14.2	10.9	30.0	28.4	29.1	22.9	20.4	11.3
MSA[1]	12.3	9.5	27.4	28.4	27.5	19.9	17.3	8.8
U.S.	13.1	9.8	29.5	23.1	25.3	20.1	18.3	12.8

Note: figures show the percent of people living below the poverty line in 1989. The average poverty threshold was $12,674 for a family of four in 1989; (1) Metropolitan Statistical Area - see Appendix A for areas included; (2) people of Hispanic origin can be of any race
Source: 1990 Census of Population and Housing, Summary Tape File 3C

EMPLOYMENT

Labor Force and Employment

Area	Civilian Labor Force			Workers Employed		
	Dec. '95	Dec. '96	% Chg.	Dec. '95	Dec. '96	% Chg.
City	680,381	703,898	3.5	655,647	684,735	4.4
MSA[1]	1,474,872	1,527,131	3.5	1,425,392	1,488,628	4.4
U.S.	134,583,000	136,742,000	1.6	127,903,000	130,785,000	2.3

Note: Data is not seasonally adjusted and covers workers 16 years of age and older; (1) Metropolitan Statistical Area - see Appendix A for areas included
Source: Bureau of Labor Statistics, http://stats.bls.gov

Phoenix was listed among the top 20 metro areas (out of 114 major areas) in terms of projected job growth from 1997 to 2002 with an annual percent change of 2.4%.
Standard & Poor's DRI, July 23, 1997

Unemployment Rate

Area	1997											
	Jan.	Feb.	Mar.	Apr.	May	Jun.	Jul.	Aug.	Sep.	Oct.	Nov.	Dec.
City	3.7	3.5	3.2	2.9	3.1	3.3	3.3	3.2	3.4	3.1	2.9	2.7
MSA[1]	3.5	3.2	2.9	2.7	2.9	3.0	3.0	3.0	3.1	2.8	2.6	2.5
U.S.	5.9	5.7	5.5	4.8	4.7	5.2	5.0	4.8	4.7	4.4	4.3	4.4

Note: Data is not seasonally adjusted and covers workers 16 years of age and older; All figures are percentages; (1) Metropolitan Statistical Area - see Appendix A for areas included
Source: Bureau of Labor Statistics, http://stats.bls.gov

Employment by Industry

Sector	MSA[1]		U.S.
	Number of Employees	Percent of Total	Percent of Total
Services	451,700	31.2	29.0
Retail Trade	270,800	18.7	18.5
Government	182,400	12.6	16.1
Manufacturing	166,400	11.5	15.0
Finance/Insurance/Real Estate	111,100	7.7	5.7
Wholesale Trade	87,800	6.1	5.4
Transportation/Public Utilities	73,400	5.1	5.3
Construction	95,200	6.6	4.5
Mining	6,800	0.5	0.5

Note: Figures cover non-farm employment as of 12/97 and are not seasonally adjusted;
(1) Metropolitan Statistical Area - see Appendix A for areas included
Source: Bureau of Labor Statistics, http://stats.bls.gov

Employment by Occupation

Occupation Category	City (%)	MSA[1] (%)	U.S. (%)
White Collar	60.9	62.6	58.1
Executive/Admin./Management	13.2	13.7	12.3
Professional	13.2	14.2	14.1
Technical & Related Support	4.1	4.2	3.7
Sales	12.4	13.1	11.8
Administrative Support/Clerical	18.1	17.4	16.3
Blue Collar	23.5	22.2	26.2
Precision Production/Craft/Repair	11.4	11.0	11.3
Machine Operators/Assem./Insp.	5.1	4.6	6.8
Transportation/Material Movers	3.4	3.3	4.1
Cleaners/Helpers/Laborers	3.6	3.4	3.9
Services	13.9	13.3	13.2
Farming/Forestry/Fishing	1.7	1.9	2.5

Note: figures cover employed persons 16 years old and over;
(1) Metropolitan Statistical Area - see Appendix A for areas included
Source: 1990 Census of Population and Housing, Summary Tape File 3C

Occupational Employment Projections: 1994 - 2005

Occupations Expected to have the Largest Job Growth (ranked by numerical growth)	Fast-Growing Occupations[1] (ranked by percent growth)
1. Salespersons, retail	1. All other computer scientists
2. Marketing & sales, supervisors	2. Computer engineers
3. General managers & top executives	3. Amusement and recreation attendants
4. Cashiers	4. Ushers/lobby attendants/ticket takers
5. Janitors/cleaners/maids, ex. priv. hshld.	5. Surveying & mapping scientists
6. Carpenters, including brattice builders	6. Helpers, brick & stone masons
7. Waiters & waitresses	7. Geologists/geophysicists/oceanographers
8. General office clerks	8. Helpers, painting & paperhanging
9. Registered nurses	9. Economists
10. Guards	10. Athletes/coaches/umpires & related workers

Projections cover the Phoenix MSA - see Appendix A for areas included.
Note: (1) Excludes occupations with employment less than 100 in 1994
Source: Arizona Department of Economic Security, Arizona Occupational Employment Forecasts, 1994-2005, Metropolitan Phoenix

Average Wages

Occupation	Wage	Occupation	Wage
Professional/Technical/Clerical	$/Week	**Health/Protective Services**	$/Week
Accountants III	750	Corrections Officers	-
Attorneys III	1,347	Firefighters	682
Budget Analysts III	892	Nurses, Licensed Practical II	-
Buyers/Contracting Specialists II	621	Nurses, Registered II	-
Clerks, Accounting III	411	Nursing Assistants II	-
Clerks, General III	364	Police Officers I	734
Computer Operators II	451	**Hourly Workers**	$/Hour
Computer Programmers II	632	Forklift Operators	10.51
Drafters II	-	General Maintenance Workers	9.34
Engineering Technicians III	-	Guards I	6.67
Engineering Technicians, Civil III	579	Janitors	6.43
Engineers III	969	Maintenance Electricians	18.96
Key Entry Operators I	310	Maintenance Electronics Techs II	15.21
Personnel Assistants III	-	Maintenance Machinists	21.41
Personnel Specialists III	782	Maintenance Mechanics, Machinery	15.40
Secretaries III	449	Material Handling Laborers	6.69
Switchboard Operator-Receptionist	310	Motor Vehicle Mechanics	15.69
Systems Analysts II	911	Shipping/Receiving Clerks	8.99
Systems Analysts Supervisor/Mgr II	1,433	Tool and Die Makers	18.64
Tax Collectors II	492	Truckdrivers, Tractor Trailer	-
Word Processors II	399	Warehouse Specialists	10.38

Note: Wage data includes full-time workers only for 4/96 and cover the Metropolitan Statistical Area (see Appendix A for areas included). Dashes indicate that data was not available.
Source: Bureau of Labor Statistics, Occupational Compensation Survey, 9/96

TAXES

Major State and Local Tax Rates

State Corp. Income (%)	State Personal Income (%)	Residential Property (effective rate per $100)	Sales & Use		State Gasoline (cents/ gallon)	State Cigarette (cents/ 20-pack)
			State (%)	Local (%)		
9.0[a]	3.0 - 5.6	1.83	5.0	1.8	18[b]	58

Note: Personal/corporate income tax rates as of 1/97. Sales, gasoline and cigarette tax rates as of 1/98; (a) Minimum tax is $50; (b) Carriers pay an additional surcharge of 8 cents
Source: Federation of Tax Administrators, www.taxadmin.org; Washington D.C. Department of Finance and Revenue, Tax Rates and Tax Burdens in the District of Columbia: A Nationwide Comparison, June 1997; Chamber of Commerce

Total Taxes Per Capita and as a Percent of Income

Area	Per Capita Income ($)	Per Capita Taxes ($)			Taxes as Pct. of Income (%)		
		Total	Federal	State/Local	Total	Federal	State/Local
Arizona	23,709	8,114	5,239	2,875	34.2	22.1	12.1
U.S.	26,187	9,205	6,127	3,078	35.2	23.4	11.8

Note: Figures are for 1997
Source: Tax Foundation, Web Site, www.taxfoundation.org

Estimated Tax Burden

Area	State Income	Local Income	Property	Sales	Total
Phoenix	1,367	0	1,800	599	3,766

Note: The numbers are estimates of taxes paid by a married couple with two kids and annual earnings of $65,000. Sales tax estimates assume they spend average amounts on food, clothing, household goods and gasoline. Property tax estimates assume they live in a $225,000 home.
Source: Kiplinger's Personal Finance Magazine, June 1997

COMMERCIAL REAL ESTATE

Office Market

Class/Location	Total Space (sq. ft.)	Vacant Space (sq. ft.)	Vac. Rate (%)	Under Constr. (sq. ft.)	Net Absorp. (sq. ft.)	Rental Rates ($/sq.ft./yr.)
Class A						
CBD	5,280,445	385,318	7.3	342,000	-22,003	19.83-24.85
Outside CBD	1,469,273	108,218	7.4	391,668	64,671	18.44-23.00
Class B						
CBD	9,991,328	596,832	6.0	n/a	81,422	14.35-20.38
Outside CBD	6,274,878	649,413	10.3	212,602	65,652	15.32-17.38

Note: Data as of 10/97 and covers Phoenix; CBD = Central Business District; n/a not available;
Source: Society of Industrial and Office Realtors, 1998 Comparative Statistics of Industrial and Office Real Estate Markets

"The Phoenix economy will remain one of the strongest in the nation, and the economic good times are expected to continue for the next 12-24 months. Aggressive recruitment of out-of-state firms by economic development agencies will keep the Phoenix growth engine in high gear in the years to come." *Society of Industrial and Office Realtors, 1998 Comparative Statistics of Industrial and Office Real Estate Markets*

Industrial Market

Location	Total Space (sq. ft.)	Vacant Space (sq. ft.)	Vac. Rate (%)	Under Constr. (sq. ft.)	Net Absorp. (sq. ft.)	Net Lease ($/sq.ft./yr.)
Central City	182,133,000	10,541,000	5.8	7,458,000	9,930,000	3.25-9.00
Suburban	n/a	n/a	n/a	n/a	n/a	n/a

Note: Data as of 10/97 and covers Phoenix. Inventory figures for central city and suburban areas are combined.; n/a not available
Source: Society of Industrial and Office Realtors, 1998 Comparative Statistics of Industrial and Office Real Estate Markets

"As in the past few years, growth prospects remain excellent. Business services, including call centers and card processing operations, have been a major growth impetus. Activity in this 'back office' sector is brisk, and new projects are built. At this point, more than seven million sq. ft. of industrial space is either under construction or in planning. This volume places Phoenix among the most active markets in the country. Financing reportedly remains a constraint, although the area's construction volume would suggest it is a constraint without much impact. Arizona's high quality of life, its strategic location close to Mexico and major Southwest markets, and cost advantages relative to California insure a vibrant industrial market in 1998." *Society of Industrial and Office Realtors, 1998 Comparative Statistics of Industrial and Office Real Estate Markets*

Retail Market

Shopping Center Inventory (sq. ft.)	Shopping Center Construction (sq. ft.)	Construction as a Percent of Inventory (%)	Torto Wheaton Rent Index[1] ($/sq. ft.)
61,623,000	1,273,000	2.1	12.27

Note: Data as of 1997 and covers the Metropolitan Statistical Area - see Appendix A for areas included; (1) Index is based on a model that predicts what the average rent should be for leases with certain characteristics, in certain locations during certain years.
Source: National Association of Realtors, 1997-1998 Market Conditions Report

"Contrary to many areas around the nation, the Phoenix retail market has experienced healthy growth. Much of the strength in the market comes from robust population growth and a booming housing industry. The area's retail rent index jumped 7.3% in 1997. The Phoenix market seems to have overcome the consolidations of two grocery store chains in 1996, as substantial absorption continues to cause vacancy rates to fall—in spite of a large amount of new construction. Development has continued on the Scottsdale Waterfront, and Barron Collier has teamed with Phoenix-based Opus Southwest Corp. to develop an office-retail project in downtown Phoenix. The MSA's retail market should continue its healthy pace through 1998," *National Association of Realtors, 1997-1998 Market Conditions Report*

COMMERCIAL UTILITIES

Typical Monthly Electric Bills

Area	Commercial Service ($/month)		Industrial Service ($/month)	
	12 kW demand 1,500 kWh	100 kW demand 30,000 kWh	1,000 kW demand 400,000 kWh	20,000 kW demand 10,000,000 kWh
City	193	2,906	28,799	561,571
U.S.	162	2,360	25,590	545,677

Note: Based on rates in effect July 1, 1997
Source: Edison Electric Institute, Typical Residential, Commercial and Industrial Bills, Summer 1997

TRANSPORTATION

Transportation Statistics

Avg. travel time to work (min.)	23.0
Interstate highways	I-10; I-17
Bus lines	
In-city	Phoenix Public Transit, 468 vehicles
Inter-city	1
Passenger air service	
Airport	Phoenix Sky Harbor International
Airlines	13
Aircraft departures	177,133 (1995)
Enplaned passengers	13,557,883 (1995)
Rail service	Amtrak Thruway Bus Connection
Motor freight carriers	n/a
Major waterways/ports	None

Source: OAG, Business Travel Planner, Summer 1997; Editor & Publisher Market Guide, 1998; FAA Airport Activity Statistics, 1996; Amtrak National Time Table, Northeast Timetable, Fall/Winter 1997-98; 1990 Census of Population and Housing, STF 3C; Chamber of Commerce/Economic Development 1997; Jane's Urban Transport Systems 1997-98; Transit Fact Book 1997

A survey of 90,000 airline passengers during the first half of 1997 ranked most of the largest airports in the U.S. Phoenix Sky Harbor International ranked number 5 out of 36. Criteria: cleanliness, quality of restaurants, attractiveness, speed of baggage delivery, ease of reaching gates, available ground transportation, ease of following signs and closeness of parking. *Plog Research Inc., First Half 1997*

Means of Transportation to Work

| Area | Car/Truck/Van | | Public Transportation | | | Bicycle | Walked | Other Means | Worked at Home |
	Drove Alone	Car-pooled	Bus	Subway	Railroad				
City	73.7	15.1	3.1	0.0	0.0	1.1	2.7	1.6	2.7
MSA[1]	75.0	14.4	2.0	0.0	0.0	1.4	2.6	1.6	2.9
U.S.	73.2	13.4	3.0	1.5	0.5	0.4	3.9	1.2	3.0

Note: figures shown are percentages and only include workers 16 years old and over;
(1) Metropolitan Statistical Area - see Appendix A for areas included
Source: 1990 Census of Population and Housing, Summary Tape File 3C

BUSINESSES

Major Business Headquarters

| Company Name | 1997 Rankings | |
	Fortune 500	Forbes 500
Forever Living Products	-	354
Phelps Dodge	362	-
Shamrock Foods	-	229

Note: Companies listed are located in the city; Dashes indicate no ranking
Fortune 500: companies that produce a 10-K are ranked 1 - 500 based on 1996 revenue
Forbes 500: private companies are ranked 1 - 500 based on 1996 revenue
Source: Forbes 12/1/97; Fortune 4/28/97

Fast-Growing Businesses

According to *Fortune*, Phoenix is home to one of America's 100 fastest-growing companies: Employee Solutions. Companies were ranked based on three years' earnings-per-share growth using least squares analysis to smooth out distortions. Criteria for inclusion: public companies with sales of least $50 million. Companies that lost money in the most recent quarter, or ended in the red for the past four quarters as a whole, were not eligible. Limited partnerships and REITs were also not considered. *Fortune, 9/29/97*

According to Deloitte & Touche LLP, Phoenix is home to one of America's 100 fastest-growing high-technology companies: Integrated Process Equipment Corp.. Companies are ranked by percentage growth in revenue over a five-year period. Criteria for inclusion: must be a U.S. company developing and/or providing technology products or services; company must have been in business for five years with 1992 revenues of at least $50,000. *Deloitte & Touche LLP, January 7, 1998*

Phoenix was ranked #23 out of 24 (#1 is best) in terms of the best-performing local stocks in 1996 according to the Money/Norby Cities Index. The index measures stocks of companies that have headquarters in 24 metro areas. *Money, 2/7/97*

Women-Owned Businesses: Number, Employment, Sales and Share

| Area | Women-Owned Businesses in 1996 | | | | Share of Women-Owned Businesses in 1996 | |
	Number	Employment	Sales ($000)	Rank[2]	Percent (%)	Rank[3]
MSA[1]	81,400	223,900	24,404,800	18	40.6	1

Note: (1) Metropolitan Statistical Area - see Appendix A for areas included; (2) Calculated on an averaging of number of businesses, employment and sales and ranges from 1 to 50 where 1 is best; (3) Ranges from 1 to 50 where 1 is best
Source: The National Foundation for Women Business Owners, 1996 Facts on Women-Owned Businesses: Trends in the Top 50 Metropolitan Areas, March 26, 1997

Women-Owned Businesses: Growth

Area	Growth in Women-Owned Businesses (% change from 1987 to 1996)				Relative Growth in the Number of Women-Owned and All Businesses (% change from 1987 to 1996)			
	Num.	Empl.	Sales	Rank[2]	Women-Owned	All Firms	Absolute Difference	Relative Difference
MSA[1]	93.9	348.1	412.9	3	93.9	51.2	42.7	1.8:1

Note: (1) Metropolitan Statistical Area - see Appendix A for areas included; (2) Calculated on an averaging of the percent growth of number of businesses, employment and sales and ranges from 1 to 50 where 1 is best
Source: The National Foundation for Women Business Owners, 1996 Facts on Women-Owned Businesses: Trends in the Top 50 Metropolitan Areas, March 26, 1997

Minority Business Opportunity

Seven of the 500 largest Hispanic-owned companies in the U.S. are located in Phoenix. *Hispanic Business, June 1997*

Phoenix is home to three companies which are on the Hispanic Business Fastest-Growing 100 list (greatest sales growth from 1992 to 1996): STAR Human Resource Group Inc. (medical insurance svcs.), Corella Cos. (elect. contract./telecom. mfg.), and International Mail Processing Inc. (mail svcs.) *Hispanic Business, July/August 1997*

Phoenix was listed among the top 25 metropolitan areas in terms of the number of Hispanic-owned companies. The city was ranked number 19 with 15,853 companies. *Hispanic Business, May 1997*

Small Business Opportunity

According to *Forbes*, Phoenix is home to four of America's 200 best small companies: Apollo Group, JDA Software Group, Knight Transportation, Viasoft. Criteria: companies must be publicly traded, U.S.-based corporations with latest 12-month sales of between $5 and $350 million. Earnings must be at least $1 million for the 12-month period. Limited partnerships, REITs and closed-end mutual funds were not considered. Banks, S&Ls and electric utilities were not included. *Forbes, November 3, 1997*

HOTELS & MOTELS

Hotels/Motels

Area	Hotels/Motels	Rooms	Luxury-Level Hotels/Motels		Average Minimum Rates ($)		
			♦♦♦♦	♦♦♦♦♦	♦♦	♦♦♦	♦♦♦♦
City	58	11,368	3	0	80	111	190
Airport	29	5,178	1	0	n/a	n/a	n/a
Suburbs	73	12,738	5	2	n/a	n/a	n/a
Total	160	29,284	9	2	n/a	n/a	n/a

Note: n/a not available; Classifications range from one diamond (budget properties with basic amenities) to five diamond (luxury properties with the finest service, rooms and facilities).
Source: OAG, Business Travel Planner, Summer 1997

Phoenix is home to one of the top 100 hotels in the world according to *Travel & Leisure*: The Phoenician. Criteria: value, rooms/ambience, location, facilities/activities and service. *Travel & Leisure, September 1997*

CONVENTION CENTERS

Major Convention Centers

Center Name	Meeting Rooms	Exhibit Space (sf)
Arizona Biltmore	17	49,000
Arizona Veterans Memorial Coliseum	n/a	225,000
El Zaribah Shrine Auditorium	n/a	n/a
Fountain Suites Hotel	12	10,000
Mountain Preserve Conference Center	n/a	11,171
Phoenix Civic Plaza Convention Center and Symphony Hall	43	330,000

Note: n/a not available
Source: Trade Shows Worldwide 1997

Living Environment

COST OF LIVING

Cost of Living Index

Composite Index	Housing	Utilities	Groceries	Health Care	Trans- portation	Misc. Goods/ Services
103.5	102.0	106.4	105.7	112.6	112.0	99.1

Note: U.S. = 100
Source: ACCRA, Cost of Living Index, 3rd Quarter 1997

HOUSING

Median Home Prices and Housing Affordability

Area	Median Price[2] 3rd Qtr. 1997 ($)	HOI[3] 3rd Qtr. 1997	Afford- ability Rank[4]
MSA[1]	116,000	66.4	117
U.S.	127,000	63.7	–

Note: (1) Metropolitan Statistical Area - see Appendix A for areas included; (2) U.S. figures calculated from the sales of 625,000 new and existing homes in 195 markets; (3) Housing Opportunity Index - percent of homes sold that were within the reach of the median income household at the prevailing mortgage interest rate; (4) Rank is from 1-195 with 1 being most affordable
Source: National Association of Home Builders, Housing Opportunity Index, 3rd Quarter 1997

It is projected that the median price of existing single-family homes in the metro area will increase by 8.7% in 1998. Nationwide, home prices are projected to increase 6.6%.
Kiplinger's Personal Finance Magazine, January 1998

Average New Home Price

Area	Price ($)
City	133,148
U.S.	135,710

Note: Figures are based on a new home with 1,800 sq. ft. of living area on an 8,000 sq. ft. lot.
Source: ACCRA, Cost of Living Index, 3rd Quarter 1997

Average Apartment Rent

Area	Rent ($/mth)
City	651
U.S.	569

Note: Figures are based on an unfurnished two bedroom, 1-1/2 or 2 bath apartment, approximately 950 sq. ft. in size, excluding all utilities except water
Source: ACCRA, Cost of Living Index, 3rd Quarter 1997

RESIDENTIAL UTILITIES

Average Residential Utility Costs

Area	All Electric ($/mth)	Part Electric ($/mth)	Other Energy ($/mth)	Phone ($/mth)
City	110.73	–	–	18.67
U.S.	109.40	55.25	43.64	19.48

Source: ACCRA, Cost of Living Index, 3rd Quarter 1997

HEALTH CARE

Average Health Care Costs

Area	Hospital ($/day)	Doctor ($/visit)	Dentist ($/visit)
City	507.38	54.70	64.33
U.S.	392.91	48.76	60.84

Note: Hospital - based on a semi-private room. Doctor - based on a general practitioner's routine exam of an established patient. Dentist - based on adult teeth cleaning and periodic oral exam.
Source: ACCRA, Cost of Living Index, 3rd Quarter 1997

Distribution of Office-Based Physicians

Area	Family/Gen. Practitioners	Specialists		
		Medical	Surgical	Other
MSA[1]	603	1,295	1,109	1,152

Note: Data as of 12/31/96; (1) Metropolitan Statistical Area - see Appendix A for areas included
Source: American Medical Assn., Physician Characteristics & Distribution in the U.S., 1997-1998

Hospitals

Phoenix has 14 general medical and surgical hospitals, 3 psychiatric, 1 other specialty, 1 children's general, 1 children's psychiatric. *AHA Guide to the Healthcare Field 1997-98*

According to *U.S. News and World Report,* Phoenix has 2 of the best hospitals in the U.S.: **Maricopa Medical Center**, noted for endocrinology; **St. Joseph's Hospital and Medical Center**, noted for AIDS, geriatrics, neurology, orthopedics, pulmonology; *U.S. News and World Report, "America's Best Hospitals", 7/28/97*

Paradise Valley Hospital is among the 100 best-run hospitals in the U.S.
Modern Healthcare, January 5, 1998

EDUCATION

Public School District Statistics

District Name	Num. Sch.	Enroll.	Classroom Teachers[1]	Pupils per Teacher	Minority Pupils (%)	Current Exp.[2] ($/pupil)
Alhambra Elementary District	11	10,503	496	21.2	n/a	n/a
Balsz Elementary District	5	2,768	n/a	n/a	n/a	n/a
Cartwright Elementary District	18	16,328	789	20.7	n/a	n/a
Creighton Elementary District	7	7,584	331	22.9	n/a	n/a
Deer Valley Unified District	20	20,420	1,008	20.3	12.0	3,766
Dept of Juvenile Corrections	4	460	n/a	n/a	n/a	n/a
Fowler Elementary District	2	1,510	49	30.8	n/a	n/a
Isaac Elementary District	8	7,616	350	21.8	n/a	n/a
Madison Elementary District	6	4,446	211	21.1	n/a	n/a
Maricopa Co Regional Dist	12	2,072	n/a	n/a	n/a	n/a
Murphy Elementary District	4	2,533	133	19.0	n/a	n/a
Osborn Elementary District	5	4,085	210	19.5	n/a	n/a
Paradise Valley Unified Distr	33	32,099	1,533	20.9	12.5	3,823
Pendergast Elementary District	6	5,621	279	20.1	n/a	n/a
Phoenix Elementary District	16	9,144	450	20.3	n/a	n/a
Phoenix Union High Sch Dist	14	21,083	n/a	n/a	72.5	6,314
Riverside Elementary District	1	183	13	14.1	n/a	n/a
Roosevelt Elementary District	19	11,598	n/a	n/a	n/a	n/a
Scottsdale Unified District	26	24,467	1,202	20.4	12.8	4,038
Washington Elementary District	32	24,587	1,358	18.1	24.7	3,693
Wilson Elementary District	2	1,194	77	15.5	n/a	n/a

Note: Data covers the 1995-1996 school year unless otherwise noted; (1) Excludes teachers reported as working in school district offices rather than in schools; (2) Based on 1993-94 enrollment collected by the Census Bureau, not the enrollment figure shown in column 3; SD = School District; ISD = Independent School District; n/a not available
Source: National Center for Education Statistics, Common Core of Data Survey; Bureau of the Census

Educational Quality

School District	Education Quotient[1]	Graduate Outcome[2]	Community Index[3]	Resource Index[4]
Phoenix	n/a	n/a	n/a	n/a

Note: Nearly 1,000 secondary school districts were rated in terms of educational quality. The scores range from a low of 50 to a high of 150; (1) Average of the Graduate Outcome, Community and Resource indexes; (2) Based on graduation rates and college board scores (SAT/ACT); (3) Based on the surrounding community's average level of education and the area's average income level; (4) Based on teacher salaries, per-pupil expenditures and student-teacher ratios.
Source: Expansion Management, Ratings Issue 1997

Educational Attainment by Race

Area	High School Graduate (%)					Bachelor's Degree (%)				
	Total	White	Black	Other	Hisp.[2]	Total	White	Black	Other	Hisp.[2]
City	78.7	82.0	71.1	53.8	47.7	19.9	21.6	11.8	9.2	5.6
MSA[1]	81.5	84.2	75.4	55.9	50.8	22.1	23.4	14.8	11.4	7.3
U.S.	75.2	77.9	63.1	60.4	49.8	20.3	21.5	11.4	19.4	9.2

Note: figures shown cover persons 25 years old and over; (1) Metropolitan Statistical Area - see Appendix A for areas included; (2) people of Hispanic origin can be of any race
Source: 1990 Census of Population and Housing, Summary Tape File 3C

School Enrollment by Type

Area	Preprimary				Elementary/High School			
	Public		Private		Public		Private	
	Enrollment	%	Enrollment	%	Enrollment	%	Enrollment	%
City	9,227	57.9	6,717	42.1	155,356	92.8	12,099	7.2
MSA[1]	20,498	57.5	15,158	42.5	329,787	93.9	21,343	6.1
U.S.	2,679,029	59.5	1,824,256	40.5	38,379,689	90.2	4,187,099	9.8

Note: figures shown cover persons 3 years old and over;
(1) Metropolitan Statistical Area - see Appendix A for areas included
Source: 1990 Census of Population and Housing, Summary Tape File 3C

School Enrollment by Race

Area	Preprimary (%)				Elementary/High School (%)			
	White	Black	Other	Hisp.[1]	White	Black	Other	Hisp.[1]
City	83.6	5.2	11.1	15.1	74.5	6.9	18.6	29.2
MSA[2]	86.1	3.5	10.4	13.4	78.3	4.7	17.0	24.3
U.S.	80.4	12.5	7.1	7.8	74.1	15.6	10.3	12.5

Note: figures shown cover persons 3 years old and over; (1) people of Hispanic origin can be of any race; (2) Metropolitan Statistical Area - see Appendix A for areas included
Source: 1990 Census of Population and Housing, Summary Tape File 3C

SAT/ACT Scores

Area/District	1995 SAT				1995 ACT	
	Percent of Graduates Tested (%)	Average Math Score	Average Verbal Score	Average Combined Score	Percent of Graduates Tested (%)	Average Composite Score
Phoenix UNHSD	n/a	n/a	n/a	973	n/a	23.1
State	27	496	448	944	29	21.0
U.S.	41	482	428	910	37	20.8

Note: Math and verbal SAT scores are out of a possible 800; ACT scores are out of a possible 36
Caution: Comparing or ranking states/cities on the basis of SAT/ACT scores alone is invalid and strongly discouraged by the The College Board and The American College Testing Program as students who take the tests are self-selected and do not represent the entire student population.
Source: Phoenix UNHSD, 1995; American College Testing Program, 1995; College Board, 1995

Classroom Teacher Salaries in Public Schools

District	B.A. Degree		M.A. Degree		Ph.D. Degree	
	Min. ($)	Max. ($)	Min. ($)	Max. ($)	Min. ($)	Max. ($)
Phoenix	24,593	34,323	25,369	43,277	n/a	n/a
Average[1]	26,120	39,270	28,175	44,667	31,643	49,825

Note: Salaries are for 1996-1997; (1) Based on all school districts covered; n/a not available
Source: American Federation of Teachers (unpublished data)

Higher Education

Two-Year Colleges		Four-Year Colleges		Medical Schools	Law Schools	Voc/ Tech
Public	Private	Public	Private			
1	2	1	9	0	0	18

Source: College Blue Book, Occupational Education 1997; Medical School Admission Requirements, 1998-99; Peterson's Guide to Two-Year Colleges, 1997; Peterson's Guide to Four-Year Colleges, 1997; Barron's Guide to Law Schools 1997

MAJOR EMPLOYERS

Major Employers

America West Airlines	Americare Employers Group
BancOne Arizona Corp.	Biltmore Hotel Partners
Blue Cross & Blue Shield of Arizona	Continental Circuits Corp.
First Interstate Bank of Arizona	John C. Lincoln Hospital & Health Center
Karstein Manufacturing Corp.	Mercy Healthcare Arizona
Mony/PSP (hotels)	Phoenix Memorial Hospital
St. Luke's Health System	Swift Transportation Co.

Note: companies listed are located in the city
Source: Dun's Business Rankings 1997; Ward's Business Directory, 1997

PUBLIC SAFETY

Crime Rate

Area	All Crimes	Violent Crimes				Property Crimes		
		Murder	Forcible Rape	Robbery	Aggrav. Assault	Burglary	Larceny -Theft	Motor Vehicle Theft
City	9,541.1	16.3	40.4	329.6	537.5	1,716.0	5,313.7	1,587.7
Suburbs[1]	6,396.6	5.2	24.4	110.5	339.6	1,175.9	3,936.3	804.8
MSA[2]	7,730.2	9.9	31.2	203.4	423.5	1,404.9	4,520.4	1,136.8
U.S.	5,078.9	7.4	36.1	202.4	388.2	943.0	2,975.9	525.9

Note: Crime rate is the number of crimes per 100,000 pop.; (1) defined as all areas within the MSA but located outside the central city; (2) Metropolitan Statistical Area - see Appendix A for areas incl.
Source: FBI Uniform Crime Reports 1996

RECREATION

Culture and Recreation

Museums	Symphony Orchestras	Opera Companies	Dance Companies	Professional Theatres	Zoos	Pro Sports Teams
10	2	1	2	1	1	4

Source: International Directory of the Performing Arts, 1996; Official Museum Directory, 1998; Chamber of Commerce/Economic Development 1997

Library System

The Maricopa County Library District has 10 branches, holdings of 496,606 volumes and a budget of $2,352,611 (1995-1996). The Phoenix Public Library has 11 branches, holdings of 1,764,965 volumes and a budget of $17,909,786 (1995-1996). *American Library Directory, 1997-1998*

MEDIA

Newspapers

Name	Type	Freq.	Distribution	Circulation
Arizona Business Gazette	n/a	1x/wk	National	16,215
Arizona Informant	Black	1x/wk	State	30,000
The Arizona Republic	General	7x/wk	Area	365,979
The Catholic Sun	Religious	2x/mo	Area	97,000
Daily Racing Form	n/a	7x/wk	International	65,000
Jewish News of Greater Phoenix	Religious	1x/wk	Local	20,000
New Times	General	1x/wk	Local	134,000

Note: Includes newspapers with circulations of 10,000 or more located in the city; n/a not available
Source: Burrelle's Media Directory, 1998 Edition

AM Radio Stations

Call Letters	Freq. (kHz)	Target Audience	Station Format	Music Format
KVVA	107	Hispanic	M/N	Adult Contemporary/Spanish
KOY	550	General	M	Adult Standards
KTAR	620	General	N/S/T	n/a
KIDR	740	General	E/M/N/S	n/a
KFYI	910	General	N/T	n/a
KOOL	960	General	M	Oldies
KXEG	1010	n/a	M/T	Christian
KDUS	1060	n/a	S/T	n/a
KRDS	1190	General	M/T	Adult Contemporary/Christian
KISO	1230	Black/Hisp	M	Urban Contemporary
KBSZ	1250	General	M	Oldies
KASR	1260	General	M/N/S	Alternative
KHEP	1280	General	M/N/S/T	Christian
KGME	1360	General	S	n/a
KSUN	1400	Hispanic	M/N/S/T	Adult Contemporary/Spanish
KOPA	1440	General	M/N	Classic Rock
KPHX	1480	Hispanic	M/N/S	Spanish
KFNN	1510	General	N/T	n/a
KASA	1540	Hispanic	M	Christian/Spanish
KCWW	1580	General	M/N/S	Country

Note: Stations included broadcast in the Phoenix metro area; n/a not available
Station Format: E = Educational; M = Music; N = News; S = Sports; T = Talk
Source: Burrelle's Media Directory, 1998 Edition

FM Radio Stations

Call Letters	Freq. (mHz)	Target Audience	Station Format	Music Format
KBAQ	89.5	n/a	M	Classical
KFLR	90.3	General	M/N/S	Christian
KKFR	92.3	n/a	M	Contemporary Top 40
KDKB	93.3	n/a	M	AOR
KBSZ	94.1	General	M	Alternative/Country
KOOL	94.5	General	M/N/S	Oldies
KYOT	95.5	General	M	Jazz
KGLQ	96.9	General	M	Oldies
KUPD	97.9	n/a	M	AOR
KKLT	98.7	General	M/N	Adult Contemporary
KESZ	99.9	General	M/N	Adult Contemporary
KHOT	100.3	General	M	Alternative
KSLX	100.7	General	M	Classic Rock
KZON	101.5	n/a	M	Alternative
KNIX	102.5	General	M/N/S	Country
KOAZ	103.5	General	M/N	Jazz/MOR/Oldies
KBZR	103.9	General	M/N/S	Contemporary Top 40/R&B
KZZP	104.7	General	M/N/S	Adult Contemporary
KRDS	105.3	n/a	M	Adult Contemporary/Adult Standards
KEDJ	106.3	General	M/N/S	Alternative
KVVA	107.1	Hispanic	M	Spanish
KMLE	107.9	General	M/N/S	Country

Note: Stations included broadcast in the Phoenix metro area; n/a not available
Station Format: E = Educational; M = Music; N = News; S = Sports; T = Talk
Music Format: AOR = Album Oriented Rock; MOR = Middle-of-the-Road
Source: Burrelle's Media Directory, 1998 Edition

Television Stations

Name	Ch.	Affiliation	Type	Owner
KTVK	3	n/a	Commercial	MAC America Communications Inc.
KPHO	5	CBS	Commercial	Meredith Corporation
KAET	8	PBS	Public	Arizona Board of Regents
KSAZ	10	Fox	Commercial	Fox Television Stations Inc.
KPNX	12	NBC	Commercial	Gannett Company Inc.
KNXV	15	ABC	Commercial	Scripps Howard Corporations
KPAZ	21	Trinity Broadcasting Network	Commercial	Paul F. Crouch
KCVA	30	n/a	Commercial	Kenneth Casey
KTVW	33	Univision	Commercial	Univision Television Group
KUTP	45	UPN	Commercial	United Television Inc.
KASW	61	n/a	Commercial	Brooks Broadcasting
KDR	64	Telemundo	Commercial	Hispanic Broadcasters of Arizona Inc.

Note: Stations included broadcast in the Phoenix metro area
Source: Burrelle's Media Directory, 1998 Edition

CLIMATE

Average and Extreme Temperatures

Temperature	Jan	Feb	Mar	Apr	May	Jun	Jul	Aug	Sep	Oct	Nov	Dec	Ann
Extreme High (°F)	88	92	100	105	113	122	118	116	118	107	93	88	122
Average High (°F)	66	70	75	84	93	103	105	103	99	88	75	67	86
Average Temp. (°F)	53	57	62	70	78	88	93	91	85	74	62	54	72
Average Low (°F)	40	44	48	55	63	72	80	78	72	60	48	41	59
Extreme Low (°F)	17	22	25	37	40	51	66	61	47	34	27	22	17

Note: Figures cover the years 1948-1990
Source: National Climatic Data Center, International Station Meteorological Climate Summary, 3/95

Average Precipitation/Snowfall/Humidity

Precip./Humidity	Jan	Feb	Mar	Apr	May	Jun	Jul	Aug	Sep	Oct	Nov	Dec	Ann
Avg. Precip. (in.)	0.7	0.6	0.8	0.3	0.1	0.1	0.8	1.0	0.7	0.6	0.6	0.9	7.3
Avg. Snowfall (in.)	Tr	Tr	0	0	0	0	0	0	0	0	0	Tr	Tr
Avg. Rel. Hum. 5am (%)	68	63	56	45	37	33	47	53	50	53	59	66	53
Avg. Rel. Hum. 5pm (%)	34	28	24	17	14	12	21	24	23	24	28	34	24

Note: Figures cover the years 1948-1990; Tr = Trace amounts (<0.05 in. of rain; <0.5 in. of snow)
Source: National Climatic Data Center, International Station Meteorological Climate Summary, 3/95

Weather Conditions

Temperature			Daytime Sky			Precipitation		
10°F & below	32°F & below	90°F & above	Clear	Partly cloudy	Cloudy	0.01 inch or more precip.	0.1 inch or more snow/ice	Thunder-storms
0	10	167	186	125	54	37	< 1	23

Note: Figures are average number of days per year and covers the years 1948-1990
Source: National Climatic Data Center, International Station Meteorological Climate Summary, 3/95

AIR & WATER QUALITY

Maximum Pollutant Concentrations

	Particulate Matter (ug/m³)	Carbon Monoxide (ppm)	Sulfur Dioxide (ppm)	Nitrogen Dioxide (ppm)	Ozone (ppm)	Lead (ug/m³)
MSA[1] Level	130	10	0.020	0.032	0.12	0.05
NAAQS[2]	150	9	0.140	0.053	0.12	1.50
Met NAAQS?	Yes	No	Yes	Yes	Yes	Yes

Note: (1) Metropolitan Statistical Area - see Appendix A for areas included; (2) National Ambient Air Quality Standards; ppm = parts per million; ug/m³ = micrograms per cubic meter; n/a not available
Source: EPA, National Air Quality and Emissions Trends Report, 1996

Pollutant Standards Index

In the Phoenix MSA (see Appendix A for areas included), the Pollutant Standards Index (PSI) exceeded 100 on 10 days in 1996. A PSI value greater than 100 indicates that air quality would be in the unhealthful range on that day. *EPA, National Air Quality and Emissions Trends Report, 1996*

Drinking Water

Water System Name	Pop. Served	Primary Water Source Type	Number of Violations in Fiscal Year 1997	Type of Violation/ Contaminants
Phoenix Muni Water Sys	1,000,000	Surface	3	(1)

Note: Data as of January 16, 1998; (1) System collected or speciated some but not all follow-up samples for compliance period under the total coliform rule (3 times in fiscal year 1997).
Source: EPA, Office of Ground Water and Drinking Water, Safe Drinking Water Information System

Phoenix tap water is alkaline, approximately 11 grains of hardness per gallon and fluoridated. *Editor & Publisher Market Guide, 1998*

Portland, Oregon

Background

Portland, Oregon is the kind of city that inspires civic pride and the desire to preserve. For who among us could be indifferent to the magnificent views of the Cascade Mountains, the mild climate, and the historical brick structures that blend so well with its more contemporary structures?

Nature is undisputedly "Queen" in Portland. The symbol of the city is embodied in "Portlandia", a statue of an earth-mother kneeling amongst her sculpture animal children. The number of activities, such as fishing, skiing, and hunting, as well as the number of outdoor activity facilities, such as the Japanese Gardens, South Park Blocks, and the Portland Zoological Gardens, attest to the mindset of the typical Portlander. To think that in 1845 Portland held the unromantic name of "Stumptown"!

For the concerned citizen looking for a place that espouses the ideals of the television series, "Northern Exposure", Portland may be its real world, big city counterpart. Portland is a major industrial and commercial center that can still boast clean air and water within its city limits as many of the factories use the electricity generated by mountain rivers. Thus little soot or smoke is belched out.

Also, Portland is a major cultural center, with art museums, such as the Portland Art Museum and the Then and Now Museum, and fine educational institutions, such as Reed College and the University of Portland.

The Portland area's regional government is referred to as Metro and it includes 24 cities and parts of three counties. Established in the late 1970's, it is the nation's first and only elected regional government. It attempts to control growth by using its authority over land use, transportation and the environment. This experiment in urban planning is designed to protect farms, forests and open space. Portland today has a downtown area that caters to pedestrians with a heavily used city park where once there was a freeway. From the air one can see a clear line against sprawl—with cities on one side and open space on the other.

Oregon's biggest city, has long been considered America's "shining example of effective sprawl control." Urban planners and visiting city officials see Portland as a "role model for 21st century urban development". The city with its seven-member Metro Council is again facing the question of whether further growth will be in the form of sprawl or of greater density on Portland and other communities inside the UGB-the urban growth boundary. On one side of the debate are the homebuilders and other advocates who want the boundary expanded and on the other side are the environmentalists, most of the regions local officials and downtown Portland interests who want to add density inside the line. The future of Portland's urban experiment may eventually depend on the actions of the Land Conservation and Development Commission which monitors all local growth boundaries in Oregon.
Governing, May 1997

Finally, its well organized mass transit system makes living in this city all the more enjoyable. This is a city that takes history, progress, and environmental protection seriously.

Portland has a very definite winter rainfall climate, with the most rain falling in the months of October through May. The winter season is marked by relatively mild temperatures, cloudy skies and rain with southeasterly surface winds predominating. Summer produces pleasantly mild temperatures with very little precipitation. Fall and spring are transitional. Fall and early winter bring the most frequent fogs. Destructive storms are infrequent with thunderstorms occurring once a month through the spring and summer. Heavy downpours are not frequent but gentle rains fall almost daily during the winter.

General Rankings and Evaluative Comments

- Portland was ranked #37 out of 300 cities by *Money's* 1997 "Survey of the Best Places to Live." Criteria used: health services, crime, economy, housing, education, transportation, weather, leisure and the arts. The city was ranked #48 in 1996 and #36 in 1995. *Money, July 1997; Money, September 1996; Money, September 1995*

- *Ladies Home Journal* ranked America's 200 largest cities based on the qualities women care about most. Portland ranked 57 out of 200. Criteria: low crime rate, good public schools, well-paying jobs, quality health and child care, the presence of women in government, proportion of women-owned businesses, size of the wage gap with men, local economy, divorce rates, the ratio of single men to single women, whether there are laws that require at least the same number of public toilets for women as men, and the probability of good hair days. *Ladies Home Journal, November 1997*

- Portland is among "The Best Places to Raise a Family". Rank: 42 out of 301 metro areas. Criteria: low crime rate, low drug and alcohol abuse, good public schools, high-quality health care, a clean environment, affordable cost of living and strong economic growth. *Reader's Digest, April 1997*

- Portland was ranked #116 out of 219 cities in terms of children's health, safety, and economic well-being. Criteria: total population, percent population change, birth rate, child immunization rate, infant mortality rate, percent low birth weight infants, percent of births to teens, physician-to-population ratio, student-to-teacher ratio, dropout rate, unemployment rate, median family income, percent of children in poverty, violent and property crime rates, number of juvenile arrests for violent crimes as a percent of the total crime index, number of days with pollution standard index (PSI) over 100, pounds toxic releases per 1,000 people and number of superfund sites. *Zero Population Growth, Children's Environmental Index 1997*

- Portland appeared on the *Utne Reader's* list of "America's 10 Most Enlightened Towns". Criteria: access to alternative health care, lively media, sense of local culture, diverse spiritual opportunities, good urban design, progressive local politics, commitment to racial equality, tolerance for gays and lesbians, and decent conditions for working-class citizens. *Utne Reader, May/June 1997*

- Portland is among the 20 most livable cities for gay men and lesbians. The list was divided between 10 cities you might expect and 10 surprises. Portland was on the cities you would expect list. Rank: 10 out of 10. Criteria: legal protection from antigay discrimination, an annual gay pride celebration, a community center, gay bookstores and publications, and an array of organizations, religious groups, and health care facilities that cater to the needs of the local gay community. The Advocate, June 1997

- Portland was selected by *Swing* magazine as being one of "The 10 Best Places to Live" in the U.S. It was also named the "Best Place to Start a Business".
The cities were selected based on census data, cost of living, economic growth, and entertainment options. Swing also read local papers, talked to industry insiders, and interviewed young people. Swing, July/August 1997

- *Conde Nast Traveler* polled 37,000 readers in terms of travel satisfaction. Cities were ranked based on the following criteria: people/friendliness, environment/ambiance, cultural enrichment, restaurants and fun/energy. Portland appeared in the top thirty, ranking number 25, with an overall rating of 58.2 out of 100 based on all the criteria. *Conde Nast Traveler, Readers' Choice Poll 1997*

- *Yahoo! Internet Life* selected "America's 100 Most Wired Cities & Towns". 50 cities were large and 50 cities were small. Portland ranked 20 out of 50 large cities. Criteria: Internet users per capita, number of networked computers, number of registered domain names, Internet backbone traffic, and the per-capita number of Web sites devoted to each city. *Yahoo! Internet Life, March 1998*

- According to *Working Mother,* "Oregon has taken a number of small steps to improve child care: A new background check on caregivers has been instituted, which includes an FBI check for criminal offenses. The state has also mandated an orientation session for anyone who wishes to open a family child care business. The two-hour briefing offers an overview of what it takes to make a home-based child care business work, and what training and support is available from the community and the state. The idea is to put the brakes on anyone who might enter the profession thinking it's an easy job and then close up shop and leave parents in the lurch—a fairly common scenario. The innovation seems to be working. Our certifier said she has not yet had to go out on a complaint for anyone who has gone through this overview.' says Janis Sabin Elliot of the state's Child Care Division.—Oregon has also stepped up its efforts to insure children's health and safety. For instance, it now has more power to revoke the licenses of child care providers in serious violation of rules.

Family child care could be improved in this state if a bill pending before the legislature becomes law. Among other things, it would require providers to have training in CPR and first aid, which should be a basic standard for any good child care program." *Working Mother, July/August 1997*

Business Environment

STATE ECONOMY

State Economic Profile

"Oregon is entering its fourth year of high growth....Income growth continues to outpace the U.S., as it has throughout the decade.

...Oregon's semiconductor industry is now large enough that it is being supplemented by a number of supplier firms moving into the state, further bolstering the economy.

Oregon's lumber and timber industry will benefit from its proximity to expanding housing markets in California and Washington, which are less likely to buckle under rising interest rates than markets elsewhere in the U.S.

Enron's takeover of Portland General Electric may benefit the economy due to the substantial rate cuts being promised by the merged utility. Lower energy costs would help preserve Oregon's competitive edge as deregulation lowers utility rates in higher cost regions of the country.

Strong economies in Washington and California may slow migration into Oregon, stifling demand for new housing. This would cause the construction industry to constrict, and house price appreciation to decelerate from current high rates. A rising dollar/yen ratio also poses a risk to export demand for Oregon's timber products.

Oregon's outlook remains good. The semiconductor industry appears to have weathered recent declines in chip prices, and all plants under construction appear headed for completion. The long-term outlook is for slower expansion, with some uncertainty as to what will replace semiconductors as the main engine of growth. The diversity of Oregon's economy minimizes this risk, however, and Oregon remains top ranked for future growth." *National Association of Realtors, Economic Profiles: The Fifty States, July 1997*

IMPORTS/EXPORTS

Total Export Sales

Area	1993 ($000)	1994 ($000)	1995 ($000)	1996 ($000)	% Chg. 1993-96	% Chg. 1995-96
MSA[1]	5,698,522	6,448,827	8,931,312	9,234,315	62.0	3.4
U.S.	464,858,354	512,415,609	583,030,524	622,827,063	34.0	6.8

Note: (1) Metropolitan Statistical Area - see Appendix A for areas included
Source: U.S. Department of Commerce, International Trade Association, Metropolitan Area Exports: An Export Performance Report on Over 250 U.S. Cities, October 1997

Imports/Exports by Port

Type	Cargo Value			Share of U.S. Total	
	1995 (US$mil.)	1996 (US$mil.)	% Change 1995-1996	1995 (%)	1996 (%)
Imports	4,356	3,995	-8.28	1.11	1.04
Exports	5,345	5,455	2.06	2.34	2.30

Source: Global Trade Information Services, WaterBorne Trade Atlas 1997

CITY FINANCES

City Government Finances

Component	FY92 ($000)	FY92 (per capita $)
Revenue	454,657	961.96
Expenditure	580,690	1,228.62
Debt Outstanding	758,688	1,605.23
Cash & Securities	524,969	1,110.73

Source: U.S. Bureau of the Census, City Government Finances: 1991-92

City Government Revenue by Source

Source	FY92 ($000)	FY92 (per capita $)	FY92 (%)
From Federal Government	11,757	24.88	2.6
From State Governments	27,597	58.39	6.1
From Local Governments	26,387	55.83	5.8
Property Taxes	138,450	292.93	30.5
General Sales Taxes	0	0.00	0.0
Selective Sales Taxes	31,344	66.32	6.9
Income Taxes	0	0.00	0.0
Current Charges	83,210	176.06	18.3
Utility/Liquor Store	51,527	109.02	11.3
Employee Retirement[1]	679	1.44	0.1
Other	83,706	177.10	18.4

Note: (1) Excludes "city contributions," classified as "nonrevenue," intragovernmental transfers.
Source: U.S. Bureau of the Census, City Government Finances: 1991-92

City Government Expenditures by Function

Function	FY92 ($000)	FY92 (per capita $)	FY92 (%)
Educational Services	0	0.00	0.0
Employee Retirement[1]	35,639	75.40	6.1
Environment/Housing	171,739	363.36	29.6
Government Administration	35,681	75.49	6.1
Interest on General Debt	42,735	90.42	7.4
Public Safety	129,564	274.13	22.3
Social Services	0	0.00	0.0
Transportation	68,306	144.52	11.8
Utility/Liquor Store	50,327	106.48	8.7
Other	46,699	98.81	8.0

Note: (1) Payments to beneficiaries including withdrawal of contributions.
Source: U.S. Bureau of the Census, City Government Finances: 1991-92

Municipal Bond Ratings

Area	Moody's	S & P
Portland	Aaa	AA+

Note: n/a not available; n/r not rated
Source: Moody's Bond Record, 2/98; Statistical Abstract of the U.S., 1997; Governing Magazine, 9/97, 3/98

POPULATION

Population Growth

Area	1980	1990	% Chg. 1980-90	July 1996 Estimate	% Chg. 1990-96
City	366,423	437,398	19.4	480,824	9.9
MSA[1]	1,105,699	1,239,842	12.1	1,758,937	41.9
U.S.	226,545,805	248,765,170	9.8	265,179,411	6.6

Note: (1) Metropolitan Statistical Area - see Appendix A for areas included
Source: 1980/1990 Census of Housing and Population, Summary Tape File 3C; Census Bureau Population Estimates

Population Characteristics

Race	City 1980 Population	%	City 1990 Population	%	% Chg. 1980-90	MSA[1] 1990 Population	%
White	319,220	87.1	371,123	84.8	16.3	1,126,742	90.9
Black	28,034	7.7	33,132	7.6	18.2	38,218	3.1
Amer Indian/Esk/Aleut	3,374	0.9	5,845	1.3	73.2	12,165	1.0
Asian/Pacific Islander	12,980	3.5	22,894	5.2	76.4	45,196	3.6
Other	2,815	0.8	4,404	1.0	56.4	17,521	1.4
Hispanic Origin[2]	7,807	2.1	13,125	3.0	68.1	42,912	3.5

Note: (1) Metropolitan Statistical Area - see Appendix A for areas included;
(2) people of Hispanic origin can be of any race
Source: 1980/1990 Census of Housing and Population, Summary Tape File 3C

Ancestry

Area	German	Irish	English	Italian	U.S.	French	Polish	Dutch
City	28.7	16.2	17.9	3.8	2.4	5.1	2.0	3.0
MSA[1]	32.2	16.2	19.9	3.5	2.6	5.6	2.0	3.8
U.S.	23.3	15.6	13.1	5.9	5.3	4.2	3.8	2.5

Note: Figures are percentages and include persons that reported multiple ancestry (eg. if a person reported being Irish and Italian, they were included in both columns); (1) Metropolitan Statistical Area - see Appendix A for areas included
Source: 1990 Census of Population and Housing, Summary Tape File 3C

Age

Area	Median Age (Years)	Under 5	Under 18	18-24	25-44	45-64	65+	80+
City	34.5	7.0	22.0	10.0	37.0	16.6	14.5	3.7
MSA[1]	33.9	7.3	25.2	9.1	35.6	17.9	12.2	2.9
U.S.	32.9	7.3	25.6	10.5	32.6	18.7	12.5	2.8

Note: (1) Metropolitan Statistical Area - see Appendix A for areas included
Source: 1990 Census of Population and Housing, Summary Tape File 3C

Male/Female Ratio

Area	Number of males per 100 females (all ages)	Number of males per 100 females (18 years old+)
City	93.9	91.4
MSA[1]	95.6	92.8
U.S.	95.0	91.9

Note: (1) Metropolitan Statistical Area - see Appendix A for areas included
Source: 1990 Census of Population, General Population Characteristics

INCOME

Per Capita/Median/Average Income

Area	Per Capita ($)	Median Household ($)	Average Household ($)
City	14,478	25,592	33,359
MSA[1]	15,286	30,930	38,482
U.S.	14,420	30,056	38,453

Note: all figures are for 1989; (1) Metropolitan Statistical Area - see Appendix A for areas included
Source: 1990 Census of Population and Housing, Summary Tape File 3C

Household Income Distribution by Race

Income ($)	City (%)					U.S. (%)				
	Total	White	Black	Other	Hisp.[1]	Total	White	Black	Other	Hisp.[1]
Less than 5,000	6.6	5.8	14.2	10.8	9.3	6.2	4.8	15.2	8.6	8.8
5,000 - 9,999	10.8	10.3	18.6	11.0	13.0	9.3	8.6	14.2	9.9	11.1
10,000 - 14,999	10.5	10.4	11.7	11.3	12.0	8.8	8.5	11.0	9.8	11.0
15,000 - 24,999	20.9	20.9	20.6	20.8	24.3	17.5	17.3	18.9	18.5	20.5
25,000 - 34,999	17.3	17.5	13.7	17.1	19.3	15.8	16.1	14.2	15.4	16.4
35,000 - 49,999	16.5	16.8	12.2	15.9	14.0	17.9	18.6	13.3	16.1	16.0
50,000 - 74,999	11.2	11.6	7.1	8.8	6.2	15.0	15.8	9.3	13.4	11.1
75,000 - 99,999	3.2	3.4	1.3	2.6	1.2	5.1	5.5	2.6	4.7	3.1
100,000+	3.0	3.3	0.6	1.7	0.8	4.4	4.8	1.3	3.7	1.9

Note: all figures are for 1989; (1) people of Hispanic origin can be of any race
Source: 1990 Census of Population and Housing, Summary Tape File 3C

Effective Buying Income

Area	Per Capita ($)	Median Household ($)	Average Household ($)
City	15,678	28,846	36,822
MSA[1]	16,965	36,471	43,923
U.S.	15,444	33,201	41,849

Note: data as of 1/1/97; (1) Metropolitan Statistical Area - see Appendix A for areas included
Source: Standard Rate & Data Service, Newspaper Advertising Source, 2/98

Effective Household Buying Income Distribution

Area	% of Households Earning						
	$10,000 -$19,999	$20,000 -$34,999	$35,000 -$49,999	$50,000 -$74,999	$75,000 -$99,000	$100,000 -$124,999	$125,000 and up
City	19.4	26.7	18.0	14.6	4.3	1.4	1.7
MSA[1]	14.7	24.0	20.2	20.4	7.0	2.2	2.2
U.S.	16.5	23.4	18.3	18.2	6.4	2.1	2.4

Note: data as of 1/1/97; (1) Metropolitan Statistical Area - see Appendix A for areas included
Source: Standard Rate & Data Service, Newspaper Advertising Source, 2/98

Poverty Rates by Race and Age

Area	Total (%)	By Race (%)				By Age (%)		
		White	Black	Other	Hisp.[2]	Under 5 years old	Under 18 years old	65 years and over
City	14.5	12.1	31.2	24.8	26.0	21.0	19.0	11.6
MSA[1]	10.0	8.7	29.3	20.1	24.9	14.7	12.3	9.4
U.S.	13.1	9.8	29.5	23.1	25.3	20.1	18.3	12.8

Note: figures show the percent of people living below the poverty line in 1989. The average poverty
threshold was $12,674 for a family of four in 1989; (1) Metropolitan Statistical Area - see Appendix A
for areas included; (2) people of Hispanic origin can be of any race
Source: 1990 Census of Population and Housing, Summary Tape File 3C

EMPLOYMENT

Labor Force and Employment

Area	Civilian Labor Force			Workers Employed		
	Dec. '95	Dec. '96	% Chg.	Dec. '95	Dec. '96	% Chg.
City	275,485	285,767	3.7	261,316	273,177	4.5
MSA[1]	1,011,531	1,053,098	4.1	966,669	1,013,762	4.9
U.S.	134,583,000	136,742,000	1.6	127,903,000	130,785,000	2.3

Note: Data is not seasonally adjusted and covers workers 16 years of age and older;
(1) Metropolitan Statistical Area - see Appendix A for areas included
Source: Bureau of Labor Statistics, http://stats.bls.gov

Portland was listed among the top 20 metro areas (out of 114 major areas) in terms of projected job growth from 1997 to 2002 with an annual percent change of 2.2%.
Standard & Poor's DRI, July 23, 1997

Unemployment Rate

Area	1997											
	Jan.	Feb.	Mar.	Apr.	May	Jun.	Jul.	Aug.	Sep.	Oct.	Nov.	Dec.
City	5.4	5.6	5.5	4.9	4.1	4.7	4.6	4.8	4.7	4.3	4.5	4.4
MSA[1]	4.6	4.8	4.7	4.2	3.5	4.0	3.9	3.9	3.9	3.6	3.8	3.7
U.S.	5.9	5.7	5.5	4.8	4.7	5.2	5.0	4.8	4.7	4.4	4.3	4.4

Note: Data is not seasonally adjusted and covers workers 16 years of age and older; All figures are percentages; (1) Metropolitan Statistical Area - see Appendix A for areas included
Source: Bureau of Labor Statistics, http://stats.bls.gov

Employment by Industry

Sector	MSA[1]		U.S.
	Number of Employees	Percent of Total	Percent of Total
Services	259,100	27.5	29.0
Retail Trade	170,700	18.1	18.5
Government	120,500	12.8	16.1
Manufacturing	149,600	15.9	15.0
Finance/Insurance/Real Estate	67,000	7.1	5.7
Wholesale Trade	68,700	7.3	5.4
Transportation/Public Utilities	53,400	5.7	5.3
Construction	52,200	5.5	4.5
Mining	1,100	0.1	0.5

Note: Figures cover non-farm employment as of 12/97 and are not seasonally adjusted;
(1) Metropolitan Statistical Area - see Appendix A for areas included
Source: Bureau of Labor Statistics, http://stats.bls.gov

Employment by Occupation

Occupation Category	City (%)	MSA[1] (%)	U.S. (%)
White Collar	61.3	60.9	58.1
Executive/Admin./Management	12.6	13.5	12.3
Professional	16.6	15.1	14.1
Technical & Related Support	3.5	3.5	3.7
Sales	11.5	12.6	11.8
Administrative Support/Clerical	17.1	16.3	16.3
Blue Collar	23.8	24.4	26.2
Precision Production/Craft/Repair	9.4	10.5	11.3
Machine Operators/Assem./Insp.	6.4	6.0	6.8
Transportation/Material Movers	3.9	4.0	4.1
Cleaners/Helpers/Laborers	4.1	3.9	3.9
Services	13.9	12.4	13.2
Farming/Forestry/Fishing	1.1	2.3	2.5

Note: figures cover employed persons 16 years old and over;
(1) Metropolitan Statistical Area - see Appendix A for areas included
Source: 1990 Census of Population and Housing, Summary Tape File 3C

Occupational Employment Projections: 1996 - 2005

Occupations Expected to have the Largest Job Growth (ranked by numerical growth)	Fast-Growing Occupations[1] (ranked by percent growth)
1. Salespersons, retail	1. Semiconductor processors
2. Semiconductor processors	2. All other computer scientists
3. General office clerks	3. Social service tech.
4. Janitors/cleaners/maids, ex. priv. hshld.	4. Home health aides
5. All other profess., paraprofess., tech.	5. Computer engineers
6. Guards	6. Amusement and recreation attendants
7. Cashiers	7. Social welfare service aids
8. Computer engineers	8. Child care workers, private household
9. Truck drivers, light	9. Detectives/investigators, private
10. First line supervisor, sales & related	10. Ushers/lobby attendants/ticket takers

Projections cover Multnomah and Washington Counties.
Note: (1) Excludes occupations with employment in the lowest 20%
Source: Oregon Employment Department, Workforce Analysis Section, Oregon Micro-OIS, 1996-2005

Average Wages

Occupation	Wage	Occupation	Wage
Professional/Technical/Clerical	$/Week	**Health/Protective Services**	$/Week
Accountants III	800	Corrections Officers	678
Attorneys III	1,289	Firefighters	768
Budget Analysts III	-	Nurses, Licensed Practical II	-
Buyers/Contracting Specialists II	648	Nurses, Registered II	-
Clerks, Accounting III	458	Nursing Assistants II	-
Clerks, General III	420	Police Officers I	800
Computer Operators II	473	**Hourly Workers**	$/Hour
Computer Programmers II	644	Forklift Operators	12.17
Drafters II	-	General Maintenance Workers	10.51
Engineering Technicians III	611	Guards I	9.26
Engineering Technicians, Civil III	616	Janitors	7.93
Engineers III	954	Maintenance Electricians	18.66
Key Entry Operators I	341	Maintenance Electronics Techs II	17.39
Personnel Assistants III	526	Maintenance Machinists	17.09
Personnel Specialists III	815	Maintenance Mechanics, Machinery	16.25
Secretaries III	548	Material Handling Laborers	-
Switchboard Operator-Receptionist	358	Motor Vehicle Mechanics	16.25
Systems Analysts II	908	Shipping/Receiving Clerks	-
Systems Analysts Supervisor/Mgr II	1,329	Tool and Die Makers	21.14
Tax Collectors II	583	Truckdrivers, Tractor Trailer	13.28
Word Processors II	416	Warehouse Specialists	-

Note: Wage data includes full-time workers only for 7/96 and cover the Metropolitan Statistical Area (see Appendix A for areas included). Dashes indicate that data was not available.
Source: Bureau of Labor Statistics, Occupational Compensation Survey, 11/96

TAXES

Major State and Local Tax Rates

State Corp. Income (%)	State Personal Income (%)	Residential Property (effective rate per $100)	Sales & Use		State Gasoline (cents/ gallon)	State Cigarette (cents/ 20-pack)
			State (%)	Local (%)		
6.6[a]	5.0 - 9.0	1.55	None	None	24[b]	68

Note: Personal/corporate income tax rates as of 1/97. Sales, gasoline and cigarette tax rates as of 1/98; (a) Minimum tax $10; (b) Does not include a 1 - 2 cents local option tax
Source: Federation of Tax Administrators, www.taxadmin.org; Washington D.C. Department of Finance and Revenue, Tax Rates and Tax Burdens in the District of Columbia: A Nationwide Comparison, June 1997; Chamber of Commerce

Total Taxes Per Capita and as a Percent of Income

Area	Per Capita Income ($)	Per Capita Taxes ($)			Taxes as Pct. of Income (%)		
		Total	Federal	State/Local	Total	Federal	State/Local
Oregon	24,918	9,062	5,799	3,263	36.4	23.3	13.1
U.S.	26,187	9,205	6,127	3,078	35.2	23.4	11.8

Note: Figures are for 1997
Source: Tax Foundation, Web Site, www.taxfoundation.org

Estimated Tax Burden

Area	State Income	Local Income	Property	Sales	Total
Portland	3,852	0	2,700	383	6,935

Note: The numbers are estimates of taxes paid by a married couple with two kids and annual earnings of $65,000. Sales tax estimates assume they spend average amounts on food, clothing, household goods and gasoline. Property tax estimates assume they live in a $225,000 home.
Source: Kiplinger's Personal Finance Magazine, June 1997

COMMERCIAL REAL ESTATE

Office Market

Class/Location	Total Space (sq. ft.)	Vacant Space (sq. ft.)	Vac. Rate (%)	Under Constr. (sq. ft.)	Net Absorp. (sq. ft.)	Rental Rates ($/sq.ft./yr.)
Class A						
CBD	7,653,256	489,923	6.4	631,179	-14,171	12.95-25.50
Outside CBD	4,635,840	344,179	7.4	476,614	376,131	16.50-25.00
Class B						
CBD	1,895,784	85,590	4.5	0	117,337	12.50-19.85
Outside CBD	3,291,701	201,397	6.1	0	71,388	12.50-19.10

Note: Data as of 10/97 and covers Portland; CBD = Central Business District; n/a not available;
Source: Society of Industrial and Office Realtors, 1998 Comparative Statistics of Industrial and Office Real Estate Markets

"More than 900,000 sq. ft. of new construction is underway in the CBD, and while more than 50% of it pre-leased, this new construction, combined with the effects of bank mergers giving back up to 200,000 sq. ft., will probably bring stratospheric rent increases back to earthly levels. Still, Portland's economy continues to surge, aided by strong gains in the high technology sector. Estimated year-to-year 1997 job growth is projected at 43%, again placing Portland among the biggest job gainers nationwide, and the metro area should continue its strong performance, albeit at somewhat slower rates, through 1998." *Society of Industrial and Office Realtors, 1998 Comparative Statistics of Industrial and Office Real Estate Markets*

Industrial Market

Location	Total Space (sq. ft.)	Vacant Space (sq. ft.)	Vac. Rate (%)	Under Constr. (sq. ft.)	Net Absorp. (sq. ft.)	Lease ($/sq.ft./yr.)
Central City	n/a	n/a	n/a	n/a	n/a	4.00-6.00
Suburban	149,051,790	7,252,261	4.9	1,988,584	11,681,628	4.00-6.00

Note: Data as of 10/97 and covers Portland; n/a not available
Source: Society of Industrial and Office Realtors, 1998 Comparative Statistics of Industrial and Office Real Estate Markets

"Most larger high-tech projects will be completed by the first quarter of 1998. Many of the multi-million, and even multi-billion dollar projects that have been announced over the past several years are nearing completion, and occupancy of these buildings is proceeding. Somewhat lost in the excitement over the glamorous chip fabrication industry is the fact that the Port of Portland continues to expand, garnering an ever-increasing share of trade with Pacific Rim nations. Rental rates will stabilize as spec building drives vacancy rates above

1997 levels. Absorption will exceed 1997 figures as Oregon's growth climate continues." *Society of Industrial and Office Realtors, 1998 Comparative Statistics of Industrial and Office Real Estate Markets*

Retail Market

Shopping Center Inventory (sq. ft.)	Shopping Center Construction (sq. ft.)	Construction as a Percent of Inventory (%)	Torto Wheaton Rent Index[1] ($/sq. ft.)
25,158,000	479,000	1.9	13.09

Note: Data as of 1997 and covers the Metropolitan Statistical Area - see Appendix A for areas included; (1) Index is based on a model that predicts what the average rent should be for leases with certain characteristics, in certain locations during certain years.
Source: National Association of Realtors, 1997-1998 Market Conditions Report

"Strong population and personal income growth have aided Portland's retail sector in recent years. The area's retail rent index surged 5.0% in 1997, thanks, in part, to limited shopping center construction. Retailers in Portland have benefitted from solid wage growth, including a 4.5% increase in 1997. The extent of the area's population growth is evidenced by a boom in multifamily housing construction. The City of Portland has taken an active role in retail development. The City and Heitman Retail Services recently completed the redevelopment of eight commercial blocks north of Lloyd Center. Continued population and wage growth should buoy the Portland retail market in 1998." *National Association of Realtors, 1997-1998 Market Conditions Report*

COMMERCIAL UTILITIES

Typical Monthly Electric Bills

Area	Commercial Service ($/month)		Industrial Service ($/month)	
	12 kW demand 1,500 kWh	100 kW demand 30,000 kWh	1,000 kW demand 400,000 kWh	20,000 kW demand 10,000,000 kWh
City	99	1,621	17,592	412,500
U.S.	162	2,360	25,590	545,677

Note: Based on rates in effect July 1, 1997
Source: Edison Electric Institute, Typical Residential, Commercial and Industrial Bills, Summer 1997

TRANSPORTATION

Transportation Statistics

Avg. travel time to work (min.)	20.3
Interstate highways	I-5; I-80
Bus lines	
In-city	Tri-County Metropolitan TD of Oregon, 642 vehicles
Inter-city	3
Passenger air service	
Airport	Portland International
Airlines	15
Aircraft departures	98,491 (1995)
Enplaned passengers	5,453,011 (1995)
Rail service	Amtrak; Light Rail
Motor freight carriers	194
Major waterways/ports	Port of Portland

Source: OAG, Business Travel Planner, Summer 1997; Editor & Publisher Market Guide, 1998; FAA Airport Activity Statistics, 1996; Amtrak National Time Table, Northeast Timetable, Fall/Winter 1997-98; 1990 Census of Population and Housing, STF 3C; Chamber of Commerce/Economic Development 1997; Jane's Urban Transport Systems 1997-98; Transit Fact Book 1997

A survey of 90,000 airline passengers during the first half of 1997 ranked most of the largest airports in the U.S. Portland International ranked number 22 out of 36. Criteria: cleanliness, quality of restaurants, attractiveness, speed of baggage delivery, ease of reaching gates, available ground transportation, ease of following signs and closeness of parking. *Plog Research Inc., First Half 1997*

Means of Transportation to Work

Area	Car/Truck/Van		Public Transportation			Bicycle	Walked	Other Means	Worked at Home
	Drove Alone	Car-pooled	Bus	Subway	Railroad				
City	65.0	12.9	10.5	0.1	0.1	1.1	5.6	1.3	3.4
MSA[1]	72.6	12.5	5.5	0.1	0.1	0.7	3.5	1.2	3.9
U.S.	73.2	13.4	3.0	1.5	0.5	0.4	3.9	1.2	3.0

Note: figures shown are percentages and only include workers 16 years old and over;
(1) Metropolitan Statistical Area - see Appendix A for areas included
Source: 1990 Census of Population and Housing, Summary Tape File 3C

BUSINESSES

Major Business Headquarters

Company Name	1997 Rankings	
	Fortune 500	Forbes 500
Fred Meyer	365	-
Hoffman Construction	-	154
KinderCare Learning Centers	-	377
North Pacific Lumber	-	175
Pacificorp	317	-
RB Pamplin	-	258
U.S. Bancorp	445	-
Willamette Industries	396	-

Note: Companies listed are located in the city; Dashes indicate no ranking
Fortune 500: companies that produce a 10-K are ranked 1 - 500 based on 1996 revenue
Forbes 500: private companies are ranked 1 - 500 based on 1996 revenue
Source: Forbes 12/1/97; Fortune 4/28/97

Women-Owned Businesses: Number, Employment, Sales and Share

Area	Women-Owned Businesses in 1996				Share of Women-Owned Businesses in 1996	
	Number	Employment	Sales ($000)	Rank[2]	Percent (%)	Rank[3]
MSA[1]	69,100	159,000	20,856,600	22	39.8	3

Note: (1) Metropolitan Statistical Area - see Appendix A for areas included; (2) Calculated on an averaging of number of businesses, employment and sales and ranges from 1 to 50 where 1 is best; (3) Ranges from 1 to 50 where 1 is best
Source: The National Foundation for Women Business Owners, 1996 Facts on Women-Owned Businesses: Trends in the Top 50 Metropolitan Areas, March 26, 1997

Women-Owned Businesses: Growth

Area	Growth in Women-Owned Businesses (% change from 1987 to 1996)				Relative Growth in the Number of Women-Owned and All Businesses (% change from 1987 to 1996)			
	Num.	Empl.	Sales	Rank[2]	Women-Owned	All Firms	Absolute Difference	Relative Difference
MSA[1]	121.2	285.0	396.1	1	121.2	88.7	32.5	1.4:1

Note: (1) Metropolitan Statistical Area - see Appendix A for areas included; (2) Calculated on an averaging of the percent growth of number of businesses, employment and sales and ranges from 1 to 50 where 1 is best
Source: The National Foundation for Women Business Owners, 1996 Facts on Women-Owned Businesses: Trends in the Top 50 Metropolitan Areas, March 26, 1997

Minority Business Opportunity

One of the 500 largest Hispanic-owned companies in the U.S. are located in Portland.
Hispanic Business, June 1997

Small Business Opportunity

Portland was included among *Entrepreneur* magazines listing of the "20 Best Cities for Small Business." It was ranked #1 among large metro areas. Criteria: risk of failure, business performance, economic growth, affordability and state attitude towards business. *Entrepreneur, 10/97*

According to *Forbes*, Portland is home to two of America's 200 best small companies: Electro Scientific Industries, Schmitt Industries. Criteria: companies must be publicly traded, U.S.-based corporations with latest 12-month sales of between $5 and $350 million. Earnings must be at least $1 million for the 12-month period. Limited partnerships, REITs and closed-end mutual funds were not considered. Banks, S&Ls and electric utilities were not included. *Forbes, November 3, 1997*

HOTELS & MOTELS

Hotels/Motels

Area	Hotels/ Motels	Rooms	Luxury-Level Hotels/Motels		Average Minimum Rates ($)		
			♦♦♦♦	♦♦♦♦♦	♦♦	♦♦♦	♦♦♦♦
City	43	6,274	4	0	84	113	166
Airport	15	2,156	0	0	n/a	n/a	n/a
Suburbs	53	5,113	0	0	n/a	n/a	n/a
Total	111	13,543	4	0	n/a	n/a	n/a

Note: n/a not available; Classifications range from one diamond (budget properties with basic amenities) to five diamond (luxury properties with the finest service, rooms and facilities). Source: OAG, Business Travel Planner, Summer 1997

CONVENTION CENTERS

Major Convention Centers

Center Name	Meeting Rooms	Exhibit Space (sf)
Oregon Convention Center	32	150,000
Portland Expo Center	4	220,000
Portland International Airport	7	n/a
Portland Memorial Coliseum/Complex Civic Stadium	7	40,000
The Rose Garden	14	32,000

Note: n/a not available
Source: Trade Shows Worldwide 1997

Living Environment

COST OF LIVING

Cost of Living Index

Composite Index	Housing	Utilities	Groceries	Health Care	Trans-portation	Misc. Goods/ Services
106.8	118.9	77.0	103.4	121.8	109.9	101.7

Note: U.S. = 100; Figures are for the Metropolitan Statistical Area - see Appendix A for areas included
Source: ACCRA, Cost of Living Index, 3rd Quarter 1997

HOUSING

Median Home Prices and Housing Affordability

Area	Median Price[2] 3rd Qtr. 1997 ($)	HOI[3] 3rd Qtr. 1997	Afford-ability Rank[4]
MSA[1]	155,000	25.5	194
U.S.	127,000	63.7	–

Note: (1) Metropolitan Statistical Area - see Appendix A for areas included; (2) U.S. figures calculated from the sales of 625,000 new and existing homes in 195 markets; (3) Housing Opportunity Index - percent of homes sold that were within the reach of the median income household at the prevailing mortgage interest rate; (4) Rank is from 1-195 with 1 being most affordable
Source: National Association of Home Builders, Housing Opportunity Index, 3rd Quarter 1997

It is projected that the median price of existing single-family homes in the metro area will increase by 8.9% in 1998. Nationwide, home prices are projected to increase 6.6%.
Kiplinger's Personal Finance Magazine, January 1998

Average New Home Price

Area	Price ($)
MSA[1]	167,600
U.S.	135,710

Note: Figures are based on a new home with 1,800 sq. ft. of living area on an 8,000 sq. ft. lot;
(1) Metropolitan Statistical Area - see Appendix A for areas included
Source: ACCRA, Cost of Living Index, 3rd Quarter 1997

Average Apartment Rent

Area	Rent ($/mth)
MSA[1]	650
U.S.	569

Note: Figures are based on an unfurnished two bedroom, 1-1/2 or 2 bath apartment, approximately 950 sq. ft. in size, excluding all utilities except water; (1) Metropolitan Statistical Area - see Appendix A for areas included
Source: ACCRA, Cost of Living Index, 3rd Quarter 1997

RESIDENTIAL UTILITIES

Average Residential Utility Costs

Area	All Electric ($/mth)	Part Electric ($/mth)	Other Energy ($/mth)	Phone ($/mth)
MSA[1]	–	35.52	38.50	20.92
U.S.	109.40	55.25	43.64	19.48

Note: (1) (1) Metropolitan Statistical Area - see Appendix A for areas included
Source: ACCRA, Cost of Living Index, 3rd Quarter 1997

HEALTH CARE

Average Health Care Costs

Area	Hospital ($/day)	Doctor ($/visit)	Dentist ($/visit)
MSA[1]	507.40	52.60	85.00
U.S.	392.91	48.76	60.84

Note: Hospital - based on a semi-private room. Doctor - based on a general practitioner's routine exam of an established patient. Dentist - based on adult teeth cleaning and periodic oral exam; (1) Metropolitan Statistical Area - see Appendix A for areas included
Source: ACCRA, Cost of Living Index, 3rd Quarter 1997

Distribution of Office-Based Physicians

Area	Family/Gen. Practitioners	Specialists		
		Medical	Surgical	Other
MSA[1]	369	1,158	848	966

Note: Data as of 12/31/96; (1) Metropolitan Statistical Area - see Appendix A for areas included
Source: American Medical Assn., Physician Characteristics & Distribution in the U.S., 1997-1998

Hospitals

Portland has 9 general medical and surgical hospitals, 1 psychiatric, 1 children's other specialty. *AHA Guide to the Healthcare Field 1997-98*

According to *U.S. News and World Report,* Portland has 1 of the best hospitals in the U.S.: **University Hospital,** noted for AIDS, endocrinology, geriatrics, gynecology, otolaryngology; *U.S. News and World Report, "America's Best Hospitals", 7/28/97*

EDUCATION

Public School District Statistics

District Name	Num. Sch.	Enroll.	Classroom Teachers[1]	Pupils per Teacher	Minority Pupils (%)	Current Exp.[2] ($/pupil)
Centennial Sch Dist 28J	8	5,583	289	19.3	n/a	n/a
David Douglas Sch Dist 40	12	7,152	362	19.8	n/a	n/a
Multnomah ESD	2	171	14	12.2	n/a	n/a
Parkrose Sch Dist 003	6	3,285	153	21.5	n/a	n/a
Portland Sch Dist 1J	101	55,130	2,785	19.8	32.3	6,588
Riverdale Sch Dist 51J	1	291	20	14.6	n/a	n/a
Sauvie Island Sch Dist 019	1	129	11	11.7	n/a	n/a

Note: Data covers the 1995-1996 school year unless otherwise noted; (1) Excludes teachers reported as working in school district offices rather than in schools; (2) Based on 1993-94 enrollment collected by the Census Bureau, not the enrollment figure shown in column 3; SD = School District; ISD = Independent School District; n/a not available
Source: National Center for Education Statistics, Common Core of Data Survey; Bureau of the Census

Educational Quality

School District	Education Quotient[1]	Graduate Outcome[2]	Community Index[3]	Resource Index[4]
Portland	109.0	90.0	103.0	134.0

Note: Nearly 1,000 secondary school districts were rated in terms of educational quality. The scores range from a low of 50 to a high of 150; (1) Average of the Graduate Outcome, Community and Resource indexes; (2) Based on graduation rates and college board scores (SAT/ACT); (3) Based on the surrounding community's average level of education and the area's average income level; (4) Based on teacher salaries, per-pupil expenditures and student-teacher ratios.
Source: Expansion Management, Ratings Issue 1997

Educational Attainment by Race

Area	High School Graduate (%)					Bachelor's Degree (%)				
	Total	White	Black	Other	Hisp.[2]	Total	White	Black	Other	Hisp.[2]
City	82.9	84.4	72.8	71.2	69.0	25.9	27.2	12.7	21.7	14.9
MSA[1]	84.6	85.6	74.2	71.7	59.7	24.8	25.2	14.0	23.3	12.8
U.S.	75.2	77.9	63.1	60.4	49.8	20.3	21.5	11.4	19.4	9.2

Note: figures shown cover persons 25 years old and over; (1) Metropolitan Statistical Area -
see Appendix A for areas included; (2) people of Hispanic origin can be of any race
Source: 1990 Census of Population and Housing, Summary Tape File 3C

School Enrollment by Type

Area	Preprimary				Elementary/High School			
	Public		Private		Public		Private	
	Enrollment	%	Enrollment	%	Enrollment	%	Enrollment	%
City	4,594	59.3	3,155	40.7	52,537	89.1	6,425	10.9
MSA[1]	13,786	57.1	10,355	42.9	181,368	91.3	17,390	8.7
U.S.	2,679,029	59.5	1,824,256	40.5	38,379,689	90.2	4,187,099	9.8

Note: figures shown cover persons 3 years old and over;
(1) Metropolitan Statistical Area - see Appendix A for areas included
Source: 1990 Census of Population and Housing, Summary Tape File 3C

School Enrollment by Race

Area	Preprimary (%)				Elementary/High School (%)			
	White	Black	Other	Hisp.[1]	White	Black	Other	Hisp.[1]
City	82.7	10.3	7.0	4.6	75.9	13.2	10.9	4.5
MSA[2]	90.3	3.9	5.9	3.6	87.6	4.5	7.8	4.9
U.S.	80.4	12.5	7.1	7.8	74.1	15.6	10.3	12.5

Note: figures shown cover persons 3 years old and over; (1) people of Hispanic origin can be of any
race; (2) Metropolitan Statistical Area - see Appendix A for areas included
Source: 1990 Census of Population and Housing, Summary Tape File 3C

SAT/ACT Scores

Area/District	1997 SAT				1997 ACT	
	Percent of Graduates Tested (%)	Average Math Score	Average Verbal Score	Average Combined Score	Percent of Graduates Tested (%)	Average Composite Score
Portland SDII	47	525	517	1,042	n/a	n/a
State	50	524	525	1,049	12	22.3
U.S.	42	511	505	1,016	36	21.0

Note: Math and verbal SAT scores are out of a possible 800; ACT scores are out of a possible 36
Caution: Comparing or ranking states/cities on the basis of SAT/ACT scores alone is invalid and
strongly discouraged by the The College Board and The American College Testing Program as
students who take the tests are self-selected and do not represent the entire student population.
Source: Portland Public Schools, Department of Research & Evaluation, 1997; College Board, 1997;
American College Testing Program, 1997

Classroom Teacher Salaries in Public Schools

District	B.A. Degree		M.A. Degree		Ph.D. Degree	
	Min. ($)	Max ($)	Min. ($)	Max. ($)	Min. ($)	Max. ($)
Portland	25,020	38,642	29,837	46,081	35,109	53,646
Average[1]	26,120	39,270	28,175	44,667	31,643	49,825

Note: Salaries are for 1996-1997; (1) Based on all school districts covered; n/a not available
Source: American Federation of Teachers (unpublished data)

Higher Education

Two-Year Colleges		Four-Year Colleges		Medical Schools	Law Schools	Voc/ Tech
Public	Private	Public	Private			
1	1	2	12	1	1	31

Source: College Blue Book, Occupational Education 1997; Medical School Admission Requirements, 1998-99; Peterson's Guide to Two-Year Colleges, 1997; Peterson's Guide to Four-Year Colleges, 1997; Barron's Guide to Law Schools 1997

MAJOR EMPLOYERS

Major Employers

Blue Cross & Blue Shield of Oregon
Emanuel Hospital
E.C. Co. (electrical work)
Gunderson Inc. (railroad equipment)
Portland Adventist Medical Center
Tri-County Metropolitan Transportation District
United Grocers
Standard Insurance

Bonneville Power Administration
Esco Corp. (mining machinery)
Freightliner Corp.
Northwest Natural Gas
Precision Castparts Corp.
US Bancorporation
Wacker Siltronic Corp. (semiconductors)

Note: companies listed are located in the city
Source: Dun's Business Rankings 1997; Ward's Business Directory, 1997

PUBLIC SAFETY

Crime Rate

Area	All Crimes	Violent Crimes				Property Crimes		
		Murder	Forcible Rape	Robbery	Aggrav. Assault	Burglary	Larceny -Theft	Motor Vehicle Theft
City	10,751.3	10.9	85.9	439.6	1,138.0	1,526.4	6,160.0	1,390.5
Suburbs[1]	4,467.5	1.9	33.7	77.5	153.4	756.6	3,003.5	440.9
MSA[2]	6,154.7	4.3	47.7	174.7	417.8	963.3	3,851.1	695.8
U.S.	5,078.9	7.4	36.1	202.4	388.2	943.0	2,975.9	525.9

Note: Crime rate is the number of crimes per 100,000 pop.; (1) defined as all areas within the MSA but located outside the central city; (2) Metropolitan Statistical Area - see Appendix A for areas incl.
Source: FBI Uniform Crime Reports 1996

RECREATION

Culture and Recreation

Museums	Symphony Orchestras	Opera Companies	Dance Companies	Professional Theatres	Zoos	Pro Sports Teams
7	1	1	2	4	1	1

Source: International Directory of the Performing Arts, 1996; Official Museum Directory, 1998; Chamber of Commerce/Economic Development 1997

Library System

The Multnomah County Library has 14 branches, holdings of 1,367,010 volumes and a budget of $21,391,719 (1994-1995). The Cedar Mill Community Library has no branches, holdings of 121,000 volumes and a budget of $1,162,600 (1996-1997). Note: n/a means not available.
American Library Directory, 1997-1998

MEDIA

Newspapers

Name	Type	Freq.	Distribution	Circulation
The Bee	General	1x/mo	Regional	14,000
Catholic Sentinel	Religious	1x/wk	State	15,700
Daily Journal of Commerce	n/a	5x/wk	Area	4,786
Daily Shipping News	n/a	5x/wk	Area	1,000
El Centinela	Hispanic	1x/mo	State	7,000
El Hispanic News	Hispanic	1x/wk	Local	10,000
The Jewish Review	Religious	2x/mo	Area	10,000
The Oregonian	General	7x/wk	Regional	333,654
Portland Observer	Black	1x/wk	Local	30,000
The Portland Skanner	Black	1x/wk	Local	21,000
Saint Johns Review	General	2x/mo	Regional	3,700
Southwest Community Connection	n/a	1x/mo	Local	10,000
The Vanguard	n/a	4x/wk	Campus & community	5,000
Willamette Week	General	1x/wk	Local	70,000

Note: Includes newspapers with circulations of 1,000 or more located in the city; n/a not available
Source: Burrelle's Media Directory, 1998 Edition

AM Radio Stations

Call Letters	Freq. (kHz)	Target Audience	Station Format	Music Format
KOTK	620	General	N/T	n/a
KXL	750	General	N/T	n/a
KPDQ	800	General	M/N/T	Christian/Country
KKSN	910	General	M	Oldies
KBBT	970	General	M	Adult Contemporary
KWJJ	1080	General	M	Country
KKEY	1150	General	T	n/a
KEX	1190	General	M/N/S/T	Adult Contemporary
KKSL	1290	Religious	M/T	Christian
KKPZ	1330	Religious	E/M/T	Christian
KBNP	1410	General	N/T	n/a
KBPS	1450	n/a	E/N	n/a
KFXX	1520	General	N/S/T	n/a

Note: Stations included broadcast in the Portland metro area; n/a not available
Station Format: E = Educational; M = Music; N = News; S = Sports; T = Talk
Source: Burrelle's Media Directory, 1998 Edition

FM Radio Stations

Call Letters	Freq. (mHz)	Target Audience	Station Format	Music Format
KMHD	89.1	n/a	M	Jazz
KBPS	89.9	General	M/N	Classical
KBOO	90.7	General	M/N/S	Jazz/R&B/Urban Contemporary
KOPB	91.5	General	E/N	n/a
KGON	92.3	General	M	Classic Rock
KPDQ	93.7	General	T	n/a
KXL	95.5	General	M	Adult Contemporary
KKSN	97.1	General	M	Oldies
KUPL	98.5	General	M	Country
KWJJ	99.5	General	M	Country
KKRZ	100.3	General	M	Contemporary Top 40
KUFO	101.1	General	M	AOR
KINK	101.9	General	M/N	AOR
KKCW	103.3	General	M/N/S	Adult Contemporary
KKRH	105.1	General	M/N/S	Classic Rock
KKJZ	106.7	General	M	Adult Contemporary/Jazz

Note: Stations included broadcast in the Portland metro area; n/a not available
Station Format: E = Educational; M = Music; N = News; S = Sports; T = Talk
Music Format: AOR = Album Oriented Rock; MOR = Middle-of-the-Road
Source: Burrelle's Media Directory, 1998 Edition

Television Stations

Name	Ch.	Affiliation	Type	Owner
KATU	2	ABC	Commercial	Fisher Broadcasting Inc.
KOAB	3	PBS	Public	Oregon Public Broadcasting
KOIN	6	CBS	Commercial	Lee Enterprises Inc.
KOAC	7	PBS	Public	Oregon Public Broadcasting
KGW	8	NBC	Commercial	A.H. Belo Corporation
KOPB	10	PBS	Public	Oregon Public Broadcasting
KPTV	12	UPN	Commercial	Chris-Craft
KTVR	13	PBS	Public	Oregon Public Broadcasting
KNMT	24	TBN	Non-Commercial	National Minority Television Inc.
KEPB	28	PBS	Public	Oregon Public Broadcasting
KPDX	49	Fox	Commercial	Meredith Broadcasting

Note: Stations included broadcast in the Portland metro area
Source: Burrelle's Media Directory, 1998 Edition

CLIMATE

Average and Extreme Temperatures

Temperature	Jan	Feb	Mar	Apr	May	Jun	Jul	Aug	Sep	Oct	Nov	Dec	Ann
Extreme High (°F)	65	71	83	93	100	102	107	107	105	92	73	64	107
Average High (°F)	45	50	56	61	68	73	80	79	74	64	53	46	62
Average Temp. (°F)	39	43	48	52	58	63	68	68	63	55	46	41	54
Average Low (°F)	34	36	39	42	48	53	57	57	52	46	40	36	45
Extreme Low (°F)	-2	-3	19	29	29	39	43	44	34	26	13	6	-3

Note: Figures cover the years 1926-1992
Source: National Climatic Data Center, International Station Meteorological Climate Summary, 3/95

Average Precipitation/Snowfall/Humidity

Precip./Humidity	Jan	Feb	Mar	Apr	May	Jun	Jul	Aug	Sep	Oct	Nov	Dec	Ann
Avg. Precip. (in.)	5.5	4.2	3.8	2.4	2.0	1.5	0.5	0.9	1.7	3.0	5.5	6.6	37.5
Avg. Snowfall (in.)	3	1	1	Tr	Tr	0	0	0	0	0	1	2	7
Avg. Rel. Hum. 7am (%)	85	86	86	84	80	78	77	81	87	90	88	87	84
Avg. Rel. Hum. 4pm (%)	75	67	60	55	53	50	45	45	49	61	74	79	59

Note: Figures cover the years 1926-1992; Tr = Trace amounts (<0.05 in. of rain; <0.5 in. of snow)
Source: National Climatic Data Center, International Station Meteorological Climate Summary, 3/95

Weather Conditions

Temperature			Daytime Sky			Precipitation		
5°F & below	32°F & below	90°F & above	Clear	Partly cloudy	Cloudy	0.01 inch or more precip.	0.1 inch or more snow/ice	Thunder-storms
< 1	37	11	67	116	182	152	4	7

Note: Figures are average number of days per year and covers the years 1926-1992
Source: National Climatic Data Center, International Station Meteorological Climate Summary, 3/95

AIR & WATER QUALITY

Maximum Pollutant Concentrations

	Particulate Matter (ug/m³)	Carbon Monoxide (ppm)	Sulfur Dioxide (ppm)	Nitrogen Dioxide (ppm)	Ozone (ppm)	Lead (ug/m³)
MSA[1] Level	70	7	n/a	n/a	0.13	0.11
NAAQS[2]	150	9	0.140	0.053	0.12	1.50
Met NAAQS?	Yes	Yes	n/a	n/a	No	Yes

Note: (1) Metropolitan Statistical Area - see Appendix A for areas included; (2) National Ambient Air Quality Standards; ppm = parts per million; ug/m³ = micrograms per cubic meter; n/a not available
Source: EPA, National Air Quality and Emissions Trends Report, 1996

Pollutant Standards Index

In the Portland MSA (see Appendix A for areas included), the Pollutant Standards Index (PSI) exceeded 100 on 4 days in 1996. A PSI value greater than 100 indicates that air quality would be in the unhealthful range on that day. *EPA, National Air Quality and Emissions Trends Report, 1996*

Drinking Water

Water System Name	Pop. Served	Primary Water Source Type	Number of Violations in Fiscal Year 1997	Type of Violation/ Contaminants
Portland Bureau of Water Works	460,000	Surface	None	None

Note: Data as of January 16, 1998
Source: EPA, Office of Ground Water and Drinking Water, Safe Drinking Water Information System

Portland tap water is neutral, very soft and not fluoridated.
Editor & Publisher Market Guide, 1998

Pueblo, Colorado

Background

James P. Beckworth, a onetime war chief of the Crow tribe, arrived in the area in 1842 and set up a trading post for Rocky Mountain fur traders and trappers. The settlement grew rapidly with the arrival of the railroads in the 1870's and the discovery of nearby coal deposits.

Located on the Arkansas River in the foothills of the Rocky Mountains, Pueblo is at the center of a network of highway and railroad connections which make it a trade and shipping center for coal, timber, livestock and farm products. Pueblo is also the industrial and commercial center of the Arkansas Valley. Its principal industry is the manufacture of steel and steel products. Other industries include meat-packing, photo-processing, and the manufacture of ski-wear.

Agriculture consists chiefly of cattle grazing on the dry plains and irrigated farming near streams. Sugar beets, corn, chili peppers and melons are the most important crops, but a variety of vegetables are grown.

Lake Pueblo, the largest body of water in southern Colorado, is located seven miles west of the city and provides a variety of water sports and fishing. The San Isabel National Forest, a wildlife preserve, provides a beautiful venue for picnicking and hiking. The countryside surrounding Pueblo consists of rolling plains, broken by normally dry arroyos, generally treeless and covered mainly with sparse bunchgrass and occasional cacti.

"Talk to the business community in Pueblo and you'll notice: The same hardy spirit that drove Fort Pueblo settlers to carve a livelihood from a harsh landscape of shale and sagebrush still lives today."

For five years, the city has fought the good fight to bring its economy out of the downturn that hit in the early '80s with the partial shutdown of CF&I (Colorado Fuel and Iron Corporation) and, consequently, of one of Pueblo's most relied-upon-industries-steel."

"Now, largely through the efforts of the Pueblo Economic Development Corp., the city's much-heralded turnaround has resulted in a diverse new business community that ranges from high-tech manufacturers Unisys and Kaiser Space Products to the brand new addition of a dog food manufacturer." *Colorado Business Magazine, 9/97*

In 1997, the city became involved in a major downtown renewal project.

Pueblo's climate is semi-arid and marked by large daily temperature variations. The temperature reaches 90 degrees or more about half the time during the summer, but the humidity is usually low. The sun shines about 76 percent of the time. Winter is comparatively mild due to the abundant sunshine and the protection afforded by the nearby mountains.

General Rankings and Evaluative Comments

- Pueblo was ranked #109 out of 300 cities by *Money's* 1997 "Survey of the Best Places to Live." Criteria used: health services, crime, economy, housing, education, transportation, weather, leisure and the arts. The city was ranked #102 in 1996 and #21 in 1995.
  Money, July 1997; Money, September 1996; Money, September 1995

- Pueblo was ranked #135 out of 219 cities in terms of children's health, safety, and economic well-being. Criteria: total population, percent population change, birth rate, child immunization rate, infant mortality rate, percent low birth weight infants, percent of births to teens, physician-to-population ratio, student-to-teacher ratio, dropout rate, unemployment rate, median family income, percent of children in poverty, violent and property crime rates, number of juvenile arrests for violent crimes as a percent of the total crime index, number of days with pollution standard index (PSI) over 100, pounds toxic releases per 1,000 people and number of superfund sites. *Zero Population Growth, Children's Environmental Index 1997*

- According to *Working Mother*, "State lawmakers developed a new funding source for child care by allowing taxpayers to check off a box on state tax forms, thereby designating part of their tax dollars for child care. The new system routes the money to the Quality Child Care Improvement Fund, which will disburse the funds to centers to buy new equipment, set up training programs for caregivers or take other steps to boost the quality of their programs. Colorado also reinstated a law giving middle-income families a tax break for child care—which could save parents hundreds of dollars a year.

  Governor Roy Romer announced a 12-point plan this year to expand and improve child care across the state. Among the more important aspects of the plan: $2 million is earmarked to help renovate child care facilities in rural areas and to increase money for child care subsides.

  Colorado also overhauled its child care licensing laws to make them more effective. State inspectors will now visit centers that have a history of problems more frequently and inspect those that have achieved accreditation less often. A new law requires all centers to post their latest inspection report so parents can see the results. (Colorado is among the 10 best states for child care.)" *Working Mother, July/August 1997*

Business Environment

STATE ECONOMY

State Economic Profile

"Colorado's economy has decelerated steadily over the past year. ....Personal bankruptcy filings are up 18%, one-half the U.S. rate of growth.

Colorado's expansion is not driven by the fortunes of a few dominant industries, as in the cases of Idaho and Nevada. Rather, a broad range of industries throughout the state are making investments and adding workers. The expansion of Colorado's market in terms of population and income has led numerous national retail chains to enter the Colorado market, providing local retailers with stiff competition and leading to casualties. At least seven retail chains have been forced to close their Colorado stores.

Declining affordability in the larger metro areas is causing growth to be pushed out to neighboring smaller metro areas. The nucleus of Colorado's growth is the Denver and Boulder areas. The current expansion of both metro areas represents moderation when compared to the growth of two years ago. Boulder's residential building restrictions and efforts to contain commercial construction are exporting growth to northern Denver and to Greeley, where housing prices are far lower.

Colorado's geographic position in the Rockies between the Plains states and the West Coast makes it a natural gateway through which the emerging western economies will increasingly channel their trade. Colorado has the population and business base in place to maintain steady long-term growth. Colorado is top-ranked for long-term growth." *National Association of Realtors, Economic Profiles: The Fifty States, July 1997*

IMPORTS/EXPORTS

Total Export Sales

Area	1993 ($000)	1994 ($000)	1995 ($000)	1996 ($000)	% Chg. 1993-96	% Chg. 1995-96
MSA[1]	n/a	n/a	n/a	n/a	n/a	n/a
U.S.	464,858,354	512,415,609	583,030,524	622,827,063	34.0	6.8

Note: (1) Metropolitan Statistical Area - see Appendix A for areas included
Source: U.S. Department of Commerce, International Trade Association, Metropolitan Area Exports: An Export Performance Report on Over 250 U.S. Cities, October 1997

Imports/Exports by Port

Type	Cargo Value			Share of U.S. Total	
	1995 (US$mil.)	1996 (US$mil.)	% Change 1995-1996	1995 (%)	1996 (%)
Imports	0	0	0	0	0
Exports	0	0	0	0	0

Source: Global Trade Information Services, WaterBorne Trade Atlas 1997

CITY FINANCES

City Government Finances

Component	FY92 ($000)	FY92 (per capita $)
Revenue	71,495	727.04
Expenditure	68,348	695.04
Debt Outstanding	98,519	1,001.85
Cash & Securities	67,389	685.29

Source: U.S. Bureau of the Census, City Government Finances: 1991-92

City Government Revenue by Source

Source	FY92 ($000)	FY92 (per capita $)	FY92 (%)
From Federal Government	3,881	39.47	5.4
From State Governments	4,046	41.14	5.7
From Local Governments	646	6.57	0.9
Property Taxes	7,050	71.69	9.9
General Sales Taxes	23,259	236.52	32.5
Selective Sales Taxes	2,705	27.51	3.8
Income Taxes	0	0.00	0.0
Current Charges	8,822	89.71	12.3
Utility/Liquor Store	14,347	145.90	20.1
Employee Retirement[1]	0	0.00	0.0
Other	6,739	68.53	9.4

Note: (1) Excludes "city contributions," classified as "nonrevenue," intragovernmental transfers.
Source: U.S. Bureau of the Census, City Government Finances: 1991-92

City Government Expenditures by Function

Function	FY92 ($000)	FY92 (per capita $)	FY92 (%)
Educational Services	1,801	18.31	2.6
Employee Retirement[1]	0	0.00	0.0
Environment/Housing	11,999	122.02	17.6
Government Administration	4,106	41.75	6.0
Interest on General Debt	6,982	71.00	10.2
Public Safety	15,577	158.40	22.8
Social Services	500	5.08	0.7
Transportation	10,964	111.49	16.0
Utility/Liquor Store	15,794	160.61	23.1
Other	625	6.36	0.9

Note: (1) Payments to beneficiaries including withdrawal of contributions.
Source: U.S. Bureau of the Census, City Government Finances: 1991-92

Municipal Bond Ratings

Area	Moody's	S & P
Pueblo	A3	n/a

Note: n/a not available; n/r not rated
Source: Moody's Bond Record, 2/98; Statistical Abstract of the U.S., 1997; Governing Magazine, 9/97, 3/98

POPULATION

Population Growth

Area	1980	1990	% Chg. 1980-90	July 1996 Estimate	% Chg. 1990-96
City	101,686	98,640	-3.0	99,406	0.8
MSA[1]	125,972	123,051	-2.3	131,217	6.6
U.S.	226,545,805	248,765,170	9.8	265,179,411	6.6

Note: (1) Metropolitan Statistical Area - see Appendix A for areas included
Source: 1980/1990 Census of Housing and Population, Summary Tape File 3C; Census Bureau Population Estimates

Population Characteristics

Race	City 1980 Population	City 1980 %	City 1990 Population	City 1990 %	% Chg. 1980-90	MSA[1] 1990 Population	MSA[1] 1990 %
White	86,250	84.8	81,951	83.1	-5.0	104,312	84.8
Black	2,359	2.3	2,006	2.0	-15.0	2,111	1.7
Amer Indian/Esk/Aleut	603	0.6	771	0.8	27.9	1,044	0.8
Asian/Pacific Islander	516	0.5	691	0.7	33.9	839	0.7
Other	11,958	11.8	13,221	13.4	10.6	14,745	12.0
Hispanic Origin[2]	36,060	35.5	38,823	39.4	7.7	43,967	35.7

Note: (1) Metropolitan Statistical Area - see Appendix A for areas included;
(2) people of Hispanic origin can be of any race
Source: 1980/1990 Census of Housing and Population, Summary Tape File 3C

Ancestry

Area	German	Irish	English	Italian	U.S.	French	Polish	Dutch
City	19.1	12.8	11.2	7.8	2.5	2.8	1.1	2.3
MSA[1]	20.5	13.3	12.3	7.9	2.5	3.0	1.3	2.3
U.S.	23.3	15.6	13.1	5.9	5.3	4.2	3.8	2.5

Note: Figures are percentages and include persons that reported multiple ancestry (eg. if a person reported being Irish and Italian, they were included in both columns); (1) Metropolitan Statistical Area - see Appendix A for areas included
Source: 1990 Census of Population and Housing, Summary Tape File 3C

Age

Area	Median Age (Years)	Under 5	Under 18	18-24	25-44	45-64	65+	80+
City	34.5	7.1	26.2	9.3	29.6	19.1	15.9	3.7
MSA[1]	34.7	7.0	26.4	9.0	29.6	20.0	15.1	3.3
U.S.	32.9	7.3	25.6	10.5	32.6	18.7	12.5	2.8

Note: (1) Metropolitan Statistical Area - see Appendix A for areas included
Source: 1990 Census of Population and Housing, Summary Tape File 3C

Male/Female Ratio

Area	Number of males per 100 females (all ages)	Number of males per 100 females (18 years old+)
City	90.9	88.4
MSA[1]	92.3	90.3
U.S.	95.0	91.9

Note: (1) Metropolitan Statistical Area - see Appendix A for areas included
Source: 1990 Census of Population, General Population Characteristics

INCOME

Per Capita/Median/Average Income

Area	Per Capita ($)	Median Household ($)	Average Household ($)
City	10,168	20,501	25,729
MSA[1]	10,347	21,553	26,651
U.S.	14,420	30,056	38,453

Note: all figures are for 1989; (1) Metropolitan Statistical Area - see Appendix A for areas included
Source: 1990 Census of Population and Housing, Summary Tape File 3C

Household Income Distribution by Race

Income ($)	City (%)					U.S. (%)				
	Total	White	Black	Other	Hisp.[1]	Total	White	Black	Other	Hisp.[1]
Less than 5,000	10.6	9.3	26.4	16.9	14.6	6.2	4.8	15.2	8.6	8.8
5,000 - 9,999	14.7	14.1	16.6	18.5	18.6	9.3	8.6	14.2	9.9	11.1
10,000 - 14,999	11.9	11.8	8.0	13.3	13.4	8.8	8.5	11.0	9.8	11.0
15,000 - 24,999	22.2	22.4	20.5	20.7	21.6	17.5	17.3	18.9	18.5	20.5
25,000 - 34,999	16.1	16.7	15.1	12.8	13.8	15.8	16.1	14.2	15.4	16.4
35,000 - 49,999	13.6	13.9	8.6	12.2	11.5	17.9	18.6	13.3	16.1	16.0
50,000 - 74,999	8.0	8.7	4.7	4.1	5.3	15.0	15.8	9.3	13.4	11.1
75,000 - 99,999	1.7	1.9	0.0	0.8	0.7	5.1	5.5	2.6	4.7	3.1
100,000+	1.2	1.3	0.0	0.8	0.5	4.4	4.8	1.3	3.7	1.9

Note: all figures are for 1989; (1) people of Hispanic origin can be of any race
Source: 1990 Census of Population and Housing, Summary Tape File 3C

Effective Buying Income

Area	Per Capita ($)	Median Household ($)	Average Household ($)
City	11,345	23,045	28,957
MSA[1]	11,852	24,769	30,765
U.S.	15,444	33,201	41,849

Note: data as of 1/1/97; (1) Metropolitan Statistical Area - see Appendix A for areas included
Source: Standard Rate & Data Service, Newspaper Advertising Source, 2/98

Effective Household Buying Income Distribution

Area	% of Households Earning						
	$10,000 -$19,999	$20,000 -$34,999	$35,000 -$49,999	$50,000 -$74,999	$75,000 -$99,000	$100,000 -$124,999	$125,000 and up
City	22.7	26.8	15.2	10.6	2.5	0.7	0.6
MSA[1]	21.6	27.1	16.2	11.9	3.0	0.8	0.7
U.S.	16.5	23.4	18.3	18.2	6.4	2.1	2.4

Note: data as of 1/1/97; (1) Metropolitan Statistical Area - see Appendix A for areas included
Source: Standard Rate & Data Service, Newspaper Advertising Source, 2/98

Poverty Rates by Race and Age

Area	Total (%)	By Race (%)				By Age (%)		
		White	Black	Other	Hisp.[2]	Under 5 years old	Under 18 years old	65 years and over
City	21.6	18.8	37.9	35.3	32.5	40.7	32.2	13.9
MSA[1]	20.2	17.7	37.7	34.0	31.4	36.8	29.6	13.6
U.S.	13.1	9.8	29.5	23.1	25.3	20.1	18.3	12.8

Note: figures show the percent of people living below the poverty line in 1989. The average poverty threshold was $12,674 for a family of four in 1989; (1) Metropolitan Statistical Area - see Appendix A for areas included; (2) people of Hispanic origin can be of any race
Source: 1990 Census of Population and Housing, Summary Tape File 3C

EMPLOYMENT

Labor Force and Employment

Area	Civilian Labor Force			Workers Employed		
	Dec. '95	Dec. '96	% Chg.	Dec. '95	Dec. '96	% Chg.
City	46,684	49,773	6.6	44,225	46,914	6.1
MSA[1]	59,217	63,123	6.6	56,217	59,635	6.1
U.S.	134,583,000	136,742,000	1.6	127,903,000	130,785,000	2.3

Note: Data is not seasonally adjusted and covers workers 16 years of age and older; (1) Metropolitan Statistical Area - see Appendix A for areas included
Source: Bureau of Labor Statistics, http://stats.bls.gov

Unemployment Rate

Area	1997											
	Jan.	Feb.	Mar.	Apr.	May	Jun.	Jul.	Aug.	Sep.	Oct.	Nov.	Dec.
City	6.0	4.9	4.9	4.2	4.8	5.6	4.8	4.6	4.4	3.7	4.1	5.7
MSA[1]	5.8	4.7	4.7	4.0	4.6	5.3	4.6	4.4	4.2	3.5	3.9	5.5
U.S.	5.9	5.7	5.5	4.8	4.7	5.2	5.0	4.8	4.7	4.4	4.3	4.4

Note: Data is not seasonally adjusted and covers workers 16 years of age and older; All figures are percentages; (1) Metropolitan Statistical Area - see Appendix A for areas included
Source: Bureau of Labor Statistics, http://stats.bls.gov

Employment by Industry

Sector	MSA[1]		U.S.
	Number of Employees	Percent of Total	Percent of Total
Services	n/a	n/a	29.0
Retail Trade	n/a	n/a	18.5
Government	n/a	n/a	16.1
Manufacturing	n/a	n/a	15.0
Finance/Insurance/Real Estate	n/a	n/a	5.7
Wholesale Trade	n/a	n/a	5.4
Transportation/Public Utilities	n/a	n/a	5.3
Construction	n/a	n/a	4.5
Mining	n/a	n/a	0.5

Note: Figures cover non-farm employment as of 12/97 and are not seasonally adjusted; (1) Metropolitan Statistical Area - see Appendix A for areas included; n/a not available
Source: Bureau of Labor Statistics, http://stats.bls.gov

Employment by Occupation

Occupation Category	City (%)	MSA[1] (%)	U.S. (%)
White Collar	55.2	53.9	58.1
Executive/Admin./Management	9.8	9.4	12.3
Professional	13.6	13.8	14.1
Technical & Related Support	3.8	3.5	3.7
Sales	12.1	11.7	11.8
Administrative Support/Clerical	15.8	15.4	16.3
Blue Collar	25.0	26.1	26.2
Precision Production/Craft/Repair	9.5	10.7	11.3
Machine Operators/Assem./Insp.	6.4	6.2	6.8
Transportation/Material Movers	4.8	5.0	4.1
Cleaners/Helpers/Laborers	4.2	4.1	3.9
Services	18.8	17.9	13.2
Farming/Forestry/Fishing	1.1	2.1	2.5

Note: figures cover employed persons 16 years old and over; (1) Metropolitan Statistical Area - see Appendix A for areas included
Source: 1990 Census of Population and Housing, Summary Tape File 3C

Occupational Employment Projections: 1994 - 2005

Occupations Expected to have the Largest Job Growth (ranked by numerical growth)	Fast-Growing Occupations (ranked by percent growth)
1. Janitors/cleaners/maids, ex. priv. hshld.	1. Computer engineers
2. Salespersons, retail	2. Systems analysts
3. Waiters & waitresses	3. Computer scientists
4. General managers & top executives	4. Amusement and recreation attendants
5. Guards	5. Personal and home care aides
6. Marketing & sales, supervisors	6. Guards
7. Truck drivers, heavy & light	7. Human services workers
8. Cashiers	8. Nursery and greenhouse managers
9. Systems analysts	9. Pruners
10. Clerical supervisors	10. Electronic pagination systems workers

Projections cover Colorado.
Source: U.S. Department of Labor, Employment and Training Administration, America's Labor Market Information System (ALMIS)

Average Wages

Occupation	Wage	Occupation	Wage
Professional/Technical/Clerical	$/Week	**Health/Protective Services**	$/Week
Accountants III	-	Corrections Officers	-
Attorneys III	-	Firefighters	-
Budget Analysts III	-	Nurses, Licensed Practical II	-
Buyers/Contracting Specialists II	-	Nurses, Registered II	-
Clerks, Accounting III	404	Nursing Assistants II	-
Clerks, General III	-	Police Officers I	-
Computer Operators II	-	**Hourly Workers**	$/Hour
Computer Programmers II	-	Forklift Operators	-
Drafters II	-	General Maintenance Workers	7.01
Engineering Technicians III	-	Guards I	-
Engineering Technicians, Civil III	-	Janitors	6.78
Engineers III	-	Maintenance Electricians	-
Key Entry Operators I	-	Maintenance Electronics Techs II	-
Personnel Assistants III	-	Maintenance Machinists	-
Personnel Specialists III	-	Maintenance Mechanics, Machinery	13.60
Secretaries III	-	Material Handling Laborers	-
Switchboard Operator-Receptionist	269	Motor Vehicle Mechanics	-
Systems Analysts II	-	Shipping/Receiving Clerks	9.56
Systems Analysts Supervisor/Mgr II	-	Tool and Die Makers	-
Tax Collectors II	-	Truckdrivers, Tractor Trailer	11.66
Word Processors II	-	Warehouse Specialists	11.50

Note: Wage data includes full-time workers only for 9/94 and cover the Metropolitan Statistical Area (see Appendix A for areas included). Dashes indicate that data was not available.
Source: Bureau of Labor Statistics, Occupational Compensation Survey

TAXES

Major State and Local Tax Rates

State Corp. Income (%)	State Personal Income (%)	Residential Property (effective rate per $100)	Sales & Use State (%)	Sales & Use Local (%)	State Gasoline (cents/ gallon)	State Cigarette (cents/ 20-pack)
5.0	5.0	n/a	3.0	4.5	22	20

Note: Personal/corporate income tax rates as of 1/97. Sales, gasoline and cigarette tax rates as of 1/98.
Source: Federation of Tax Administrators, www.taxadmin.org; Washington D.C. Department of Finance and Revenue, Tax Rates and Tax Burdens in the District of Columbia: A Nationwide Comparison, June 1997; Chamber of Commerce

Total Taxes Per Capita and as a Percent of Income

Area	Per Capita Income ($)	Per Capita Taxes ($)			Taxes as Pct. of Income (%)		
		Total	Federal	State/Local	Total	Federal	State/Local
Colorado	27,624	9,705	6,521	3,184	35.1	23.6	11.5
U.S.	26,187	9,205	6,127	3,078	35.2	23.4	11.8

Note: Figures are for 1997
Source: Tax Foundation, Web Site, www.taxfoundation.org

Estimated Tax Burden

Area	State Income	Local Income	Property	Sales	Total
Pueblo	2,220	0	2,250	638	5,108

Note: The numbers are estimates of taxes paid by a married couple with two kids and annual earnings of $65,000. Sales tax estimates assume they spend average amounts on food, clothing, household goods and gasoline. Property tax estimates assume they live in a $225,000 home.
Source: Kiplinger's Personal Finance Magazine, June 1997

COMMERCIAL REAL ESTATE

Data not available at time of publication.

COMMERCIAL UTILITIES

Typical Monthly Electric Bills

Area	Commercial Service ($/month)		Industrial Service ($/month)	
	12 kW demand 1,500 kWh	100 kW demand 30,000 kWh	1,000 kW demand 400,000 kWh	20,000 kW demand 10,000,000 kWh
City	n/a	n/a	n/a	n/a
U.S.	162	2,360	25,590	545,677

Note: Based on rates in effect July 1, 1997; n/a not available
Source: Edison Electric Institute, Typical Residential, Commercial and Industrial Bills, Summer 1997

TRANSPORTATION

Transportation Statistics

Avg. travel time to work (min.)	16.1
Interstate highways	I-25
Bus lines	
In-city	Pueblo Transit
Inter-city	2
Passenger air service	
Airport	Pueblo Memorial
Airlines	1
Aircraft departures	n/a
Enplaned passengers	n/a
Rail service	Amtrak Thruway Motorcoach Connections
Motor freight carriers	8
Major waterways/ports	None

Source: OAG, Business Travel Planner, Summer 1997; Editor & Publisher Market Guide, 1998; FAA Airport Activity Statistics, 1996; Amtrak National Time Table, Northeast Timetable, Fall/Winter 1997-98; 1990 Census of Population and Housing, STF 3C; Chamber of Commerce/Economic Development 1997; Jane's Urban Transport Systems 1997-98; Transit Fact Book 1997

Means of Transportation to Work

Area	Car/Truck/Van		Public Transportation			Bicycle	Walked	Other Means	Worked at Home
	Drove Alone	Car-pooled	Bus	Subway	Railroad				
City	80.1	13.4	1.0	0.0	0.0	0.3	2.9	0.7	1.5
MSA[1]	80.4	13.0	0.9	0.0	0.0	0.3	2.6	0.7	2.0
U.S.	73.2	13.4	3.0	1.5	0.5	0.4	3.9	1.2	3.0

Note: figures shown are percentages and only include workers 16 years old and over;
(1) Metropolitan Statistical Area - see Appendix A for areas included
Source: 1990 Census of Population and Housing, Summary Tape File 3C

BUSINESSES

Major Business Headquarters

Company Name	1997 Rankings	
	Fortune 500	Forbes 500

No companies listed.

Note: Companies listed are located in the city; Dashes indicate no ranking
Fortune 500: companies that produce a 10-K are ranked 1 - 500 based on 1996 revenue
Forbes 500: private companies are ranked 1 - 500 based on 1996 revenue
Source: Forbes 12/1/97; Fortune 4/28/97

HOTELS & MOTELS

Hotels/Motels

Area	Hotels/ Motels	Rooms	Luxury-Level Hotels/Motels		Average Minimum Rates ($)		
			♦♦♦♦	♦♦♦♦♦	♦♦	♦♦♦	♦♦♦♦
City	5	463	0	0	n/a	n/a	n/a

Note: n/a not available; Classifications range from one diamond (budget properties with basic amenities) to five diamond (luxury properties with the finest service, rooms and facilities).
Source: OAG, Business Travel Planner, Summer 1997

CONVENTION CENTERS

Major Convention Centers

Center Name	Meeting Rooms	Exhibit Space (sf)

None listed in city
Source: Trade Shows Worldwide 1997

Living Environment

COST OF LIVING

Cost of Living Index

Composite Index	Housing	Utilities	Groceries	Health Care	Trans- portation	Misc. Goods/ Services
89.4	82.5	76.7	104.9	107.9	91.7	86.8

Note: U.S. = 100
Source: ACCRA, Cost of Living Index, 3rd Quarter 1997

HOUSING

Median Home Prices and Housing Affordability

Area	Median Price[2] 3rd Qtr. 1997 ($)	HOI[3] 3rd Qtr. 1997	Afford- ability Rank[4]
MSA[1]	92,000	58.2	156
U.S.	127,000	63.7	--

Note: (1) Metropolitan Statistical Area - see Appendix A for areas included; (2) U.S. figures calculated from the sales of 625,000 new and existing homes in 195 markets; (3) Housing Opportunity Index - percent of homes sold that were within the reach of the median income household at the prevailing mortgage interest rate; (4) Rank is from 1-195 with 1 being most affordable
Source: National Association of Home Builders, Housing Opportunity Index, 3rd Quarter 1997

Average New Home Price

Area	Price ($)
City	111,675
U.S.	135,710

Note: Figures are based on a new home with 1,800 sq. ft. of living area on an 8,000 sq. ft. lot.
Source: ACCRA, Cost of Living Index, 3rd Quarter 1997

Average Apartment Rent

Area	Rent ($/mth)
City	455
U.S.	569

Note: Figures are based on an unfurnished two bedroom, 1-1/2 or 2 bath apartment, approximately 950 sq. ft. in size, excluding all utilities except water
Source: ACCRA, Cost of Living Index, 3rd Quarter 1997

RESIDENTIAL UTILITIES

Average Residential Utility Costs

Area	All Electric ($/mth)	Part Electric ($/mth)	Other Energy ($/mth)	Phone ($/mth)
City	--	42.63	31.16	20.86
U.S.	109.40	55.25	43.64	19.48

Source: ACCRA, Cost of Living Index, 3rd Quarter 1997

HEALTH CARE

Average Health Care Costs

Area	Hospital ($/day)	Doctor ($/visit)	Dentist ($/visit)
City	342.50	62.60	61.80
U.S.	392.91	48.76	60.84

Note: Hospital - based on a semi-private room. Doctor - based on a general practitioner's routine exam of an established patient. Dentist - based on adult teeth cleaning and periodic oral exam.
Source: ACCRA, Cost of Living Index, 3rd Quarter 1997

Distribution of Office-Based Physicians

Area	Family/Gen. Practitioners	Specialists		
		Medical	Surgical	Other
MSA[1]	45	69	62	68

Note: Data as of 12/31/96; (1) Metropolitan Statistical Area - see Appendix A for areas included
Source: American Medical Assn., Physician Characteristics & Distribution in the U.S., 1997-1998

Hospitals

Pueblo has 2 general medical and surgical hospitals, 1 psychiatric. *AHA Guide to the Healthcare Field 1997-98*

EDUCATION

Public School District Statistics

District Name	Num. Sch.	Enroll.	Classroom Teachers[1]	Pupils per Teacher	Minority Pupils (%)	Current Exp.[2] ($/pupil)
Pueblo City 60	35	17,817	948	18.8	n/a	n/a
Pueblo County Rural 70	17	5,160	261	19.8	n/a	n/a

Note: Data covers the 1995-1996 school year unless otherwise noted; (1) Excludes teachers reported as working in school district offices rather than in schools; (2) Based on 1993-94 enrollment collected by the Census Bureau, not the enrollment figure shown in column 3; SD = School District; ISD = Independent School District; n/a not available
Source: National Center for Education Statistics, Common Core of Data Survey; Bureau of the Census

Educational Quality

School District	Education Quotient[1]	Graduate Outcome[2]	Community Index[3]	Resource Index[4]
Pueblo City	82.0	84.0	76.0	85.0

Note: Nearly 1,000 secondary school districts were rated in terms of educational quality. The scores range from a low of 50 to a high of 150; (1) Average of the Graduate Outcome, Community and Resource indexes; (2) Based on graduation rates and college board scores (SAT/ACT); (3) Based on the surrounding community's average level of education and the area's average income level; (4) Based on teacher salaries, per-pupil expenditures and student-teacher ratios.
Source: Expansion Management, Ratings Issue 1997

Educational Attainment by Race

Area	High School Graduate (%)					Bachelor's Degree (%)				
	Total	White	Black	Other	Hisp.[2]	Total	White	Black	Other	Hisp.[2]
City	73.2	74.1	71.3	66.9	62.2	13.8	14.9	11.2	5.9	5.1
MSA[1]	73.9	75.0	70.1	66.4	61.8	14.0	15.1	10.5	6.1	5.0
U.S.	75.2	77.9	63.1	60.4	49.8	20.3	21.5	11.4	19.4	9.2

Note: figures shown cover persons 25 years old and over; (1) Metropolitan Statistical Area - see Appendix A for areas included; (2) people of Hispanic origin can be of any race
Source: 1990 Census of Population and Housing, Summary Tape File 3C

School Enrollment by Type

Area	Preprimary				Elementary/High School			
	Public		Private		Public		Private	
	Enrollment	%	Enrollment	%	Enrollment	%	Enrollment	%
City	1,434	76.2	447	23.8	16,721	96.5	604	3.5
MSA[1]	1,658	74.5	567	25.5	21,367	96.6	762	3.4
U.S.	2,679,029	59.5	1,824,256	40.5	38,379,689	90.2	4,187,099	9.8

Note: figures shown cover persons 3 years old and over;
(1) Metropolitan Statistical Area - see Appendix A for areas included
Source: 1990 Census of Population and Housing, Summary Tape File 3C

School Enrollment by Race

Area	Preprimary (%)				Elementary/High School (%)			
	White	Black	Other	Hisp.[1]	White	Black	Other	Hisp.[1]
City	80.2	2.3	17.5	48.5	78.1	1.8	20.0	50.7
MSA[2]	81.5	1.9	16.5	44.4	80.6	1.5	17.8	45.4
U.S.	80.4	12.5	7.1	7.8	74.1	15.6	10.3	12.5

Note: figures shown cover persons 3 years old and over; (1) people of Hispanic origin can be of any race; (2) Metropolitan Statistical Area - see Appendix A for areas included
Source: 1990 Census of Population and Housing, Summary Tape File 3C

SAT/ACT Scores

Area/District	1997 SAT				1997 ACT	
	Percent of Graduates Tested (%)	Average Math Score	Average Verbal Score	Average Combined Score	Percent of Graduates Tested (%)	Average Composite Score
Pueblo SD60	5	553	546	1,099	51	20.1
State	30	539	536	1,075	62	21.5
U.S.	42	511	505	1,016	36	21.0

Note: Math and verbal SAT scores are out of a possible 800; ACT scores are out of a possible 36
Caution: Comparing or ranking states/cities on the basis of SAT/ACT scores alone is invalid and strongly discouraged by the The College Board and The American College Testing Program as students who take the tests are self-selected and do not represent the entire student population.
Source: Pueblo School District #60, Media/Technology Services, 1997; American College Testing Program, 1997; College Board, 1997

Classroom Teacher Salaries in Public Schools

District	B.A. Degree		M.A. Degree		Ph.D. Degree	
	Min. ($)	Max ($)	Min. ($)	Max. ($)	Min. ($)	Max. ($)
Pueblo	n/a	n/a	n/a	n/a	n/a	n/a
Average[1]	26,120	39,270	28,175	44,667	31,643	49,825

Note: Salaries are for 1996-1997; (1) Based on all school districts covered; n/a not available
Source: American Federation of Teachers (unpublished data)

Higher Education

Two-Year Colleges		Four-Year Colleges		Medical Schools	Law Schools	Voc/ Tech
Public	Private	Public	Private			
1	1	1	0	0	0	1

Source: College Blue Book, Occupational Education 1997; Medical School Admission Requirements, 1998-99; Peterson's Guide to Two-Year Colleges, 1997; Peterson's Guide to Four-Year Colleges, 1997; Barron's Guide to Law Schools 1997

MAJOR EMPLOYERS

Major Employers

CF&I Steel	St. Mary-Corwin Hospital
Industrial Gas Products & Supply	Minnequa Bank of Pueblo
Pueblo Bank & Trust	Gobins Inc. (office furniture)

Note: companies listed are located in the city
Source: Dun's Business Rankings 1997; Ward's Business Directory, 1997

PUBLIC SAFETY

Crime Rate

Area	All Crimes	Violent Crimes				Property Crimes		
		Murder	Forcible Rape	Robbery	Aggrav. Assault	Burglary	Larceny -Theft	Motor Vehicle Theft
City	7,016.1	11.4	70.4	186.6	1,050.8	1,283.1	4,097.7	316.0
Suburbs[1]	3,414.8	3.5	17.6	10.6	70.3	847.5	2,342.2	123.1
MSA[2]	6,249.0	9.7	59.2	149.1	842.0	1,190.3	3,723.8	274.9
U.S.	5,078.9	7.4	36.1	202.4	388.2	943.0	2,975.9	525.9

Note: Crime rate is the number of crimes per 100,000 pop.; (1) defined as all areas within the MSA but located outside the central city; (2) Metropolitan Statistical Area - see Appendix A for areas incl.
Source: FBI Uniform Crime Reports 1996

RECREATION

Culture and Recreation

Museums	Symphony Orchestras	Opera Companies	Dance Companies	Professional Theatres	Zoos	Pro Sports Teams
5	1	0	1	1	1	0

Source: International Directory of the Performing Arts, 1996; Official Museum Directory, 1998; Chamber of Commerce/Economic Development 1997

Library System

The Pueblo Library District has two branches, holdings of 294,611 volumes and a budget of $4,214,250 (1996). *American Library Directory, 1997-1998*

MEDIA

Newspapers

Name	Type	Freq.	Distribution	Circulation
The Pueblo Chieftain	n/a	7x/wk	Area	51,205

Note: Includes newspapers with circulations of 500 or more located in the city; n/a not available
Source: Burrelle's Media Directory, 1998 Edition

AM Radio Stations

Call Letters	Freq. (kHz)	Target Audience	Station Format	Music Format
KCSJ	590	General	N/S/T	n/a
KRMX	690	Hispanic	M/N	Spanish
KFEL	970	Religious	E/M/N/S/T	Christian
KGHF	1350	General	M	MOR
KRRU	1480	Hispanic	N/T	n/a

Note: Stations included broadcast in the Pueblo metro area; n/a not available
Station Format: E = Educational; M = Music; N = News; S = Sports; T = Talk
Music Format: AOR = Album Oriented Rock; MOR = Middle-of-the-Road
Source: Burrelle's Media Directory, 1998 Edition

FM Radio Stations

Call Letters	Freq. (mHz)	Target Audience	Station Format	Music Format
KTSC	89.5	General	M/N/S/T	AOR/Alternative
KSPZ	92.9	n/a	M	Oldies
KCCY	96.9	General	M	Country
KYZX	104.5	General	M/N/S	Country
KNKN	107.1	Hispanic	M	Spanish
KDZA	107.9	General	M	Oldies

Note: Stations included broadcast in the Pueblo metro area; n/a not available
Station Format: E = Educational; M = Music; N = News; S = Sports; T = Talk
Music Format: AOR = Album Oriented Rock; MOR = Middle-of-the-Road
Source: Burrelle's Media Directory, 1998 Edition

Television Stations

Name	Ch.	Affiliation	Type	Owner
KTSC	8	PBS	Public	University of Southern Colorado

Note: Stations included broadcast in the Pueblo metro area
Source: Burrelle's Media Directory, 1998 Edition

CLIMATE

Average and Extreme Temperatures

Temperature	Jan	Feb	Mar	Apr	May	Jun	Jul	Aug	Sep	Oct	Nov	Dec	Ann
Extreme High (°F)	78	81	86	93	98	108	106	104	100	94	84	82	108
Average High (°F)	45	50	57	67	77	88	92	90	82	70	56	47	69
Average Temp. (°F)	30	35	42	52	61	71	77	74	66	54	40	32	53
Average Low (°F)	14	19	26	36	46	55	61	59	50	37	24	16	37
Extreme Low (°F)	-28	-24	-10	2	26	37	47	40	27	13	-17	-28	-28

Note: Figures cover the years 1954-1992
Source: National Climatic Data Center, International Station Meteorological Climate Summary, 3/95

Average Precipitation/Snowfall/Humidity

Precip./Humidity	Jan	Feb	Mar	Apr	May	Jun	Jul	Aug	Sep	Oct	Nov	Dec	Ann
Avg. Precip. (in.)	0.3	0.3	0.8	0.9	1.4	1.3	2.0	2.0	0.9	0.8	0.5	0.4	11.6
Avg. Snowfall (in.)	6	4	6	3	1	0	0	0	1	2	4	5	32
Avg. Rel. Hum. 5am (%)	69	69	67	65	69	70	71	74	70	67	73	68	69
Avg. Rel. Hum. 5pm (%)	49	40	35	29	32	29	32	34	31	32	44	50	36

Note: Figures cover the years 1954-1992; Tr = Trace amounts (<0.05 in. of rain; <0.5 in. of snow)
Source: National Climatic Data Center, International Station Meteorological Climate Summary, 3/95

Weather Conditions

Temperature			Daytime Sky			Precipitation		
32°F & below	45°F & below	90°F & above	Clear	Partly cloudy	Cloudy	0.01 inch or more precip.	0.1 inch or more snow/ice	Thunder-storms
156	228	64	118	160	87	70	24	39

Note: Figures are average number of days per year and covers the years 1954-1992
Source: National Climatic Data Center, International Station Meteorological Climate Summary, 3/95

AIR & WATER QUALITY

Maximum Pollutant Concentrations

	Particulate Matter (ug/m^3)	Carbon Monoxide (ppm)	Sulfur Dioxide (ppm)	Nitrogen Dioxide (ppm)	Ozone (ppm)	Lead (ug/m^3)
MSA[1] Level	49	n/a	n/a	n/a	n/a	n/a
NAAQS[2]	150	9	0.140	0.053	0.12	1.50
Met NAAQS?	Yes	n/a	n/a	n/a	n/a	n/a

Note: (1) Metropolitan Statistical Area - see Appendix A for areas included; (2) National Ambient Air Quality Standards; ppm = parts per million; ug/m^3 = micrograms per cubic meter; n/a not available
Source: EPA, National Air Quality and Emissions Trends Report, 1996

Pollutant Standards Index

Data not available. *EPA, National Air Quality and Emissions Trends Report, 1996*

Drinking Water

Water System Name	Pop. Served	Primary Water Source Type	Number of Violations in Fiscal Year 1997	Type of Violation/ Contaminants
Pueblo Board of Water Works	100,000	Surface	None	None

Note: Data as of January 16, 1998
Source: EPA, Office of Ground Water and Drinking Water, Safe Drinking Water Information System

Pueblo tap water is alkaline, hard, naturally fluoridated. *Editor & Publisher Mkt. Guide, 1998*

Riverside, California

Background

Riverside is a beautiful city on the Santa Ana River between the low and the high California desert, about 53 miles east of Los Angeles. In an area called the Inland Empire, Riverside is surrounded by some of the richest agricultural land in the nation.

The town was founded in 1870 by John North on land that was once a Spanish rancho. English and Canadian investors moved into the area and brought with them the activities and traditions of their former countries. The first golf course and polo grounds in Southern California were built in Riverside. In fact, Riverside is a veritable city of firsts. In 1872, Eliza Tibbets received a gift of two Brazilian navel orange trees from a friend and planted them at her Riverside home. All navel oranges grown in the United States are descendants of those two trees, one of which still produces. In 1909, Riverside was the nation's first community to hold an interdenominational open-air sunrise service on Easter Sunday and later became the first to use electric lights to decorate the community's Christmas tree. Gone with the Wind was first shown to audiences at the Riverside Fox Theater in 1939 and the nearby March Air Reserve Base was the first Air Force base on the West Coast.

While Riverside may be home to many "firsts," it is also home to many "largests," especially in business. Toro Inc. has one of the world's largest irrigation equipment manufacturing facilities in the world. Luxfer USA Limited is the largest manufacturer of high pressure gas cylinders in the world. Fleetwood Enterprises is the largest manufacturer in both the recreational vehicle and manufactured housing industries. The company manufactures one in three recreational vehicles on the road today. Rohr is a leading producer of aerospace components for commercial and military aircraft, while Bourns, Inc. specializes in the design, manufacture and marketing of high technology products for the electronic components industry. Riverside is also home to two Anheuser-Busch facilities, the Hunter Business Park, and, of course, extensive citrus-packing plants.

But all work and no play does not lead to a centered life. In and around Riverside there is a great deal to do. With snow-topped, lake-filled mountains and desert playgrounds, it has been a popular resort area since the 1890's. Colorful gliders dot the sky as enthusiasts soar on the mountain air currents while slower hot-air balloons drift over mountainsides and orange groves. Bicycle trails connect to the famous "Crest to Coast" route along the Santa Ana River and golfers can choose from six public and three private courses. Almost three dozen county parks and two state parks offer hiking, biking, horseback riding, watersports, picnic facilities and more. For those who prefer faster action, the Riverside International Raceway holds some of the nation's most important stock-car and off-road races.

Riverside is not only a great place to find a job and enjoy the outdoors, it is also a good place to get a great education. The various schools include the University of California at Riverside, California Baptist College, the La Sierra campus of Loma Linda University, Riverside City College, California School for the Deaf, the Citrus Belt Law School, and Pepperdine University-Riverside Center. The Sherman Indian High School draws students from six nearby states.

From the mountains to the desert, from the employment opportunities to the educational offerings, Riverside, California is a great place to be.

General Rankings and Evaluative Comments

- Riverside was ranked #91 out of 300 cities by *Money's* 1997 "Survey of the Best Places to Live." Criteria used: health services, crime, economy, housing, education, transportation, weather, leisure and the arts. The city was ranked #127 in 1996 and #118 in 1995. *Money, July 1997; Money, September 1996; Money, September 1995*

- *Ladies Home Journal* ranked America's 200 largest cities based on the qualities women care about most. Riverside ranked 151 out of 200. Criteria: low crime rate, good public schools, well-paying jobs, quality health and child care, the presence of women in government, proportion of women-owned businesses, size of the wage gap with men, local economy, divorce rates, the ratio of single men to single women, whether there are laws that require at least the same number of public toilets for women as men, and the probability of good hair days. *Ladies Home Journal, November 1997*

- Riverside was ranked #180 out of 219 cities in terms of children's health, safety, and economic well-being. Criteria: total population, percent population change, birth rate, child immunization rate, infant mortality rate, percent low birth weight infants, percent of births to teens, physician-to-population ratio, student-to-teacher ratio, dropout rate, unemployment rate, median family income, percent of children in poverty, violent and property crime rates, number of juvenile arrests for violent crimes as a percent of the total crime index, number of days with pollution standard index (PSI) over 100, pounds toxic releases per 1,000 people and number of superfund sites. *Zero Population Growth, Children's Environmental Index 1997*

- According to *Working Mother*, "Lawmakers here—on both sides of the aisle—have agreed that the state must kick in more money to help working parents find and pay for child care. To that end, Governor Pete Wilson has proposed a significant expansion of the state's child care budget—an additional $277 million in state and federal funds. The new money would pay for care for about 90,000 more kids a year; and for preschool for another 13,000. In addition, some $45 million will be spent on recruiting and training caregivers for infants and toddlers.

  To help parents become more informed consumers, California passed a law that many consider a step backward. It allows family child care providers to care for two more kids, without hiring additional help. This means a family child care provider can now care for up to eight kids, instead of six, without additional help. The new rule also worries child care advocates because it may limit infant care in California. When caregivers take in the two extra older children, they must reduce the number of babies in their care. (California is among the 10 best states for child care.)" *Working Mother, July/August 1997*

Business Environment

STATE ECONOMY

State Economic Profile

"California's expansion is strong and stable....Entertainment and filmmaking remain steady contributors to the state's improved income growth and labor markets....

California's banking industry is consolidating and shedding workers. Improved credit conditions and healthy balance sheets make many remaining California thrifts likely takeover targets for out-of-state banks.

Delinquency rates on consumer credit have declined for the past two years and are well below the U.S. average. Mortgage foreclosure rates remain high, but they are down from the peak of one year ago when mortgage lenders took advantage of the improved housing market to shed nonperforming loans. California consumers remain cautious, however. Retail sales growth last year of 5% was no better than the national average.

Housing prices are up in northern California, and the number of units sold is rising throughout the state. Multifamily units dominated construction activity last year. With population growth accelerating and income growth outpacing the U.S. for the first time this decade, demand for single-family homes will strengthen.

Housing prices are up in northern California, and the number of units sold is rising throughout the state. Multifamily units dominated construction activity last year. With population growth accelerating the income growth outpacing the U.S. for the first time this decade, demand for single-family homes will strengthen.

Construction will contribute to the near-term expansion as home building accelerates. The greatest risk to the California economy is that the rising dollar could choke off foreign demand for California's export products. Longer term there will be some consolidation among high-tech firms, and high costs will limit the breadth of industrial development. California will remain an average performer over the long term." *National Association of Realtors, Economic Profiles: The Fifty States, July 1997*

IMPORTS/EXPORTS

Total Export Sales

Area	1993 ($000)	1994 ($000)	1995 ($000)	1996 ($000)	% Chg. 1993-96	% Chg. 1995-96
MSA[1]	1,093,799	1,458,850	1,856,457	1,982,060	81.2	6.8
U.S.	464,858,354	512,415,609	583,030,524	622,827,063	34.0	6.8

Note: (1) Metropolitan Statistical Area - see Appendix A for areas included
Source: U.S. Department of Commerce, International Trade Association, Metropolitan Area Exports: An Export Performance Report on Over 250 U.S. Cities, October 1997

Imports/Exports by Port

Type	Cargo Value			Share of U.S. Total	
	1995 (US$mil.)	1996 (US$mil.)	% Change 1995-1996	1995 (%)	1996 (%)
Imports	0	0	0	0	0
Exports	0	0	0	0	0

Source: Global Trade Information Services, WaterBorne Trade Atlas 1997

CITY FINANCES

City Government Finances

Component	FY92 ($000)	FY92 (per capita $)
Revenue	413,680	1,707.38
Expenditure	398,434	1,644.45
Debt Outstanding	726,619	2,998.96
Cash & Securities	603,626	2,491.34

Source: U.S. Bureau of the Census, City Government Finances: 1991-92

City Government Revenue by Source

Source	FY92 ($000)	FY92 (per capita $)	FY92 (%)
From Federal Government	4,100	16.92	1.0
From State Governments	25,695	106.05	6.2
From Local Governments	1,959	8.09	0.5
Property Taxes	25,061	103.43	6.1
General Sales Taxes	22,463	92.71	5.4
Selective Sales Taxes	19,271	79.54	4.7
Income Taxes	0	0.00	0.0
Current Charges	40,201	165.92	9.7
Utility/Liquor Store	197,476	815.04	47.7
Employee Retirement[1]	0	0.00	0.0
Other	77,454	319.67	18.7

Note: (1) Excludes "city contributions," classified as "nonrevenue," intragovernmental transfers.
Source: U.S. Bureau of the Census, City Government Finances: 1991-92

City Government Expenditures by Function

Function	FY92 ($000)	FY92 (per capita $)	FY92 (%)
Educational Services	11,730	48.41	2.9
Employee Retirement[1]	0	0.00	0.0
Environment/Housing	68,205	281.50	17.1
Government Administration	4,798	19.80	1.2
Interest on General Debt	29,213	120.57	7.3
Public Safety	57,761	238.40	14.5
Social Services	1,066	4.40	0.3
Transportation	29,098	120.10	7.3
Utility/Liquor Store	179,723	741.77	45.1
Other	16,840	69.50	4.2

Note: (1) Payments to beneficiaries including withdrawal of contributions.
Source: U.S. Bureau of the Census, City Government Finances: 1991-92

Municipal Bond Ratings

Area	Moody's	S & P
Riverside	n/r	n/r

Note: n/a not available; n/r not rated
Source: Moody's Bond Record, 2/98; Statistical Abstract of the U.S., 1997;
Governing Magazine, 9/97, 3/98

POPULATION

Population Growth

Area	1980	1990	% Chg. 1980-90	July 1996 Estimate	% Chg. 1990-96
City	170,876	226,505	32.6	255,069	12.6
MSA[1]	1,558,215	2,588,793	66.1	3,015,783	16.5
U.S.	226,545,805	248,765,170	9.8	265,179,411	6.6

Note: (1) Metropolitan Statistical Area - see Appendix A for areas included
Source: 1980/1990 Census of Housing and Population, Summary Tape File 3C;
Census Bureau Population Estimates

Population Characteristics

Race	City 1980 Population	%	City 1990 Population	%	% Chg. 1980-90	MSA[1] 1990 Population	%
White	139,098	81.4	160,640	70.9	15.5	1,932,332	74.6
Black	11,812	6.9	16,848	7.4	42.6	178,698	6.9
Amer Indian/Esk/Aleut	2,212	1.3	1,984	0.9	-10.3	25,938	1.0
Asian/Pacific Islander	3,553	2.1	11,694	5.2	229.1	100,232	3.9
Other	14,201	8.3	35,339	15.6	148.8	351,593	13.6
Hispanic Origin[2]	27,507	16.1	57,741	25.5	109.9	675,918	26.1

Note: (1) Metropolitan Statistical Area - see Appendix A for areas included;
(2) people of Hispanic origin can be of any race
Source: 1980/1990 Census of Housing and Population, Summary Tape File 3C

Ancestry

Area	German	Irish	English	Italian	U.S.	French	Polish	Dutch
City	19.6	12.6	13.5	4.1	3.1	4.2	2.1	2.4
MSA[1]	19.6	13.3	13.5	4.4	3.2	4.1	1.9	2.8
U.S.	23.3	15.6	13.1	5.9	5.3	4.2	3.8	2.5

Note: Figures are percentages and include persons that reported multiple ancestry (eg. if a person reported being Irish and Italian, they were included in both columns); (1) Metropolitan Statistical Area - see Appendix A for areas included
Source: 1990 Census of Population and Housing, Summary Tape File 3C

Age

Area	Median Age (Years)	Age Distribution (%) Under 5	Under 18	18-24	25-44	45-64	65+	80+
City	29.0	8.8	28.9	13.0	34.1	15.0	9.0	2.0
MSA[1]	30.3	9.3	29.8	10.3	33.3	15.8	10.7	2.1
U.S.	32.9	7.3	25.6	10.5	32.6	18.7	12.5	2.8

Note: (1) Metropolitan Statistical Area - see Appendix A for areas included
Source: 1990 Census of Population and Housing, Summary Tape File 3C

Male/Female Ratio

Area	Number of males per 100 females (all ages)	Number of males per 100 females (18 years old+)
City	98.6	95.7
MSA[1]	100.0	98.3
U.S.	95.0	91.9

Note: (1) Metropolitan Statistical Area - see Appendix A for areas included
Source: 1990 Census of Population, General Population Characteristics

INCOME

Per Capita/Median/Average Income

Area	Per Capita ($)	Median Household ($)	Average Household ($)
City	14,235	34,801	42,016
MSA[1]	13,879	33,279	40,721
U.S.	14,420	30,056	38,453

Note: all figures are for 1989; (1) Metropolitan Statistical Area - see Appendix A for areas included
Source: 1990 Census of Population and Housing, Summary Tape File 3C

Household Income Distribution by Race

Income ($)	City (%)					U.S. (%)				
	Total	White	Black	Other	Hisp.[1]	Total	White	Black	Other	Hisp.[1]
Less than 5,000	4.2	3.6	5.3	6.9	3.8	6.2	4.8	15.2	8.6	8.8
5,000 - 9,999	7.2	6.9	11.1	7.1	6.8	9.3	8.6	14.2	9.9	11.1
10,000 - 14,999	7.6	6.9	11.2	9.2	9.8	8.8	8.5	11.0	9.8	11.0
15,000 - 24,999	15.2	14.0	18.7	19.3	21.2	17.5	17.3	18.9	18.5	20.5
25,000 - 34,999	15.9	15.7	14.9	17.5	19.1	15.8	16.1	14.2	15.4	16.4
35,000 - 49,999	20.4	21.0	16.6	19.4	20.1	17.9	18.6	13.3	16.1	16.0
50,000 - 74,999	18.4	19.8	13.4	14.4	14.1	15.0	15.8	9.3	13.4	11.1
75,000 - 99,999	6.2	6.7	6.3	4.1	3.4	5.1	5.5	2.6	4.7	3.1
100,000+	4.7	5.4	2.6	2.2	1.8	4.4	4.8	1.3	3.7	1.9

Note: all figures are for 1989; (1) people of Hispanic origin can be of any race
Source: 1990 Census of Population and Housing, Summary Tape File 3C

Effective Buying Income

Area	Per Capita ($)	Median Household ($)	Average Household ($)
City	12,455	32,777	38,830
MSA[1]	12,434	32,054	38,539
U.S.	15,444	33,201	41,849

Note: data as of 1/1/97; (1) Metropolitan Statistical Area - see Appendix A for areas included
Source: Standard Rate & Data Service, Newspaper Advertising Source, 2/98

Effective Household Buying Income Distribution

Area	% of Households Earning						
	$10,000 -$19,999	$20,000 -$34,999	$35,000 -$49,999	$50,000 -$74,999	$75,000 -$99,000	$100,000 -$124,999	$125,000 and up
City	16.4	25.3	21.5	17.5	4.5	1.4	1.7
MSA[1]	17.7	24.6	20.1	17.8	4.7	1.2	1.6
U.S.	16.5	23.4	18.3	18.2	6.4	2.1	2.4

Note: data as of 1/1/97; (1) Metropolitan Statistical Area - see Appendix A for areas included
Source: Standard Rate & Data Service, Newspaper Advertising Source, 2/98

Poverty Rates by Race and Age

Area	Total (%)	By Race (%)				By Age (%)		
		White	Black	Other	Hisp.[2]	Under 5 years old	Under 18 years old	65 years and over
City	11.9	8.8	21.9	18.9	16.6	15.3	15.0	6.9
MSA[1]	12.2	9.7	20.4	19.2	19.4	18.1	17.0	7.8
U.S.	13.1	9.8	29.5	23.1	25.3	20.1	18.3	12.8

Note: figures show the percent of people living below the poverty line in 1989. The average poverty threshold was $12,674 for a family of four in 1989; (1) Metropolitan Statistical Area - see Appendix A for areas included; (2) people of Hispanic origin can be of any race
Source: 1990 Census of Population and Housing, Summary Tape File 3C

EMPLOYMENT

Labor Force and Employment

Area	Civilian Labor Force			Workers Employed		
	Dec. '95	Dec. '96	% Chg.	Dec. '95	Dec. '96	% Chg.
City	132,553	135,428	2.2	123,294	127,543	3.4
MSA[1]	1,321,636	1,353,315	2.4	1,238,518	1,281,208	3.4
U.S.	134,583,000	136,742,000	1.6	127,903,000	130,785,000	2.3

Note: Data is not seasonally adjusted and covers workers 16 years of age and older; (1) Metropolitan Statistical Area - see Appendix A for areas included
Source: Bureau of Labor Statistics, http://stats.bls.gov

Riverside was listed among the top 20 metro areas (out of 114 major areas) in terms of projected job growth from 1997 to 2002 with an annual percent change of 2.6%.
Standard & Poor's DRI, July 23, 1997

Unemployment Rate

Area	1997											
	Jan.	Feb.	Mar.	Apr.	May	Jun.	Jul.	Aug.	Sep.	Oct.	Nov.	Dec.
City	8.0	7.6	6.8	6.8	6.5	7.2	9.1	8.8	8.7	8.0	6.8	5.8
MSA[1]	7.5	7.0	6.5	6.5	6.4	7.0	8.1	7.7	7.6	7.1	6.1	5.3
U.S.	5.9	5.7	5.5	4.8	4.7	5.2	5.0	4.8	4.7	4.4	4.3	4.4

Note: Data is not seasonally adjusted and covers workers 16 years of age and older; All figures are percentages; (1) Metropolitan Statistical Area - see Appendix A for areas included
Source: Bureau of Labor Statistics, http://stats.bls.gov

Employment by Industry

Sector	MSA[1]		U.S.
	Number of Employees	Percent of Total	Percent of Total
Services	227,300	26.2	29.0
Retail Trade	187,500	21.6	18.5
Government	174,500	20.1	16.1
Manufacturing	107,400	12.4	15.0
Finance/Insurance/Real Estate	30,700	3.5	5.7
Wholesale Trade	40,100	4.6	5.4
Transportation/Public Utilities	44,400	5.1	5.3
Construction	53,200	6.1	4.5
Mining	1,100	0.1	0.5

Note: Figures cover non-farm employment as of 12/97 and are not seasonally adjusted;
(1) Metropolitan Statistical Area - see Appendix A for areas included
Source: Bureau of Labor Statistics, http://stats.bls.gov

Employment by Occupation

Occupation Category	City (%)	MSA[1] (%)	U.S. (%)
White Collar	58.0	54.8	58.1
Executive/Admin./Management	11.8	11.7	12.3
Professional	14.5	11.7	14.1
Technical & Related Support	3.7	3.1	3.7
Sales	11.8	12.4	11.8
Administrative Support/Clerical	16.3	15.9	16.3
Blue Collar	28.3	29.2	26.2
Precision Production/Craft/Repair	13.5	14.4	11.3
Machine Operators/Assem./Insp.	6.6	5.4	6.8
Transportation/Material Movers	4.0	4.7	4.1
Cleaners/Helpers/Laborers	4.2	4.5	3.9
Services	11.9	13.1	13.2
Farming/Forestry/Fishing	1.8	2.9	2.5

Note: figures cover employed persons 16 years old and over;
(1) Metropolitan Statistical Area - see Appendix A for areas included
Source: 1990 Census of Population and Housing, Summary Tape File 3C

Occupational Employment Projections: 1994 - 2001

Occupations Expected to have the Largest Job Growth (ranked by numerical growth)	Fast-Growing Occupations[1] (ranked by percent growth)
1. General office clerks	1. Home health aides
2. Salespersons, retail	2. Computer engineers
3. Waiters & waitresses	3. Systems analysts
4. Cashiers	4. Instructors/coaches, sports/phys. train.
5. Food preparation workers	5. Plastic molding/casting mach. oper.
6. Registered nurses	6. Food service workers
7. Teachers, secondary school	7. Baggage porters & bellhops
8. Instructional aides	8. Merchandise displayers/window trimmers
9. Gardeners & groundskeepers	9. Laundry/dryclean mach. oper.
10. Truck drivers, light	10. Printing/binding mach. oper.

Projections cover Riverside County.
Note: (1) Excludes occupations with employment of less than 200 in 2001
Source: State of California, Employment Development Department, Labor Market Information Division, Information Services Group

Average Wages

Occupation	Wage	Occupation	Wage
Professional/Technical/Clerical	$/Week	**Health/Protective Services**	$/Week
Accountants III	790	Corrections Officers	767
Attorneys III	1,232	Firefighters	817
Budget Analysts III	753	Nurses, Licensed Practical II	500
Buyers/Contracting Specialists II	576	Nurses, Registered II	770
Clerks, Accounting III	479	Nursing Assistants II	304
Clerks, General III	376	Police Officers I	833
Computer Operators II	492	**Hourly Workers**	$/Hour
Computer Programmers II	650	Forklift Operators	12.23
Drafters II	552	General Maintenance Workers	14.44
Engineering Technicians III	625	Guards I	10.03
Engineering Technicians, Civil III	690	Janitors	8.91
Engineers III	889	Maintenance Electricians	16.57
Key Entry Operators I	331	Maintenance Electronics Techs II	17.48
Personnel Assistants III	534	Maintenance Machinists	15.88
Personnel Specialists III	741	Maintenance Mechanics, Machinery	16.65
Secretaries III	566	Material Handling Laborers	8.33
Switchboard Operator-Receptionist	317	Motor Vehicle Mechanics	17.97
Systems Analysts II	882	Shipping/Receiving Clerks	8.33
Systems Analysts Supervisor/Mgr II	-	Tool and Die Makers	18.35
Tax Collectors II	-	Truckdrivers, Tractor Trailer	17.29
Word Processors II	515	Warehouse Specialists	11.51

Note: Wage data includes full-time workers only for 4/95 and cover the Metropolitan Statistical Area (see Appendix A for areas included). Dashes indicate that data was not available.
Source: Bureau of Labor Statistics, Occupational Compensation Survey, 11/95

TAXES

Major State and Local Tax Rates

State Corp. Income (%)	State Personal Income (%)	Residential Property (effective rate per $100)	Sales & Use State (%)	Sales & Use Local (%)	State Gasoline (cents/ gallon)	State Cigarette (cents/ 20-pack)
8.84[a]	1.0 - 9.3	n/a	6.0	1.75	18[b]	37

Note: Personal/corporate income tax rates as of 1/97. Sales, gasoline and cigarette tax rates as of 1/98; (a) Minimum tax is $800. The tax rate on S-Corporations is 1.5%; (b) Does not include 1 cent local option tax
Source: Federation of Tax Administrators, www.taxadmin.org; Washington D.C. Department of Finance and Revenue, Tax Rates and Tax Burdens in the District of Columbia: A Nationwide Comparison, June 1997; Chamber of Commerce

Total Taxes Per Capita and as a Percent of Income

Area	Per Capita Income ($)	Per Capita Taxes ($)			Taxes as Pct. of Income (%)		
		Total	Federal	State/Local	Total	Federal	State/Local
California	27,117	9,321	6,287	3,034	34.4	23.2	11.2
U.S.	26,187	9,205	6,127	3,078	35.2	23.4	11.8

Note: Figures are for 1997
Source: Tax Foundation, Web Site, www.taxfoundation.org

COMMERCIAL REAL ESTATE

Data not available at time of publication.

COMMERCIAL UTILITIES

Typical Monthly Electric Bills

Area	Commercial Service ($/month)		Industrial Service ($/month)	
	12 kW demand 1,500 kWh	100 kW demand 30,000 kWh	1,000 kW demand 400,000 kWh	20,000 kW demand 10,000,000 kWh
City	191	3,689	49,032	815,632
U.S.	162	2,360	25,590	545,677

Note: Based on rates in effect July 1, 1997
Source: Edison Electric Institute, Typical Residential, Commercial and Industrial Bills, Summer 1997

TRANSPORTATION

Transportation Statistics

Avg. travel time to work (min.)	26.4
Interstate highways	I-215 connecting with I-15
Bus lines	
In-city	Riverside Transit Agency
Inter-city	3
Passenger air service	
Airport	Ontario International (18 miles east); Palm Springs Regional (2 miles east)
Airlines	12
Aircraft departures	51,931 (1995)
Enplaned passengers	3,193,612 (1995)
Rail service	Amtrak Thruway Motorcoach Connection; Metrolink
Motor freight carriers	n/a
Major waterways/ports	none

Source: OAG, Business Travel Planner, Summer 1997; Editor & Publisher Market Guide, 1998; FAA Airport Activity Statistics, 1996; Amtrak National Time Table, Northeast Timetable, Fall/Winter 1997-98; 1990 Census of Population and Housing, STF 3C; Chamber of Commerce/Economic Development 1997; Jane's Urban Transport Systems 1997-98; Transit Fact Book 1997

Means of Transportation to Work

Area	Car/Truck/Van		Public Transportation			Bicycle	Walked	Other Means	Worked at Home
	Drove Alone	Car-pooled	Bus	Subway	Railroad				
City	73.9	16.3	1.5	0.0	0.0	1.2	3.5	1.3	2.4
MSA[1]	74.6	17.2	0.8	0.0	0.0	0.6	2.7	1.5	2.7
U.S.	73.2	13.4	3.0	1.5	0.5	0.4	3.9	1.2	3.0

Note: figures shown are percentages and only include workers 16 years old and over;
(1) Metropolitan Statistical Area - see Appendix A for areas included
Source: 1990 Census of Population and Housing, Summary Tape File 3C

BUSINESSES

Major Business Headquarters

Company Name	1997 Rankings	
	Fortune 500	Forbes 500
Fleetwood Enterprises	467	-

Note: Companies listed are located in the city; Dashes indicate no ranking
Fortune 500: companies that produce a 10-K are ranked 1 - 500 based on 1996 revenue
Forbes 500: private companies are ranked 1 - 500 based on 1996 revenue
Source: Forbes 12/1/97; Fortune 4/28/97

Women-Owned Businesses: Number, Employment, Sales and Share

Area	Women-Owned Businesses in 1996				Share of Women-Owned Businesses in 1996	
	Number	Employment	Sales ($000)	Rank[2]	Percent (%)	Rank[3]
MSA[1]	82,600	127,100	15,195,200	25	38.5	12

Note: (1) Metropolitan Statistical Area - see Appendix A for areas included; (2) Calculated on an averaging of number of businesses, employment and sales and ranges from 1 to 50 where 1 is best; (3) Ranges from 1 to 50 where 1 is best
Source: The National Foundation for Women Business Owners, 1996 Facts on Women-Owned Businesses: Trends in the Top 50 Metropolitan Areas, March 26, 1997

Women-Owned Businesses: Growth

Area	Growth in Women-Owned Businesses (% change from 1987 to 1996)				Relative Growth in the Number of Women-Owned and All Businesses (% change from 1987 to 1996)			
	Num.	Empl.	Sales	Rank[2]	Women-Owned	All Firms	Absolute Difference	Relative Difference
MSA[1]	121.8	254.9	249.8	11	121.8	63.1	58.7	1.9:1

Note: (1) Metropolitan Statistical Area - see Appendix A for areas included; (2) Calculated on an averaging of the percent growth of number of businesses, employment and sales and ranges from 1 to 50 where 1 is best
Source: The National Foundation for Women Business Owners, 1996 Facts on Women-Owned Businesses: Trends in the Top 50 Metropolitan Areas, March 26, 1997

Minority Business Opportunity

One of the 500 largest Hispanic-owned companies in the U.S. are located in Riverside. *Hispanic Business, June 1997*

Riverside was listed among the top 25 metropolitan areas in terms of the number of Hispanic-owned companies. The city was ranked number 5 with 43,277 companies. *Hispanic Business, May 1997*

HOTELS & MOTELS

Hotels/Motels

Area	Hotels/ Motels	Rooms	Luxury-Level Hotels/Motels		Average Minimum Rates ($)		
			◆◆◆◆	◆◆◆◆◆	◆◆	◆◆◆	◆◆◆◆
City	7	863	0	0	n/a	n/a	n/a
Airport	1	116	0	0	n/a	n/a	n/a
Suburbs	2	57	0	0	n/a	n/a	n/a
Total	10	1,036	0	0	n/a	n/a	n/a

Note: n/a not available; Classifications range from one diamond (budget properties with basic amenities) to five diamond (luxury properties with the finest service, rooms and facilities).
Source: OAG, Business Travel Planner, Summer 1997

CONVENTION CENTERS

Major Convention Centers

Center Name	Meeting Rooms	Exhibit Space (sf)
None listed in city		

Source: Trade Shows Worldwide 1997

Living Environment

COST OF LIVING

Cost of Living Index

Composite Index	Housing	Utilities	Groceries	Health Care	Trans-portation	Misc. Goods/ Services
106.6	108.3	101.2	101.0	126.4	107.0	105.5

Note: U.S. = 100
Source: ACCRA, Cost of Living Index, 3rd Quarter 1997

HOUSING

Median Home Prices and Housing Affordability

Area	Median Price[2] 3rd Qtr. 1997 ($)	HOI[3] 3rd Qtr. 1997	Afford-ability Rank[4]
MSA[1]	115,000	70.7	90
U.S.	127,000	63.7	--

Note: (1) Metropolitan Statistical Area - see Appendix A for areas included; (2) U.S. figures calculated from the sales of 625,000 new and existing homes in 195 markets; (3) Housing Opportunity Index - percent of homes sold that were within the reach of the median income household at the prevailing mortgage interest rate; (4) Rank is from 1-195 with 1 being most affordable
Source: National Association of Home Builders, Housing Opportunity Index, 3rd Quarter 1997

It is projected that the median price of existing single-family homes in the metro area will increase by 11.9% in 1998. Nationwide, home prices are projected to increase 6.6%.
Kiplinger's Personal Finance Magazine, January 1998

Average New Home Price

Area	Price ($)
City	146,661
U.S.	135,710

Note: Figures are based on a new home with 1,800 sq. ft. of living area on an 8,000 sq. ft. lot.
Source: ACCRA, Cost of Living Index, 3rd Quarter 1997

Average Apartment Rent

Area	Rent ($/mth)
City	617
U.S.	569

Note: Figures are based on an unfurnished two bedroom, 1-1/2 or 2 bath apartment, approximately 950 sq. ft. in size, excluding all utilities except water
Source: ACCRA, Cost of Living Index, 3rd Quarter 1997

RESIDENTIAL UTILITIES

Average Residential Utility Costs

Area	All Electric ($/mth)	Part Electric ($/mth)	Other Energy ($/mth)	Phone ($/mth)
City	--	71.52	34.95	16.31
U.S.	109.40	55.25	43.64	19.48

Source: ACCRA, Cost of Living Index, 3rd Quarter 1997

HEALTH CARE

Average Health Care Costs

Area	Hospital ($/day)	Doctor ($/visit)	Dentist ($/visit)
City	645.67	48.00	85.60
U.S.	392.91	48.76	60.84

Note: Hospital - based on a semi-private room. Doctor - based on a general practitioner's routine exam of an established patient. Dentist - based on adult teeth cleaning and periodic oral exam.
Source: ACCRA, Cost of Living Index, 3rd Quarter 1997

Distribution of Office-Based Physicians

Area	Family/Gen. Practitioners	Specialists		
		Medical	Surgical	Other
MSA[1]	602	1,054	846	862

Note: Data as of 12/31/96; (1) Metropolitan Statistical Area - see Appendix A for areas included
Source: American Medical Assn., Physician Characteristics & Distribution in the U.S., 1997-1998

Hospitals

Riverside has 4 general medical and surgical hospitals. *AHA Guide to the Healthcare Field 1997-98*

EDUCATION

Public School District Statistics

District Name	Num. Sch.	Enroll.	Classroom Teachers[1]	Pupils per Teacher	Minority Pupils (%)	Current Exp.[2] ($/pupil)
Alvord Unified	17	16,356	609	26.9	n/a	n/a
California School for the Deaf	1	465	116	4.0	n/a	n/a
Jurupa Unified	22	17,305	665	26.0	n/a	n/a
Riverside Co. Office of Educ	3	2,813	230	12.2	n/a	n/a
Riverside Unified	42	35,055	1,386	25.3	54.1	4,213

Note: Data covers the 1995-1996 school year unless otherwise noted; (1) Excludes teachers reported as working in school district offices rather than in schools; (2) Based on 1993-94 enrollment collected by the Census Bureau, not the enrollment figure shown in column 3; SD = School District; ISD = Independent School District; n/a not available
Source: National Center for Education Statistics, Common Core of Data Survey; Bureau of the Census

Educational Quality

School District	Education Quotient[1]	Graduate Outcome[2]	Community Index[3]	Resource Index[4]
Riverside	85.0	71.0	74.0	110.0

Note: Nearly 1,000 secondary school districts were rated in terms of educational quality. The scores range from a low of 50 to a high of 150; (1) Average of the Graduate Outcome, Community and Resource indexes; (2) Based on graduation rates and college board scores (SAT/ACT); (3) Based on the surrounding community's average level of education and the area's average income level; (4) Based on teacher salaries, per-pupil expenditures and student-teacher ratios.
Source: Expansion Management, Ratings Issue 1997

Educational Attainment by Race

Area	High School Graduate (%)					Bachelor's Degree (%)				
	Total	White	Black	Other	Hisp.[2]	Total	White	Black	Other	Hisp.[2]
City	77.8	82.6	79.0	56.2	50.5	19.3	20.8	16.9	13.9	7.2
MSA[1]	74.8	78.1	78.7	55.6	49.4	14.8	15.4	13.5	11.7	5.6
U.S.	75.2	77.9	63.1	60.4	49.8	20.3	21.5	11.4	19.4	9.2

Note: figures shown cover persons 25 years old and over; (1) Metropolitan Statistical Area - see Appendix A for areas included; (2) people of Hispanic origin can be of any race
Source: 1990 Census of Population and Housing, Summary Tape File 3C

School Enrollment by Type

Area	Preprimary				Elementary/High School			
	Public		Private		Public		Private	
	Enrollment	%	Enrollment	%	Enrollment	%	Enrollment	%
City	2,112	54.7	1,751	45.3	39,240	91.4	3,703	8.6
MSA[1]	26,476	59.0	18,382	41.0	466,755	93.0	35,180	7.0
U.S.	2,679,029	59.5	1,824,256	40.5	38,379,689	90.2	4,187,099	9.8

Note: figures shown cover persons 3 years old and over;
(1) Metropolitan Statistical Area - see Appendix A for areas included
Source: 1990 Census of Population and Housing, Summary Tape File 3C

School Enrollment by Race

Area	Preprimary (%)				Elementary/High School (%)			
	White	Black	Other	Hisp.[1]	White	Black	Other	Hisp.[1]
City	73.1	9.2	17.7	24.3	63.9	8.6	27.5	34.5
MSA[2]	75.9	7.8	16.3	23.7	67.4	8.5	24.1	35.1
U.S.	80.4	12.5	7.1	7.8	74.1	15.6	10.3	12.5

Note: figures shown cover persons 3 years old and over; (1) people of Hispanic origin can be of any race; (2) Metropolitan Statistical Area - see Appendix A for areas included
Source: 1990 Census of Population and Housing, Summary Tape File 3C

SAT/ACT Scores

Area/District	1997 SAT				1997 ACT	
	Percent of Graduates Tested (%)	Average Math Score	Average Verbal Score	Average Combined Score	Percent of Graduates Tested (%)	Average Composite Score
Riverside USD	47	496	482	978	10	20.7
State	45	514	496	1,010	11	21.0
U.S.	42	511	505	1,016	36	21.0

Note: Math and verbal SAT scores are out of a possible 800; ACT scores are out of a possible 36
Caution: Comparing or ranking states/cities on the basis of SAT/ACT scores alone is invalid and strongly discouraged by the The College Board and The American College Testing Program as students who take the tests are self-selected and do not represent the entire student population.
Source: Riverside USD, Educational Accountability, 1997; American College Testing Program, 1997; College Board, 1997

Classroom Teacher Salaries in Public Schools

District	B.A. Degree		M.A. Degree		Ph.D. Degree	
	Min. ($)	Max ($)	Min. ($)	Max. ($)	Min. ($)	Max. ($)
Riverside	30,549	39,124	31,394	49,979	34,894	55,851
Average[1]	26,120	39,270	28,175	44,667	31,643	49,825

Note: Salaries are for 1996-1997; (1) Based on all school districts covered; n/a not available
Source: American Federation of Teachers (unpublished data)

Higher Education

Two-Year Colleges		Four-Year Colleges		Medical Schools	Law Schools	Voc/ Tech
Public	Private	Public	Private			
1	0	1	2	0	1	7

Source: College Blue Book, Occupational Education 1997; Medical School Admission Requirements, 1998-99; Peterson's Guide to Two-Year Colleges, 1997; Peterson's Guide to Four-Year Colleges, 1997; Barron's Guide to Law Schools 1997

MAJOR EMPLOYERS

Major Employers

Riverside Community Hospital
Press Enterprise

Fleetwood Holidays Inc. (utility trailers)
Riverside Transit Agency

Parkview Community Hospital Med. Ctr.
Fleetwood Enterprises (prefabricated wood buildings)
Electro Pneumatic Corp.
E.L. Yeager Construction

Note: companies listed are located in the city
Source: Dun's Business Rankings 1997; Ward's Business Directory, 1997

PUBLIC SAFETY

Crime Rate

Area	All Crimes	Violent Crimes				Property Crimes		
		Murder	Forcible Rape	Robbery	Aggrav. Assault	Burglary	Larceny -Theft	Motor Vehicle Theft
City	6,321.6	7.3	46.9	356.6	882.2	1,180.8	2,905.6	942.1
Suburbs[1]	5,491.2	10.3	32.0	234.8	493.9	1,404.1	2,474.1	842.1
MSA[2]	5,560.6	10.1	33.2	245.0	526.3	1,385.4	2,510.1	850.5
U.S.	5,078.9	7.4	36.1	202.4	388.2	943.0	2,975.9	525.9

Note: Crime rate is the number of crimes per 100,000 pop.; (1) defined as all areas within the MSA but located outside the central city; (2) Metropolitan Statistical Area - see Appendix A for areas incl.
Source: FBI Uniform Crime Reports 1996

RECREATION

Culture and Recreation

Museums	Symphony Orchestras	Opera Companies	Dance Companies	Professional Theatres	Zoos	Pro Sports Teams
6	1	1	2	3	0	0

Source: International Directory of the Performing Arts, 1996; Official Museum Directory, 1998; Chamber of Commerce/Economic Development 1997

Library System

The Riverside City & County Public Library has 28 branches, holdings of n/a volumes and a budget of $11,181,067 (1995-1996). Note: n/a means not available. *American Library Directory, 1997-1998*

MEDIA

Newspapers

Name	Type	Freq.	Distribution	Circulation
Black Voice News	Black	1x/wk	Area	7,500
The Press-Enterprise	n/a	7x/wk	Local	167,958

Note: Includes newspapers with circulations of 1,000 or more located in the city; n/a not available
Source: Burrelle's Media Directory, 1998 Edition

AM Radio Stations

Call Letters	Freq. (kHz)	Target Audience	Station Format	Music Format
KDES	920	General	N/T	n/a
KCLB	970	Hispanic	M/N/S	Spanish
KPSL	1010	General	E/M/N/S/T	n/a
KCMJ	1140	General	M	Adult Standards/Oldies
KNWZ	1270	General	N/T	n/a
KMRZ	1290	General	M/N/S	Oldies/R&B
KSDT	1320	General	M	Oldies
KWXY	1340	General	M/N/S	Adult Contemporary/Big Band/Easy Listening
KCKC	1350	n/a	M/N/S	Country
KWRM	1370	Hispanic	M	Spanish
KESQ	1400	Hispanic	M/N	Adult Standards
KDIF	1440	Hispanic	M/N/S	n/a
KPSI	1450	General	N/T	n/a
KNSE	1510	Hispanic	M/N/S	Spanish
KPRO	1570	Religious	M/N	Christian

Note: Stations included broadcast in the Riverside metro area; n/a not available
Station Format: E = Educational; M = Music; N = News; S = Sports; T = Talk
Source: Burrelle's Media Directory, 1998 Edition

FM Radio Stations

Call Letters	Freq. (mHz)	Target Audience	Station Format	Music Format
KUCR	88.3	General	E/M/N/S/T	Alternative/Christian/Classical/Jazz/Oldies/Spanish/Urban Contemporary
KRTM	88.9	General	M/N/S/T	Alternative
KSGN	89.7	Religious	E/M/N	Christian
KCMJ	92.7	General	M	Classic Rock/Oldies
KCLB	93.7	General	M/N/S/T	AOR
KLOB	94.7	Hispanic	M	n/a
KFRG	95.1	n/a	M	Country
KUNA	96.7	Hispanic	M/N/S	Spanish
KWXY	98.5	General	M/N	Adult Standards/Easy Listening/Oldies
KGGI	99.1	General	M	Adult Contemporary
KOLA	99.9	General	M	Oldies
KJMB	100.3	n/a	M/N	Adult Contemporary
KPSI	100.5	General	M	Contemporary Top 40
KATY	101.3	General	M	Adult Contemporary
KJJZ	102.3	General	M	Jazz
KEZN	103.1	General	M/N/S	Adult Contemporary
KDES	104.7	General	M	Oldies
KXRS	105.7	Hispanic	M	Spanish
KPLM	106.1	General	M	Country

Note: Stations included broadcast in the Riverside metro area; n/a not available
Station Format: E = Educational; M = Music; N = News; S = Sports; T = Talk
Music Format: AOR = Album Oriented Rock; MOR = Middle-of-the-Road
Source: Burrelle's Media Directory, 1998 Edition

Television Stations

Name	Ch.	Affiliation	Type	Owner
KMIR	36	NBC	Commercial	Desert Empire Television Corp.
KESQ	42	ABC	Commercial	News-Press & Gazette Co.

Note: Stations included broadcast in the Riverside metro area
Source: Burrelle's Media Directory, 1998 Edition

CLIMATE

Average and Extreme Temperatures

Temperature	Jan	Feb	Mar	Apr	May	Jun	Jul	Aug	Sep	Oct	Nov	Dec	Ann
Extreme High (°F)	90	89	97	110	107	114	114	114	112	110	95	99	114
Average High (°F)	66	68	68	75	79	86	92	92	89	83	73	67	78
Average Temp. (°F)	54	57	58	63	67	73	78	78	76	70	61	55	66
Average Low (°F)	42	45	47	50	55	59	63	64	62	56	47	42	53
Extreme Low (°F)	25	29	30	35	38	43	52	51	47	40	31	24	24

Note: Figures cover the years 1973-1993
Source: National Climatic Data Center, International Station Meteorological Climate Summary, 3/95

Average Precipitation/Snowfall/Humidity

Precip./Humidity	Jan	Feb	Mar	Apr	May	Jun	Jul	Aug	Sep	Oct	Nov	Dec	Ann
Avg. Precip. (in.)	n/a	n/a	n/a	n/a	n/a	n/a	n/a	n/a	n/a	n/a	n/a	n/a	n/a
Avg. Snowfall (in.)	n/a	n/a	n/a	n/a	n/a	n/a	n/a	n/a	n/a	n/a	n/a	n/a	n/a
Avg. Rel. Hum. 6am (%)	45	44	50	42	44	39	35	36	38	37	36	39	40
Avg. Rel. Hum. 3pm (%)	74	75	79	75	77	76	73	72	71	73	69	70	74

Note: Figures cover the years 1973-1993
Source: National Climatic Data Center, International Station Meteorological Climate Summary, 3/95

Weather Conditions

Temperature			Daytime Sky			Precipitation		
10°F & below	32°F & below	90°F & above	Clear	Partly cloudy	Cloudy	0.01 inch or more precip.	0.1 inch or more snow/ice	Thunder-storms
0	4	82	124	178	63	n/a	n/a	5

Note: Figures are average number of days per year and covers the years 1973-1993
Source: National Climatic Data Center, International Station Meteorological Climate Summary, 3/95

AIR & WATER QUALITY

Maximum Pollutant Concentrations

	Particulate Matter (ug/m^3)	Carbon Monoxide (ppm)	Sulfur Dioxide (ppm)	Nitrogen Dioxide (ppm)	Ozone (ppm)	Lead (ug/m^3)
MSA[1] Level	155	7	0.005	0.038	0.22	0.04
NAAQS[2]	150	9	0.140	0.053	0.12	1.50
Met NAAQS?	No	Yes	Yes	Yes	No	Yes

Note: (1) Metropolitan Statistical Area - see Appendix A for areas included; (2) National Ambient Air Quality Standards; ppm = parts per million; ug/m^3 = micrograms per cubic meter; n/a not available
Source: EPA, National Air Quality and Emissions Trends Report, 1996

Pollutant Standards Index

In the Riverside MSA (see Appendix A for areas included), the Pollutant Standards Index (PSI) exceeded 100 on 94 days in 1996. A PSI value greater than 100 indicates that air quality would be in the unhealthful range on that day. *EPA, National Air Quality and Emissions Trends Report, 1996*

Drinking Water

Water System Name	Pop. Served	Primary Water Source Type	Number of Violations in Fiscal Year 1997	Type of Violation/ Contaminants
City of Riverside	245,000	Ground	None	None

Note: Data as of January 16, 1998
Source: EPA, Office of Ground Water and Drinking Water, Safe Drinking Water Information System

Riverside tap water is alkaline, medium hard and naturally fluoridated.
Editor & Publisher Market Guide, 1998

Salem, Oregon

Background

Salem is the capital of Oregon and located on the Willamette River, 45 minutes southwest of Portland. The third largest city in Oregon, Salem is in the heart of the fertile Willamette Valley, midway between the Cascade Mountains and the Oregon coast, which lies about 60 miles to the west. Founded by Methodist missionary James Lee in 1840, Salem is the anglicized form of the Hebrew word Shalom meaning "peace." The new settlement sold land for homes to finance the Oregon Institute, a religious school for Native Americans that later became Willamette University. As traffic along the Oregon Trail increased, the prosperity of Salem grew. The town became the territorial capital in 1851 and when Oregon was admitted to the Union on Feb. 14, 1859, Salem became the capital of the new 33rd state.

The town became a distribution center for goods shipped via the Willamette River. When railroads made their way to the town in the 1870's, Salem's continued growth was assured. Salem became the food-processing center for the diversified agricultural products grown in the surrounding valley which include livestock, dairy cattle, poultry, grain, hay and seed crops, and fruit, nuts and vegetables. A recent addition to the Salem area is the art of wine making. Six wineries are located within a few miles of the city.

Salem's principal non-food related industries include machinery, electrical products and batteries, sand, gravel, concrete products, textiles, and lumber and wood products. Trees hold a special place in the hearts of Oregonians and especially the citizens of Salem. The largest black cottonwood in the nation (27 feet in circumference and 147 feet tall) is located in Salem. Waldo Park, cited by Ripley as the World's Smallest Park, was built to protect a Sierra Redwood planted by the son of an 1840 pioneer, while five Sequoia Redwoods were planted on the Willamette University campus in 1942 to celebrate the school's 100th anniversary. So it is not surprising that Salem has again been named a Tree City USA by The National Arbor Day Foundation for the twenty-first consecutive year. In fact, Salem is a charter member and was the first Oregon city to receive this award.

Salem also receives high marks for education. Six institutions of higher education are located in Salem including Willamette University, Tokyo International University of America, Oregon School for the Deaf, Western Oregon University, Chemeketa Community College, and Western Baptist College.

The Salem climate is mild, but the seasons do exist. In general 70% of the total annual rainfall of 42" occurs from November through March, with only 6% occurring during the summer months. The average maximum high temperature for the year occurs in August (81.9 F) and the average minimum low occurs in December (33.6 F). Such mild overall temperature allow Salem residents to enjoy the beautiful Willamette Valley wildlife. Fishing for steelhead salmon and rainbow trout is a favorite activity, as is hunting. For those who prefer to watch, rather than catch, patient birdwatchers will be rewarded with bald eagles, tundra swans, sandhill cranes and more.

General Rankings and Evaluative Comments

- Salem was ranked #102 out of 300 cities by *Money's* 1997 "Survey of the Best Places to Live." Criteria used: health services, crime, economy, housing, education, transportation, weather, leisure and the arts. The city was ranked #164 in 1996 and #158 in 1995. *Money, July 1997; Money, September 1996; Money, September 1995*

- *Ladies Home Journal* ranked America's 200 largest cities based on the qualities women care about most. Salem ranked 107 out of 200. Criteria: low crime rate, good public schools, well-paying jobs, quality health and child care, the presence of women in government, proportion of women-owned businesses, size of the wage gap with men, local economy, divorce rates, the ratio of single men to single women, whether there are laws that require at least the same number of public toilets for women as men, and the probability of good hair days. *Ladies Home Journal, November 1997*

- Salem is among "The Best Places to Raise a Family". Rank: 32 out of 301 metro areas. Criteria: low crime rate, low drug and alcohol abuse, good public schools, high-quality health care, a clean environment, affordable cost of living and strong economic growth. *Reader's Digest, April 1997*

- Salem was ranked #68 out of 219 cities in terms of children's health, safety, and economic well-being. Criteria: total population, percent population change, birth rate, child immunization rate, infant mortality rate, percent low birth weight infants, percent of births to teens, physician-to-population ratio, student-to-teacher ratio, dropout rate, unemployment rate, median family income, percent of children in poverty, violent and property crime rates, number of juvenile arrests for violent crimes as a percent of the total crime index, number of days with pollution standard index (PSI) over 100, pounds toxic releases per 1,000 people and number of superfund sites. *Zero Population Growth, Children's Environmental Index 1997*

- According to *Working Mother,* "Oregon has taken a number of small steps to improve child care: A new background check on caregivers has been instituted, which includes an FBI check for criminal offenses. The state has also mandated an orientation session for anyone who wishes to open a family child care business. The two-hour briefing offers an overview of what it takes to make a home-based child care business work, and what training and support is available from the community and the state. The idea is to put the brakes on anyone who might enter the profession thinking it's an easy job and then close up shop and leave parents in the lurch—a fairly common scenario. The innovation seems to be working. Our certifier said she has not yet had to go out on a complaint for anyone who has gone through this overview.' says Janis Sabin Elliot of the state's Child Care Division.—Oregon has also stepped up its efforts to insure children's health and safety. For instance, it now has more power to revoke the licenses of child care providers in serious violation of rules.

  Family child care could be improved in this state if a bill pending before the legislature becomes law. Among other things, it would require providers to have training in CPR and first aid, which should be a basic standard for any good child care program." *Working Mother, July/August 1997*

Business Environment

STATE ECONOMY

State Economic Profile

"Oregon is entering its fourth year of high growth....Income growth continues to outpace the U.S., as it has throughout the decade.

...Oregon's semiconductor industry is now large enough that it is being supplemented by a number of supplier firms moving into the state, further bolstering the economy.

Oregon's lumber and timber industry will benefit from its proximity to expanding housing markets in California and Washington, which are less likely to buckle under rising interest rates than markets elsewhere in the U.S.

Enron's takeover of Portland General Electric may benefit the economy due to the substantial rate cuts being promised by the merged utility. Lower energy costs would help preserve Oregon's competitive edge as deregulation lowers utility rates in higher cost regions of the country.

Strong economies in Washington and California may slow migration into Oregon, stifling demand for new housing. This would cause the construction industry to constrict, and house price appreciation to decelerate from current high rates. A rising dollar/yen ratio also poses a risk to export demand for Oregon's timber products.

Oregon's outlook remains good. The semiconductor industry appears to have weathered recent declines in chip prices, and all plants under construction appear headed for completion. The long-term outlook is for slower expansion, with some uncertainty as to what will replace semiconductors as the main engine of growth. The diversity of Oregon's economy minimizes this risk, however, and Oregon remains top ranked for future growth." *National Association of Realtors, Economic Profiles: The Fifty States, July 1997*

IMPORTS/EXPORTS

Total Export Sales

Area	1993 ($000)	1994 ($000)	1995 ($000)	1996 ($000)	% Chg. 1993-96	% Chg. 1995-96
MSA[1]	66,294	72,944	111,956	123,013	85.6	9.9
U.S.	464,858,354	512,415,609	583,030,524	622,827,063	34.0	6.8

Note: (1) Metropolitan Statistical Area - see Appendix A for areas included
Source: U.S. Department of Commerce, International Trade Association, Metropolitan Area Exports: An Export Performance Report on Over 250 U.S. Cities, October 1997

Imports/Exports by Port

Type	Cargo Value			Share of U.S. Total	
	1995 (US$mil.)	1996 (US$mil.)	% Change 1995-1996	1995 (%)	1996 (%)
Imports	0	0	0	0	0
Exports	0	0	0	0	0

Source: Global Trade Information Services, WaterBorne Trade Atlas 1997

CITY FINANCES

City Government Finances

Component	FY92 ($000)	FY92 (per capita $)
Revenue	76,821	678.97
Expenditure	82,726	731.16
Debt Outstanding	59,403	525.03
Cash & Securities	36,811	325.35

Source: U.S. Bureau of the Census, City Government Finances: 1991-92

City Government Revenue by Source

Source	FY92 ($000)	FY92 (per capita $)	FY92 (%)
From Federal Government	953	8.42	1.2
From State Governments	6,706	59.27	8.7
From Local Governments	1,393	12.31	1.8
Property Taxes	28,899	255.42	37.6
General Sales Taxes	0	0.00	0.0
Selective Sales Taxes	5,580	49.32	7.3
Income Taxes	0	0.00	0.0
Current Charges	17,521	154.86	22.8
Utility/Liquor Store	6,471	57.19	8.4
Employee Retirement[1]	0	0.00	0.0
Other	9,298	82.18	12.1

Note: (1) Excludes "city contributions," classified as "nonrevenue," intragovernmental transfers.
Source: U.S. Bureau of the Census, City Government Finances: 1991-92

City Government Expenditures by Function

Function	FY92 ($000)	FY92 (per capita $)	FY92 (%)
Educational Services	2,381	21.04	2.9
Employee Retirement[1]	0	0.00	0.0
Environment/Housing	18,006	159.14	21.8
Government Administration	6,342	56.05	7.7
Interest on General Debt	4,143	36.62	5.0
Public Safety	21,390	189.05	25.9
Social Services	1,927	17.03	2.3
Transportation	8,241	72.84	10.0
Utility/Liquor Store	5,271	46.59	6.4
Other	15,025	132.80	18.2

Note: (1) Payments to beneficiaries including withdrawal of contributions.
Source: U.S. Bureau of the Census, City Government Finances: 1991-92

Municipal Bond Ratings

Area	Moody's	S & P
Salem	A1	n/a

Note: n/a not available; n/r not rated
Source: Moody's Bond Record, 2/98; Statistical Abstract of the U.S., 1997;
Governing Magazine, 9/97, 3/98

POPULATION

Population Growth

Area	1980	1990	% Chg. 1980-90	July 1996 Estimate	% Chg. 1990-96
City	89,233	107,786	20.8	122,566	13.7
MSA[1]	249,895	278,024	11.3	319,420	14.9
U.S.	226,545,805	248,765,170	9.8	265,179,411	6.6

Note: (1) Metropolitan Statistical Area - see Appendix A for areas included
Source: 1980/1990 Census of Housing and Population, Summary Tape File 3C;
Census Bureau Population Estimates

Population Characteristics

Race	City				% Chg. 1980-90	MSA[1]	
	1980		1990			1990	
	Population	%	Population	%		Population	%
White	84,227	94.4	98,343	91.2	16.8	255,295	91.8
Black	1,038	1.2	1,497	1.4	44.2	2,210	0.8
Amer Indian/Esk/Aleut	1,183	1.3	1,875	1.7	58.5	4,300	1.5
Asian/Pacific Islander	1,587	1.8	2,634	2.4	66.0	4,702	1.7
Other	1,198	1.3	3,437	3.2	186.9	11,517	4.1
Hispanic Origin[2]	2,900	3.2	6,207	5.8	114.0	20,181	7.3

Note: (1) Metropolitan Statistical Area - see Appendix A for areas included;
(2) people of Hispanic origin can be of any race
Source: 1980/1990 Census of Housing and Population, Summary Tape File 3C

Ancestry

Area	German	Irish	English	Italian	U.S.	French	Polish	Dutch
City	31.0	15.3	19.4	2.5	3.4	5.1	1.6	3.9
MSA[1]	32.5	15.3	18.5	2.1	3.7	5.3	1.4	4.2
U.S.	23.3	15.6	13.1	5.9	5.3	4.2	3.8	2.5

Note: Figures are percentages and include persons that reported multiple ancestry (eg. if a person reported being Irish and Italian, they were included in both columns); (1) Metropolitan Statistical Area - see Appendix A for areas included
Source: 1990 Census of Population and Housing, Summary Tape File 3C

Age

Area	Median Age (Years)	Age Distribution (%)						
		Under 5	Under 18	18-24	25-44	45-64	65+	80+
City	33.4	7.3	24.3	10.5	34.3	16.2	14.7	4.0
MSA[1]	33.8	7.3	26.4	9.7	31.2	18.1	14.5	3.6
U.S.	32.9	7.3	25.6	10.5	32.6	18.7	12.5	2.8

Note: (1) Metropolitan Statistical Area - see Appendix A for areas included
Source: 1990 Census of Population and Housing, Summary Tape File 3C

Male/Female Ratio

Area	Number of males per 100 females (all ages)	Number of males per 100 females (18 years old+)
City	98.7	97.3
MSA[1]	97.2	94.7
U.S.	95.0	91.9

Note: (1) Metropolitan Statistical Area - see Appendix A for areas included
Source: 1990 Census of Population, General Population Characteristics

INCOME

Per Capita/Median/Average Income

Area	Per Capita ($)	Median Household ($)	Average Household ($)
City	12,641	25,236	31,928
MSA[1]	12,260	26,771	32,756
U.S.	14,420	30,056	38,453

Note: all figures are for 1989; (1) Metropolitan Statistical Area - see Appendix A for areas included
Source: 1990 Census of Population and Housing, Summary Tape File 3C

Household Income Distribution by Race

Income ($)	City (%)					U.S. (%)				
	Total	White	Black	Other	Hisp.[1]	Total	White	Black	Other	Hisp.[1]
Less than 5,000	6.1	5.7	17.4	13.0	11.6	6.2	4.8	15.2	8.6	8.8
5,000 - 9,999	11.0	11.0	23.0	9.5	12.5	9.3	8.6	14.2	9.9	11.1
10,000 - 14,999	10.7	10.7	10.8	10.6	13.8	8.8	8.5	11.0	9.8	11.0
15,000 - 24,999	21.7	21.5	18.8	26.9	25.5	17.5	17.3	18.9	18.5	20.5
25,000 - 34,999	17.0	17.1	14.1	15.8	14.3	15.8	16.1	14.2	15.4	16.4
35,000 - 49,999	16.9	17.0	7.5	16.0	12.1	17.9	18.6	13.3	16.1	16.0
50,000 - 74,999	11.7	12.0	8.5	5.8	8.5	15.0	15.8	9.3	13.4	11.1
75,000 - 99,999	2.7	2.7	0.0	2.2	0.0	5.1	5.5	2.6	4.7	3.1
100,000+	2.2	2.3	0.0	0.3	1.7	4.4	4.8	1.3	3.7	1.9

Note: all figures are for 1989; (1) people of Hispanic origin can be of any race
Source: 1990 Census of Population and Housing, Summary Tape File 3C

Effective Buying Income

Area	Per Capita ($)	Median Household ($)	Average Household ($)
City	13,699	28,225	36,099
MSA[1]	13,569	30,342	37,261
U.S.	15,444	33,201	41,849

Note: data as of 1/1/97; (1) Metropolitan Statistical Area - see Appendix A for areas included
Source: Standard Rate & Data Service, Newspaper Advertising Source, 2/98

Effective Household Buying Income Distribution

Area	% of Households Earning						
	$10,000 -$19,999	$20,000 -$34,999	$35,000 -$49,999	$50,000 -$74,999	$75,000 -$99,000	$100,000 -$124,999	$125,000 and up
City	20.0	27.5	18.3	14.9	3.5	1.1	1.1
MSA[1]	18.4	27.9	19.7	16.2	3.8	1.2	1.2
U.S.	16.5	23.4	18.3	18.2	6.4	2.1	2.4

Note: data as of 1/1/97; (1) Metropolitan Statistical Area - see Appendix A for areas included
Source: Standard Rate & Data Service, Newspaper Advertising Source, 2/98

Poverty Rates by Race and Age

Area	Total (%)	By Race (%)				By Age (%)		
		White	Black	Other	Hisp.[2]	Under 5 years old	Under 18 years old	65 years and over
City	14.5	13.1	39.5	29.2	34.5	25.9	19.0	8.9
MSA[1]	13.2	11.9	34.5	28.7	32.7	21.3	17.3	9.6
U.S.	13.1	9.8	29.5	23.1	25.3	20.1	18.3	12.8

Note: figures show the percent of people living below the poverty line in 1989. The average poverty threshold was $12,674 for a family of four in 1989; (1) Metropolitan Statistical Area - see Appendix A for areas included; (2) people of Hispanic origin can be of any race
Source: 1990 Census of Population and Housing, Summary Tape File 3C

EMPLOYMENT

Labor Force and Employment

Area	Civilian Labor Force			Workers Employed		
	Dec. '95	Dec. '96	% Chg.	Dec. '95	Dec. '96	% Chg.
City	61,256	62,176	1.5	57,320	58,718	2.4
MSA[1]	161,676	164,182	1.6	151,656	155,355	2.4
U.S.	134,583,000	136,742,000	1.6	127,903,000	130,785,000	2.3

Note: Data is not seasonally adjusted and covers workers 16 years of age and older; (1) Metropolitan Statistical Area - see Appendix A for areas included
Source: Bureau of Labor Statistics, http://stats.bls.gov

Unemployment Rate

Area	1997											
	Jan.	Feb.	Mar.	Apr.	May	Jun.	Jul.	Aug.	Sep.	Oct.	Nov.	Dec.
City	6.8	6.8	6.9	6.2	5.0	5.5	5.2	4.9	4.6	4.5	5.3	5.6
MSA[1]	6.6	6.5	6.7	5.9	4.8	5.3	5.0	4.7	4.5	4.3	5.1	5.4
U.S.	5.9	5.7	5.5	4.8	4.7	5.2	5.0	4.8	4.7	4.4	4.3	4.4

Note: Data is not seasonally adjusted and covers workers 16 years of age and older; All figures are percentages; (1) Metropolitan Statistical Area - see Appendix A for areas included
Source: Bureau of Labor Statistics, http://stats.bls.gov

Employment by Industry

Sector	MSA[1]		U.S.
	Number of Employees	Percent of Total	Percent of Total
Services	31,600	23.9	29.0
Retail Trade	24,600	18.6	18.5
Government	37,100	28.0	16.1
Manufacturing	16,700	12.6	15.0
Finance/Insurance/Real Estate	6,600	5.0	5.7
Wholesale Trade	4,100	3.1	5.4
Transportation/Public Utilities	3,500	2.6	5.3
Construction	7,900	6.0	4.5
Mining	200	0.2	0.5

Note: Figures cover non-farm employment as of 12/97 and are not seasonally adjusted;
(1) Metropolitan Statistical Area - see Appendix A for areas included
Source: Bureau of Labor Statistics, http://stats.bls.gov

Employment by Occupation

Occupation Category	City (%)	MSA[1] (%)	U.S. (%)
White Collar	61.3	55.0	58.1
Executive/Admin./Management	14.1	12.1	12.3
Professional	15.4	13.6	14.1
Technical & Related Support	3.6	3.1	3.7
Sales	11.6	10.4	11.8
Administrative Support/Clerical	16.5	15.7	16.3
Blue Collar	20.1	24.0	26.2
Precision Production/Craft/Repair	8.7	10.2	11.3
Machine Operators/Assem./Insp.	5.1	5.9	6.8
Transportation/Material Movers	2.8	4.0	4.1
Cleaners/Helpers/Laborers	3.5	3.9	3.9
Services	15.7	15.0	13.2
Farming/Forestry/Fishing	2.9	6.0	2.5

Note: figures cover employed persons 16 years old and over;
(1) Metropolitan Statistical Area - see Appendix A for areas included
Source: 1990 Census of Population and Housing, Summary Tape File 3C

Occupational Employment Projections: 1996 - 2005

Occupations Expected to have the Largest Job Growth (ranked by numerical growth)	Fast-Growing Occupations[1] (ranked by percent growth)
1. Salespersons, retail	1. Home health aides
2. Waiters & waitresses	2. Data processing equipment repairers
3. General office clerks	3. Social welfare service aids
4. Cashiers	4. Engineers, other
5. Food preparation workers	5. Semiconductor processors
6. Truck drivers, heavy & tractor trailer	6. Athletes/coaches/umpires & related workers
7. Student workers	7. Guards
8. Janitors/cleaners/maids, ex. priv. hshld.	8. Gaming supervisor
9. General managers & top executives	9. Engineers, electrical & electronic
10. Home health aides	10. Screen printing machine setters

Projections cover Marion, Polk and Yamhill Counties.
Note: (1) Excludes occupations with employment in the lowest 20%
Source: Oregon Employment Department, Workforce Analysis Section, Oregon Micro-OIS, 1996-2005

Average Wages

Occupation	Wage	Occupation	Wage
Professional/Technical/Clerical	$/Week	**Health/Protective Services**	$/Week
Accountants III	647	Corrections Officers	521
Attorneys III	-	Firefighters	618
Budget Analysts III	757	Nurses, Licensed Practical II	-
Buyers/Contracting Specialists II	616	Nurses, Registered II	-
Clerks, Accounting III	442	Nursing Assistants II	-
Clerks, General III	378	Police Officers I	740
Computer Operators II	481	**Hourly Workers**	$/Hour
Computer Programmers II	540	Forklift Operators	10.45
Drafters II	-	General Maintenance Workers	11.64
Engineering Technicians III	-	Guards I	-
Engineering Technicians, Civil III	494	Janitors	8.59
Engineers III	799	Maintenance Electricians	15.19
Key Entry Operators I	334	Maintenance Electronics Techs II	-
Personnel Assistants III	-	Maintenance Machinists	-
Personnel Specialists III	749	Maintenance Mechanics, Machinery	-
Secretaries III	483	Material Handling Laborers	-
Switchboard Operator-Receptionist	318	Motor Vehicle Mechanics	13.11
Systems Analysts II	766	Shipping/Receiving Clerks	8.96
Systems Analysts Supervisor/Mgr II	-	Tool and Die Makers	-
Tax Collectors II	550	Truckdrivers, Tractor Trailer	-
Word Processors II	-	Warehouse Specialists	9.65

Note: Wage data includes full-time workers only for 1/94 and cover the Metropolitan Statistical Area (see Appendix A for areas included). Dashes indicate that data was not available.
Source: Bureau of Labor Statistics, Occupational Compensation Survey

TAXES

Major State and Local Tax Rates

State Corp. Income (%)	State Personal Income (%)	Residential Property (effective rate per $100)	Sales & Use		State Gasoline (cents/ gallon)	State Cigarette (cents/ 20-pack)
			State (%)	Local (%)		
6.6[a]	5.0 - 9.0	n/a	None	None	24[b]	68

Note: Personal/corporate income tax rates as of 1/97. Sales, gasoline and cigarette tax rates as of 1/98; (a) Minimum tax $10; (b) Does not include a 1 - 2 cents local option tax
Source: Federation of Tax Administrators, www.taxadmin.org; Washington D.C. Department of Finance and Revenue, Tax Rates and Tax Burdens in the District of Columbia: A Nationwide Comparison, June 1997; Chamber of Commerce

Total Taxes Per Capita and as a Percent of Income

Area	Per Capita Income ($)	Per Capita Taxes ($)			Taxes as Pct. of Income (%)		
		Total	Federal	State/Local	Total	Federal	State/Local
Oregon	24,918	9,062	5,799	3,263	36.4	23.3	13.1
U.S.	26,187	9,205	6,127	3,078	35.2	23.4	11.8

Note: Figures are for 1997
Source: Tax Foundation, Web Site, www.taxfoundation.org

Estimated Tax Burden

Area	State Income	Local Income	Property	Sales	Total
Salem	3,852	0	3,825	383	8,060

Note: The numbers are estimates of taxes paid by a married couple with two kids and annual earnings of $65,000. Sales tax estimates assume they spend average amounts on food, clothing, household goods and gasoline. Property tax estimates assume they live in a $225,000 home.
Source: Kiplinger's Personal Finance Magazine, June 1997

COMMERCIAL REAL ESTATE

Data not available at time of publication.

COMMERCIAL UTILITIES

Typical Monthly Electric Bills

Area	Commercial Service ($/month)		Industrial Service ($/month)	
	12 kW demand 1,500 kWh	100 kW demand 30,000 kWh	1,000 kW demand 400,000 kWh	20,000 kW demand 10,000,000 kWh
City	99	1,621	17,592	412,500
U.S.	162	2,360	25,590	545,677

Note: Based on rates in effect July 1, 1997
Source: Edison Electric Institute, Typical Residential, Commercial and Industrial Bills, Summer 1997

TRANSPORTATION

Transportation Statistics

Avg. travel time to work (min.)	17.9
Interstate highways	I-5
Bus lines	
In-city	Cherriots Bus Service
Inter-city	1
Passenger air service	
Airport	Portland International (50 miles north)
Airlines	n/a
Aircraft departures	n/a
Enplaned passengers	n/a
Rail service	Amtrak
Motor freight carriers	20
Major waterways/ports	Willamette River

Source: OAG, Business Travel Planner, Summer 1997; Editor & Publisher Market Guide, 1998; FAA Airport Activity Statistics, 1996; Amtrak National Time Table, Northeast Timetable, Fall/Winter 1997-98; 1990 Census of Population and Housing, STF 3C; Chamber of Commerce/Economic Development 1997; Jane's Urban Transport Systems 1997-98; Transit Fact Book 1997

Means of Transportation to Work

Area	Car/Truck/Van		Public Transportation			Bicycle	Walked	Other Means	Worked at Home
	Drove Alone	Car-pooled	Bus	Subway	Railroad				
City	72.5	15.3	2.4	0.0	0.0	1.3	4.3	1.4	2.8
MSA[1]	73.3	15.2	1.4	0.0	0.0	0.8	4.0	1.2	4.2
U.S.	73.2	13.4	3.0	1.5	0.5	0.4	3.9	1.2	3.0

Note: figures shown are percentages and only include workers 16 years old and over;
(1) Metropolitan Statistical Area - see Appendix A for areas included
Source: 1990 Census of Population and Housing, Summary Tape File 3C

BUSINESSES

Major Business Headquarters

Company Name	1997 Rankings	
	Fortune 500	Forbes 500

No companies listed.

Note: Companies listed are located in the city; Dashes indicate no ranking
Fortune 500: companies that produce a 10-K are ranked 1 - 500 based on 1996 revenue
Forbes 500: private companies are ranked 1 - 500 based on 1996 revenue
Source: Forbes 12/1/97; Fortune 4/28/97

Minority Business Opportunity

One of the 500 largest Hispanic-owned companies in the U.S. are located in Salem.
Hispanic Business, June 1997

HOTELS & MOTELS

Hotels/Motels

Area	Hotels/ Motels	Rooms	Luxury-Level Hotels/Motels		Average Minimum Rates ($)		
			♦♦♦♦	♦♦♦♦♦	♦♦	♦♦♦	♦♦♦♦
City	7	644	0	0	n/a	n/a	n/a
Airport	1	42	0	0	n/a	n/a	n/a
Total	8	686	0	0	n/a	n/a	n/a

Note: n/a not available; Classifications range from one diamond (budget properties with basic amenities) to five diamond (luxury properties with the finest service, rooms and facilities).
Source: OAG, Business Travel Planner, Summer 1997

CONVENTION CENTERS

Major Convention Centers

Center Name	Meeting Rooms	Exhibit Space (sf)
Oregon State Fair & Expo Center	3	84,000

Source: Trade Shows Worldwide 1997

Living Environment

COST OF LIVING

Cost of Living Index

Composite Index	Housing	Utilities	Groceries	Health Care	Trans-portation	Misc. Goods/ Services
105.1	120.7	75.3	93.9	119.5	106.5	101.4

Note: U.S. = 100
Source: ACCRA, Cost of Living Index, 4th Quarter 1996

HOUSING

Median Home Prices and Housing Affordability

Area	Median Price[2] 3rd Qtr. 1997 ($)	HOI[3] 3rd Qtr. 1997	Afford-ability Rank[4]
MSA[1]	120,000	35.8	189
U.S.	127,000	63.7	–

Note: (1) Metropolitan Statistical Area - see Appendix A for areas included; (2) U.S. figures calculated from the sales of 625,000 new and existing homes in 195 markets; (3) Housing Opportunity Index - percent of homes sold that were within the reach of the median income household at the prevailing mortgage interest rate; (4) Rank is from 1-195 with 1 being most affordable
Source: National Association of Home Builders, Housing Opportunity Index, 3rd Quarter 1997

Average New Home Price

Area	Price ($)
City	170,598
U.S.	133,063

Note: Figures are based on a new home with 1,800 sq. ft. of living area on an 8,000 sq. ft. lot.
Source: ACCRA, Cost of Living Index, 4th Quarter 1996

Average Apartment Rent

Area	Rent ($/mth)
City	502
U.S.	562

Note: Figures are based on an unfurnished two bedroom, 1-1/2 or 2 bath apartment, approximately 950 sq. ft. in size, excluding all utilities except water
Source: ACCRA, Cost of Living Index, 4th Quarter 1996

RESIDENTIAL UTILITIES

Average Residential Utility Costs

Area	All Electric ($/mth)	Part Electric ($/mth)	Other Energy ($/mth)	Phone ($/mth)
City	–	36.97	37.02	18.36
U.S.	111.56	55.48	42.49	19.46

Source: ACCRA, Cost of Living Index, 4th Quarter 1996

HEALTH CARE

Average Health Care Costs

Area	Hospital ($/day)	Doctor ($/visit)	Dentist ($/visit)
City	390.00	48.92	85.80
U.S.	385.60	47.03	58.35

Note: Hospital - based on a semi-private room. Doctor - based on a general practitioner's routine exam of an established patient. Dentist - based on adult teeth cleaning and periodic oral exam.
Source: ACCRA, Cost of Living Index, 4th Quarter 1996

Distribution of Office-Based Physicians

Area	Family/Gen. Practitioners	Specialists Medical	Specialists Surgical	Specialists Other
MSA[1]	102	98	102	106

Note: Data as of 12/31/96; (1) Metropolitan Statistical Area - see Appendix A for areas included
Source: American Medical Assn., Physician Characteristics & Distribution in the U.S., 1997-1998

Hospitals

Salem has 1 general medical and surgical hospital and 1 psychiatric. *AHA Guide to the Healthcare Field 1997-98*

EDUCATION

Public School District Statistics

District Name	Num. Sch.	Enroll.	Classroom Teachers[1]	Pupils per Teacher	Minority Pupils (%)	Current Exp.[2] ($/pupil)
Bureau Of Indian Affairs	1	405	24	16.9	n/a	n/a
Oregon State Dept of Education	2	161	31	5.2	n/a	n/a
Pratum Sch Dist 50	1	64	4	16.0	n/a	n/a
Salem/Keizer Sch Dist 24J	52	31,364	1,290	24.3	15.9	5,094

Note: Data covers the 1995-1996 school year unless otherwise noted; (1) Excludes teachers reported as working in school district offices rather than in schools; (2) Based on 1993-94 enrollment collected by the Census Bureau, not the enrollment figure shown in column 3; SD = School District; ISD = Independent School District; n/a not available
Source: National Center for Education Statistics, Common Core of Data Survey; Bureau of the Census

Educational Quality

School District	Education Quotient[1]	Graduate Outcome[2]	Community Index[3]	Resource Index[4]
Salem/Keizer	85.0	78.0	88.0	88.0

Note: Nearly 1,000 secondary school districts were rated in terms of educational quality. The scores range from a low of 50 to a high of 150; (1) Average of the Graduate Outcome, Community and Resource indexes; (2) Based on graduation rates and college board scores (SAT/ACT); (3) Based on the surrounding community's average level of education and the area's average income level; (4) Based on teacher salaries, per-pupil expenditures and student-teacher ratios.
Source: Expansion Management, Ratings Issue 1997

Educational Attainment by Race

Area	High School Graduate (%) Total	White	Black	Other	Hisp.[2]	Bachelor's Degree (%) Total	White	Black	Other	Hisp.[2]
City	81.5	82.6	82.3	63.5	51.8	21.7	22.5	10.7	10.9	8.4
MSA[1]	78.9	80.2	79.5	56.4	43.0	18.2	18.7	13.6	9.2	6.6
U.S.	75.2	77.9	63.1	60.4	49.8	20.3	21.5	11.4	19.4	9.2

Note: figures shown cover persons 25 years old and over; (1) Metropolitan Statistical Area - see Appendix A for areas included; (2) people of Hispanic origin can be of any race
Source: 1990 Census of Population and Housing, Summary Tape File 3C

School Enrollment by Type

Area	Preprimary Public Enrollment	%	Preprimary Private Enrollment	%	Elementary/High School Public Enrollment	%	Elementary/High School Private Enrollment	%
City	1,004	55.2	816	44.8	15,355	92.4	1,258	7.6
MSA[1]	2,955	60.5	1,933	39.5	44,108	92.5	3,582	7.5
U.S.	2,679,029	59.5	1,824,256	40.5	38,379,689	90.2	4,187,099	9.8

Note: figures shown cover persons 3 years old and over; (1) Metropolitan Statistical Area - see Appendix A for areas included
Source: 1990 Census of Population and Housing, Summary Tape File 3C

School Enrollment by Race

Area	Preprimary (%)				Elementary/High School (%)			
	White	Black	Other	Hisp.[1]	White	Black	Other	Hisp.[1]
City	93.4	0.0	6.6	5.2	87.9	1.8	10.3	8.5
MSA[2]	93.1	0.8	6.2	5.8	89.3	1.1	9.7	10.5
U.S.	80.4	12.5	7.1	7.8	74.1	15.6	10.3	12.5

Note: figures shown cover persons 3 years old and over; (1) people of Hispanic origin can be of any race; (2) Metropolitan Statistical Area - see Appendix A for areas included
Source: 1990 Census of Population and Housing, Summary Tape File 3C

SAT/ACT Scores

Area/District	1997 SAT				1997 ACT	
	Percent of Graduates Tested (%)	Average Math Score	Average Verbal Score	Average Combined Score	Percent of Graduates Tested (%)	Average Composite Score
Salem-Keizer PS	48	546	532	1,078	n/a	n/a
State	50	524	525	1,049	12	22.3
U.S.	42	511	505	1,016	36	21.0

Note: Math and verbal SAT scores are out of a possible 800; ACT scores are out of a possible 36
Caution: Comparing or ranking states/cities on the basis of SAT/ACT scores alone is invalid and strongly discouraged by the The College Board and The American College Testing Program as students who take the tests are self-selected and do not represent the entire student population.
Source: Salem-Keizer Public Schools, 1997; American College Testing Program, 1997; College Board, 1997

Classroom Teacher Salaries in Public Schools

District	B.A. Degree		M.A. Degree		Ph.D. Degree	
	Min. ($)	Max. ($)	Min. ($)	Max. ($)	Min. ($)	Max. ($)
Salem	24,789	41,145	28,757	46,081	n/a	n/a
Average[1]	26,120	39,270	28,175	44,667	31,643	49,825

Note: Salaries are for 1996-1997; (1) Based on all school districts covered; n/a not available
Source: American Federation of Teachers (unpublished data)

Higher Education

Two-Year Colleges		Four-Year Colleges		Medical Schools	Law Schools	Voc/ Tech
Public	Private	Public	Private			
1	0	0	2	0	1	10

Source: College Blue Book, Occupational Education 1997; Medical School Admission Requirements, 1998-99; Peterson's Guide to Two-Year Colleges, 1997; Peterson's Guide to Four-Year Colleges, 1997; Barron's Guide to Law Schools 1997

MAJOR EMPLOYERS

Major Employers

HMO Oregon
SAIF Corp. (insurance)
Eagle Newspapers
First Pacific Corp. (management services)

Morrow Snowboards
Salem Hospital
Capital City Companies (petroleum products)
Microflect Co. (microwave communications equip.)

Note: companies listed are located in the city
Source: Dun's Business Rankings 1997; Ward's Business Directory, 1997

PUBLIC SAFETY

Crime Rate

Area	All Crimes	Violent Crimes				Property Crimes		
		Murder	Forcible Rape	Robbery	Aggrav. Assault	Burglary	Larceny -Theft	Motor Vehicle Theft
City	8,956.6	5.8	78.4	159.4	85.1	1,069.9	6,935.3	622.6
Suburbs[1]	5,125.0	2.0	35.0	53.7	161.7	806.4	3,681.1	385.2
MSA[2]	6,572.7	3.5	51.4	93.7	132.8	905.9	4,910.6	474.9
U.S.	5,078.9	7.4	36.1	202.4	388.2	943.0	2,975.9	525.9

Note: Crime rate is the number of crimes per 100,000 pop.; (1) defined as all areas within the MSA but located outside the central city; (2) Metropolitan Statistical Area - see Appendix A for areas incl. Source: FBI Uniform Crime Reports 1996

RECREATION

Culture and Recreation

Museums	Symphony Orchestras	Opera Companies	Dance Companies	Professional Theatres	Zoos	Pro Sports Teams
7	1	0	0	2	0	0

Source: International Directory of the Performing Arts, 1996; Official Museum Directory, 1998; Chamber of Commerce/Economic Development 1997

Library System

The Salem Public Library has one branch, holdings of 301,344 volumes and a budget of $2,994,961 (1995-1996). *American Library Directory, 1997-1998*

MEDIA

Newspapers

Name	Type	Freq.	Distribution	Circulation
Statesman-Journal	General	7x/wk	Area	62,000

Note: Includes newspapers with circulations of 500 or more located in the city; Source: Burrelle's Media Directory, 1998 Edition

AM Radio Stations

Call Letters	Freq. (kHz)	Target Audience	Station Format	Music Format
KWBY	940	Hispanic	M/N/S	n/a
KCCS	1220	Religious	M/N/S	Christian/MOR
KSLM	1390	General	M/N/S	Oldies
KYKN	1430	Religious	N/S/T	n/a
KCKX	1460	General	M	Country
KBZY	1490	General	M/S	Adult Contemporary

*Note: Stations included broadcast in the Salem metro area; n/a not available
Station Format: E = Educational; M = Music; N = News; S = Sports; T = Talk
Music Format: AOR = Album Oriented Rock; MOR = Middle-of-the-Road
Source: Burrelle's Media Directory, 1998 Edition*

FM Radio Stations

Call Letters	Freq. (mHz)	Target Audience	Station Format	Music Format

No stations listed.

*Note: Stations included broadcast in the Salem metro area
Station Format: E = Educational; M = Music; N = News; S = Sports; T = Talk
Source: Burrelle's Media Directory, 1998 Edition*

Television Stations

Name	Ch.	Affiliation	Type	Owner
KBSP	22	HSN	Commercial	Blackstar of Salem Inc.

*Note: Stations included broadcast in the Salem metro area
Source: Burrelle's Media Directory, 1998 Edition*

CLIMATE

Average and Extreme Temperatures

Temperature	Jan	Feb	Mar	Apr	May	Jun	Jul	Aug	Sep	Oct	Nov	Dec	Ann
Extreme High (°F)	65	72	75	88	100	102	106	108	104	93	72	66	108
Average High (°F)	46	51	55	61	67	74	82	81	76	64	53	47	63
Average Temp. (°F)	39	43	46	50	55	61	66	67	62	53	45	41	52
Average Low (°F)	32	34	36	38	43	48	51	51	47	41	37	34	41
Extreme Low (°F)	-10	-4	12	23	25	32	37	36	26	23	9	-12	-12

Note: Figures cover the years 1948-1990
Source: National Climatic Data Center, International Station Meteorological Climate Summary, 3/95

Average Precipitation/Snowfall/Humidity

Precip./Humidity	Jan	Feb	Mar	Apr	May	Jun	Jul	Aug	Sep	Oct	Nov	Dec	Ann
Avg. Precip. (in.)	6.5	4.9	4.3	2.4	2.0	1.4	0.5	0.7	1.5	3.3	6.1	6.8	40.2
Avg. Snowfall (in.)	3	1	1	Tr	Tr	0	0	0	0	Tr	Tr	2	7
Avg. Rel. Hum. 7am (%)	87	89	89	85	81	77	75	79	86	92	90	89	85
Avg. Rel. Hum. 4pm (%)	76	70	62	56	53	50	40	40	45	61	76	81	59

Note: Figures cover the years 1948-1990; Tr = Trace amounts (<0.05 in. of rain; <0.5 in. of snow)
Source: National Climatic Data Center, International Station Meteorological Climate Summary, 3/95

Weather Conditions

Temperature			Daytime Sky			Precipitation		
5°F & below	32°F & below	90°F & above	Clear	Partly cloudy	Cloudy	0.01 inch or more precip.	0.1 inch or more snow/ice	Thunder-storms
< 1	66	16	78	119	168	146	6	5

Note: Figures are average number of days per year and covers the years 1948-1990
Source: National Climatic Data Center, International Station Meteorological Climate Summary, 3/95

AIR & WATER QUALITY

Maximum Pollutant Concentrations

	Particulate Matter (ug/m³)	Carbon Monoxide (ppm)	Sulfur Dioxide (ppm)	Nitrogen Dioxide (ppm)	Ozone (ppm)	Lead (ug/m³)
MSA[1] Level	n/a	7	n/a	n/a	0.12	n/a
NAAQS[2]	150	9	0.140	0.053	0.12	1.50
Met NAAQS?	n/a	Yes	n/a	n/a	Yes	n/a

Note: (1) Metropolitan Statistical Area - see Appendix A for areas included; (2) National Ambient Air Quality Standards; ppm = parts per million; ug/m³ = micrograms per cubic meter; n/a not available
Source: EPA, National Air Quality and Emissions Trends Report, 1996

Pollutant Standards Index

Data not available.   *EPA, National Air Quality and Emissions Trends Report, 1996*

Drinking Water

Water System Name	Pop. Served	Primary Water Source Type	Number of Violations in Fiscal Year 1997	Type of Violation/ Contaminants
Salem Public Works	116,000	Surface	1	(1)

Note: Data as of January 16, 1998; (1) System did not perform the required treatment technique under the Surface Water Treatment Rule.
Source: EPA, Office of Ground Water and Drinking Water, Safe Drinking Water Information System

Salem tap water is soft mountain water.
Editor & Publisher Market Guide, 1998

Salt Lake City, Utah

Background

One cannot disassociate Salt Lake City, the largest city in Utah, and its state capital, from its Mormon, or Church of Jesus Christ of Latter Day Saints, origins. The city was founded by Brigham Young on July 24, 1847, as a place of refuge from mainstream ostracism for their polygamous lifestyle. Brigham Young decided to lead his people to a "land that nobody wanted", so they could exercise their form of worship in peace.

Two scouts, Orson Pratt and Erastus Snow, located the site for Brigham Young, and their leader declared that "this is the place". The site that was to be called Salt Lake City was breathtaking. The area was bordered on the east and southwest by the dramatic peaks of the Wasatch Range, and bordered on the northwest by the great Salt Lake.

The land was too dry and hard for farming. Nevertheless Mormon industry diverted the flow of mountain streams to irrigate the land, and the valley turned into a prosperous agricultural region.

A little more than 10 years after its incorporation as a city, the U.S. government was still suspicious of the Mormons. Fort Douglas was erected in 1862, manned by Federal troops, to keep an eye on the Mormons and their polygamous practices.

In 1869 the completion of the Transcontinental Railroad brought mining, industry, and other non-Mormon interests to Salt Lake City. As for polygamy, the Mormon Church made it illegal in 1890.

While mining played a major role in the early development of Salt Lake City, today the major industry sectors are construction, trade, transportation, communications, finance, insurance and real estate.

According to the Association of University Related Research Parks, The University of Utah Research Park, located in Salt Lake City is ranked #10 out of the top 10 research parks in the U. S. with 46 companies. *World Trade 4/97*

The mountain ranges, which surround the city, and the Great Salt Lake greatly influence climatic conditions. Temperatures are moderated by the lake in winter and storm activity is enhanced by both lake and mountains.

Salt Lake City normally has a semi-arid continental climate with four well-defined seasons. Summers are hot and dry, while winters are cold, but generally not severe. Mountains to the north and east act as a barrier to frequent invasions of cold air. Heavy fog can develop when there is a temperature inversion in winter and may persist for several days at a time.

General Rankings and Evaluative Comments

- Salt Lake City was ranked #99 out of 300 cities by *Money's* 1997 "Survey of the Best Places to Live." Criteria used: health services, crime, economy, housing, education, transportation, weather, leisure and the arts. The city was ranked #77 in 1996 and #62 in 1995. *Money, July 1997; Money, September 1996; Money, September 1995*

- *Ladies Home Journal* ranked America's 200 largest cities based on the qualities women care about most. Salt Lake City ranked 39 out of 200. Criteria: low crime rate, good public schools, well-paying jobs, quality health and child care, the presence of women in government, proportion of women-owned businesses, size of the wage gap with men, local economy, divorce rates, the ratio of single men to single women, whether there are laws that require at least the same number of public toilets for women as men, and the probability of good hair days. *Ladies Home Journal, November 1997*

- Salt Lake City is among "The Best Places to Raise a Family". Rank: 31 out of 301 metro areas. Criteria: low crime rate, low drug and alcohol abuse, good public schools, high-quality health care, a clean environment, affordable cost of living and strong economic growth. *Reader's Digest, April 1997*

- Salt Lake City was ranked #136 out of 219 cities in terms of children's health, safety, and economic well-being. Criteria: total population, percent population change, birth rate, child immunization rate, infant mortality rate, percent low birth weight infants, percent of births to teens, physician-to-population ratio, student-to-teacher ratio, dropout rate, unemployment rate, median family income, percent of children in poverty, violent and property crime rates, number of juvenile arrests for violent crimes as a percent of the total crime index, number of days with pollution standard index (PSI) over 100, pounds toxic releases per 1,000 people and number of superfund sites. *Zero Population Growth, Children's Environmental Index 1997*

- Salt Lake City appeared on *New Mobility's* list of "10 Disability Friendly Cities". Rank: 7 out of 10. Criteria: affordable and accessible housing, transportation, quality medical care, personal assistance services and strong advocacy.

  "...Both the mainline transit system (70 percent accessible) and Flex Trans, the paratransit service, run six days a week. Housing is difficult, since inflated costs have made Section 8 and other HUD certificates virtually useless. Salt lake City is the home of the Utah Independent Living Center—which offers a strong advocacy program and helps consumers living in their own homes through its Community Action Program—and of the Disabled Rights Action Committee, aggressive litigants in ADA and fair housing cases....

  There's a lot to do here—the Delta Center meets ADA standards. you can take in professional rodeo, hockey and basketball, or check out adaptive skiing and whitewater programs. If you move here, try to stick to 'The Avenue' if you need accessible bus lines, though a roof over your head may be pricey...." *New Mobility, December 1997*

- *Conde Nast Traveler* polled 37,000 readers in terms of travel satisfaction. Cities were ranked based on the following criteria: people/friendliness, environment/ambiance, cultural enrichment, restaurants and fun/energy. Salt Lake City appeared in the top thirty, ranking number 15, with an overall rating of 65.9 out of 100 based on all the criteria. The cities were also ranked in each category separately. Salt Lake City appeared in the top 10 based on people/friendliness, ranking number 8 with a rating of 73.5 out of 100. Salt Lake City appeared in the top 10 based on environment/ambiance, ranking number 7 with a rating of 82.4 out of 100. Salt Lake City appeared in the top 10 based on cultural enrichment, ranking number 8 with a rating of 64.7 out of 100. *Conde Nast Traveler, Readers' Choice Poll 1997*

■ According to *Working Mother,* "Utah has delayed new child care standards, after a fractious battle over them. The state recently shifted child care oversight to a new government agency— the department of health, and officials must now start the rule-revision process from scratch.

In a more positive move, Utah officials are exploring ways to expand care for school-age kids. One interesting proposal: the state will offer $500,000 to communities willing to put up matching funds to create new slots for school-age care. Half the money would be for programs run by private caregivers. This is an interesting approach, since it uses both public and private resources to help kids." *Working Mother, July/August 1997*

Business Environment

STATE ECONOMY

State Economic Profile

"Utah's manufacturing establishments have been making large capital investments due in part to the state's exemption of new or expanding operations from a portion of sales taxes on machinery and equipment. In addition to this incentive, Utah's low business costs have spurred relocations and expansions. For manufacturers selling to the local residential market, the past few years have reflected boom conditions, and strong sales growth is contributing to capital purchasing. Continued globalization of manufacturing production has increased competitive pressures, forcing firms to continually upgrade their equipment. As these pressures are unlikely to abate in the next few years, Utah's pattern of investment augurs well for the competitive ability of its manufacturing industries.

Due to rapid job and income growth in the state, Utah is emerging as an important new market, attracting the attention of both national retail chains and financial firms. Moreover, the private investment of numerous hotel and food chains is accelerating in anticipation of the 2002 Olympics and the resulting tourism industry.

Strong population trends will continue to be an important driver of growth for the state. Utah has had six consecutive years of net in-migration that have supported the strong growth of its labor force and population. The tight labor market and rising income growth have attracted Utah residents into the labor force.

Strong demographic trends and below-average business costs are two important comparative advantages for the state. The major downside risks to Utah's outlook are continued weakness in the semiconductor chip market and the specter of overbuilding, particularly in the upper price ranges. Upside risks include further expansion of Utah's information industries and the increased publicity, and retail and construction spending brought on by the 2002 Winter Olympics. Utah is top-ranked for both short-and long-term growth." *National Association of Realtors, Economic Profiles: The Fifty States, July 1997*

IMPORTS/EXPORTS

Total Export Sales

Area	1993 ($000)	1994 ($000)	1995 ($000)	1996 ($000)	% Chg. 1993-96	% Chg. 1995-96
MSA[1]	1,660,879	1,808,673	1,838,151	2,111,534	27.1	14.9
U.S.	464,858,354	512,415,609	583,030,524	622,827,063	34.0	6.8

Note: (1) Metropolitan Statistical Area - see Appendix A for areas included
Source: U.S. Department of Commerce, International Trade Association, Metropolitan Area Exports: An Export Performance Report on Over 250 U.S. Cities, October 1997

Imports/Exports by Port

Type	Cargo Value 1995 (US$mil.)	1996 (US$mil.)	% Change 1995-1996	Share of U.S. Total 1995 (%)	1996 (%)
Imports	0	0	0	0	0
Exports	0	0	0	0	0

Source: Global Trade Information Services, WaterBorne Trade Atlas 1997

CITY FINANCES

City Government Finances

Component	FY92 ($000)	FY92 (per capita $)
Revenue	212,925	1,277.32
Expenditure	244,611	1,467.40
Debt Outstanding	297,769	1,786.29
Cash & Securities	133,460	800.61

Source: U.S. Bureau of the Census, City Government Finances: 1991-92

City Government Revenue by Source

Source	FY92 ($000)	FY92 (per capita $)	FY92 (%)
From Federal Government	4,483	26.89	2.1
From State Governments	7,260	43.55	3.4
From Local Governments	0	0.00	0.0
Property Taxes	43,531	261.14	20.4
General Sales Taxes	23,651	141.88	11.1
Selective Sales Taxes	14,916	89.48	7.0
Income Taxes	0	0.00	0.0
Current Charges	73,532	441.11	34.5
Utility/Liquor Store	23,737	142.40	11.1
Employee Retirement[1]	0	0.00	0.0
Other	21,815	130.87	10.2

Note: (1) Excludes "city contributions," classified as "nonrevenue," intragovernmental transfers.
Source: U.S. Bureau of the Census, City Government Finances: 1991-92

City Government Expenditures by Function

Function	FY92 ($000)	FY92 (per capita $)	FY92 (%)
Educational Services	6,338	38.02	2.6
Employee Retirement[1]	0	0.00	0.0
Environment/Housing	48,568	291.35	19.9
Government Administration	13,297	79.77	5.4
Interest on General Debt	19,774	118.62	8.1
Public Safety	42,992	257.91	17.6
Social Services	88	0.53	0.0
Transportation	74,651	447.82	30.5
Utility/Liquor Store	32,169	192.98	13.2
Other	6,734	40.40	2.8

Note: (1) Payments to beneficiaries including withdrawal of contributions.
Source: U.S. Bureau of the Census, City Government Finances: 1991-92

Municipal Bond Ratings

Area	Moody's	S & P
Salt Lake City	Aaa	n/a

Note: n/a not available; n/r not rated
Source: Moody's Bond Record, 2/98; Statistical Abstract of the U.S., 1997;
Governing Magazine, 9/97, 3/98

POPULATION

Population Growth

Area	1980	1990	% Chg. 1980-90	July 1996 Estimate	% Chg. 1990-96
City	163,033	159,936	-1.9	172,575	7.9
MSA[1]	910,222	1,072,227	17.8	1,217,842	13.6
U.S.	226,545,805	248,765,170	9.8	265,179,411	6.6

Note: (1) Metropolitan Statistical Area - see Appendix A for areas included
Source: 1980/1990 Census of Housing and Population, Summary Tape File 3C;
Census Bureau Population Estimates

Population Characteristics

Race	City 1980 Population	%	City 1990 Population	%	% Chg. 1980-90	MSA[1] 1990 Population	%
White	146,886	90.1	139,420	87.2	-5.1	1,001,049	93.4
Black	2,557	1.6	2,620	1.6	2.5	10,057	0.9
Amer Indian/Esk/Aleut	1,982	1.2	2,696	1.7	36.0	8,514	0.8
Asian/Pacific Islander	5,204	3.2	7,512	4.7	44.4	25,212	2.4
Other	6,404	3.9	7,688	4.8	20.0	27,395	2.6
Hispanic Origin[2]	12,311	7.6	15,220	9.5	23.6	61,269	5.7

Note: (1) Metropolitan Statistical Area - see Appendix A for areas included;
(2) people of Hispanic origin can be of any race
Source: 1980/1990 Census of Housing and Population, Summary Tape File 3C

Ancestry

Area	German	Irish	English	Italian	U.S.	French	Polish	Dutch
City	17.2	9.0	33.7	3.0	2.8	3.2	1.2	2.8
MSA[1]	18.3	8.5	41.2	3.0	3.7	3.1	1.0	3.7
U.S.	23.3	15.6	13.1	5.9	5.3	4.2	3.8	2.5

Note: Figures are percentages and include persons that reported multiple ancestry (eg. if a person reported being Irish and Italian, they were included in both columns); (1) Metropolitan Statistical Area - see Appendix A for areas included
Source: 1990 Census of Population and Housing, Summary Tape File 3C

Age

Area	Median Age (Years)	Age Distribution (%) Under 5	Under 18	18-24	25-44	45-64	65+	80+
City	31.0	8.3	25.1	12.3	33.7	14.4	14.5	4.0
MSA[1]	27.5	9.7	35.6	10.2	30.9	14.9	8.4	1.8
U.S.	32.9	7.3	25.6	10.5	32.6	18.7	12.5	2.8

Note: (1) Metropolitan Statistical Area - see Appendix A for areas included
Source: 1990 Census of Population and Housing, Summary Tape File 3C

Male/Female Ratio

Area	Number of males per 100 females (all ages)	Number of males per 100 females (18 years old+)
City	96.8	94.8
MSA[1]	98.5	95.4
U.S.	95.0	91.9

Note: (1) Metropolitan Statistical Area - see Appendix A for areas included
Source: 1990 Census of Population, General Population Characteristics

INCOME

Per Capita/Median/Average Income

Area	Per Capita ($)	Median Household ($)	Average Household ($)
City	13,482	22,697	32,046
MSA[1]	12,029	30,882	36,866
U.S.	14,420	30,056	38,453

Note: all figures are for 1989; (1) Metropolitan Statistical Area - see Appendix A for areas included
Source: 1990 Census of Population and Housing, Summary Tape File 3C

Household Income Distribution by Race

Income ($)	City (%)					U.S. (%)				
	Total	White	Black	Other	Hisp.[1]	Total	White	Black	Other	Hisp.[1]
Less than 5,000	7.4	6.5	19.0	13.6	12.5	6.2	4.8	15.2	8.6	8.8
5,000 - 9,999	12.9	12.4	25.2	16.4	13.8	9.3	8.6	14.2	9.9	11.1
10,000 - 14,999	12.8	12.5	11.6	16.4	15.8	8.8	8.5	11.0	9.8	11.0
15,000 - 24,999	21.1	21.0	21.5	21.9	23.9	17.5	17.3	18.9	18.5	20.5
25,000 - 34,999	15.6	16.0	7.9	13.4	15.2	15.8	16.1	14.2	15.4	16.4
35,000 - 49,999	14.2	14.6	6.4	12.0	12.0	17.9	18.6	13.3	16.1	16.0
50,000 - 74,999	9.5	10.1	3.1	4.7	5.8	15.0	15.8	9.3	13.4	11.1
75,000 - 99,999	3.2	3.4	4.0	1.1	0.7	5.1	5.5	2.6	4.7	3.1
100,000+	3.4	3.7	1.2	0.6	0.3	4.4	4.8	1.3	3.7	1.9

Note: all figures are for 1989; (1) people of Hispanic origin can be of any race
Source: 1990 Census of Population and Housing, Summary Tape File 3C

Effective Buying Income

Area	Per Capita ($)	Median Household ($)	Average Household ($)
City	15,522	27,235	37,224
MSA[1]	14,155	36,897	43,478
U.S.	15,444	33,201	41,849

Note: data as of 1/1/97; (1) Metropolitan Statistical Area - see Appendix A for areas included
Source: Standard Rate & Data Service, Newspaper Advertising Source, 2/98

Effective Household Buying Income Distribution

Area	% of Households Earning						
	$10,000 -$19,999	$20,000 -$34,999	$35,000 -$49,999	$50,000 -$74,999	$75,000 -$99,000	$100,000 -$124,999	$125,000 and up
City	21.9	25.5	15.6	13.3	4.7	1.7	2.4
MSA[1]	14.0	24.8	21.2	21.1	6.7	2.0	2.0
U.S.	16.5	23.4	18.3	18.2	6.4	2.1	2.4

Note: data as of 1/1/97; (1) Metropolitan Statistical Area - see Appendix A for areas included
Source: Standard Rate & Data Service, Newspaper Advertising Source, 2/98

Poverty Rates by Race and Age

Area	Total (%)	By Race (%)				By Age (%)		
		White	Black	Other	Hisp.[2]	Under 5 years old	Under 18 years old	65 years and over
City	16.4	13.3	39.4	37.5	32.4	25.8	21.6	9.8
MSA[1]	9.4	8.3	29.1	24.9	22.0	14.2	11.3	7.7
U.S.	13.1	9.8	29.5	23.1	25.3	20.1	18.3	12.8

Note: figures show the percent of people living below the poverty line in 1989. The average poverty threshold was $12,674 for a family of four in 1989; (1) Metropolitan Statistical Area - see Appendix A for areas included; (2) people of Hispanic origin can be of any race
Source: 1990 Census of Population and Housing, Summary Tape File 3C

EMPLOYMENT

Labor Force and Employment

Area	Civilian Labor Force			Workers Employed		
	Dec. '95	Dec. '96	% Chg.	Dec. '95	Dec. '96	% Chg.
City	102,428	107,450	4.9	99,558	104,753	5.2
MSA[1]	651,751	683,365	4.9	634,216	667,307	5.2
U.S.	134,583,000	136,742,000	1.6	127,903,000	130,785,000	2.3

Note: Data is not seasonally adjusted and covers workers 16 years of age and older; (1) Metropolitan Statistical Area - see Appendix A for areas included
Source: Bureau of Labor Statistics, http://stats.bls.gov

Salt Lake City was listed among the top 20 metro areas (out of 114 major areas) in terms of projected job growth from 1997 to 2002 with an annual percent change of 1.9%.
Standard & Poor's DRI, July 23, 1997

Unemployment Rate

Area	1997											
	Jan.	Feb.	Mar.	Apr.	May	Jun.	Jul.	Aug.	Sep.	Oct.	Nov.	Dec.
City	3.2	3.5	2.9	3.1	3.1	3.8	3.1	3.4	2.8	3.0	3.0	2.5
MSA[1]	2.9	3.1	2.6	2.7	2.7	3.3	2.8	3.2	2.8	2.9	2.8	2.3
U.S.	5.9	5.7	5.5	4.8	4.7	5.2	5.0	4.8	4.7	4.4	4.3	4.4

Note: Data is not seasonally adjusted and covers workers 16 years of age and older; All figures are percentages; (1) Metropolitan Statistical Area - see Appendix A for areas included
Source: Bureau of Labor Statistics, http://stats.bls.gov

Employment by Industry

Sector	MSA[1]		U.S.
	Number of Employees	Percent of Total	Percent of Total
Services	185,400	26.9	29.0
Retail Trade	132,600	19.2	18.5
Government	112,200	16.2	16.1
Manufacturing	83,300	12.1	15.0
Finance/Insurance/Real Estate	44,800	6.5	5.7
Wholesale Trade	39,700	5.7	5.4
Transportation/Public Utilities	46,200	6.7	5.3
Construction	43,300	6.3	4.5
Mining	3,000	0.4	0.5

Note: Figures cover non-farm employment as of 12/97 and are not seasonally adjusted; (1) Metropolitan Statistical Area - see Appendix A for areas included
Source: Bureau of Labor Statistics, http://stats.bls.gov

Employment by Occupation

Occupation Category	City (%)	MSA[1] (%)	U.S. (%)
White Collar	64.8	62.6	58.1
Executive/Admin./Management	11.9	13.3	12.3
Professional	20.6	14.4	14.1
Technical & Related Support	4.9	4.3	3.7
Sales	11.1	12.6	11.8
Administrative Support/Clerical	16.4	18.1	16.3
Blue Collar	19.6	24.3	26.2
Precision Production/Craft/Repair	7.4	11.0	11.3
Machine Operators/Assem./Insp.	5.5	6.0	6.8
Transportation/Material Movers	3.3	3.7	4.1
Cleaners/Helpers/Laborers	3.5	3.7	3.9
Services	14.6	12.1	13.2
Farming/Forestry/Fishing	1.0	1.0	2.5

Note: figures cover employed persons 16 years old and over; (1) Metropolitan Statistical Area - see Appendix A for areas included
Source: 1990 Census of Population and Housing, Summary Tape File 3C

Occupational Employment Projections: 1994 - 2005

Occupations Expected to have the Largest Job Growth (ranked by numerical growth)	Fast-Growing Occupations (ranked by percent growth)
1. Salespersons, retail	1. Child care workers, private household
2. Janitors/cleaners/maids, ex. priv. hshld.	2. Dentists
3. General managers & top executives	3. Residential counselors
4. Secretaries, except legal & medical	4. Home health aides
5. Truck drivers, heavy & light	5. Physical therapy assistants and aides
6. Cashiers	6. Dental lab techs., precision
7. Registered nurses	7. Dental hygienists
8. Waiters & waitresses	8. Dental assistants
9. General office clerks	9. Human services workers
10. Food service workers	10. Recreational therapists

Projections cover Utah.
Source: U.S. Department of Labor, Employment and Training Administration, America's Labor Market Information System (ALMIS)

Average Wages

Occupation	Wage	Occupation	Wage
Professional/Technical/Clerical	$/Week	**Health/Protective Services**	$/Week
Accountants III	758	Corrections Officers	458
Attorneys III	1,065	Firefighters	609
Budget Analysts III	800	Nurses, Licensed Practical II	406
Buyers/Contracting Specialists II	640	Nurses, Registered II	664
Clerks, Accounting III	421	Nursing Assistants II	266
Clerks, General III	336	Police Officers I	581
Computer Operators II	399	**Hourly Workers**	$/Hour
Computer Programmers II	640	Forklift Operators	9.76
Drafters II	461	General Maintenance Workers	9.70
Engineering Technicians III	570	Guards I	5.99
Engineering Technicians, Civil III	501	Janitors	6.64
Engineers III	912	Maintenance Electricians	15.36
Key Entry Operators I	302	Maintenance Electronics Techs II	16.94
Personnel Assistants III	444	Maintenance Machinists	15.73
Personnel Specialists III	743	Maintenance Mechanics, Machinery	15.20
Secretaries III	489	Material Handling Laborers	10.45
Switchboard Operator-Receptionist	317	Motor Vehicle Mechanics	15.24
Systems Analysts II	898	Shipping/Receiving Clerks	8.49
Systems Analysts Supervisor/Mgr II	-	Tool and Die Makers	16.78
Tax Collectors II	548	Truckdrivers, Tractor Trailer	14.73
Word Processors II	441	Warehouse Specialists	10.96

Note: Wage data includes full-time workers only for 8/95 and cover the Metropolitan Statistical Area (see Appendix A for areas included). Dashes indicate that data was not available.
Source: Bureau of Labor Statistics, Occupational Compensation Survey, 2/96

TAXES

Major State and Local Tax Rates

State Corp. Income (%)	State Personal Income (%)	Residential Property (effective rate per $100)	Sales & Use State (%)	Sales & Use Local (%)	State Gasoline (cents/ gallon)	State Cigarette (cents/ 20-pack)
5.0[a]	2.3 - 7.0	1.55	4.75	1.25	24.5	51.5

Note: Personal/corporate income tax rates as of 1/97. Sales, gasoline and cigarette tax rates as of 1/98; (a) Minimum tax $100
Source: Federation of Tax Administrators, www.taxadmin.org; Washington D.C. Department of Finance and Revenue, Tax Rates and Tax Burdens in the District of Columbia: A Nationwide Comparison, June 1997; Chamber of Commerce

Total Taxes Per Capita and as a Percent of Income

Area	Per Capita Income ($)	Per Capita Taxes ($)			Taxes as Pct. of Income (%)		
		Total	Federal	State/Local	Total	Federal	State/Local
Utah	21,298	7,341	4,699	2,642	34.5	22.1	12.4
U.S.	26,187	9,205	6,127	3,078	35.2	23.4	11.8

Note: Figures are for 1997
Source: Tax Foundation, Web Site, www.taxfoundation.org

Estimated Tax Burden

Area	State Income	Local Income	Property	Sales	Total
Salt Lake City	2,951	0	2,700	839	6,490

Note: The numbers are estimates of taxes paid by a married couple with two kids and annual earnings of $65,000. Sales tax estimates assume they spend average amounts on food, clothing, household goods and gasoline. Property tax estimates assume they live in a $225,000 home.
Source: Kiplinger's Personal Finance Magazine, June 1997

COMMERCIAL REAL ESTATE

Office Market

Class/Location	Total Space (sq. ft.)	Vacant Space (sq. ft.)	Vac. Rate (%)	Under Constr. (sq. ft.)	Net Absorp. (sq. ft.)	Rental Rates ($/sq.ft./yr.)
Class A						
CBD	3,100,000	110,000	3.5	200,000	190,000	18.00-24.00
Outside CBD	9,500,000	100,000	1.1	400,000	300,000	18.00-24.00
Class B						
CBD	2,000,000	50,000	2.5	100,000	300,000	15.00-18.00
Outside CBD	3,000,000	200,000	6.7	100,000	50,000	15.00-18.00

Note: Data as of 10/97 and covers Salt Lake City; CBD = Central Business District; n/a not available;
Source: Society of Industrial and Office Realtors, 1998 Comparative Statistics of Industrial and Office Real Estate Markets

"Preparation for the 2002 Winter Olympics will provide yet another catalyst to growth. Currently 600,000 sq. ft. of Class 'A' office space is under construction, but considering the market is absorbing space at rates approaching 1,000,000 sq. ft. per year it would seem that overbuilding poses only minimal risk at present. the Salt Lake Valley now appears brightly on institutional investor's 'radar screens', as the market seems to have reached a wholly arbitrary but no less real size threshold that allows pension funds, REITs, and the like, to now consider the market alongside larger investment destinations such as Phoenix, Denver, and Dallas."
Society of Industrial and Office Realtors, 1998 Comparative Statistics of Industrial and Office Real Estate Markets

Industrial Market

Location	Total Space (sq. ft.)	Vacant Space (sq. ft.)	Vac. Rate (%)	Under Constr. (sq. ft.)	Net Absorp. (sq. ft.)	Lease ($/sq.ft./yr.)
Central City	6,612,000	153,000	2.3	0	43,000	2.53-4.00
Suburban	79,181,000	5,624,000	7.1	1,670,000	2,311,000	3.30-5.16

Note: Data as of 10/97 and covers Salt Lake City; n/a not available
Source: Society of Industrial and Office Realtors, 1998 Comparative Statistics of Industrial and Office Real Estate Markets

"Overall vacancies have nestled comfortably in the four percent to seven percent range for several years. These vacancies have remained stable despite new construction, attesting to the depth of demand in the Salt Lake market. Much of Salt Lake's recent construction has centered in the West Valley, home to Centennial and Pioneer Business Parks and the Salt Lake International Center. Heavy industry remains concentrated in northwest Salt Lake, near the airport and rail yards. Recently, gross demand totals have ranged between three and four million sq. ft. per year. With the construction and infrastructure improvements associated with the upcoming Olympic Winter Games in 2002 and a buoyant, diversified economy, Salt Lake's industrial market would seem to have excellent prospects." *Society of Industrial and Office Realtors, 1998 Comparative Statistics of Industrial and Office Real Estate Markets*

Retail Market

Shopping Center Inventory (sq. ft.)	Shopping Center Construction (sq. ft.)	Construction as a Percent of Inventory (%)	Torto Wheaton Rent Index[1] ($/sq. ft.)
19,911,000	493,000	2.5	10.03

Note: Data as of 1997 and covers the Metropolitan Statistical Area - see Appendix A for areas included; (1) Index is based on a model that predicts what the average rent should be for leases with certain characteristics, in certain locations during certain years.
Source: National Association of Realtors, 1997-1998 Market Conditions Report

"The retail market is performing relatively well. Since 1994, construction has been steady, while rents, unlike other Western MSAs, have appreciated. However, Salt Lake's rents remain among the lowest in the nation. Compared to the last four years, employment growth will cool, but will still remain above the national average. The MSA's slowdown does not indicate any shortcomings or weakness in the local economy, but rather a natural slowdown from the high growth rates experienced in the early to mid-90s. This will be offset by the forthcoming Winter Olympics hosted by Salt Lake City in 2002, which are expected to boost tourism. In order to meet the rising demands from the travel industry, an $87 million renovation of the Salt Palace Convention Center is planned." *National Association of Realtors, 1997-1998 Market Conditions Report*

COMMERCIAL UTILITIES

Typical Monthly Electric Bills

Area	Commercial Service ($/month)		Industrial Service ($/month)	
	12 kW demand 1,500 kWh	120 kW demand 30,000 kWh	1,000 kW demand 400,000 kWh	20,000 kW demand 10,000,000 kWh
City[1]	123	1,992	15,393	353,628
U.S.[2]	162	2,360[a]	25,590	545,677

Note: (1) Based on rates in effect January 1, 1997; (2) Based on rates in effect July 1, 1997; (a) Based on 100 kW demand and 30,000 kWh usage.
Source: Memphis Light, Gas and Water, 1997 Utility Bill Comparisons for Selected U.S. Cities; Edison Electric Institute, Typical Residential, Commercial and Industrial Bills, Summer 1997

TRANSPORTATION

Transportation Statistics

Avg. travel time to work (min.)	17.1
Interstate highways	I-15; I-80; I-84
Bus lines	
In-city	Utah TA, 446 vehicles
Inter-city	5
Passenger air service	
Airport	Salt Lake City International
Airlines	10
Aircraft departures	94,189 (1995)
Enplaned passengers	8,238,765 (1995)
Rail service	Amtrak; Light rail under construction
Motor freight carriers	40
Major waterways/ports	None

Source: OAG, Business Travel Planner, Summer 1997; Editor & Publisher Market Guide, 1998; FAA Airport Activity Statistics, 1996; Amtrak National Time Table, Northeast Timetable, Fall/Winter 1997-98; 1990 Census of Population and Housing, STF 3C; Chamber of Commerce/Economic Development 1997; Jane's Urban Transport Systems 1997-98; Transit Fact Book 1997

A survey of 90,000 airline passengers during the first half of 1997 ranked most of the largest airports in the U.S. Salt Lake City International ranked number 8 out of 36. Criteria:

cleanliness, quality of restaurants, attractiveness, speed of baggage delivery, ease of reaching gates, available ground transportation, ease of following signs and closeness of parking. *Plog Research Inc., First Half 1997*

Means of Transportation to Work

Area	Car/Truck/Van		Public Transportation			Bicycle	Walked	Other Means	Worked at Home
	Drove Alone	Car-pooled	Bus	Subway	Railroad				
City	69.6	13.4	5.5	0.0	0.0	1.5	6.0	1.0	2.8
MSA[1]	76.3	14.0	2.9	0.0	0.0	0.5	2.3	0.9	3.1
U.S.	73.2	13.4	3.0	1.5	0.5	0.4	3.9	1.2	3.0

Note: figures shown are percentages and only include workers 16 years old and over;
(1) Metropolitan Statistical Area - see Appendix A for areas included
Source: 1990 Census of Population and Housing, Summary Tape File 3C

BUSINESSES

Major Business Headquarters

Company Name	1997 Rankings	
	Fortune 500	Forbes 500
American Stores	56	-
Deseret Management	-	342
Huntsman	-	30
Sinclair Oil	-	100
Smith's Food & Drug Centers	461	-
Steiner	-	365

Note: Companies listed are located in the city; Dashes indicate no ranking
Fortune 500: companies that produce a 10-K are ranked 1 - 500 based on 1996 revenue
Forbes 500: private companies are ranked 1 - 500 based on 1996 revenue
Source: Forbes 12/1/97; Fortune 4/28/97

Fast-Growing Businesses

According to *Inc.*, Salt Lake City is home to one of America's 100 fastest-growing private companies: Cablelink. Criteria for inclusion: must be an independent, privately-held, U.S. corporation, proprietorship or partnership; sales of at least $200,000 in 1993; five-year operating/sales history; increase in 1997 sales over 1996 sales; holding companies, regulated banks, and utilities were excluded. *Inc. 500, 1997*

Women-Owned Businesses: Number, Employment, Sales and Share

Area	Women-Owned Businesses in 1996				Share of Women-Owned Businesses in 1996	
	Number	Employment	Sales ($000)	Rank[2]	Percent (%)	Rank[3]
MSA[1]	39,500	65,500	10,289,400	42	38.0	15

Note: (1) Metropolitan Statistical Area - see Appendix A for areas included; (2) Calculated on an averaging of number of businesses, employment and sales and ranges from 1 to 50 where 1 is best; (3) Ranges from 1 to 50 where 1 is best
Source: The National Foundation for Women Business Owners, 1996 Facts on Women-Owned Businesses: Trends in the Top 50 Metropolitan Areas, March 26, 1997

Women-Owned Businesses: Growth

Area	Growth in Women-Owned Businesses (% change from 1987 to 1996)				Relative Growth in the Number of Women-Owned and All Businesses (% change from 1987 to 1996)			
	Num.	Empl.	Sales	Rank[2]	Women-Owned	All Firms	Absolute Difference	Relative Difference
MSA[1]	86.9	160.4	386.7	20	86.9	50.9	36.0	1.7:1

Note: (1) Metropolitan Statistical Area - see Appendix A for areas included; (2) Calculated on an averaging of the percent growth of number of businesses, employment and sales and ranges from 1 to 50 where 1 is best
Source: The National Foundation for Women Business Owners, 1996 Facts on Women-Owned Businesses: Trends in the Top 50 Metropolitan Areas, March 26, 1997

Small Business Opportunity

Salt Lake City was included among *Entrepreneur* magazines listing of the "20 Best Cities for Small Business." It was ranked #9 among large metro areas. Criteria: risk of failure, business performance, economic growth, affordability and state attitude towards business. *Entrepreneur, 10/97*

According to *Forbes*, Salt Lake City is home to one of America's 200 best small companies: SOS Staffing Services. Criteria: companies must be publicly traded, U.S.-based corporations with latest 12-month sales of between $5 and $350 million. Earnings must be at least $1 million for the 12-month period. Limited partnerships, REITs and closed-end mutual funds were not considered. Banks, S&Ls and electric utilities were not included. *Forbes, November 3, 1997*

HOTELS & MOTELS

Hotels/Motels

Area	Hotels/Motels	Rooms	Luxury-Level Hotels/Motels		Average Minimum Rates ($)		
			♦♦♦♦	♦♦♦♦♦	♦♦	♦♦♦	♦♦♦♦
City	34	6,236	0	0	80	98	n/a
Airport	9	1,093	0	0	n/a	n/a	n/a
Suburbs	16	1,421	0	0	n/a	n/a	n/a
Total	59	8,750	0	0	n/a	n/a	n/a

Note: n/a not available; Classifications range from one diamond (budget properties with basic amenities) to five diamond (luxury properties with the finest service, rooms and facilities).
Source: OAG, Business Travel Planner, Summer 1997

CONVENTION CENTERS

Major Convention Centers

Center Name	Meeting Rooms	Exhibit Space (sf)
ExpoMart Salt Lake	5	37,000
Salt Palace Convention Center	30	200,832

Source: Trade Shows Worldwide 1997

Living Environment

COST OF LIVING

Cost of Living Index

Composite Index	Housing	Utilities	Groceries	Health Care	Trans-portation	Misc. Goods/ Services
102.1	107.2	80.2	103.6	95.3	117.4	99.4

Note: U.S. = 100
Source: ACCRA, Cost of Living Index, 3rd Quarter 1997

HOUSING

Median Home Prices and Housing Affordability

Area	Median Price[2] 3rd Qtr. 1997 ($)	HOI[3] 3rd Qtr. 1997	Afford-ability Rank[4]
MSA[1]	155,000	44.1	181
U.S.	127,000	63.7	–

Note: (1) Metropolitan Statistical Area - see Appendix A for areas included; (2) U.S. figures calculated from the sales of 625,000 new and existing homes in 195 markets; (3) Housing Opportunity Index - percent of homes sold that were within the reach of the median income household at the prevailing mortgage interest rate; (4) Rank is from 1-195 with 1 being most affordable
Source: National Association of Home Builders, Housing Opportunity Index, 3rd Quarter 1997

It is projected that the median price of existing single-family homes in the metro area will increase by 2.7% in 1998. Nationwide, home prices are projected to increase 6.6%.
Kiplinger's Personal Finance Magazine, January 1998

Average New Home Price

Area	Price ($)
City	139,040
U.S.	135,710

Note: Figures are based on a new home with 1,800 sq. ft. of living area on an 8,000 sq. ft. lot.
Source: ACCRA, Cost of Living Index, 3rd Quarter 1997

Average Apartment Rent

Area	Rent ($/mth)
City	656
U.S.	569

Note: Figures are based on an unfurnished two bedroom, 1-1/2 or 2 bath apartment, approximately 950 sq. ft. in size, excluding all utilities except water
Source: ACCRA, Cost of Living Index, 3rd Quarter 1997

RESIDENTIAL UTILITIES

Average Residential Utility Costs

Area	All Electric ($/mth)	Part Electric ($/mth)	Other Energy ($/mth)	Phone ($/mth)
City	–	42.08	38.15	17.97
U.S.	109.40	55.25	43.64	19.48

Source: ACCRA, Cost of Living Index, 3rd Quarter 1997

HEALTH CARE

Average Health Care Costs

Area	Hospital ($/day)	Doctor ($/visit)	Dentist ($/visit)
City	396.20	43.20	57.40
U.S.	392.91	48.76	60.84

Note: Hospital - based on a semi-private room. Doctor - based on a general practitioner's routine exam of an established patient. Dentist - based on adult teeth cleaning and periodic oral exam.
Source: ACCRA, Cost of Living Index, 3rd Quarter 1997

Distribution of Office-Based Physicians

| Area | Family/Gen. Practitioners | Specialists | | |
		Medical	Surgical	Other
MSA[1]	231	633	567	615

Note: Data as of 12/31/96; (1) Metropolitan Statistical Area - see Appendix A for areas included
Source: American Medical Assn., Physician Characteristics & Distribution in the U.S., 1997-1998

Hospitals

Salt Lake City has 5 general medical and surgical hospitals, 2 psychiatric, 1 alcoholism and other chemical dependency, 2 children's other specialty. *AHA Guide to the Healthcare Field 1997-98*

According to *U.S. News and World Report,* Salt Lake City has one of the best hospitals in the U.S.: **University of Utah Hospitals and Clinics**, noted for cardiology, gynecology, orthopedics, pulmonology. *U.S. News and World Report, "America's Best Hospitals", 7/28/97*

EDUCATION

Public School District Statistics

District Name	Num. Sch.	Enroll.	Classroom Teachers[1]	Pupils per Teacher	Minority Pupils (%)	Current Exp.[2] ($/pupil)
Granite School District	97	77,106	3,496	22.1	13.0	3,208
Salt Lake City School District	40	25,712	1,294	19.9	32.5	4,035

Note: Data covers the 1995-1996 school year unless otherwise noted; (1) Excludes teachers reported as working in school district offices rather than in schools; (2) Based on 1993-94 enrollment collected by the Census Bureau, not the enrollment figure shown in column 3; SD = School District; ISD = Independent School District; n/a not available
Source: National Center for Education Statistics, Common Core of Data Survey; Bureau of the Census

Educational Quality

School District	Education Quotient[1]	Graduate Outcome[2]	Community Index[3]	Resource Index[4]
Salt Lake City	122.0	120.0	129.0	117.0

Note: Nearly 1,000 secondary school districts were rated in terms of educational quality. The scores range from a low of 50 to a high of 150; (1) Average of the Graduate Outcome, Community and Resource indexes; (2) Based on graduation rates and college board scores (SAT/ACT); (3) Based on the surrounding community's average level of education and the area's average income level; (4) Based on teacher salaries, per-pupil expenditures and student-teacher ratios.
Source: Expansion Management, Ratings Issue 1997

Educational Attainment by Race

| Area | High School Graduate (%) | | | | | Bachelor's Degree (%) | | | | |
	Total	White	Black	Other	Hisp.[2]	Total	White	Black	Other	Hisp.[2]
City	83.0	85.0	67.3	66.3	57.2	30.4	31.7	14.8	20.6	10.6
MSA[1]	85.6	86.6	76.1	68.4	62.1	22.9	23.4	15.5	15.5	8.9
U.S.	75.2	77.9	63.1	60.4	49.8	20.3	21.5	11.4	19.4	9.2

Note: figures shown cover persons 25 years old and over; (1) Metropolitan Statistical Area - see Appendix A for areas included; (2) people of Hispanic origin can be of any race
Source: 1990 Census of Population and Housing, Summary Tape File 3C

School Enrollment by Type

| Area | Preprimary | | | | Elementary/High School | | | |
| | Public | | Private | | Public | | Private | |
	Enrollment	%	Enrollment	%	Enrollment	%	Enrollment	%
City	1,786	57.0	1,348	43.0	23,141	93.5	1,608	6.5
MSA[1]	17,219	63.6	9,848	36.4	246,375	96.8	8,205	3.2
U.S.	2,679,029	59.5	1,824,256	40.5	38,379,689	90.2	4,187,099	9.8

Note: figures shown cover persons 3 years old and over;
(1) Metropolitan Statistical Area - see Appendix A for areas included
Source: 1990 Census of Population and Housing, Summary Tape File 3C

School Enrollment by Race

Area	Preprimary (%)				Elementary/High School (%)			
	White	Black	Other	Hisp.[1]	White	Black	Other	Hisp.[1]
City	86.1	1.9	12.1	9.8	82.2	1.9	15.9	14.6
MSA[2]	94.5	1.1	4.4	5.2	93.2	0.9	6.0	6.4
U.S.	80.4	12.5	7.1	7.8	74.1	15.6	10.3	12.5

Note: figures shown cover persons 3 years old and over; (1) people of Hispanic origin can be of any race; (2) Metropolitan Statistical Area - see Appendix A for areas included
Source: 1990 Census of Population and Housing, Summary Tape File 3C

SAT/ACT Scores

Area/District	1997 SAT				1997 ACT	
	Percent of Graduates Tested (%)	Average Math Score	Average Verbal Score	Average Combined Score	Percent of Graduates Tested (%)	Average Composite Score
Salt Lake City SD	12	570	583	1,153	54	22.5
State	4	570	576	1,146	69	21.5
U.S.	42	511	505	1,016	36	21.0

Note: Math and verbal SAT scores are out of a possible 800; ACT scores are out of a possible 36
Caution: Comparing or ranking states/cities on the basis of SAT/ACT scores alone is invalid and strongly discouraged by the The College Board and The American College Testing Program as students who take the tests are self-selected and do not represent the entire student population.
Source: Salt Lake City School District, Curriculum Department, 1997; American College Testing Program, 1997; College Board, 1997

Classroom Teacher Salaries in Public Schools

District	B.A. Degree		M.A. Degree		Ph.D. Degree	
	Min. ($)	Max ($)	Min. ($)	Max. ($)	Min. ($)	Max. ($)
Salt Lake City	24,110	34,277	27,343	41,333	n/a	n/a
Average1	26,120	39,270	28,175	44,667	31,643	49,825

Note: Salaries are for 1996-1997; (1) Based on all school districts covered; n/a not available
Source: American Federation of Teachers (unpublished data)

Higher Education

Two-Year Colleges		Four-Year Colleges		Medical Schools	Law Schools	Voc/ Tech
Public	Private	Public	Private			
0	0	1	1	1	1	17

Source: College Blue Book, Occupational Education 1997; Medical School Admission Requirements, 1998-99; Peterson's Guide to Two-Year Colleges, 1997; Peterson's Guide to Four-Year Colleges, 1997; Barron's Guide to Law Schools 1997

MAJOR EMPLOYERS

Major Employers

Associated Food Stores
Compaq International (computers)
Franklin Quest Co. (publishing)
Huish Detergents
Megahertz Corp. (pumps)
Renco Metals
University of Utah Hospital

Blue Cross & Blue Shield of Utah
First Security Service
HCA Health Services of Utah
Huntsman Family Corp. (plastics)
Pioneer Valley Hospital
O.C. Tanner Co. (jewelry)
Utah Transit Authority

Note: companies listed are located in the city
Source: Dun's Business Rankings 1997; Ward's Business Directory, 1997

PUBLIC SAFETY

Crime Rate

Area	All Crimes	Violent Crimes				Property Crimes		
		Murder	Forcible Rape	Robbery	Aggrav. Assault	Burglary	Larceny -Theft	Motor Vehicle Theft
City	12,367.1	11.1	84.4	328.0	409.6	1,673.3	8,268.4	1,592.3
Suburbs[1]	6,127.4	3.0	40.6	62.8	244.8	850.4	4,524.1	401.7
MSA[2]	7,037.6	4.2	47.0	101.5	268.9	970.4	5,070.3	575.4
U.S.	5,078.9	7.4	36.1	202.4	388.2	943.0	2,975.9	525.9

Note: Crime rate is the number of crimes per 100,000 pop.; (1) defined as all areas within the MSA but located outside the central city; (2) Metropolitan Statistical Area - see Appendix A for areas incl.
Source: FBI Uniform Crime Reports 1996

RECREATION

Culture and Recreation

Museums	Symphony Orchestras	Opera Companies	Dance Companies	Professional Theatres	Zoos	Pro Sports Teams
6	3	1	2	3	1	1

Source: International Directory of the Performing Arts, 1996; Official Museum Directory, 1998; Chamber of Commerce/Economic Development 1997

Library System

The Salt Lake City Public Library has five branches, holdings of 495,738 volumes and a budget of $n/a (1995). The Salt Lake County Library System has 16 branches, holdings of 1,385,765 volumes and a budget of $15,394,596 (1995). Note: n/a means not available.
American Library Directory, 1997-1998

MEDIA

Newspapers

Name	Type	Freq.	Distribution	Circulation
The Deseret News	n/a	7x/wk	State	63,000
The Event	n/a	26x/yr	Local	36,000
Intermountain Catholic	Religious	1x/wk	State	13,667
The Salt Lake Tribune	n/a	7x/wk	Area	186,824
Utah Chronicle	n/a	5x/wk	Campus	community & alumni
The West Valley Eagle	n/a	1x/wk	Local	20,000

Note: Includes newspapers with circulations of 1,000 or more located in the city; n/a not available
Source: Burrelle's Media Directory, 1998 Edition

AM Radio Stations

Call Letters	Freq. (kHz)	Target Audience	Station Format	Music Format
KTKK	630	General	E/N/T	n/a
KFAM	700	General	M	Easy Listening
KCNR	860	General	n/a	n/a
KALL	910	General	N/S/T	n/a
KKDS	1060	General	M	n/a
KANN	1120	Religious	E/M/N	Christian
KSL	1160	General	N/T	n/a
KMGR	1230	Hispanic	M	Oldies
KDYL	1280	General	M	MOR
KFNZ	1320	General	S	n/a
KSOP	1370	General	M	Country

Note: Stations included broadcast in the Salt Lake City metro area; n/a not available
Station Format: E = Educational; M = Music; N = News; S = Sports; T = Talk
Music Format: AOR = Album Oriented Rock; MOR = Middle-of-the-Road
Source: Burrelle's Media Directory, 1998 Edition

FM Radio Stations

Call Letters	Freq. (mHz)	Target Audience	Station Format	Music Format
KUER	90.1	General	M/N	Classical/Jazz
KRCL	90.9	General	M/N	n/a
KUFR	91.7	n/a	E/M/N/T	Christian
KMGR	92.1	General	M/N/S	Adult Contemporary
KUBL	93.3	General	M/N/S	Country
KODJ	94.1	General	M	Oldies
KZHT	94.9	General	M	Contemporary Top 40
KXRK	96.3	Alternative	M	Adult Contemporary
KISN	97.1	n/a	M	Adult Contemporary
KBZN	97.9	General	M	Jazz
KBEE	98.7	General	M/N/S	Adult Contemporary
KURR	99.5	Nat. Amer.	M/N/S	Alternative
KSFI	100.3	General	M	Adult Contemporary
KBER	101.1	n/a	M/N/S	AOR/Alternative
KKAT	101.9	General	M/N/S	Country
KQMB	102.7	General	M	Adult Contemporary/Country
KRSP	103.5	General	M	AOR
KSOP	104.3	General	M/N/S	Country
KUMT	105.7	General	M	Easy Listening
KENZ	107.5	General	M	Alternative

Note: Stations included broadcast in the Salt Lake City metro area; n/a not available
Station Format: E = Educational; M = Music; N = News; S = Sports; T = Talk
Music Format: AOR = Album Oriented Rock; MOR = Middle-of-the-Road
Source: Burrelle's Media Directory, 1998 Edition

Television Stations

Name	Ch.	Affiliation	Type	Owner
KUTV	2	CBS	Commercial	Westinghouse Broadcasting Company/CBS
KTVX	4	ABC	Commercial	Chris Craft
KSL	5	NBC	Commercial	Bonneville International Corporation
KUED	7	PBS	Public	University of Utah
KULC	9	PBS	Public	Utah State Board of Regents
KSTU	13	Fox	Commercial	Fox Television Stations Inc.
KJZZ	14	UPN	Commercial	Larry H. Miller Communications

Note: Stations included broadcast in the Salt Lake City metro area
Source: Burrelle's Media Directory, 1998 Edition

CLIMATE

Average and Extreme Temperatures

Temperature	Jan	Feb	Mar	Apr	May	Jun	Jul	Aug	Sep	Oct	Nov	Dec	Ann
Extreme High (°F)	62	69	78	85	93	104	107	104	100	89	75	67	107
Average High (°F)	37	43	52	62	72	83	93	90	80	66	50	38	64
Average Temp. (°F)	28	34	41	50	59	69	78	76	65	53	40	30	52
Average Low (°F)	19	24	31	38	46	54	62	61	51	40	30	22	40
Extreme Low (°F)	-22	-14	2	15	25	35	40	37	27	16	-14	-15	-22

Note: Figures cover the years 1948-1990
Source: National Climatic Data Center, International Station Meteorological Climate Summary, 3/95

Average Precipitation/Snowfall/Humidity

Precip./Humidity	Jan	Feb	Mar	Apr	May	Jun	Jul	Aug	Sep	Oct	Nov	Dec	Ann
Avg. Precip. (in.)	1.3	1.2	1.8	2.0	1.7	0.9	0.8	0.9	1.1	1.3	1.3	1.4	15.6
Avg. Snowfall (in.)	13	10	11	6	1	Tr	0	0	Tr	2	6	13	63
Avg. Rel. Hum. 5am (%)	79	77	71	67	66	60	53	54	60	68	75	79	67
Avg. Rel. Hum. 5pm (%)	69	59	47	38	33	26	22	23	28	40	59	71	43

Note: Figures cover the years 1948-1990; Tr = Trace amounts (<0.05 in. of rain; <0.5 in. of snow)
Source: National Climatic Data Center, International Station Meteorological Climate Summary, 3/95

Weather Conditions

Temperature			Daytime Sky			Precipitation		
5°F & below	32°F & below	90°F & above	Clear	Partly cloudy	Cloudy	0.01 inch or more precip.	0.1 inch or more snow/ice	Thunder-storms
7	128	56	94	152	119	92	38	38

Note: Figures are average number of days per year and covers the years 1948-1990
Source: National Climatic Data Center, International Station Meteorological Climate Summary, 3/95

AIR & WATER QUALITY

Maximum Pollutant Concentrations

	Particulate Matter (ug/m³)	Carbon Monoxide (ppm)	Sulfur Dioxide (ppm)	Nitrogen Dioxide (ppm)	Ozone (ppm)	Lead (ug/m³)
MSA[1] Level	157	7	0.021	0.026	0.12	0.03
NAAQS[2]	150	9	0.140	0.053	0.12	1.50
Met NAAQS?	No	Yes	Yes	Yes	Yes	Yes

Note: (1) Metropolitan Statistical Area - see Appendix A for areas included; (2) National Ambient Air Quality Standards; ppm = parts per million; ug/m³ = micrograms per cubic meter; n/a not available
Source: EPA, National Air Quality and Emissions Trends Report, 1996

Pollutant Standards Index

In the Salt Lake City MSA (see Appendix A for areas included), the Pollutant Standards Index (PSI) exceeded 100 on 6 days in 1996. A PSI value greater than 100 indicates that air quality would be in the unhealthful range on that day. *EPA, National Air Quality and Emissions Trends Report, 1996*

Drinking Water

Water System Name	Pop. Served	Primary Water Source Type	Number of Violations in Fiscal Year 1997	Type of Violation/ Contaminants
Metropolitan WD of Salt Lake City	700,000	Surface	None	None
Salt Lake City Water System	305,835	Surface	45	(1)

Note: Data as of January 16, 1998; (1) System failed to conduct initial or repeat sampling, or to accurately report an analytical result for specific contaminants (nitrate, endrin, aldicarb, aldicarb sulfone, aldicarb sulfoxide, barium, arsenic, dioxin, simazine, picloram, oxamyl (Vydate), hexachlorocyclopentadiene, hexachlorobenzene (HCB), total thallium, cyanide, total beryllium, total antimony, fluoride, selenium, mercury, chromium, cadmium, glyphosate, endothall, diquat, dinoseb, di(2-ethylhexyl) phthalate), di(2-ethylhexyl) adipate, dalapon, benzo (A) pyrene, pentachlorophenol, total polychlorinated biphenyls (PCB), heptachlor epoxide, heptachlor, ethylene dibromide (EDB), 1,2 dibromo-3-chloropropane (DBCP), chlordane, carbofuran, atrazine, alachlor (Lasso), methoxychlor, toxaphene, 2,4,5-TP (Silvex), 2,4-D and BHC-gamma (Lindane).
Source: EPA, Office of Ground Water and Drinking Water, Safe Drinking Water Information System

Salt Lake City tap water is alkaline, hard and fluoridated.
Editor & Publisher Market Guide, 1998

San Diego, California

Background

San Diego is the archetypal southern California city. Located 100 miles south of Los Angeles, near the Mexican border, San Diego is characterized by bright, sunny days; an excellent harbor; a populous citizenry that alludes to its Spanish heritage; and recreational activities that demand enjoyment of its ideal weather conditions.

San Diego was first claimed in 1542 for Spain by Juan Rodriguez Cabrillo, a Portuguese navigator in the service of the Spanish Crown. The site remained uneventful until 1769, when Spanish colonizer, Gaspar de Portola, established a permanent settlement there. It was the first European settlement in California. Accompanying de Portola was a Franciscan monk named Junipero Serra, who established the Mission Basilica San Diego de Alcala, the first of a chain of missions along the California coast.

After San Diego fell under the U.S. flag during the Mexican War of 1846, the city existed in relative isolation, deferring status and importance to its sister cities in the north: Los Angeles and San Francisco. Even when San Francisco businessman, Alonzo Horton, bought 1,000 acres of land near the harbor in 1867, to establish a logical and practical downtown there, San Diego remained secondary to Los Angeles and San Francisco. The city saw a decrease in population from 40,000 in 1880 to 17,000 at the turn of the century.

World War II repopulated the city, when the Navy moved one of its bases from Pearl Harbor to San Diego. The naval base brought personnel and a number of related industries, such as nuclear and oceanographic research, and aviation development.

Today, San Diego is the second most populous city in California with plenty of outdoor activities, jobs, fine educational institutions, theaters, and museums with which to attract new residents, young and old alike.

The San Diego area has also become a center for wireless industries being led by Qualcomm with 7,500 employees and net sales of over $800 million in 1996. It is also the home base of a new digital cellular transmission standard known as C.D. M.A., now the fastest-growing wireless technology in the U.S. The intellectual brains behind this technology is the University of California at San Diego's School of Engineering's Center for Wireless Communications founded in 1995. *New York Times 3/24/97*

According to the February 1998 issue of *Worth Magazine,* the western part of the U.S. from Seattle to Silicon Valley, from San Diego to Denver is becoming the center for all the hot growth industries namely telecommunications, biomedical products, software, financial services to name a few. San Diego leads the country in biotechnology companies that are attracting venture capital.

Still, San Diego has its problems. It needs a larger airport, more and larger commercial piers, better rail connections and a better water supply. *New York Times, 8/11/96*

San Diego's summers are cool and winters are warm in comparison with other locations along the same general latitude. The Pacific Ocean is responsible for these great weather conditions.

A marked feature of the climate, is the wide variation in temperature within short distances. In nearby valleys, for example, daytimes temperatures are much warmer in summer and nights noticeably cooler in winter. As is usual on the Pacific Coast, nighttime and early morning cloudiness is the norm. Considerable fog occurs along the coast, especially during the winter months.

General Rankings and Evaluative Comments

- San Diego was ranked #28 out of 300 cities by *Money's* 1997 "Survey of the Best Places to Live." Criteria used: health services, crime, economy, housing, education, transportation, weather, leisure and the arts. The city was ranked #16 in 1996 and #86 in 1995. *Money, July 1997; Money, September 1996; Money, September 1995*

- *Ladies Home Journal* ranked America's 200 largest cities based on the qualities women care about most. San Diego ranked 42 out of 200. Criteria: low crime rate, good public schools, well-paying jobs, quality health and child care, the presence of women in government, proportion of women-owned businesses, size of the wage gap with men, local economy, divorce rates, the ratio of single men to single women, whether there are laws that require at least the same number of public toilets for women as men, and the probability of good hair days. *Ladies Home Journal, November 1997*

- San Diego was ranked #66 out of 219 cities in terms of children's health, safety, and economic well-being. Criteria: total population, percent population change, birth rate, child immunization rate, infant mortality rate, percent low birth weight infants, percent of births to teens, physician-to-population ratio, student-to-teacher ratio, dropout rate, unemployment rate, median family income, percent of children in poverty, violent and property crime rates, number of juvenile arrests for violent crimes as a percent of the total crime index, number of days with pollution standard index (PSI) over 100, pounds toxic releases per 1,000 people and number of superfund sites. *Zero Population Growth, Children's Environmental Index 1997*

- *Conde Nast Traveler* polled 37,000 readers in terms of travel satisfaction. Cities were ranked based on the following criteria: people/friendliness, environment/ambiance, cultural enrichment, restaurants and fun/energy. San Diego appeared in the top thirty, ranking number 17, with an overall rating of 64.3 out of 100 based on all the criteria. The cities were also ranked in each category separately. San Diego appeared in the top 10 based on environment/ambiance, ranking number 10 with a rating of 78.9 out of 100. San Diego appeared in the top 10 based on fun/energy, ranking number 10 with a rating of 70.6 out of 100. *Conde Nast Traveler, Readers' Choice Poll 1997*

- *Yahoo! Internet Life* selected "America's 100 Most Wired Cities & Towns". 50 cities were large and 50 cities were small. San Diego ranked 12 out of 50 large cities. Criteria: Internet users per capita, number of networked computers, number of registered domain names, Internet backbone traffic, and the per-capita number of Web sites devoted to each city. *Yahoo! Internet Life, March 1998*

- According to *Working Mother*, "Lawmakers here—on both sides of the aisle—have agreed that the state must kick in more money to help working parents find and pay for child care. To that end, Governor Pete Wilson has proposed a significant expansion of the state's child care budget—an additional $277 million in state and federal funds. The new money would pay for care for about 90,000 more kids a year; and for preschool for another 13,000. In addition, some $45 million will be spent on recruiting and training caregivers for infants and toddlers.

  To help parents become more informed consumers, California passed a law that many consider a step backward. It allows family child care providers to care for two more kids, without hiring additional help. This means a family child care provider can now care for up to eight kids, instead of six, without additional help. The new rule also worries child care advocates because it may limit infant care in California. When caregivers take in the two extra older children, they must reduce the number of babies in their care. (California is among the 10 best states for child care.)" *Working Mother, July/August 1997*

Business Environment

STATE ECONOMY

State Economic Profile

"California's expansion is strong and stable....Entertainment and filmmaking remain steady contributors to the state's improved income growth and labor markets....

California's banking industry is consolidating and shedding workers. Improved credit conditions and healthy balance sheets make many remaining California thrifts likely takeover targets for out-of-state banks.

Delinquency rates on consumer credit have declined for the past two years and are well below the U.S. average. Mortgage foreclosure rates remain high, but they are down from the peak of one year ago when mortgage lenders took advantage of the improved housing market to shed nonperforming loans. California consumers remain cautious, however. Retail sales growth last year of 5% was no better than the national average.

Housing prices are up in northern California, and the number of units sold is rising throughout the state. Multifamily units dominated construction activity last year. With population growth accelerating and income growth outpacing the U.S. for the first time this decade, demand for single-family homes will strengthen.

Housing prices are up in northern California, and the number of units sold is rising throughout the state. Multifamily units dominated construction activity last year. With population growth accelerating the income growth outpacing the U.S. for the first time this decade, demand for single-family homes will strengthen.

Construction will contribute to the near-term expansion as home building accelerates. The greatest risk to the California economy is that the rising dollar could choke off foreign demand for California's export products. Longer term there will be some consolidation among high-tech firms, and high costs will limit the breadth of industrial development. California will remain an average performer over the long term." *National Association of Realtors, Economic Profiles: The Fifty States, July 1997*

IMPORTS/EXPORTS

Total Export Sales

Area	1993 ($000)	1994 ($000)	1995 ($000)	1996 ($000)	% Chg. 1993-96	% Chg. 1995-96
MSA[1]	4,357,749	4,867,278	5,860,940	6,719,405	54.2	14.6
U.S.	464,858,354	512,415,609	583,030,524	622,827,063	34.0	6.8

Note: (1) Metropolitan Statistical Area - see Appendix A for areas included
Source: U.S. Department of Commerce, International Trade Association, Metropolitan Area Exports: An Export Performance Report on Over 250 U.S. Cities, October 1997

Imports/Exports by Port

Type	Cargo Value			Share of U.S. Total	
	1995 (US$mil.)	1996 (US$mil.)	% Change 1995-1996	1995 (%)	1996 (%)
Imports	324	714	120.03	0.08	0.19
Exports	346	135	-61.05	0.15	0.06

Source: Global Trade Information Services, WaterBorne Trade Atlas 1997

CITY FINANCES

City Government Finances

Component	FY94 ($000)	FY94 (per capita $)
Revenue	1,476,593	1,278.09
Expenditure	1,379,738	1,194.26
Debt Outstanding	1,807,021	1,564.10
Cash & Securities	3,262,071	2,823.55

Source: U.S. Bureau of the Census, City Government Finances: 1993-94

City Government Revenue by Source

Source	FY94 ($000)	FY94 (per capita $)	FY94 (%)
From Federal Government	111,085	96.15	7.5
From State Governments	106,325	92.03	7.2
From Local Governments	54,400	47.09	3.7
Property Taxes	138,122	119.55	9.4
General Sales Taxes	126,300	109.32	8.6
Selective Sales Taxes	77,301	66.91	5.2
Income Taxes	0	0.00	0.0
Current Charges	248,924	215.46	16.9
Utility/Liquor Store	155,782	134.84	10.6
Employee Retirement[1]	111,030	96.10	7.5
Other	347,324	300.63	23.5

Note: (1) Excludes "city contributions," classified as "nonrevenue," intragovernmental transfers.
Source: U.S. Bureau of the Census, City Government Finances: 1993-94

City Government Expenditures by Function

Function	FY94 ($000)	FY94 (per capita $)	FY94 (%)
Educational Services	21,212	18.36	1.5
Employee Retirement[1]	58,109	50.30	4.2
Environment/Housing	505,852	437.85	36.7
Government Administration	69,661	60.30	5.0
Interest on General Debt	132,001	114.26	9.6
Public Safety	257,671	223.03	18.7
Social Services	1,181	1.02	0.1
Transportation	81,661	70.68	5.9
Utility/Liquor Store	207,380	179.50	15.0
Other	45,010	38.96	3.3

Note: (1) Payments to beneficiaries including withdrawal of contributions.
Source: U.S. Bureau of the Census, City Government Finances: 1993-94

Municipal Bond Ratings

Area	Moody's	S & P
San Diego	Aa1	AA

Note: n/a not available; n/r not rated
Source: Moody's Bond Record, 2/98; Statistical Abstract of the U.S., 1997;
Governing Magazine, 9/97, 3/98

POPULATION

Population Growth

Area	1980	1990	% Chg. 1980-90	July 1996 Estimate	% Chg. 1990-96
City	875,538	1,110,549	26.8	1,171,121	5.5
MSA[1]	1,861,846	2,498,016	34.2	2,655,463	6.3
U.S.	226,545,805	248,765,170	9.8	265,179,411	6.6

Note: (1) Metropolitan Statistical Area - see Appendix A for areas included
Source: 1980/1990 Census of Housing and Population, Summary Tape File 3C;
Census Bureau Population Estimates

Population Characteristics

Race	City 1980 Population	%	City 1990 Population	%	% Chg. 1980-90	MSA[1] 1990 Population	%
White	674,268	77.0	746,381	67.2	10.7	1,875,517	75.1
Black	77,508	8.9	103,668	9.3	33.8	157,495	6.3
Amer Indian/Esk/Aleut	5,833	0.7	7,252	0.7	24.3	21,509	0.9
Asian/Pacific Islander	61,655	7.0	131,444	11.8	113.2	198,675	8.0
Other	56,274	6.4	121,804	11.0	116.4	244,820	9.8
Hispanic Origin[2]	130,613	14.9	223,616	20.1	71.2	498,578	20.0

Note: (1) Metropolitan Statistical Area - see Appendix A for areas included;
(2) people of Hispanic origin can be of any race
Source: 1980/1990 Census of Housing and Population, Summary Tape File 3C

Ancestry

Area	German	Irish	English	Italian	U.S.	French	Polish	Dutch
City	17.8	11.8	12.4	4.7	2.2	3.5	2.4	1.7
MSA[1]	20.8	13.6	14.5	4.9	2.6	4.2	2.5	2.2
U.S.	23.3	15.6	13.1	5.9	5.3	4.2	3.8	2.5

Note: Figures are percentages and include persons that reported multiple ancestry (eg. if a person reported being Irish and Italian, they were included in both columns); (1) Metropolitan Statistical Area - see Appendix A for areas included
Source: 1990 Census of Population and Housing, Summary Tape File 3C

Age

Area	Median Age (Years)	Age Distribution (%) Under 5	Under 18	18-24	25-44	45-64	65+	80+
City	30.5	7.3	23.1	14.4	36.6	15.7	10.2	2.1
MSA[1]	30.8	7.7	24.5	13.2	35.4	16.0	10.9	2.3
U.S.	32.9	7.3	25.6	10.5	32.6	18.7	12.5	2.8

Note: (1) Metropolitan Statistical Area - see Appendix A for areas included
Source: 1990 Census of Population and Housing, Summary Tape File 3C

Male/Female Ratio

Area	Number of males per 100 females (all ages)	Number of males per 100 females (18 years old+)
City	104.2	103.7
MSA[1]	103.8	103.5
U.S.	95.0	91.9

Note: (1) Metropolitan Statistical Area - see Appendix A for areas included
Source: 1990 Census of Population, General Population Characteristics

INCOME

Per Capita/Median/Average Income

Area	Per Capita ($)	Median Household ($)	Average Household ($)
City	16,401	33,686	43,627
MSA[1]	16,220	35,022	44,375
U.S.	14,420	30,056	38,453

Note: all figures are for 1989; (1) Metropolitan Statistical Area - see Appendix A for areas included
Source: 1990 Census of Population and Housing, Summary Tape File 3C

Household Income Distribution by Race

Income ($)	City (%)					U.S. (%)				
	Total	White	Black	Other	Hisp.[1]	Total	White	Black	Other	Hisp.[1]
Less than 5,000	4.0	3.2	7.4	6.2	5.8	6.2	4.8	15.2	8.6	8.8
5,000 - 9,999	7.7	6.8	13.5	9.0	11.8	9.3	8.6	14.2	9.9	11.1
10,000 - 14,999	7.8	7.1	10.7	9.3	11.8	8.8	8.5	11.0	9.8	11.0
15,000 - 24,999	16.6	15.6	20.2	19.3	21.6	17.5	17.3	18.9	18.5	20.5
25,000 - 34,999	15.7	15.4	16.3	16.3	16.4	15.8	16.1	14.2	15.4	16.4
35,000 - 49,999	18.3	18.8	15.9	17.4	16.2	17.9	18.6	13.3	16.1	16.0
50,000 - 74,999	17.3	18.4	11.4	15.3	11.3	15.0	15.8	9.3	13.4	11.1
75,000 - 99,999	6.7	7.5	3.2	4.7	3.2	5.1	5.5	2.6	4.7	3.1
100,000+	5.9	7.2	1.3	2.4	1.9	4.4	4.8	1.3	3.7	1.9

Note: all figures are for 1989; (1) people of Hispanic origin can be of any race
Source: 1990 Census of Population and Housing, Summary Tape File 3C

Effective Buying Income

Area	Per Capita ($)	Median Household ($)	Average Household ($)
City	15,139	33,339	42,602
MSA[1]	15,323	35,379	44,536
U.S.	15,444	33,201	41,849

Note: data as of 1/1/97; (1) Metropolitan Statistical Area - see Appendix A for areas included
Source: Standard Rate & Data Service, Newspaper Advertising Source, 2/98

Effective Household Buying Income Distribution

Area	% of Households Earning						
	$10,000 -$19,999	$20,000 -$34,999	$35,000 -$49,999	$50,000 -$74,999	$75,000 -$99,000	$100,000 -$124,999	$125,000 and up
City	16.8	24.5	18.8	18.3	6.1	2.0	2.4
MSA[1]	15.7	24.1	19.2	19.8	6.8	2.2	2.6
U.S.	16.5	23.4	18.3	18.2	6.4	2.1	2.4

Note: data as of 1/1/97; (1) Metropolitan Statistical Area - see Appendix A for areas included
Source: Standard Rate & Data Service, Newspaper Advertising Source, 2/98

Poverty Rates by Race and Age

Area	Total (%)	By Race (%)				By Age (%)		
		White	Black	Other	Hisp.[2]	Under 5 years old	Under 18 years old	65 years and over
City	13.4	9.3	23.1	21.3	25.6	20.8	19.8	7.4
MSA[1]	11.3	8.4	21.3	19.9	22.8	17.2	16.2	6.3
U.S.	13.1	9.8	29.5	23.1	25.3	20.1	18.3	12.8

Note: figures show the percent of people living below the poverty line in 1989. The average poverty
threshold was $12,674 for a family of four in 1989; (1) Metropolitan Statistical Area - see Appendix A
for areas included; (2) people of Hispanic origin can be of any race
Source: 1990 Census of Population and Housing, Summary Tape File 3C

EMPLOYMENT

Labor Force and Employment

Area	Civilian Labor Force			Workers Employed		
	Dec. '95	Dec. '96	% Chg.	Dec. '95	Dec. '96	% Chg.
City	565,302	575,958	1.9	541,976	557,491	2.9
MSA[1]	1,232,606	1,256,057	1.9	1,182,656	1,216,513	2.9
U.S.	134,583,000	136,742,000	1.6	127,903,000	130,785,000	2.3

Note: Data is not seasonally adjusted and covers workers 16 years of age and older;
(1) Metropolitan Statistical Area - see Appendix A for areas included
Source: Bureau of Labor Statistics, http://stats.bls.gov

Unemployment Rate

Area	1997											
	Jan.	Feb.	Mar.	Apr.	May	Jun.	Jul.	Aug.	Sep.	Oct.	Nov.	Dec.
City	5.0	4.7	4.5	4.4	4.4	4.6	4.8	4.6	4.7	4.3	3.7	3.2
MSA[1]	5.0	4.6	4.4	4.4	4.3	4.5	4.7	4.6	4.6	4.2	3.6	3.1
U.S.	5.9	5.7	5.5	4.8	4.7	5.2	5.0	4.8	4.7	4.4	4.3	4.4

Note: Data is not seasonally adjusted and covers workers 16 years of age and older; All figures are percentages; (1) Metropolitan Statistical Area - see Appendix A for areas included
Source: Bureau of Labor Statistics, http://stats.bls.gov

Employment by Industry

Sector	MSA[1]		U.S.
	Number of Employees	Percent of Total	Percent of Total
Services	344,400	32.0	29.0
Retail Trade	204,900	19.1	18.5
Government	197,400	18.4	16.1
Manufacturing	124,000	11.5	15.0
Finance/Insurance/Real Estate	61,900	5.8	5.7
Wholesale Trade	45,000	4.2	5.4
Transportation/Public Utilities	42,400	3.9	5.3
Construction	54,900	5.1	4.5
Mining	400	0.0	0.5

Note: Figures cover non-farm employment as of 12/97 and are not seasonally adjusted;
(1) Metropolitan Statistical Area - see Appendix A for areas included
Source: Bureau of Labor Statistics, http://stats.bls.gov

Employment by Occupation

Occupation Category	City (%)	MSA[1] (%)	U.S. (%)
White Collar	66.5	63.4	58.1
Executive/Admin./Management	14.9	14.6	12.3
Professional	17.6	15.5	14.1
Technical & Related Support	5.0	4.4	3.7
Sales	12.7	13.0	11.8
Administrative Support/Clerical	16.3	15.9	16.3
Blue Collar	18.2	21.1	26.2
Precision Production/Craft/Repair	9.4	11.1	11.3
Machine Operators/Assem./Insp.	3.7	3.9	6.8
Transportation/Material Movers	2.3	2.7	4.1
Cleaners/Helpers/Laborers	2.7	3.3	3.9
Services	13.9	13.4	13.2
Farming/Forestry/Fishing	1.4	2.1	2.5

Note: figures cover employed persons 16 years old and over;
(1) Metropolitan Statistical Area - see Appendix A for areas included
Source: 1990 Census of Population and Housing, Summary Tape File 3C

Occupational Employment Projections: 1994 - 2001

Occupations Expected to have the Largest Job Growth (ranked by numerical growth)	Fast-Growing Occupations[1] (ranked by percent growth)
1. Salespersons, retail	1. Computer engineers
2. Cashiers	2. Systems analysts
3. General managers & top executives	3. Home health aides
4. Waiters & waitresses	4. Ushers/lobby attendants/ticket takers
5. Instructional aides	5. Food service and lodging managers
6. Guards	6. Demonstrators/promoters/models
7. Systems analysts	7. Chemists, exc. biochemists
8. Receptionists and information clerks	8. Occupational therapists
9. Janitors/cleaners/maids, ex. priv. hshld.	9. Corrections officers & jailers
10. Secretaries, except legal & medical	10. Amusement and recreation attendants

Projections cover San Diego County.
Note: (1) Excludes occupations with employment of less than 700 in 2001
Source: State of California, Employment Development Department, Labor Market Information Division, Information Services Group

Average Wages

Occupation	Wage	Occupation	Wage
Professional/Technical/Clerical	$/Week	**Health/Protective Services**	$/Week
Accountants III	842	Corrections Officers	695
Attorneys III	1,333	Firefighters	818
Budget Analysts III	-	Nurses, Licensed Practical II	-
Buyers/Contracting Specialists II	670	Nurses, Registered II	-
Clerks, Accounting III	456	Nursing Assistants II	-
Clerks, General III	414	Police Officers I	840
Computer Operators II	471	**Hourly Workers**	$/Hour
Computer Programmers II	-	Forklift Operators	-
Drafters II	545	General Maintenance Workers	9.53
Engineering Technicians III	-	Guards I	6.31
Engineering Technicians, Civil III	694	Janitors	8.38
Engineers III	893	Maintenance Electricians	18.25
Key Entry Operators I	339	Maintenance Electronics Techs II	17.48
Personnel Assistants III	518	Maintenance Machinists	-
Personnel Specialists III	819	Maintenance Mechanics, Machinery	19.28
Secretaries III	585	Material Handling Laborers	-
Switchboard Operator-Receptionist	351	Motor Vehicle Mechanics	16.25
Systems Analysts II	954	Shipping/Receiving Clerks	7.92
Systems Analysts Supervisor/Mgr II	-	Tool and Die Makers	20.41
Tax Collectors II	-	Truckdrivers, Tractor Trailer	-
Word Processors II	488	Warehouse Specialists	-

Note: Wage data includes full-time workers only for 7/96 and cover the Metropolitan Statistical Area (see Appendix A for areas included). Dashes indicate that data was not available.
Source: Bureau of Labor Statistics, Occupational Compensation Survey, 1/97

TAXES

Major State and Local Tax Rates

State Corp. Income (%)	State Personal Income (%)	Residential Property (effective rate per $100)	Sales & Use		State Gasoline (cents/ gallon)	State Cigarette (cents/ 20-pack)
			State (%)	Local (%)		
8.84[a]	1.0 - 9.3	n/a	6.0	1.75	18[b]	37

Note: Personal/corporate income tax rates as of 1/97. Sales, gasoline and cigarette tax rates as of 1/98; (a) Minimum tax is $800. The tax rate on S-Corporations is 1.5%; (b) Does not include 1 cent local option tax
Source: Federation of Tax Administrators, www.taxadmin.org; Washington D.C. Department of Finance and Revenue, Tax Rates and Tax Burdens in the District of Columbia: A Nationwide Comparison, June 1997; Chamber of Commerce

Total Taxes Per Capita and as a Percent of Income

Area	Per Capita Income ($)	Per Capita Taxes ($)			Taxes as Pct. of Income (%)		
		Total	Federal	State/Local	Total	Federal	State/Local
California	27,117	9,321	6,287	3,034	34.4	23.2	11.2
U.S.	26,187	9,205	6,127	3,078	35.2	23.4	11.8

Note: Figures are for 1997
Source: Tax Foundation, Web Site, www.taxfoundation.org

COMMERCIAL REAL ESTATE

Office Market

Class/Location	Total Space (sq. ft.)	Vacant Space (sq. ft.)	Vac. Rate (%)	Under Constr. (sq. ft.)	Net Absorp. (sq. ft.)	Rental Rates ($/sq.ft./yr.)
Class A						
CBD	10,440,325	1,503,407	14.4	n/a	219,247	19.80-21.60
Outside CBD	29,395,358	2,116,456	7.2	240,000	789,164	18.00-25.00
Class B						
CBD	5,872,682	875,030	14.9	n/a	93,963	14.40-16.20
Outside CBD	13,759,135	1,018,176	7.4	n/a	275,183	16.75-18.00

Note: Data as of 10/97 and covers San Diego; CBD = Central Business District; n/a not available;
Source: Society of Industrial and Office Realtors, 1998 Comparative Statistics of Industrial and Office Real Estate Markets

"Despite strong absorption over the past couple of years, San Diego has yet to see new speculative construction on a widespread basis. Most of the 250,000 sq. ft. of speculative space currently under construction is in the northern part of the city of San Diego, or in San Diego's 'North County.' Build-to-suit development is relatively active, especially for San Diego's wide array of high-tech companies. San Diego's strengthening economy, led by high technology, a still-imposing Navy presence, and ever-increasing trade with Mexico, should cause moderate increases in rental rates and reductions in vacancies over the next year. Most new office construction will be of the build-to-suit variety for owner users." *Society of Industrial and Office Realtors, 1998 Comparative Statistics of Industrial and Office Real Estate Markets*

Industrial Market

Location	Total Space (sq. ft.)	Vacant Space (sq. ft.)	Vac. Rate (%)	Under Constr. (sq. ft.)	Net Absorp. (sq. ft.)	Net Lease ($/sq.ft./yr.)
Central City	38,087,560	4,063,078	10.7	962,494	-426,518	3.60-7.10
Suburban	44,224,150	4,441,236	10.0	619,298	1,067,914	3.20-6.80

Note: Data as of 10/97 and covers San Diego; n/a not available
Source: Society of Industrial and Office Realtors, 1998 Comparative Statistics of Industrial and Office Real Estate Markets

"1998 should see more than three million sq. ft. of development, primarily in suburban markets where land is affordable. Carlsbad and Poway will continue to be hot markets. Traffic congestion on major freeways will force siting decisions on some companies as they try to locate closer to housing. Money for spec projects remains tight, as lenders look for substantial pre-leasing requirements. Many cities are reducing permit fees to spur affordable development. On the acquisition front, REITs will continue to set the upper limits of value as they continue their feverish pitch for ownership of prime industrial investment properties. Lower capital gain rates will force older industrial parks to market where they can be rehabbed and converted to leasable space to satisfy excess demand in some area." *Society of Industrial and Office Realtors, 1998 Comparative Statistics of Industrial and Office Real Estate Markets*

Retail Market

Shopping Center Inventory (sq. ft.)	Shopping Center Construction (sq. ft.)	Construction as a Percent of Inventory (%)	Torto Wheaton Rent Index[1] ($/sq. ft.)
54,735,000	180,000	0.3	14.31

Note: Data as of 1997 and covers the Metropolitan Statistical Area - see Appendix A for areas included; (1) Index is based on a model that predicts what the average rent should be for leases with certain characteristics, in certain locations during certain years.
Source: National Association of Realtors, 1997-1998 Market Conditions Report

"Although completions have been trending down since 1993, the decline has been on par with national and Western MSAs. Similar to other Western cities, rents have been flat. Since 1995, employment growth has strengthened and should continue to increase slowly. Changing demographics have been a drawback for San Diego; net migration has been negative for several years, which has put a strain on household formations. Thus, construction should remain low through 2000." *National Association of Realtors, 1997-1998 Market Conditions Report*

COMMERCIAL UTILITIES

Typical Monthly Electric Bills

Area	Commercial Service ($/month)		Industrial Service ($/month)	
	12 kW demand 1,500 kWh	100 kW demand 30,000 kWh	1,000 kW demand 400,000 kWh	20,000 kW demand 10,000,000 kWh
City	182	4,050	44,010	719,918
U.S.	162	2,360	25,590	545,677

Note: Based on rates in effect July 1, 1997
Source: Edison Electric Institute, Typical Residential, Commercial and Industrial Bills, Summer 1997

TRANSPORTATION

Transportation Statistics

Avg. travel time to work (min.)	20.4
Interstate highways	I-5; I-8; I-15
Bus lines	
In-city	San Diego Transit, 285 vehicles
Inter-city	1
Passenger air service	
Airport	San Diego International/Lindbergh Field
Airlines	17
Aircraft departures	76,414 (1995)
Enplaned passengers	6,335,713 (1995)
Rail service	Amtrak; Light Rail
Motor freight carriers	42
Major waterways/ports	San Diego Harbor

Source: OAG, Business Travel Planner, Summer 1997; Editor & Publisher Market Guide, 1998; FAA Airport Activity Statistics, 1996; Amtrak National Time Table, Northeast Timetable, Fall/Winter 1997-98; 1990 Census of Population and Housing, STF 3C; Chamber of Commerce/Economic Development 1997; Jane's Urban Transport Systems 1997-98; Transit Fact Book 1997

Means of Transportation to Work

Area	Car/Truck/Van		Public Transportation			Bicycle	Walked	Other Means	Worked at Home
	Drove Alone	Car-pooled	Bus	Subway	Railroad				
City	70.7	12.8	4.0	0.0	0.0	1.1	4.9	2.0	4.6
MSA[1]	70.9	13.8	3.0	0.0	0.0	0.9	4.5	2.0	5.0
U.S.	73.2	13.4	3.0	1.5	0.5	0.4	3.9	1.2	3.0

Note: figures shown are percentages and only include workers 16 years old and over; (1) Metropolitan Statistical Area - see Appendix A for areas included
Source: 1990 Census of Population and Housing, Summary Tape File 3C

BUSINESSES

Major Business Headquarters

Company Name	1997 Rankings	
	Fortune 500	Forbes 500
Science Applications Intl.	-	55

Note: Companies listed are located in the city; Dashes indicate no ranking
Fortune 500: companies that produce a 10-K are ranked 1 - 500 based on 1996 revenue
Forbes 500: private companies are ranked 1 - 500 based on 1996 revenue
Source: Forbes 12/1/97; Fortune 4/28/97

Fast-Growing Businesses

According to *Inc.*, San Diego is home to one of America's 100 fastest-growing private companies: High Technology Solutions. Criteria for inclusion: must be an independent, privately-held, U.S. corporation, proprietorship or partnership; sales of at least $200,000 in 1993; five-year operating/sales history; increase in 1997 sales over 1996 sales; holding companies, regulated banks, and utilities were excluded. *Inc. 500, 1997*

San Diego is home to three of *Business Week's* "hot growth" companies: Document Sciences, Overland Data and Encad. Criteria: sales and earnings, return on capital and stock price. *Business Week, 5/26/97*

According to *Fortune*, San Diego is home to one of America's 100 fastest-growing companies: Thermotrex. Companies were ranked based on three years' earnings-per-share growth using least squares analysis to smooth out distortions. Criteria for inclusion: public companies with sales of least $50 million. Companies that lost money in the most recent quarter, or ended in the red for the past four quarters as a whole, were not eligible. Limited partnerships and REITs were also not considered. *Fortune, 9/29/97*

According to Deloitte & Touche LLP, San Diego is home to one of America's 100 fastest-growing high-technology companies: Amylin Pharmaceuticals Inc. Companies are ranked by percentage growth in revenue over a five-year period. Criteria for inclusion: must be a U.S. company developing and/or providing technology products or services; company must have been in business for five years with 1992 revenues of at least $50,000. *Deloitte & Touche LLP, January 7, 1998*

San Diego was ranked #1 out of 24 (#1 is best) in terms of the best-performing local stocks in 1996 according to the Money/Norby Cities Index. The index measures stocks of companies that have headquarters in 24 metro areas. *Money, 2/7/97*

Women-Owned Businesses: Number, Employment, Sales and Share

Area	Women-Owned Businesses in 1996				Share of Women-Owned Businesses in 1996	
	Number	Employment	Sales ($000)	Rank[2]	Percent (%)	Rank[3]
MSA[1]	89,900	285,400	25,048,500	14	38.2	13

Note: (1) Metropolitan Statistical Area - see Appendix A for areas included; (2) Calculated on an averaging of number of businesses, employment and sales and ranges from 1 to 50 where 1 is best; (3) Ranges from 1 to 50 where 1 is best
Source: The National Foundation for Women Business Owners, 1996 Facts on Women-Owned Businesses: Trends in the Top 50 Metropolitan Areas, March 26, 1997

Women-Owned Businesses: Growth

Area	Growth in Women-Owned Businesses (% change from 1987 to 1996)				Relative Growth in the Number of Women-Owned and All Businesses (% change from 1987 to 1996)			
	Num.	Empl.	Sales	Rank[2]	Women-Owned	All Firms	Absolute Difference	Relative Difference
MSA[1]	74.2	458.0	364.5	10	74.2	44.5	29.7	1.7:1

Note: (1) Metropolitan Statistical Area - see Appendix A for areas included; (2) Calculated on an averaging of the percent growth of number of businesses, employment and sales and ranges from 1 to 50 where 1 is best
Source: The National Foundation for Women Business Owners, 1996 Facts on Women-Owned Businesses: Trends in the Top 50 Metropolitan Areas, March 26, 1997

Minority Business Opportunity

Eight of the 500 largest Hispanic-owned companies in the U.S. are located in San Diego. *Hispanic Business, June 1997*

San Diego is home to one company which is on the Hispanic Business Fastest-Growing 100 list (greatest sales growth from 1992 to 1996): Casas International Customs Brokerage Inc. (customs brokerage) *Hispanic Business, July/August 1997*

San Diego was listed among the top 25 metropolitan areas in terms of the number of Hispanic-owned companies. The city was ranked number 7 with 37,352 companies. *Hispanic Business, May 1997*

Small Business Opportunity

According to *Forbes*, San Diego is home to three of America's 200 best small companies: HNC Software, ResMed, Safeskin. Criteria: companies must be publicly traded, U.S.-based corporations with latest 12-month sales of between $5 and $350 million. Earnings must be at least $1 million for the 12-month period. Limited partnerships, REITs and closed-end mutual funds were not considered. Banks, S&Ls and electric utilities were not included. *Forbes, November 3, 1997*

HOTELS & MOTELS

Hotels/Motels

Area	Hotels/Motels	Rooms	Luxury-Level Hotels/Motels		Average Minimum Rates ($)		
			♦♦♦♦	♦♦♦♦♦	♦♦	♦♦♦	♦♦♦♦
City	121	23,548	4	0	70	109	161
Airport	5	1,337	0	0	n/a	n/a	n/a
Suburbs	94	9,900	4	0	n/a	n/a	n/a
Total	220	34,785	8	0	n/a	n/a	n/a

Note: n/a not available; Classifications range from one diamond (budget properties with basic amenities) to five diamond (luxury properties with the finest service, rooms and facilities).
Source: OAG, Business Travel Planner, Summer 1997

CONVENTION CENTERS

Major Convention Centers

Center Name	Meeting Rooms	Exhibit Space (sf)
San Diego Concourse Convention & Performing Arts Center	18	67,700
San Diego Convention Center	32	354,000
Town and Country Hotel/Convention Center	42	160,000

Source: Trade Shows Worldwide 1997

Living Environment

COST OF LIVING

Cost of Living Index

Composite Index	Housing	Utilities	Groceries	Health Care	Trans-portation	Misc. Goods/ Services
119.9	147.5	101.3	112.1	122.2	120.4	104.3

Note: U.S. = 100
Source: ACCRA, Cost of Living Index, 3rd Quarter 1997

HOUSING

Median Home Prices and Housing Affordability

Area	Median Price[2] 3rd Qtr. 1997 ($)	HOI[3] 3rd Qtr. 1997	Afford-ability Rank[4]
MSA[1]	176,000	41.4	185
U.S.	127,000	63.7	--

Note: (1) Metropolitan Statistical Area - see Appendix A for areas included; (2) U.S. figures calculated from the sales of 625,000 new and existing homes in 195 markets; (3) Housing Opportunity Index - percent of homes sold that were within the reach of the median income household at the prevailing mortgage interest rate; (4) Rank is from 1-195 with 1 being most affordable
Source: National Association of Home Builders, Housing Opportunity Index, 3rd Quarter 1997

It is projected that the median price of existing single-family homes in the metro area will increase by 8.7% in 1998. Nationwide, home prices are projected to increase 6.6%.
Kiplinger's Personal Finance Magazine, January 1998

Average New Home Price

Area	Price ($)
City	205,998
U.S.	135,710

Note: Figures are based on a new home with 1,800 sq. ft. of living area on an 8,000 sq. ft. lot.
Source: ACCRA, Cost of Living Index, 3rd Quarter 1997

Average Apartment Rent

Area	Rent ($/mth)
City	803
U.S.	569

Note: Figures are based on an unfurnished two bedroom, 1-1/2 or 2 bath apartment, approximately 950 sq. ft. in size, excluding all utilities except water
Source: ACCRA, Cost of Living Index, 3rd Quarter 1997

RESIDENTIAL UTILITIES

Average Residential Utility Costs

Area	All Electric ($/mth)	Part Electric ($/mth)	Other Energy ($/mth)	Phone ($/mth)
City	--	72.92	33.80	16.07
U.S.	109.40	55.25	43.64	19.48

Source: ACCRA, Cost of Living Index, 3rd Quarter 1997

HEALTH CARE

Average Health Care Costs

Area	Hospital ($/day)	Doctor ($/visit)	Dentist ($/visit)
City	659.12	49.25	75.60
U.S.	392.91	48.76	60.84

Note: Hospital - based on a semi-private room. Doctor - based on a general practitioner's routine exam of an established patient. Dentist - based on adult teeth cleaning and periodic oral exam.
Source: ACCRA, Cost of Living Index, 3rd Quarter 1997

Distribution of Office-Based Physicians

Area	Family/Gen. Practitioners	Specialists		
		Medical	Surgical	Other
MSA[1]	671	1,564	1,221	1,384

Note: Data as of 12/31/96; (1) Metropolitan Statistical Area - see Appendix A for areas included
Source: American Medical Assn., Physician Characteristics & Distribution in the U.S., 1997-1998

Hospitals

San Diego has 12 general medical and surgical hospitals, 3 psychiatric, 1 children's general, 1 children's psychiatric, 1 children's other specialty. *AHA Guide to the Healthcare Field 1997-98*

According to *U.S. News and World Report,* San Diego has 1 of the best hospitals in the U.S.: **UCSD Medical Center**, noted for AIDS, cardiology, orthopedics, pulmonology, urology; *U.S. News and World Report, "America's Best Hospitals", 7/28/97*

EDUCATION

Public School District Statistics

District Name	Num. Sch.	Enroll.	Classroom Teachers[1]	Pupils per Teacher	Minority Pupils (%)	Current Exp.[2] ($/pupil)
San Diego City Unified	164	130,360	5,527	23.6	70.0	5,145
San Diego Co. Office of Educ	3	2,657	148	18.0	n/a	n/a

Note: Data covers the 1995-1996 school year unless otherwise noted; (1) Excludes teachers reported as working in school district offices rather than in schools; (2) Based on 1993-94 enrollment collected by the Census Bureau, not the enrollment figure shown in column 3; SD = School District; ISD = Independent School District; n/a not available
Source: National Center for Education Statistics, Common Core of Data Survey; Bureau of the Census

Educational Quality

School District	Education Quotient[1]	Graduate Outcome[2]	Community Index[3]	Resource Index[4]
San Diego City	95.0	76.0	101.0	107.0

Note: Nearly 1,000 secondary school districts were rated in terms of educational quality. The scores range from a low of 50 to a high of 150; (1) Average of the Graduate Outcome, Community and Resource indexes; (2) Based on graduation rates and college board scores (SAT/ACT); (3) Based on the surrounding community's average level of education and the area's average income level; (4) Based on teacher salaries, per-pupil expenditures and student-teacher ratios.
Source: Expansion Management, Ratings Issue 1997

Educational Attainment by Race

Area	High School Graduate (%)					Bachelor's Degree (%)				
	Total	White	Black	Other	Hisp.[2]	Total	White	Black	Other	Hisp.[2]
City	82.3	87.6	80.3	62.9	51.9	29.8	34.3	14.0	19.3	10.7
MSA[1]	81.9	85.7	82.0	62.3	52.5	25.3	27.6	14.1	17.0	9.5
U.S.	75.2	77.9	63.1	60.4	49.8	20.3	21.5	11.4	19.4	9.2

Note: figures shown cover persons 25 years old and over; (1) Metropolitan Statistical Area - see Appendix A for areas included; (2) people of Hispanic origin can be of any race
Source: 1990 Census of Population and Housing, Summary Tape File 3C

School Enrollment by Type

Area	Preprimary				Elementary/High School			
	Public		Private		Public		Private	
	Enrollment	%	Enrollment	%	Enrollment	%	Enrollment	%
City	10,602	58.2	7,618	41.8	156,497	91.9	13,744	8.1
MSA[1]	26,048	59.1	18,027	40.9	367,435	92.4	30,352	7.6
U.S.	2,679,029	59.5	1,824,256	40.5	38,379,689	90.2	4,187,099	9.8

Note: figures shown cover persons 3 years old and over; (1) Metropolitan Statistical Area - see Appendix A for areas included
Source: 1990 Census of Population and Housing, Summary Tape File 3C

School Enrollment by Race

Area	Preprimary (%)				Elementary/High School (%)			
	White	Black	Other	Hisp.[1]	White	Black	Other	Hisp.[1]
City	67.6	12.0	20.4	20.3	51.0	12.3	36.7	32.3
MSA[2]	77.2	7.4	15.4	19.8	65.1	7.5	27.4	30.5
U.S.	80.4	12.5	7.1	7.8	74.1	15.6	10.3	12.5

Note: figures shown cover persons 3 years old and over; (1) people of Hispanic origin can be of any race; (2) Metropolitan Statistical Area - see Appendix A for areas included
Source: 1990 Census of Population and Housing, Summary Tape File 3C

SAT/ACT Scores

Area/District	1997 SAT				1997 ACT	
	Percent of Graduates Tested (%)	Average Math Score	Average Verbal Score	Average Combined Score	Percent of Graduates Tested (%)	Average Composite Score
San Diego City	48	500	487	987	11	20.2
State	45	514	496	1,010	11	21.0
U.S.	42	511	505	1,016	36	21.0

Note: Math and verbal SAT scores are out of a possible 800; ACT scores are out of a possible 36
Caution: Comparing or ranking states/cities on the basis of SAT/ACT scores alone is invalid and strongly discouraged by the The College Board and The American College Testing Program as students who take the tests are self-selected and do not represent the entire student population.
Source: San Diego City Schools, Testing Unit, 1997; American College Testing Program, 1997; College Board, 1997

Classroom Teacher Salaries in Public Schools

District	B.A. Degree		M.A. Degree		Ph.D. Degree	
	Min. ($)	Max ($)	Min. ($)	Max. ($)	Min. ($)	Max. ($)
San Diego	27,089	39,303	28,742	42,462	33,702	52,310
Average[1]	26,120	39,270	28,175	44,667	31,643	49,825

Note: Salaries are for 1996-1997; (1) Based on all school districts covered
Source: American Federation of Teachers (unpublished data)

Higher Education

Two-Year Colleges		Four-Year Colleges		Medical Schools	Law Schools	Voc/ Tech
Public	Private	Public	Private			
3	3	1	7	1	3	30

Source: College Blue Book, Occupational Education 1997; Medical School Admission Requirements, 1998-99; Peterson's Guide to Two-Year Colleges, 1997; Peterson's Guide to Four-Year Colleges, 1997; Barron's Guide to Law Schools 1997

MAJOR EMPLOYERS

Major Employers

Atlas Hotels
Golden Eagle Insurance
National Dispatch Center
Scripps Institutions of Medicine & Science
San Diego Gas & Electric
Science Applications International
Staffpro Services
Trizec Centers (real estate)

Children's Hospital-San Diego
Kyocera International (semiconductors)
National Steel & Shipbuilding
Qualcomm (broadcasting equipment)
San Diego Marriott & Marina
Solar Turbines
Zoological Society of San Diego
Tar-Car (auto dealers)

Note: companies listed are located in the city
Source: Dun's Business Rankings 1997; Ward's Business Directory, 1997

PUBLIC SAFETY

Crime Rate

Area	All Crimes	Violent Crimes				Property Crimes		
		Murder	Forcible Rape	Robbery	Aggrav. Assault	Burglary	Larceny -Theft	Motor Vehicle Theft
City	5,270.1	6.8	31.5	256.6	573.7	736.8	2,712.2	952.5
Suburbs[1]	4,120.8	5.7	29.8	164.4	386.6	883.5	2,020.2	630.6
MSA[2]	4,623.8	6.2	30.5	204.8	468.5	819.3	2,323.0	771.5
U.S.	5,078.9	7.4	36.1	202.4	388.2	943.0	2,975.9	525.9

Note: Crime rate is the number of crimes per 100,000 pop.; (1) defined as all areas within the MSA but located outside the central city; (2) Metropolitan Statistical Area - see Appendix A for areas incl.
Source: FBI Uniform Crime Reports 1996

RECREATION

Culture and Recreation

Museums	Symphony Orchestras	Opera Companies	Dance Companies	Professional Theatres	Zoos	Pro Sports Teams
21	1	1	2	5	1	2

Source: International Directory of the Performing Arts, 1996; Official Museum Directory, 1998; Chamber of Commerce/Economic Development 1997

Library System

The San Diego County Library has 32 branches, holdings of 1,099,557 volumes and a budget of $8,466,698 (1995-1996). The San Diego Public Library has 32 branches, holdings of 2,473,994 volumes and a budget of $19,388,403 (1995-1996). *American Library Directory, 1997-1998*

MEDIA

Newspapers

Name	Type	Freq.	Distribution	Circulation
La Prensa San Diego	Hispanic	1x/wk	Local	30,000
Navy Dispatch at Ease	n/a	1x/wk	Local	30,000
Old San Diego Gazette	General	1x/mo	Local	75,000
San Diego Navy Dispatch	n/a	1x/wk	Local	25,000
San Diego Reader	n/a	51x/yr	Local	158,000
The San Diego Union-Tribune	General	7x/wk	Area	379,705
Southern Cross	Religious	2x/mo	Area	25,000

Note: Includes newspapers with circulations of 25,000 or more located in the city; n/a not available
Source: Burrelle's Media Directory, 1998 Edition

AM Radio Stations

Call Letters	Freq. (kHz)	Target Audience	Station Format	Music Format
KOGO	600	General	T	n/a
XTRA	690	Hispanic	N/S/T	n/a
KFMB	760	General	M/N/S	Contemporary Top 40
XEMM	800	Hispanic	M/N/S/T	Country
KECR	910	Religious	E/M	Christian
KCLB	970	Hispanic	M/N/S	Spanish
KCEO	1000	General	E/N/T	n/a
KURS	1040	Hispanic	E/M/N/S/T	Spanish
KSDO	1130	General	N/T	n/a
KCBQ	1170	General	T	n/a
KPRZ	1210	Hisp/Relig	M/N/T	Christian/Spanish
KSON	1240	General	M	Country
KKLQ	1320	n/a	M/N/S	Contemporary Top 40
KKSM	1320	General	M/N/S	AOR/Adult Contemporary/Alternative
KPOP	1360	General	M/N/T	Contemporary Top 40/Oldies
KSPA	1450	General	M	Oldies
XEBG	1550	Hispanic	M/N/S/T	Adult Contemporary

Note: Stations included broadcast in the San Diego metro area; n/a not available
Station Format: E = Educational; M = Music; N = News; S = Sports; T = Talk
Music Format: AOR = Album Oriented Rock; MOR = Middle-of-the-Road
Source: Burrelle's Media Directory, 1998 Edition

FM Radio Stations

Call Letters	Freq. (mHz)	Target Audience	Station Format	Music Format
KSDS	88.3	General	M/N	n/a
KPBS	89.5	General	N/T	n/a
XTRA	91.1	General	M/T	AOR/Alternative
KOWF	92.1	General	M	Classical
XHRM	92.5	Nat. Amer.	M	Alternative
KHTS	93.3	n/a	M	Contemporary Top 40
KFSD	94.1	n/a	M	Classical
KBZT	94.9	General	M/N/S	Oldies
KMCG	95.7	General	M	Adult Contemporary
KYXY	96.5	General	M/N	Adult Contemporary/Easy Listening
KSON	97.3	General	M/N	Country
KIFM	98.1	General	M	Jazz
XHMORE	98.9	Hispanic	M	Classic Rock/Easy Listening
XHKY	99.3	Hispanic	M	Country
KFMB	100.7	General	M	Adult Contemporary
KGB	101.5	General	M	Classic Rock
KIOZ	102.1	n/a	M	AOR
KXST	102.1	General	M	Alternative
KKBH	102.9	General	M	Adult Contemporary
KOST	103.5	General	M	Adult Contemporary
KPLN	103.7	General	M	Adult Contemporary/Classic Rock
XLTN	104.5	Hispanic	M	Adult Contemporary/Spanish
KKLQ	106.5	General	M	Contemporary Top 40

Note: Stations included broadcast in the San Diego metro area; n/a not available
Station Format: E = Educational; M = Music; N = News; S = Sports; T = Talk
Music Format: AOR = Album Oriented Rock; MOR = Middle-of-the-Road
Source: Burrelle's Media Directory, 1998 Edition

Television Stations

Name	Ch.	Affiliation	Type	Owner
XETV	6	Fox	Commercial	Grupo Televisa
KFMB	8	CBS	Commercial	Midwest TV Stations
KGTV	10	ABC	Commercial	McGraw-Hill
KPBS	15	PBS	Public	San Diego State University
KNSD	39	NBC	Commercial	General Electric Company
XHBJ	45	n/a	Commercial	Mario Mayans
KUSI	51	UPN	Commercial	McKinnon Broadcasting Company
KSWB	69	WB	Commercial	Tribune Company

Note: Stations included broadcast in the San Diego metro area
Source: Burrelle's Media Directory, 1998 Edition

CLIMATE

Average and Extreme Temperatures

Temperature	Jan	Feb	Mar	Apr	May	Jun	Jul	Aug	Sep	Oct	Nov	Dec	Ann
Extreme High (°F)	88	88	93	98	96	101	95	98	111	107	97	88	111
Average High (°F)	65	66	66	68	69	72	76	77	77	74	71	66	71
Average Temp. (°F)	57	58	59	62	64	67	71	72	71	67	62	58	64
Average Low (°F)	48	50	52	55	58	61	65	66	65	60	53	49	57
Extreme Low (°F)	29	36	39	44	48	51	55	58	51	43	38	34	29

Note: Figures cover the years 1948-1990
Source: National Climatic Data Center, International Station Meteorological Climate Summary, 3/95

Average Precipitation/Snowfall/Humidity

Precip./Humidity	Jan	Feb	Mar	Apr	May	Jun	Jul	Aug	Sep	Oct	Nov	Dec	Ann
Avg. Precip. (in.)	1.9	1.4	1.7	0.8	0.2	0.1	Tr	0.1	0.2	0.4	1.2	1.4	9.5
Avg. Snowfall (in.)	Tr	0	0	0	0	0	0	0	0	0	0	Tr	Tr
Avg. Rel. Hum. 7am (%)	70	72	73	72	73	77	79	79	78	74	69	68	74
Avg. Rel. Hum. 4pm (%)	57	58	59	59	63	66	65	66	65	63	60	58	62

Note: Figures cover the years 1948-1990; Tr = Trace amounts (<0.05 in. of rain; <0.5 in. of snow)
Source: National Climatic Data Center, International Station Meteorological Climate Summary, 3/95

Weather Conditions

Temperature			Daytime Sky			Precipitation		
10°F & below	32°F & below	90°F & above	Clear	Partly cloudy	Cloudy	0.01 inch or more precip.	0.1 inch or more snow/ice	Thunder-storms
0	< 1	4	115	126	124	40	0	5

Note: Figures are average number of days per year and covers the years 1948-1990
Source: National Climatic Data Center, International Station Meteorological Climate Summary, 3/95

AIR & WATER QUALITY

Maximum Pollutant Concentrations

	Particulate Matter (ug/m³)	Carbon Monoxide (ppm)	Sulfur Dioxide (ppm)	Nitrogen Dioxide (ppm)	Ozone (ppm)	Lead (ug/m³)
MSA[1] Level	92	6	0.017	0.022	0.13	0.02
NAAQS[2]	150	9	0.140	0.053	0.12	1.50
Met NAAQS?	Yes	Yes	Yes	Yes	No	Yes

Note: (1) Metropolitan Statistical Area - see Appendix A for areas included; (2) National Ambient Air Quality Standards; ppm = parts per million; ug/m³ = micrograms per cubic meter; n/a not available
Source: EPA, National Air Quality and Emissions Trends Report, 1996

Pollutant Standards Index

In the San Diego MSA (see Appendix A for areas included), the Pollutant Standards Index (PSI) exceeded 100 on 4 days in 1996. A PSI value greater than 100 indicates that air quality would be in the unhealthful range on that day. *EPA, National Air Quality and Emissions Trends Report, 1996*

Drinking Water

Water System Name	Pop. Served	Primary Water Source Type	Number of Violations in Fiscal Year 1997	Type of Violation/ Contaminants
City of San Diego	1,177,400	Surface	None	None

Note: Data as of January 16, 1998
Source: EPA, Office of Ground Water and Drinking Water, Safe Drinking Water Information System

San Diego tap water is hard and not fluoridated.
Editor & Publisher Market Guide, 1998

San Francisco, California

Background

San Francisco is one of the most beautiful cities in the world. The city is blessed with a mild climate; one of the best landlocked harbors in the world; and a strong sense of civic pride shaped by its unique history. According to the May 1993 issue of Travel and Leisure, San Francisco is, "Paris, but populated with Americans, most of them smiling."

The hilly peninsula known today as San Francisco, and its bay, was largely ignored by explorers during the 16th and 17th centuries. Until the 1760's, no one had seen the "Golden Gate", or the narrow strip of water, leading into what was to become one of the greatest harbors in the world. However, even with the eventual discovery of that prime piece of real estate, San Francisco remained a quiet and pastoral settlement for nearly 90 years.

The discovery of gold in the Sierra Nevada foothills in 1848 changed San Francisco forever. Every hopeful adventurer from around the world docked in San Francisco, aspiring to make his fortune. San Francisco had entered its phase as a rowdy, frontier, gold-prospecting town, with plenty of bachelor males, amusing themselves at the gambling houses and saloons.

When the supply of gold dwindled, many of the men went back to their native countries, but many stayed and continued to live in the ethnic neighborhoods they had created. Some of these neighborhoods still exist today like Chinatown, the Italian District, and the Japan Center.

The charm of San Francisco lies in its cosmopolitan, yet cohesive, flavor. Ever mindful of its citizenry, newspapers in San Francisco range from English, Irish, Spanish and Swiss to Chinese, Japanese, and Korean, with many community newspapers in between.

One of the major economic regions of the United States, the San Francisco Bay Area has one of the highest percentages of college-educated adults in the nation, which translates into a high per capita real income. The Bay Area is also home to 20% of California's environmental companies and leads the state with the largest concentration of biotech companies. A former warehouse district in San Francisco has become the center for nearly 400 fast-growing multimedia and Internet-related companies. This industry cluster, combined with the concentration of multimedia activity in the Bay Area, has produced jobs for nearly 60,000 people. In terms of world trade, high-tech exports from the Silicon Valley Area account for almost one-third of the nation's high-technology exports. This has helped make San Francisco the fourth largest port in the United States.

San Francisco is known as the "Air-Conditioned City" with cool pleasant summers and mild winters. It has greater climatic variability than any other urban area of the same size in the country.

Sea fogs, and associated low stratus clouds are most common in the summertime, when it is not unusual to see a low cloud perched on the Golden Gate Bridge while the sun forms a glow about it.

General Rankings and Evaluative Comments

■ San Francisco was ranked #13 out of 300 cities by *Money's* 1997 "Survey of the Best Places to Live." Criteria used: health services, crime, economy, housing, education, transportation, weather, leisure and the arts. The city was ranked #13 in 1996 and #24 in 1995. *Money, July 1997; Money, September 1996; Money, September 1995*

■ *Ladies Home Journal* ranked America's 200 largest cities based on the qualities women care about most. San Francisco ranked 116 out of 200. Criteria: low crime rate, good public schools, well-paying jobs, quality health and child care, the presence of women in government, proportion of women-owned businesses, size of the wage gap with men, local economy, divorce rates, the ratio of single men to single women, whether there are laws that require at least the same number of public toilets for women as men, and the probability of good hair days. *Ladies Home Journal, November 1997*

■ San Francisco was ranked #76 out of 219 cities in terms of children's health, safety, and economic well-being. Criteria: total population, percent population change, birth rate, child immunization rate, infant mortality rate, percent low birth weight infants, percent of births to teens, physician-to-population ratio, student-to-teacher ratio, dropout rate, unemployment rate, median family income, percent of children in poverty, violent and property crime rates, number of juvenile arrests for violent crimes as a percent of the total crime index, number of days with pollution standard index (PSI) over 100, pounds toxic releases per 1,000 people and number of superfund sites. *Zero Population Growth, Children's Environmental Index 1997*

■ San Francisco appeared on *Ebony's* list of the best cities for African-Americans Rank: 2 out of 4. The cities were selected based on a survey of the 100 Most Influential Black Americans. They were asked which city offered the best overall experience for African-Americans, and which dream city they would select if they could live anywhere they wanted to. *Ebony* also asked opinion-makers which cities offered the best cultural experiences, the best schools and the most diversity.

"The Black population of San Francisco now stands at around 10 percent, which is below the national average of 12 percent. Among some Blacks, the city still has image problems to overcome. During the late 1960s and early 1970s, Blacks were all but forced out of the Bay Side city by an urban renewal project in the City's Fillmore District. But Willie Brown, the city's first Black mayor, has brought new optimism to the city. 'San Francisco provides an excellent environment for advancement,' says William Lucy, president of the Coalition of Black Trade Unionists, 'socially, politically and economically.'" *Ebony, 9/97*

■ San Francisco is among the 20 most livable cities for gay men and lesbians. The list was divided between 10 cities you might expect and 10 surprises. San Francisco was on the cities you would expect list. Rank: 1 out of 10. Criteria: legal protection from antigay discrimination, an annual gay pride celebration, a community center, gay bookstores and publications, and an array of organizations, religious groups, and health care facilities that cater to the needs of the local gay community. *The Advocate, June 1997*

■ San Francisco appeared on *Travel & Leisure's* list of the world's best cities. Rank: 4 out of 25. Criteria: activities/attractions, culture/arts, people, restaurants/food, and value. *Travel & Leisure, September 1997*

■ *Conde Nast Traveler* polled 37,000 readers in terms of travel satisfaction. Cities were ranked based on the following criteria: people/friendliness, environment/ambiance, cultural enrichment, restaurants and fun/energy. San Francisco appeared in the top thirty, ranking number 1, with an overall rating of 83.7 out of 100 based on all the criteria. The cities were also ranked in each category separately. San Francisco appeared in the top 10 based on environment/ambiance, ranking number 2 with a rating of 89.6 out of 100. San Francisco appeared in the top 10 based on cultural enrichment, ranking number 4 with a rating of 85.5 out of 100. San Francisco appeared in the top 10 based on restaurants, ranking number 1 with a rating of 91.8 out of 100. San Francisco appeared in the top 10 based on fun/energy, ranking number 3 with a rating of 87.3 out of 100. *Conde Nast Traveler, Readers' Choice Poll 1997*

- *Yahoo! Internet Life* selected "America's 100 Most Wired Cities & Towns". 50 cities were large and 50 cities were small. San Francisco ranked 1 out of 50 large cities. Criteria: Internet users per capita, number of networked computers, number of registered domain names, Internet backbone traffic, and the per-capita number of Web sites devoted to each city.San Francisco was highlighted as having the most online business, most access and most users. *Yahoo! Internet Life, March 1998*

- *Reader's Digest* non-scientifically ranked the 12 largest U.S. metropolitan areas in terms of having the worst drivers. The San Francisco-Oakland metro area ranked number 12. The areas were selected by asking approximately 1,200 readers on the *Reader's Digest* Web site and 200 interstate bus drivers and long-haul truckers which metro areas have the worst drivers. Their responses were factored in with fatality, insurance and rental-car rates to create the rankings. *Reader's Digest, March 1998*

- San Francisco appeared on *Sales & Marketing Management's* list of the 20 hottest domestic markets to do business in. Rank: 14 out of 20. America's 320 Metropolitan Statistical Areas were ranked based on the market's potential to buy products in certain industries like high-tech, manufacturing, office equipment and business services, as well as population and household income growth. The study had nine criteria in all.

  "Money is the driver of this market as financial institutions lead the economy. Also San Francisco is a prime retail market, as it's among the richest cities in the country, with household effective buying income at more than $55,000, almost $15,000 more than the national average." *Sales & Marketing Management, January 1998*

- Morrison & Foerster (law firm), headquartered in San Francisco, is among the "100 Best Companies to Work for in America." Criteria: trust in management, pride in work/company, camaraderie, company responses to the Hewitt People Practices Inventory, and employee responses to their Great Place to Work survey. The companies also had to be at least 10 years old and have a minimum of 500 employees. *Fortune, January 12, 1998*

- Genentech, Inc., headquartered in San Francisco, is among the "100 Best Companies for Working Mothers." Criteria: pay compared with competition, opportunities for women to advance, support for child care, flexible work schedules and family-friendly benefits. *Working Mother, October 1997*

- According to *Working Mother,* "Lawmakers here—on both sides of the aisle—have agreed that the state must kick in more money to help working parents find and pay for child care. To that end, Governor Pete Wilson has proposed a significant expansion of the state's child care budget—an additional $277 million in state and federal funds. The new money would pay for care for about 90,000 more kids a year; and for preschool for another 13,000. In addition, some $45 million will be spent on recruiting and training caregivers for infants and toddlers.

  To help parents become more informed consumers, California passed a law that many consider a step backward. It allows family child care providers to care for two more kids, without hiring additional help. This means a family child care provider can now care for up to eight kids, instead of six, without additional help. The new rule also worries child care advocates because it may limit infant care in California. When caregivers take in the two extra older children, they must reduce the number of babies in their care. (California is among the 10 best states for child care.)" *Working Mother, July/August 1997*

Business Environment

STATE ECONOMY

State Economic Profile

"California's expansion is strong and stable....Entertainment and filmmaking remain steady contributors to the state's improved income growth and labor markets....

California's banking industry is consolidating and shedding workers. Improved credit conditions and healthy balance sheets make many remaining California thrifts likely takeover targets for out-of-state banks.

Delinquency rates on consumer credit have declined for the past two years and are well below the U.S. average. Mortgage foreclosure rates remain high, but they are down from the peak of one year ago when mortgage lenders took advantage of the improved housing market to shed nonperforming loans. California consumers remain cautious, however. Retail sales growth last year of 5% was no better than the national average.

Housing prices are up in northern California, and the number of units sold is rising throughout the state. Multifamily units dominated construction activity last year. With population growth accelerating and income growth outpacing the U.S. for the first time this decade, demand for single-family homes will strengthen.

Housing prices are up in northern California, and the number of units sold is rising throughout the state. Multifamily units dominated construction activity last year. With population growth accelerating the income growth outpacing the U.S. for the first time this decade, demand for single-family homes will strengthen.

Construction will contribute to the near-term expansion as home building accelerates. The greatest risk to the California economy is that the rising dollar could choke off foreign demand for California's export products. Longer term there will be some consolidation among high-tech firms, and high costs will limit the breadth of industrial development. California will remain an average performer over the long term." *National Association of Realtors, Economic Profiles: The Fifty States, July 1997*

IMPORTS/EXPORTS

Total Export Sales

Area	1993 ($000)	1994 ($000)	1995 ($000)	1996 ($000)	% Chg. 1993-96	% Chg. 1995-96
MSA[1]	9,264,899	9,303,816	8,133,685	8,560,407	-7.6	5.2
U.S.	464,858,354	512,415,609	583,030,524	622,827,063	34.0	6.8

Note: (1) Metropolitan Statistical Area - see Appendix A for areas included
Source: U.S. Department of Commerce, International Trade Association, Metropolitan Area Exports: An Export Performance Report on Over 250 U.S. Cities, October 1997

Imports/Exports by Port

Type	Cargo Value			Share of U.S. Total	
	1995 (US$mil.)	1996 (US$mil.)	% Change 1995-1996	1995 (%)	1996 (%)
Imports	673	399	-40.75	0.17	0.10
Exports	763	253	-66.84	0.33	0.11

Source: Global Trade Information Services, WaterBorne Trade Atlas 1997

CITY FINANCES

City Government Finances

Component	FY94 ($000)	FY94 (per capita $)
Revenue	3,745,702	5,136.78
Expenditure	3,585,304	4,916.81
Debt Outstanding	3,523,058	4,831.45
Cash & Securities	8,534,982	11,704.70

Source: U.S. Bureau of the Census, City Government Finances: 1993-94

City Government Revenue by Source

Source	FY94 ($000)	FY94 (per capita $)	FY94 (%)
From Federal Government	136,857	187.68	3.7
From State Governments	977,651	1,340.73	26.1
From Local Governments	14,375	19.71	0.4
Property Taxes	473,979	650.00	12.7
General Sales Taxes	84,711	116.17	2.3
Selective Sales Taxes	141,676	194.29	3.8
Income Taxes	0	0.00	0.0
Current Charges	585,121	802.42	15.6
Utility/Liquor Store	254,753	349.36	6.8
Employee Retirement[1]	528,161	724.31	14.1
Other	548,418	752.09	14.6

Note: (1) Excludes "city contributions," classified as "nonrevenue," intragovernmental transfers.
Source: U.S. Bureau of the Census, City Government Finances: 1993-94

City Government Expenditures by Function

Function	FY94 ($000)	FY94 (per capita $)	FY94 (%)
Educational Services	124,234	170.37	3.5
Employee Retirement[1]	272,292	373.42	7.6
Environment/Housing	423,028	580.13	11.8
Government Administration	211,060	289.44	5.9
Interest on General Debt	170,221	233.44	4.7
Public Safety	413,464	567.02	11.5
Social Services	986,087	1,352.30	27.5
Transportation	241,100	330.64	6.7
Utility/Liquor Store	550,906	755.50	15.4
Other	192,912	264.56	5.4

Note: (1) Payments to beneficiaries including withdrawal of contributions.
Source: U.S. Bureau of the Census, City Government Finances: 1993-94

Municipal Bond Ratings

Area	Moody's	S & P
San Francisco	Aa3	AA-

Note: n/a not available; n/r not rated
Source: Moody's Bond Record, 2/98; Statistical Abstract of the U.S., 1997;
Governing Magazine, 9/97, 3/98

POPULATION

Population Growth

Area	1980	1990	% Chg. 1980-90	July 1996 Estimate	% Chg. 1990-96
City	678,974	723,959	6.6	735,315	1.6
MSA[1]	1,488,871	1,603,678	7.7	1,655,454	3.2
U.S.	226,545,805	248,765,170	9.8	265,179,411	6.6

Note: (1) Metropolitan Statistical Area - see Appendix A for areas included
Source: 1980/1990 Census of Housing and Population, Summary Tape File 3C;
Census Bureau Population Estimates

Population Characteristics

Race	City 1980 Population	%	City 1990 Population	%	% Chg. 1980-90	MSA[1] 1990 Population	%
White	402,131	59.2	388,341	53.6	-3.4	1,060,840	66.2
Black	86,190	12.7	78,931	10.9	-8.4	121,509	7.6
Amer Indian/Esk/Aleut	3,566	0.5	3,354	0.5	-5.9	7,407	0.5
Asian/Pacific Islander	149,269	22.0	211,000	29.1	41.4	329,499	20.5
Other	37,818	5.6	42,333	5.8	11.9	84,423	5.3
Hispanic Origin[2]	83,373	12.3	96,640	13.3	15.9	226,734	14.1

Note: (1) Metropolitan Statistical Area - see Appendix A for areas included;
(2) people of Hispanic origin can be of any race
Source: 1980/1990 Census of Housing and Population, Summary Tape File 3C

Ancestry

Area	German	Irish	English	Italian	U.S.	French	Polish	Dutch
City	10.6	10.2	8.1	5.6	1.1	2.8	2.1	1.0
MSA[1]	14.1	12.4	11.2	7.7	1.3	3.4	2.2	1.3
U.S.	23.3	15.6	13.1	5.9	5.3	4.2	3.8	2.5

Note: Figures are percentages and include persons that reported multiple ancestry (eg. if a person reported being Irish and Italian, they were included in both columns); (1) Metropolitan Statistical Area - see Appendix A for areas included
Source: 1990 Census of Population and Housing, Summary Tape File 3C

Age

Area	Median Age (Years)	Age Distribution (%) Under 5	Under 18	18-24	25-44	45-64	65+	80+
City	35.7	4.9	16.1	9.8	40.2	19.3	14.5	3.7
MSA[1]	35.7	5.8	18.8	9.2	38.2	20.5	13.3	3.1
U.S.	32.9	7.3	25.6	10.5	32.6	18.7	12.5	2.8

Note: (1) Metropolitan Statistical Area - see Appendix A for areas included
Source: 1990 Census of Population and Housing, Summary Tape File 3C

Male/Female Ratio

Area	Number of males per 100 females (all ages)	Number of males per 100 females (18 years old+)
City	100.1	99.4
MSA[1]	98.9	97.2
U.S.	95.0	91.9

Note: (1) Metropolitan Statistical Area - see Appendix A for areas included
Source: 1990 Census of Population, General Population Characteristics

INCOME

Per Capita/Median/Average Income

Area	Per Capita ($)	Median Household ($)	Average Household ($)
City	19,695	33,414	45,664
MSA[1]	22,049	40,494	54,162
U.S.	14,420	30,056	38,453

Note: all figures are for 1989; (1) Metropolitan Statistical Area - see Appendix A for areas included
Source: 1990 Census of Population and Housing, Summary Tape File 3C

Household Income Distribution by Race

Income ($)	City (%)					U.S. (%)				
	Total	White	Black	Other	Hisp.[1]	Total	White	Black	Other	Hisp.[1]
Less than 5,000	5.1	3.9	10.6	5.8	4.8	6.2	4.8	15.2	8.6	8.8
5,000 - 9,999	9.3	7.7	18.7	9.9	9.4	9.3	8.6	14.2	9.9	11.1
10,000 - 14,999	7.4	6.8	9.3	8.1	9.6	8.8	8.5	11.0	9.8	11.0
15,000 - 24,999	15.1	14.9	16.5	15.0	17.9	17.5	17.3	18.9	18.5	20.5
25,000 - 34,999	15.0	15.3	13.6	14.9	16.5	15.8	16.1	14.2	15.4	16.4
35,000 - 49,999	17.2	17.7	13.7	17.4	19.1	17.9	18.6	13.3	16.1	16.0
50,000 - 74,999	16.5	17.1	11.2	17.1	15.4	15.0	15.8	9.3	13.4	11.1
75,000 - 99,999	6.9	7.3	3.8	7.3	4.4	5.1	5.5	2.6	4.7	3.1
100,000+	7.4	9.3	2.5	4.4	2.9	4.4	4.8	1.3	3.7	1.9

Note: all figures are for 1989; (1) people of Hispanic origin can be of any race
Source: 1990 Census of Population and Housing, Summary Tape File 3C

Effective Buying Income

Area	Per Capita ($)	Median Household ($)	Average Household ($)
City	20,120	36,735	48,562
MSA[1]	22,131	44,024	56,451
U.S.	15,444	33,201	41,849

Note: data as of 1/1/97; (1) Metropolitan Statistical Area - see Appendix A for areas included
Source: Standard Rate & Data Service, Newspaper Advertising Source, 2/98

Effective Household Buying Income Distribution

Area	% of Households Earning						
	$10,000 -$19,999	$20,000 -$34,999	$35,000 -$49,999	$50,000 -$74,999	$75,000 -$99,000	$100,000 -$124,999	$125,000 and up
City	14.5	21.4	17.4	19.0	8.3	3.3	4.3
MSA[1]	11.4	19.1	17.5	22.1	10.8	4.5	5.9
U.S.	16.5	23.4	18.3	18.2	6.4	2.1	2.4

Note: data as of 1/1/97; (1) Metropolitan Statistical Area - see Appendix A for areas included
Source: Standard Rate & Data Service, Newspaper Advertising Source, 2/98

Poverty Rates by Race and Age

Area	Total (%)	By Race (%)				By Age (%)		
		White	Black	Other	Hisp.[2]	Under 5 years old	Under 18 years old	65 years and over
City	12.7	9.3	26.2	13.7	16.4	17.7	18.6	9.9
MSA[1]	9.0	6.5	22.5	11.7	14.2	11.3	11.9	8.0
U.S.	13.1	9.8	29.5	23.1	25.3	20.1	18.3	12.8

Note: figures show the percent of people living below the poverty line in 1989. The average poverty threshold was $12,674 for a family of four in 1989; (1) Metropolitan Statistical Area - see Appendix A for areas included; (2) people of Hispanic origin can be of any race
Source: 1990 Census of Population and Housing, Summary Tape File 3C

EMPLOYMENT

Labor Force and Employment

Area	Civilian Labor Force			Workers Employed		
	Dec. '95	Dec. '96	% Chg.	Dec. '95	Dec. '96	% Chg.
City	406,753	411,647	1.2	392,806	398,274	1.4
MSA[1]	921,320	930,753	1.0	894,480	906,931	1.4
U.S.	134,583,000	136,742,000	1.6	127,903,000	130,785,000	2.3

Note: Data is not seasonally adjusted and covers workers 16 years of age and older;
(1) Metropolitan Statistical Area - see Appendix A for areas included
Source: Bureau of Labor Statistics, http://stats.bls.gov

Unemployment Rate

Area	1997											
	Jan.	Feb.	Mar.	Apr.	May	Jun.	Jul.	Aug.	Sep.	Oct.	Nov.	Dec.
City	4.2	3.8	3.7	3.8	3.9	4.3	4.7	4.5	4.5	4.2	3.6	3.2
MSA[1]	3.5	3.3	3.2	3.2	3.2	3.5	3.8	3.6	3.6	3.3	2.9	2.6
U.S.	5.9	5.7	5.5	4.8	4.7	5.2	5.0	4.8	4.7	4.4	4.3	4.4

Note: Data is not seasonally adjusted and covers workers 16 years of age and older; All figures are percentages; (1) Metropolitan Statistical Area - see Appendix A for areas included
Source: Bureau of Labor Statistics, http://stats.bls.gov

Employment by Industry

Sector	MSA[1]		U.S.
	Number of Employees	Percent of Total	Percent of Total
Services	371,400	36.8	29.0
Retail Trade	166,300	16.5	18.5
Government	123,000	12.2	16.1
Manufacturing	78,100	7.7	15.0
Finance/Insurance/Real Estate	103,300	10.2	5.7
Wholesale Trade	49,200	4.9	5.4
Transportation/Public Utilities	80,000	7.9	5.3
Construction	36,100	3.6	4.5
Mining	500	0.0	0.5

Note: Figures cover non-farm employment as of 12/97 and are not seasonally adjusted;
(1) Metropolitan Statistical Area - see Appendix A for areas included
Source: Bureau of Labor Statistics, http://stats.bls.gov

Employment by Occupation

Occupation Category	City (%)	MSA[1] (%)	U.S. (%)
White Collar	68.6	69.1	58.1
Executive/Admin./Management	16.0	17.0	12.3
Professional	18.6	17.5	14.1
Technical & Related Support	3.8	3.8	3.7
Sales	11.9	12.9	11.8
Administrative Support/Clerical	18.2	17.8	16.3
Blue Collar	15.3	16.5	26.2
Precision Production/Craft/Repair	6.3	7.9	11.3
Machine Operators/Assem./Insp.	4.1	3.4	6.8
Transportation/Material Movers	2.4	2.5	4.1
Cleaners/Helpers/Laborers	2.5	2.7	3.9
Services	15.7	13.3	13.2
Farming/Forestry/Fishing	0.5	1.1	2.5

Note: figures cover employed persons 16 years old and over;
(1) Metropolitan Statistical Area - see Appendix A for areas included
Source: 1990 Census of Population and Housing, Summary Tape File 3C

Occupational Employment Projections: 1994 - 2001

Occupations Expected to have the Largest Job Growth (ranked by numerical growth)	Fast-Growing Occupations (ranked by percent growth)
1. Systems analysts	1. Computer engineers
2. Janitors/cleaners/maids, ex. priv. hshld.	2. Home health aides
3. Guards	3. Electronic pagination systems workers
4. General managers & top executives	4. Systems analysts
5. Waiters & waitresses	5. Patternmakers and layout workers
6. Receptionists and information clerks	6. Corrections officers & jailers
7. Computer engineers	7. Personal and home care aides
8. Cashiers	8. Employment interviewers
9. Financial managers	9. Technical writers
10. Sales agents, business services	10. Food service and lodging managers

Projections cover San Francisco County.
Source: State of California, Employment Development Department, Labor Market Information Division, Information Services Group

Average Wages

Occupation	Wage	Occupation	Wage
Professional/Technical/Clerical	$/Week	**Health/Protective Services**	$/Week
Accountants III	907	Corrections Officers	823
Attorneys III	1,523	Firefighters	-
Budget Analysts III	924	Nurses, Licensed Practical II	-
Buyers/Contracting Specialists II	749	Nurses, Registered II	-
Clerks, Accounting III	533	Nursing Assistants II	-
Clerks, General III	511	Police Officers I	955
Computer Operators II	598	**Hourly Workers**	$/Hour
Computer Programmers II	723	Forklift Operators	-
Drafters II	573	General Maintenance Workers	10.69
Engineering Technicians III	680	Guards I	7.81
Engineering Technicians, Civil III	878	Janitors	-
Engineers III	1,056	Maintenance Electricians	22.43
Key Entry Operators I	-	Maintenance Electronics Techs II	19.83
Personnel Assistants III	638	Maintenance Machinists	19.37
Personnel Specialists III	910	Maintenance Mechanics, Machinery	20.78
Secretaries III	668	Material Handling Laborers	7.41
Switchboard Operator-Receptionist	438	Motor Vehicle Mechanics	20.55
Systems Analysts II	1,071	Shipping/Receiving Clerks	11.80
Systems Analysts Supervisor/Mgr II	1,571	Tool and Die Makers	-
Tax Collectors II	664	Truckdrivers, Tractor Trailer	-
Word Processors II	589	Warehouse Specialists	-

Note: Wage data includes full-time workers only for 3/96 and cover the Metropolitan Statistical Area (see Appendix A for areas included). Dashes indicate that data was not available.
Source: Bureau of Labor Statistics, Occupational Compensation Survey, 8/96

TAXES

Major State and Local Tax Rates

State Corp. Income (%)	State Personal Income (%)	Residential Property (effective rate per $100)	Sales & Use		State Gasoline (cents/ gallon)	State Cigarette (cents/ 20-pack)
			State (%)	Local (%)		
8.84[a]	1.0 - 9.3	n/a	6.0	2.50	18[b]	37

Note: Personal/corporate income tax rates as of 1/97. Sales, gasoline and cigarette tax rates as of 1/98; (a) Minimum tax is $800. The tax rate on S-Corporations is 1.5%; (b) Does not include 1 cent local option tax
Source: Federation of Tax Administrators, www.taxadmin.org; Washington D.C. Department of Finance and Revenue, Tax Rates and Tax Burdens in the District of Columbia: A Nationwide Comparison, June 1997; Chamber of Commerce

Total Taxes Per Capita and as a Percent of Income

Area	Per Capita Income ($)	Per Capita Taxes ($)			Taxes as Pct. of Income (%)		
		Total	Federal	State/Local	Total	Federal	State/Local
California	27,117	9,321	6,287	3,034	34.4	23.2	11.2
U.S.	26,187	9,205	6,127	3,078	35.2	23.4	11.8

Note: Figures are for 1997
Source: Tax Foundation, Web Site, www.taxfoundation.org

Estimated Tax Burden

Area	State Income	Local Income	Property	Sales	Total
San Francisco	1,824	0	2,700	723	5,247

Note: The numbers are estimates of taxes paid by a married couple with two kids and annual earnings of $65,000. Sales tax estimates assume they spend average amounts on food, clothing, household goods and gasoline. Property tax estimates assume they live in a $225,000 home.
Source: Kiplinger's Personal Finance Magazine, June 1997

COMMERCIAL REAL ESTATE

Office Market

Class/Location	Total Space (sq. ft.)	Vacant Space (sq. ft.)	Vac. Rate (%)	Under Constr. (sq. ft.)	Net Absorp. (sq. ft.)	Rental Rates ($/sq.ft./yr.)
Class A						
CBD	32,683,694	1,346,951	4.1	567,122	1,054,773	20.76-51.96
Outside CBD	10,330,671	1,544,788	15.0	n/a	150,020	12.96-33.00
Class B						
CBD	4,035,675	243,255	6.0	n/a	137,251	14.04-36.00
Outside CBD	4,483,533	294,687	6.6	n/a	377,704	10.80-30.00

Note: Data as of 10/97 and covers San Francisco; CBD = Central Business District; n/a not available;
Source: Society of Industrial and Office Realtors, 1998 Comparative Statistics of Industrial and Office Real Estate Markets

"San Francisco will remain one of the tightest, and expensive, CBDs in the nation during 1998. With no new construction deliveries for at least the next two years and continued strong demand for space, vacancies are likely to decline even more. Some relief for space-seekers is on the way, however. More than 500,000 sq. ft. of new construction is expected to commence in 1998, including 150 California Street, a 220,000 sq. ft. property expected to break ground in the first quarter. It will take at least two years until this and other new properties are available for occupancy. Despite some conversion and rehabilitation of Class 'B' and 'C' properties, especially in the South of Market sub-market, the San Francisco office sector will remain a 'landlord's market' through the millennium." *Society of Industrial and Office Realtors, 1998 Comparative Statistics of Industrial and Office Real Estate Markets*

Retail Market

Shopping Center Inventory (sq. ft.)	Shopping Center Construction (sq. ft.)	Construction as a Percent of Inventory (%)	Torto Wheaton Rent Index[1] ($/sq. ft.)
14,897,000	318,000	2.1	17.20

Note: Data as of 1997 and covers the Metropolitan Statistical Area - see Appendix A for areas included; (1) Index is based on a model that predicts what the average rent should be for leases with certain characteristics, in certain locations during certain years.
Source: National Association of Realtors, 1997-1998 Market Conditions Report

"The retail sector is performing in line with Western MSAs. During the last two years, construction has been the highest since the early 90s. Meanwhile, rents have been flat but still compare favorably to Western MSAs which have seen drops in rents over the last five years. Currently, rents are the second highest in the nation. The metro area is building momentum and this is evident in the spread of job gains beyond services. Services had accounted for the lion's share of the jobs during the past two years. San Francisco is one of the nation's most affluent areas, and real incomes are expected to increase over 1.5% per year through 2000." National Association of Realtors, 1997-1998 Market Conditions Report

COMMERCIAL UTILITIES

Typical Monthly Electric Bills

Area	Commercial Service ($/month)		Industrial Service ($/month)	
	12 kW demand 1,500 kWh	100 kW demand 30,000 kWh	1,000 kW demand 400,000 kWh	20,000 kW demand 10,000,000 kWh
City	231	3,420	41,622	565,537
U.S.	162	2,360	25,590	545,677

Note: Based on rates in effect July 1, 1997
Source: Edison Electric Institute, Typical Residential, Commercial and Industrial Bills, Summer 1997

TRANSPORTATION

Transportation Statistics

Avg. travel time to work (min.)	26.9
Interstate highways	I-80
Bus lines	
In-city	Golden Gate Transit, 265 vehicles; San Francisco Municipal Railway (Muni), 455 vehicles
Inter-city	16
Passenger air service	
Airport	San Francisco International
Airlines	49
Aircraft departures	142,598 (1995)
Enplaned passengers	15,013,265 (1995)
Rail service	Amtrak Thruway Motorcoach Connection; BART; Muni Metro (light rail)
Motor freight carriers	1,991 (San Francisco/Oakland PMSA)
Major waterways/ports	Port of San Francisco

Source: OAG, Business Travel Planner, Summer 1997; Editor & Publisher Market Guide, 1998; FAA Airport Activity Statistics, 1996; Amtrak National Time Table, Northeast Timetable, Fall/Winter 1997-98; 1990 Census of Population and Housing, STF 3C; Chamber of Commerce/Economic Development 1997; Jane's Urban Transport Systems 1997-98; Transit Fact Book 1997

A survey of 90,000 airline passengers during the first half of 1997 ranked most of the largest airports in the U.S. San Francisco International ranked number 21 out of 36. Criteria: cleanliness, quality of restaurants, attractiveness, speed of baggage delivery, ease of reaching gates, available ground transportation, ease of following signs and closeness of parking. *Plog Research Inc., First Half 1997*

Means of Transportation to Work

Area	Car/Truck/Van		Public Transportation			Bicycle	Walked	Other Means	Worked at Home
	Drove Alone	Car-pooled	Bus	Subway	Railroad				
City	38.5	11.5	24.4	5.2	0.4	1.0	9.8	5.5	3.8
MSA[1]	56.3	12.2	13.6	3.0	0.8	0.8	5.9	3.4	3.8
U.S.	73.2	13.4	3.0	1.5	0.5	0.4	3.9	1.2	3.0

Note: figures shown are percentages and only include workers 16 years old and over;
(1) Metropolitan Statistical Area - see Appendix A for areas included
Source: 1990 Census of Population and Housing, Summary Tape File 3C

BUSINESSES

Major Business Headquarters

Company Name	1997 Rankings	
	Fortune 500	Forbes 500
BankAmerica	38	-
Bechtel Group	-	11
Chevron	15	-
Chronicle Publishing	-	451
Del Monte Foods	-	149
Gap	269	-
Levi Strauss & Co.	-	16
McKesson	90	-
Pacific Gas & Electric	153	-
Pacific Telesis Group	154	-
Shorenstein	-	350
Swinerton	-	431
Transamerica	230	-
Wells Fargo	169	-
Wilbur-Ellis	-	227

Note: Companies listed are located in the city; Dashes indicate no ranking
Fortune 500: companies that produce a 10-K are ranked 1 - 500 based on 1996 revenue
Forbes 500: private companies are ranked 1 - 500 based on 1996 revenue
Source: Forbes 12/1/97; Fortune 4/28/97

Fast-Growing Businesses

According to *Inc.*, San Francisco is home to one of America's 100 fastest-growing private companies: MediaTel Corporation. Criteria for inclusion: must be an independent, privately-held, U.S. corporation, proprietorship or partnership; sales of at least $200,000 in 1993; five-year operating/sales history; increase in 1997 sales over 1996 sales; holding companies, regulated banks, and utilities were excluded. *Inc. 500, 1997*

San Francisco is home to one of *Business Week's* "hot growth" companies: Indus Group. Criteria: sales and earnings, return on capital and stock price. *Business Week, 5/26/97*

According to *Fortune*, San Francisco is home to one of America's 100 fastest-growing companies: URS. Companies were ranked based on three years' earnings-per-share growth using least squares analysis to smooth out distortions. Criteria for inclusion: public companies with sales of least $50 million. Companies that lost money in the most recent quarter, or ended in the red for the past four quarters as a whole, were not eligible. Limited partnerships and REITs were also not considered. *Fortune, 9/29/97*

San Francisco was ranked #7 out of 24 (#1 is best) in terms of the best-performing local stocks in 1996 according to the Money/Norby Cities Index. The index measures stocks of companies that have headquarters in 24 metro areas. *Money, 2/7/97*

Women-Owned Businesses: Number, Employment, Sales and Share

Area	Women-Owned Businesses in 1996				Share of Women-Owned Businesses in 1996	
	Number	Employment	Sales ($000)	Rank[2]	Percent (%)	Rank[3]
MSA[1]	80,800	217,000	31,562,900	17	39.0	9

Note: (1) Metropolitan Statistical Area - see Appendix A for areas included; (2) Calculated on an averaging of number of businesses, employment and sales and ranges from 1 to 50 where 1 is best; (3) Ranges from 1 to 50 where 1 is best
Source: The National Foundation for Women Business Owners, 1996 Facts on Women-Owned Businesses: Trends in the Top 50 Metropolitan Areas, March 26, 1997

Women-Owned Businesses: Growth

Area	Growth in Women-Owned Businesses (% change from 1987 to 1996)				Relative Growth in the Number of Women-Owned and All Businesses (% change from 1987 to 1996)			
	Num.	Empl.	Sales	Rank[2]	Women-Owned	All Firms	Absolute Difference	Relative Difference
MSA[1]	61.4	233.8	295.8	27	61.4	39.7	21.7	1.5:1

Note: (1) Metropolitan Statistical Area - see Appendix A for areas included; (2) Calculated on an averaging of the percent growth of number of businesses, employment and sales and ranges from 1 to 50 where 1 is best
Source: The National Foundation for Women Business Owners, 1996 Facts on Women-Owned Businesses: Trends in the Top 50 Metropolitan Areas, March 26, 1997

Minority Business Opportunity

Four of the 500 largest Hispanic-owned companies in the U.S. are located in San Francisco. *Hispanic Business, June 1997*

San Francisco is home to one company which is on the Hispanic Business Fastest-Growing 100 list (greatest sales growth from 1992 to 1996): A. Ruiz Construction Co. & Assoc. Inc. (general contracting and engineering) *Hispanic Business, July/August 1997*

San Francisco was listed among the top 25 metropolitan areas in terms of the number of Hispanic-owned companies. The city was ranked number 11 with 23,662 companies. *Hispanic Business, May 1997*

Small Business Opportunity

According to *Forbes*, San Francisco is home to one of America's 200 best small companies: Indus International. Criteria: companies must be publicly traded, U.S.-based corporations with latest 12-month sales of between $5 and $350 million. Earnings must be at least $1 million for the 12-month period. Limited partnerships, REITs and closed-end mutual funds were not considered. Banks, S&Ls and electric utilities were not included. *Forbes, November 3, 1997*

HOTELS & MOTELS

Hotels/Motels

Area	Hotels/Motels	Rooms	Luxury-Level Hotels/Motels		Average Minimum Rates ($)		
			♦♦♦♦	♦♦♦♦♦	♦♦	♦♦♦	♦♦♦♦
City	159	23,816	9	3	93	144	216
Airport	31	6,517	1	0	n/a	n/a	n/a
Suburbs	26	2,940	0	0	n/a	n/a	n/a
Total	216	33,273	10	3	n/a	n/a	n/a

Note: n/a not available; Classifications range from one diamond (budget properties with basic amenities) to five diamond (luxury properties with the finest service, rooms and facilities).
Source: OAG, Business Travel Planner, Summer 1997

San Francisco is home to one of the top 100 hotels in the world according to *Travel & Leisure*: Ritz-Carlton. Criteria: value, rooms/ambience, location, facilities/activities and service. *Travel & Leisure, September 1997*

CONVENTION CENTERS   **Major Convention Centers**

Center Name	Meeting Rooms	Exhibit Space (sf)
Brooks Hall Civic Auditorium	42	138,200
Concourse Exhibition Center	n/a	n/a
Cow Palace	n/a	300,000
Fairmont Hotel San Francisco	19	n/a
Moscone Center	60	442,000
Pacific Telesis Center	n/a	n/a

Note: n/a not available
Source: Trade Shows Worldwide 1997

Living Environment

COST OF LIVING

Cost of Living Index

Composite Index	Housing	Utilities	Groceries	Health Care	Trans-portation	Misc. Goods/ Services
152.5	223.4	99.3	123.6	172.8	143.7	118.0

Note: U.S. = 100
Source: ACCRA, Cost of Living Index, 2nd Quarter 1997

HOUSING

Median Home Prices and Housing Affordability

Area	Median Price[2] 3rd Qtr. 1997 ($)	HOI[3] 3rd Qtr. 1997	Afford-ability Rank[4]
MSA[1]	315,000	20.7	195
U.S.	127,000	63.7	–

Note: (1) Metropolitan Statistical Area - see Appendix A for areas included; (2) U.S. figures calculated from the sales of 625,000 new and existing homes in 195 markets; (3) Housing Opportunity Index - percent of homes sold that were within the reach of the median income household at the prevailing mortgage interest rate; (4) Rank is from 1-195 with 1 being most affordable
Source: National Association of Home Builders, Housing Opportunity Index, 3rd Quarter 1997

It is projected that the median price of existing single-family homes in the metro area will increase by 9.6% in 1998. Nationwide, home prices are projected to increase 6.6%. Kiplinger's Personal Finance Magazine, January 1998

Average New Home Price

Area	Price ($)
City	279,900
U.S.	135,150

Note: Figures are based on a new home with 1,800 sq. ft. of living area on an 8,000 sq. ft. lot.
Source: ACCRA, Cost of Living Index, 2nd Quarter 1997

Average Apartment Rent

Area	Rent ($/mth)
City	1,576
U.S.	575

Note: Figures are based on an unfurnished two bedroom, 1-1/2 or 2 bath apartment, approximately 950 sq. ft. in size, excluding all utilities except water
Source: ACCRA, Cost of Living Index, 2nd Quarter 1997

RESIDENTIAL UTILITIES

Average Residential Utility Costs

Area	All Electric ($/mth)	Part Electric ($/mth)	Other Energy ($/mth)	Phone ($/mth)
City	–	66.03	35.43	20.75
U.S.	108.38	56.32	44.12	19.66

Source: ACCRA, Cost of Living Index, 2nd Quarter 1997

HEALTH CARE

Average Health Care Costs

Area	Hospital ($/day)	Doctor ($/visit)	Dentist ($/visit)
City	1,288.75	60.75	96.80
U.S.	390.32	48.32	60.14

Note: Hospital - based on a semi-private room. Doctor - based on a general practitioner's routine exam of an established patient. Dentist - based on adult teeth cleaning and periodic oral exam.
Source: ACCRA, Cost of Living Index, 2nd Quarter 1997

Distribution of Office-Based Physicians

Area	Family/Gen. Practitioners	Specialists		
		Medical	Surgical	Other
MSA[1]	363	1,966	1,235	1,729

Note: Data as of 12/31/96; (1) Metropolitan Statistical Area - see Appendix A for areas included
Source: American Medical Assn., Physician Characteristics & Distribution in the U.S., 1997-1998

Hospitals

San Francisco has 11 general medical and surgical hospitals, 1 chronic disease, 1 other specialty, 1 children's other specialty. *AHA Guide to the Healthcare Field 1997-98*

According to *U.S. News and World Report,* San Francisco has 2 of the best hospitals in the U.S.:
San Francisco General Hospital Medical Center, noted for AIDS; **University of California, San Francisco Medical Center**, noted for AIDS, cancer, cardiology, endocrinology, gastroenterology, geriatrics, gynecology, neurology, ophthalmology, orthopedics, otolaryngology, pediatrics, psychiatry, pulmonology, urology

U.S. News and World Report, "America's Best Hospitals", 7/28/97

UCSF Stanford Health Care is among the 100 best-run hospitals in the U.S.
Modern Healthcare, January 5, 1998

EDUCATION

Public School District Statistics

District Name	Num. Sch.	Enroll.	Classroom Teachers[1]	Pupils per Teacher	Minority Pupils (%)	Current Exp.[2] ($/pupil)
San Francisco Co. Off. of Educ	3	941	57	16.5	n/a	n/a
San Francisco Unified	111	61,889	2,849	21.7	86.9	4,898

Note: Data covers the 1995-1996 school year unless otherwise noted; (1) Excludes teachers reported as working in school district offices rather than in schools; (2) Based on 1993-94 enrollment collected by the Census Bureau, not the enrollment figure shown in column 3; SD = School District; ISD = Independent School District; n/a not available
Source: National Center for Education Statistics, Common Core of Data Survey; Bureau of the Census

Educational Quality

School District	Education Quotient[1]	Graduate Outcome[2]	Community Index[3]	Resource Index[4]
San Francisco	110.0	97.0	122.0	111.0

Note: Nearly 1,000 secondary school districts were rated in terms of educational quality. The scores range from a low of 50 to a high of 150; (1) Average of the Graduate Outcome, Community and Resource indexes; (2) Based on graduation rates and college board scores (SAT/ACT); (3) Based on the surrounding community's average level of education and the area's average income level; (4) Based on teacher salaries, per-pupil expenditures and student-teacher ratios.
Source: Expansion Management, Ratings Issue 1997

Educational Attainment by Race

Area	High School Graduate (%)					Bachelor's Degree (%)				
	Total	White	Black	Other	Hisp.[2]	Total	White	Black	Other	Hisp.[2]
City	78.0	86.8	72.4	63.7	60.7	35.0	44.6	14.9	23.7	15.1
MSA[1]	82.4	87.6	74.1	69.4	60.7	34.9	39.4	15.6	27.1	13.8
U.S.	75.2	77.9	63.1	60.4	49.8	20.3	21.5	11.4	19.4	9.2

Note: figures shown cover persons 25 years old and over; (1) Metropolitan Statistical Area - see Appendix A for areas included; (2) people of Hispanic origin can be of any race
Source: 1990 Census of Population and Housing, Summary Tape File 3C

School Enrollment by Type

Area	Preprimary				Elementary/High School			
	Public		Private		Public		Private	
	Enrollment	%	Enrollment	%	Enrollment	%	Enrollment	%
City	4,493	51.4	4,256	48.6	65,078	77.5	18,853	22.5
MSA[1]	12,034	47.4	13,331	52.6	165,447	80.7	39,665	19.3
U.S.	2,679,029	59.5	1,824,256	40.5	38,379,689	90.2	4,187,099	9.8

Note: figures shown cover persons 3 years old and over;
(1) Metropolitan Statistical Area - see Appendix A for areas included
Source: 1990 Census of Population and Housing, Summary Tape File 3C

School Enrollment by Race

Area	Preprimary (%)				Elementary/High School (%)			
	White	Black	Other	Hisp.[1]	White	Black	Other	Hisp.[1]
City	43.8	16.6	39.7	14.8	30.9	16.1	52.9	21.2
MSA[2]	66.5	9.1	24.4	13.5	52.9	10.5	36.6	21.8
U.S.	80.4	12.5	7.1	7.8	74.1	15.6	10.3	12.5

Note: figures shown cover persons 3 years old and over; (1) people of Hispanic origin can be of any race; (2) Metropolitan Statistical Area - see Appendix A for areas included
Source: 1990 Census of Population and Housing, Summary Tape File 3C

SAT/ACT Scores

Area/District	1997 SAT				1997 ACT	
	Percent of Graduates Tested (%)	Average Math Score	Average Verbal Score	Average Combined Score	Percent of Graduates Tested (%)	Average Composite Score
San Francisco USD	n/a	517	456	973	n/a	20.0
State	45	514	496	1,010	11	21.0
U.S.	42	511	505	1,016	36	21.0

Note: Math and verbal SAT scores are out of a possible 800; ACT scores are out of a possible 36
Caution: Comparing or ranking states/cities on the basis of SAT/ACT scores alone is invalid and strongly discouraged by the The College Board and The American College Testing Program as students who take the tests are self-selected and do not represent the entire student population.
Source: San Francisco Unified School District, Assessment & Accountability, 1997; American College Testing Program, 1997; College Board, 1997

Classroom Teacher Salaries in Public Schools

District	B.A. Degree		M.A. Degree		Ph.D. Degree	
	Min. ($)	Max ($)	Min. ($)	Max. ($)	Min. ($)	Max. ($)
San Francisco	28,297	38,741	n/a	n/a	n/a	n/a
Average[1]	26,120	39,270	28,175	44,667	31,643	49,825

Note: Salaries are for 1996-1997; (1) Based on all school districts covered; n/a not available
Source: American Federation of Teachers (unpublished data)

Higher Education

Two-Year Colleges		Four-Year Colleges		Medical Schools	Law Schools	Voc/ Tech
Public	Private	Public	Private			
1	2	1	8	1	5	35

Source: College Blue Book, Occupational Education 1997; Medical School Admission Requirements, 1998-99; Peterson's Guide to Two-Year Colleges, 1997; Peterson's Guide to Four-Year Colleges, 1997; Barron's Guide to Law Schools 1997

MAJOR EMPLOYERS

Major Employers

BankAmerica Corp.	Bechtel Group (engineering services)
California Pacific Medical Center	California State Automobile Association
Charles Schwab & Co.	Chevron Corp.
Federal Reserve Bank of SF	Levi Strauss & Co.
Macy's West	Pacific Gas & Electric
Pacific Telesis Group	Southern Pacific Transportation
St. Mary's Hospital & Medical Center	State Compensation Insurance Fund

Note: companies listed are located in the city
Source: Dun's Business Rankings 1997; Ward's Business Directory, 1997

PUBLIC SAFETY

Crime Rate

Area	All Crimes	Violent Crimes				Property Crimes		
		Murder	Forcible Rape	Robbery	Aggrav. Assault	Burglary	Larceny -Theft	Motor Vehicle Theft
City	7,594.9	11.0	40.0	743.4	532.4	950.0	4,168.7	1,149.5
Suburbs[1]	3,597.1	1.5	19.3	117.7	239.2	497.4	2,377.3	344.7
MSA[2]	5,381.6	5.8	28.5	397.0	370.1	699.4	3,176.9	703.9
U.S.	5,078.9	7.4	36.1	202.4	388.2	943.0	2,975.9	525.9

Note: Crime rate is the number of crimes per 100,000 pop.; (1) defined as all areas within the MSA but located outside the central city; (2) Metropolitan Statistical Area - see Appendix A for areas incl.
Source: FBI Uniform Crime Reports 1996

RECREATION

Culture and Recreation

Museums	Symphony Orchestras	Opera Companies	Dance Companies	Professional Theatres	Zoos	Pro Sports Teams
25	2	4	6	4	1	2

Source: International Directory of the Performing Arts, 1996; Official Museum Directory, 1998; Chamber of Commerce/Economic Development 1997

Library System

The San Francisco Public Library has 26 branches, holdings of 2,008,619 volumes and a budget of $n/a (1995). Note: n/a means not available. *American Library Directory, 1997-1998*

MEDIA

Newspapers

Name	Type	Freq.	Distribution	Circulation
California Voice	Black	1x/wk	Local	37,325
Chinese Times	Asian	7x/wk	Area	10,000
El Bohemio News	Hispanic	1x/wk	Local	30,000
El Mensajero	Hispanic	1x/wk	Local	75,000
El Tecolote	Hispanic	1x/mo	Local	10,000
Hokubei Mainichi	Asian	5x/wk	National	10,000
Jewish Bulletin of Northern California	Religious	1x/wk	Local	29,000
Nuevo Horizonte	Hispanic	2x/mo	Area	20,000
Oakland Metro Reporter	Black	1x/wk	Local	32,645
Philippine News	Asian	1x/wk	National	138,817
The San Francisco Bay Guardian	General	1x/wk	Area	137,000
San Francisco Bay View	Black	2x/mo	Local	35,000
San Francisco Beacon	General	1x/wk	Local	10,000
San Francisco Chronicle	General	7x/wk	Area	495,286
San Francisco Examiner	General	7x/wk	Area	128,736
San Francisco Metro Reporter	Black	1x/wk	Local	22,325
San Jose/Peninsula Reporter	Black	1x/wk	Local	19,575
The Sun Reporter	Black	1x/wk	Local	16,000
Tiempo Latino	Hispanic	1x/wk	Regional	30,000

Note: Includes newspapers with circulations of 10,000 or more located in the city; Source: Burrelle's Media Directory, 1998 Edition

AM Radio Stations

Call Letters	Freq. (kHz)	Target Audience	Station Format	Music Format
KSFO	560	General	N/T	n/a
KFRC	610	n/a	M/S	MOR
KNBR	680	General	S/T	n/a
KCBS	740	General	N	n/a
KGO	810	n/a	E/N/S/T	n/a
KNEW	910	General	M	Country
KABL	960	n/a	M	Adult Standards
KIQI	1010	Hispanic	M/N/S/T	n/a
KOFY	1050	Hispanic	M/N	Spanish
KDFC	1220	General	M	Classical
KOIT	1260	n/a	M/N/S	Adult Contemporary
KDIA	1310	Black	M	Christian/R&B
KEST	1450	Asian	N/T	n/a
KKHI	1510	General	M	Classical
KPIX	1550	n/a	M/N/S	n/a

Note: Stations included broadcast in the San Francisco metro area; n/a not available
Station Format: E = Educational; M = Music; N = News; S = Sports; T = Talk
Music Format: AOR = Album Oriented Rock; MOR = Middle-of-the-Road
Source: Burrelle's Media Directory, 1998 Edition

FM Radio Stations

Call Letters	Freq. (mHz)	Target Audience	Station Format	Music Format
KQED	88.5	General	E/N/T	n/a
KPOO	89.5	n/a	M/N/S	Jazz/R&B
KFJC	89.7	General	M	Alternative
KUSF	90.3	General	E/M/S/T	Alternative/Classical/Country/Hard Rock/Jazz/Oldies/R&B/Urban Contemporary
KALW	91.7	General	E/M/N	n/a
KZSF	92.7	Hispanic	M/T	Spanish
KYCY	93.3	General	M	Country
KYLD	94.9	General	M	Contemporary Top 40
KOIT	96.5	n/a	M	Adult Contemporary
KLLC	97.3	General	M/N/S	AOR
KPIX	97.7	n/a	M/N/S	n/a
KBGG	98.1	n/a	M	Classic Rock
KSOL	98.9	General	M/N/S	Spanish
KFRC	99.7	General	M/S	Oldies
KBAY	100.3	General	M	Adult Contemporary
KKHI	100.7	General	M	Classical
KIOI	101.3	n/a	M/N/S	Adult Contemporary
KDFC	102.1	General	M/N	Classical
KBLX	102.9	General	M/N/S	Adult Contemporary
KKSF	103.7	n/a	M	Adult Contemporary/Jazz
KFOG	104.5	General	M/N/S	AOR
KBRG	104.9	Hispanic	M/N	Adult Contemporary
KITS	105.3	n/a	M/N	Alternative
KMEL	106.1	General	M	Contemporary Top 40
KSAN	107.7	General	M	Classic Rock

Note: Stations included broadcast in the San Francisco metro area; n/a not available
Station Format: E = Educational; M = Music; N = News; S = Sports; T = Talk
Music Format: AOR = Album Oriented Rock; MOR = Middle-of-the-Road
Source: Burrelle's Media Directory, 1998 Edition

Television Stations

Name	Ch.	Affiliation	Type	Owner
KTVU	2	Fox	Commercial	Cox Enterprises Inc.
KRON	4	NBC	Commercial	Chronicle Broadcasting Inc.
KPIX	5	CBS	Commercial	Westinghouse Broadcasting Company
KGO	7	ABC	Commercial	ABC Inc.
KQED	9	PBS	Public	KQED Inc.
KDTV	14	Univision	Commercial	Christian Television Group
KOFY	20	WB	Commercial	Pacific FM Inc.
KTSF	26	n/a	Commercial	Lincoln Broadcasting Company
KMTP	32	PBS	Public	Minority Television Project
KCNS	38	n/a	Commercial	Global Broadcasting Systems Inc.
KBHK	44	UPN	Commercial	UTV of San Francisco Inc.
KCSM	60	PBS	Public	San Mateo County Community College District
KPST	66	HSN	Commercial	Whitehead Media, Inc.

Note: Stations included broadcast in the San Francisco metro area
Source: Burrelle's Media Directory, 1998 Edition

CLIMATE

Average and Extreme Temperatures

Temperature	Jan	Feb	Mar	Apr	May	Jun	Jul	Aug	Sep	Oct	Nov	Dec	Ann
Extreme High (°F)	72	77	85	92	97	106	105	98	103	99	85	75	106
Average High (°F)	56	59	61	64	66	70	71	72	73	70	63	56	65
Average Temp. (°F)	49	52	53	56	58	61	63	63	64	61	55	50	57
Average Low (°F)	42	44	45	47	49	52	53	54	54	51	47	42	49
Extreme Low (°F)	26	30	31	36	39	43	44	45	41	37	31	24	24

Note: Figures cover the years 1948-1990
Source: National Climatic Data Center, International Station Meteorological Climate Summary, 3/95

Average Precipitation/Snowfall/Humidity

Precip./Humidity	Jan	Feb	Mar	Apr	May	Jun	Jul	Aug	Sep	Oct	Nov	Dec	Ann
Avg. Precip. (in.)	4.3	3.1	2.9	1.4	0.3	0.1	Tr	Tr	0.2	1.0	2.5	3.4	19.3
Avg. Snowfall (in.)	Tr	Tr	Tr	0	0	0	0	0	0	0	0	Tr	Tr
Avg. Rel. Hum. 7am (%)	86	85	82	79	78	77	81	83	83	83	85	86	82
Avg. Rel. Hum. 4pm (%)	67	65	63	61	61	60	60	62	60	60	64	68	63

Note: Figures cover the years 1948-1990; Tr = Trace amounts (<0.05 in. of rain; <0.5 in. of snow)
Source: National Climatic Data Center, International Station Meteorological Climate Summary, 3/95

Weather Conditions

Temperature			Daytime Sky			Precipitation		
10°F & below	32°F & below	90°F & above	Clear	Partly cloudy	Cloudy	0.01 inch or more precip.	0.1 inch or more snow/ice	Thunder-storms
0	6	4	136	130	99	63	< 1	5

Note: Figures are average number of days per year and covers the years 1948-1990
Source: National Climatic Data Center, International Station Meteorological Climate Summary, 3/95

AIR & WATER QUALITY

Maximum Pollutant Concentrations

	Particulate Matter (ug/m³)	Carbon Monoxide (ppm)	Sulfur Dioxide (ppm)	Nitrogen Dioxide (ppm)	Ozone (ppm)	Lead (ug/m³)
MSA[1] Level	59	5	0.007	0.022	0.10	0.01
NAAQS[2]	150	9	0.140	0.053	0.12	1.50
Met NAAQS?	Yes	Yes	Yes	Yes	Yes	Yes

Note: (1) Metropolitan Statistical Area - see Appendix A for areas included; (2) National Ambient Air Quality Standards; ppm = parts per million; ug/m³ = micrograms per cubic meter; n/a not available
Source: EPA, National Air Quality and Emissions Trends Report, 1996

Pollutant Standards Index

In the San Francisco MSA (see Appendix A for areas included), the Pollutant Standards Index (PSI) exceeded 100 on 0 days in 1996. A PSI value greater than 100 indicates that air quality would be in the unhealthful range on that day. *EPA, National Air Quality and Emissions Trends Report, 1996*

Drinking Water

Water System Name	Pop. Served	Primary Water Source Type	Number of Violations in Fiscal Year 1997	Type of Violation/ Contaminants
East Bay MUD	1,300,000	Surface	None	None

Note: Data as of January 16, 1998
Source: EPA, Office of Ground Water and Drinking Water, Safe Drinking Water Information System

San Francisco tap water is alkaline, very soft and fluoridated.
Editor & Publisher Market Guide, 1998

San Jose, California

Background

Like many cities in the valleys of northern California, San Jose is an abundant cornucopia of wine grapes and produce. Situated only seven miles from the southernmost tip of San Francisco, San Jose is flanked by the Santa Cruz Mountains to the west, and the Mount Hamilton arm of the Diablo Range to the east. The Coyote and Guadalupe Rivers gently cut through this landscape, carrying water only in the spring.

San Jose was founded on November 29, 1777 by Spanish colonizers, and can rightfully claim to be the oldest civic settlement in California. Like its present day role, San Jose was established by the Spanish to be a produce and cattle supplier to the nearby communities/presidios of San Francisco and Monterey.

After U.S. troops wrested the territory of California from Mexican rule, San Jose became its state capital. At the same time, the city served as a supply base to gold prospectors.

Today, San Jose retains much of its history in its present day life. As in the past, San Jose is still a major shipping and processing center for agricultural produce. Also, San Jose produces some of the best table wines in the country. To remind its citizens of its Spanish heritage, a replica of the Mission of Santa Clara stands on the grounds of the University of Santa Clara.

Due to annexations of surrounding communities after World War II, the population of San Jose has increased more than ten-fold. With the additional industries of national aeronautics and space administration research, and electronic components and electric motors production to attract people to the area, San Jose is rapidly becoming a family-oriented community of housing developments and shopping malls.

San Jose is home to more than half of Silicon Valley's leading semiconductor, networking and telecommunications companies. The city also has more Fortune 500 firms than any other city on the west coast. The newly renovated downtown recently became the new world headquarters of Adobe Systems, a major developer of computer software. *Site Selection Oct/Nov 1997*

San Jose enjoys a Mediterranean or dry summer subtropical climate. Winter rains account for approximately 80% of the annual precipitation during the months of November through March. Severe winter storms with gale winds and heavy rain are occasional occurrences. The summer weather is dominated by night and morning stratus clouds along with sea breezes blowing from the cold waters of the bay. During the winter months fog is common causing difficult flying conditions. Inversions causing pollution are not common during the summer months but become more frequent during the fall and winter.

General Rankings and Evaluative Comments

■ San Jose was ranked #8 out of 300 cities by *Money's* 1997 "Survey of the Best Places to Live." Criteria used: health services, crime, economy, housing, education, transportation, weather, leisure and the arts. The city was ranked #19 in 1996 and #44 in 1995.
Money, July 1997; Money, September 1996; Money, September 1995

"You may think of San Jose and the rest of Silicon Valley as the home of America's sharpest computer wonks....But San Jose, an hours drive south of San Francisco, rose from No. 19 last year largely because of the things locals do when they log off. There are so many diversions here, you can understand why First Kid Chelsea Clinton decided to call the county's Stanford University her home for the next four years.

Blessed with an average summer temperature of 74 degrees fahrenheit, Santa Clara County has more than 100,000 acres of parkland perfect for biking, roller-blading and picnics. San Jose's SoFA (South of First Street Area) district offers coffeehouses, comfortable clubs and pool halls. And for cultural outing, you can visit the Tech Museum of Innovation, which lets kids 'fly' over the surface of Mars....The area has rebounded nicely from the defense cutbacks and computer industry slowdown of the early 90s. Local firms added 38,000 jobs last year alone,....While San Jose was tops in our survey for housing-permit growth last year (up 84%), the cost of buying a home can be daunting...." *Money, July 1997*

■ *Ladies Home Journal* ranked America's 200 largest cities based on the qualities women care about most. San Jose ranked 33 out of 200. Criteria: low crime rate, good public schools, well-paying jobs, quality health and child care, the presence of women in government, proportion of women-owned businesses, size of the wage gap with men, local economy, divorce rates, the ratio of single men to single women, whether there are laws that require at least the same number of public toilets for women as men, and the probability of good hair days. *Ladies Home Journal, November 1997*

■ San Jose was ranked #53 out of 219 cities in terms of children's health, safety, and economic well-being. Criteria: total population, percent population change, birth rate, child immunization rate, infant mortality rate, percent low birth weight infants, percent of births to teens, physician-to-population ratio, student-to-teacher ratio, dropout rate, unemployment rate, median family income, percent of children in poverty, violent and property crime rates, number of juvenile arrests for violent crimes as a percent of the total crime index, number of days with pollution standard index (PSI) over 100, pounds toxic releases per 1,000 people and number of superfund sites. *Zero Population Growth, Children's Environmental Index 1997*

■ San Jose appeared on *New Mobility's* list of "10 Disability Friendly Cities". Rank: 6 out of 10. Criteria: affordable and accessible housing, transportation, quality medical care, personal assistance services and strong advocacy.

"San Jose..., the Santa Clara Valley's largest and most accessible city, reports good attitudes resulting from government and business taking active roles in disability issues. Mainline transportation is accessible except for a few express commuter routes lacking voice announcement systems. The light rail—running north-to-south through Silicon Valley—is completely accessible, and the paratransit system Outreach offers unlimited rides with its share of headaches.

Valley Medical has a well-known spinal cord injury program, including community and school education and advocacy. Personal assistance services are available through California's mammoth—but usually workable—IHSS program.

...The high cost of living, inadequate housing and poor air quality are major deterrents, but the easy climate can offset a lot of negatives." *New Mobility, December 1997*

■ *Yahoo! Internet Life* selected "America's 100 Most Wired Cities & Towns". 50 cities were large and 50 cities were small. San Jose ranked 18 out of 50 large cities. Criteria: Internet users per capita, number of networked computers, number of registered domain names, Internet backbone traffic, and the per-capita number of Web sites devoted to each city. *Yahoo! Internet Life, March 1998*

- San Jose appeared on *Sales & Marketing Management's* list of the 20 hottest domestic markets to do business in. Rank: 3 out of 20. America's 320 Metropolitan Statistical Areas were ranked based on the market's potential to buy products in certain industries like high-tech, manufacturing, office equipment and business services, as well as population and household income growth. The study had nine criteria in all.

  "It's no secret why San Jose ranks so high on S&MM's list of 20 hot markets to sell in; after all, Silicon Valley is one of the best places to do business these days.

  ...technology, of course, is San Jose's pacesetter. Home to such giants as Cisco Systems and IBM, California's third largest city boasts more than 1,500 of Silicon Valley's largest electronics firms.

  ...San Jose's technology companies run the gamut from Web site developers to laptop computers to medical technology.

  Of course, all those high-tech corporations need techno-savvy office space—and lots of it—which has led to a construction boom...." *Sales & Marketing Management, January 1998*

- Cisco Systems (computer network hardware) and Adobe Systems (computer software), headquartered in San Jose, are among the "100 Best Companies to Work for in America." Criteria: trust in management, pride in work/company, camaraderie, company responses to the Hewitt People Practices Inventory, and employee responses to their Great Place to Work survey. The companies also had to be at least 10 years old and have a minimum of 500 employees. *Fortune, January 12, 1998*

- According to *Working Mother*, "Lawmakers here—on both sides of the aisle—have agreed that the state must kick in more money to help working parents find and pay for child care. To that end, Governor Pete Wilson has proposed a significant expansion of the state's child care budget—an additional $277 million in state and federal funds. The new money would pay for care for about 90,000 more kids a year; and for preschool for another 13,000. In addition, some $45 million will be spent on recruiting and training caregivers for infants and toddlers.

  To help parents become more informed consumers, California passed a law that many consider a step backward. It allows family child care providers to care for two more kids, without hiring additional help. This means a family child care provider can now care for up to eight kids, instead of six, without additional help. The new rule also worries child care advocates because it may limit infant care in California. When caregivers take in the two extra older children, they must reduce the number of babies in their care. (California is among the 10 best states for child care.)" *Working Mother, July/August 1997*

Business Environment

STATE ECONOMY

State Economic Profile

"California's expansion is strong and stable....Entertainment and filmmaking remain steady contributors to the state's improved income growth and labor markets....

California's banking industry is consolidating and shedding workers. Improved credit conditions and healthy balance sheets make many remaining California thrifts likely takeover targets for out-of-state banks.

Delinquency rates on consumer credit have declined for the past two years and are well below the U.S. average. Mortgage foreclosure rates remain high, but they are down from the peak of one year ago when mortgage lenders took advantage of the improved housing market to shed nonperforming loans. California consumers remain cautious, however. Retail sales growth last year of 5% was no better than the national average.

Housing prices are up in northern California, and the number of units sold is rising throughout the state. Multifamily units dominated construction activity last year. With population growth accelerating and income growth outpacing the U.S. for the first time this decade, demand for single-family homes will strengthen.

Housing prices are up in northern California, and the number of units sold is rising throughout the state. Multifamily units dominated construction activity last year. With population growth accelerating the income growth outpacing the U.S. for the first time this decade, demand for single-family homes will strengthen.

Construction will contribute to the near-term expansion as home building accelerates. The greatest risk to the California economy is that the rising dollar could choke off foreign demand for California's export products. Longer term there will be some consolidation among high-tech firms, and high costs will limit the breadth of industrial development. California will remain an average performer over the long term." *National Association of Realtors, Economic Profiles: The Fifty States, July 1997*

IMPORTS/EXPORTS

Total Export Sales

Area	1993 ($000)	1994 ($000)	1995 ($000)	1996 ($000)	% Chg. 1993-96	% Chg. 1995-96
MSA[1]	16,171,568	19,942,678	26,822,812	29,331,297	81.4	9.4
U.S.	464,858,354	512,415,609	583,030,524	622,827,063	34.0	6.8

Note: (1) Metropolitan Statistical Area - see Appendix A for areas included
Source: U.S. Department of Commerce, International Trade Association, Metropolitan Area Exports: An Export Performance Report on Over 250 U.S. Cities, October 1997

Imports/Exports by Port

Type	Cargo Value			Share of U.S. Total	
	1995 (US$mil.)	1996 (US$mil.)	% Change 1995-1996	1995 (%)	1996 (%)
Imports	0	0	0	0	0
Exports	0	0	0	0	0

Source: Global Trade Information Services, WaterBorne Trade Atlas 1997

CITY FINANCES

City Government Finances

Component	FY94 ($000)	FY94 (per capita $)
Revenue	885,407	1,087.49
Expenditure	846,003	1,039.10
Debt Outstanding	1,513,178	1,858.55
Cash & Securities	2,160,607	2,653.75

Source: U.S. Bureau of the Census, City Government Finances: 1993-94

City Government Revenue by Source

Source	FY94 ($000)	FY94 (per capita $)	FY94 (%)
From Federal Government	14,541	17.86	1.6
From State Governments	54,477	66.91	6.2
From Local Governments	28,627	35.16	3.2
Property Taxes	124,031	152.34	14.0
General Sales Taxes	80,624	99.03	9.1
Selective Sales Taxes	73,074	89.75	8.3
Income Taxes	0	0.00	0.0
Current Charges	221,404	271.94	25.0
Utility/Liquor Store	10,323	12.68	1.2
Employee Retirement[1]	132,177	162.35	14.9
Other	146,129	179.48	16.5

Note: (1) Excludes "city contributions," classified as "nonrevenue," intragovernmental transfers.
Source: U.S. Bureau of the Census, City Government Finances: 1993-94

City Government Expenditures by Function

Function	FY94 ($000)	FY94 (per capita $)	FY94 (%)
Educational Services	15,531	19.08	1.8
Employee Retirement[1]	52,294	64.23	6.2
Environment/Housing	313,504	385.06	37.1
Government Administration	61,677	75.75	7.3
Interest on General Debt	68,226	83.80	8.1
Public Safety	186,632	229.23	22.1
Social Services	2,053	2.52	0.2
Transportation	89,137	109.48	10.5
Utility/Liquor Store	27,707	34.03	3.3
Other	29,242	35.92	3.5

Note: (1) Payments to beneficiaries including withdrawal of contributions.
Source: U.S. Bureau of the Census, City Government Finances: 1993-94

Municipal Bond Ratings

Area	Moody's	S & P
San Jose	Aa	n/r

Note: n/a not available; n/r not rated
Source: Moody's Bond Record, 2/98; Statistical Abstract of the U.S., 1997; Governing Magazine, 9/97, 3/98

POPULATION

Population Growth

Area	1980	1990	% Chg. 1980-90	July 1996 Estimate	% Chg. 1990-96
City	629,442	782,225	24.3	838,744	7.2
MSA[1]	1,295,071	1,497,577	15.6	1,599,604	6.8
U.S.	226,545,805	248,765,170	9.8	265,179,411	6.6

Note: (1) Metropolitan Statistical Area - see Appendix A for areas included
Source: 1980/1990 Census of Housing and Population, Summary Tape File 3C; Census Bureau Population Estimates

Population Characteristics

Race	City 1980 Population	%	City 1990 Population	%	% Chg. 1980-90	MSA[1] 1990 Population	%
White	470,458	74.7	492,692	63.0	4.7	1,035,029	69.1
Black	28,792	4.6	36,397	4.7	26.4	55,365	3.7
Amer Indian/Esk/Aleut	5,801	0.9	5,323	0.7	-8.2	9,130	0.6
Asian/Pacific Islander	53,205	8.5	152,926	19.6	187.4	261,574	17.5
Other	71,186	11.3	94,887	12.1	33.3	136,479	9.1
Hispanic Origin[2]	140,529	22.3	204,012	26.1	45.2	307,113	20.5

Note: (1) Metropolitan Statistical Area - see Appendix A for areas included;
(2) people of Hispanic origin can be of any race
Source: 1980/1990 Census of Housing and Population, Summary Tape File 3C

Ancestry

Area	German	Irish	English	Italian	U.S.	French	Polish	Dutch
City	14.0	9.8	10.3	6.8	1.9	2.9	1.6	1.5
MSA[1]	16.7	11.2	12.7	6.8	1.9	3.4	2.0	1.7
U.S.	23.3	15.6	13.1	5.9	5.3	4.2	3.8	2.5

Note: Figures are percentages and include persons that reported multiple ancestry (eg. if a person
reported being Irish and Italian, they were included in both columns); (1) Metropolitan Statistical Area -
see Appendix A for areas included
Source: 1990 Census of Population and Housing, Summary Tape File 3C

Age

Area	Median Age (Years)	Age Distribution (%) Under 5	Under 18	18-24	25-44	45-64	65+	80+
City	30.4	8.3	26.7	11.2	37.7	17.3	7.1	1.5
MSA[1]	31.8	7.4	23.9	11.0	37.9	18.6	8.6	1.8
U.S.	32.9	7.3	25.6	10.5	32.6	18.7	12.5	2.8

Note: (1) Metropolitan Statistical Area - see Appendix A for areas included
Source: 1990 Census of Population and Housing, Summary Tape File 3C

Male/Female Ratio

Area	Number of males per 100 females (all ages)	Number of males per 100 females (18 years old+)
City	102.9	102.8
MSA[1]	102.7	102.1
U.S.	95.0	91.9

Note: (1) Metropolitan Statistical Area - see Appendix A for areas included
Source: 1990 Census of Population, General Population Characteristics

INCOME

Per Capita/Median/Average Income

Area	Per Capita ($)	Median Household ($)	Average Household ($)
City	16,905	46,206	52,091
MSA[1]	20,423	48,115	57,913
U.S.	14,420	30,056	38,453

Note: all figures are for 1989; (1) Metropolitan Statistical Area - see Appendix A for areas included
Source: 1990 Census of Population and Housing, Summary Tape File 3C

Household Income Distribution by Race

Income ($)	City (%)					U.S. (%)				
	Total	White	Black	Other	Hisp.[1]	Total	White	Black	Other	Hisp.[1]
Less than 5,000	2.5	2.0	3.4	3.5	3.1	6.2	4.8	15.2	8.6	8.8
5,000 - 9,999	4.7	4.5	7.4	4.9	6.6	9.3	8.6	14.2	9.9	11.1
10,000 - 14,999	4.7	4.4	5.8	5.3	6.7	8.8	8.5	11.0	9.8	11.0
15,000 - 24,999	10.9	10.5	12.7	11.5	15.0	17.5	17.3	18.9	18.5	20.5
25,000 - 34,999	12.6	12.4	16.2	12.6	16.1	15.8	16.1	14.2	15.4	16.4
35,000 - 49,999	19.0	19.0	19.7	19.2	21.0	17.9	18.6	13.3	16.1	16.0
50,000 - 74,999	25.0	25.4	19.9	24.9	20.9	15.0	15.8	9.3	13.4	11.1
75,000 - 99,999	12.5	12.9	10.1	11.9	7.2	5.1	5.5	2.6	4.7	3.1
100,000+	8.0	8.8	4.7	6.2	3.3	4.4	4.8	1.3	3.7	1.9

Note: all figures are for 1989; (1) people of Hispanic origin can be of any race
Source: 1990 Census of Population and Housing, Summary Tape File 3C

Effective Buying Income

Area	Per Capita ($)	Median Household ($)	Average Household ($)
City	17,024	50,006	54,728
MSA[1]	20,744	53,384	61,794
U.S.	15,444	33,201	41,849

Note: data as of 1/1/97; (1) Metropolitan Statistical Area - see Appendix A for areas included
Source: Standard Rate & Data Service, Newspaper Advertising Source, 2/98

Effective Household Buying Income Distribution

Area	% of Households Earning						
	$10,000 -$19,999	$20,000 -$34,999	$35,000 -$49,999	$50,000 -$74,999	$75,000 -$99,000	$100,000 -$124,999	$125,000 and up
City	9.2	16.7	18.0	27.5	14.6	5.0	3.0
MSA[1]	8.3	15.5	16.9	26.0	15.4	6.6	5.8
U.S.	16.5	23.4	18.3	18.2	6.4	2.1	2.4

Note: data as of 1/1/97; (1) Metropolitan Statistical Area - see Appendix A for areas included
Source: Standard Rate & Data Service, Newspaper Advertising Source, 2/98

Poverty Rates by Race and Age

Area	Total (%)	By Race (%)				By Age (%)		
		White	Black	Other	Hisp.[2]	Under 5 years old	Under 18 years old	65 years and over
City	9.3	6.4	14.4	14.3	15.5	12.7	13.1	7.1
MSA[1]	7.5	5.3	12.7	12.3	14.3	10.3	10.5	6.2
U.S.	13.1	9.8	29.5	23.1	25.3	20.1	18.3	12.8

Note: figures show the percent of people living below the poverty line in 1989. The average poverty threshold was $12,674 for a family of four in 1989; (1) Metropolitan Statistical Area - see Appendix A for areas included; (2) people of Hispanic origin can be of any race
Source: 1990 Census of Population and Housing, Summary Tape File 3C

EMPLOYMENT

Labor Force and Employment

Area	Civilian Labor Force			Workers Employed		
	Dec. '95	Dec. '96	% Chg.	Dec. '95	Dec. '96	% Chg.
City	459,515	475,439	3.5	443,467	462,483	4.3
MSA[1]	904,156	936,614	3.6	877,359	914,980	4.3
U.S.	134,583,000	136,742,000	1.6	127,903,000	130,785,000	2.3

Note: Data is not seasonally adjusted and covers workers 16 years of age and older;
(1) Metropolitan Statistical Area - see Appendix A for areas included
Source: Bureau of Labor Statistics, http://stats.bls.gov

Unemployment Rate

Area	1997											
	Jan.	Feb.	Mar.	Apr.	May	Jun.	Jul.	Aug.	Sep.	Oct.	Nov.	Dec.
City	4.1	3.9	3.7	3.7	3.6	3.7	3.9	3.6	3.7	3.4	3.0	2.7
MSA[1]	3.5	3.3	3.1	3.1	3.1	3.1	3.3	3.0	3.1	2.9	2.5	2.3
U.S.	5.9	5.7	5.5	4.8	4.7	5.2	5.0	4.8	4.7	4.4	4.3	4.4

Note: Data is not seasonally adjusted and covers workers 16 years of age and older; All figures are percentages; (1) Metropolitan Statistical Area - see Appendix A for areas included
Source: Bureau of Labor Statistics, http://stats.bls.gov

Employment by Industry

Sector	MSA[1]		U.S.
	Number of Employees	Percent of Total	Percent of Total
Services	310,100	32.5	29.0
Retail Trade	136,400	14.3	18.5
Government	89,200	9.3	16.1
Manufacturing	260,500	27.3	15.0
Finance/Insurance/Real Estate	31,100	3.3	5.7
Wholesale Trade	58,500	6.1	5.4
Transportation/Public Utilities	28,700	3.0	5.3
Construction	40,600	4.2	4.5
Mining	200	0.0	0.5

Note: Figures cover non-farm employment as of 12/97 and are not seasonally adjusted;
(1) Metropolitan Statistical Area - see Appendix A for areas included
Source: Bureau of Labor Statistics, http://stats.bls.gov

Employment by Occupation

Occupation Category	City (%)	MSA[1] (%)	U.S. (%)
White Collar	62.0	67.7	58.1
Executive/Admin./Management	13.9	16.3	12.3
Professional	14.8	18.6	14.1
Technical & Related Support	5.7	6.1	3.7
Sales	10.6	10.7	11.8
Administrative Support/Clerical	16.9	15.9	16.3
Blue Collar	25.3	21.1	26.2
Precision Production/Craft/Repair	12.5	10.6	11.3
Machine Operators/Assem./Insp.	6.7	5.4	6.8
Transportation/Material Movers	2.7	2.3	4.1
Cleaners/Helpers/Laborers	3.3	2.8	3.9
Services	11.5	9.9	13.2
Farming/Forestry/Fishing	1.3	1.4	2.5

Note: figures cover employed persons 16 years old and over;
(1) Metropolitan Statistical Area - see Appendix A for areas included
Source: 1990 Census of Population and Housing, Summary Tape File 3C

Occupational Employment Projections: 1994 - 2001

Occupations Expected to have the Largest Job Growth (ranked by numerical growth)	Fast-Growing Occupations[1] (ranked by percent growth)
1. Computer engineers	1. Systems analysts
2. Engineers, electrical & electronic	2. Numerical control machine tool oper.
3. Systems analysts	3. Computer engineers
4. General managers & top executives	4. Data processing equipment repairers
5. Computer programmers	5. Demonstrators/promoters/models
6. Janitors/cleaners/maids, ex. priv. hshld.	6. Employment interviewers
7. Waiters & waitresses	7. Technical writers
8. Guards	8. Paving/surfacing/tamping equipment oper.
9. Engineers, other	9. Electrical powerline installers
10. Receptionists and information clerks	10. Home health aides

Projections cover Santa Clara County.
Note: (1) Excludes occupations with employment of less than 400 in 2001
Source: State of California, Employment Development Department, Labor Market Information Division, Information Services Group

Average Wages

Occupation	Wage	Occupation	Wage
Professional/Technical/Clerical	$/Week	**Health/Protective Services**	$/Week
Accountants III	-	Corrections Officers	-
Attorneys III	-	Firefighters	-
Budget Analysts III	-	Nurses, Licensed Practical II	-
Buyers/Contracting Specialists II	-	Nurses, Registered II	982
Clerks, Accounting III	503	Nursing Assistants II	-
Clerks, General III	470	Police Officers I	-
Computer Operators II	506	**Hourly Workers**	$/Hour
Computer Programmers II	701	Forklift Operators	-
Drafters II	529	General Maintenance Workers	11.06
Engineering Technicians III	625	Guards I	7.96
Engineering Technicians, Civil III	-	Janitors	8.72
Engineers III	-	Maintenance Electricians	22.47
Key Entry Operators I	349	Maintenance Electronics Techs II	16.97
Personnel Assistants III	-	Maintenance Machinists	22.60
Personnel Specialists III	-	Maintenance Mechanics, Machinery	18.47
Secretaries III	601	Material Handling Laborers	8.83
Switchboard Operator-Receptionist	412	Motor Vehicle Mechanics	18.74
Systems Analysts II	942	Shipping/Receiving Clerks	10.87
Systems Analysts Supervisor/Mgr II	-	Tool and Die Makers	23.07
Tax Collectors II	-	Truckdrivers, Tractor Trailer	14.52
Word Processors II	573	Warehouse Specialists	11.09

Note: Wage data includes full-time workers only for 4/94 and cover the Metropolitan Statistical Area (see Appendix A for areas included). Dashes indicate that data was not available.
Source: Bureau of Labor Statistics, Occupational Compensation Survey, 7/94

TAXES

Major State and Local Tax Rates

State Corp. Income (%)	State Personal Income (%)	Residential Property (effective rate per $100)	Sales & Use		State Gasoline (cents/ gallon)	State Cigarette (cents/ 20-pack)
			State (%)	Local (%)		
8.84[a]	1.0 - 9.3	n/a	6.0	2.25	18[b]	37

Note: Personal/corporate income tax rates as of 1/97. Sales, gasoline and cigarette tax rates as of 1/98; (a) Minimum tax is $800. The tax rate on S-Corporations is 1.5%; (b) Does not include 1 cent local option tax
Source: Federation of Tax Administrators, www.taxadmin.org; Washington D.C. Department of Finance and Revenue, Tax Rates and Tax Burdens in the District of Columbia: A Nationwide Comparison, June 1997; Chamber of Commerce

Total Taxes Per Capita and as a Percent of Income

Area	Per Capita Income ($)	Per Capita Taxes ($)			Taxes as Pct. of Income (%)		
		Total	Federal	State/Local	Total	Federal	State/Local
California	27,117	9,321	6,287	3,034	34.4	23.2	11.2
U.S.	26,187	9,205	6,127	3,078	35.2	23.4	11.8

Note: Figures are for 1997
Source: Tax Foundation, Web Site, www.taxfoundation.org

COMMERCIAL REAL ESTATE

Office Market

Class/ Location	Total Space (sq. ft.)	Vacant Space (sq. ft.)	Vac. Rate (%)	Under Constr. (sq. ft.)	Net Absorp. (sq. ft.)	Rental Rates ($/sq.ft./yr.)
Class A						
CBD	2,049,146	81,402	4.0	0	21,140	22.80-30.00
Outside CBD	2,894,481	161,874	5.6	568,000	69,922	18.00-35.40
Class B						
CBD	3,130,197	266,907	8.5	0	80,551	15.00-28.80
Outside CBD	7,443,391	182,164	2.4	0	71,404	17.20-30.00

Note: Data as of 10/97 and covers San Jose; CBD = Central Business District; n/a not available;
Source: Society of Industrial and Office Realtors, 1998 Comparative Statistics of Industrial and Office Real Estate Markets

"In addition to the speculative development in the San Jose Airport area, developers are eyeing three parcels in downtown San Jose, though none has committed to a start date without significant pre-leasing. Acquisition interest is high. REITs have been, and will likely continue to be, the primary buyers of quality properties, the most active being Carr America, Spicker Properties, and Beacon Properties. The San Jose office market will continue to be very tight through 1998. Demand is high, and new supply is still lagging far behind the demand in this dynamic market." *Society of Industrial and Office Realtors, 1998 Comparative Statistics of Industrial and Office Real Estate Markets*

Industrial Market

Location	Total Space (sq. ft.)	Vacant Space (sq. ft.)	Vac. Rate (%)	Under Constr. (sq. ft.)	Net Absorp. (sq. ft.)	Net Lease ($/sq.ft./yr.)
Central City	n/a	n/a	n/a	n/a	n/a	n/a
Suburban	73,878,989	2,135,402	2.9	1,500,000	2,337,328	9.00-13.80

Note: Data as of 10/97 and covers San Jose (Silicon Valley); n/a not available
Source: Society of Industrial and Office Realtors, 1998 Comparative Statistics of Industrial and Office Real Estate Markets

"In an effort to control their own destinies, many large high-tech companies, including Intel, Cisco, and Sun Micro, are aggressively seeking to construct or expand their own campus-style facilities. REITs have arrived in force, and will be involved in the purchase of existing assets as well as the funding of speculative new construction. Lease and sales prices will rise, although the rate of such increases will slow as pricing in Silicon Valley has long since reached a stage where achievable rents now exceed replacement cost." *Society of Industrial and Office Realtors, 1998 Comparative Statistics of Industrial and Office Real Estate Markets*

Retail Market

Shopping Center Inventory (sq. ft.)	Shopping Center Construction (sq. ft.)	Construction as a Percent of Inventory (%)	Torto Wheaton Rent Index1 ($/sq. ft.)
30,508,000	377,000	1.2	14.55

Note: Data as of 1997 and covers the Metropolitan Statistical Area - see Appendix A for areas included; (1) Index is based on a model that predicts what the average rent should be for leases with certain characteristics, in certain locations during certain years.
Source: National Association of Realtors, 1997-1998 Market Conditions Report

"Although employment and confidence have grown considerably during the last two years, they have not impacted the retail market. Rents have remained at virtually the same level over the past five years. However, the sluggish rents are consistent with other Western MSAs. Although the area is currently boasting strong employment growth and high incomes, the retail market is expected to perform similar to the pattern of the previous few years."
National Association of Realtors, 1997-1998 Market Conditions Report

COMMERCIAL UTILITIES

Typical Monthly Electric Bills

Area	Commercial Service ($/month)		Industrial Service ($/month)	
	12 kW demand 1,500 kWh	100 kW demand 30,000 kWh	1,000 kW demand 400,000 kWh	20,000 kW demand 10,000,000 kWh
City	231	3,420	41,622	565,537
U.S.	162	2,360	25,590	545,677

Note: Based on rates in effect July 1, 1997
Source: Edison Electric Institute, Typical Residential, Commercial and Industrial Bills, Summer 1997

TRANSPORTATION

Transportation Statistics

Avg. travel time to work (min.)	25.5
Interstate highways	I-80
Bus lines	
In-city	Santa Clara Valley TA
Inter-city	1
Passenger air service	
Airport	San Jose International
Airlines	14
Aircraft departures	52,846 (1995)
Enplaned passengers	4,267,071 (1995)
Rail service	Amtrak; Light Rail
Motor freight carriers	n/a
Major waterways/ports	None

Source: OAG, Business Travel Planner, Summer 1997; Editor & Publisher Market Guide, 1998; FAA Airport Activity Statistics, 1996; Amtrak National Time Table, Northeast Timetable, Fall/Winter 1997-98; 1990 Census of Population and Housing, STF 3C; Chamber of Commerce/Economic Development 1997; Jane's Urban Transport Systems 1997-98; Transit Fact Book 1997

Means of Transportation to Work

Area	Car/Truck/Van		Public Transportation			Bicycle	Walked	Other Means	Worked at Home
	Drove Alone	Car-pooled	Bus	Subway	Railroad				
City	76.9	14.6	3.1	0.1	0.3	0.6	1.6	0.9	1.9
MSA[1]	77.7	12.3	2.4	0.1	0.4	1.5	2.1	1.0	2.5
U.S.	73.2	13.4	3.0	1.5	0.5	0.4	3.9	1.2	3.0

Note: figures shown are percentages and only include workers 16 years old and over;
(1) Metropolitan Statistical Area - see Appendix A for areas included
Source: 1990 Census of Population and Housing, Summary Tape File 3C

BUSINESSES

Major Business Headquarters

Company Name	1997 Rankings	
	Fortune 500	Forbes 500
Cisco Systems	332	-
Fry's Electronics	-	155

Note: Companies listed are located in the city; Dashes indicate no ranking
Fortune 500: companies that produce a 10-K are ranked 1 - 500 based on 1996 revenue
Forbes 500: private companies are ranked 1 - 500 based on 1996 revenue
Source: Forbes 12/1/97; Fortune 4/28/97

Fast-Growing Businesses

San Jose is home to two of *Business Week's* "hot growth" companies: Rockshox and Micrel. Criteria: sales and earnings, return on capital and stock price. *Business Week, 5/26/97*

According to *Fortune*, San Jose is home to six of America's 100 fastest-growing companies: Altera, Atmel, Chips & Technologies, KLA-Tencor, Sanmina, and Ultratech Stepper. Companies were ranked based on three years' earnings-per-share growth using least squares analysis to smooth out distortions. Criteria for inclusion: public companies with sales of least $50 million. Companies that lost money in the most recent quarter, or ended in the red for the past four quarters as a whole, were not eligible. Limited partnerships and REITs were also not considered. *Fortune, 9/29/97*

According to Deloitte & Touche LLP, San Jose is home to four of America's 100 fastest-growing high-technology companies: Pericom Semiconductor Corp., Alliance Semiconductor Corp., Clarify Inc., and ArrayComm Inc. Companies are ranked by percentage growth in revenue over a five-year period. Criteria for inclusion: must be a U.S. company developing and/or providing technology products or services; company must have been in business for five years with 1992 revenues of at least $50,000. *Deloitte & Touche LLP, January 7, 1998*

Women-Owned Businesses: Number, Employment, Sales and Share

Area	Women-Owned Businesses in 1996				Share of Women-Owned Businesses in 1996	
	Number	Employment	Sales ($000)	Rank[2]	Percent (%)	Rank[3]
MSA[1]	53,800	104,800	14,191,300	32	37.7	18

Note: (1) Metropolitan Statistical Area - see Appendix A for areas included; (2) Calculated on an averaging of number of businesses, employment and sales and ranges from 1 to 50 where 1 is best; (3) Ranges from 1 to 50 where 1 is best
Source: The National Foundation for Women Business Owners, 1996 Facts on Women-Owned Businesses: Trends in the Top 50 Metropolitan Areas, March 26, 1997

Women-Owned Businesses: Growth

Area	Growth in Women-Owned Businesses (% change from 1987 to 1996)				Relative Growth in the Number of Women-Owned and All Businesses (% change from 1987 to 1996)			
	Num.	Empl.	Sales	Rank[2]	Women-Owned	All Firms	Absolute Difference	Relative Difference
MSA[1]	59.2	258.6	313.9	22	59.2	38.3	20.9	1.5:1

Note: (1) Metropolitan Statistical Area - see Appendix A for areas included; (2) Calculated on an averaging of the percent growth of number of businesses, employment and sales and ranges from 1 to 50 where 1 is best
Source: The National Foundation for Women Business Owners, 1996 Facts on Women-Owned Businesses: Trends in the Top 50 Metropolitan Areas, March 26, 1997

Minority Business Opportunity

Six of the 500 largest Hispanic-owned companies in the U.S. are located in San Jose. *Hispanic Business, June 1997*

San Jose was listed among the top 25 metropolitan areas in terms of the number of Hispanic-owned companies. The city was ranked number 17 with 16,057 companies. *Hispanic Business, May 1997*

Small Business Opportunity

According to *Forbes*, San Jose is home to one of America's 200 best small companies: Micrel. Criteria: companies must be publicly traded, U.S.-based corporations with latest 12-month sales of between $5 and $350 million. Earnings must be at least $1 million for the 12-month period. Limited partnerships, REITs and closed-end mutual funds were not considered. Banks, S&Ls and electric utilities were not included. *Forbes, November 3, 1997*

HOTELS & MOTELS

Hotels/Motels

Area	Hotels/ Motels	Rooms	Luxury-Level Hotels/Motels		Average Minimum Rates ($)		
			♦♦♦♦	♦♦♦♦♦	♦♦	♦♦♦	♦♦♦♦
City	19	2,226	1	0	56	128	179
Airport	30	5,436	0	0	n/a	n/a	n/a
Suburbs	88	9,192	0	0	n/a	n/a	n/a
Total	137	16,854	1	0	n/a	n/a	n/a

Note: n/a not available; Classifications range from one diamond (budget properties with basic amenities) to five diamond (luxury properties with the finest service, rooms and facilities).
Source: OAG, Business Travel Planner, Summer 1997

CONVENTION CENTERS

Major Convention Centers

Center Name	Meeting Rooms	Exhibit Space (sf)
Civic Auditorium Complex/San Jose	33	265,000
San Jose McEnergy Convention Center	30	200,000

Source: Trade Shows Worldwide 1997

Living Environment

COST OF LIVING

Cost of Living Index

Composite Index	Housing	Utilities	Groceries	Health Care	Trans-portation	Misc. Goods/ Services
n/a	n/a	n/a	n/a	n/a	n/a	n/a

Note: U.S. = 100; n/a not available
Source: ACCRA, Cost of Living Index, 3rd Quarter 1997

HOUSING

Median Home Prices and Housing Affordability

Area	Median Price[2] 3rd Qtr. 1997 ($)	HOI[3] 3rd Qtr. 1997	Afford-ability Rank[4]
MSA[1]	280,000	34.6	190
U.S.	127,000	63.7	--

Note: (1) Metropolitan Statistical Area - see Appendix A for areas included; (2) U.S. figures calculated from the sales of 625,000 new and existing homes in 195 markets; (3) Housing Opportunity Index - percent of homes sold that were within the reach of the median income household at the prevailing mortgage interest rate; (4) Rank is from 1-195 with 1 being most affordable
Source: National Association of Home Builders, Housing Opportunity Index, 3rd Quarter 1997

It is projected that the median price of existing single-family homes in the metro area will increase by 10.6% in 1998. Nationwide, home prices are projected to increase 6.6%.
Kiplinger's Personal Finance Magazine, January 1998

Average New Home Price

Area	Price ($)
City	n/a
U.S.	135,710

Note: n/a not available
Source: ACCRA, Cost of Living Index, 3rd Quarter 1997

Average Apartment Rent

Area	Rent ($/mth)
City	n/a
U.S.	569

Note: n/a not available
Source: ACCRA, Cost of Living Index, 3rd Quarter 1997

RESIDENTIAL UTILITIES

Average Residential Utility Costs

Area	All Electric ($/mth)	Part Electric ($/mth)	Other Energy ($/mth)	Phone ($/mth)
City	n/a	n/a	n/a	n/a
U.S.	109.40	55.25	43.64	19.48

Note: n/a not available
Source: ACCRA, Cost of Living Index, 3rd Quarter 1997

HEALTH CARE

Average Health Care Costs

Area	Hospital ($/day)	Doctor ($/visit)	Dentist ($/visit)
City	n/a	n/a	n/a
U.S.	392.91	48.76	60.84

Note: n/a not available
Source: ACCRA, Cost of Living Index, 3rd Quarter 1997

Distribution of Office-Based Physicians

| Area | Family/Gen. Practitioners | Specialists | | |
		Medical	Surgical	Other
MSA[1]	312	1,217	819	915

Note: Data as of 12/31/96; (1) Metropolitan Statistical Area - see Appendix A for areas included
Source: American Medical Assn., Physician Characteristics & Distribution in the U.S., 1997-1998

Hospitals

San Jose has 6 general medical and surgical hospitals. *AHA Guide to the Healthcare Field 1997-98*

According to *U.S. News and World Report,* San Jose has 1 of the best hospitals in the U.S.: **Santa Clara Valley Medical Center**, noted for rehabilitation; *U.S. News and World Report, "America's Best Hospitals", 7/28/97*

EDUCATION

Public School District Statistics

District Name	Num. Sch.	Enroll.	Classroom Teachers[1]	Pupils per Teacher	Minority Pupils (%)	Current Exp.[2] ($/pupil)
Alum Rock Union Elementary	25	15,834	541	29.3	n/a	n/a
Berryessa Union Elementary	13	9,011	353	25.5	n/a	n/a
Cambrian Elementary	5	2,773	112	24.8	n/a	n/a
Campbell Union High	5	6,477	272	23.8	n/a	n/a
East Side Union High	14	22,082	954	23.1	79.7	5,186
Evergreen Elementary	15	11,052	418	26.4	n/a	n/a
Franklin-Mckinley Elementary	13	10,643	386	27.6	n/a	n/a
Luther Burbank Elementary	1	403	17	23.7	n/a	n/a
Moreland Elementary	9	4,446	183	24.3	n/a	n/a
Mt. Pleasant Elementary	5	2,737	110	24.9	n/a	n/a
Oak Grove Elementary	20	12,231	487	25.1	n/a	n/a
Orchard Elementary	1	523	23	22.7	n/a	n/a
San Jose Unified	49	32,160	1,375	23.4	67.2	5,229
Santa Clara Co. Off. of Educ	2	2,611	247	10.6	n/a	n/a
Union Elementary	10	4,839	212	22.8	n/a	n/a

Note: Data covers the 1995-1996 school year unless otherwise noted; (1) Excludes teachers reported as working in school district offices rather than in schools; (2) Based on 1993-94 enrollment collected by the Census Bureau, not the enrollment figure shown in column 3; SD = School District; ISD = Independent School District; n/a not available
Source: National Center for Education Statistics, Common Core of Data Survey; Bureau of the Census

Educational Quality

School District	Education Quotient[1]	Graduate Outcome[2]	Community Index[3]	Resource Index[4]
San Jose	128.0	105.0	146.0	134.0

Note: Nearly 1,000 secondary school districts were rated in terms of educational quality. The scores range from a low of 50 to a high of 150; (1) Average of the Graduate Outcome, Community and Resource indexes; (2) Based on graduation rates and college board scores (SAT/ACT); (3) Based on the surrounding community's average level of education and the area's average income level; (4) Based on teacher salaries, per-pupil expenditures and student-teacher ratios.
Source: Expansion Management, Ratings Issue 1997

Educational Attainment by Race

| Area | High School Graduate (%) | | | | | Bachelor's Degree (%) | | | | |
	Total	White	Black	Other	Hisp.[2]	Total	White	Black	Other	Hisp.[2]
City	77.2	81.2	82.9	66.9	50.5	25.3	26.1	21.4	24.2	7.1
MSA[1]	82.0	85.3	84.3	71.9	54.1	32.6	33.8	23.3	30.3	9.3
U.S.	75.2	77.9	63.1	60.4	49.8	20.3	21.5	11.4	19.4	9.2

Note: figures shown cover persons 25 years old and over; (1) Metropolitan Statistical Area - see Appendix A for areas included; (2) people of Hispanic origin can be of any race
Source: 1990 Census of Population and Housing, Summary Tape File 3C

School Enrollment by Type

Area	Preprimary Public Enrollment	Preprimary Public %	Preprimary Private Enrollment	Preprimary Private %	Elementary/High School Public Enrollment	Elementary/High School Public %	Elementary/High School Private Enrollment	Elementary/High School Private %
City	7,378	55.5	5,909	44.5	126,273	90.9	12,573	9.1
MSA[1]	14,196	52.6	12,816	47.4	213,645	90.1	23,398	9.9
U.S.	2,679,029	59.5	1,824,256	40.5	38,379,689	90.2	4,187,099	9.8

Note: figures shown cover persons 3 years old and over;
(1) Metropolitan Statistical Area - see Appendix A for areas included
Source: 1990 Census of Population and Housing, Summary Tape File 3C

School Enrollment by Race

Area	Preprimary (%) White	Preprimary (%) Black	Preprimary (%) Other	Preprimary (%) Hisp.[1]	Elementary/High School (%) White	Elementary/High School (%) Black	Elementary/High School (%) Other	Elementary/High School (%) Hisp.[1]
City	65.4	4.7	29.9	22.2	54.5	5.3	40.2	34.6
MSA[2]	69.3	3.5	27.2	17.2	60.1	4.5	35.4	29.6
U.S.	80.4	12.5	7.1	7.8	74.1	15.6	10.3	12.5

Note: figures shown cover persons 3 years old and over; (1) people of Hispanic origin can be of any race; (2) Metropolitan Statistical Area - see Appendix A for areas included
Source: 1990 Census of Population and Housing, Summary Tape File 3C

SAT/ACT Scores

Area/District	1996 SAT Percent of Graduates Tested (%)	1996 SAT Average Math Score	1996 SAT Average Verbal Score	1996 SAT Average Combined Score	1996 ACT Percent of Graduates Tested (%)	1996 ACT Average Composite Score
San Jose USD	39	533	513	1,046	7	21.7
State	45	511	495	1,006	11	21.0
U.S.	41	508	505	1,013	35	20.9

Note: Math and verbal SAT scores are out of a possible 800; ACT scores are out of a possible 36
Caution: Comparing or ranking states/cities on the basis of SAT/ACT scores alone is invalid and strongly discouraged by the The College Board and The American College Testing Program as students who take the tests are self-selected and do not represent the entire student population. 1996 SAT scores cannot be compared to previous years due to recentering.
Source: San Jose Unified School District, 1995-96; American College Testing Program, 1996; College Board, 1996

Classroom Teacher Salaries in Public Schools

District	B.A. Degree Min. ($)	B.A. Degree Max. ($)	M.A. Degree Min. ($)	M.A. Degree Max. ($)	Ph.D. Degree Min. ($)	Ph.D. Degree Max. ($)
San Jose	27,075	38,317	28,681	39,923	33,499	47,953
Average[1]	26,120	39,270	28,175	44,667	31,643	49,825

Note: Salaries are for 1996-1997; (1) Based on all school districts covered
Source: American Federation of Teachers (unpublished data)

Higher Education

Two-Year Colleges Public	Two-Year Colleges Private	Four-Year Colleges Public	Four-Year Colleges Private	Medical Schools	Law Schools	Voc/ Tech
2	1	1	2	0	0	19

Source: College Blue Book, Occupational Education 1997; Medical School Admission Requirements, 1998-99; Peterson's Guide to Two-Year Colleges, 1997; Peterson's Guide to Four-Year Colleges, 1997; Barron's Guide to Law Schools 1997

MAJOR EMPLOYERS

Major Employers

Alexian Brothers of San Jose
Cadence Design Systems
Seagate Peripherals (computers)
Fujitsu America (computers)
KLA Instruments Corp.
O'Connor Hospital
Sutter's Place (amusement services)
XILINX Inc. (semiconductors)

Altera Corp. (semiconductors)
Cisco Systems (computers)
Cypress Semiconductor
Garden City Inc. (amusement services)
VLSI Technology (semiconductors)
Stratacom (telephone apparatus)
Viking Freight
Silicon Valley Group

Note: companies listed are located in the city
Source: Dun's Business Rankings 1997; Ward's Business Directory, 1997

PUBLIC SAFETY

Crime Rate

Area	All Crimes	Violent Crimes				Property Crimes		
		Murder	Forcible Rape	Robbery	Aggrav. Assault	Burglary	Larceny -Theft	Motor Vehicle Theft
City	4,129.1	4.8	41.1	132.2	553.5	566.0	2,383.6	447.9
Suburbs[1]	3,899.7	1.1	27.0	86.0	260.1	563.7	2,696.9	265.0
MSA[2]	4,020.3	3.0	34.4	110.3	414.3	564.9	2,532.2	361.2
U.S.	5,078.9	7.4	36.1	202.4	388.2	943.0	2,975.9	525.9

Note: Crime rate is the number of crimes per 100,000 pop.; (1) defined as all areas within the MSA but located outside the central city; (2) Metropolitan Statistical Area - see Appendix A for areas incl.
Source: FBI Uniform Crime Reports 1996

RECREATION

Culture and Recreation

Museums	Symphony Orchestras	Opera Companies	Dance Companies	Professional Theatres	Zoos	Pro Sports Teams
6	1	1	1	3	1	1

Source: International Directory of the Performing Arts, 1996; Official Museum Directory, 1998; Chamber of Commerce/Economic Development 1997

Library System

The San Jose Public Library has 17 branches, holdings of 1,385,619 volumes and a budget of $16,848,908 (1994-1995). *American Library Directory, 1997-1998*

MEDIA

Newspapers

Name	Type	Freq.	Distribution	Circulation
El Observador	Hispanic	1x/wk	Area	23,000
La Oferta Review	Hispanic	1x/wk	Local	102,000
Metro	General	1x/wk	Area	90,000
Nuevo Mundo	Hispanic	1x/wk	Area	39,000
San Jose Mercury News	General	7x/wk	Area	290,115
Willow Glen Resident	General	1x/wk	Local	19,000

Note: Includes newspapers with circulations of 10,000 or more located in the city; Source: Burrelle's Media Directory, 1998 Edition

AM Radio Stations

Call Letters	Freq. (kHz)	Target Audience	Station Format	Music Format
KLOK	1170	Hispanic	M	Spanish
KAZA	1290	Hispanic	M/N/S	Spanish
KKSJ	1370	General	M/N/S	Adult Standards
KNTA	1430	Hispanic	M/N/S	n/a
KSJX	1500	n/a	M/N/S	n/a
KLIV	1590	n/a	N	n/a

Note: Stations included broadcast in the San Jose metro area; n/a not available
Station Format: E = Educational; M = Music; N = News; S = Sports; T = Talk
Source: Burrelle's Media Directory, 1998 Edition

FM Radio Stations

Call Letters	Freq. (mHz)	Target Audience	Station Format	Music Format
KLEL	89.3	n/a	M/N/S	AOR
KFJC	89.7	General	M	Alternative
KZSU	90.1	General	E/M/N/S	Alternative/Big Band/Christian/Classic Rock/Classical/Country/Jazz/Oldies/R&B/Urban Contemporary
KSFH	90.5	General	M	n/a
KSJS	90.5	n/a	M	Alternative/Big Band/Christian/Jazz/Oldies/R&B/Spanish
KKUP	91.5	General	E/M/T	n/a
KSJO	92.3	General	M	AOR
KUFX	94.5	n/a	M/N/S	Classic Rock
KRTY	95.3	General	M/N/S	Country
KOME	98.5	General	M	Alternative
KBAY	100.3	General	M	Adult Contemporary
KSCU	103.3	n/a	M/N/S	n/a
KARA	105.7	n/a	M	Adult Contemporary
KEZR	106.5	General	M/N/S	Adult Contemporary

Note: Stations included broadcast in the San Jose metro area; n/a not available
Station Format: E = Educational; M = Music; N = News; S = Sports; T = Talk
Music Format: AOR = Album Oriented Rock; MOR = Middle-of-the-Road
Source: Burrelle's Media Directory, 1998 Edition

Television Stations

Name	Ch.	Affiliation	Type	Owner
KNTV	11	ABC	Commercial	Granite Broadcasting Corporation
KCU	15	Telemundo	Commercial	Telemundo Group Inc.
KICU	36	n/a	Commercial	KICU, Inc.
KDQ	47	Telemundo	Commercial	Telemundo Group Inc.
KSTS	48	Telemundo	Commercial	Telemundo Group Inc.
KTEH	54	PBS	Public	KTEH Foundation

Note: Stations included broadcast in the San Jose metro area
Source: Burrelle's Media Directory, 1998 Edition

CLIMATE

Average and Extreme Temperatures

Temperature	Jan	Feb	Mar	Apr	May	Jun	Jul	Aug	Sep	Oct	Nov	Dec	Ann
Extreme High (°F)	76	82	83	95	103	104	105	101	105	100	87	76	105
Average High (°F)	57	61	63	67	70	74	75	75	76	72	65	58	68
Average Temp. (°F)	50	53	55	58	61	65	66	67	66	63	56	50	59
Average Low (°F)	42	45	46	48	51	55	57	58	57	53	47	42	50
Extreme Low (°F)	21	26	30	32	38	43	45	47	41	33	29	23	21

Note: Figures cover the years 1945-1993
Source: National Climatic Data Center, International Station Meteorological Climate Summary, 3/95

Average Precipitation/Snowfall/Humidity

Precip./Humidity	Jan	Feb	Mar	Apr	May	Jun	Jul	Aug	Sep	Oct	Nov	Dec	Ann
Avg. Precip. (in.)	2.7	2.3	2.2	0.9	0.3	0.1	Tr	Tr	0.2	0.7	1.7	2.3	13.5
Avg. Snowfall (in.)	Tr	Tr	Tr	0	0	0	0	0	0	0	0	Tr	Tr
Avg. Rel. Hum. 7am (%)	82	82	80	76	74	73	77	79	79	79	81	82	79
Avg. Rel. Hum. 4pm (%)	62	59	56	52	53	54	58	58	55	54	59	63	57

Note: Figures cover the years 1945-1993; Tr = Trace amounts (<0.05 in. of rain; <0.5 in. of snow)
Source: National Climatic Data Center, International Station Meteorological Climate Summary, 3/95

Weather Conditions

Temperature			Daytime Sky			Precipitation		
10°F & below	32°F & below	90°F & above	Clear	Partly cloudy	Cloudy	0.01 inch or more precip.	0.1 inch or more snow/ice	Thunder-storms
0	5	5	106	180	79	57	< 1	6

Note: Figures are average number of days per year and covers the years 1945-1993
Source: National Climatic Data Center, International Station Meteorological Climate Summary, 3/95

AIR & WATER QUALITY

Maximum Pollutant Concentrations

	Particulate Matter (ug/m^3)	Carbon Monoxide (ppm)	Sulfur Dioxide (ppm)	Nitrogen Dioxide (ppm)	Ozone (ppm)	Lead (ug/m^3)
MSA[1] Level	68	6	n/a	0.025	0.12	0.01
NAAQS[2]	150	9	0.140	0.053	0.12	1.50
Met NAAQS?	Yes	Yes	n/a	Yes	Yes	Yes

Note: (1) Metropolitan Statistical Area - see Appendix A for areas included; (2) National Ambient Air Quality Standards; ppm = parts per million; ug/m^3 = micrograms per cubic meter; n/a not available
Source: EPA, National Air Quality and Emissions Trends Report, 1996

Pollutant Standards Index

In the San Jose MSA (see Appendix A for areas included), the Pollutant Standards Index (PSI) exceeded 100 on 2 days in 1996. A PSI value greater than 100 indicates that air quality would be in the unhealthful range on that day. *EPA, National Air Quality and Emissions Trends Report, 1996*

Drinking Water

Water System Name	Pop. Served	Primary Water Source Type	Number of Violations in Fiscal Year 1997	Type of Violation/ Contaminants
San Jose Water Company	928,000	Ground	None	None

Note: Data as of January 16, 1998
Source: EPA, Office of Ground Water and Drinking Water, Safe Drinking Water Information System

San Jose tap water is alkaline, very hard and not fluoridated.
Editor & Publisher Market Guide, 1998

Santa Rosa, California

Background

The city of Santa Rosa is the seat of Sonoma County in Northern California, about 15 miles east of the Pacific coast and 50 miles north-northwest of San Francisco. Located on Santa Rosa Creek, at the foot of the Sonoma Mountains, Santa Rosa was founded in 1833 by Mariano Guadalupe Vallejo and presumably named for St. Rose of Lima. Called "the chosen spot of all the earth as far as nature is concerned" by the famed horticulturist Luther Burbank, Santa Rosa and Sonoma County is a beautiful place to live.

Luther Burbank, whose home and Memorial Gardens are open to the public, is a famous son of Santa Rosa. Living in the city from 1875 until his death in 1926, Burbank developed the Shasta daisy, the Russet potato, an edible raspberry, as well as a multitude of other new horticultural varieties. Agriculture remains a major factor in the area and Santa Rosa is the processing and shipping center for the produce of the region. The surrounding Sonoma County is famous for its vineyards, which produce some of the finest California vintages. More than 145 wineries and 31,000 acres of wine grapes are located within the county. The city's principal industries outside of agriculture and viniculture are lumber, fish packing, optical coating, and the manufacture of machinery, clothing and shoes.

Another famous son of Santa Rosa is Robert L. Ripley, of Believe It or Not fame. The Ripley Museum, located in town, was made from one giant redwood that stood 275 feet high with an 18 foot diameter. Ripley, living in Santa Rosa, sold his first cartoon to Life magazine for eight dollars. In true "believe it or not" fashion, Charles Schultz sold his first cartoon to Ripley for the same amount. Mr. Schultz continues to write his famous Peanuts cartoons from his studio in Santa Rosa.

Santa Rosa, Sonoma County and its lovely countryside can be enjoyed in a multitude of ways. Golf is a favorite pastime and six courses are located in the city. Ballooning provides views from the air, while bicycles and horseback riding give an up-close look. Just to the north of the city is the Petrified Forest, containing silicified and opalized redwood trees, while northwest of the city is the Armstrong Redwoods State Park and its live giant redwoods. Of course, the glorious Northern California Pacific coastline lies just 15 miles to the west. For those who prefer indoor entertainment, the Luther Burbank Center for the Arts hosts a wide variety of musical and theatrical entertainments.

General Rankings and Evaluative Comments

- Santa Rosa was ranked #97 out of 300 cities by *Money's* 1997 "Survey of the Best Places to Live." Criteria used: health services, crime, economy, housing, education, transportation, weather, leisure and the arts. The city was ranked #97 in 1996 and #64 in 1995. *Money, July 1997; Money, September 1996; Money, September 1995*

- *Ladies Home Journal* ranked America's 200 largest cities based on the qualities women care about most. Santa Rosa ranked 45 out of 200. Criteria: low crime rate, good public schools, well-paying jobs, quality health and child care, the presence of women in government, proportion of women-owned businesses, size of the wage gap with men, local economy, divorce rates, the ratio of single men to single women, whether there are laws that require at least the same number of public toilets for women as men, and the probability of good hair days. *Ladies Home Journal, November 1997*

- Santa Rosa was ranked #20 out of 219 cities in terms of children's health, safety, and economic well-being. Criteria: total population, percent population change, birth rate, child immunization rate, infant mortality rate, percent low birth weight infants, percent of births to teens, physician-to-population ratio, student-to-teacher ratio, dropout rate, unemployment rate, median family income, percent of children in poverty, violent and property crime rates, number of juvenile arrests for violent crimes as a percent of the total crime index, number of days with pollution standard index (PSI) over 100, pounds toxic releases per 1,000 people and number of superfund sites. *Zero Population Growth, Children's Environmental Index 1997*

- According to *Working Mother,* "Lawmakers here—on both sides of the aisle—have agreed that the state must kick in more money to help working parents find and pay for child care. To that end, Governor Pete Wilson has proposed a significant expansion of the state's child care budget—an additional $277 million in state and federal funds. The new money would pay for care for about 90,000 more kids a year; and for preschool for another 13,000. In addition, some $45 million will be spent on recruiting and training caregivers for infants and toddlers.

  To help parents become more informed consumers, California passed a law that many consider a step backward. It allows family child care providers to care for two more kids, without hiring additional help. This means a family child care provider can now care for up to eight kids, instead of six, without additional help. The new rule also worries child care advocates because it may limit infant care in California. When caregivers take in the two extra older children, they must reduce the number of babies in their care. (California is among the 10 best states for child care.)" *Working Mother, July/August 1997*

Business Environment

STATE ECONOMY

State Economic Profile

"California's expansion is strong and stable....Entertainment and filmmaking remain steady contributors to the state's improved income growth and labor markets....

California's banking industry is consolidating and shedding workers. Improved credit conditions and healthy balance sheets make many remaining California thrifts likely takeover targets for out-of-state banks.

Delinquency rates on consumer credit have declined for the past two years and are well below the U.S. average. Mortgage foreclosure rates remain high, but they are down from the peak of one year ago when mortgage lenders took advantage of the improved housing market to shed nonperforming loans. California consumers remain cautious, however. Retail sales growth last year of 5% was no better than the national average.

Housing prices are up in northern California, and the number of units sold is rising throughout the state. Multifamily units dominated construction activity last year. With population growth accelerating and income growth outpacing the U.S. for the first time this decade, demand for single-family homes will strengthen.

Housing prices are up in northern California, and the number of units sold is rising throughout the state. Multifamily units dominated construction activity last year. With population growth accelerating the income growth outpacing the U.S. for the first time this decade, demand for single-family homes will strengthen.

Construction will contribute to the near-term expansion as home building accelerates. The greatest risk to the California economy is that the rising dollar could choke off foreign demand for California's export products. Longer term there will be some consolidation among high-tech firms, and high costs will limit the breadth of industrial development. California will remain an average performer over the long term." *National Association of Realtors, Economic Profiles: The Fifty States, July 1997*

IMPORTS/EXPORTS

Total Export Sales

Area	1993 ($000)	1994 ($000)	1995 ($000)	1996 ($000)	% Chg. 1993-96	% Chg. 1995-96
MSA[1]	409,067	485,151	572,939	681,825	66.7	19.0
U.S.	464,858,354	512,415,609	583,030,524	622,827,063	34.0	6.8

Note: (1) Metropolitan Statistical Area - see Appendix A for areas included
Source: U.S. Department of Commerce, International Trade Association, Metropolitan Area Exports: An Export Performance Report on Over 250 U.S. Cities, October 1997

Imports/Exports by Port

Type	Cargo Value			Share of U.S. Total	
	1995 (US$mil.)	1996 (US$mil.)	% Change 1995-1996	1995 (%)	1996 (%)
Imports	0	0	0	0	0
Exports	0	0	0	0	0

Source: Global Trade Information Services, WaterBorne Trade Atlas 1997

CITY FINANCES

City Government Finances

Component	FY92 ($000)	FY92 (per capita $)
Revenue	132,924	1,132.55
Expenditure	135,635	1,155.65
Debt Outstanding	218,731	1,863.65
Cash & Securities	245,163	2,088.86

Source: U.S. Bureau of the Census, City Government Finances: 1991-92

City Government Revenue by Source

Source	FY92 ($000)	FY92 (per capita $)	FY92 (%)
From Federal Government	2,509	21.38	1.9
From State Governments	16,319	139.04	12.3
From Local Governments	0	0.00	0.0
Property Taxes	13,538	115.35	10.2
General Sales Taxes	18,355	156.39	13.8
Selective Sales Taxes	9,040	77.02	6.8
Income Taxes	0	0.00	0.0
Current Charges	28,162	239.95	21.2
Utility/Liquor Store	13,173	112.24	9.9
Employee Retirement[1]	0	0.00	0.0
Other	31,828	271.18	23.9

Note: (1) Excludes "city contributions," classified as "nonrevenue," intragovernmental transfers.
Source: U.S. Bureau of the Census, City Government Finances: 1991-92

City Government Expenditures by Function

Function	FY92 ($000)	FY92 (per capita $)	FY92 (%)
Educational Services	0	0.00	0.0
Employee Retirement[1]	0	0.00	0.0
Environment/Housing	41,525	353.80	30.6
Government Administration	19,565	166.70	14.4
Interest on General Debt	13,400	114.17	9.9
Public Safety	24,868	211.88	18.3
Social Services	405	3.45	0.3
Transportation	12,939	110.24	9.5
Utility/Liquor Store	17,054	145.30	12.6
Other	5,879	50.09	4.3

Note: (1) Payments to beneficiaries including withdrawal of contributions.
Source: U.S. Bureau of the Census, City Government Finances: 1991-92

Municipal Bond Ratings

Area	Moody's	S & P
Santa Rosa	Aa	n/a

Note: n/a not available; n/r not rated
Source: Moody's Bond Record, 2/98; Statistical Abstract of the U.S., 1997;
Governing Magazine, 9/97, 3/98

POPULATION

Population Growth

Area	1980	1990	% Chg. 1980-90	July 1996 Estimate	% Chg. 1990-96
City	83,320	113,313	36.0	121,879	7.6
MSA[1]	299,681	388,222	29.5	420,872	8.4
U.S.	226,545,805	248,765,170	9.8	265,179,411	6.6

Note: (1) Metropolitan Statistical Area - see Appendix A for areas included
Source: 1980/1990 Census of Housing and Population, Summary Tape File 3C;
Census Bureau Population Estimates

Population Characteristics

Race	City 1980 Population	%	City 1990 Population	%	% Chg. 1980-90	MSA[1] 1990 Population	%
White	77,831	93.4	101,387	89.5	30.3	351,983	90.7
Black	1,224	1.5	2,101	1.9	71.7	5,554	1.4
Amer Indian/Esk/Aleut	1,108	1.3	1,307	1.2	18.0	4,513	1.2
Asian/Pacific Islander	1,433	1.7	3,837	3.4	167.8	10,881	2.8
Other	1,724	2.1	4,681	4.1	171.5	15,291	3.9
Hispanic Origin[2]	4,690	5.6	10,565	9.3	125.3	39,537	10.2

Note: (1) Metropolitan Statistical Area - see Appendix A for areas included;
(2) people of Hispanic origin can be of any race
Source: 1980/1990 Census of Housing and Population, Summary Tape File 3C

Ancestry

Area	German	Irish	English	Italian	U.S.	French	Polish	Dutch
City	24.4	17.5	19.1	9.9	2.7	5.3	2.1	2.8
MSA[1]	24.3	18.5	18.5	10.6	2.6	5.2	2.0	2.6
U.S.	23.3	15.6	13.1	5.9	5.3	4.2	3.8	2.5

Note: Figures are percentages and include persons that reported multiple ancestry (eg. if a person reported being Irish and Italian, they were included in both columns); (1) Metropolitan Statistical Area - see Appendix A for areas included
Source: 1990 Census of Population and Housing, Summary Tape File 3C

Age

Area	Median Age (Years)	Age Distribution (%) Under 5	Under 18	18-24	25-44	45-64	65+	80+
City	35.0	7.1	23.7	9.6	33.9	16.5	16.3	4.1
MSA[1]	34.8	7.3	24.6	8.8	35.4	17.7	13.5	3.0
U.S.	32.9	7.3	25.6	10.5	32.6	18.7	12.5	2.8

Note: (1) Metropolitan Statistical Area - see Appendix A for areas included
Source: 1990 Census of Population and Housing, Summary Tape File 3C

Male/Female Ratio

Area	Number of males per 100 females (all ages)	Number of males per 100 females (18 years old+)
City	91.4	87.3
MSA[1]	96.1	92.9
U.S.	95.0	91.9

Note: (1) Metropolitan Statistical Area - see Appendix A for areas included
Source: 1990 Census of Population, General Population Characteristics

INCOME

Per Capita/Median/Average Income

Area	Per Capita ($)	Median Household ($)	Average Household ($)
City	17,259	35,237	42,288
MSA[1]	17,239	36,299	44,331
U.S.	14,420	30,056	38,453

Note: all figures are for 1989; (1) Metropolitan Statistical Area - see Appendix A for areas included
Source: 1990 Census of Population and Housing, Summary Tape File 3C

Household Income Distribution by Race

Income ($)	City (%)					U.S. (%)				
	Total	White	Black	Other	Hisp.[1]	Total	White	Black	Other	Hisp.[1]
Less than 5,000	2.3	2.2	7.5	2.1	2.4	6.2	4.8	15.2	8.6	8.8
5,000 - 9,999	7.8	7.6	9.7	9.3	5.8	9.3	8.6	14.2	9.9	11.1
10,000 - 14,999	6.8	6.9	10.1	5.2	4.7	8.8	8.5	11.0	9.8	11.0
15,000 - 24,999	16.7	16.3	18.4	21.6	26.3	17.5	17.3	18.9	18.5	20.5
25,000 - 34,999	16.0	15.9	15.3	17.2	16.4	15.8	16.1	14.2	15.4	16.4
35,000 - 49,999	20.6	20.5	24.0	21.9	23.1	17.9	18.6	13.3	16.1	16.0
50,000 - 74,999	18.8	19.2	9.8	15.5	14.4	15.0	15.8	9.3	13.4	11.1
75,000 - 99,999	6.3	6.3	5.2	5.8	6.3	5.1	5.5	2.6	4.7	3.1
100,000+	4.7	5.0	0.0	1.4	0.6	4.4	4.8	1.3	3.7	1.9

Note: all figures are for 1989; (1) people of Hispanic origin can be of any race
Source: 1990 Census of Population and Housing, Summary Tape File 3C

Effective Buying Income

Area	Per Capita ($)	Median Household ($)	Average Household ($)
City	16,826	35,818	42,135
MSA[1]	17,158	38,158	45,374
U.S.	15,444	33,201	41,849

Note: data as of 1/1/97; (1) Metropolitan Statistical Area - see Appendix A for areas included
Source: Standard Rate & Data Service, Newspaper Advertising Source, 2/98

Effective Household Buying Income Distribution

Area	% of Households Earning						
	$10,000 -$19,999	$20,000 -$34,999	$35,000 -$49,999	$50,000 -$74,999	$75,000 -$99,000	$100,000 -$124,999	$125,000 and up
City	15.3	24.5	20.7	20.5	6.2	1.8	2.0
MSA[1]	14.1	23.0	20.3	22.4	7.3	2.3	2.3
U.S.	16.5	23.4	18.3	18.2	6.4	2.1	2.4

Note: data as of 1/1/97; (1) Metropolitan Statistical Area - see Appendix A for areas included
Source: Standard Rate & Data Service, Newspaper Advertising Source, 2/98

Poverty Rates by Race and Age

Area	Total (%)	By Race (%)				By Age (%)		
		White	Black	Other	Hisp.[2]	Under 5 years old	Under 18 years old	65 years and over
City	8.3	7.0	18.2	20.0	16.4	12.9	11.7	5.4
MSA[1]	7.6	6.8	15.5	15.7	15.6	9.5	9.7	5.7
U.S.	13.1	9.8	29.5	23.1	25.3	20.1	18.3	12.8

Note: figures show the percent of people living below the poverty line in 1989. The average poverty
threshold was $12,674 for a family of four in 1989; (1) Metropolitan Statistical Area - see Appendix A
for areas included; (2) people of Hispanic origin can be of any race
Source: 1990 Census of Population and Housing, Summary Tape File 3C

EMPLOYMENT

Labor Force and Employment

Area	Civilian Labor Force			Workers Employed		
	Dec. '95	Dec. '96	% Chg.	Dec. '95	Dec. '96	% Chg.
City	66,165	67,911	2.6	63,877	65,875	3.1
MSA[1]	231,216	237,282	2.6	222,983	229,955	3.1
U.S.	134,583,000	136,742,000	1.6	127,903,000	130,785,000	2.3

Note: Data is not seasonally adjusted and covers workers 16 years of age and older;
(1) Metropolitan Statistical Area - see Appendix A for areas included
Source: Bureau of Labor Statistics, http://stats.bls.gov

Unemployment Rate

Area	1997											
	Jan.	Feb.	Mar.	Apr.	May	Jun.	Jul.	Aug.	Sep.	Oct.	Nov.	Dec.
City	4.4	4.3	3.9	3.8	3.5	3.7	4.1	3.8	3.5	3.3	3.2	3.0
MSA[1]	4.6	4.4	4.0	3.9	3.6	3.8	4.2	3.9	3.6	3.4	3.3	3.1
U.S.	5.9	5.7	5.5	4.8	4.7	5.2	5.0	4.8	4.7	4.4	4.3	4.4

Note: Data is not seasonally adjusted and covers workers 16 years of age and older; All figures are percentages; (1) Metropolitan Statistical Area - see Appendix A for areas included
Source: Bureau of Labor Statistics, http://stats.bls.gov

Employment by Industry

Sector	MSA[1]		U.S.
	Number of Employees	Percent of Total	Percent of Total
Services	48,400	28.7	29.0
Retail Trade	35,200	20.9	18.5
Government	26,000	15.4	16.1
Manufacturing	25,800	15.3	15.0
Finance/Insurance/Real Estate	9,500	5.6	5.7
Wholesale Trade	7,700	4.6	5.4
Transportation/Public Utilities	6,400	3.8	5.3
Construction	9,100	5.4	4.5
Mining	400	0.2	0.5

Note: Figures cover non-farm employment as of 12/97 and are not seasonally adjusted;
(1) Metropolitan Statistical Area - see Appendix A for areas included
Source: Bureau of Labor Statistics, http://stats.bls.gov

Employment by Occupation

Occupation Category	City (%)	MSA[1] (%)	U.S. (%)
White Collar	62.9	59.8	58.1
Executive/Admin./Management	13.1	13.4	12.3
Professional	15.5	14.7	14.1
Technical & Related Support	3.7	3.6	3.7
Sales	13.9	12.7	11.8
Administrative Support/Clerical	16.7	15.4	16.3
Blue Collar	22.5	23.6	26.2
Precision Production/Craft/Repair	11.0	12.3	11.3
Machine Operators/Assem./Insp.	4.3	4.0	6.8
Transportation/Material Movers	3.0	3.3	4.1
Cleaners/Helpers/Laborers	4.2	4.0	3.9
Services	12.7	13.0	13.2
Farming/Forestry/Fishing	1.9	3.5	2.5

Note: figures cover employed persons 16 years old and over;
(1) Metropolitan Statistical Area - see Appendix A for areas included
Source: 1990 Census of Population and Housing, Summary Tape File 3C

Occupational Employment Projections: 1994 - 2001

Occupations Expected to have the Largest Job Growth (ranked by numerical growth)	Fast-Growing Occupations[1] (ranked by percent growth)
1. Salespersons, retail	1. Computer engineers
2. Cashiers	2. Personal and home care aides
3. General managers & top executives	3. Amusement and recreation attendants
4. Teachers, elementary school	4. Systems analysts
5. Teachers, secondary school	5. Home health aides
6. Waiters & waitresses	6. Food service and lodging managers
7. General office clerks	7. Management analyst
8. Secretaries, except legal & medical	8. Hotel desk clerks
9. Receptionists and information clerks	9. Employment interviewers
10. Sales reps, non-technical, exc retail	10. Nursery workers

Projections cover Sonoma County.
Note: (1) Excludes occupations with employment of less than 100 in 2001
Source: State of California, Employment Development Department, Labor Market Information Division, Information Services Group

Wages

Occupation	Wage Range ($/hour)		
	No Experience	Experienced	3 Years With Firm
Automotive Mechanics	4.25-9.50	10.00-20.50	15.00-23.50
Bookkeepers	8.00-10.75	8.50-19.50	10.50-24.25
Child Care Workers	5.00-8.00	5.25-9.00	7.00-9.75
Computer Engineers	11.00-16.75	15.50-25.00	20.75-36.00
Data Processing Equip. Repairers	7.50-13.00	7.50-15.75	11.50-20.50
Dental Assistants	8.50-13.00	9.25-15.50	13.50-17.00
Drafters	8.00-14.50	11.00-17.75	14.00-26.25
Electrical/Electronic Assemblers	5.75-8.00	6.75-10.00	8.00-15.50
Electrical/Electronic Engr. Tech.	6.50-13.25	10.00-17.50	12.25-21.75
Food Preparation Workers	4.50-6.00	5.25-6.75	7.00-10.00
General Office Clerks	7.00-8.50	7.75-12.75	8.50-15.00
Hazardous Materials/Waste Tech.	6.50-12.00	9.00-15.00	12.50-18.00
Home Health Care Workers	5.75-9.50	7.00-14.00	8.00-16.00
Licensed Vocational Nurses	12.50-15.00	12.50-15.00	14.00-18.00
Maintenance Repairers, Gen. Util.	6.00-11.25	7.50-15.50	9.25-20.00
Mktg./Advertising/Pub. Rel. Mgr.	9.50-15.00	13.25-19.25	14.50-25.25
Medical Assistants	6.50-9.00	8.00-12.00	9.00-15.00
Nursery Workers	4.25-6.50	4.50-9.00	7.00-12.00
Secretaries, General	9.00-11.00	9.00-12.00	10.25-13.75
Secretaries, Medical	7.25-9.00	8.75-12.25	10.00-15.00
Stock Clerks	5.50-6.75	5.75-9.00	7.50-14.50
Truck Drivers, Light	5.00-10.00	5.50-10.50	7.00-15.50

Note: Figures are for 1995 and cover Sonoma County
Source: California Employment Development Department, Labor Market Information, 1996

TAXES

Major State and Local Tax Rates

State Corp. Income (%)	State Personal Income (%)	Residential Property (effective rate per $100)	Sales & Use		State Gasoline (cents/ gallon)	State Cigarette (cents/ 20-pack)
			State (%)	Local (%)		
8.84[a]	1.0 - 9.3	n/a	6.0	1.5	18[b]	37

Note: Personal/corporate income tax rates as of 1/97. Sales, gasoline and cigarette tax rates as of 1/98; (a) Minimum tax is $800. The tax rate on S-Corporations is 1.5%; (b) Does not include 1 cent local option tax
Source: Federation of Tax Administrators, www.taxadmin.org; Washington D.C. Department of Finance and Revenue, Tax Rates and Tax Burdens in the District of Columbia: A Nationwide Comparison, June 1997; Chamber of Commerce

Total Taxes Per Capita and as a Percent of Income

Area	Per Capita Income ($)	Per Capita Taxes ($)			Taxes as Pct. of Income (%)		
		Total	Federal	State/Local	Total	Federal	State/Local
California	27,117	9,321	6,287	3,034	34.4	23.2	11.2
U.S.	26,187	9,205	6,127	3,078	35.2	23.4	11.8

Note: Figures are for 1997
Source: Tax Foundation, Web Site, www.taxfoundation.org

COMMERCIAL REAL ESTATE

Office Market

Class/ Location	Total Space (sq. ft.)	Vacant Space (sq. ft.)	Vac. Rate (%)	Under Constr. (sq. ft.)	Net Absorp. (sq. ft.)	Rental Rates ($/sq.ft./yr.)
Class A						
CBD	867,423	52,045	6.0	0	39,410	17.40-23.40
Outside CBD	n/a	n/a	n/a	n/a	n/a	17.40-21.00
Class B						
CBD	3,469,691	312,272	9.0	0	67,267	13.20-16.20
Outside CBD	n/a	n/a	n/a	n/a	n/a	12.00-18.00

Note: Data as of 10/97 and covers Sonoma County; CBD = Central Business District; n/a not available;
Source: Society of Industrial and Office Realtors, 1998 Comparative Statistics of Industrial and Office Real Estate Markets

"While most activity will come from existing Sonoma County companies expanding operations, roughly a third will likely be generated by new entrants. Very little new construction is on the drawing boards, which will keep the market conditions taut. Economic growth in Sonoma County is actually expected to outpace that of the Bay Area as a whole over the next several years, according to local economists. Increasingly, Sonoma County is no longer perceived as a hinterland, but is becoming more fully integrated into the regional Bay Area economy. With this shift, institutional money is finding its way here on a more regular basis." *Society of Industrial and Office Realtors, 1998 Comparative Statistics of Industrial and Office Real Estate Markets*

Industrial Market

Location	Total Space (sq. ft.)	Vacant Space (sq. ft.)	Vac. Rate (%)	Under Constr. (sq. ft.)	Net Absorp. (sq. ft.)	Net Lease ($/sq.ft./yr.)
Central City	n/a	n/a	n/a	n/a	n/a	n/a
Suburban	18,457,597	963,879	5.2	457,372	1,033,405	4.00-7.00

Note: Data as of 10/97 and covers Santa Rosa; n/a not available
Source: Society of Industrial and Office Realtors, 1998 Comparative Statistics of Industrial and Office Real Estate Markets

"With vacancies far under the 10 percent mark, the area has a shortage of space. Construction of new development is a relatively difficult and lengthy process, however. Both Santa Rosa and Sonoma County exhibit strong and well-established slow growth sentiments. Nevertheless, the local economy is growing at a fairly rapid rate, with annual job growth topping the three percent mark each of the past three years. Approximately 450,000 sq. ft. is currently under construction,an amount that should be rapidly absorbed. Sonoma County's industrial market, though small, should enjoy continued rising lease and sales prices for some time to come." *Society of Industrial and Office Realtors, 1998 Comparative Statistics of Industrial and Office Real Estate Markets*

COMMERCIAL UTILITIES

Typical Monthly Electric Bills

Area	Commercial Service ($/month)		Industrial Service ($/month)	
	12 kW demand 1,500 kWh	100 kW demand 30,000 kWh	1,000 kW demand 400,000 kWh	20,000 kW demand 10,000,000 kWh
City	231	3,420	41,622	565,537
U.S.	162	2,360	25,590	545,677

Note: Based on rates in effect July 1, 1997
Source: Edison Electric Institute, Typical Residential, Commercial and Industrial Bills, Summer 1997

TRANSPORTATION

Transportation Statistics

Avg. travel time to work (min.)	20.1
Interstate highways	None
Bus lines	
In-city	Sonoma County Transit; Santa Rosa Municipal Transit
Inter-city	3
Passenger air service	
Airport	Sonoma County Airport; San Francisco International (60 miles south)
Airlines	1
Aircraft departures	n/a
Enplaned passengers	n/a
Rail service	Amtrak Thruway Motorcoach Services
Motor freight carriers	38
Major waterways/ports	None

Source: OAG, Business Travel Planner, Summer 1997; Editor & Publisher Market Guide, 1998; FAA Airport Activity Statistics, 1996; Amtrak National Time Table, Northeast Timetable, Fall/Winter 1997-98; 1990 Census of Population and Housing, STF 3C; Chamber of Commerce/Economic Development 1997; Jane's Urban Transport Systems 1997-98; Transit Fact Book 1997

Means of Transportation to Work

Area	Car/Truck/Van		Public Transportation			Bicycle	Walked	Other Means	Worked at Home
	Drove Alone	Car-pooled	Bus	Subway	Railroad				
City	76.8	11.4	2.2	0.0	0.0	1.6	2.9	1.2	3.8
MSA[1]	74.6	13.0	2.2	0.0	0.0	1.0	3.3	1.0	4.9
U.S.	73.2	13.4	3.0	1.5	0.5	0.4	3.9	1.2	3.0

Note: figures shown are percentages and only include workers 16 years old and over;
(1) Metropolitan Statistical Area - see Appendix A for areas included
Source: 1990 Census of Population and Housing, Summary Tape File 3C

BUSINESSES

Major Business Headquarters

Company Name	1997 Rankings	
	Fortune 500	Forbes 500

No companies listed.

Note: Companies listed are located in the city; Dashes indicate no ranking
Fortune 500: companies that produce a 10-K are ranked 1 - 500 based on 1996 revenue
Forbes 500: private companies are ranked 1 - 500 based on 1996 revenue
Source: Forbes 12/1/97; Fortune 4/28/97

Minority Business Opportunity

Three of the 500 largest Hispanic-owned companies in the U.S. are located in Santa Rosa.
Hispanic Business, June 1997

HOTELS & MOTELS

Hotels/Motels

Area	Hotels/ Motels	Rooms	Luxury-Level Hotels/Motels		Average Minimum Rates ($)		
			♦♦♦♦	♦♦♦♦♦	♦♦	♦♦♦	♦♦♦♦
City	10	970	0	0	n/a	n/a	n/a
Airport	4	258	0	0	n/a	n/a	n/a
Suburbs	1	100	0	0	n/a	n/a	n/a
Total	15	1,328	0	0	n/a	n/a	n/a

Note: n/a not available; Classifications range from one diamond (budget properties with basic amenities) to five diamond (luxury properties with the finest service, rooms and facilities).
Source: OAG, Business Travel Planner, Summer 1997

CONVENTION CENTERS

Major Convention Centers

Center Name	Meeting Rooms	Exhibit Space (sf)
None listed in city		

Source: Trade Shows Worldwide 1997

Living Environment

COST OF LIVING

Cost of Living Index

Composite Index	Housing	Utilities	Groceries	Health Care	Trans-portation	Misc. Goods/ Services
137.9	196.6	99.3	117.5	135.9	122.4	111.9

Note: U.S. = 100
Source: ACCRA, Cost of Living Index, 2nd Quarter 1997

HOUSING

Median Home Prices and Housing Affordability

Area	Median Price[2] 3rd Qtr. 1997 ($)	HOI[3] 3rd Qtr. 1997	Afford-ability Rank[4]
MSA[1]	198,000	34.0	191
U.S.	127,000	63.7	–

Note: (1) Metropolitan Statistical Area - see Appendix A for areas included; (2) U.S. figures calculated from the sales of 625,000 new and existing homes in 195 markets; (3) Housing Opportunity Index - percent of homes sold that were within the reach of the median income household at the prevailing mortgage interest rate; (4) Rank is from 1-195 with 1 being most affordable
Source: National Association of Home Builders, Housing Opportunity Index, 3rd Quarter 1997

Average New Home Price

Area	Price ($)
City	273,975
U.S.	135,150

Note: Figures are based on a new home with 1,800 sq. ft. of living area on an 8,000 sq. ft. lot.
Source: ACCRA, Cost of Living Index, 2nd Quarter 1997

Average Apartment Rent

Area	Rent ($/mth)
City	876
U.S.	575

Note: Figures are based on an unfurnished two bedroom, 1-1/2 or 2 bath apartment, approximately 950 sq. ft. in size, excluding all utilities except water
Source: ACCRA, Cost of Living Index, 2nd Quarter 1997

RESIDENTIAL UTILITIES

Average Residential Utility Costs

Area	All Electric ($/mth)	Part Electric ($/mth)	Other Energy ($/mth)	Phone ($/mth)
City	–	66.03	35.43	20.75
U.S.	108.38	56.32	44.12	19.66

Source: ACCRA, Cost of Living Index, 2nd Quarter 1997

HEALTH CARE

Average Health Care Costs

Area	Hospital ($/day)	Doctor ($/visit)	Dentist ($/visit)
City	698.33	52.17	91.00
U.S.	390.32	48.32	60.14

Note: Hospital - based on a semi-private room. Doctor - based on a general practitioner's routine exam of an established patient. Dentist - based on adult teeth cleaning and periodic oral exam.
Source: ACCRA, Cost of Living Index, 2nd Quarter 1997

Distribution of Office-Based Physicians

Area	Family/Gen. Practitioners	Specialists		
		Medical	Surgical	Other
MSA[1]	190	212	198	226

Note: Data as of 12/31/96; (1) Metropolitan Statistical Area - see Appendix A for areas included
Source: American Medical Assn., Physician Characteristics & Distribution in the U.S., 1997-1998

Hospitals

Santa Rosa has 5 general medical and surgical hospitals. *AHA Guide to the Healthcare Field 1997-98*

EDUCATION

Public School District Statistics

District Name	Num. Sch.	Enroll.	Classroom Teachers[1]	Pupils per Teacher	Minority Pupils (%)	Current Exp.[2] ($/pupil)
Bellevue Union Elementary	2	1,378	59	23.4	n/a	n/a
Bennett Valley Union Elem	2	883	33	26.8	n/a	n/a
Mark West Union Elementary	3	1,538	61	25.2	n/a	n/a
Oak Grove Union Elementary	2	590	27	21.9	n/a	n/a
Piner-Olivet Union Elementary	3	1,529	58	26.4	n/a	n/a
Rincon Valley Union Elementary	7	2,631	101	26.0	n/a	n/a
Roseland Elementary	2	1,146	45	25.5	n/a	n/a
Santa Rosa Elementary	13	5,122	219	23.4	n/a	n/a
Santa Rosa High	14	11,278	484	23.3	n/a	n/a
Sonoma Co. Office of Education	2	1,093	72	15.2	n/a	n/a
Wright Elementary	3	1,266	51	24.8	n/a	n/a

Note: Data covers the 1995-1996 school year unless otherwise noted; (1) Excludes teachers reported as working in school district offices rather than in schools; (2) Based on 1993-94 enrollment collected by the Census Bureau, not the enrollment figure shown in column 3; SD = School District; ISD = Independent School District; n/a not available
Source: National Center for Education Statistics, Common Core of Data Survey; Bureau of the Census

Educational Quality

School District	Education Quotient[1]	Graduate Outcome[2]	Community Index[3]	Resource Index[4]
Santa Rosa	120.0	118.0	125.0	117.0

Note: Nearly 1,000 secondary school districts were rated in terms of educational quality. The scores range from a low of 50 to a high of 150; (1) Average of the Graduate Outcome, Community and Resource indexes; (2) Based on graduation rates and college board scores (SAT/ACT); (3) Based on the surrounding community's average level of education and the area's average income level; (4) Based on teacher salaries, per-pupil expenditures and student-teacher ratios.
Source: Expansion Management, Ratings Issue 1997

Educational Attainment by Race

Area	High School Graduate (%)					Bachelor's Degree (%)				
	Total	White	Black	Other	Hisp.[2]	Total	White	Black	Other	Hisp.[2]
City	85.7	87.4	79.8	63.0	58.8	26.9	27.8	14.6	16.7	13.0
MSA[1]	84.4	85.8	78.8	64.6	55.4	24.5	25.1	17.7	16.8	11.1
U.S.	75.2	77.9	63.1	60.4	49.8	20.3	21.5	11.4	19.4	9.2

Note: figures shown cover persons 25 years old and over; (1) Metropolitan Statistical Area - see Appendix A for areas included; (2) people of Hispanic origin can be of any race
Source: 1990 Census of Population and Housing, Summary Tape File 3C

School Enrollment by Type

Area	Preprimary				Elementary/High School			
	Public		Private		Public		Private	
	Enrollment	%	Enrollment	%	Enrollment	%	Enrollment	%
City	1,134	51.3	1,078	48.7	15,834	91.4	1,481	8.6
MSA[1]	4,350	53.9	3,719	46.1	56,495	92.0	4,896	8.0
U.S.	2,679,029	59.5	1,824,256	40.5	38,379,689	90.2	4,187,099	9.8

Note: figures shown cover persons 3 years old and over;
(1) Metropolitan Statistical Area - see Appendix A for areas included
Source: 1990 Census of Population and Housing, Summary Tape File 3C

School Enrollment by Race

Area	Preprimary (%)				Elementary/High School (%)			
	White	Black	Other	Hisp.[1]	White	Black	Other	Hisp.[1]
City	89.6	4.1	6.2	12.5	84.7	2.7	12.6	13.1
MSA[2]	90.8	2.3	6.9	10.6	87.2	2.1	10.7	14.4
U.S.	80.4	12.5	7.1	7.8	74.1	15.6	10.3	12.5

Note: figures shown cover persons 3 years old and over; (1) people of Hispanic origin can be of any race; (2) Metropolitan Statistical Area - see Appendix A for areas included
Source: 1990 Census of Population and Housing, Summary Tape File 3C

SAT/ACT Scores

Area/District	1996 SAT				1996 ACT	
	Percent of Graduates Tested (%)	Average Math Score	Average Verbal Score	Average Combined Score	Percent of Graduates Tested (%)	Average Composite Score
Santa Rosa CSD	31	541	522	1,063	6	23.6
State	45	511	495	1,006	11	21.0
U.S.	41	508	505	1,013	35	20.9

Note: Math and verbal SAT scores are out of a possible 800; ACT scores are out of a possible 36
Caution: Comparing or ranking states/cities on the basis of SAT/ACT scores alone is invalid and strongly discouraged by the The College Board and The American College Testing Program as students who take the tests are self-selected and do not represent the entire student population. 1996 SAT scores cannot be compared to previous years due to recentering.
Source: Santa Rosa Community School District, Educational Services, 1996; American College Testing Program, 1996; College Board, 1996

Classroom Teacher Salaries in Public Schools

District	B.A. Degree		M.A. Degree		Ph.D. Degree	
	Min. ($)	Max ($)	Min. ($)	Max. ($)	Min. ($)	Max. ($)
Santa Rosa	24,635	26,940	26,385	39,120	31,125	47,685
Average[1]	26,120	39,270	28,175	44,667	31,643	49,825

Note: Salaries are for 1996-1997; (1) Based on all school districts covered
Source: American Federation of Teachers (unpublished data)

Higher Education

Two-Year Colleges		Four-Year Colleges		Medical Schools	Law Schools	Voc/ Tech
Public	Private	Public	Private			
0	1	0	0	0	1	5

Source: College Blue Book, Occupational Education 1997; Medical School Admission Requirements, 1998-99; Peterson's Guide to Two-Year Colleges, 1997; Peterson's Guide to Four-Year Colleges, 1997; Barron's Guide to Law Schools 1997

MAJOR EMPLOYERS

Major Employers

Optical Coating Laboratory
Flex Products (lens coating equip.)
Komag Material Technology (disk drives)
Gateway Industries (mirrored glass)

Santa Rosa Memorial Hospital
Discovery Enterprises (photocopy machines)
Microsource (microwave components)

Note: companies listed are located in the city
Source: Dun's Business Rankings 1997; Ward's Business Directory, 1997

PUBLIC SAFETY

Crime Rate

Area	All Crimes	Violent Crimes				Property Crimes		
		Murder	Forcible Rape	Robbery	Aggrav. Assault	Burglary	Larceny -Theft	Motor Vehicle Theft
City	5,820.9	1.7	68.3	143.3	345.6	775.6	4,131.5	354.9
Suburbs[1]	3,582.5	5.0	30.9	52.5	314.7	874.3	2,120.8	184.3
MSA[2]	4,220.7	4.1	41.6	78.4	323.5	846.1	2,694.1	232.9
U.S.	5,078.9	7.4	36.1	202.4	388.2	943.0	2,975.9	525.9

Note: Crime rate is the number of crimes per 100,000 pop.; (1) defined as all areas within the MSA but located outside the central city; (2) Metropolitan Statistical Area - see Appendix A for areas incl.
Source: FBI Uniform Crime Reports 1996

RECREATION

Culture and Recreation

Museums	Symphony Orchestras	Opera Companies	Dance Companies	Professional Theatres	Zoos	Pro Sports Teams
4	1	0	1	0	0	0

Source: International Directory of the Performing Arts, 1996; Official Museum Directory, 1998; Chamber of Commerce/Economic Development 1997

Library System

The Sonoma County Library has 11 branches, holdings of 693,185 volumes and a budget of $6,931,425 (1995-1996). *American Library Directory, 1997-1998*

MEDIA

Newspapers

Name	Type	Freq.	Distribution	Circulation
The Press Democrat	General	7x/wk	Area	94,365
Sonoma County Daily Herald-Recorder	n/a	5x/wk	Local	500
Sonoma County Independent	n/a	1x/wk	Local	30,000

Note: Includes newspapers with circulations of 500 or more located in the city; n/a not available
Source: Burrelle's Media Directory, 1998 Edition

AM Radio Stations

Call Letters	Freq. (kHz)	Target Audience	Station Format	Music Format
KMXN	1150	Hispanic	M	Spanish
KSRO	1350	General	N/T	n/a
KRRS	1460	Hispanic	M/N/S	Adult Contemporary/Country/Spanish
KTOB	1490	General	M/N/S	Classic Rock/Oldies

Note: Stations included broadcast in the Santa Rosa metro area; n/a not available
Station Format: E = Educational; M = Music; N = News; S = Sports; T = Talk
Source: Burrelle's Media Directory, 1998 Edition

FM Radio Stations

Call Letters	Freq. (mHz)	Target Audience	Station Format	Music Format
KBBF	89.1	Hispanic	M/N/S	Jazz/R&B/Spanish
KRCB	91.1	General	E/M/N	Alternative/Classical/Jazz
KLVR	91.9	General	E/M	Adult Contemporary/Christian
KLCQ	92.9	n/a	M	Country
KJZY	93.7	General	M/N	Jazz
KMGG	97.7	n/a	M	Oldies
KZST	100.1	General	M/N/S	Adult Contemporary
KXFX	101.7	General	M	AOR

Note: Stations included broadcast in the Santa Rosa metro area; n/a not available
Station Format: E = Educational; M = Music; N = News; S = Sports; T = Talk
Music Format: AOR = Album Oriented Rock; MOR = Middle-of-the-Road
Source: Burrelle's Media Directory, 1998 Edition

Television Stations

Name	Ch.	Affiliation	Type	Owner
KRCB	22	PBS	Public	Rural California Broadcasting Corp.
KFTY	50	n/a	Commercial	Ackerley Communications Inc.

Note: Stations included broadcast in the Santa Rosa metro area
Source: Burrelle's Media Directory, 1998 Edition

CLIMATE

Average and Extreme Temperatures

Temperature	Jan	Feb	Mar	Apr	May	Jun	Jul	Aug	Sep	Oct	Nov	Dec	Ann
Extreme High (°F)	69	72	83	89	99	102	103	105	109	94	85	73	109
Average High (°F)	56	61	65	69	74	79	81	84	84	75	65	58	71
Average Temp. (°F)	46	50	51	55	60	63	65	66	65	60	52	47	57
Average Low (°F)	35	38	36	41	45	47	49	47	46	44	39	35	42
Extreme Low (°F)	24	26	25	29	32	36	41	40	36	32	28	23	23

Note: Figures cover the years 1948-1990
Source: National Climatic Data Center, International Station Meteorological Climate Summary, 3/95

Average Precipitation/Snowfall/Humidity

Precip./Humidity	Jan	Feb	Mar	Apr	May	Jun	Jul	Aug	Sep	Oct	Nov	Dec	Ann
Avg. Precip. (in.)	5.6	6.2	4.5	0.7	0.9	0.1	0.0	0.0	0.0	2.3	4.7	4.0	29.0
Avg. Snowfall (in.)	n/a	n/a	n/a	0	0	0	0	0	0	0	n/a	n/a	n/a
Avg. Rel. Hum. (%)	85	74	70	69	68	63	71	68	66	74	81	82	73

Note: Figures cover the years 1948-1990
Source: National Climatic Data Center, International Station Meteorological Climate Summary, 3/95

Weather Conditions

Temperature			Daytime Sky			Precipitation		
0°F & below	32°F & below	90°F & above	Clear	Partly cloudy	Cloudy	0.01 inch or more precip.	0.1 inch or more snow/ice	Thunder-storms
0	43	30	n/a	n/a	n/a	n/a	n/a	2

Note: Figures are average number of days per year and covers the years 1948-1990
Source: National Climatic Data Center, International Station Meteorological Climate Summary, 3/95

AIR & WATER QUALITY

Maximum Pollutant Concentrations

	Particulate Matter (ug/m³)	Carbon Monoxide (ppm)	Sulfur Dioxide (ppm)	Nitrogen Dioxide (ppm)	Ozone (ppm)	Lead (ug/m³)
MSA[1] Level	39	3	n/a	0.014	0.09	n/a
NAAQS[2]	150	9	0.140	0.053	0.12	1.50
Met NAAQS?	Yes	Yes	n/a	Yes	Yes	n/a

Note: (1) Metropolitan Statistical Area - see Appendix A for areas included; (2) National Ambient Air Quality Standards; ppm = parts per million; ug/m³ = micrograms per cubic meter; n/a not available
Source: EPA, National Air Quality and Emissions Trends Report, 1996

Pollutant Standards Index

Data not available. *EPA, National Air Quality and Emissions Trends Report, 1996*

Drinking Water

Water System Name	Pop. Served	Primary Water Source Type	Number of Violations in Fiscal Year 1997	Type of Violation/ Contaminants
City of Santa Rosa	128,000	Ground	None	None

Note: Data as of January 16, 1998
Source: EPA, Office of Ground Water and Drinking Water, Safe Drinking Water Information System

Santa Rosa tap water is alkaline, hard and not fluoridated.
Editor & Publisher Market Guide, 1998

Seattle, Washington

Background

Thomas Hoving, the former Director of the Metropolitan Museum of Art in New York City, once wrote that one could not interchange one U.S. city for another. For example, the essence of Pittsburgh is not reciprocal with the essence of New Orleans. Taking that into consideration, can one imagine that the virgin hinterlands and wide curving arch of Elliot Bay of present day Seattle was once named New York?

In 1853, two years after its first five families from Illinois had settled into the narrow strip of land between Puget Sound and Lake Washington, "New York" was changed to "Seattle", named for the Native American Chief Seattle.

The lush green forests of the "Emerald City", created by the infamously frequent rains and its many natural waterways, gave birth to Seattle's first major industry: lumber. However, this industry only bred a society of bearded, diamond-in-the-rough, plaid-wearing, bachelor men. To alleviate that problem, Asa Mercer, President of the Territorial University, which was later to be called the University of Washington, trekked back East, and recruited marriageable women. Among those "Mercer girls" was Mrs. Mercer herself.

Today, Seattle does not rely on lumber as its major industry. Instead, Seattle has expanded to commercial aircraft production and missile research, due to the presence of Boeing on the outskirts of the city. In addition to the revenue brought by Boeing, import/export is a major source of revenue as well. As the closest U.S. mainland port to Asia, Seattle has become a key trade center for goods as diverse as cars, forest products, electronic equipment, bananas, and petroleum products.

Seattle is another major American city that is undergoing a cultural and commercial re-emergence of its downtown. Tourists and locals are being drawn here by new hotels, restaurants, a new 16-screen movie theater and other entertainment-oriented businesses, and the first in a nationwide chain of Game Works, computerized playgrounds for adults. *USA Today, August 4, 1997*

Meanwhile on the technology front, Seattle could be moving in the direction of becoming the next Silicon Valley. Right now it is predominantly a software town dominated by one software company, Microsoft, with its more than 20,000 employees. At this point analysts differ as to the ability of the Microsoft founders to translate new ideas and entrepreneurial energy into the creation of a concentration of computer giants to rival Silicon Valley's. There are signs that Seattle is ready for more expansion and innovation with an increase in the rise of young firms. In the end the voters of Seattle may have the last say. *Fortune 7/7/97*

Seattle's summer has pleasant temperatures. But rain gear is a necessity from October through April for that's when the city receives about 80% of its rainfall.

Seattle's dedication to education and to the arts is magnificent. The city has a number of excellent public and private schools. Their fine arts and natural history museums ranks have obtained notable rank on the Pacific coast.

General Rankings and Evaluative Comments

- Seattle was ranked #11 out of 300 cities by *Money's* 1997 "Survey of the Best Places to Live." Criteria used: health services, crime, economy, housing, education, transportation, weather, leisure and the arts. The city was ranked #9 in 1996 and #4 in 1995.
Money, July 1997; Money, September 1996; Money, September 1995

- Seattle appeared on *Fortune's* list of "North America's Most Improved Cities"
Rank: 4 out of 10. The selected cities satisfied basic business-location needs and also demonstrated improvement over a five- to ten-year period in a number of business and quality-of-life measures.

    "Unless you've been living under a rock, you have some idea why Seattle has attracted so much attention during the past few years. It's the city that's awash in rivers of Starbucks coffee and microbrewed beer, the city in which every day is casual Friday, the city that's surrounded with breathtaking nature but still leaping ahead in its high-technology industries....

    Back around 1991...the downtown area was almost completely abandoned. Now it's the new home of the Seattle Art Museum. Across the street, the city's orchestra is building a new concert hall, scheduled to open in the fall of 1998....

    A newer twist to Seattle's business community is the uptick in locally based venture capital firms. Until now most of the startup capital for the city's fledgling biotech companies...has been shipped to Seattle from Silicon Valley and beyond. Now a cluster of local firms is stepping in....

    One thing that's stayed the same is the city's legendary quality of life....

    As long as Seattle's software-coding/Starbucks-sipping-loving zeitgeist doesn't fall out of fashion as quickly as grunge did, chances are you'll be hearing about this city for years to come." *Fortune, 11/24/97*

- *Ladies Home Journal* ranked America's 200 largest cities based on the qualities women care about most. Seattle ranked 15 out of 200. Criteria: low crime rate, good public schools, well-paying jobs, quality health and child care, the presence of women in government, proportion of women-owned businesses, size of the wage gap with men, local economy, divorce rates, the ratio of single men to single women, whether there are laws that require at least the same number of public toilets for women as men, and the probability of good hair days. *Ladies Home Journal, November 1997*

- Seattle is among the 10 healthiest cities for women. Rank: 5 out of 10.
Criteria: 1) number of doctors, psychologists and dietitians; 2) quality of hospital gynecology departments; 3) number of working mothers; 4) rate of violent crimes; 5) cleanliness of air and water; 6) number of fitness opportunities; 7) quality of public schools.
American Health, January/February 1997

- Seattle was ranked #70 out of 219 cities in terms of children's health, safety, and economic well-being. Criteria: total population, percent population change, birth rate, child immunization rate, infant mortality rate, percent low birth weight infants, percent of births to teens, physician-to-population ratio, student-to-teacher ratio, dropout rate, unemployment rate, median family income, percent of children in poverty, violent and property crime rates, number of juvenile arrests for violent crimes as a percent of the total crime index, number of days with pollution standard index (PSI) over 100, pounds toxic releases per 1,000 people and number of superfund sites. *Zero Population Growth, Children's Environmental Index 1997*

- Seattle appeared on *New Mobility's* list of "10 Disability Friendly Cities". Rank: 3 out of 10. Criteria: affordable and accessible housing, transportation, quality medical care, personal assistance services and strong advocacy.

    "...The weather is mild, services are available, transportation is great, cultural events are plentiful and companies are hiring. The King County metro bus system has been accessible for 20 years, thanks in large part to the Washington Coalition for Citizens with Disabilities, which operates as the area CIL. A highly visible disability community translates to positive attitudes and high employability at Boeing and Microsoft and in the tourism industry. The University of Washington and Harborview both offer spinal cord injury programs and support." *New Mobility, December 1997*

■ Seattle is among the 20 most livable cities for gay men and lesbians. The list was divided between 10 cities you might expect and 10 surprises. Seattle was on the cities you would expect list. Rank: 6 out of 10. Criteria: legal protection from antigay discrimination, an annual gay pride celebration, a community center, gay bookstores and publications, and an array of organizations, religious groups, and health care facilities that cater to the needs of the local gay community. *The Advocate, June 1997*

■ *Conde Nast Traveler* polled 37,000 readers in terms of travel satisfaction. Cities were ranked based on the following criteria: people/friendliness, environment/ambiance, cultural enrichment, restaurants and fun/energy. Seattle appeared in the top thirty, ranking number 7, with an overall rating of 70.8 out of 100 based on all the criteria. The cities were also ranked in each category separately. Seattle appeared in the top 10 based on people/friendliness, ranking number 10 with a rating of 73.0 out of 100. Seattle appeared in the top 10 based on restaurants, ranking number 8 with a rating of 73.9 out of 100. *Conde Nast Traveler, Readers' Choice Poll 1997*

■ *Yahoo! Internet Life* selected "America's 100 Most Wired Cities & Towns". 50 cities were large and 50 cities were small. Seattle ranked 5 out of 50 large cities. Criteria: Internet users per capita, number of networked computers, number of registered domain names, Internet backbone traffic, and the per-capita number of Web sites devoted to each city. *Yahoo! Internet Life, March 1998*

■ Nordstrom (upscale department store chain) and Starbucks (coffee bar chain), headquartered in Seattle, are among the "100 Best Companies to Work for in America." Criteria: trust in management, pride in work/company, camaraderie, company responses to the Hewitt People Practices Inventory, and employee responses to their Great Place to Work survey. The companies also had to be at least 10 years old and have a minimum of 500 employees. *Fortune, January 12, 1998*

■ The Seattle Times, headquartered in Seattle, is among the "100 Best Companies for Working Mothers." Criteria: pay compared with competition, opportunities for women to advance, support for child care, flexible work schedules and family-friendly benefits. *Working Mother, October 1997*

■ According to *Working Mother,* "Washington State officials are working hard to expand the supply of child care this year. Governor Gary Locke's proposed budget earmarked $350 million for child care, including $100 million in new dollars and $9 million for nontraditional care, such as off-hours programs for parents who work swing shift or nights. This is an especially important innovation; child care advocates across the country report that parents with nontraditional hours find it nearly impossible to obtain care for their children. Last year, state lawmakers earmarked about $10 million in state funds to eliminate a waiting list for state-sponsored child care.

New funds have been made available for resource and referral, caregiver training and parent-education efforts. Training requirements for all caregivers have been strengthened as part of the program. All providers in the state will soon have to have 20 hours of training during their first year on the job, and 10 hours annually after that. Currently, most caregivers need no training at all before they start caring for kids." *Working Mother, July/August 1997*

Business Environment

STATE ECONOMY

State Economic Profile

"Washington's economy is accelerating....Income has returned to above average growth after lagging for nearly two years.

Boeing's current expansion is accelerating beyond previous estimates, with production planned to increase to 40 planes per month by the end of 1997, and to 48 per month by 1999. The uptick of the aircraft cycle makes up for a recent slowdown in the expansion of software/data processing employment. Prospects remain good over the long term for continued expansion of the software industry, as applications expand to Internet management and telecommunications.

The new governor's budget proposal for the 1997-1999 biennium is reduced slightly from earlier estimates in order to meet Initiative 601, which limits increases in state general-fund spending to the combined rates of inflation and population growth. Governor Locke has proposed reductions in residential property taxes and a reduction of the business and occupation tax to pre-1993 levels. Washington's state and local tax burden currently ranks third highest in the nation.

Near-term risks are focused on the upside, with considerable potential for further hiring at Boeing. Continued expansion of aircraft production is based on assumptions that airlines will remain in good financial condition; that economic conditions remain stable in the U.S. and Asia, while improving in Europe; that cargo and passenger traffic continue to increase; that there are no substantial increase in fuel costs; and finally that European deregulation does not significantly reduce the number of airlines. A rising dollar/yen ratio also poses some near-term risk to Washington's seafood industry, wood products makers, and fruit growers.

The Washington economy will continue to expand strongly this year. The cyclical upturn in aircraft and expanding high-tech hardware, software, and semiconductors will support western Washington, while central Washington's agriculture will benefit from freer trade and worldwide income growth. Eastern Washington will also benefit from aircraft parts production. Washington is ranked as a top performer over the long term but is at risk of a downturn early next decade." National Association of Realtors, Economic Profiles: The Fifty States, July 1997

IMPORTS/EXPORTS

Total Export Sales

Area	1993 ($000)	1994 ($000)	1995 ($000)	1996 ($000)	% Chg. 1993-96	% Chg. 1995-96
MSA[1]	23,815,649	21,752,982	17,815,388	21,391,133	-10.2	20.1
U.S.	464,858,354	512,415,609	583,030,524	622,827,063	34.0	6.8

Note: (1) Metropolitan Statistical Area - see Appendix A for areas included
Source: U.S. Department of Commerce, International Trade Association, Metropolitan Area Exports: An Export Performance Report on Over 250 U.S. Cities, October 1997

Imports/Exports by Port

Type	Cargo Value			Share of U.S. Total	
	1995 (US$mil.)	1996 (US$mil.)	% Change 1995-1996	1995 (%)	1996 (%)
Imports	25,997	22,402	-13.83	6.64	5.84
Exports	12,061	11,558	-4.17	5.27	4.88

Source: Global Trade Information Services, WaterBorne Trade Atlas 1997

CITY FINANCES

City Government Finances

Component	FY94 ($000)	FY94 (per capita $)
Revenue	1,266,418	2,420.11
Expenditure	1,330,432	2,542.44
Debt Outstanding	1,319,472	2,521.50
Cash & Securities	1,036,300	1,980.36

Source: U.S. Bureau of the Census, City Government Finances: 1993-94

City Government Revenue by Source

Source	FY94 ($000)	FY94 (per capita $)	FY94 (%)
From Federal Government	25,782	49.27	2.0
From State Governments	97,543	186.40	7.7
From Local Governments	5,745	10.98	0.5
Property Taxes	136,881	261.58	10.8
General Sales Taxes	86,788	165.85	6.9
Selective Sales Taxes	84,700	161.86	6.7
Income Taxes	0	0.00	0.0
Current Charges	214,655	410.20	16.9
Utility/Liquor Store	377,607	721.60	29.8
Employee Retirement[1]	72,307	138.18	5.7
Other	164,410	314.19	13.0

Note: (1) Excludes "city contributions," classified as "nonrevenue," intragovernmental transfers.
Source: U.S. Bureau of the Census, City Government Finances: 1993-94

City Government Expenditures by Function

Function	FY94 ($000)	FY94 (per capita $)	FY94 (%)
Educational Services	22,963	43.88	1.7
Employee Retirement[1]	63,902	122.12	4.8
Environment/Housing	302,772	578.59	22.8
Government Administration	69,761	133.31	5.2
Interest on General Debt	19,698	37.64	1.5
Public Safety	210,061	401.42	15.8
Social Services	16,811	32.13	1.3
Transportation	71,245	136.15	5.4
Utility/Liquor Store	482,709	922.45	36.3
Other	70,510	134.74	5.3

Note: (1) Payments to beneficiaries including withdrawal of contributions.
Source: U.S. Bureau of the Census, City Government Finances: 1993-94

Municipal Bond Ratings

Area	Moody's	S & P
Seattle	Aa1	AA+

Note: n/a not available; n/r not rated
Source: Moody's Bond Record, 2/98; Statistical Abstract of the U.S., 1997;
Governing Magazine, 9/97, 3/98

POPULATION

Population Growth

Area	1980	1990	% Chg. 1980-90	July 1996 Estimate	% Chg. 1990-96
City	493,846	516,259	4.5	524,704	1.6
MSA[1]	1,607,469	1,972,961	22.7	2,234,707	13.3
U.S.	226,545,805	248,765,170	9.8	265,179,411	6.6

Note: (1) Metropolitan Statistical Area - see Appendix A for areas included
Source: 1980/1990 Census of Housing and Population, Summary Tape File 3C;
Census Bureau Population Estimates

Population Characteristics

Race	City 1980 Population	%	City 1990 Population	%	% Chg. 1980-90	MSA[1] 1990 Population	%
White	396,275	80.2	389,304	75.4	-1.8	1,715,208	86.9
Black	46,565	9.4	51,652	10.0	10.9	79,433	4.0
Amer Indian/Esk/Aleut	6,821	1.4	7,406	1.4	8.6	24,552	1.2
Asian/Pacific Islander	38,936	7.9	61,293	11.9	57.4	135,468	6.9
Other	5,249	1.1	6,604	1.3	25.8	18,300	0.9
Hispanic Origin[2]	12,646	2.6	17,058	3.3	34.9	51,624	2.6

Note: (1) Metropolitan Statistical Area - see Appendix A for areas included;
(2) people of Hispanic origin can be of any race
Source: 1980/1990 Census of Housing and Population, Summary Tape File 3C

Ancestry

Area	German	Irish	English	Italian	U.S.	French	Polish	Dutch
City	21.1	14.1	16.3	3.4	1.8	4.6	2.1	2.2
MSA[1]	27.1	15.6	18.6	3.7	2.7	5.4	2.2	3.2
U.S.	23.3	15.6	13.1	5.9	5.3	4.2	3.8	2.5

Note: Figures are percentages and include persons that reported multiple ancestry (eg. if a person reported being Irish and Italian, they were included in both columns); (1) Metropolitan Statistical Area - see Appendix A for areas included
Source: 1990 Census of Population and Housing, Summary Tape File 3C

Age

Area	Median Age (Years)	Age Distribution (%) Under 5	Under 18	18-24	25-44	45-64	65+	80+
City	34.9	5.6	16.3	11.9	39.9	16.6	15.2	3.9
MSA[1]	33.3	7.3	23.8	9.6	37.7	18.2	10.7	2.3
U.S.	32.9	7.3	25.6	10.5	32.6	18.7	12.5	2.8

Note: (1) Metropolitan Statistical Area - see Appendix A for areas included
Source: 1990 Census of Population and Housing, Summary Tape File 3C

Male/Female Ratio

Area	Number of males per 100 females (all ages)	Number of males per 100 females (18 years old+)
City	95.1	94.0
MSA[1]	97.4	95.7
U.S.	95.0	91.9

Note: (1) Metropolitan Statistical Area - see Appendix A for areas included
Source: 1990 Census of Population, General Population Characteristics

INCOME

Per Capita/Median/Average Income

Area	Per Capita ($)	Median Household ($)	Average Household ($)
City	18,308	29,353	38,895
MSA[1]	17,921	36,338	44,338
U.S.	14,420	30,056	38,453

Note: all figures are for 1989; (1) Metropolitan Statistical Area - see Appendix A for areas included
Source: 1990 Census of Population and Housing, Summary Tape File 3C

Household Income Distribution by Race

Income ($)	City (%)					U.S. (%)				
	Total	White	Black	Other	Hisp.[1]	Total	White	Black	Other	Hisp.[1]
Less than 5,000	5.6	4.3	12.1	10.1	6.6	6.2	4.8	15.2	8.6	8.8
5,000 - 9,999	9.3	8.5	14.6	10.8	12.0	9.3	8.6	14.2	9.9	11.1
10,000 - 14,999	8.9	8.6	12.3	8.8	8.2	8.8	8.5	11.0	9.8	11.0
15,000 - 24,999	18.7	18.7	18.8	19.1	21.5	17.5	17.3	18.9	18.5	20.5
25,000 - 34,999	16.2	16.4	14.4	16.0	16.9	15.8	16.1	14.2	15.4	16.4
35,000 - 49,999	17.2	17.6	14.4	16.0	16.7	17.9	18.6	13.3	16.1	16.0
50,000 - 74,999	14.2	14.9	9.7	13.1	11.6	15.0	15.8	9.3	13.4	11.1
75,000 - 99,999	5.0	5.4	2.4	4.1	3.4	5.1	5.5	2.6	4.7	3.1
100,000+	4.8	5.5	1.3	1.9	3.1	4.4	4.8	1.3	3.7	1.9

Note: all figures are for 1989; (1) people of Hispanic origin can be of any race
Source: 1990 Census of Population and Housing, Summary Tape File 3C

Effective Buying Income

Area	Per Capita ($)	Median Household ($)	Average Household ($)
City	21,988	36,128	48,120
MSA[1]	21,971	45,918	55,509
U.S.	15,444	33,201	41,849

Note: data as of 1/1/97; (1) Metropolitan Statistical Area - see Appendix A for areas included
Source: Standard Rate & Data Service, Newspaper Advertising Source, 2/98

Effective Household Buying Income Distribution

Area	% of Households Earning						
	$10,000 -$19,999	$20,000 -$34,999	$35,000 -$49,999	$50,000 -$74,999	$75,000 -$99,000	$100,000 -$124,999	$125,000 and up
City	15.2	22.5	17.4	18.4	8.5	3.1	4.0
MSA[1]	10.7	19.0	18.7	23.9	11.9	4.6	4.7
U.S.	16.5	23.4	18.3	18.2	6.4	2.1	2.4

Note: data as of 1/1/97; (1) Metropolitan Statistical Area - see Appendix A for areas included
Source: Standard Rate & Data Service, Newspaper Advertising Source, 2/98

Poverty Rates by Race and Age

Area	Total (%)	By Race (%)				By Age (%)		
		White	Black	Other	Hisp.[2]	Under 5 years old	Under 18 years old	65 years and over
City	12.4	9.0	25.2	21.0	22.3	15.9	16.2	9.0
MSA[1]	7.6	6.1	21.7	15.9	13.9	10.4	9.5	7.2
U.S.	13.1	9.8	29.5	23.1	25.3	20.1	18.3	12.8

Note: figures show the percent of people living below the poverty line in 1989. The average poverty threshold was $12,674 for a family of four in 1989; (1) Metropolitan Statistical Area - see Appendix A for areas included; (2) people of Hispanic origin can be of any race
Source: 1990 Census of Population and Housing, Summary Tape File 3C

EMPLOYMENT

Labor Force and Employment

Area	Civilian Labor Force			Workers Employed		
	Dec. '95	Dec. '96	% Chg.	Dec. '95	Dec. '96	% Chg.
City	340,364	362,205	6.4	323,266	350,363	8.4
MSA[1]	1,304,171	1,391,352	6.7	1,247,353	1,351,910	8.4
U.S.	134,583,000	136,742,000	1.6	127,903,000	130,785,000	2.3

Note: Data is not seasonally adjusted and covers workers 16 years of age and older;
(1) Metropolitan Statistical Area - see Appendix A for areas included
Source: Bureau of Labor Statistics, http://stats.bls.gov

Unemployment Rate

Area	1997											
	Jan.	Feb.	Mar.	Apr.	May	Jun.	Jul.	Aug.	Sep.	Oct.	Nov.	Dec.
City	5.0	4.8	4.5	4.1	3.8	4.0	3.9	3.7	3.8	3.6	3.4	3.3
MSA[1]	4.4	4.2	3.9	3.5	3.3	3.4	3.3	3.1	3.2	3.1	2.9	2.8
U.S.	5.9	5.7	5.5	4.8	4.7	5.2	5.0	4.8	4.7	4.4	4.3	4.4

Note: Data is not seasonally adjusted and covers workers 16 years of age and older; All figures are percentages; (1) Metropolitan Statistical Area - see Appendix A for areas included
Source: Bureau of Labor Statistics, http://stats.bls.gov

Employment by Industry

Sector	MSA[1]		U.S.
	Number of Employees	Percent of Total	Percent of Total
Services	386,400	28.8	29.0
Retail Trade	229,400	17.1	18.5
Government	181,900	13.5	16.1
Manufacturing	226,200	16.8	15.0
Finance/Insurance/Real Estate	81,200	6.0	5.7
Wholesale Trade	89,900	6.7	5.4
Transportation/Public Utilities	80,100	6.0	5.3
Construction	67,600	5.0	4.5
Mining	700	0.1	0.5

Note: Figures cover non-farm employment as of 12/97 and are not seasonally adjusted; (1) Metropolitan Statistical Area - see Appendix A for areas included
Source: Bureau of Labor Statistics, http://stats.bls.gov

Employment by Occupation

Occupation Category	City (%)	MSA[1] (%)	U.S. (%)
White Collar	69.3	65.2	58.1
Executive/Admin./Management	15.0	14.7	12.3
Professional	21.3	16.8	14.1
Technical & Related Support	4.9	4.4	3.7
Sales	11.6	12.7	11.8
Administrative Support/Clerical	16.6	16.6	16.3
Blue Collar	16.6	22.2	26.2
Precision Production/Craft/Repair	7.0	11.1	11.3
Machine Operators/Assem./Insp.	4.2	4.7	6.8
Transportation/Material Movers	2.6	3.3	4.1
Cleaners/Helpers/Laborers	2.8	3.1	3.9
Services	12.9	11.2	13.2
Farming/Forestry/Fishing	1.1	1.4	2.5

Note: figures cover employed persons 16 years old and over; (1) Metropolitan Statistical Area - see Appendix A for areas included
Source: 1990 Census of Population and Housing, Summary Tape File 3C

Occupational Employment Projections: 1994 - 2005

Occupations Expected to have the Largest Job Growth (ranked by numerical growth)	Fast-Growing Occupations (ranked by percent growth)
1. Waiters & waitresses	1. Computer scientists
2. Salespersons, retail	2. Computer engineers
3. General managers & top executives	3. Electronic pagination systems workers
4. Systems analysts	4. Personal and home care aides
5. Cashiers	5. Residential counselors
6. Registered nurses	6. Patternmakers and layout workers
7. Computer engineers	7. Machine assemblers
8. Receptionists and information clerks	8. Human services workers
9. Truck drivers, heavy & light	9. Systems analysts
10. Janitors/cleaners/maids, ex. priv. hshld.	10. Occupational therapists

Projections cover Washington.
Source: U.S. Department of Labor, Employment and Training Administration, America's Labor Market Information System (ALMIS)

Average Wages

Occupation	Wage	Occupation	Wage
Professional/Technical/Clerical	$/Week	**Health/Protective Services**	$/Week
Accountants III	827	Corrections Officers	624
Attorneys III	1,443	Firefighters	925
Budget Analysts III	822	Nurses, Licensed Practical II	-
Buyers/Contracting Specialists II	671	Nurses, Registered II	-
Clerks, Accounting III	463	Nursing Assistants II	-
Clerks, General III	434	Police Officers I	854
Computer Operators II	470	**Hourly Workers**	$/Hour
Computer Programmers II	626	Forklift Operators	14.41
Drafters II	525	General Maintenance Workers	12.46
Engineering Technicians III	708	Guards I	6.56
Engineering Technicians, Civil III	788	Janitors	7.84
Engineers III	912	Maintenance Electricians	22.23
Key Entry Operators I	430	Maintenance Electronics Techs II	20.58
Personnel Assistants III	514	Maintenance Machinists	19.97
Personnel Specialists III	816	Maintenance Mechanics, Machinery	20.09
Secretaries III	582	Material Handling Laborers	7.41
Switchboard Operator-Receptionist	396	Motor Vehicle Mechanics	18.71
Systems Analysts II	955	Shipping/Receiving Clerks	18.48
Systems Analysts Supervisor/Mgr II	1,350	Tool and Die Makers	-
Tax Collectors II	635	Truckdrivers, Tractor Trailer	13.90
Word Processors II	475	Warehouse Specialists	-

Note: Wage data includes full-time workers only for 11/95 and cover the Metropolitan Statistical Area (see Appendix A for areas included). Dashes indicate that data was not available.
Source: Bureau of Labor Statistics, Occupational Compensation Survey, 5/96

TAXES

Major State and Local Tax Rates

State Corp. Income (%)	State Personal Income (%)	Residential Property (effective rate per $100)	Sales & Use		State Gasoline (cents/ gallon)	State Cigarette (cents/ 20-pack)
			State (%)	Local (%)		
None	None	1.14	6.5	1.7	23	82.5

Note: Personal/corporate income tax rates as of 1/97. Sales, gasoline and cigarette tax rates as of 1/98.
Source: Federation of Tax Administrators, www.taxadmin.org; Washington D.C. Department of Finance and Revenue, Tax Rates and Tax Burdens in the District of Columbia: A Nationwide Comparison, June 1997; Chamber of Commerce

Total Taxes Per Capita and as a Percent of Income

Area	Per Capita Income ($)	Per Capita Taxes ($)			Taxes as Pct. of Income (%)		
		Total	Federal	State/Local	Total	Federal	State/Local
Washington	27,086	9,881	6,572	3,309	36.5	24.3	12.2
U.S.	26,187	9,205	6,127	3,078	35.2	23.4	11.8

Note: Figures are for 1997
Source: Tax Foundation, Web Site, www.taxfoundation.org

Estimated Tax Burden

Area	State Income	Local Income	Property	Sales	Total
Seattle	0	0	2,475	731	3,206

Note: The numbers are estimates of taxes paid by a married couple with two kids and annual earnings of $65,000. Sales tax estimates assume they spend average amounts on food, clothing, household goods and gasoline. Property tax estimates assume they live in a $225,000 home.
Source: Kiplinger's Personal Finance Magazine, June 1997

COMMERCIAL REAL ESTATE

Office Market

Class/Location	Total Space (sq. ft.)	Vacant Space (sq. ft.)	Vac. Rate (%)	Under Constr. (sq. ft.)	Net Absorp. (sq. ft.)	Rental Rates ($/sq.ft./yr.)
Class A						
CBD	18,790,037	1,001,158	5.3	300,000	196,078	13.00-32.00
Outside CBD	3,792,839	230,421	6.1	0	412,711	12.00-18.90
Class B						
CBD	4,509,380	507,562	11.3	0	392,723	10.00-21.00
Outside CBD	1,709,648	255,156	14.9	0	400,131	10.50-21.25

Note: Data as of 10/97 and covers Seattle; CBD = Central Business District; n/a not available;
Source: Society of Industrial and Office Realtors, 1998 Comparative Statistics of Industrial and Office Real Estate Markets

"Tight market concessions and rising rents have prompted plans for new development to be taken seriously, following several years of relative inactivity. Overall vacancy in the downtown's 18.8 million sq. ft. Class 'A' market is just above five percent, and downtown's direct vacancy (i.e., subtracting sublease availabilities) is a miniscule 3.3 percent. Developers with sharpened pencils have proposed up to six million sq. ft. of new development. It is likely that only a small portion of that will be built, however. Lender insistence on pre-leasing requirements should keep vacancies low and rental rates rising for the foreseeable future."
Society of Industrial and Office Realtors, 1998 Comparative Statistics of Industrial and Office Real Estate Markets

Industrial Market

Location	Total Space (sq. ft.)	Vacant Space (sq. ft.)	Vac. Rate (%)	Under Constr. (sq. ft.)	Net Absorp. (sq. ft.)	Lease ($/sq.ft./yr.)
Central City	40,146,588	1,016,631	2.5	138,890	-550,092	3.84-5.16
Suburban	80,425,462	4,218,653	5.2	1,711,000	1,356,255	3.48-4.80

Note: Data as of 10/97 and covers Seattle-South; n/a not available
Source: Society of Industrial and Office Realtors, 1998 Comparative Statistics of Industrial and Office Real Estate Markets

"Seattle's local economy is very strong, and likely to remain so for the foreseeable future. Boeing and Microsoft are the biggest players, but a host of suppliers and spin-offs are booming as well. Demolition of numerous industrial buildings just south of downtown have been initiated by the Port of Seattle, as part of a $1.2 billion expansion of port facilities. The port will relocate another one million sq. ft. of users in 1998, most of whom are considering sites on less expensive land further south, in the Kent/Auburn area, or even in Pierce County near Tacoma. Furthermore, the Mariners Stadium Authority is proceeding with acquisition plans for a new baseball park, which would displace more industrial tenants to the benefit of 'southside' markets.'' *Society of Industrial and Office Realtors, 1998 Comparative Statistics of Industrial and Office Real Estate Markets*

Retail Market

Shopping Center Inventory (sq. ft.)	Shopping Center Construction (sq. ft.)	Construction as a Percent of Inventory (%)	Torto Wheaton Rent Index[1] ($/sq. ft.)
33,612,000	1,288,000	3.8	12.11

Note: Data as of 1997 and covers the Metropolitan Statistical Area - see Appendix A for areas included; (1) Index is based on a model that predicts what the average rent should be for leases with certain characteristics, in certain locations during certain years.
Source: National Association of Realtors, 1997-1998 Market Conditions Report

"Stronger employment growth spurred real income increases of nearly 4.0% in 1996 and 1997. Relative to other MSAs, Seattle has experienced healthy construction levels during the last three years, but rent inflation has increased only slightly. Efforts are underway to revitalize the Pine Street area. These include the opening of Nike Town and construction of a new symphony hall—which will further ignite retail construction. Also looming is Nordstrom's $100 million plan to renovate the old Frederik & Nelson building. The retail market is somewhat vulnerable to swings in the economy due to the heavy reliance on the volatile aerospace and software industries." *National Association of Realtors, 1997-1998 Market Conditions Report*

COMMERCIAL UTILITIES

Typical Monthly Electric Bills

Area	Commercial Service ($/month)		Industrial Service ($/month)	
	12 kW demand 1,500 kWh	120 kW demand 30,000 kWh	1,000 kW demand 400,000 kWh	20,000 kW demand 10,000,000 kWh
City[1]	75	1,571	16,263	396,900
U.S.[2]	162	2,360[a]	25,590	545,677

Note: (1) Based on rates in effect January 1, 1997; (2) Based on rates in effect July 1, 1997; (a) Based on 100 kW demand and 30,000 kWh usage.
Source: Memphis Light, Gas and Water, 1997 Utility Bill Comparisons for Selected U.S. Cities; Edison Electric Institute, Typical Residential, Commercial and Industrial Bills, Summer 1997

TRANSPORTATION

Transportation Statistics

Avg. travel time to work (min.)	22.0
Interstate highways	I-50; I-90
Bus lines	
In-city	METRO (Metropolitan Seattle Transit), 892 vehicles
Inter-city	1
Passenger air service	
Airport	Seattle-Tacoma International
Airlines	35
Aircraft departures	154,656 (1995)
Enplaned passengers	10,731,233 (1995)
Rail service	Amtrak; Light Rail
Motor freight carriers	155
Major waterways/ports	Puget Sound (Port of Seattle)

Source: OAG, Business Travel Planner, Summer 1997; Editor & Publisher Market Guide, 1998; FAA Airport Activity Statistics, 1996; Amtrak National Time Table, Northeast Timetable, Fall/Winter 1997-98; 1990 Census of Population and Housing, STF 3C; Chamber of Commerce/Economic Development 1997; Jane's Urban Transport Systems 1997-98; Transit Fact Book 1997

A survey of 90,000 airline passengers during the first half of 1997 ranked most of the largest airports in the U.S. Seattle-Tacoma International ranked number 13 out of 36. Criteria: cleanliness, quality of restaurants, attractiveness, speed of baggage delivery, ease of reaching gates, available ground transportation, ease of following signs and closeness of parking. *Plog Research Inc., First Half 1997*

Means of Transportation to Work

Area	Car/Truck/Van		Public Transportation			Bicycle	Walked	Other Means	Worked at Home
	Drove Alone	Car-pooled	Bus	Subway	Railroad				
City	58.7	11.8	15.6	0.0	0.0	1.5	7.2	1.3	3.8
MSA[1]	72.8	11.6	7.2	0.0	0.0	0.6	3.3	1.1	3.4
U.S.	73.2	13.4	3.0	1.5	0.5	0.4	3.9	1.2	3.0

Note: figures shown are percentages and only include workers 16 years old and over;
(1) Metropolitan Statistical Area - see Appendix A for areas included
Source: 1990 Census of Population and Housing, Summary Tape File 3C

BUSINESSES

Major Business Headquarters

Company Name	1997 Rankings	
	Fortune 500	Forbes 500
Baugh Enterprises	-	498
Boeing	36	-
Nordstrom	310	-
Safeco	346	-
Services Group of America	-	126
Simpson Investment	-	110
Stevedoring Services of America	-	263
Washington Mutual	398	-

Note: Companies listed are located in the city; Dashes indicate no ranking
Fortune 500: companies that produce a 10-K are ranked 1 - 500 based on 1996 revenue
Forbes 500: private companies are ranked 1 - 500 based on 1996 revenue
Source: Forbes 12/1/97; Fortune 4/28/97

Fast-Growing Businesses

According to *Inc.*, Seattle is home to two of America's 100 fastest-growing private companies: Photo Disc and CSI Digital. Criteria for inclusion: must be an independent, privately-held, U.S. corporation, proprietorship or partnership; sales of at least $200,000 in 1993; five-year operating/sales history; increase in 1997 sales over 1996 sales; holding companies, regulated banks, and utilities were excluded. *Inc. 500, 1997*

Seattle is home to one of *Business Week's* "hot growth" companies: Seattle Filmworks. Criteria: sales and earnings, return on capital and stock price. *Business Week, 5/26/97*

According to *Fortune*, Seattle is home to one of America's 100 fastest-growing companies: Starbucks. Companies were ranked based on three years' earnings-per-share growth using least squares analysis to smooth out distortions. Criteria for inclusion: public companies with sales of least $50 million. Companies that lost money in the most recent quarter, or ended in the red for the past four quarters as a whole, were not eligible. Limited partnerships and REITs were also not considered. *Fortune, 9/29/97*

Seattle was ranked #4 out of 24 (#1 is best) in terms of the best-performing local stocks in 1996 according to the Money/Norby Cities Index. The index measures stocks of companies that have headquarters in 24 metro areas. *Money, 2/7/97*

Women-Owned Businesses: Number, Employment, Sales and Share

Area	Women-Owned Businesses in 1996				Share of Women-Owned Businesses in 1996	
	Number	Employment	Sales ($000)	Rank[2]	Percent (%)	Rank[3]
MSA[1]	91,000	311,300	37,971,800	7	40.0	2

Note: (1) Metropolitan Statistical Area - see Appendix A for areas included; (2) Calculated on an averaging of number of businesses, employment and sales and ranges from 1 to 50 where 1 is best; (3) Ranges from 1 to 50 where 1 is best
Source: The National Foundation for Women Business Owners, 1996 Facts on Women-Owned Businesses: Trends in the Top 50 Metropolitan Areas, March 26, 1997

Women-Owned Businesses: Growth

Area	Growth in Women-Owned Businesses (% change from 1987 to 1996)				Relative Growth in the Number of Women-Owned and All Businesses (% change from 1987 to 1996)			
	Num.	Empl.	Sales	Rank[2]	Women-Owned	All Firms	Absolute Difference	Relative Difference
MSA[1]	88.3	501.8	650.8	2	88.3	56.5	31.8	1.6:1

Note: (1) Metropolitan Statistical Area - see Appendix A for areas included; (2) Calculated on an averaging of the percent growth of number of businesses, employment and sales and ranges from 1 to 50 where 1 is best
Source: The National Foundation for Women Business Owners, 1996 Facts on Women-Owned Businesses: Trends in the Top 50 Metropolitan Areas, March 26, 1997

Minority Business Opportunity

One of the 500 largest Hispanic-owned companies in the U.S. are located in Seattle. *Hispanic Business, June 1997*

Small Business Opportunity

Seattle was included among *Entrepreneur* magazines listing of the "20 Best Cities for Small Business." It was ranked #3 among large metro areas. Criteria: risk of failure, business performance, economic growth, affordability and state attitude towards business. *Entrepreneur, 10/97*

HOTELS & MOTELS

Hotels/Motels

Area	Hotels/Motels	Rooms	Luxury-Level Hotels/Motels		Average Minimum Rates ($)		
			♦♦♦♦	♦♦♦♦♦	♦♦	♦♦♦	♦♦♦♦
City	60	8,865	4	0	92	134	179
Airport	42	6,462	0	0	n/a	n/a	n/a
Suburbs	55	5,725	0	0	n/a	n/a	n/a
Total	157	21,052	4	0	n/a	n/a	n/a

Note: n/a not available; Classifications range from one diamond (budget properties with basic amenities) to five diamond (luxury properties with the finest service, rooms and facilities).
Source: OAG, Business Travel Planner, Summer 1997

Seattle is home to one of the top 100 hotels in the world according to *Travel & Leisure*: Four Seasons Olympic Hotel. Criteria: value, rooms/ambience, location, facilities/activities and service. *Travel & Leisure, September 1997*

CONVENTION CENTERS

Major Convention Centers

Center Name	Meeting Rooms	Exhibit Space (sf)
The Kingdome	5	280,480
Seattle Gift Center	1	15,600
Seattle Center	4	85,000
Seattle International Trade Center	6	75,000
Sheraton Seattle Hotel and Towers	25	n/a
Washington State Convention and Trade Center	54	100,000
The Westin Hotel	24	n/a

Note: n/a not available
Source: Trade Shows Worldwide 1997

Living Environment

COST OF LIVING

Cost of Living Index

Composite Index	Housing	Utilities	Groceries	Health Care	Trans-portation	Misc. Goods/ Services
113.9	125.7	77.9	112.1	143.6	108.2	109.5

Note: U.S. = 100
Source: ACCRA, Cost of Living Index, 2nd Quarter 1997

HOUSING

Median Home Prices and Housing Affordability

Area	Median Price[2] 3rd Qtr. 1997 ($)	HOI[3] 3rd Qtr. 1997	Afford-ability Rank[4]
MSA[1]	171,000	53.5	168
U.S.	127,000	63.7	--

Note: (1) Metropolitan Statistical Area - see Appendix A for areas included; (2) U.S. figures calculated from the sales of 625,000 new and existing homes in 195 markets; (3) Housing Opportunity Index - percent of homes sold that were within the reach of the median income household at the prevailing mortgage interest rate; (4) Rank is from 1-195 with 1 being most affordable
Source: National Association of Home Builders, Housing Opportunity Index, 3rd Quarter 1997

It is projected that the median price of existing single-family homes in the metro area will increase by 7.5% in 1998. Nationwide, home prices are projected to increase 6.6%.
Kiplinger's Personal Finance Magazine, January 1998

Average New Home Price

Area	Price ($)
City	169,000
U.S.	135,150

Note: Figures are based on a new home with 1,800 sq. ft. of living area on an 8,000 sq. ft. lot.
Source: ACCRA, Cost of Living Index, 2nd Quarter 1997

Average Apartment Rent

Area	Rent ($/mth)
City	789
U.S.	575

Note: Figures are based on an unfurnished two bedroom, 1-1/2 or 2 bath apartment, approximately 950 sq. ft. in size, excluding all utilities except water
Source: ACCRA, Cost of Living Index, 2nd Quarter 1997

RESIDENTIAL UTILITIES

Average Residential Utility Costs

Area	All Electric ($/mth)	Part Electric ($/mth)	Other Energy ($/mth)	Phone ($/mth)
City	80.43	--	--	15.29
U.S.	108.38	56.32	44.12	19.66

Source: ACCRA, Cost of Living Index, 2nd Quarter 1997

HEALTH CARE

Average Health Care Costs

Area	Hospital ($/day)	Doctor ($/visit)	Dentist ($/visit)
City	569.40	62.22	101.75
U.S.	390.32	48.32	60.14

Note: Hospital - based on a semi-private room. Doctor - based on a general practitioner's routine exam of an established patient. Dentist - based on adult teeth cleaning and periodic oral exam.
Source: ACCRA, Cost of Living Index, 2nd Quarter 1997

Distribution of Office-Based Physicians

Area	Family/Gen. Practitioners	Specialists		
		Medical	Surgical	Other
MSA[1]	867	1,425	1,170	1,450

Note: Data as of 12/31/96; (1) Metropolitan Statistical Area - see Appendix A for areas included
Source: American Medical Assn., Physician Characteristics & Distribution in the U.S., 1997-1998

Hospitals

Seattle has 9 general medical and surgical hospitals, 1 alcoholism and other chemical dependency, 1 children's general. *AHA Guide to the Healthcare Field 1997-98*

According to *U.S. News and World Report,* Seattle has 3 of the best hospitals in the U.S.: **University of Washington Medical Center**, noted for AIDS, cancer, cardiology, geriatrics, gynecology, orthopedics, otolaryngology, pulmonology, rehabilitation, rheumatology, urology; **Harborview Medical Center**, noted for AIDS; **Children's Hospital and Medical Center**, noted for pediatrics; *U.S. News and World Report, "America's Best Hospitals",* 7/28/97

EDUCATION

Public School District Statistics

District Name	Num. Sch.	Enroll.	Classroom Teachers[1]	Pupils per Teacher	Minority Pupils (%)	Current Exp.[2] ($/pupil)
Highline	38	18,209	853	21.3	n/a	n/a
Seattle	114	46,757	2,417	19.3	58.9	6,444
Shoreline	18	9,929	489	20.3	n/a	n/a
South Central	6	2,163	107	20.2	n/a	n/a

Note: Data covers the 1995-1996 school year unless otherwise noted; (1) Excludes teachers reported as working in school district offices rather than in schools; (2) Based on 1993-94 enrollment collected by the Census Bureau, not the enrollment figure shown in column 3; SD = School District; ISD = Independent School District; n/a not available
Source: National Center for Education Statistics, Common Core of Data Survey; Bureau of the Census

Educational Quality

School District	Education Quotient[1]	Graduate Outcome[2]	Community Index[3]	Resource Index[4]
Seattle	106.0	84.0	137.0	97.0

Note: Nearly 1,000 secondary school districts were rated in terms of educational quality. The scores range from a low of 50 to a high of 150; (1) Average of the Graduate Outcome, Community and Resource indexes; (2) Based on graduation rates and college board scores (SAT/ACT); (3) Based on the surrounding community's average level of education and the area's average income level; (4) Based on teacher salaries, per-pupil expenditures and student-teacher ratios.
Source: Expansion Management, Ratings Issue 1997

Educational Attainment by Race

Area	High School Graduate (%)					Bachelor's Degree (%)				
	Total	White	Black	Other	Hisp.[2]	Total	White	Black	Other	Hisp.[2]
City	86.4	89.7	75.5	72.8	77.7	37.9	41.8	14.4	28.4	25.4
MSA[1]	87.7	88.8	79.5	78.1	79.0	29.8	30.3	16.4	30.0	20.3
U.S.	75.2	77.9	63.1	60.4	49.8	20.3	21.5	11.4	19.4	9.2

Note: figures shown cover persons 25 years old and over; (1) Metropolitan Statistical Area - see Appendix A for areas included; (2) people of Hispanic origin can be of any race
Source: 1990 Census of Population and Housing, Summary Tape File 3C

School Enrollment by Type

Area	Preprimary				Elementary/High School			
	Public		Private		Public		Private	
	Enrollment	%	Enrollment	%	Enrollment	%	Enrollment	%
City	3,889	42.2	5,327	57.8	39,423	78.6	10,741	21.4
MSA[1]	22,997	51.8	21,435	48.2	264,909	90.2	28,825	9.8
U.S.	2,679,029	59.5	1,824,256	40.5	38,379,689	90.2	4,187,099	9.8

Note: figures shown cover persons 3 years old and over;
(1) Metropolitan Statistical Area - see Appendix A for areas included
Source: 1990 Census of Population and Housing, Summary Tape File 3C

School Enrollment by Race

Area	Preprimary (%)				Elementary/High School (%)			
	White	Black	Other	Hisp.[1]	White	Black	Other	Hisp.[1]
City	72.3	13.2	14.5	5.2	55.7	20.3	24.0	5.2
MSA[2]	86.9	4.4	8.7	3.0	82.4	5.6	12.0	3.7
U.S.	80.4	12.5	7.1	7.8	74.1	15.6	10.3	12.5

Note: figures shown cover persons 3 years old and over; (1) people of Hispanic origin can be of any race; (2) Metropolitan Statistical Area - see Appendix A for areas included
Source: 1990 Census of Population and Housing, Summary Tape File 3C

SAT/ACT Scores

Area/District	1997 SAT				1997 ACT	
	Percent of Graduates Tested (%)	Average Math Score	Average Verbal Score	Average Combined Score	Percent of Graduates Tested (%)	Average Composite Score
Seattle SD1	45	518	519	1,037	n/a	n/a
State	46	523	523	1,046	16	22.4
U.S.	42	511	505	1,016	36	21.0

Note: Math and verbal SAT scores are out of a possible 800; ACT scores are out of a possible 36
Caution: Comparing or ranking states/cities on the basis of SAT/ACT scores alone is invalid and strongly discouraged by the The College Board and The American College Testing Program as students who take the tests are self-selected and do not represent the entire student population.
Source: Seattle Public Schools, Student Information Services, 1997; American College Testing Program, 1997; College Board, 1997

Classroom Teacher Salaries in Public Schools

District	B.A. Degree		M.A. Degree		Ph.D. Degree	
	Min. ($)	Max. ($)	Min. ($)	Max. ($)	Min. ($)	Max. ($)
Seattle	22,347	24,917	26,714	35,881	28,762	47,638
Average[1]	26,120	39,270	28,175	44,667	31,643	49,825

Note: Salaries are for 1996-1997; (1) Based on all school districts covered; n/a not available
Source: American Federation of Teachers (unpublished data)

Higher Education

Two-Year Colleges		Four-Year Colleges		Medical Schools	Law Schools	Voc/Tech
Public	Private	Public	Private			
4	1	1	6	1	1	33

Source: College Blue Book, Occupational Education 1997; Medical School Admission Requirements, 1998-99; Peterson's Guide to Two-Year Colleges, 1997; Peterson's Guide to Four-Year Colleges, 1997; Barron's Guide to Law Schools 1997

MAJOR EMPLOYERS

Major Employers

Airborne Freight Corp.	Alaska Airlines
Associated Grocers	Boeing Co.
Children's Hospital & Medical Center	Holland America Line-Westtours
King County Medical Blue Shield	Nordstrom
Safeco Corp.	Baugh Construction
Seattle Times	Starbucks Corp.
Swedish Health Services	Virginia Mason Medical Center
Todd Pacific Shipyards	Immunex Research & Development

Note: companies listed are located in the city
Source: Dun's Business Rankings 1997; Ward's Business Directory, 1997

PUBLIC SAFETY

Crime Rate

Area	All Crimes	Violent Crimes				Property Crimes		
		Murder	Forcible Rape	Robbery	Aggrav. Assault	Burglary	Larceny -Theft	Motor Vehicle Theft
City	10,310.8	6.9	48.4	363.8	422.9	1,455.7	6,835.4	1,177.7
Suburbs[1]	n/a	n/a	n/a	n/a	n/a	n/a	n/a	n/a
MSA[2]	n/a	n/a	n/a	n/a	n/a	n/a	n/a	n/a
U.S.	5,078.9	7.4	36.1	202.4	388.2	943.0	2,975.9	525.9

Note: Crime rate is the number of crimes per 100,000 pop.; (1) defined as all areas within the MSA but located outside the central city; (2) Metropolitan Statistical Area - see Appendix A for areas incl.
Source: FBI Uniform Crime Reports 1996

RECREATION

Culture and Recreation

Museums	Symphony Orchestras	Opera Companies	Dance Companies	Professional Theatres	Zoos	Pro Sports Teams
14	2	2	2	9	1	3

Source: International Directory of the Performing Arts, 1996; Official Museum Directory, 1998; Chamber of Commerce/Economic Development 1997

Library System

The King County Library System has 39 branches, holdings of 2,871,833 volumes and a budget of $45,184,308 (1995). The Seattle Public Library has 22 branches, holdings of 1,800,000 volumes and a budget of $24,564,928 (1997). *American Library Directory, 1997-1998*

MEDIA

Newspapers

Name	Type	Freq.	Distribution	Circulation
Ballard Tribune	General	1x/wk	Local	18,000
Beacon Hill News	General	1x/wk	Local	20,000
Capitol Hill Times	General	1x/wk	Local	17,000
The Catholic Northwest Progress	Religious	1x/wk	Local	15,516
The Daily of the University of Washington	n/a	5x/wk	Campus & community	18,000
Eastsideweek	General	1x/wk	Local	36,794
Facts	Black	1x/wk	Local	55,000
Hispanic News	Hispanic	1x/wk	Local	10,000
International Examiner	Asian	2x/mo	Local	12,000
Northwest Asian Weekly	Asian	1x/wk	Local	10,000
Portland Medium	General	1x/wk	Area	13,500
Queen Anne/Magnolia News	General	1x/wk	Local	21,000
Seattle Chinese Post	Asian	1x/wk	Local	15,000
Seattle Gay News	n/a	1x/wk	Local	30,000
Seattle Medium	Black	1x/wk	Area	45,000
Seattle Post-Intelligencer	General	7x/wk	Area	203,000
The Seattle Skanner	Black	1x/wk	Local	10,000
The Seattle Times	n/a	7x/wk	Area	226,287
Seattle Weekly	General	1x/wk	Area	77,013
South District Journal	General	1x/wk	Local	18,000
Tacoma True Citizen	Black	1x/wk	Local	16,000
University Herald	General	1x/wk	Local	11,500
West Seattle Herald	General	1x/wk	Local	30,000
White Center News	n/a	1x/wk	Local	28,000

Note: Includes newspapers with circulations of 10,000 or more located in the city; n/a not available
Source: Burrelle's Media Directory, 1998 Edition

AM Radio Stations

Call Letters	Freq. (kHz)	Target Audience	Station Format	Music Format
KVI	570	General	N/T	n/a
KCIS	630	Religious	M/N/S/T	Christian
KIRO	710	General	N/S/T	n/a
KNWX	770	General	N/T	n/a
KGNW	820	General	M	Christian
KIXI	880	General	M	Oldies
KJR	950	General	S	n/a
KOMO	1000	General	M	Adult Contemporary/Oldies
KBLE	1050	General	M/T	Christian
KRPM	1090	General	M/N/S	Country
KEZX	1150	General	T	n/a
KBSG	1210	General	E/M/N	Oldies
KMPS	1300	General	M/N/S	Country
KRIZ	1420	General	M/N/T	R&B/Urban Contemporary
KARR	1460	General	M	Christian
KBLV	1540	n/a	M/N/S	Country
KZIZ	1560	General	M/N/T	Christian/R&B/Urban Contemporary

Note: Stations included broadcast in the Seattle metro area; n/a not available
Station Format: E = Educational; M = Music; N = News; S = Sports; T = Talk
Source: Burrelle's Media Directory, 1998 Edition

FM Radio Stations

Call Letters	Freq. (mHz)	Target Audience	Station Format	Music Format
KPLU	88.5	General	M/N	Jazz
KASB	89.3	n/a	M/N/S	Alternative
KNHC	89.5	General	E/M/N/S	Christian/Contemporary Top 40
KGRG	89.9	General	M/N/S	Alternative
KCMU	90.3	General	M	Alternative
KBCS	91.3	n/a	E/M	n/a
KLSY	92.5	General	M	Adult Contemporary
KUBE	93.3	General	M	Contemporary Top 40
KMPS	94.1	n/a	M	Country
KUOW	94.9	General	E/M/N/S/T	Big Band/Classical
KJR	95.7	General	M	Adult Contemporary
KYCW	96.5	n/a	M	Country
KBSG	97.3	General	E/M/N	Oldies
KING	98.1	General	M	Classical
KISW	99.9	General	M	AOR
KIRO	100.7	General	N/T	n/a
KPLZ	101.5	General	M/N/S	Adult Contemporary
KZOK	102.5	General	M/N	Classic Rock
KMTT	103.7	General	M	Alternative
KMIH	104.5	General	E/M/S	Alternative
KCMS	105.3	General	M	Adult Contemporary/Christian
KRPM	106.1	General	M/N/S	Contemporary Top 40/Country
KRWM	106.9	General	M	Adult Contemporary
KNDD	107.7	General	M	Alternative

Note: Stations included broadcast in the Seattle metro area; n/a not available
Station Format: E = Educational; M = Music; N = News; S = Sports; T = Talk
Music Format: AOR = Album Oriented Rock; MOR = Middle-of-the-Road
Source: Burrelle's Media Directory, 1998 Edition

Television Stations

Name	Ch.	Affiliation	Type	Owner
KOMO	4	ABC	Commercial	Fisher Broadcasting Inc.
KING	5	NBC	Commercial	A.H. Belo Corporation
KIRO	7	UPN	Commercial	A.H. Belo Corporation
KCTS	9	PBS	Public	KCTS
KSTW	11	UPN	Commercial	Viacom/Paramount
KCPQ	13	Fox	Commercial	Kelly Television Company
KTZZ	22	WB	Commercial	Dudley Broadcast Management

Note: Stations included broadcast in the Seattle metro area
Source: Burrelle's Media Directory, 1998 Edition

CLIMATE

Average and Extreme Temperatures

Temperature	Jan	Feb	Mar	Apr	May	Jun	Jul	Aug	Sep	Oct	Nov	Dec	Ann
Extreme High (°F)	64	70	75	85	93	96	98	99	98	89	74	63	99
Average High (°F)	44	48	52	57	64	69	75	74	69	59	50	45	59
Average Temp. (°F)	39	43	45	49	55	61	65	65	60	52	45	41	52
Average Low (°F)	34	36	38	41	46	51	54	55	51	45	39	36	44
Extreme Low (°F)	0	1	11	29	28	38	43	44	35	28	6	6	0

Note: Figures cover the years 1948-1990
Source: National Climatic Data Center, International Station Meteorological Climate Summary, 3/95

Average Precipitation/Snowfall/Humidity

Precip./Humidity	Jan	Feb	Mar	Apr	May	Jun	Jul	Aug	Sep	Oct	Nov	Dec	Ann
Avg. Precip. (in.)	5.7	4.2	3.7	2.4	1.7	1.4	0.8	1.1	1.9	3.5	5.9	5.9	38.4
Avg. Snowfall (in.)	5	2	1	Tr	Tr	0	0	0	0	Tr	1	3	13
Avg. Rel. Hum. 7am (%)	83	83	84	83	80	79	79	84	87	88	85	85	83
Avg. Rel. Hum. 4pm (%)	76	69	63	57	54	54	49	51	57	68	76	79	63

Note: Figures cover the years 1948-1990; Tr = Trace amounts (<0.05 in. of rain; <0.5 in. of snow)
Source: National Climatic Data Center, International Station Meteorological Climate Summary, 3/95

Weather Conditions

Temperature			Daytime Sky			Precipitation		
5°F & below	32°F & below	90°F & above	Clear	Partly cloudy	Cloudy	0.01 inch or more precip.	0.1 inch or more snow/ice	Thunder-storms
< 1	38	3	57	121	187	157	8	8

Note: Figures are average number of days per year and covers the years 1948-1990
Source: National Climatic Data Center, International Station Meteorological Climate Summary, 3/95

AIR & WATER QUALITY

Maximum Pollutant Concentrations

	Particulate Matter (ug/m3)	Carbon Monoxide (ppm)	Sulfur Dioxide (ppm)	Nitrogen Dioxide (ppm)	Ozone (ppm)	Lead (ug/m3)
MSA[1] Level	93	7	0.019	0.020	0.12	n/a
NAAQS[2]	150	9	0.140	0.053	0.12	1.50
Met NAAQS?	Yes	Yes	Yes	Yes	Yes	n/a

Note: (1) Metropolitan Statistical Area - see Appendix A for areas included; (2) National Ambient Air Quality Standards; ppm = parts per million; ug/m3 = micrograms per cubic meter; n/a not available
Source: EPA, National Air Quality and Emissions Trends Report, 1996

Pollutant Standards Index

In the Seattle MSA (see Appendix A for areas included), the Pollutant Standards Index (PSI) exceeded 100 on 1 day in 1996. A PSI value greater than 100 indicates that air quality would be in the unhealthful range on that day. *EPA, National Air Quality and Emissions Trends Report, 1996*

Drinking Water

Water System Name	Pop. Served	Primary Water Source Type	Number of Violations in Fiscal Year 1997	Type of Violation/ Contaminants
Seattle Public Utilities	587,000	Surface	1	Lead & copper rule[1]

Note: Data as of January 16, 1998; (1) System failed to complete Optimum Corrosion Control Treatment Study recommendation on time, submit an applicable study on time, or provide sufficient information to make a treatment decision as required under the lead and copper rule.
Source: EPA, Office of Ground Water and Drinking Water, Safe Drinking Water Information System

Seattle tap water is alkaline, very soft.
Editor & Publisher Market Guide, 1998

Tacoma, Washington

Background

Between the Olympic Mountains in the northwest and snow-capped Mt. Rainier in the east, Tacoma, with its natural harbor, offers a breathtaking panorama.

Captain George Vancouver became the first white explorer in the area in 1792. (The Puyallup and Nisqwually tribes were already resident.) The Charles Wilkes expedition arrived in 1841. The first settlement, however, took place in 1852, when lumber attracted immigrants and entrepreneurs. Nicholas De Lin, a Swedish immigrant, constructed the first water-driven mill.

In 1868 General Morton M. McCarver established a town on the west shore calling it Commencement Bay. The name was later changed to Tacoma, the Native American word for Mt. Rainier.

The arrival of the Northern Pacific Railway in 1887 gave rise to the city's rapid growth in the 1880's and early 90's, but literally stopped during the depression of 1893. Further growth proceeded slowly after World War II.

Incorporated in 1884, Tacoma has become the third largest city in the state, a leading port, and an industrial and wholesale center. Shipbuilding and steel are major industries. Other products include electrochemicals, wool, men's clothing and a variety of forest products. It is also a chemical center.

For the outdoors people, the area offers many recreational activities.

Tacoma's climate is characterized by mild temperatures, a pronounced rainy season and considerable cloudiness during the winter. Local summer afternoon showers and a few thunderstorms occur, but do not add significantly to the total accumulation. Fog or low clouds form over southern Puget Sound and often dominate the nocturnal weather conditions during late summer, fall and early winter months.

General Rankings and Evaluative Comments

- Tacoma was ranked #42 out of 300 cities by *Money's* 1997 "Survey of the Best Places to Live." Criteria used: health services, crime, economy, housing, education, transportation, weather, leisure and the arts. The city was ranked #51 in 1996 and #42 in 1995. *Money, July 1997; Money, September 1996; Money, September 1995*

- *Ladies Home Journal* ranked America's 200 largest cities based on the qualities women care about most. Tacoma ranked 95 out of 200. Criteria: low crime rate, good public schools, well-paying jobs, quality health and child care, the presence of women in government, proportion of women-owned businesses, size of the wage gap with men, local economy, divorce rates, the ratio of single men to single women, whether there are laws that require at least the same number of public toilets for women as men, and the probability of good hair days. *Ladies Home Journal, November 1997*

- Tacoma was ranked #141 out of 219 cities in terms of children's health, safety, and economic well-being. Criteria: total population, percent population change, birth rate, child immunization rate, infant mortality rate, percent low birth weight infants, percent of births to teens, physician-to-population ratio, student-to-teacher ratio, dropout rate, unemployment rate, median family income, percent of children in poverty, violent and property crime rates, number of juvenile arrests for violent crimes as a percent of the total crime index, number of days with pollution standard index (PSI) over 100, pounds toxic releases per 1,000 people and number of superfund sites. *Zero Population Growth, Children's Environmental Index 1997*

- According to *Working Mother,* "Washington State officials are working hard to expand the supply of child care this year. Governor Gary Locke's proposed budget earmarked $350 million for child care, including $100 million in new dollars and $9 million for nontraditional care, such as off-hours programs for parents who work swing shift or nights. This is an especially important innovation; child care advocates across the country report that parents with nontraditional hours find it nearly impossible to obtain care for their children. Last year, state lawmakers earmarked about $10 million in state funds to eliminate a waiting list for state-sponsored child care.

  New funds have been made available for resource and referral, caregiver training and parent-education efforts. Training requirements for all caregivers have been strengthened as part of the program. All providers in the state will soon have to have 20 hours of training during their first year on the job, and 10 hours annually after that. Currently, most caregivers need no training at all before they start caring for kids." *Working Mother, July/August 1997*

Business Environment

STATE ECONOMY

State Economic Profile

"Washington's economy is accelerating....Income has returned to above average growth after lagging for nearly two years.

Boeing's current expansion is accelerating beyond previous estimates, with production planned to increase to 40 planes per month by the end of 1997, and to 48 per month by 1999. The uptick of the aircraft cycle makes up for a recent slowdown in the expansion of software/data processing employment. Prospects remain good over the long term for continued expansion of the software industry, as applications expand to Internet management and telecommunications.

The new governor's budget proposal for the 1997-1999 biennium is reduced slightly from earlier estimates in order to meet Initiative 601, which limits increases in state general-fund spending to the combined rates of inflation and population growth. Governor Locke has proposed reductions in residential property taxes and a reduction of the business and occupation tax to pre-1993 levels. Washington's state and local tax burden currently ranks third highest in the nation.

Near-term risks are focused on the upside, with considerable potential for further hiring at Boeing. Continued expansion of aircraft production is based on assumptions that airlines will remain in good financial condition; that economic conditions remain stable in the U.S. and Asia, while improving in Europe; that cargo and passenger traffic continue to increase; that there are no substantial increase in fuel costs; and finally that European deregulation does not significantly reduce the number of airlines. A rising dollar/yen ratio also poses some near-term risk to Washington's seafood industry, wood products makers, and fruit growers.

The Washington economy will continue to expand strongly this year. The cyclical upturn in aircraft and expanding high-tech hardware, software, and semiconductors will support western Washington, while central Washington's agriculture will benefit from freer trade and worldwide income growth. Eastern Washington will also benefit from aircraft parts production. Washington is ranked as a top performer over the long term but is at risk of a downturn early next decade." *National Association of Realtors, Economic Profiles: The Fifty States, July 1997*

IMPORTS/EXPORTS

Total Export Sales

Area	1993 ($000)	1994 ($000)	1995 ($000)	1996 ($000)	% Chg. 1993-96	% Chg. 1995-96
MSA[1]	1,115,321	774,869	1,098,921	1,179,693	5.8	7.4
U.S.	464,858,354	512,415,609	583,030,524	622,827,063	34.0	6.8

Note: (1) Metropolitan Statistical Area - see Appendix A for areas included
Source: U.S. Department of Commerce, International Trade Association, Metropolitan Area Exports: An Export Performance Report on Over 250 U.S. Cities, October 1997

Imports/Exports by Port

Type	Cargo Value			Share of U.S. Total	
	1995 (US$mil.)	1996 (US$mil.)	% Change 1995-1996	1995 (%)	1996 (%)
Imports	18,963	15,951	-15.88	4.84	4.16
Exports	3,951	4,586	16.05	1.73	1.94

Source: Global Trade Information Services, WaterBorne Trade Atlas 1997

CITY FINANCES

City Government Finances

Component	FY92 ($000)	FY92 (per capita $)
Revenue	517,992	2,874.04
Expenditure	497,476	2,760.21
Debt Outstanding	568,488	3,154.22
Cash & Securities	505,459	2,804.51

Source: U.S. Bureau of the Census, City Government Finances: 1991-92

City Government Revenue by Source

Source	FY92 ($000)	FY92 (per capita $)	FY92 (%)
From Federal Government	3,213	17.83	0.6
From State Governments	15,276	84.76	2.9
From Local Governments	509	2.82	0.1
Property Taxes	24,891	138.11	4.8
General Sales Taxes	22,282	123.63	4.3
Selective Sales Taxes	26,540	147.26	5.1
Income Taxes	0	0.00	0.0
Current Charges	59,188	328.40	11.4
Utility/Liquor Store	264,136	1,465.54	51.0
Employee Retirement[1]	49,494	274.61	9.6
Other	52,463	291.09	10.1

Note: (1) Excludes "city contributions," classified as "nonrevenue," intragovernmental transfers.
Source: U.S. Bureau of the Census, City Government Finances: 1991-92

City Government Expenditures by Function

Function	FY92 ($000)	FY92 (per capita $)	FY92 (%)
Educational Services	7,242	40.18	1.5
Employee Retirement[1]	15,293	84.85	3.1
Environment/Housing	101,346	562.31	20.4
Government Administration	18,445	102.34	3.7
Interest on General Debt	13,471	74.74	2.7
Public Safety	46,725	259.25	9.4
Social Services	4,342	24.09	0.9
Transportation	11,152	61.88	2.2
Utility/Liquor Store	265,073	1,470.74	53.3
Other	14,387	79.83	2.9

Note: (1) Payments to beneficiaries including withdrawal of contributions.
Source: U.S. Bureau of the Census, City Government Finances: 1991-92

Municipal Bond Ratings

Area	Moody's	S & P
Tacoma	A1	n/a

Note: n/a not available; n/r not rated
Source: Moody's Bond Record, 2/98; Statistical Abstract of the U.S., 1997;
Governing Magazine, 9/97, 3/98

POPULATION

Population Growth

Area	1980	1990	% Chg. 1980-90	July 1996 Estimate	% Chg. 1990-96
City	158,501	176,664	11.5	179,114	1.4
MSA[1]	485,643	586,203	20.7	657,272	12.1
U.S.	226,545,805	248,765,170	9.8	265,179,411	6.6

Note: (1) Metropolitan Statistical Area - see Appendix A for areas included
Source: 1980/1990 Census of Housing and Population, Summary Tape File 3C;
Census Bureau Population Estimates

Population Characteristics

Race	City 1980 Population	%	City 1990 Population	%	% Chg. 1980-90	MSA[1] 1990 Population	%
White	133,745	84.4	138,449	78.4	3.5	499,371	85.2
Black	14,439	9.1	20,193	11.4	39.9	42,269	7.2
Amer Indian/Esk/Aleut	2,919	1.8	3,410	1.9	16.8	8,428	1.4
Asian/Pacific Islander	5,647	3.6	12,295	7.0	117.7	28,918	4.9
Other	1,751	1.1	2,317	1.3	32.3	7,217	1.2
Hispanic Origin[2]	4,159	2.6	6,270	3.5	50.8	19,445	3.3

Note: (1) Metropolitan Statistical Area - see Appendix A for areas included;
(2) people of Hispanic origin can be of any race
Source: 1980/1990 Census of Housing and Population, Summary Tape File 3C

Ancestry

Area	German	Irish	English	Italian	U.S.	French	Polish	Dutch
City	24.4	15.1	14.8	3.3	3.2	4.9	2.1	2.7
MSA[1]	28.2	15.4	16.5	3.5	3.4	5.3	2.2	2.9
U.S.	23.3	15.6	13.1	5.9	5.3	4.2	3.8	2.5

Note: Figures are percentages and include persons that reported multiple ancestry (eg. if a person reported being Irish and Italian, they were included in both columns); (1) Metropolitan Statistical Area - see Appendix A for areas included
Source: 1990 Census of Population and Housing, Summary Tape File 3C

Age

Area	Median Age (Years)	Age Distribution (%) Under 5	Under 18	18-24	25-44	45-64	65+	80+
City	31.8	8.2	25.9	10.9	33.4	16.1	13.7	3.7
MSA[1]	31.2	8.2	27.2	11.2	33.6	17.6	10.4	2.2
U.S.	32.9	7.3	25.6	10.5	32.6	18.7	12.5	2.8

Note: (1) Metropolitan Statistical Area - see Appendix A for areas included
Source: 1990 Census of Population and Housing, Summary Tape File 3C

Male/Female Ratio

Area	Number of males per 100 females (all ages)	Number of males per 100 females (18 years old+)
City	93.8	90.1
MSA[1]	99.8	97.8
U.S.	95.0	91.9

Note: (1) Metropolitan Statistical Area - see Appendix A for areas included
Source: 1990 Census of Population, General Population Characteristics

INCOME

Per Capita/Median/Average Income

Area	Per Capita ($)	Median Household ($)	Average Household ($)
City	12,272	25,333	30,620
MSA[1]	13,439	30,412	35,767
U.S.	14,420	30,056	38,453

Note: all figures are for 1989; (1) Metropolitan Statistical Area - see Appendix A for areas included
Source: 1990 Census of Population and Housing, Summary Tape File 3C

Household Income Distribution by Race

Income ($)	City (%)					U.S. (%)				
	Total	White	Black	Other	Hisp.[1]	Total	White	Black	Other	Hisp.[1]
Less than 5,000	6.7	5.9	9.0	12.9	5.9	6.2	4.8	15.2	8.6	8.8
5,000 - 9,999	12.3	11.7	16.4	13.3	13.2	9.3	8.6	14.2	9.9	11.1
10,000 - 14,999	10.9	10.8	10.5	13.2	8.2	8.8	8.5	11.0	9.8	11.0
15,000 - 24,999	19.5	19.5	18.9	20.0	23.8	17.5	17.3	18.9	18.5	20.5
25,000 - 34,999	16.9	17.0	17.0	15.9	23.3	15.8	16.1	14.2	15.4	16.4
35,000 - 49,999	18.0	18.7	15.9	13.0	13.9	17.9	18.6	13.3	16.1	16.0
50,000 - 74,999	11.3	11.6	9.6	9.6	8.6	15.0	15.8	9.3	13.4	11.1
75,000 - 99,999	2.7	2.9	2.1	1.4	1.9	5.1	5.5	2.6	4.7	3.1
100,000+	1.7	1.9	0.6	0.7	1.2	4.4	4.8	1.3	3.7	1.9

Note: all figures are for 1989; (1) people of Hispanic origin can be of any race
Source: 1990 Census of Population and Housing, Summary Tape File 3C

Effective Buying Income

Area	Per Capita ($)	Median Household ($)	Average Household ($)
City	14,929	31,005	37,994
MSA[1]	16,993	38,836	46,554
U.S.	15,444	33,201	41,849

Note: data as of 1/1/97; (1) Metropolitan Statistical Area - see Appendix A for areas included
Source: Standard Rate & Data Service, Newspaper Advertising Source, 2/98

Effective Household Buying Income Distribution

Area	% of Households Earning						
	$10,000 -$19,999	$20,000 -$34,999	$35,000 -$49,999	$50,000 -$74,999	$75,000 -$99,000	$100,000 -$124,999	$125,000 and up
City	18.7	23.2	18.7	17.5	5.3	1.5	1.3
MSA[1]	14.0	22.1	19.4	21.9	8.8	2.5	2.4
U.S.	16.5	23.4	18.3	18.2	6.4	2.1	2.4

Note: data as of 1/1/97; (1) Metropolitan Statistical Area - see Appendix A for areas included
Source: Standard Rate & Data Service, Newspaper Advertising Source, 2/98

Poverty Rates by Race and Age

Area	Total (%)	By Race (%)				By Age (%)		
		White	Black	Other	Hisp.[2]	Under 5 years old	Under 18 years old	65 years and over
City	16.8	13.1	26.8	34.0	23.0	26.3	23.4	12.3
MSA[1]	11.4	9.5	22.6	22.5	17.0	18.3	15.5	9.1
U.S.	13.1	9.8	29.5	23.1	25.3	20.1	18.3	12.8

Note: figures show the percent of people living below the poverty line in 1989. The average poverty
threshold was $12,674 for a family of four in 1989; (1) Metropolitan Statistical Area - see Appendix A
for areas included; (2) people of Hispanic origin can be of any race
Source: 1990 Census of Population and Housing, Summary Tape File 3C

EMPLOYMENT

Labor Force and Employment

Area	Civilian Labor Force			Workers Employed		
	Dec. '95	Dec. '96	% Chg.	Dec. '95	Dec. '96	% Chg.
City	97,410	100,082	2.7	91,108	95,326	4.6
MSA[1]	324,815	334,531	3.0	306,570	320,762	4.6
U.S.	134,583,000	136,742,000	1.6	127,903,000	130,785,000	2.3

Note: Data is not seasonally adjusted and covers workers 16 years of age and older;
(1) Metropolitan Statistical Area - see Appendix A for areas included
Source: Bureau of Labor Statistics, http://stats.bls.gov

Unemployment Rate

Area	1997											
	Jan.	Feb.	Mar.	Apr.	May	Jun.	Jul.	Aug.	Sep.	Oct.	Nov.	Dec.
City	6.7	6.5	6.0	5.4	5.1	5.5	5.2	4.8	5.1	5.1	5.0	4.8
MSA[1]	5.8	5.6	5.2	4.7	4.4	4.8	4.5	4.2	4.4	4.4	4.3	4.1
U.S.	5.9	5.7	5.5	4.8	4.7	5.2	5.0	4.8	4.7	4.4	4.3	4.4

Note: Data is not seasonally adjusted and covers workers 16 years of age and older; All figures are percentages; (1) Metropolitan Statistical Area - see Appendix A for areas included
Source: Bureau of Labor Statistics, http://stats.bls.gov

Employment by Industry

Sector	MSA[1]		U.S.
	Number of Employees	Percent of Total	Percent of Total
Services	65,000	28.0	29.0
Retail Trade	46,500	20.0	18.5
Government	48,200	20.8	16.1
Manufacturing	25,700	11.1	15.0
Finance/Insurance/Real Estate	11,800	5.1	5.7
Wholesale Trade	12,900	5.6	5.4
Transportation/Public Utilities	9,300	4.0	5.3
Construction	12,600	5.4	4.5
Mining	200	0.1	0.5

Note: Figures cover non-farm employment as of 12/97 and are not seasonally adjusted; (1) Metropolitan Statistical Area - see Appendix A for areas included
Source: Bureau of Labor Statistics, http://stats.bls.gov

Employment by Occupation

Occupation Category	City (%)	MSA[1] (%)	U.S. (%)
White Collar	54.4	55.8	58.1
Executive/Admin./Management	10.1	11.1	12.3
Professional	12.9	13.3	14.1
Technical & Related Support	4.0	3.9	3.7
Sales	11.5	11.6	11.8
Administrative Support/Clerical	15.9	15.8	16.3
Blue Collar	27.5	28.1	26.2
Precision Production/Craft/Repair	11.9	13.2	11.3
Machine Operators/Assem./Insp.	6.3	5.8	6.8
Transportation/Material Movers	4.2	4.6	4.1
Cleaners/Helpers/Laborers	5.1	4.5	3.9
Services	16.5	14.3	13.2
Farming/Forestry/Fishing	1.6	1.8	2.5

Note: figures cover employed persons 16 years old and over; (1) Metropolitan Statistical Area - see Appendix A for areas included
Source: 1990 Census of Population and Housing, Summary Tape File 3C

Occupational Employment Projections: 1994 - 2005

Occupations Expected to have the Largest Job Growth (ranked by numerical growth)	Fast-Growing Occupations (ranked by percent growth)
1. Waiters & waitresses	1. Computer scientists
2. Salespersons, retail	2. Computer engineers
3. General managers & top executives	3. Electronic pagination systems workers
4. Systems analysts	4. Personal and home care aides
5. Cashiers	5. Residential counselors
6. Registered nurses	6. Patternmakers and layout workers
7. Computer engineers	7. Machine assemblers
8. Receptionists and information clerks	8. Human services workers
9. Truck drivers, heavy & light	9. Systems analysts
10. Janitors/cleaners/maids, ex. priv. hshld.	10. Occupational therapists

Projections cover Washington.
Source: U.S. Department of Labor, Employment and Training Administration, America's Labor Market Information System (ALMIS)

Average Wages

Occupation	Wage	Occupation	Wage
Professional/Technical/Clerical	$/Week	**Health/Protective Services**	$/Week
Accountants III	-	Corrections Officers	-
Attorneys III	-	Firefighters	-
Budget Analysts III	-	Nurses, Licensed Practical II	-
Buyers/Contracting Specialists II	-	Nurses, Registered II	-
Clerks, Accounting III	414	Nursing Assistants II	-
Clerks, General III	-	Police Officers I	-
Computer Operators II	441	**Hourly Workers**	$/Hour
Computer Programmers II	571	Forklift Operators	13.49
Drafters II	-	General Maintenance Workers	9.07
Engineering Technicians III	-	Guards I	5.38
Engineering Technicians, Civil III	-	Janitors	6.98
Engineers III	-	Maintenance Electricians	17.77
Key Entry Operators I	286	Maintenance Electronics Techs II	-
Personnel Assistants III	-	Maintenance Machinists	-
Personnel Specialists III	-	Maintenance Mechanics, Machinery	13.88
Secretaries III	499	Material Handling Laborers	-
Switchboard Operator-Receptionist	334	Motor Vehicle Mechanics	14.23
Systems Analysts II	811	Shipping/Receiving Clerks	10.91
Systems Analysts Supervisor/Mgr II	-	Tool and Die Makers	-
Tax Collectors II	-	Truckdrivers, Tractor Trailer	13.88
Word Processors II	-	Warehouse Specialists	10.26

Note: Wage data includes full-time workers only for 2/93 and cover the Metropolitan Statistical Area (see Appendix A for areas included). Dashes indicate that data was not available.
Source: Bureau of Labor Statistics, Occupational Compensation Survey

TAXES

Major State and Local Tax Rates

State Corp. Income (%)	State Personal Income (%)	Residential Property (effective rate per $100)	Sales & Use		State Gasoline (cents/ gallon)	State Cigarette (cents/ 20-pack)
			State (%)	Local (%)		
None	None	n/a	6.5	1.5	23	82.5

Note: Personal/corporate income tax rates as of 1/97. Sales, gasoline and cigarette tax rates as of 1/98.
Source: Federation of Tax Administrators, www.taxadmin.org; Washington D.C. Department of Finance and Revenue, Tax Rates and Tax Burdens in the District of Columbia: A Nationwide Comparison, June 1997; Chamber of Commerce

Total Taxes Per Capita and as a Percent of Income

Area	Per Capita Income ($)	Per Capita Taxes ($)			Taxes as Pct. of Income (%)		
		Total	Federal	State/Local	Total	Federal	State/Local
Washington	27,086	9,881	6,572	3,309	36.5	24.3	12.2
U.S.	26,187	9,205	6,127	3,078	35.2	23.4	11.8

Note: Figures are for 1997
Source: Tax Foundation, Web Site, www.taxfoundation.org

Industrial Market

Location	Total Space (sq. ft.)	Vacant Space (sq. ft.)	Vac. Rate (%)	Under Constr. (sq. ft.)	Net Absorp. (sq. ft.)	Net Lease ($/sq.ft./yr.)
Central City	22,513,818	1,674,175	7.4	447,700	-545,275	3.00-4.20
Suburban	n/a	n/a	n/a	n/a	n/a	n/a

Note: Data as of 10/97 and covers Tacoma; n/a not available
Source: Society of Industrial and Office Realtors, 1998 Comparative Statistics of Industrial and Office Real Estate Markets

"Large blocks of space more than 100,000 sq. ft. are attracting interest from companies based in neighboring metro Seattle. This activity and increased traffic through the port of Tacoma should lead to an uptick in absorption. Further, Pierce County should begin to experience the multiplier effects from a new Intel semi-conductor manufacturing plant and Matsushita's semiconductor plant expansion. Demand should also be generated by construction contracts expected in conjunction with expansion of McChord Air Force Base, as it prepares for its accommodation of the C-17 transport planes that will arrive at the end of the decade." *Society of Industrial and Office Realtors, 1998 Comparative Statistics of Industrial and Office Real Estate Markets*

COMMERCIAL UTILITIES

Typical Monthly Electric Bills

Area	Commercial Service ($/month)		Industrial Service ($/month)	
	12 kW demand 1,500 kWh	100 kW demand 30,000 kWh	1,000 kW demand 400,000 kWh	20,000 kW demand 10,000,000 kWh
City	n/a	n/a	n/a	n/a
U.S.	162	2,360	25,590	545,677

Note: Based on rates in effect July 1, 1997; n/a not available
Source: Edison Electric Institute, Typical Residential, Commercial and Industrial Bills, Summer 1997

TRANSPORTATION

Transportation Statistics

Avg. travel time to work (min.)	21.9
Interstate highways	I-5
Bus lines	
In-city	Pierce Transit
Inter-city	8
Passenger air service	
Airport	Seattle-Tacoma International
Airlines	24
Aircraft departures	154,656 (1995)
Enplaned passengers	10,731,233 (1995)
Rail service	Amtrak
Motor freight carriers	240+
Major waterways/ports	Puget Sound (Port of Tacoma)

Source: OAG, Business Travel Planner, Summer 1997; Editor & Publisher Market Guide, 1998; FAA Airport Activity Statistics, 1996; Amtrak National Time Table, Northeast Timetable, Fall/Winter 1997-98; 1990 Census of Population and Housing, STF 3C; Chamber of Commerce/Economic Development 1997; Jane's Urban Transport Systems 1997-98; Transit Fact Book 1997

A survey of 90,000 airline passengers during the first half of 1997 ranked most of the largest airports in the U.S. Seattle-Tacoma International ranked number 13 out of 36. Criteria:

cleanliness, quality of restaurants, attractiveness, speed of baggage delivery, ease of reaching gates, available ground transportation, ease of following signs and closeness of parking. *Plog Research Inc., First Half 1997*

Means of Transportation to Work

Area	Car/Truck/Van		Public Transportation			Bicycle	Walked	Other Means	Worked at Home
	Drove Alone	Car-pooled	Bus	Subway	Railroad				
City	74.6	13.5	3.7	0.0	0.0	0.4	3.8	1.0	3.0
MSA[1]	75.9	13.2	1.9	0.0	0.0	0.3	4.3	1.1	3.3
U.S.	73.2	13.4	3.0	1.5	0.5	0.4	3.9	1.2	3.0

Note: figures shown are percentages and only include workers 16 years old and over;
(1) Metropolitan Statistical Area - see Appendix A for areas included
Source: 1990 Census of Population and Housing, Summary Tape File 3C

BUSINESSES

Major Business Headquarters

Company Name	1997 Rankings	
	Fortune 500	Forbes 500

No companies listed.

Note: Companies listed are located in the city; Dashes indicate no ranking
Fortune 500: companies that produce a 10-K are ranked 1 - 500 based on 1996 revenue
Forbes 500: private companies are ranked 1 - 500 based on 1996 revenue
Source: Forbes 12/1/97; Fortune 4/28/97

Small Business Opportunity

Tacoma was included among *Entrepreneur* magazines listing of the "20 Best Cities for Small Business." It was ranked #2 among mid-size metro areas. Criteria: risk of failure, business performance, economic growth, affordability and state attitude towards business. *Entrepreneur, 10/97*

HOTELS & MOTELS

Hotels/Motels

Area	Hotels/ Motels	Rooms	Luxury-Level Hotels/Motels		Average Minimum Rates ($)		
			♦♦♦♦	♦♦♦♦♦	♦♦	♦♦♦	♦♦♦♦
City	12	1,665	0	0	n/a	n/a	n/a
Suburbs	15	1,085	0	0	n/a	n/a	n/a
Total	27	2,750	0	0	n/a	n/a	n/a

Note: n/a not available; Classifications range from one diamond (budget properties with basic amenities) to five diamond (luxury properties with the finest service, rooms and facilities).
Source: OAG, Business Travel Planner, Summer 1997

CONVENTION CENTERS

Major Convention Centers

Center Name	Meeting Rooms	Exhibit Space (sf)
Sheraton Tacoma Hotel and Convention Center	28	n/a
Tacoma Convention Center & Bicentennial Pavilion	n/a	24,000
Tacoma Dome Arena and Convention Hall	3	126,000

Note: n/a not available
Source: Trade Shows Worldwide 1997

Living Environment

COST OF LIVING

Cost of Living Index

Composite Index	Housing	Utilities	Groceries	Health Care	Trans-portation	Misc. Goods/Services
101.0	103.3	70.8	100.7	140.4	102.8	98.8

Note: U.S. = 100
Source: ACCRA, Cost of Living Index, 3rd Quarter 1997

HOUSING

Median Home Prices and Housing Affordability

Area	Median Price[2] 3rd Qtr. 1997 ($)	HOI[3] 3rd Qtr. 1997	Afford-ability Rank[4]
MSA[1]	127,000	59.4	152
U.S.	127,000	63.7	–

Note: (1) Metropolitan Statistical Area - see Appendix A for areas included; (2) U.S. figures calculated from the sales of 625,000 new and existing homes in 195 markets; (3) Housing Opportunity Index - percent of homes sold that were within the reach of the median income household at the prevailing mortgage interest rate; (4) Rank is from 1-195 with 1 being most affordable
Source: National Association of Home Builders, Housing Opportunity Index, 3rd Quarter 1997

Average New Home Price

Area	Price ($)
City	139,000
U.S.	135,710

Note: Figures are based on a new home with 1,800 sq. ft. of living area on an 8,000 sq. ft. lot.
Source: ACCRA, Cost of Living Index, 3rd Quarter 1997

Average Apartment Rent

Area	Rent ($/mth)
City	612
U.S.	569

Note: Figures are based on an unfurnished two bedroom, 1-1/2 or 2 bath apartment, approximately 950 sq. ft. in size, excluding all utilities except water
Source: ACCRA, Cost of Living Index, 3rd Quarter 1997

RESIDENTIAL UTILITIES

Average Residential Utility Costs

Area	All Electric ($/mth)	Part Electric ($/mth)	Other Energy ($/mth)	Phone ($/mth)
City	–	29.10	38.45	19.96
U.S.	109.40	55.25	43.64	19.48

Source: ACCRA, Cost of Living Index, 3rd Quarter 1997

HEALTH CARE

Average Health Care Costs

Area	Hospital ($/day)	Doctor ($/visit)	Dentist ($/visit)
City	421.80	62.00	110.00
U.S.	392.91	48.76	60.84

Note: Hospital - based on a semi-private room. Doctor - based on a general practitioner's routine exam of an established patient. Dentist - based on adult teeth cleaning and periodic oral exam.
Source: ACCRA, Cost of Living Index, 3rd Quarter 1997

Distribution of Office-Based Physicians

Area	Family/Gen. Practitioners	Specialists		
		Medical	Surgical	Other
MSA[1]	169	244	226	239

Note: Data as of 12/31/96; (1) Metropolitan Statistical Area - see Appendix A for areas included
Source: American Medical Assn., Physician Characteristics & Distribution in the U.S., 1997-1998

Hospitals

Tacoma has 5 general medical and surgical hospitals, 1 children's general. *AHA Guide to the Healthcare Field 1997-98*

St. Joseph Medical Center is among the 100 best-run hospitals in the U.S.
Modern Healthcare, January 5, 1998

EDUCATION

Public School District Statistics

District Name	Num. Sch.	Enroll.	Classroom Teachers[1]	Pupils per Teacher	Minority Pupils (%)	Current Exp.[2] ($/pupil)
Clover Park	31	13,692	660	20.7	n/a	n/a
Fife	4	2,589	120	21.6	n/a	n/a
Franklin Pierce	14	6,655	320	20.8	n/a	n/a
Tacoma	71	31,596	1,710	18.5	39.3	6,163
University Place	9	5,070	255	19.9	n/a	n/a

Note: Data covers the 1995-1996 school year unless otherwise noted; (1) Excludes teachers reported as working in school district offices rather than in schools; (2) Based on 1993-94 enrollment collected by the Census Bureau, not the enrollment figure shown in column 3; SD = School District; ISD = Independent School District; n/a not available
Source: National Center for Education Statistics, Common Core of Data Survey; Bureau of the Census

Educational Quality

School District	Education Quotient[1]	Graduate Outcome[2]	Community Index[3]	Resource Index[4]
Tacoma	107.0	71.0	107.0	144.0

Note: Nearly 1,000 secondary school districts were rated in terms of educational quality. The scores range from a low of 50 to a high of 150; (1) Average of the Graduate Outcome, Community and Resource indexes; (2) Based on graduation rates and college board scores (SAT/ACT); (3) Based on the surrounding community's average level of education and the area's average income level; (4) Based on teacher salaries, per-pupil expenditures and student-teacher ratios.
Source: Expansion Management, Ratings Issue 1997

Educational Attainment by Race

Area	High School Graduate (%)					Bachelor's Degree (%)				
	Total	White	Black	Other	Hisp.[2]	Total	White	Black	Other	Hisp.[2]
City	79.3	80.5	79.6	65.6	75.2	15.8	16.9	9.9	11.0	10.1
MSA[1]	83.2	83.9	84.7	73.1	80.2	17.5	18.1	13.3	12.9	12.1
U.S.	75.2	77.9	63.1	60.4	49.8	20.3	21.5	11.4	19.4	9.2

Note: figures shown cover persons 25 years old and over; (1) Metropolitan Statistical Area - see Appendix A for areas included; (2) people of Hispanic origin can be of any race
Source: 1990 Census of Population and Housing, Summary Tape File 3C

School Enrollment by Type

| Area | Preprimary | | | | Elementary/High School | | | |
| | Public | | Private | | Public | | Private | |
	Enrollment	%	Enrollment	%	Enrollment	%	Enrollment	%
City	2,357	65.7	1,233	34.3	25,891	91.4	2,451	8.6
MSA[1]	7,622	63.2	4,437	36.8	95,627	93.7	6,376	6.3
U.S.	2,679,029	59.5	1,824,256	40.5	38,379,689	90.2	4,187,099	9.8

Note: figures shown cover persons 3 years old and over;
(1) Metropolitan Statistical Area - see Appendix A for areas included
Source: 1990 Census of Population and Housing, Summary Tape File 3C

School Enrollment by Race

| Area | Preprimary (%) | | | | Elementary/High School (%) | | | |
	White	Black	Other	Hisp.[1]	White	Black	Other	Hisp.[1]
City	75.1	13.8	11.1	4.5	67.4	16.6	16.0	5.7
MSA[2]	83.2	8.6	8.2	4.0	81.1	9.0	9.9	4.5
U.S.	80.4	12.5	7.1	7.8	74.1	15.6	10.3	12.5

Note: figures shown cover persons 3 years old and over; (1) people of Hispanic origin can be of any race; (2) Metropolitan Statistical Area - see Appendix A for areas included
Source: 1990 Census of Population and Housing, Summary Tape File 3C

SAT/ACT Scores

| Area/District | 1997 SAT | | | | 1997 ACT | |
	Percent of Graduates Tested (%)	Average Math Score	Average Verbal Score	Average Combined Score	Percent of Graduates Tested (%)	Average Composite Score
Tacoma PS	43	504	510	1,014	n/a	n/a
State	46	523	523	1,046	16	22.4
U.S.	42	511	505	1,016	36	21.0

Note: Math and verbal SAT scores are out of a possible 800; ACT scores are out of a possible 36
Caution: Comparing or ranking states/cities on the basis of SAT/ACT scores alone is invalid and strongly discouraged by the The College Board and The American College Testing Program as students who take the tests are self-selected and do not represent the entire student population.
Source: Tacoma Public Schools, Research & Evaluation, 1997; College Board, 1997; American College Testing Program, 1997

Classroom Teacher Salaries in Public Schools

| District | B.A. Degree | | M.A. Degree | | Ph.D. Degree | |
	Min. ($)	Max. ($)	Min. ($)	Max. ($)	Min. ($)	Max. ($)
Tacoma	22,608	35,042	27,129	41,824	31,650	48,605
Average[1]	26,120	39,270	28,175	44,667	31,643	49,825

Note: Salaries are for 1996-1997; (1) Based on all school districts covered; n/a not available
Source: American Federation of Teachers (unpublished data)

Higher Education

| Two-Year Colleges | | Four-Year Colleges | | Medical Schools | Law Schools | Voc/ Tech |
Public	Private	Public	Private			
2	0	0	2	0	1	9

Source: College Blue Book, Occupational Education 1997; Medical School Admission Requirements, 1998-99; Peterson's Guide to Two-Year Colleges, 1997; Peterson's Guide to Four-Year Colleges, 1997; Barron's Guide to Law Schools 1997

MAJOR EMPLOYERS

Major Employers

First Healthcare Corp.	Frank Russell Co. (insurance)
Milgard Manufacturing (plastics)	Morning Sun
Multicare Health System	Pederson's Fryer Farms
Pierce County Medical Bureau	Pierce Transit
Simpson Tacoma Kraft Co.	St. Joseph Medical Center
Tacoma Center Hotel Associates	Tacoma Goodwill Industries Rehab. Ctr.
Tacoma Lutheran Home & Retirement Community	

Note: companies listed are located in the city
Source: Dun's Business Rankings 1997; Ward's Business Directory, 1997

PUBLIC SAFETY

Crime Rate

Area	All Crimes	Violent Crimes				Property Crimes		
		Murder	Forcible Rape	Robbery	Aggrav. Assault	Burglary	Larceny -Theft	Motor Vehicle Theft
City	10,625.7	10.6	72.3	417.8	968.5	1,732.4	5,937.2	1,487.1
Suburbs[1]	5,429.4	5.3	36.4	92.5	311.7	1,006.3	3,485.8	491.3
MSA[2]	6,917.9	6.8	46.7	185.7	499.9	1,214.3	4,188.0	776.5
U.S.	5,078.9	7.4	36.1	202.4	388.2	943.0	2,975.9	525.9

Note: Crime rate is the number of crimes per 100,000 pop.; (1) defined as all areas within the MSA but located outside the central city; (2) Metropolitan Statistical Area - see Appendix A for areas incl.
Source: FBI Uniform Crime Reports 1996

RECREATION

Culture and Recreation

Museums	Symphony Orchestras	Opera Companies	Dance Companies	Professional Theatres	Zoos	Pro Sports Teams
6	2	1	2	1	1	0

Source: International Directory of the Performing Arts, 1996; Official Museum Directory, 1998; Chamber of Commerce/Economic Development 1997

Library System

The Pierce County Rural Library District has 16 branches, holdings of 1,165,825 volumes and a budget of $9,143,926 (1994). The Tacoma Public Library has nine branches, holdings of 1,005,354 volumes and a budget of $8,052,430 (1994). *American Library Directory, 1997-1998*

MEDIA

Newspapers

Name	Type	Freq.	Distribution	Circulation
The News Tribune	n/a	7x/wk	Area	126,000
The Northwest Dispatch	n/a	1x/wk	Local	15,000
The Tacoma Daily Index	n/a	5x/wk	Local	1,300

Note: Includes newspapers with circulations of 1,000 or more located in the city; n/a not available
Source: Burrelle's Media Directory, 1998 Edition

AM Radio Stations

Call Letters	Freq. (kHz)	Target Audience	Station Format	Music Format
KLAY	1180	General	M/N/S	n/a
KKMO	1360	Hispanic	M/N/T	Easy Listening/Jazz/Spanish
KNTB	1480	Religious	M	n/a

Note: Stations included broadcast in the Tacoma metro area; n/a not available
Station Format: E = Educational; M = Music; N = News; S = Sports; T = Talk
Source: Burrelle's Media Directory, 1998 Edition

FM Radio Stations

Call Letters	Freq. (mHz)	Target Audience	Station Format	Music Format
KPLU	88.5	General	M/N	Jazz
KUPS	90.1	General	E/M/N	AOR/Alternative/Classic Rock/Jazz/R&B/Spanish
KVTI	90.9	General	M/N/S	Contemporary Top 40
KBTC	91.7	General	E/M	Classic Rock
KKBY	104.9	General	M	Country

Note: Stations included broadcast in the Tacoma metro area
Station Format: E = Educational; M = Music; N = News; S = Sports; T = Talk
Music Format: AOR = Album Oriented Rock; MOR = Middle-of-the-Road
Source: Burrelle's Media Directory, 1998 Edition

Television Stations

Name	Ch.	Affiliation	Type	Owner
KSTW	11	UPN	Commercial	Viacom/Paramount
KCKA	15	PBS	Public	State Board for Community and Technical Colleges
KBTC	28	PBS	Public	State Board for Community and Technical Colleges

Note: Stations included broadcast in the Tacoma metro area
Source: Burrelle's Media Directory, 1998 Edition

CLIMATE

Average and Extreme Temperatures

Temperature	Jan	Feb	Mar	Apr	May	Jun	Jul	Aug	Sep	Oct	Nov	Dec	Ann
Extreme High (°F)	64	70	75	85	93	96	98	99	98	89	74	63	99
Average High (°F)	44	48	52	57	64	69	75	74	69	59	50	45	59
Average Temp. (°F)	39	43	45	49	55	61	65	65	60	52	45	41	52
Average Low (°F)	34	36	38	41	46	51	54	55	51	45	39	36	44
Extreme Low (°F)	0	1	11	29	28	38	43	44	35	28	6	6	0

Note: Figures cover the years 1948-1990
Source: National Climatic Data Center, International Station Meteorological Climate Summary, 3/95

Average Precipitation/Snowfall/Humidity

Precip./Humidity	Jan	Feb	Mar	Apr	May	Jun	Jul	Aug	Sep	Oct	Nov	Dec	Ann
Avg. Precip. (in.)	5.7	4.2	3.7	2.4	1.7	1.4	0.8	1.1	1.9	3.5	5.9	5.9	38.4
Avg. Snowfall (in.)	5	2	1	Tr	Tr	0	0	0	0	Tr	1	3	13
Avg. Rel. Hum. 7am (%)	83	83	84	83	80	79	79	84	87	88	85	85	83
Avg. Rel. Hum. 4pm (%)	76	69	63	57	54	54	49	51	57	68	76	79	63

Note: Figures cover the years 1948-1990; Tr = Trace amounts (<0.05 in. of rain; <0.5 in. of snow)
Source: National Climatic Data Center, International Station Meteorological Climate Summary, 3/95

Weather Conditions

Temperature			Daytime Sky			Precipitation		
5°F & below	32°F & below	90°F & above	Clear	Partly cloudy	Cloudy	0.01 inch or more precip.	0.1 inch or more snow/ice	Thunderstorms
< 1	38	3	57	121	187	157	8	8

Note: Figures are average number of days per year and covers the years 1948-1990
Source: National Climatic Data Center, International Station Meteorological Climate Summary, 3/95

AIR & WATER QUALITY

Maximum Pollutant Concentrations

	Particulate Matter (ug/m³)	Carbon Monoxide (ppm)	Sulfur Dioxide (ppm)	Nitrogen Dioxide (ppm)	Ozone (ppm)	Lead (ug/m³)
MSA[1] Level	74	6	0.028	n/a	0.10	n/a
NAAQS[2]	150	9	0.140	0.053	0.12	1.50
Met NAAQS?	Yes	Yes	Yes	n/a	Yes	n/a

Note: (1) Metropolitan Statistical Area - see Appendix A for areas included; (2) National Ambient Air Quality Standards; ppm = parts per million; ug/m³ = micrograms per cubic meter; n/a not available
Source: EPA, National Air Quality and Emissions Trends Report, 1996

Pollutant Standards Index

In the Tacoma MSA (see Appendix A for areas included), the Pollutant Standards Index (PSI) exceeded 100 on 0 days in 1996. A PSI value greater than 100 indicates that air quality would be in the unhealthful range on that day. *EPA, National Air Quality and Emissions Trends Report, 1996*

Drinking Water

Water System Name	Pop. Served	Primary Water Source Type	Number of Violations in Fiscal Year 1997	Type of Violation/ Contaminants
City of Tacoma Water Division	262,500	Surface	2	(1), (2)

Note: Data as of January 16, 1998; (1) System did not perform the required treatment technique under the Surface Water Treatment Rule; (2) System failed to complete Optimum Corrosion Control Treatment Study recommendation on time, submit an applicable study on time, or provide sufficient information to make a treatment decision as required under the lead and copper rule.
Source: EPA, Office of Ground Water and Drinking Water, Safe Drinking Water Information System

Tacoma tap water is neutral, very soft mountain river water, stand-by aquifer well supply, relatively hard and not fluoridated.
Editor & Publisher Market Guide, 1998

Tucson, Arizona

Background

Tucson lies in a high desert valley which was once the floor of an ancient inland sea. Surrounded by four mountain ranges Tucson has much sunshine, dry air and rich desert vegetation.

The city is both an industrial center and a health resort. Its name derives from the Papago tribes' term for the ancient settlement, Stukshon, which in Spanish became Tuquisón.

It is believed that the Spanish Jesuit Eusebio Francesco Kino was the first European to visit the area in 1700. He established the San Xavier Mission. Spanish prospectors who came after Father Kino were driven out by the native tribes trying to protect their territory.

Tucson came under Mexican jurisdiction in 1821, when Mexico was no longer ruled by Spain. The city became a military outpost established for defense against the Apaches in 1709. In 1853 Mexico sold the area to the U.S. and soon after, overland stage service from San Antonio was instituted.

The Civil War interrupted travel along this route to California. After the war, Tucson continued as a supply and distribution point, first for the army and then for miners. From 1867-77 it was the capital of the territory.

Tucson grew slowly until World War II when it became more industrialized. Aircraft and missile manufacturing as well as electronics research comprise Tucson's chief economic components. Along with tourism Tucson is also the retailing center of the region.

Despite its increased industrialization, Tucson has not lost touch with its Native American and Mexican roots.

General Rankings and Evaluative Comments

■ Tucson was ranked #39 out of 300 cities by *Money's* 1997 "Survey of the Best Places to Live." Criteria used: health services, crime, economy, housing, education, transportation, weather, leisure and the arts. The city was ranked #47 in 1996 and #60 in 1995. *Money, July 1997; Money, September 1996; Money, September 1995*

■ *Ladies Home Journal* ranked America's 200 largest cities based on the qualities women care about most. Tucson ranked 130 out of 200. Criteria: low crime rate, good public schools, well-paying jobs, quality health and child care, the presence of women in government, proportion of women-owned businesses, size of the wage gap with men, local economy, divorce rates, the ratio of single men to single women, whether there are laws that require at least the same number of public toilets for women as men, and the probability of good hair days. *Ladies Home Journal, November 1997*

■ Tucson was ranked #123 out of 219 cities in terms of children's health, safety, and economic well-being. Criteria: total population, percent population change, birth rate, child immunization rate, infant mortality rate, percent low birth weight infants, percent of births to teens, physician-to-population ratio, student-to-teacher ratio, dropout rate, unemployment rate, median family income, percent of children in poverty, violent and property crime rates, number of juvenile arrests for violent crimes as a percent of the total crime index, number of days with pollution standard index (PSI) over 100, pounds toxic releases per 1,000 people and number of superfund sites. *Zero Population Growth, Children's Environmental Index 1997*

■ Green Valley, located 25 miles south of Tucson, is among America's best retirement communities. Criteria: communities must have state-of-the-art facilities, newly built homes for sale, and give you the most value for your money in every price range. Communities must also welcome newcomers of all races and religions. *New Choices, July/August 1997*

■ Tucson is among the 20 most livable cities for gay men and lesbians. The list was divided between 10 cities you might expect and 10 surprises. Tucson was on the cities you wouldn't expect list. Rank: 4 out of 10. Criteria: legal protection from antigay discrimination, an annual gay pride celebration, a community center, gay bookstores and publications, and an array of organizations, religious groups, and health care facilities that cater to the needs of the local gay community. *The Advocate, June 1997*

■ *Conde Nast Traveler* polled 37,000 readers in terms of travel satisfaction. Cities were ranked based on the following criteria: people/friendliness, environment/ambiance, cultural enrichment, restaurants and fun/energy. Tucson appeared in the top thirty, ranking number 6, with an overall rating of 71.1 out of 100 based on all the criteria. The cities were also ranked in each category separately. Tucson appeared in the top 10 based on people/friendliness, ranking number 3 with a rating of 79.4 out of 100. Tucson appeared in the top 10 based on environment/ambiance, ranking number 9 with a rating of 79.4 out of 100. *Conde Nast Traveler, Readers' Choice Poll 1997*

■ *Yahoo! Internet Life* selected "America's 100 Most Wired Cities & Towns". 50 cities were large and 50 cities were small. Tucson ranked 37 out of 50 large cities. Criteria: Internet users per capita, number of networked computers, number of registered domain names, Internet backbone traffic, and the per-capita number of Web sites devoted to each city. *Yahoo! Internet Life, March 1998*

■ According to *Working Mother*, "Arizona has lively advocates who have produced wonderful studies showing how kids benefit from high-quality child care. And these advocates have made some progress. This year, for example, they convinced reluctant lawmakers to pass a bill that requires all school-age programs to be licensed. Yet the legislature still refused to fund additional inspectors to oversee these programs. Without funds for new staff, the average inspector's job caseload jumps by a third—giving them each more than 100 programs to visit." *Working Mother, July/August 1997*

Business Environment

STATE ECONOMY

State Economic Profile

"Arizona's economy is maintaining its strong expansion....Growth in personal bankruptcy filings is 30%, about the U.S. pace of growth....

Arizona communities close to the Mexican border are benefiting from the North American Free Trade Agreement (NAFTA) through increased trade links with Mexico. However, workers imported from other parts of the nation have filled many of the newly created positions. This is because the new jobs being created on the U.S. side require skills that do not match the skills of many of the local residents. In the near term, Southern Arizona communities will benefit since the new job opportunities will attract in-migrants who will support the growth of local services and the housing market. To date there is little evidence of a large outflow of Arizona firms over the border; however, the Arizona Department of Economic Security estimates that sixteen companies have left Arizona for Mexico, representing nearly 1,000 jobs statewide.

Over the last few years, call centers and other back-office operations have fueled expansion. Business services employment in the state is growing at a 12% year-over-year pace currently, and has posted double-digit growth for 32 months. However, business services is cyclical. This development is worrisome for an economy already vulnerable to national business cycles. While enjoying the upside of this dependence during the current expansion, Arizona may suffer inordinately in the next recession.

Arizona is expected to remain one of the nation's fastest-growing states through the remainder of the decade. However, growth is expected to slow from its torrid pace of recent years. Where in the past Arizona's risks were driven by its dependence on natural resource industries (citrus, copper, cattle) and tourism, it is now facing a new pattern of risk due to its concentration in high-tech manufacturing and business services. Migration and business relocations from California will slow as that state's recovery matures. Nonetheless, Arizona is top-ranked for long-term growth." *National Association of Realtors, Economic Profiles: The Fifty States, July 1997*

IMPORTS/EXPORTS

Total Export Sales

Area	1993 ($000)	1994 ($000)	1995 ($000)	1996 ($000)	% Chg. 1993-96	% Chg. 1995-96
MSA[1]	487,123	638,118	671,723	800,052	64.2	19.1
U.S.	464,858,354	512,415,609	583,030,524	622,827,063	34.0	6.8

Note: (1) Metropolitan Statistical Area - see Appendix A for areas included
Source: U.S. Department of Commerce, International Trade Association, Metropolitan Area Exports: An Export Performance Report on Over 250 U.S. Cities, October 1997

Imports/Exports by Port

Type	Cargo Value			Share of U.S. Total	
	1995 (US$mil.)	1996 (US$mil.)	% Change 1995-1996	1995 (%)	1996 (%)
Imports	0	0	0	0	0
Exports	0	0	0	0	0

Source: Global Trade Information Services, WaterBorne Trade Atlas 1997

CITY FINANCES

City Government Finances

Component	FY92 ($000)	FY92 (per capita $)
Revenue	455,490	1,080.71
Expenditure	462,682	1,097.78
Debt Outstanding	824,821	1,957.01
Cash & Securities	686,182	1,628.06

Source: U.S. Bureau of the Census, City Government Finances: 1991-92

City Government Revenue by Source

Source	FY92 ($000)	FY92 (per capita $)	FY92 (%)
From Federal Government	22,111	52.46	4.9
From State Governments	91,016	215.95	20.0
From Local Governments	6,535	15.51	1.4
Property Taxes	23,537	55.84	5.2
General Sales Taxes	89,412	212.14	19.6
Selective Sales Taxes	14,189	33.67	3.1
Income Taxes	0	0.00	0.0
Current Charges	45,193	107.23	9.9
Utility/Liquor Store	76,443	181.37	16.8
Employee Retirement[1]	17,803	42.24	3.9
Other	69,251	164.31	15.2

Note: (1) Excludes "city contributions," classified as "nonrevenue," intragovernmental transfers.
Source: U.S. Bureau of the Census, City Government Finances: 1991-92

City Government Expenditures by Function

Function	FY92 ($000)	FY92 (per capita $)	FY92 (%)
Educational Services	10,127	24.03	2.2
Employee Retirement[1]	9,675	22.96	2.1
Environment/Housing	80,857	191.84	17.5
Government Administration	35,540	84.32	7.7
Interest on General Debt	54,366	128.99	11.8
Public Safety	78,066	185.22	16.9
Social Services	2,872	6.81	0.6
Transportation	68,146	161.69	14.7
Utility/Liquor Store	110,313	261.73	23.8
Other	12,720	30.18	2.7

Note: (1) Payments to beneficiaries including withdrawal of contributions.
Source: U.S. Bureau of the Census, City Government Finances: 1991-92

Municipal Bond Ratings

Area	Moody's	S & P
Tucson	Aa3	AA

Note: n/a not available; n/r not rated
Source: Moody's Bond Record, 2/98; Statistical Abstract of the U.S., 1997;
Governing Magazine, 9/97, 3/98

POPULATION

Population Growth

Area	1980	1990	% Chg. 1980-90	July 1996 Estimate	% Chg. 1990-96
City	330,537	405,390	22.6	449,002	10.8
MSA[1]	531,443	666,880	25.5	767,873	15.1
U.S.	226,545,805	248,765,170	9.8	265,179,411	6.6

Note: (1) Metropolitan Statistical Area - see Appendix A for areas included
Source: 1980/1990 Census of Housing and Population, Summary Tape File 3C;
Census Bureau Population Estimates

Population Characteristics

Race	City 1980 Population	%	City 1990 Population	%	% Chg. 1980-90	MSA[1] 1990 Population	%
White	274,750	83.1	305,847	75.4	11.3	526,404	78.9
Black	11,587	3.5	17,564	4.3	51.6	20,856	3.1
Amer Indian/Esk/Aleut	4,578	1.4	6,371	1.6	39.2	20,034	3.0
Asian/Pacific Islander	3,427	1.0	8,803	2.2	156.9	12,149	1.8
Other	36,195	11.0	66,805	16.5	84.6	87,437	13.1
Hispanic Origin[2]	82,106	24.8	117,267	28.9	42.8	161,053	24.2

Note: (1) Metropolitan Statistical Area - see Appendix A for areas included;
(2) people of Hispanic origin can be of any race
Source: 1980/1990 Census of Housing and Population, Summary Tape File 3C

Ancestry

Area	German	Irish	English	Italian	U.S.	French	Polish	Dutch
City	21.8	13.8	13.5	4.2	2.2	4.1	2.8	2.3
MSA[1]	23.8	14.3	15.2	4.4	2.2	4.3	2.8	2.5
U.S.	23.3	15.6	13.1	5.9	5.3	4.2	3.8	2.5

Note: Figures are percentages and include persons that reported multiple ancestry (eg. if a person
reported being Irish and Italian, they were included in both columns); (1) Metropolitan Statistical Area -
see Appendix A for areas included
Source: 1990 Census of Population and Housing, Summary Tape File 3C

Age

Area	Median Age (Years)	Age Distribution (%) Under 5	Under 18	18-24	25-44	45-64	65+	80+
City	30.6	7.7	24.4	14.3	33.0	15.7	12.6	2.9
MSA[1]	32.7	7.4	24.9	11.6	32.1	17.8	13.7	2.8
U.S.	32.9	7.3	25.6	10.5	32.6	18.7	12.5	2.8

Note: (1) Metropolitan Statistical Area - see Appendix A for areas included
Source: 1990 Census of Population and Housing, Summary Tape File 3C

Male/Female Ratio

Area	Number of males per 100 females (all ages)	Number of males per 100 females (18 years old+)
City	94.3	91.9
MSA[1]	95.2	93.0
U.S.	95.0	91.9

Note: (1) Metropolitan Statistical Area - see Appendix A for areas included
Source: 1990 Census of Population, General Population Characteristics

INCOME

Per Capita/Median/Average Income

Area	Per Capita ($)	Median Household ($)	Average Household ($)
City	11,184	21,748	27,435
MSA[1]	13,177	25,401	33,127
U.S.	14,420	30,056	38,453

Note: all figures are for 1989; (1) Metropolitan Statistical Area - see Appendix A for areas included
Source: 1990 Census of Population and Housing, Summary Tape File 3C

Household Income Distribution by Race

Income ($)	City (%) Total	White	Black	Other	Hisp.[1]	U.S. (%) Total	White	Black	Other	Hisp.[1]
Less than 5,000	9.3	7.9	17.4	15.0	11.9	6.2	4.8	15.2	8.6	8.8
5,000 - 9,999	12.3	11.7	14.0	15.4	14.2	9.3	8.6	14.2	9.9	11.1
10,000 - 14,999	12.6	12.7	13.3	12.3	12.3	8.8	8.5	11.0	9.8	11.0
15,000 - 24,999	22.0	22.0	20.9	22.7	23.7	17.5	17.3	18.9	18.5	20.5
25,000 - 34,999	16.7	16.8	13.1	16.7	17.2	15.8	16.1	14.2	15.4	16.4
35,000 - 49,999	14.7	15.5	13.9	10.8	12.3	17.9	18.6	13.3	16.1	16.0
50,000 - 74,999	8.8	9.6	5.4	5.6	6.5	15.0	15.8	9.3	13.4	11.1
75,000 - 99,999	2.0	2.2	1.5	0.9	1.2	5.1	5.5	2.6	4.7	3.1
100,000+	1.5	1.7	0.6	0.6	0.7	4.4	4.8	1.3	3.7	1.9

Note: all figures are for 1989; (1) people of Hispanic origin can be of any race
Source: 1990 Census of Population and Housing, Summary Tape File 3C

Effective Buying Income

Area	Per Capita ($)	Median Household ($)	Average Household ($)
City	11,886	23,550	29,615
MSA[1]	14,146	27,783	36,011
U.S.	15,444	33,201	41,849

Note: data as of 1/1/97; (1) Metropolitan Statistical Area - see Appendix A for areas included
Source: Standard Rate & Data Service, Newspaper Advertising Source, 2/98

Effective Household Buying Income Distribution

Area	% of Households Earning $10,000 -$19,999	$20,000 -$34,999	$35,000 -$49,999	$50,000 -$74,999	$75,000 -$99,000	$100,000 -$124,999	$125,000 and up
City	23.5	27.2	15.9	10.5	2.3	0.8	0.7
MSA[1]	20.2	25.9	17.0	14.1	4.3	1.4	1.8
U.S.	16.5	23.4	18.3	18.2	6.4	2.1	2.4

Note: data as of 1/1/97; (1) Metropolitan Statistical Area - see Appendix A for areas included
Source: Standard Rate & Data Service, Newspaper Advertising Source, 2/98

Poverty Rates by Race and Age

Area	Total (%)	By Race (%) White	Black	Other	Hisp.[2]	By Age (%) Under 5 years old	Under 18 years old	65 years and over
City	20.2	15.9	29.3	34.0	29.9	30.2	26.3	12.1
MSA[1]	17.2	12.8	27.5	34.6	28.2	26.9	23.5	10.0
U.S.	13.1	9.8	29.5	23.1	25.3	20.1	18.3	12.8

Note: figures show the percent of people living below the poverty line in 1989. The average poverty threshold was $12,674 for a family of four in 1989; (1) Metropolitan Statistical Area - see Appendix A for areas included; (2) people of Hispanic origin can be of any race
Source: 1990 Census of Population and Housing, Summary Tape File 3C

EMPLOYMENT

Labor Force and Employment

Area	Civilian Labor Force Dec. '95	Dec. '96	% Chg.	Workers Employed Dec. '95	Dec. '96	% Chg.
City	237,890	235,752	-0.9	228,664	228,311	-0.2
MSA[1]	382,504	379,338	-0.8	369,088	368,518	-0.2
U.S.	134,583,000	136,742,000	1.6	127,903,000	130,785,000	2.3

Note: Data is not seasonally adjusted and covers workers 16 years of age and older;
(1) Metropolitan Statistical Area - see Appendix A for areas included
Source: Bureau of Labor Statistics, http://stats.bls.gov

Tucson was listed among the top 20 metro areas (out of 114 major areas) in terms of projected job growth from 1997 to 2002 with an annual percent change of 2.1%.
Standard & Poor's DRI, July 23, 1997

Unemployment Rate

Area	1997											
	Jan.	Feb.	Mar.	Apr.	May	Jun.	Jul.	Aug.	Sep.	Oct.	Nov.	Dec.
City	4.0	3.7	3.4	3.2	3.4	3.7	3.8	3.7	3.9	3.5	3.2	3.2
MSA[1]	3.6	3.3	3.1	2.9	3.1	3.4	3.4	3.3	3.5	3.2	2.9	2.9
U.S.	5.9	5.7	5.5	4.8	4.7	5.2	5.0	4.8	4.7	4.4	4.3	4.4

Note: Data is not seasonally adjusted and covers workers 16 years of age and older; All figures are percentages; (1) Metropolitan Statistical Area - see Appendix A for areas included
Source: Bureau of Labor Statistics, http://stats.bls.gov

Employment by Industry

Sector	MSA[1]		U.S.
	Number of Employees	Percent of Total	Percent of Total
Services	101,000	31.4	29.0
Retail Trade	59,900	18.6	18.5
Government	73,600	22.9	16.1
Manufacturing	28,400	8.8	15.0
Finance/Insurance/Real Estate	12,100	3.8	5.7
Wholesale Trade	11,000	3.4	5.4
Transportation/Public Utilities	13,200	4.1	5.3
Construction	19,900	6.2	4.5
Mining	2,400	0.7	0.5

Note: Figures cover non-farm employment as of 12/97 and are not seasonally adjusted;
(1) Metropolitan Statistical Area - see Appendix A for areas included
Source: Bureau of Labor Statistics, http://stats.bls.gov

Employment by Occupation

Occupation Category	City (%)	MSA[1] (%)	U.S. (%)
White Collar	59.1	61.1	58.1
Executive/Admin./Management	10.6	12.0	12.3
Professional	15.7	16.5	14.1
Technical & Related Support	4.7	4.6	3.7
Sales	12.7	13.3	11.8
Administrative Support/Clerical	15.4	14.7	16.3
Blue Collar	21.2	20.9	26.2
Precision Production/Craft/Repair	10.8	10.8	11.3
Machine Operators/Assem./Insp.	3.8	3.5	6.8
Transportation/Material Movers	3.2	3.3	4.1
Cleaners/Helpers/Laborers	3.4	3.2	3.9
Services	18.2	16.3	13.2
Farming/Forestry/Fishing	1.6	1.7	2.5

Note: figures cover employed persons 16 years old and over;
(1) Metropolitan Statistical Area - see Appendix A for areas included
Source: 1990 Census of Population and Housing, Summary Tape File 3C

Occupational Employment Projections: 1994 - 2005

Occupations Expected to have the Largest Job Growth (ranked by numerical growth)	Fast-Growing Occupations[1] (ranked by percent growth)
1. Salespersons, retail	1. All other computer scientists
2. Waiters & waitresses	2. Computer engineers
3. Janitors/cleaners/maids, ex. priv. hshld.	3. Painting/coating/decorating, hand
4. General managers & top executives	4. Systems analysts
5. General office clerks	5. Solderers/brazers
6. Cashiers	6. Economists
7. Marketing & sales, supervisors	7. Data processing equipment repairers
8. Secretaries, except legal & medical	8. All other sales reps. & services
9. Guards	9. Paving/surfacing/tamping equipment oper.
10. Registered nurses	10. Pest controllers & assistants

Projections cover Pima County.
Note: (1) Excludes occupations with employment less than 50 in 1994
Source: Arizona Department of Economic Security, Arizona Occupational Employment Forecasts, 1994-2005, Pima County

Average Wages

Occupation	Wage	Occupation	Wage
Professional/Technical/Clerical	$/Week	**Health/Protective Services**	$/Week
Accountants III	-	Corrections Officers	-
Attorneys III	-	Firefighters	-
Budget Analysts III	-	Nurses, Licensed Practical II	-
Buyers/Contracting Specialists II	-	Nurses, Registered II	-
Clerks, Accounting III	358	Nursing Assistants II	-
Clerks, General III	338	Police Officers I	-
Computer Operators II	384	**Hourly Workers**	$/Hour
Computer Programmers II	590	Forklift Operators	6.27
Drafters II	-	General Maintenance Workers	7.88
Engineering Technicians III	-	Guards I	4.82
Engineering Technicians, Civil III	-	Janitors	5.29
Engineers III	-	Maintenance Electricians	17.07
Key Entry Operators I	-	Maintenance Electronics Techs II	15.61
Personnel Assistants III	-	Maintenance Machinists	-
Personnel Specialists III	-	Maintenance Mechanics, Machinery	15.63
Secretaries III	-	Material Handling Laborers	-
Switchboard Operator-Receptionist	267	Motor Vehicle Mechanics	-
Systems Analysts II	761	Shipping/Receiving Clerks	7.78
Systems Analysts Supervisor/Mgr II	-	Tool and Die Makers	-
Tax Collectors II	-	Truckdrivers, Tractor Trailer	-
Word Processors II	-	Warehouse Specialists	8.95

Note: Wage data includes full-time workers only for 2/94 and cover the Metropolitan Statistical Area (see Appendix A for areas included). Dashes indicate that data was not available.
Source: Bureau of Labor Statistics, Occupational Compensation Survey

TAXES

Major State and Local Tax Rates

State Corp. Income (%)	State Personal Income (%)	Residential Property (effective rate per $100)	Sales & Use State (%)	Sales & Use Local (%)	State Gasoline (cents/ gallon)	State Cigarette (cents/ 20-pack)
9.0[a]	3.0 - 5.6	n/a	5.0	2.0	18[b]	58

Note: Personal/corporate income tax rates as of 1/97. Sales, gasoline and cigarette tax rates as of 1/98; (a) Minimum tax is $50; (b) Carriers pay an additional surcharge of 8 cents
Source: Federation of Tax Administrators, www.taxadmin.org; Washington D.C. Department of Finance and Revenue, Tax Rates and Tax Burdens in the District of Columbia: A Nationwide Comparison, June 1997; Chamber of Commerce

Total Taxes Per Capita and as a Percent of Income

Area	Per Capita Income ($)	Per Capita Taxes ($)			Taxes as Pct. of Income (%)		
		Total	Federal	State/Local	Total	Federal	State/Local
Arizona	23,709	8,114	5,239	2,875	34.2	22.1	12.1
U.S.	26,187	9,205	6,127	3,078	35.2	23.4	11.8

Note: Figures are for 1997
Source: Tax Foundation, Web Site, www.taxfoundation.org

Estimated Tax Burden

Area	State Income	Local Income	Property	Sales	Total
Tucson	1,367	0	2,025	595	3,987

Note: The numbers are estimates of taxes paid by a married couple with two kids and annual earnings of $65,000. Sales tax estimates assume they spend average amounts on food, clothing, household goods and gasoline. Property tax estimates assume they live in a $225,000 home.
Source: Kiplinger's Personal Finance Magazine, June 1997

COMMERCIAL REAL ESTATE

Office Market

Class/Location	Total Space (sq. ft.)	Vacant Space (sq. ft.)	Vac. Rate (%)	Under Constr. (sq. ft.)	Net Absorp. (sq. ft.)	Rental Rates ($/sq.ft./yr.)
Class A						
CBD	490,423	61,270	12.5	0	21,284	16.50-20.50
Outside CBD	2,448,482	103,642	4.2	65,000	151,843	16.50-22.50
Class B						
CBD	941,800	149,400	15.9	0	19,858	12.50-15.50
Outside CBD	2,383,447	104,977	4.4	0	41,929	14.50-17.50

Note: Data as of 10/97 and covers Tucson; CBD = Central Business District; n/a not available;
Source: Society of Industrial and Office Realtors, 1998 Comparative Statistics of Industrial and Office Real Estate Markets

"Despite marketwide vacancy rates dipping below the 10 percent level, very little speculative development is occurring except in Tucson's foothills and northern suburban areas. Within these submarkets four projects are expected to deliver up to 900,000 sq. ft. in the market over the next several years. New construction is somewhat stymied by rental rates which, while from their low point in 1992, have yet to improve to the point where large scale office construction becomes economically viable. Only within the telemarketing/back office segment, currently Tucson's strongest and fastest growing business sector, are the economics right for new construction." *Society of Industrial and Office Realtors, 1998 Comparative Statistics of Industrial and Office Real Estate Markets*

Industrial Market

Location	Total Space (sq. ft.)	Vacant Space (sq. ft.)	Vac. Rate (%)	Under Constr. (sq. ft.)	Net Absorp. (sq. ft.)	Net Lease ($/sq.ft./yr.)
Central City	29,684,908	1,707,935	5.8	330,000	1,241,775	4.08-5.16
Suburban	n/a	n/a	n/a	n/a	n/a	n/a

Note: Data as of 10/97 and covers Tucson; n/a not available
Source: Society of Industrial and Office Realtors, 1998 Comparative Statistics of Industrial and Office Real Estate Markets

"Growth in the 'teleservices' sectors continue to boost demand for industrial properties, and especially for 'flex space'. Tucson's average vacancy rate fluctuates between six percent and eight percent, depending on the timing of new construction. Most experts expect between 500,000 and one million sq. ft. of development in 1998, an amount consistent with previous years. Some shortages have been reported and no subsector is reporting significant oversupply. Land parcels are abundant and reasonably priced in Tucson. Rent increases are expected to be moderate without the sharp spikes that characterize some other western markets." *Society of Industrial and Office Realtors, 1998 Comparative Statistics of Industrial and Office Real Estate Markets*

Retail Market

Shopping Center Inventory (sq. ft.)	Shopping Center Construction (sq. ft.)	Construction as a Percent of Inventory (%)	Torto Wheaton Rent Index[1] ($/sq. ft.)
13,789,000	49,000	0.4	10.97

Note: Data as of 1997 and covers the Metropolitan Statistical Area - see Appendix A for areas included; (1) Index is based on a model that predicts what the average rent should be for leases with certain characteristics, in certain locations during certain years.
Source: National Association of Realtors, 1997-1998 Market Conditions Report

"Tucson's tremendous growth in the early 90s was a boon to the retail market. Its retail rent index has risen by over 32% during the past five years—an increase that is much higher than the national or Western averages. However, at $10.97 per square foot, Tucson's rent still falls well below the national average of $13.15. A very low unemployment rate and strong wage growth should continue to fuel rent inflation at rates well in excess of the nation through the year 2000." *National Association of Realtors, 1997-1998 Market Conditions Report*

COMMERCIAL UTILITIES

Typical Monthly Electric Bills

Area	Commercial Service ($/month)		Industrial Service ($/month)	
	12 kW demand 1,500 kWh	100 kW demand 30,000 kWh	1,000 kW demand 400,000 kWh	20,000 kW demand 10,000,000 kWh
City	186	3,228	33,938	696,420
U.S.	162	2,360	25,590	545,677

Note: Based on rates in effect July 1, 1997
Source: Edison Electric Institute, Typical Residential, Commercial and Industrial Bills, Summer 1997

TRANSPORTATION

Transportation Statistics

Avg. travel time to work (min.)	19.7
Interstate highways	I-10; I-19
Bus lines	
In-city	Sun Tran Transit
Inter-city	2
Passenger air service	
Airport	Tucson International
Airlines	11
Aircraft departures	21,556 (1995)
Enplaned passengers	1,660,934 (1995)
Rail service	Amtrak
Motor freight carriers	32
Major waterways/ports	None

Source: OAG, Business Travel Planner, Summer 1997; Editor & Publisher Market Guide, 1998; FAA Airport Activity Statistics, 1996; Amtrak National Time Table, Northeast Timetable, Fall/Winter 1997-98; 1990 Census of Population and Housing, STF 3C; Chamber of Commerce/Economic Development 1997; Jane's Urban Transport Systems 1997-98; Transit Fact Book 1997

Means of Transportation to Work

Area	Car/Truck/Van		Public Transportation			Bicycle	Walked	Other Means	Worked at Home
	Drove Alone	Car-pooled	Bus	Subway	Railroad				
City	69.8	14.8	4.1	0.0	0.0	2.7	4.0	1.8	2.8
MSA[1]	71.9	15.0	3.1	0.0	0.0	1.9	3.2	1.7	3.2
U.S.	73.2	13.4	3.0	1.5	0.5	0.4	3.9	1.2	3.0

Note: figures shown are percentages and only include workers 16 years old and over;
(1) Metropolitan Statistical Area - see Appendix A for areas included
Source: 1990 Census of Population and Housing, Summary Tape File 3C

BUSINESSES

Major Business Headquarters

Company Name	1997 Rankings	
	Fortune 500	Forbes 500
Sundt	-	496

Note: Companies listed are located in the city; Dashes indicate no ranking
Fortune 500: companies that produce a 10-K are ranked 1 - 500 based on 1996 revenue
Forbes 500: private companies are ranked 1 - 500 based on 1996 revenue
Source: Forbes 12/1/97; Fortune 4/28/97

Minority Business Opportunity

One of the 500 largest Hispanic-owned companies in the U.S. are located in Tucson.
Hispanic Business, June 1997

Small Business Opportunity

Tucson was ranked #3 out of 219 in terms of the best cities to start and grow a home-based business by *Home Office Computing*. Criteria: economic growth, population growth, industrial diversity, business climate, market access systems, work flexibility, lifestyle, education level, intellectual capital, age, and home-based business score (zoning flexibility, community support, regulatory streamlining). "The desert is fertile ground when it comes to growing home-based businesses. To help sow the seeds, Tucson's mayor and city council appointed a Small Business Commission with the mandate to make city government more user-friendly to small businesses. The Commission also publishes the Guide to Operating a Business in the City of Tucson and actively campaigns on behalf of small and home-based businesses regarding signs, zoning, excessive regulations, and so on. The chamber of commerce's Web site mentions home-based businesses and provides information about regulations and steps for obtaining a home occupation permit. And the home-based business community actively networks through organizations such as the Tucson Business Coalition." *Home Office Computing, December 1997*

HOTELS & MOTELS

Hotels/Motels

Area	Hotels/ Motels	Rooms	Luxury-Level Hotels/Motels		Average Minimum Rates ($)		
			♦♦♦♦	♦♦♦♦♦	♦♦	♦♦♦	♦♦♦♦
City	68	7,988	6	0	69	113	207
Airport	8	1,391	0	0	n/a	n/a	n/a
Suburbs	2	216	0	0	n/a	n/a	n/a
Total	78	9,595	6	0	n/a	n/a	n/a

Note: n/a not available; Classifications range from one diamond (budget properties with basic amenities) to five diamond (luxury properties with the finest service, rooms and facilities).
Source: OAG, Business Travel Planner, Summer 1997

Tucson is home to one of the top 100 hotels in the world according to *Travel & Leisure*: Loews Ventana Canyon Resort. Criteria: value, rooms/ambience, location, facilities/activities and service. *Travel & Leisure, September 1997*

CONVENTION CENTERS

Major Convention Centers

Center Name	Meeting Rooms	Exhibit Space (sf)
Hotel Park Tucson & Conference Center	n/a	4,200
Tucson Convention Center	8	93,000

Note: n/a not available
Source: Trade Shows Worldwide 1997

Living Environment

COST OF LIVING

Cost of Living Index

Composite Index	Housing	Utilities	Groceries	Health Care	Trans- portation	Misc. Goods/ Services
97.3	95.6	104.2	103.1	105.3	97.0	93.0

Note: U.S. = 100
Source: ACCRA, Cost of Living Index, 3rd Quarter 1997

HOUSING

Median Home Prices and Housing Affordability

Area	Median Price[2] 3rd Qtr. 1997 ($)	HOI[3] 3rd Qtr. 1997	Afford- ability Rank[4]
MSA[1]	107,000	62.5	133
U.S.	127,000	63.7	–

Note: (1) Metropolitan Statistical Area - see Appendix A for areas included; (2) U.S. figures calculated from the sales of 625,000 new and existing homes in 195 markets; (3) Housing Opportunity Index - percent of homes sold that were within the reach of the median income household at the prevailing mortgage interest rate; (4) Rank is from 1-195 with 1 being most affordable
Source: National Association of Home Builders, Housing Opportunity Index, 3rd Quarter 1997

It is projected that the median price of existing single-family homes in the metro area will increase by 4.8% in 1998. Nationwide, home prices are projected to increase 6.6%.
Kiplinger's Personal Finance Magazine, January 1998

Average New Home Price

Area	Price ($)
City	125,500
U.S.	135,710

Note: Figures are based on a new home with 1,800 sq. ft. of living area on an 8,000 sq. ft. lot.
Source: ACCRA, Cost of Living Index, 3rd Quarter 1997

Average Apartment Rent

Area	Rent ($/mth)
City	586
U.S.	569

Note: Figures are based on an unfurnished two bedroom, 1-1/2 or 2 bath apartment, approximately 950 sq. ft. in size, excluding all utilities except water
Source: ACCRA, Cost of Living Index, 3rd Quarter 1997

RESIDENTIAL UTILITIES

Average Residential Utility Costs

Area	All Electric ($/mth)	Part Electric ($/mth)	Other Energy ($/mth)	Phone ($/mth)
City	–	75.23	32.87	18.68
U.S.	109.40	55.25	43.64	19.48

Source: ACCRA, Cost of Living Index, 3rd Quarter 1997

HEALTH CARE

Average Health Care Costs

Area	Hospital ($/day)	Doctor ($/visit)	Dentist ($/visit)
City	622.50	47.50	53.75
U.S.	392.91	48.76	60.84

Note: Hospital - based on a semi-private room. Doctor - based on a general practitioner's routine exam of an established patient. Dentist - based on adult teeth cleaning and periodic oral exam.
Source: ACCRA, Cost of Living Index, 3rd Quarter 1997

Distribution of Office-Based Physicians

| Area | Family/Gen. Practitioners | Specialists | | |
		Medical	Surgical	Other
MSA[1]	175	532	390	485

Note: Data as of 12/31/96; (1) Metropolitan Statistical Area - see Appendix A for areas included
Source: American Medical Assn., Physician Characteristics & Distribution in the U.S., 1997-1998

Hospitals

Tucson has 9 general medical and surgical hospitals, 1 rehabilitation, 1 children's psychiatric. *AHA Guide to the Healthcare Field 1997-98*

According to *U.S. News and World Report,* Tucson has 1 of the best hospitals in the U.S.: **University Medical Center**, noted for cancer, cardiology, urology; *U.S. News and World Report, "America's Best Hospitals", 7/28/97*

EDUCATION

Public School District Statistics

District Name	Num. Sch.	Enroll.	Classroom Teachers[1]	Pupils per Teacher	Minority Pupils (%)	Current Exp.[2] ($/pupil)
Altar Valley Elementary Dist	1	807	42	19.2	n/a	n/a
Amphitheater Unified District	18	15,451	n/a	n/a	n/a	n/a
Catalina Foothills Unif Dist	7	4,581	233	19.7	n/a	n/a
Flowing Wells Unified District	8	6,028	284	21.2	n/a	n/a
Sunnyside Unified District	18	14,476	727	19.9	n/a	n/a
Tanque Verde Unified District	3	1,500	85	17.6	n/a	n/a
Tucson Unified District	110	62,317	n/a	n/a	53.5	4,037

Note: Data covers the 1995-1996 school year unless otherwise noted; (1) Excludes teachers reported as working in school district offices rather than in schools; (2) Based on 1993-94 enrollment collected by the Census Bureau, not the enrollment figure shown in column 3; SD = School District; ISD = Independent School District; n/a not available
Source: National Center for Education Statistics, Common Core of Data Survey; Bureau of the Census

Educational Quality

School District	Education Quotient[1]	Graduate Outcome[2]	Community Index[3]	Resource Index[4]
Tucson	87.0	79.0	89.0	94.0

Note: Nearly 1,000 secondary school districts were rated in terms of educational quality. The scores range from a low of 50 to a high of 150; (1) Average of the Graduate Outcome, Community and Resource indexes; (2) Based on graduation rates and college board scores (SAT/ACT); (3) Based on the surrounding community's average level of education and the area's average income level; (4) Based on teacher salaries, per-pupil expenditures and student-teacher ratios.
Source: Expansion Management, Ratings Issue 1997

Educational Attainment by Race

| Area | High School Graduate (%) | | | | | Bachelor's Degree (%) | | | | |
	Total	White	Black	Other	Hisp.[2]	Total	White	Black	Other	Hisp.[2]
City	78.6	83.0	75.6	57.5	56.2	20.7	23.4	11.9	9.5	8.1
MSA[1]	80.5	84.5	76.1	57.6	58.0	23.3	25.9	13.6	9.7	8.7
U.S.	75.2	77.9	63.1	60.4	49.8	20.3	21.5	11.4	19.4	9.2

Note: figures shown cover persons 25 years old and over; (1) Metropolitan Statistical Area - see Appendix A for areas included; (2) people of Hispanic origin can be of any race
Source: 1990 Census of Population and Housing, Summary Tape File 3C

School Enrollment by Type

Area	Preprimary				Elementary/High School			
	Public		Private		Public		Private	
	Enrollment	%	Enrollment	%	Enrollment	%	Enrollment	%
City	3,333	54.7	2,756	45.3	57,306	91.9	5,043	8.1
MSA[1]	5,794	55.5	4,645	44.5	100,154	92.5	8,110	7.5
U.S.	2,679,029	59.5	1,824,256	40.5	38,379,689	90.2	4,187,099	9.8

Note: figures shown cover persons 3 years old and over;
(1) Metropolitan Statistical Area - see Appendix A for areas included
Source: 1990 Census of Population and Housing, Summary Tape File 3C

School Enrollment by Race

Area	Preprimary (%)				Elementary/High School (%)			
	White	Black	Other	Hisp.[1]	White	Black	Other	Hisp.[1]
City	76.1	4.5	19.4	28.0	63.8	6.0	30.2	43.7
MSA[2]	79.2	2.8	18.0	23.8	68.8	4.2	27.1	35.9
U.S.	80.4	12.5	7.1	7.8	74.1	15.6	10.3	12.5

Note: figures shown cover persons 3 years old and over; (1) people of Hispanic origin can be of any race; (2) Metropolitan Statistical Area - see Appendix A for areas included
Source: 1990 Census of Population and Housing, Summary Tape File 3C

SAT/ACT Scores

Area/District	1997 SAT				1997 ACT	
	Percent of Graduates Tested (%)	Average Math Score	Average Verbal Score	Average Combined Score	Percent of Graduates Tested (%)	Average Composite Score
Tucson USD	34	521	520	1,041	16	21.7
State	29	522	523	1,045	27	21.2
U.S.	42	511	505	1,016	36	21.0

Note: Math and verbal SAT scores are out of a possible 800; ACT scores are out of a possible 36
Caution: Comparing or ranking states/cities on the basis of SAT/ACT scores alone is invalid and strongly discouraged by the The College Board and The American College Testing Program as students who take the tests are self-selected and do not represent the entire student population.
Source: Tucson Unified School District, Department of Planning & Assessment, 1997; American College Testing Program, 1997; College Board, 1997

Classroom Teacher Salaries in Public Schools

District	B.A. Degree		M.A. Degree		Ph.D. Degree	
	Min. ($)	Max. ($)	Min. ($)	Max. ($)	Min. ($)	Max. ($)
Tucson	21,750	36,750	24,500	45,000	26,500	45,750
Average[1]	26,120	39,270	28,175	44,667	31,643	49,825

Note: Salaries are for 1996-1997; (1) Based on all school districts covered; n/a not available
Source: American Federation of Teachers (unpublished data)

Higher Education

Two-Year Colleges		Four-Year Colleges		Medical Schools	Law Schools	Voc/ Tech
Public	Private	Public	Private			
1	3	1	0	1	1	12

Source: College Blue Book, Occupational Education 1997; Medical School Admission Requirements, 1998-99; Peterson's Guide to Two-Year Colleges, 1997; Peterson's Guide to Four-Year Colleges, 1997; Barron's Guide to Law Schools 1997

MAJOR EMPLOYERS

Major Employers

Burr-Brown Corp. (semiconductors)	Canyon Ranch
Carondelet Health Care Corp.	Dependable Nurses
Hughes Missile Systems	Southwest Canning & Packaging
TNI Partners (newspapers)	Thomas-Davis Medical Center
Tucson Electric Power	Tucson General Hospital
Tucson Medical Center	University Medical Center
Weiser Lock Corp.	El Conquistador Hotel Associates

Note: companies listed are located in the city
Source: Dun's Business Rankings 1997; Ward's Business Directory, 1997

PUBLIC SAFETY

Crime Rate

Area	All Crimes	Violent Crimes				Property Crimes		
		Murder	Forcible Rape	Robbery	Aggrav. Assault	Burglary	Larceny -Theft	Motor Vehicle Theft
City	9,819.3	9.7	59.7	272.7	758.5	1,420.5	6,024.7	1,273.5
Suburbs[1]	4,974.4	9.0	30.1	86.2	257.0	820.4	3,189.1	582.6
MSA[2]	7,853.6	9.4	47.7	197.0	555.0	1,177.0	4,874.2	993.2
U.S.	5,078.9	7.4	36.1	202.4	388.2	943.0	2,975.9	525.9

Note: Crime rate is the number of crimes per 100,000 pop.; (1) defined as all areas within the MSA but located outside the central city; (2) Metropolitan Statistical Area - see Appendix A for areas incl.
Source: FBI Uniform Crime Reports 1996

RECREATION

Culture and Recreation

Museums	Symphony Orchestras	Opera Companies	Dance Companies	Professional Theatres	Zoos	Pro Sports Teams
12	1	1	3	2	1	0

Source: International Directory of the Performing Arts, 1996; Official Museum Directory, 1998; Chamber of Commerce/Economic Development 1997

Library System

The Tucson-Pima Public Library has 19 branches, holdings of 1,172,100 volumes and a budget of $14,034,130 (1996-1997). *American Library Directory, 1997-1998*

MEDIA

Newspapers

Name	Type	Freq.	Distribution	Circulation
The Arizona Daily Star	n/a	7x/wk	Area	98,050
Arizona Daily Wildcat	n/a	5x/wk	Campus	community & alumni
Arizona Jewish Post	Religious	2x/mo	Local	7,500
The Daily Territorial	n/a	5x/wk	Local	1,048
The Desert Airman	n/a	1x/wk	Local	10,500
DesertLeaf	n/a	1x/mo	Local	41,000
Explorer	n/a	1x/wk	Local	25,000
Inside Tucson Business	General	1x/wk	Local	8,400
Tucson Citizen	General	6x/wk	Area	50,000
Tucson Weekly	General	1x/wk	Local	40,000

Note: Includes newspapers with circulations of 1,000 or more located in the city; n/a not available
Source: Burrelle's Media Directory, 1998 Edition

AM Radio Stations

Call Letters	Freq. (kHz)	Target Audience	Station Format	Music Format
KVOI	690	General	E/M/N	Christian
KNST	790	n/a	N/T	n/a
KFLT	830	Religious	M	Christian
KTKT	990	General	N	n/a
KGVY	1080	General	M/N/S	Big Band
KQTL	1210	Hispanic	M	Spanish
KCUB	1290	n/a	M/N	Country
KTUC	1400	General	N/S/T	n/a
KTZR	1450	Hispanic	M/N/S	Spanish
KFFN	1490	General	M/N/S/T	Alternative
KUAT	1550	General	M/N	Jazz
KXEW	1600	Hispanic	M	Christian

Note: Stations included broadcast in the Tucson metro area; n/a not available
Station Format: E = Educational; M = Music; N = News; S = Sports; T = Talk
Source: Burrelle's Media Directory, 1998 Edition

FM Radio Stations

Call Letters	Freq. (mHz)	Target Audience	Station Format	Music Format
KUAZ	89.1	General	M/N/S	Jazz
KUAT	90.5	General	M	Classical
KXCI	91.3	Black/Hisp/Relig	M/N/T	n/a
KFMA	92.1	General	M	Alternative
KWFM	92.9	General	M	Oldies
KRQQ	93.7	General	M	Contemporary Top 40
KMXZ	94.9	n/a	M/N	Adult Contemporary
KLPX	96.1	General	M/N/S	AOR
KGMS	97.1	Religious	M	Christian
KSJM	97.5	n/a	M/N/S	Spanish
KOHT	98.3	Hispanic	M/N	Adult Contemporary/Oldies/Spanish
KIIM	99.5	General	M	Country
KKHG	104.1	General	M/N	Classic Rock
KHYT	107.5	General	M/N	Oldies

Note: Stations included broadcast in the Tucson metro area; n/a not available
Station Format: E = Educational; M = Music; N = News; S = Sports; T = Talk
Music Format: AOR = Album Oriented Rock; MOR = Middle-of-the-Road
Source: Burrelle's Media Directory, 1998 Edition

Television Stations

Name	Ch.	Affiliation	Type	Owner
KVOA	4	NBC	Commercial	Evening Post Publishing Company
KUAT	6	PBS	Public	University of Arizona
KGUN	9	ABC	Commercial	Lee Enterprises Inc.
KMSB	11	Fox	Commercial	A.H. Belo Corporation
KOLD	13	CBS	Commercial	Raycom Media Inc.
KTTU	18	Fox	Commercial	Clear Channel Communications
KUAS	27	PBS	Public	University of Arizona
KHRR	40	Telemundo	Commercial	Hispanic Broadcasters of Tucson Inc.

Note: Stations included broadcast in the Tucson metro area
Source: Burrelle's Media Directory, 1998 Edition

CLIMATE

Average and Extreme Temperatures

Temperature	Jan	Feb	Mar	Apr	May	Jun	Jul	Aug	Sep	Oct	Nov	Dec	Ann
Extreme High (°F)	87	92	99	104	107	117	114	108	107	101	90	84	117
Average High (°F)	64	68	73	81	89	99	99	96	94	84	73	65	82
Average Temp. (°F)	51	54	59	66	74	84	86	84	81	71	59	52	69
Average Low (°F)	38	40	44	51	58	68	74	72	67	57	45	39	55
Extreme Low (°F)	16	20	20	33	38	47	62	61	44	26	24	16	16

Note: Figures cover the years 1946-1990
Source: National Climatic Data Center, International Station Meteorological Climate Summary, 3/95

Average Precipitation/Snowfall/Humidity

Precip./Humidity	Jan	Feb	Mar	Apr	May	Jun	Jul	Aug	Sep	Oct	Nov	Dec	Ann
Avg. Precip. (in.)	0.9	0.7	0.7	0.3	0.1	0.2	2.5	2.2	1.4	0.9	0.6	0.9	11.6
Avg. Snowfall (in.)	Tr	Tr	Tr	Tr	0	0	0	0	0	0	Tr	Tr	2
Avg. Rel. Hum. 5am (%)	62	58	52	41	34	32	58	65	55	52	54	61	52
Avg. Rel. Hum. 5pm (%)	31	26	22	16	13	13	29	32	26	24	27	33	24

Note: Figures cover the years 1946-1990; Tr = Trace amounts (<0.05 in. of rain; <0.5 in. of snow)
Source: National Climatic Data Center, International Station Meteorological Climate Summary, 3/95

Weather Conditions

Temperature			Daytime Sky			Precipitation		
10°F & below	32°F & below	90°F & above	Clear	Partly cloudy	Cloudy	0.01 inch or more precip.	0.1 inch or more snow/ice	Thunder-storms
0	18	140	177	119	69	54	2	42

Note: Figures are average number of days per year and covers the years 1946-1990
Source: National Climatic Data Center, International Station Meteorological Climate Summary, 3/95

AIR & WATER QUALITY

Maximum Pollutant Concentrations

	Particulate Matter (ug/m³)	Carbon Monoxide (ppm)	Sulfur Dioxide (ppm)	Nitrogen Dioxide (ppm)	Ozone (ppm)	Lead (ug/m³)
MSA[1] Level	81	5	0.004	0.019	0.09	0.05
NAAQS[2]	150	9	0.140	0.053	0.12	1.50
Met NAAQS?	Yes	Yes	Yes	Yes	Yes	Yes

Note: (1) Metropolitan Statistical Area - see Appendix A for areas included; (2) National Ambient Air Quality Standards; ppm = parts per million; ug/m³ = micrograms per cubic meter; n/a not available
Source: EPA, National Air Quality and Emissions Trends Report, 1996

Pollutant Standards Index

In the Tucson MSA (see Appendix A for areas included), the Pollutant Standards Index (PSI) exceeded 100 on 0 days in 1996. A PSI value greater than 100 indicates that air quality would be in the unhealthful range on that day. *EPA, National Air Quality and Emissions Trends Report, 1996*

Drinking Water

Water System Name	Pop. Served	Primary Water Source Type	Number of Violations in Fiscal Year 1997	Type of Violation/ Contaminants
Tucson Muni Water Dept	550,000	Surface	7	(1)

Note: Data as of January 16, 1998; (1) System collected or speciated some but not all follow-up samples for compliance period under the total coliform rule (7 times in fiscal year 1997).
Source: EPA, Office of Ground Water and Drinking Water, Safe Drinking Water Information System

Tucson tap water is alkaline and very hard from South Side Reservoir No. 1 and alkaline, soft and not fluoridated from North Side Reservoir No. 3.
Editor & Publisher Market Guide, 1998

Comparative Statistics

Population Growth: City

City	Population			% Change	
	1980	1990	1996[1]	1980-90	1990-96
Colo. Spgs.	215,150	281,140	345,127	30.7	22.8
Denver	492,365	467,610	497,840	-5.0	6.5
Eugene	105,624	112,669	123,718	6.7	9.8
Las Vegas	164,674	258,295	376,906	56.9	45.9
Los Angeles	2,966,850	3,485,398	3,553,638	17.5	2.0
Oakland	339,337	372,242	367,230	9.7	-1.3
Phoenix	789,704	983,403	1,159,014	24.5	17.9
Portland	366,423	437,398	480,824	19.4	9.9
Pueblo	101,686	98,640	99,406	-3.0	0.8
Riverside	170,876	226,505	255,069	32.6	12.6
Salem	89,233	107,786	122,566	20.8	13.7
Salt Lake City	163,033	159,936	172,575	-1.9	7.9
San Diego	875,538	1,110,549	1,171,121	26.8	5.5
San Francisco	678,974	723,959	735,315	6.6	1.6
San Jose	629,442	782,225	838,744	24.3	7.2
Santa Rosa	83,320	113,313	121,879	36.0	7.6
Seattle	493,846	516,259	524,704	4.5	1.6
Tacoma	158,501	176,664	179,114	11.5	1.4
Tucson	330,537	405,390	449,002	22.6	10.8
U.S.	**226,545,805**	**248,765,170**	**265,179,411**	**9.8**	**6.6**

Note: (1) Census Bureau estimate as of 7/96
Source: 1980 Census; 1990 Census of Population and Housing, Summary Tape File 3C

Population Growth: Metro Area

MSA[1]	Population			% Change	
	1980	1990	1996[2]	1980-90	1990-96
Colo. Spgs.	309,424	397,014	472,924	28.3	19.1
Denver	1,428,836	1,622,980	1,866,978	13.6	15.0
Eugene	275,226	282,912	306,862	2.8	8.5
Las Vegas	463,087	741,459	1,201,073	60.1	62.0
Los Angeles	7,477,503	8,863,164	9,127,751	18.5	3.0
Oakland	(a)	2,082,914	2,209,629	(a)	6.1
Phoenix	1,509,052	2,122,101	2,746,703	40.6	29.4
Portland	1,105,699	1,239,842	1,758,937	12.1	41.9
Pueblo	125,972	123,051	131,217	-2.3	6.6
Riverside	1,558,215	2,588,793	3,015,783	66.1	16.5
Salem	249,895	278,024	319,420	11.3	14.9
Salt Lake City	910,222	1,072,227	1,217,842	17.8	13.6
San Diego	1,861,846	2,498,016	2,655,463	34.2	6.3
San Francisco	1,488,871	1,603,678	1,655,454	7.7	3.2
San Jose	1,295,071	1,497,577	1,599,604	15.6	6.8
Santa Rosa	299,681	388,222	420,872	29.5	8.4
Seattle	1,607,469	1,972,961	2,234,707	22.7	13.3
Tacoma	485,643	586,203	657,272	20.7	12.1
Tucson	531,443	666,880	767,873	25.5	15.1
U.S.	**226,545,805**	**248,765,170**	**265,179,411**	**9.8**	**6.6**

Note: (1) Metropolitan Statistical Area - see Appendix A for areas included; (2) Census Bureau estimate as of 7/96; (a) Oakland was part of the San Francisco-Oakland MSA in 1980
Source: 1980 Census; 1990 Census of Population and Housing, Summary Tape File 3C

Population Characteristics: City

City	1990 Percent of Total (%)					
	White	Black	American Indian/ Esk./Aleut.	Asian/ Pacific Islander	Other	Hispanic Origin[1]
Colo. Spgs.	86.1	7.0	0.9	2.4	3.7	8.9
Denver	72.2	12.9	1.1	2.3	11.5	22.8
Eugene	93.3	1.2	0.9	3.5	1.1	2.9
Las Vegas	78.4	11.4	0.9	3.6	5.6	12.1
Los Angeles	52.9	13.9	0.4	9.8	22.9	39.3
Oakland	32.5	43.9	0.6	14.9	8.1	13.2
Phoenix	81.7	5.2	1.9	1.6	9.6	19.7
Portland	84.8	7.6	1.3	5.2	1.0	3.0
Pueblo	83.1	2.0	0.8	0.7	13.4	39.4
Riverside	70.9	7.4	0.9	5.2	15.6	25.5
Salem	91.2	1.4	1.7	2.4	3.2	5.8
Salt Lake City	87.2	1.6	1.7	4.7	4.8	9.5
San Diego	67.2	9.3	0.7	11.8	11.0	20.1
San Francisco	53.6	10.9	0.5	29.1	5.8	13.3
San Jose	63.0	4.7	0.7	19.6	12.1	26.1
Santa Rosa	89.5	1.9	1.2	3.4	4.1	9.3
Seattle	75.4	10.0	1.4	11.9	1.3	3.3
Tacoma	78.4	11.4	1.9	7.0	1.3	3.5
Tucson	75.4	4.3	1.6	2.2	16.5	28.9
U.S.	**80.3**	**12.0**	**0.8**	**2.9**	**3.9**	**8.8**

Note: (1) People of Hispanic origin can be of any race
Source: 1990 Census of Population and Housing, Summary Tape File 3C

Population Characteristics: Metro Area

MSA[1]	1990 Percent of Total (%)					
	White	Black	American Indian/ Esk./Aleut.	Asian/ Pacific Islander	Other	Hispanic Origin[2]
Colo. Spgs.	86.2	7.1	0.9	2.4	3.4	8.4
Denver	85.7	5.9	0.8	2.3	5.4	12.8
Eugene	95.3	0.7	1.1	2.0	0.9	2.5
Las Vegas	81.3	9.5	0.9	3.5	4.7	10.9
Los Angeles	56.9	11.2	0.5	10.8	20.6	37.3
Oakland	66.0	14.6	0.7	13.0	5.8	12.8
Phoenix	84.9	3.5	1.8	1.7	8.1	16.0
Portland	90.9	3.1	1.0	3.6	1.4	3.5
Pueblo	84.8	1.7	0.8	0.7	12.0	35.7
Riverside	74.6	6.9	1.0	3.9	13.6	26.1
Salem	91.8	0.8	1.5	1.7	4.1	7.3
Salt Lake City	93.4	0.9	0.8	2.4	2.6	5.7
San Diego	75.1	6.3	0.9	8.0	9.8	20.0
San Francisco	66.2	7.6	0.5	20.5	5.3	14.1
San Jose	69.1	3.7	0.6	17.5	9.1	20.5
Santa Rosa	90.7	1.4	1.2	2.8	3.9	10.2
Seattle	86.9	4.0	1.2	6.9	0.9	2.6
Tacoma	85.2	7.2	1.4	4.9	1.2	3.3
Tucson	78.9	3.1	3.0	1.8	13.1	24.2
U.S.	**80.3**	**12.0**	**0.8**	**2.9**	**3.9**	**8.8**

Note: (1) Metropolitan Statistical Area - see Appendix A for areas included;
(2) People of Hispanic origin can be of any race
Source: 1990 Census of Population and Housing, Summary Tape File 3C

Age: City

City	Median Age (Years)	Age Distribution (%)						
		Under 5	Under 18	18-24	25-44	45-64	65+	80+
Colo. Spgs.	31.0	8.5	26.7	10.9	36.6	16.7	9.2	1.9
Denver	33.8	7.3	21.8	9.5	37.6	17.4	13.7	3.5
Eugene	32.2	5.9	21.1	16.7	34.1	15.4	12.7	3.4
Las Vegas	32.5	8.2	24.8	9.9	35.4	19.7	10.3	1.5
Los Angeles	30.6	8.0	24.7	12.7	36.0	16.6	9.9	2.2
Oakland	32.6	8.0	24.8	10.1	36.1	16.8	12.2	3.0
Phoenix	31.0	8.5	27.1	10.5	35.2	17.5	9.7	1.8
Portland	34.5	7.0	22.0	10.0	37.0	16.6	14.5	3.7
Pueblo	34.5	7.1	26.2	9.3	29.6	19.1	15.9	3.7
Riverside	29.0	8.8	28.9	13.0	34.1	15.0	9.0	2.0
Salem	33.4	7.3	24.3	10.5	34.3	16.2	14.7	4.0
Salt Lake City	31.0	8.3	25.1	12.3	33.7	14.4	14.5	4.0
San Diego	30.5	7.3	23.1	14.4	36.6	15.7	10.2	2.1
San Francisco	35.7	4.9	16.1	9.8	40.2	19.3	14.5	3.7
San Jose	30.4	8.3	26.7	11.2	37.7	17.3	7.1	1.5
Santa Rosa	35.0	7.1	23.7	9.6	33.9	16.5	16.3	4.1
Seattle	34.9	5.6	16.3	11.9	39.9	16.6	15.2	3.9
Tacoma	31.8	8.2	25.9	10.9	33.4	16.1	13.7	3.7
Tucson	30.6	7.7	24.4	14.3	33.0	15.7	12.6	2.9
U.S.	**32.9**	**7.3**	**25.6**	**10.5**	**32.6**	**18.7**	**12.5**	**2.8**

Source: 1990 Census of Population and Housing, Summary Tape File 3C

Age: Metro Area

MSA[1]	Median Age (Years)	Age Distribution (%)						
		Under 5	Under 18	18-24	25-44	45-64	65+	80+
Colo. Spgs.	30.2	8.5	27.5	12.0	35.8	16.7	8.0	1.6
Denver	32.7	7.8	25.9	8.8	37.8	18.2	9.3	2.0
Eugene	33.9	6.6	24.4	11.7	32.7	18.2	13.1	2.8
Las Vegas	33.0	7.6	24.4	10.0	34.5	20.7	10.5	1.4
Los Angeles	30.6	8.2	26.2	11.9	35.1	17.1	9.7	2.1
Oakland	33.2	7.5	24.2	10.0	36.4	18.7	10.7	2.3
Phoenix	32.0	8.0	26.1	10.5	33.5	17.4	12.5	2.6
Portland	33.9	7.3	25.2	9.1	35.6	17.9	12.2	2.9
Pueblo	34.7	7.0	26.4	9.0	29.6	20.0	15.1	3.3
Riverside	30.3	9.3	29.8	10.3	33.3	15.8	10.7	2.1
Salem	33.8	7.3	26.4	9.7	31.2	18.1	14.5	3.6
Salt Lake City	27.5	9.7	35.6	10.2	30.9	14.9	8.4	1.8
San Diego	30.8	7.7	24.5	13.2	35.4	16.0	10.9	2.3
San Francisco	35.7	5.8	18.8	9.2	38.2	20.5	13.3	3.1
San Jose	31.8	7.4	23.9	11.0	37.9	18.6	8.6	1.8
Santa Rosa	34.8	7.3	24.6	8.8	35.4	17.7	13.5	3.0
Seattle	33.3	7.3	23.8	9.6	37.7	18.2	10.7	2.3
Tacoma	31.2	8.2	27.2	11.2	33.6	17.6	10.4	2.2
Tucson	32.7	7.4	24.9	11.6	32.1	17.8	13.7	2.8
U.S.	**32.9**	**7.3**	**25.6**	**10.5**	**32.6**	**18.7**	**12.5**	**2.8**

Note: (1) Metropolitan Statistical Area - see Appendix A for areas included
Source: 1990 Census of Population and Housing, Summary Tape File 3C

Male/Female Ratio: City

City	Number of males per 100 females (all ages)	Number of males per 100 females (18 years old+)
Colo. Spgs.	95.8	92.8
Denver	95.1	92.0
Eugene	92.5	89.7
Las Vegas	102.2	102.4
Los Angeles	100.7	99.6
Oakland	91.4	89.2
Phoenix	98.0	96.0
Portland	93.9	91.4
Pueblo	90.9	88.4
Riverside	98.6	95.7
Salem	98.7	97.3
Salt Lake City	96.8	94.8
San Diego	104.2	103.7
San Francisco	100.1	99.4
San Jose	102.9	102.8
Santa Rosa	91.4	87.3
Seattle	95.1	94.0
Tacoma	93.8	90.1
Tucson	94.3	91.9
U.S.	**95.0**	**91.9**

Source: 1990 Census of Population, General Population Characteristics

Male/Female Ratio: Metro Area

MSA[1]	Number of males per 100 females (all ages)	Number of males per 100 females (18 years old+)
Colo. Spgs.	100.5	99.4
Denver	96.5	93.6
Eugene	95.1	92.0
Las Vegas	103.0	102.4
Los Angeles	99.5	97.7
Oakland	96.0	94.2
Phoenix	96.9	94.6
Portland	95.6	92.8
Pueblo	92.3	90.3
Riverside	100.0	98.3
Salem	97.2	94.7
Salt Lake City	98.5	95.4
San Diego	103.8	103.5
San Francisco	98.9	97.2
San Jose	102.7	102.1
Santa Rosa	96.1	92.9
Seattle	97.4	95.7
Tacoma	99.8	97.8
Tucson	95.2	93.0
U.S.	**95.0**	**91.9**

Note: (1) Metropolitan Statistical Area - see Appendix A for areas included
Source: 1990 Census of Population, General Population Characteristics

Educational Attainment by Race: City

City	High School Graduate (%)					Bachelor's Degree (%)				
	Total	White	Black	Other	Hisp.[1]	Total	White	Black	Other	Hisp.[1]
Colo. Spgs.	87.8	89.1	86.6	70.7	69.2	27.5	29.3	16.3	13.3	12.1
Denver	79.2	83.5	75.0	54.0	50.4	29.0	33.9	14.5	10.3	6.9
Eugene	88.6	88.7	90.0	84.9	80.1	34.9	34.7	42.1	38.6	25.8
Las Vegas	76.3	79.4	68.1	57.0	49.8	13.4	14.0	9.4	11.5	6.2
Los Angeles	67.0	75.8	69.9	47.2	33.0	23.0	28.8	13.3	15.5	5.6
Oakland	74.4	85.9	73.3	54.6	45.6	27.2	46.0	14.1	17.9	10.8
Phoenix	78.7	82.0	71.1	53.8	47.7	19.9	21.6	11.8	9.2	5.6
Portland	82.9	84.4	72.8	71.2	69.0	25.9	27.2	12.7	21.7	14.9
Pueblo	73.2	74.1	71.3	66.9	62.2	13.8	14.9	11.2	5.9	5.1
Riverside	77.8	82.6	79.0	56.2	50.5	19.3	20.8	16.9	13.9	7.2
Salem	81.5	82.6	82.3	63.5	51.8	21.7	22.5	10.7	10.9	8.4
Salt Lake City	83.0	85.0	67.3	66.3	57.2	30.4	31.7	14.8	20.6	10.6
San Diego	82.3	87.6	80.3	62.9	51.9	29.8	34.3	14.0	19.3	10.7
San Francisco	78.0	86.8	72.4	63.7	60.7	35.0	44.6	14.9	23.7	15.1
San Jose	77.2	81.2	82.9	66.9	50.5	25.3	26.1	21.4	24.2	7.1
Santa Rosa	85.7	87.4	79.8	63.0	58.8	26.9	27.8	14.6	16.7	13.0
Seattle	86.4	89.7	75.5	72.8	77.7	37.9	41.8	14.4	28.4	25.4
Tacoma	79.3	80.5	79.6	65.6	75.2	15.8	16.9	9.9	11.0	10.1
Tucson	78.6	83.0	75.6	57.5	56.2	20.7	23.4	11.9	9.5	8.1
U.S.	**75.2**	**77.9**	**63.1**	**60.4**	**49.8**	**20.3**	**21.5**	**11.4**	**19.4**	**9.2**

Note: Figures shown cover persons 25 years old and over; (1) people of Hispanic origin can be of any race
Source: 1990 Census of Population and Housing, Summary Tape File 3C

Educational Attainment by Race: Metro Area

MSA[1]	High School Graduate (%)					Bachelor's Degree (%)				
	Total	White	Black	Other	Hisp.[2]	Total	White	Black	Other	Hisp.[2]
Colo. Spgs.	88.3	89.5	88.1	71.7	71.3	25.8	27.4	15.7	12.8	11.8
Denver	85.5	87.6	79.1	64.2	60.2	28.9	30.8	17.2	14.3	9.6
Eugene	83.0	83.2	86.4	77.7	75.1	22.2	22.0	32.3	25.3	16.4
Las Vegas	77.3	79.6	70.6	60.0	53.4	13.8	14.4	9.0	12.3	7.0
Los Angeles	70.0	76.7	73.8	53.2	39.2	22.3	25.6	14.8	17.7	6.0
Oakland	83.4	87.1	76.3	73.7	63.3	29.9	32.7	15.6	29.3	12.9
Phoenix	81.5	84.2	75.4	55.9	50.8	22.1	23.4	14.8	11.4	7.3
Portland	84.6	85.6	74.2	71.7	59.7	24.8	25.2	14.0	23.3	12.8
Pueblo	73.9	75.0	70.1	66.4	61.8	14.0	15.1	10.5	6.1	5.0
Riverside	74.8	78.1	78.7	55.6	49.4	14.8	15.4	13.5	11.7	5.6
Salem	78.9	80.2	79.5	56.4	43.0	18.2	18.7	13.6	9.2	6.6
Salt Lake City	85.6	86.6	76.1	68.4	62.1	22.9	23.4	15.5	15.5	8.9
San Diego	81.9	85.7	82.0	62.3	52.5	25.3	27.6	14.1	17.0	9.5
San Francisco	82.4	87.6	74.1	69.4	60.7	34.9	39.4	15.6	27.1	13.8
San Jose	82.0	85.3	84.3	71.9	54.1	32.6	33.8	23.3	30.3	9.3
Santa Rosa	84.4	85.8	78.8	64.6	55.4	24.5	25.1	17.7	16.8	11.1
Seattle	87.7	88.8	79.5	78.1	79.0	29.8	30.3	16.4	30.0	20.3
Tacoma	83.2	83.9	84.7	73.1	80.2	17.5	18.1	13.3	12.9	12.1
Tucson	80.5	84.5	76.1	57.6	58.0	23.3	25.9	13.6	9.7	8.7
U.S.	**75.2**	**77.9**	**63.1**	**60.4**	**49.8**	**20.3**	**21.5**	**11.4**	**19.4**	**9.2**

Note: Figures shown cover persons 25 years old and over; (1) Metropolitan Statistical Area - see Appendix A for areas included; (2) people of Hispanic origin can be of any race
Source: 1990 Census of Population and Housing, Summary Tape File 3C

Per Capita/Median/Average Income: City

City	Per Capita ($)	Median Household ($)	Average Household ($)
Colo. Spgs.	14,243	28,928	35,709
Denver	15,590	25,106	33,983
Eugene	13,886	25,369	33,056
Las Vegas	14,737	30,590	37,719
Los Angeles	16,188	30,925	45,701
Oakland	14,676	27,095	37,100
Phoenix	14,096	29,291	37,159
Portland	14,478	25,592	33,359
Pueblo	10,168	20,501	25,729
Riverside	14,235	34,801	42,016
Salem	12,641	25,236	31,928
Salt Lake City	13,482	22,697	32,046
San Diego	16,401	33,686	43,627
San Francisco	19,695	33,414	45,664
San Jose	16,905	46,206	52,091
Santa Rosa	17,259	35,237	42,288
Seattle	18,308	29,353	38,895
Tacoma	12,272	25,333	30,620
Tucson	11,184	21,748	27,435
U.S.	**14,420**	**30,056**	**38,453**

Note: Figures are for 1989
Source: 1990 Census of Population and Housing, Summary Tape File 3C

Per Capita/Median/Average Income: Metro Area

MSA[1]	Per Capita ($)	Median Household ($)	Average Household ($)
Colo. Spgs.	13,664	29,604	35,989
Denver	16,539	32,852	40,841
Eugene	12,570	25,268	31,613
Las Vegas	15,109	30,746	38,595
Los Angeles	16,149	34,965	47,252
Oakland	18,782	40,621	49,478
Phoenix	14,970	30,797	38,996
Portland	15,286	30,930	38,482
Pueblo	10,347	21,553	26,651
Riverside	13,879	33,279	40,721
Salem	12,260	26,771	32,756
Salt Lake City	12,029	30,882	36,866
San Diego	16,220	35,022	44,375
San Francisco	22,049	40,494	54,162
San Jose	20,423	48,115	57,913
Santa Rosa	17,239	36,299	44,331
Seattle	17,921	36,338	44,338
Tacoma	13,439	30,412	35,767
Tucson	13,177	25,401	33,127
U.S.	**14,420**	**30,056**	**38,453**

Note: Figures are for 1989; (1) Metropolitan Statistical Area - see Appendix A for areas included
Source: 1990 Census of Population and Housing, Summary Tape File 3C

Household Income Distribution: City

City	Less than $5,000	$5,000 -$9,999	$10,000 -$14,999	$15,000 -$24,999	$25,000 -$34,999	$35,000 -$49,999	$50,000 -$74,999	$75,000 -$99,999	$100,000 and up
				% of Households Earning					
Colo. Spgs.	4.6	7.7	9.8	20.6	17.7	18.3	14.0	4.1	3.0
Denver	7.6	11.3	10.8	20.1	16.0	15.3	11.5	3.5	3.9
Eugene	8.3	12.3	10.2	18.4	15.5	16.3	12.3	3.3	3.3
Las Vegas	5.1	8.0	8.8	17.8	17.8	19.7	14.8	4.4	3.5
Los Angeles	6.0	9.6	8.7	16.7	14.5	15.7	14.6	6.3	7.9
Oakland	6.4	12.8	9.5	17.5	15.1	15.0	13.1	5.6	4.9
Phoenix	5.7	8.0	9.1	19.4	16.9	18.2	14.2	4.6	3.9
Portland	6.6	10.8	10.5	20.9	17.3	16.5	11.2	3.2	3.0
Pueblo	10.6	14.7	11.9	22.2	16.1	13.6	8.0	1.7	1.2
Riverside	4.2	7.2	7.6	15.2	15.9	20.4	18.4	6.2	4.7
Salem	6.1	11.0	10.7	21.7	17.0	16.9	11.7	2.7	2.2
Salt Lake City	7.4	12.9	12.8	21.1	15.6	14.2	9.5	3.2	3.4
San Diego	4.0	7.7	7.8	16.6	15.7	18.3	17.3	6.7	5.9
San Francisco	5.1	9.3	7.4	15.1	15.0	17.2	16.5	6.9	7.4
San Jose	2.5	4.7	4.7	10.9	12.6	19.0	25.0	12.5	8.0
Santa Rosa	2.3	7.8	6.8	16.7	16.0	20.6	18.8	6.3	4.7
Seattle	5.6	9.3	8.9	18.7	16.2	17.2	14.2	5.0	4.8
Tacoma	6.7	12.3	10.9	19.5	16.9	18.0	11.3	2.7	1.7
Tucson	9.3	12.3	12.6	22.0	16.7	14.7	8.8	2.0	1.5
U.S.	**6.2**	**9.3**	**8.8**	**17.5**	**15.8**	**17.9**	**15.0**	**5.1**	**4.4**

Note: Figures are for 1989
Source: 1990 Census of Population and Housing, Summary Tape File 3C

Household Income Distribution: Metro Area

MSA[1]	Less than $5,000	$5,000 -$9,999	$10,000 -$14,999	$15,000 -$24,999	$25,000 -$34,999	$35,000 -$49,999	$50,000 -$74,999	$75,000 -$99,999	$100,000 and up
				% of Households Earning					
Colo. Spgs.	4.4	7.1	9.3	20.9	18.0	18.9	14.3	4.2	2.9
Denver	4.7	7.1	7.9	17.0	16.4	19.4	17.2	5.8	4.7
Eugene	6.6	11.3	10.7	20.8	17.4	17.0	11.1	2.7	2.4
Las Vegas	4.8	6.9	8.8	19.1	17.7	19.4	14.8	4.7	3.7
Los Angeles	4.8	8.0	7.5	15.2	14.5	17.3	17.3	7.5	7.9
Oakland	3.5	6.8	6.1	12.9	13.5	18.4	21.1	9.7	8.1
Phoenix	5.1	7.4	8.7	18.7	16.8	18.9	15.3	5.0	4.2
Portland	4.5	8.0	8.5	18.6	17.5	19.4	15.3	4.6	3.8
Pueblo	9.7	13.9	11.6	21.9	16.8	14.5	8.6	1.9	1.3
Riverside	4.0	8.3	8.3	16.1	15.5	19.4	18.0	6.1	4.2
Salem	5.3	9.6	10.0	21.6	18.0	18.7	11.9	2.7	2.2
Salt Lake City	4.1	7.3	8.4	18.9	18.8	20.6	15.1	4.0	2.9
San Diego	3.4	7.0	7.5	16.4	15.7	18.9	18.2	7.0	6.0
San Francisco	3.8	6.6	5.8	12.8	13.9	17.8	19.4	9.2	10.5
San Jose	2.4	4.4	4.4	10.2	12.3	18.3	23.9	12.8	11.4
Santa Rosa	2.6	7.2	6.9	15.5	15.8	20.1	20.1	6.8	5.2
Seattle	3.4	6.2	6.6	15.5	16.1	20.9	19.2	6.7	5.4
Tacoma	4.6	8.4	8.8	18.7	17.4	20.1	15.5	3.8	2.7
Tucson	7.5	10.4	11.0	20.4	16.6	16.1	11.6	3.4	3.1
U.S.	**6.2**	**9.3**	**8.8**	**17.5**	**15.8**	**17.9**	**15.0**	**5.1**	**4.4**

Note: Figures are for 1989; (1) Metropolitan Statistical Area - see Appendix A for areas included
Source: 1990 Census of Population and Housing, Summary Tape File 3C

Effective Buying Income: City

City	Per Capita ($)	Median Household ($)	Average Household ($)
Colo. Spgs.	14,457	29,398	36,235
Denver	16,812	27,453	36,768
Eugene	14,879	27,854	36,082
Las Vegas	16,736	35,593	43,567
Los Angeles	14,176	29,515	41,879
Oakland	14,519	28,788	38,516
Phoenix	14,294	30,184	38,004
Portland	15,678	28,846	36,822
Pueblo	11,345	23,045	28,957
Riverside	12,455	32,777	38,830
Salem	13,699	28,225	36,099
Salt Lake City	15,522	27,235	37,224
San Diego	15,139	33,339	42,602
San Francisco	20,120	36,735	48,562
San Jose	17,024	50,006	54,728
Santa Rosa	16,826	35,818	42,135
Seattle	21,988	36,128	48,120
Tacoma	14,929	31,005	37,994
Tucson	11,886	23,550	29,615
U.S.	**15,444**	**33,201**	**41,849**

Note: Data as of 1/1/97
Source: Standard Rate & Data Service, Newspaper Advertising Source, 2/98

Effective Buying Income: Metro Area

MSA[1]	Per Capita ($)	Median Household ($)	Average Household ($)
Colo. Spgs.	14,302	30,928	38,128
Denver	18,348	37,622	45,521
Eugene	13,992	28,759	35,559
Las Vegas	17,275	35,632	44,843
Los Angeles	14,521	34,165	44,632
Oakland	18,754	43,519	51,401
Phoenix	15,241	32,216	40,254
Portland	16,965	36,471	43,923
Pueblo	11,852	24,769	30,765
Riverside	12,434	32,054	38,539
Salem	13,569	30,342	37,261
Salt Lake City	14,155	36,897	43,478
San Diego	15,323	35,379	44,536
San Francisco	22,131	44,024	56,451
San Jose	20,744	53,384	61,794
Santa Rosa	17,158	38,158	45,374
Seattle	21,971	45,918	55,509
Tacoma	16,993	38,836	46,554
Tucson	14,146	27,783	36,011
U.S.	**15,444**	**33,201**	**41,849**

Note: Data as of 1/1/97; (1) Metropolitan Statistical Area - see Appendix A for areas included
Source: Standard Rate & Data Service, Newspaper Advertising Source, 2/98

Effective Household Buying Income Distribution: City

City	% of Households Earning						
	$10,000 -$19,999	$20,000 -$34,999	$35,000 -$49,999	$50,000 -$74,999	$75,000 -$99,000	$100,000 -$124,999	$125,000 and up
Colo. Spgs.	19.8	27.9	18.7	15.5	4.1	1.3	1.3
Denver	20.2	25.3	16.3	13.8	4.4	1.8	2.2
Eugene	19.6	24.0	17.2	14.9	4.1	1.3	1.9
Las Vegas	15.4	23.2	19.9	19.3	7.0	2.1	2.5
Los Angeles	18.6	23.4	16.2	14.8	5.7	2.1	3.6
Oakland	18.7	23.6	15.4	15.1	6.1	2.2	2.3
Phoenix	18.4	26.4	18.3	16.0	4.9	1.6	1.8
Portland	19.4	26.7	18.0	14.6	4.3	1.4	1.7
Pueblo	22.7	26.8	15.2	10.6	2.5	0.7	0.6
Riverside	16.4	25.3	21.5	17.5	4.5	1.4	1.7
Salem	20.0	27.5	18.3	14.9	3.5	1.1	1.1
Salt Lake City	21.9	25.5	15.6	13.3	4.7	1.7	2.4
San Diego	16.8	24.5	18.8	18.3	6.1	2.0	2.4
San Francisco	14.5	21.4	17.4	19.0	8.3	3.3	4.3
San Jose	9.2	16.7	18.0	27.5	14.6	5.0	3.0
Santa Rosa	15.3	24.5	20.7	20.5	6.2	1.8	2.0
Seattle	15.2	22.5	17.4	18.4	8.5	3.1	4.0
Tacoma	18.7	23.2	18.7	17.5	5.3	1.5	1.3
Tucson	23.5	27.2	15.9	10.5	2.3	0.8	0.7
U.S.	**16.5**	**23.4**	**18.3**	**18.2**	**6.4**	**2.1**	**2.4**

Note: Data as of 1/1/97
Source: Standard Rate & Data Service, Newspaper Advertising Source, 2/98

Effective Household Buying Income Distribution: Metro Area

MSA[1]	% of Households Earning						
	$10,000 -$19,999	$20,000 -$34,999	$35,000 -$49,999	$50,000 -$74,999	$75,000 -$99,000	$100,000 -$124,999	$125,000 and up
Colo. Spgs.	18.4	28.0	19.5	16.4	4.7	1.3	1.4
Denver	14.2	22.9	19.3	21.1	7.8	2.7	2.7
Eugene	19.4	27.0	18.2	15.0	3.7	1.1	1.5
Las Vegas	15.3	24.2	19.3	19.1	7.3	2.5	2.7
Los Angeles	16.0	22.8	17.8	18.3	6.9	2.4	3.4
Oakland	11.9	19.0	17.9	23.6	11.0	4.0	3.8
Phoenix	17.3	25.5	19.0	17.3	5.5	1.9	2.1
Portland	14.7	24.0	20.2	20.4	7.0	2.2	2.2
Pueblo	21.6	27.1	16.2	11.9	3.0	0.8	0.7
Riverside	17.7	24.6	20.1	17.8	4.7	1.2	1.6
Salem	18.4	27.9	19.7	16.2	3.8	1.2	1.2
Salt Lake City	14.0	24.8	21.2	21.1	6.7	2.0	2.0
San Diego	15.7	24.1	19.2	19.8	6.8	2.2	2.6
San Francisco	11.4	19.1	17.5	22.1	10.8	4.5	5.9
San Jose	8.3	15.5	16.9	26.0	15.4	6.6	5.8
Santa Rosa	14.1	23.0	20.3	22.4	7.3	2.3	2.3
Seattle	10.7	19.0	18.7	23.9	11.9	4.6	4.7
Tacoma	14.0	22.1	19.4	21.9	8.8	2.5	2.4
Tucson	20.2	25.9	17.0	14.1	4.3	1.4	1.8
U.S.	**16.5**	**23.4**	**18.3**	**18.2**	**6.4**	**2.1**	**2.4**

Note: Data as of 1/1/97; (1) Metropolitan Statistical Area - see Appendix A for areas included
Source: Standard Rate & Data Service, Newspaper Advertising Source, 2/98

Poverty Rates by Race and Age: City

City	Total (%)	By Race (%)				By Age (%)		
		White	Black	Other	Hisp.[1]	Under 5 years old	Under 18 years old	65 years and over
Colo. Spgs.	10.9	9.1	22.4	21.0	21.0	19.3	15.3	7.8
Denver	17.1	12.4	27.0	31.3	30.6	29.4	27.4	12.7
Eugene	17.0	15.9	30.5	34.2	26.9	18.3	14.3	8.1
Las Vegas	11.5	8.8	25.8	16.7	19.5	17.2	15.9	10.8
Los Angeles	18.9	13.1	25.3	25.4	28.2	27.7	27.8	10.5
Oakland	18.8	9.0	23.9	22.6	21.7	32.1	30.3	11.0
Phoenix	14.2	10.9	30.0	28.4	29.1	22.9	20.4	11.3
Portland	14.5	12.1	31.2	24.8	26.0	21.0	19.0	11.6
Pueblo	21.6	18.8	37.9	35.3	32.5	40.7	32.2	13.9
Riverside	11.9	8.8	21.9	18.9	16.6	15.3	15.0	6.9
Salem	14.5	13.1	39.5	29.2	34.5	25.9	19.0	8.9
Salt Lake City	16.4	13.3	39.4	37.5	32.4	25.8	21.6	9.8
San Diego	13.4	9.3	23.1	21.3	25.6	20.8	19.8	7.4
San Francisco	12.7	9.3	26.2	13.7	16.4	17.7	18.6	9.9
San Jose	9.3	6.4	14.4	14.3	15.5	12.7	13.1	7.1
Santa Rosa	8.3	7.0	18.2	20.0	16.4	12.9	11.7	5.4
Seattle	12.4	9.0	25.2	21.0	22.3	15.9	16.2	9.0
Tacoma	16.8	13.1	26.8	34.0	23.0	26.3	23.4	12.3
Tucson	20.2	15.9	29.3	34.0	29.9	30.2	26.3	12.1
U.S.	**13.1**	**9.8**	**29.5**	**23.1**	**25.3**	**20.1**	**18.3**	**12.8**

Note: Figures show the percent of people living below the poverty line in 1989. The average poverty threshold was $12,674 for a family of four in 1989; (1) People of Hispanic origin can be of any race
Source: 1990 Census of Population and Housing, Summary Tape File 3C

Poverty Rates by Race and Age: Metro Area

MSA[1]	Total (%)	By Race (%)				By Age (%)		
		White	Black	Other	Hisp.[2]	Under 5 years old	Under 18 years old	65 years and over
Colo. Spgs.	10.4	8.9	19.7	19.6	19.6	18.0	14.4	8.1
Denver	9.7	7.5	24.6	22.6	22.3	15.9	13.5	9.5
Eugene	14.5	13.8	28.4	29.5	24.0	21.4	16.1	9.0
Las Vegas	10.5	8.4	23.8	15.7	17.1	16.2	14.4	9.1
Los Angeles	15.1	10.6	21.2	20.9	22.9	22.0	21.9	9.2
Oakland	9.3	5.9	21.1	12.4	13.2	14.7	13.7	7.0
Phoenix	12.3	9.5	27.4	28.4	27.5	19.9	17.3	8.8
Portland	10.0	8.7	29.3	20.1	24.9	14.7	12.3	9.4
Pueblo	20.2	17.7	37.7	34.0	31.4	36.8	29.6	13.6
Riverside	12.2	9.7	20.4	19.2	19.4	18.1	17.0	7.8
Salem	13.2	11.9	34.5	28.7	32.7	21.3	17.3	9.6
Salt Lake City	9.4	8.3	29.1	24.9	22.0	14.2	11.3	7.7
San Diego	11.3	8.4	21.3	19.9	22.8	17.2	16.2	6.3
San Francisco	9.0	6.5	22.5	11.7	14.2	11.3	11.9	8.0
San Jose	7.5	5.3	12.7	12.3	14.3	10.3	10.5	6.2
Santa Rosa	7.6	6.8	15.5	15.7	15.6	9.5	9.7	5.7
Seattle	7.6	6.1	21.7	15.9	13.9	10.4	9.5	7.2
Tacoma	11.4	9.5	22.6	22.5	17.0	18.3	15.5	9.1
Tucson	17.2	12.8	27.5	34.6	28.2	26.9	23.5	10.0
U.S.	**13.1**	**9.8**	**29.5**	**23.1**	**25.3**	**20.1**	**18.3**	**12.8**

Note: Figures show the percent of people living below the poverty line in 1989. The average poverty threshold was $12,674 for a family of four in 1989; (1) Metropolitan Statistical Area - see Appendix A for areas included; (2) People of Hispanic origin can be of any race
Source: 1990 Census of Population and Housing, Summary Tape File 3C

Major State and Local Tax Rates

City	State Corp. Income (%)	State Personal Income (%)	Residential Property (effective rate per $100)	Sales & Use State (%)	Sales & Use Local (%)	State Gasoline (cents/ gallon)	State Cigarette (cents/ 20-pack)
Colo. Springs	5.0	5.0	n/a	3.0	3.0	22	20
Denver	5.0	5.0	0.84	3.0	4.3	22	20
Eugene	6.6[a]	5.0 - 9.0	n/a	None	None	24[b]	68
Las Vegas	None	None	1.00	6.5	0.5	23[c]	35
Los Angeles	8.84[d]	1.0 - 9.3	0.74	6.0	2.25	18[e]	37
Oakland	8.84[d]	1.0 - 9.3	n/a	6.0	2.25	18[e]	37
Phoenix	9.0[f]	3.0 - 5.6	1.83	5.0	1.8	18[g]	58
Portland	6.6[a]	5.0 - 9.0	1.55	None	None	24[b]	68
Pueblo	5.0	5.0	n/a	3.0	4.5	22	20
Riverside	8.84[d]	1.0 - 9.3	n/a	6.0	1.75	18[e]	37
Salem	6.6[a]	5.0 - 9.0	n/a	None	None	24[b]	68
Salt Lake City	5.0[h]	2.3 - 7.0	1.55	4.75	1.25	24.5	51.5
San Diego	8.84[d]	1.0 - 9.3	n/a	6.0	1.75	18[e]	37
San Francisco	8.84[d]	1.0 - 9.3	n/a	6.0	2.50	18[e]	37
San Jose	8.84[d]	1.0 - 9.3	n/a	6.0	2.25	18[e]	37
Santa Rosa	8.84[d]	1.0 - 9.3	n/a	6.0	1.5	18[e]	37
Seattle	None	None	1.14	6.5	1.7	23	82.5
Tacoma	None	None	n/a	6.5	1.5	23	82.5
Tucson	9.0[f]	3.0 - 5.6	n/a	5.0	2.0	18[g]	58

Note: (a) Minimum tax $10; (b) Does not include a 1 - 2 cents local option tax; (c) Does not include a local option tax of 1 - 10 cents; (d) Minimum tax is $800. The tax rate on S-Corporations is 1.5%; (e) Does not include 1 cent local option tax; (f) Minimum tax is $50; (g) Carriers pay an additional surcharge of 8 cents; (h) Minimum tax $100
Source: Source: Federation of Tax Administrators, www.taxadmin.org; Washington D.C. Department of Finance and Revenue, Tax Rates and Tax Burdens in the District of Columbia: A Nationwide Comparison, June 1997; Chambers of Commerce

Employment by Industry

MSA[1]	Services	Retail	Gov't.	Manuf.	Finance/ Ins./R.E.	Whole- sale	Transp./ Utilities	Constr.	Mining
Colo. Spgs.	32.2	20.1	16.0	12.5	5.3	2.7	5.5	5.7	(a)
Denver	30.6	18.3	13.7	8.7	8.0	6.4	7.9	5.8	0.6
Eugene	26.6	21.3	18.4	15.0	5.3	4.6	3.4	5.3	0.1
Las Vegas	44.6	17.4	10.8	3.4	4.8	3.3	5.1	10.2	0.3
Los Angeles	32.7	15.7	13.8	17.0	5.6	6.8	5.4	2.9	0.1
Oakland	29.6	16.6	17.7	12.4	5.7	6.2	6.3	5.2	0.2
Phoenix	31.2	18.7	12.6	11.5	7.7	6.1	5.1	6.6	0.5
Portland	27.5	18.1	12.8	15.9	7.1	7.3	5.7	5.5	0.1
Pueblo	n/a	n/a	n/a	n/a	n/a	n/a	n/a	n/a	n/a
Riverside	26.2	21.6	20.1	12.4	3.5	4.6	5.1	6.1	0.1
Salem	23.9	18.6	28.0	12.6	5.0	3.1	2.6	6.0	0.2
Salt Lake City	26.9	19.2	16.2	12.1	6.5	5.7	6.7	6.3	0.4
San Diego	32.0	19.1	18.4	11.5	5.8	4.2	3.9	5.1	0.0
San Francisco	36.8	16.5	12.2	7.7	10.2	4.9	7.9	3.6	0.0
San Jose	32.5	14.3	9.3	27.3	3.3	6.1	3.0	4.2	0.0
Santa Rosa	28.7	20.9	15.4	15.3	5.6	4.6	3.8	5.4	0.2
Seattle	28.8	17.1	13.5	16.8	6.0	6.7	6.0	5.0	0.1
Tacoma	28.0	20.0	20.8	11.1	5.1	5.6	4.0	5.4	0.1
Tucson	31.4	18.6	22.9	8.8	3.8	3.4	4.1	6.2	0.7
U.S.	**29.0**	**18.5**	**16.1**	**15.0**	**5.7**	**5.4**	**5.3**	**4.5**	**0.5**

Note: Figures cover non-farm employment as of 12/97 and are not seasonally adjusted; (1) Metropolitan Statistical Area - see Appendix A for areas included; (a) Mining is included with construction
Source: Bureau of Labor Statistics, http://stats.bls.gov

Labor Force, Employment and Job Growth: City

Area	Civilian Labor Force			Workers Employed		
	Dec. '95	Dec. '96	% Chg.	Dec. '95	Dec. '96	% Chg.
Colo. Spgs.	176,712	187,138	5.9	169,813	181,864	7.1
Denver	272,124	283,534	4.2	260,366	274,874	5.6
Eugene	66,722	68,982	3.4	63,137	65,837	4.3
Las Vegas	203,293	214,971	5.7	193,076	207,154	7.3
Los Angeles	1,768,027	1,823,759	3.2	1,627,652	1,702,838	4.6
Oakland	179,282	181,581	1.3	168,157	171,948	2.3
Phoenix	680,381	703,898	3.5	655,647	684,735	4.4
Portland	275,485	285,767	3.7	261,316	273,177	4.5
Pueblo	46,684	49,773	6.6	44,225	46,914	6.1
Riverside	132,553	135,428	2.2	123,294	127,543	3.4
Salem	61,256	62,176	1.5	57,320	58,718	2.4
Salt Lake City	102,428	107,450	4.9	99,558	104,753	5.2
San Diego	565,302	575,958	1.9	541,976	557,491	2.9
San Francisco	406,753	411,647	1.2	392,806	398,274	1.4
San Jose	459,515	475,439	3.5	443,467	462,483	4.3
Santa Rosa	66,165	67,911	2.6	63,877	65,875	3.1
Seattle	340,364	362,205	6.4	323,266	350,363	8.4
Tacoma	97,410	100,082	2.7	91,108	95,326	4.6
Tucson	237,890	235,752	-0.9	228,664	228,311	-0.2
U.S.	**134,583,000**	**136,742,000**	**1.6**	**127,903,000**	**130,785,000**	**2.3**

Note: Data is not seasonally adjusted and covers workers 16 years of age and older
Source: Bureau of Labor Statistics, http://stats.bls.gov

Labor Force, Employment and Job Growth: Metro Area

Area	Civilian Labor Force			Workers Employed		
	Dec. '95	Dec. '96	% Chg.	Dec. '95	Dec. '96	% Chg.
Colo. Spgs.	237,860	251,905	5.9	228,612	244,836	7.1
Denver	1,047,752	1,095,077	4.5	1,013,776	1,070,262	5.6
Eugene	159,349	164,589	3.3	149,828	156,237	4.3
Las Vegas	652,679	686,165	5.1	618,370	660,642	6.8
Los Angeles	4,413,112	4,557,466	3.3	4,103,659	4,284,946	4.4
Oakland	1,143,540	1,161,695	1.6	1,098,419	1,123,181	2.3
Phoenix	1,474,872	1,527,131	3.5	1,425,392	1,488,628	4.4
Portland	1,011,531	1,053,098	4.1	966,669	1,013,762	4.9
Pueblo	59,217	63,123	6.6	56,217	59,635	6.1
Riverside	1,321,636	1,353,315	2.4	1,238,518	1,281,208	3.4
Salem	161,676	164,182	1.6	151,656	155,355	2.4
Salt Lake City	651,751	683,365	4.9	634,216	667,307	5.2
San Diego	1,232,606	1,256,057	1.9	1,182,656	1,216,513	2.9
San Francisco	921,320	930,753	1.0	894,480	906,931	1.4
San Jose	904,156	936,614	3.6	877,359	914,980	4.3
Santa Rosa	231,216	237,282	2.6	222,983	229,955	3.1
Seattle	1,304,171	1,391,352	6.7	1,247,353	1,351,910	8.4
Tacoma	324,815	334,531	3.0	306,570	320,762	4.6
Tucson	382,504	379,338	-0.8	369,088	368,518	-0.2
U.S.	**134,583,000**	**136,742,000**	**1.6**	**127,903,000**	**130,785,000**	**2.3**

Note: Data is not seasonally adjusted and covers workers 16 years of age and older;
(1) Metropolitan Statistical Area - see Appendix A for areas included
Source: Bureau of Labor Statistics, http://stats.bls.gov

Unemployment Rate: City

Area	1997											
	Jan.	Feb.	Mar.	Apr.	May	Jun.	Jul.	Aug.	Sep.	Oct.	Nov.	Dec.
Colo. Spgs.	4.4	3.9	3.8	3.3	3.8	4.5	3.8	3.6	3.5	3.1	3.3	2.8
Denver	5.0	4.2	4.1	3.5	3.8	4.4	3.6	3.7	3.5	3.1	3.4	3.1
Eugene	5.7	5.9	5.8	5.0	4.0	4.4	4.3	4.3	4.2	4.1	4.5	4.6
Las Vegas	4.5	4.2	4.0	4.1	4.0	4.9	4.8	4.5	4.6	4.1	3.8	3.6
Los Angeles	9.0	8.6	8.2	8.1	7.7	8.0	8.6	7.9	7.5	7.1	7.0	6.6
Oakland	7.7	7.3	6.9	6.9	6.9	7.3	7.9	7.5	7.4	6.9	6.0	5.3
Phoenix	3.7	3.5	3.2	2.9	3.1	3.3	3.3	3.2	3.4	3.1	2.9	2.7
Portland	5.4	5.6	5.5	4.9	4.1	4.7	4.6	4.8	4.7	4.3	4.5	4.4
Pueblo	6.0	4.9	4.9	4.2	4.8	5.6	4.8	4.6	4.4	3.7	4.1	5.7
Riverside	8.0	7.6	6.8	6.8	6.5	7.2	9.1	8.8	8.7	8.0	6.8	5.8
Salem	6.8	6.8	6.9	6.2	5.0	5.5	5.2	4.9	4.6	4.5	5.3	5.6
Salt Lake City	3.2	3.5	2.9	3.1	3.1	3.8	3.1	3.4	2.8	3.0	3.0	2.5
San Diego	5.0	4.7	4.5	4.4	4.4	4.6	4.8	4.6	4.7	4.3	3.7	3.2
San Francisco	4.2	3.8	3.7	3.8	3.9	4.3	4.7	4.5	4.5	4.2	3.6	3.2
San Jose	4.1	3.9	3.7	3.7	3.6	3.7	3.9	3.6	3.7	3.4	3.0	2.7
Santa Rosa	4.4	4.3	3.9	3.8	3.5	3.7	4.1	3.8	3.5	3.3	3.2	3.0
Seattle	5.0	4.8	4.5	4.1	3.8	4.0	3.9	3.7	3.8	3.6	3.4	3.3
Tacoma	6.7	6.5	6.0	5.4	5.1	5.5	5.2	4.8	5.1	5.1	5.0	4.8
Tucson	4.0	3.7	3.4	3.2	3.4	3.7	3.8	3.7	3.9	3.5	3.2	3.2
U.S.	**5.9**	**5.7**	**5.5**	**4.8**	**4.7**	**5.2**	**5.0**	**4.8**	**4.7**	**4.4**	**4.3**	**4.4**

Note: All figures are percentages, are not seasonally adjusted and covers workers 16 years of age and older
Source: Bureau of Labor Statistics, http://stats.bls.gov

Unemployment Rate: Metro Area

Area	1997											
	Jan.	Feb.	Mar.	Apr.	May	Jun.	Jul.	Aug.	Sep.	Oct.	Nov.	Dec.
Colo. Spgs.	4.4	3.9	3.8	3.3	3.8	4.5	3.8	3.6	3.5	3.1	3.3	2.8
Denver	3.7	3.1	3.1	2.7	3.0	3.4	2.8	2.8	2.7	2.4	2.6	2.3
Eugene	6.3	6.6	6.4	5.6	4.4	4.9	4.8	4.8	4.7	4.6	5.0	5.1
Las Vegas	4.8	4.5	4.1	4.1	4.1	4.9	4.9	4.5	4.6	4.2	3.8	3.7
Los Angeles	7.8	7.5	6.9	6.8	6.7	6.8	7.5	7.0	6.6	6.3	6.3	6.0
Oakland	4.9	4.6	4.3	4.3	4.3	4.6	4.9	4.6	4.5	4.2	3.7	3.3
Phoenix	3.5	3.2	2.9	2.7	2.9	3.0	3.0	3.0	3.1	2.8	2.6	2.5
Portland	4.6	4.8	4.7	4.2	3.5	4.0	3.9	3.9	3.9	3.6	3.8	3.7
Pueblo	5.8	4.7	4.7	4.0	4.6	5.3	4.6	4.4	4.2	3.5	3.9	5.5
Riverside	7.5	7.0	6.5	6.5	6.4	7.0	8.1	7.7	7.6	7.1	6.1	5.3
Salem	6.6	6.5	6.7	5.9	4.8	5.3	5.0	4.7	4.5	4.3	5.1	5.4
Salt Lake City	2.9	3.1	2.6	2.7	2.7	3.3	2.8	3.2	2.8	2.9	2.8	2.3
San Diego	5.0	4.6	4.4	4.4	4.3	4.5	4.7	4.6	4.6	4.2	3.6	3.1
San Francisco	3.5	3.3	3.2	3.2	3.2	3.5	3.8	3.6	3.6	3.3	2.9	2.6
San Jose	3.5	3.3	3.1	3.1	3.1	3.1	3.3	3.0	3.1	2.9	2.5	2.3
Santa Rosa	4.6	4.4	4.0	3.9	3.6	3.8	4.2	3.9	3.6	3.4	3.3	3.1
Seattle	4.4	4.2	3.9	3.5	3.3	3.4	3.3	3.1	3.2	3.1	2.9	2.8
Tacoma	5.8	5.6	5.2	4.7	4.4	4.8	4.5	4.2	4.4	4.4	4.3	4.1
Tucson	3.6	3.3	3.1	2.9	3.1	3.4	3.4	3.3	3.5	3.2	2.9	2.9
U.S.	**5.9**	**5.7**	**5.5**	**4.8**	**4.7**	**5.2**	**5.0**	**4.8**	**4.7**	**4.4**	**4.3**	**4.4**

Note: All figures are percentages, are not seasonally adjusted and covers workers 16 years of age and older
(1) Metropolitan Statistical Area - see Appendix A for areas included
Source: Bureau of Labor Statistics, http://stats.bls.gov

Average Wages: Selected Professional Occupations

MSA[1] (Month/Year)	Accountant III	Attorney III	Computer Program. II	Engineer III	Systems Analyst II	Systems Analyst Supv./Mgr. II
Colo. Spgs. (8/96)	-	-	657	-	939	-
Denver (1/96)	808	1,322	681	956	958	1,317
Eugene (3/95)	-	-	-	-	877	-
Las Vegas (12/92)	-	-	612	-	912	-
Los Angeles (12/95)	860	-	677	999	1,002	1,575
Oakland (1/95)	881	1,461	663	1,031	1,020	-
Phoenix (4/96)	750	1,347	632	969	911	1,433
Portland (7/96)	800	1,289	644	954	908	1,329
Pueblo (9/94)	-	-	-	-	-	-
Riverside (4/95)	790	1,232	650	889	882	-
Salem (1/94)	647	-	540	799	766	-
Salt Lake City (8/95)	758	1,065	640	912	898	-
San Diego (7/96)	842	1,333	-	893	954	-
San Francisco (3/96)	907	1,523	723	1,056	1,071	1,571
San Jose (4/94)	-	-	701	-	942	-
Santa Rosa	-	-	-	-	-	-
Seattle (11/95)	827	1,443	626	912	955	1,350
Tacoma (2/93)	-	-	571	-	811	-
Tucson (2/94)	-	-	590	-	761	-

Notes: Figures are average weekly earnings; Dashes indicate that data was not available;
(1) Metropolitan Statistical Area - see Appendix A for areas included
Source: Bureau of Labor Statistics, Occupational Compensation Surveys

Average Wages: Selected Technical and Clerical Occupations

MSA[1] (Month/Year)	Accounting Clerk III	General Clerk II	Computer Operator II	Key Entry Operator I	Secretary III	Switchboard Operator/ Receptionist
Colo. Spgs. (8/96)	420	404	-	-	513	297
Denver (1/96)	478	396	450	362	553	357
Eugene (3/95)	406	351	-	250	473	327
Las Vegas (12/92)	414	463	444	332	519	335
Los Angeles (12/95)	506	482	497	-	637	371
Oakland (1/95)	517	490	521	363	620	407
Phoenix (4/96)	411	364	451	310	449	310
Portland (7/96)	458	420	473	341	548	358
Pueblo (9/94)	404	-	-	-	-	269
Riverside (4/95)	479	376	492	331	566	317
Salem (1/94)	442	378	481	334	483	318
Salt Lake City (8/95)	421	336	399	302	489	317
San Diego (7/96)	456	414	471	339	585	351
San Francisco (3/96)	533	511	598	-	668	438
San Jose (4/94)	503	470	506	349	601	412
Santa Rosa	-	-	-	-	-	-
Seattle (11/95)	463	434	470	430	582	396
Tacoma (2/93)	414	-	441	286	499	334
Tucson (2/94)	358	338	384	-	-	267

Notes: Figures are average weekly earnings; Dashes indicate that data was not available;
(1) Metropolitan Statistical Area - see Appendix A for areas included
Source: Bureau of Labor Statistics, Occupational Compensation Surveys

Average Wages: Selected Health and Protective Service Occupations

MSA[1] (Month/Year)	Corrections Officer	Firefighter	Lic. Prac. Nurse II	Registered Nurse II	Nursing Assistant II	Police Officer I
Colo. Spgs. (8/96)	-	-	-	-	-	-
Denver (1/96)	566	751	-	-	-	733
Eugene (3/95)	-	-	-	-	-	-
Las Vegas (12/92)	-	-	-	-	-	-
Los Angeles (12/95)	746	-	-	-	-	928
Oakland (1/95)	710	905	653	1,034	367	938
Phoenix (4/96)	-	682	-	-	-	734
Portland (7/96)	678	768	-	-	-	800
Pueblo (9/94)	-	-	-	-	-	-
Riverside (4/95)	767	817	500	770	304	833
Salem (1/94)	521	618	-	-	-	740
Salt Lake City (8/95)	458	609	406	664	266	581
San Diego (7/96)	695	818	-	-	-	840
San Francisco (3/96)	823	-	-	-	-	955
San Jose (4/94)	-	-	-	982	-	-
Santa Rosa	-	-	-	-	-	-
Seattle (11/95)	624	925	-	-	-	854
Tacoma (2/93)	-	-	-	-	-	-
Tucson (2/94)	-	-	-	-	-	-

Notes: Figures are average weekly earnings; Dashes indicate that data was not available;
(1) Metropolitan Statistical Area - see Appendix A for areas included
Source: Bureau of Labor Statistics, Occupational Compensation Surveys

Average Wages: Selected Maintenance, Material Movement and Custodial Occupations

MSA[1] (Month/Year)	General Maintenance	Guard I	Janitor	Maintenance Electrician	Motor Vehicle Mechanic	Truckdriver (Trac. Trail.)
Colo. Spgs. (8/96)	8.41	6.13	6.54	-	15.16	-
Denver (1/96)	11.20	6.49	7.62	18.41	16.00	15.98
Eugene (3/95)	9.93	5.26	6.76	14.93	12.91	10.69
Las Vegas (12/92)	9.12	6.41	9.29	18.61	18.37	16.09
Los Angeles (12/95)	-	6.85	7.70	20.30	18.70	15.67
Oakland (1/95)	11.37	7.35	9.79	20.43	19.98	16.31
Phoenix (4/96)	9.34	6.67	6.43	18.96	15.69	-
Portland (7/96)	10.51	9.26	7.93	18.66	16.25	13.28
Pueblo (9/94)	7.01	-	6.78	-	-	11.66
Riverside (4/95)	14.44	10.03	8.91	16.57	17.97	17.29
Salem (1/94)	11.64	-	8.59	15.19	13.11	-
Salt Lake City (8/95)	9.70	5.99	6.64	15.36	15.24	14.73
San Diego (7/96)	9.53	6.31	8.38	18.25	16.25	-
San Francisco (3/96)	10.69	7.81	-	22.43	20.55	-
San Jose (4/94)	11.06	7.96	8.72	22.47	18.74	14.52
Santa Rosa	-	-	-	-	-	-
Seattle (11/95)	12.46	6.56	7.84	22.23	18.71	13.90
Tacoma (2/93)	9.07	5.38	6.98	17.77	14.23	13.88
Tucson (2/94)	7.88	4.82	5.29	17.07	-	-

Notes: Figures are average hourly earnings; Dashes indicate that data was not available;
(1) Metropolitan Statistical Area - see Appendix A for areas included
Source: Bureau of Labor Statistics, Occupational Compensation Surveys

Means of Transportation to Work: City

| City | Car/Truck/Van | | Public Transportation | | | Bicycle | Walked | Other Means | Worked at Home |
	Drove Alone	Car-pooled	Bus	Subway	Railroad				
Colo. Spgs.	77.9	12.9	1.2	0.0	0.0	0.5	3.2	0.9	3.4
Denver	68.6	13.1	7.8	0.0	0.0	0.9	5.3	1.0	3.4
Eugene	69.0	9.9	3.3	0.0	0.0	5.8	6.9	1.0	4.0
Las Vegas	74.0	15.8	2.8	0.0	0.0	0.7	3.6	1.7	1.5
Los Angeles	65.2	15.4	10.4	0.0	0.0	0.6	3.9	1.4	3.1
Oakland	57.0	14.1	11.5	5.9	0.2	1.1	4.9	1.8	3.6
Phoenix	73.7	15.1	3.1	0.0	0.0	1.1	2.7	1.6	2.7
Portland	65.0	12.9	10.5	0.1	0.1	1.1	5.6	1.3	3.4
Pueblo	80.1	13.4	1.0	0.0	0.0	0.3	2.9	0.7	1.5
Riverside	73.9	16.3	1.5	0.0	0.0	1.2	3.5	1.3	2.4
Salem	72.5	15.3	2.4	0.0	0.0	1.3	4.3	1.4	2.8
Salt Lake City	69.6	13.4	5.5	0.0	0.0	1.5	6.0	1.0	2.8
San Diego	70.7	12.8	4.0	0.0	0.0	1.1	4.9	2.0	4.6
San Francisco	38.5	11.5	24.4	5.2	0.4	1.0	9.8	5.5	3.8
San Jose	76.9	14.6	3.1	0.1	0.3	0.6	1.6	0.9	1.9
Santa Rosa	76.8	11.4	2.2	0.0	0.0	1.6	2.9	1.2	3.8
Seattle	58.7	11.8	15.6	0.0	0.0	1.5	7.2	1.3	3.8
Tacoma	74.6	13.5	3.7	0.0	0.0	0.4	3.8	1.0	3.0
Tucson	69.8	14.8	4.1	0.0	0.0	2.7	4.0	1.8	2.8
U.S.	**73.2**	**13.4**	**3.0**	**1.5**	**0.5**	**0.4**	**3.9**	**1.2**	**3.0**

Note: Figures shown are percentages and only include workers 16 years old and over
Source: 1990 Census of Population and Housing, Summary Tape File 3C

Means of Transportation to Work: Metro Area

| MSA[1] | Car/Truck/Van | | Public Transportation | | | Bicycle | Walked | Other Means | Worked at Home |
	Drove Alone	Car-pooled	Bus	Subway	Railroad				
Colo. Spgs.	74.6	13.3	1.0	0.0	0.0	0.4	6.2	1.0	3.5
Denver	75.6	12.6	4.3	0.0	0.0	0.4	3.0	0.8	3.4
Eugene	73.4	11.4	2.3	0.0	0.0	2.9	4.5	1.1	4.4
Las Vegas	74.8	15.4	1.9	0.0	0.0	0.8	3.7	2.1	1.5
Los Angeles	70.1	15.5	6.4	0.0	0.0	0.6	3.3	1.3	2.7
Oakland	68.6	13.2	3.9	4.7	0.4	1.0	3.1	1.4	3.7
Phoenix	75.0	14.4	2.0	0.0	0.0	1.4	2.6	1.6	2.9
Portland	72.6	12.5	5.5	0.1	0.1	0.7	3.5	1.2	3.9
Pueblo	80.4	13.0	0.9	0.0	0.0	0.3	2.6	0.7	2.0
Riverside	74.6	17.2	0.8	0.0	0.0	0.6	2.7	1.5	2.7
Salem	73.3	15.2	1.4	0.0	0.0	0.8	4.0	1.2	4.2
Salt Lake City	76.3	14.0	2.9	0.0	0.0	0.5	2.3	0.9	3.1
San Diego	70.9	13.8	3.0	0.0	0.0	0.9	4.5	2.0	5.0
San Francisco	56.3	12.2	13.6	3.0	0.8	0.8	5.9	3.4	3.8
San Jose	77.7	12.3	2.4	0.1	0.4	1.5	2.1	1.0	2.5
Santa Rosa	74.6	13.0	2.2	0.0	0.0	1.0	3.3	1.0	4.9
Seattle	72.8	11.6	7.2	0.0	0.0	0.6	3.3	1.1	3.4
Tacoma	75.9	13.2	1.9	0.0	0.0	0.3	4.3	1.1	3.3
Tucson	71.9	15.0	3.1	0.0	0.0	1.9	3.2	1.7	3.2
U.S.	**73.2**	**13.4**	**3.0**	**1.5**	**0.5**	**0.4**	**3.9**	**1.2**	**3.0**

Note: Figures shown are percentages and only include workers 16 years old and over;
(1) Metropolitan Statistical Area - see Appendix A for areas included
Source: 1990 Census of Population and Housing, Summary Tape File 3C

Cost of Living Index

Area	Composite	Groceries	Health	Housing	Misc.	Transp.	Utilities
Colo. Springs	102.0	98.8	127.4	115.8	94.1	105.2	70.5
Denver[1]	106.4	101.4	122.4	119.6	98.6	112.7	82.9
Eugene	105.5	94.7	120.0	122.6	101.2	105.7	73.6
Las Vegas	106.2	107.4	124.2	110.1	105.9	107.5	76.1
Los Angeles[1]	116.1	113.1	111.1	131.9	107.6	107.4	115.5
Oakland	n/a	n/a	n/a	n/a	n/a	n/a	n/a
Phoenix	103.5	105.7	112.6	102.0	99.1	112.0	106.4
Portland[1]	106.8	103.4	121.8	118.9	101.7	109.9	77.0
Pueblo	89.4	104.9	107.9	82.5	86.8	91.7	76.7
Riverside	106.6	101.0	126.4	108.3	105.5	107.0	101.2
Salem[2]	105.1	93.9	119.5	120.7	101.4	106.5	75.3
Salt Lake City	102.1	103.6	95.3	107.2	99.4	117.4	80.2
San Diego	119.9	112.1	122.2	147.5	104.3	120.4	101.3
San Francisco[3]	152.5	123.6	172.8	223.4	118.0	143.7	99.3
San Jose	n/a	n/a	n/a	n/a	n/a	n/a	n/a
Santa Rosa[3]	137.9	117.5	135.9	196.6	111.9	122.4	99.3
Seattle[3]	113.9	112.1	143.6	125.7	109.5	108.2	77.9
Tacoma	101.0	100.7	140.4	103.3	98.8	102.8	70.8
Tucson	97.3	103.1	105.3	95.6	93.0	97.0	104.2
U.S.	**100.0**	**100.0**	**100.0**	**100.0**	**100.0**	**100.0**	**100.0**

Note: n/a not available; (1) Metropolitan Statistical Area (MSA) - see Appendix A for areas included;
(2) 4th Quarter 1996; (3) 2nd Quarter 1997
Source: ACCRA, Cost of Living Index, 3rd Quarter 1997 unless otherwise noted

Median Home Prices and Housing Affordability

MSA[1]	Median Price[2] 3rd Qtr. 1997 ($)	HOI[3] 3rd Qtr. 1997	Afford-ability Rank[4]
Colo. Spgs.	130,000	58.8	154
Denver	138,000	68.0	105
Eugene	n/a	n/a	n/a
Las Vegas	125,000	65.6	121
Los Angeles	165,000	47.2	178
Oakland	220,000	41.8	184
Phoenix	116,000	66.4	117
Portland	155,000	25.5	194
Pueblo	92,000	58.2	156
Riverside	115,000	70.7	90
Salem	120,000	35.8	189
Salt Lake City	155,000	44.1	181
San Diego	176,000	41.4	185
San Francisco	315,000	20.7	195
San Jose	280,000	34.6	190
Santa Rosa	198,000	34.0	191
Seattle	171,000	53.5	168
Tacoma	127,000	59.4	152
Tucson	107,000	62.5	133
U.S.	**127,000**	**63.7**	–

Note: (1) Metropolitan Statistical Area - see Appendix A for areas included; (2) U.S. figures calculated from the sales of 625,000 new and existing homes in 195 markets; (3) Housing Opportunity Index - percent of homes sold that were within the reach of the median income household at the prevailing mortgage interest rate; (4) Rank is from 1-195 with 1 being most affordable; n/a not available
Source: National Association of Home Builders, Housing News Service, 3rd Quarter 1997

Average Home Prices

Area	Price ($)
Colo. Springs	154,231
Denver[1]	163,750
Eugene	172,267
Las Vegas	142,667
Los Angeles[1]	172,920
Oakland	n/a
Phoenix	133,148
Portland[1]	167,600
Pueblo	111,675
Riverside	146,661
Salem[2]	170,598
Salt Lake City	139,040
San Diego	205,998
San Francisco[3]	279,900
San Jose	n/a
Santa Rosa[3]	273,975
Seattle[3]	169,000
Tacoma	139,000
Tucson	125,500
U.S.	**135,710**

Note: Figures are based on a new home with 1,800 sq. ft. of living area on an 8,000 sq. ft. lot; n/a not available; (1) Metropolitan Statistical Area (MSA) - see Appendix A for areas included; (2) 4th Quarter 1996; (3) 2nd Quarter 1997 Source: ACCRA, Cost of Living Index, 3rd Quarter 1997 unless otherwise noted

Average Apartment Rent

Area	Rent ($/mth)
Colo. Springs	707
Denver[1]	731
Eugene	626
Las Vegas	764
Los Angeles[1]	724
Oakland	n/a
Phoenix	651
Portland[1]	650
Pueblo	455
Riverside	617
Salem[2]	502
Salt Lake City	656
San Diego	803
San Francisco[3]	1,576
San Jose	n/a
Santa Rosa[3]	876
Seattle[3]	789
Tacoma	612
Tucson	586
U.S.	**569**

Note: Figures are based on an unfurnished two bedroom, 1-1/2 or 2 bath apartment, approximately 950 sq. ft. in size, excluding all utilities except water; n/a not available; (1) Metropolitan Statistical Area (MSA) - see Appendix A for areas included; (2) 4th Quarter 1996; (3) 2nd Quarter 1997 Source: ACCRA, Cost of Living Index, 3rd Quarter 1997 unless otherwise noted

Average Residential Utility Costs

Area	All Electric ($/mth)	Part Electric ($/mth)	Other Energy ($/mth)	Phone ($/mth)
Colo. Springs	-	35.29	31.49	20.39
Denver[1]	-	43.33	37.58	21.07
Eugene	71.50	-	-	19.18
Las Vegas	-	51.89	28.86	11.42
Los Angeles[1]	-	90.03	30.33	19.94
Oakland	n/a	n/a	n/a	n/a
Phoenix	110.73	-	-	18.67
Portland[1]	-	35.52	38.50	20.92
Pueblo	-	42.63	31.16	20.86
Riverside	-	71.52	34.95	16.31
Salem[2]	-	36.97	37.02	18.36
Salt Lake City	-	42.08	38.15	17.97
San Diego	-	72.92	33.80	16.07
San Francisco[3]	-	66.03	35.43	20.75
San Jose	n/a	n/a	n/a	n/a
Santa Rosa[3]	-	66.03	35.43	20.75
Seattle[3]	80.43	-	-	15.29
Tacoma	-	29.10	38.45	19.96
Tucson	-	75.23	32.87	18.68
U.S.	**109.40**	**55.25**	**43.64**	**19.48**

Note: Dashes indicate data not applicable; n/a not available;
(1) Metropolitan Statistical Area (MSA) - see Appendix A for areas included; (2) 4th Quarter 1996; (3) 2nd Quarter 1997
Source: ACCRA, Cost of Living Index, 3rd Quarter 1997 unless otherwise noted

Average Health Care Costs

Area	Hospital ($/day)	Doctor ($/visit)	Dentist ($/visit)
Colo. Springs	542.50	65.11	75.40
Denver[1]	498.30	62.71	73.29
Eugene	387.50	54.05	89.40
Las Vegas	351.50	58.75	91.00
Los Angeles[1]	602.80	55.00	54.00
Oakland	n/a	n/a	n/a
Phoenix	507.38	54.70	64.33
Portland[1]	507.40	52.60	85.00
Pueblo	342.50	62.60	61.80
Riverside	645.67	48.00	85.60
Salem[2]	390.00	48.92	85.80
Salt Lake City	396.20	43.20	57.40
San Diego	659.12	49.25	75.60
San Francisco[3]	1,288.75	60.75	96.80
San Jose	n/a	n/a	n/a
Santa Rosa[3]	698.33	52.17	91.00
Seattle[3]	569.40	62.22	101.75
Tacoma	421.80	62.00	110.00
Tucson	622.50	47.50	53.75
U.S.	**392.91**	**48.76**	**60.84**

Note: n/a not available; Hospital - based on a semi-private room. Doctor - based on a general practitioner's routine exam of an established patient. Dentist - based on adult teeth cleaning and periodic oral exam; (1) Metropolitan Statistical Area (MSA) - see Appendix A for areas included; (2) 4th Quarter 1996; (3) 2nd Quarter 1997
Source: ACCRA, Cost of Living Index, 3rd Quarter 1997 unless otherwise noted

Distribution of Office-Based Physicians

MSA[1]	General Practitioners	Specialists		
		Medical	Surgical	Other
Colo. Spgs.	79	167	183	205
Denver	437	1,234	923	1,054
Eugene	117	157	135	134
Las Vegas	200	508	426	427
Los Angeles	2,043	5,992	4,212	4,674
Oakland	474	1,527	945	1,188
Phoenix	603	1,295	1,109	1,152
Portland	369	1,158	848	966
Pueblo	45	69	62	68
Riverside	602	1,054	846	862
Salem	102	98	102	106
Salt Lake City	231	633	567	615
San Diego	671	1,564	1,221	1,384
San Francisco	363	1,966	1,235	1,729
San Jose	312	1,217	819	915
Santa Rosa	190	212	198	226
Seattle	867	1,425	1,170	1,450
Tacoma	169	244	226	239
Tucson	175	532	390	485

Note: Data as of 12/31/96; (1) Metropolitan Statistical Area - see Appendix A for areas included
Source: Physician Characteristics & Distribution in the U.S. 1997-98

Educational Quality

City	School District	Education Quotient[1]	Graduate Outcome[2]	Community Index[3]	Resource Index[4]
Colo. Springs	Academy-Colo. Springs	129.0	147.0	124.0	115.0
Denver	Denver County	93.0	62.0	97.0	121.0
Eugene	Eugene	117.0	129.0	94.0	129.0
Las Vegas	Las Vegas	87.0	101.0	98.0	61.0
Los Angeles	Los Angeles	82.0	55.0	67.0	123.0
Oakland	Oakland	81.0	53.0	118.0	71.0
Phoenix	Phoenix	n/a	n/a	n/a	n/a
Portland	Portland	109.0	90.0	103.0	134.0
Pueblo	Pueblo City	82.0	84.0	76.0	85.0
Riverside	Riverside	85.0	71.0	74.0	110.0
Salem	Salem/Keizer	85.0	78.0	88.0	88.0
Salt Lake City	Salt Lake City	122.0	120.0	129.0	117.0
San Diego	San Diego City	95.0	76.0	101.0	107.0
San Francisco	San Francisco	110.0	97.0	122.0	111.0
San Jose	San Jose	128.0	105.0	146.0	134.0
Santa Rosa	Santa Rosa	120.0	118.0	125.0	117.0
Seattle	Seattle	106.0	84.0	137.0	97.0
Tacoma	Tacoma	107.0	71.0	107.0	144.0
Tucson	Tucson	87.0	79.0	89.0	94.0

Note: Nearly 1,000 secondary school districts were rated in terms of educational quality. The scores range from a low of 50 to a high of 150; (1) Average of the Graduate Outcome, Community and Resource indexes; (2) Based on graduation rates and college board scores (SAT/ACT); (3) Based on the surrounding community's average level of education and the area's average income level; (4) Based on teacher salaries, per-pupil expenditures and student-teacher ratios.
Source: Expansion Management, Ratings Issue 1997

School Enrollment by Type: City

City	Preprimary				Elementary/High School			
	Public		Private		Public		Private	
	Enrollment	%	Enrollment	%	Enrollment	%	Enrollment	%
Colo. Spgs.	3,038	55.2	2,466	44.8	43,594	93.6	2,979	6.4
Denver	4,579	57.3	3,410	42.7	55,388	85.9	9,065	14.1
Eugene	1,195	52.5	1,083	47.5	14,203	92.7	1,121	7.3
Las Vegas	2,190	53.4	1,914	46.6	36,848	93.0	2,781	7.0
Los Angeles	25,962	52.4	23,600	47.6	531,302	86.8	80,848	13.2
Oakland	3,366	60.8	2,169	39.2	53,247	86.7	8,167	13.3
Phoenix	9,227	57.9	6,717	42.1	155,356	92.8	12,099	7.2
Portland	4,594	59.3	3,155	40.7	52,537	89.1	6,425	10.9
Pueblo	1,434	76.2	447	23.8	16,721	96.5	604	3.5
Riverside	2,112	54.7	1,751	45.3	39,240	91.4	3,703	8.6
Salem	1,004	55.2	816	44.8	15,355	92.4	1,258	7.6
Salt Lake City	1,786	57.0	1,348	43.0	23,141	93.5	1,608	6.5
San Diego	10,602	58.2	7,618	41.8	156,497	91.9	13,744	8.1
San Francisco	4,493	51.4	4,256	48.6	65,078	77.5	18,853	22.5
San Jose	7,378	55.5	5,909	44.5	126,273	90.9	12,573	9.1
Santa Rosa	1,134	51.3	1,078	48.7	15,834	91.4	1,481	8.6
Seattle	3,889	42.2	5,327	57.8	39,423	78.6	10,741	21.4
Tacoma	2,357	65.7	1,233	34.3	25,891	91.4	2,451	8.6
Tucson	3,333	54.7	2,756	45.3	57,306	91.9	5,043	8.1
U.S.	**2,679,029**	**59.5**	**1,824,256**	**40.5**	**38,379,689**	**90.2**	**4,187,099**	**9.8**

Note: Figures shown cover persons 3 years old and over
Source: 1990 Census of Population and Housing, Summary Tape File 3C

School Enrollment by Type: Metro Area

MSA[1]	Preprimary				Elementary/High School			
	Public		Private		Public		Private	
	Enrollment	%	Enrollment	%	Enrollment	%	Enrollment	%
Colo. Spgs.	4,421	57.8	3,225	42.2	64,283	94.1	4,008	5.9
Denver	19,953	57.9	14,488	42.1	248,623	91.8	22,151	8.2
Eugene	3,211	58.8	2,246	41.2	42,499	94.5	2,469	5.5
Las Vegas	6,818	61.6	4,254	38.4	108,051	94.3	6,526	5.7
Los Angeles	74,476	54.3	62,585	45.7	1,430,190	88.5	185,714	11.5
Oakland	22,693	54.3	19,124	45.7	293,406	89.3	35,303	10.7
Phoenix	20,498	57.5	15,158	42.5	329,787	93.9	21,343	6.1
Portland	13,786	57.1	10,355	42.9	181,368	91.3	17,390	8.7
Pueblo	1,658	74.5	567	25.5	21,367	96.6	762	3.4
Riverside	26,476	59.0	18,382	41.0	466,755	93.0	35,180	7.0
Salem	2,955	60.5	1,933	39.5	44,108	92.5	3,582	7.5
Salt Lake City	17,219	63.6	9,848	36.4	246,375	96.8	8,205	3.2
San Diego	26,048	59.1	18,027	40.9	367,435	92.4	30,352	7.6
San Francisco	12,034	47.4	13,331	52.6	165,447	80.7	39,665	19.3
San Jose	14,196	52.6	12,816	47.4	213,645	90.1	23,398	9.9
Santa Rosa	4,350	53.9	3,719	46.1	56,495	92.0	4,896	8.0
Seattle	22,997	51.8	21,435	48.2	264,909	90.2	28,825	9.8
Tacoma	7,622	63.2	4,437	36.8	95,627	93.7	6,376	6.3
Tucson	5,794	55.5	4,645	44.5	100,154	92.5	8,110	7.5
U.S.	**2,679,029**	**59.5**	**1,824,256**	**40.5**	**38,379,689**	**90.2**	**4,187,099**	**9.8**

Note: Figures shown cover persons 3 years old and over;
(1) Metropolitan Statistical Area - see Appendix A for areas included
Source: 1990 Census of Population and Housing, Summary Tape File 3C

School Enrollment by Race: City

City	Preprimary (%) White	Black	Other	Hisp.[1]	Elementary/High School (%) White	Black	Other	Hisp.[1]
Colo. Spgs.	85.3	8.2	6.5	8.8	82.8	8.9	8.2	11.0
Denver	70.2	14.0	15.7	27.6	55.5	18.7	25.8	39.3
Eugene	95.4	0.7	3.9	3.5	92.3	1.6	6.2	3.8
Las Vegas	79.8	13.2	6.9	8.7	71.3	15.8	12.9	17.6
Los Angeles	55.2	17.0	27.8	34.2	41.3	14.5	44.2	57.5
Oakland	27.9	52.3	19.8	11.6	16.1	52.1	31.8	18.0
Phoenix	83.6	5.2	11.1	15.1	74.5	6.9	18.6	29.2
Portland	82.7	10.3	7.0	4.6	75.9	13.2	10.9	4.5
Pueblo	80.2	2.3	17.5	48.5	78.1	1.8	20.0	50.7
Riverside	73.1	9.2	17.7	24.3	63.9	8.6	27.5	34.5
Salem	93.4	0.0	6.6	5.2	87.9	1.8	10.3	8.5
Salt Lake City	86.1	1.9	12.1	9.8	82.2	1.9	15.9	14.6
San Diego	67.6	12.0	20.4	20.3	51.0	12.3	36.7	32.3
San Francisco	43.8	16.6	39.7	14.8	30.9	16.1	52.9	21.2
San Jose	65.4	4.7	29.9	22.2	54.5	5.3	40.2	34.6
Santa Rosa	89.6	4.1	6.2	12.5	84.7	2.7	12.6	13.1
Seattle	72.3	13.2	14.5	5.2	55.7	20.3	24.0	5.2
Tacoma	75.1	13.8	11.1	4.5	67.4	16.6	16.0	5.7
Tucson	76.1	4.5	19.4	28.0	63.8	6.0	30.2	43.7
U.S.	**80.4**	**12.5**	**7.1**	**7.8**	**74.1**	**15.6**	**10.3**	**12.5**

Note: Figures shown cover persons 3 years old and over; (1) People of Hispanic origin can be of any race
Source: 1990 Census of Population and Housing, Summary Tape File 3C

School Enrollment by Race: Metro Area

MSA[1]	Preprimary (%) White	Black	Other	Hisp.[2]	Elementary/High School (%) White	Black	Other	Hisp.[2]
Colo. Spgs.	85.7	7.4	6.8	8.8	83.2	8.8	7.9	10.5
Denver	87.3	5.1	7.5	12.3	81.1	7.3	11.7	18.2
Eugene	96.3	0.6	3.2	3.1	94.4	1.0	4.6	3.7
Las Vegas	84.1	9.8	6.1	8.2	74.9	13.7	11.4	14.9
Los Angeles	58.1	14.5	27.5	32.1	46.5	11.9	41.6	52.3
Oakland	68.2	14.7	17.1	13.0	56.9	18.2	24.8	17.5
Phoenix	86.1	3.5	10.4	13.4	78.3	4.7	17.0	24.3
Portland	90.3	3.9	5.9	3.6	87.6	4.5	7.8	4.9
Pueblo	81.5	1.9	16.5	44.4	80.6	1.5	17.8	45.4
Riverside	75.9	7.8	16.3	23.7	67.4	8.5	24.1	35.1
Salem	93.1	0.8	6.2	5.8	89.3	1.1	9.7	10.5
Salt Lake City	94.5	1.1	4.4	5.2	93.2	0.9	6.0	6.4
San Diego	77.2	7.4	15.4	19.8	65.1	7.5	27.4	30.5
San Francisco	66.5	9.1	24.4	13.5	52.9	10.5	36.6	21.8
San Jose	69.3	3.5	27.2	17.2	60.1	4.5	35.4	29.6
Santa Rosa	90.8	2.3	6.9	10.6	87.2	2.1	10.7	14.4
Seattle	86.9	4.4	8.7	3.0	82.4	5.6	12.0	3.7
Tacoma	83.2	8.6	8.2	4.0	81.1	9.0	9.9	4.5
Tucson	79.2	2.8	18.0	23.8	68.8	4.2	27.1	35.9
U.S.	**80.4**	**12.5**	**7.1**	**7.8**	**74.1**	**15.6**	**10.3**	**12.5**

Note: Figures shown cover persons 3 years old and over; (1) Metropolitan Statistical Area - see Appendix A for areas included; (2) People of Hispanic origin can be of any race
Source: 1990 Census of Population and Housing, Summary Tape File 3C

Crime Rate: City

City	All Crimes	Violent Crimes				Property Crimes		
		Murder	Forcible Rape	Robbery	Aggrav. Assault	Burglary	Larceny -Theft	Motor Vehicle Theft
Colo. Spgs.	6,199.9	3.6	71.9	136.8	269.5	998.1	4,304.3	415.7
Denver	6,647.1	12.4	69.3	257.1	403.5	1,508.6	3,345.3	1,050.9
Eugene	9,932.6	1.6	40.8	221.0	339.2	1,560.7	7,147.1	622.2
Las Vegas	6,849.8	19.4	57.1	439.1	496.0	1,402.1	3,482.7	953.4
Los Angeles	6,725.3	20.3	41.8	720.1	1,014.2	1,025.3	2,717.7	1,185.9
Oakland	10,526.5	25.0	86.5	973.3	1,110.1	1,627.9	5,341.5	1,362.4
Phoenix	9,541.1	16.3	40.4	329.6	537.5	1,716.0	5,313.7	1,587.7
Portland	10,751.3	10.9	85.9	439.6	1,138.0	1,526.4	6,160.0	1,390.5
Pueblo	7,016.1	11.4	70.4	186.6	1,050.8	1,283.1	4,097.7	316.0
Riverside	6,321.6	7.3	46.9	356.6	882.2	1,180.8	2,905.6	942.1
Salem	8,956.6	5.8	78.4	159.4	85.1	1,069.9	6,935.3	622.6
Salt Lake City	12,367.1	11.1	84.4	328.0	409.6	1,673.3	8,268.4	1,592.3
San Diego	5,270.1	6.8	31.5	256.6	573.7	736.8	2,712.2	952.5
San Francisco	7,594.9	11.0	40.0	743.4	532.4	950.0	4,168.7	1,149.5
San Jose	4,129.1	4.8	41.1	132.2	553.5	566.0	2,383.6	447.9
Santa Rosa	5,820.9	1.7	68.3	143.3	345.6	775.6	4,131.5	354.9
Seattle	10,310.8	6.9	48.4	363.8	422.9	1,455.7	6,835.4	1,177.7
Tacoma	10,625.7	10.6	72.3	417.8	968.5	1,732.4	5,937.2	1,487.1
Tucson	9,819.3	9.7	59.7	272.7	758.5	1,420.5	6,024.7	1,273.5
U.S.	**5,078.9**	**7.4**	**36.1**	**202.4**	**388.2**	**943.0**	**2,975.9**	**525.9**

Note: Crime rate is the number of crimes per 100,000 population; n/a not available;
Source: FBI Uniform Crime Reports 1996

Crime Rate: Suburbs

Suburbs[1]	All Crimes	Violent Crimes				Property Crimes		
		Murder	Forcible Rape	Robbery	Aggrav. Assault	Burglary	Larceny -Theft	Motor Vehicle Theft
Colo. Spgs.	2,589.6	5.6	18.3	19.0	205.4	625.4	1,544.2	171.7
Denver	4,946.4	3.1	38.0	97.7	214.2	800.0	3,425.5	368.0
Eugene	4,916.3	4.8	39.9	74.6	169.3	1,064.5	3,174.4	388.7
Las Vegas	6,353.8	13.7	42.4	191.3	478.6	1,501.4	3,488.8	637.5
Los Angeles	4,666.2	11.9	27.2	362.9	562.3	889.8	1,963.6	848.4
Oakland	5,386.0	6.5	26.9	220.3	349.9	900.2	3,274.8	607.4
Phoenix	6,396.6	5.2	24.4	110.5	339.6	1,175.9	3,936.3	804.8
Portland	4,467.5	1.9	33.7	77.5	153.4	756.6	3,003.5	440.9
Pueblo	3,414.8	3.5	17.6	10.6	70.3	847.5	2,342.2	123.1
Riverside	5,491.2	10.3	32.0	234.8	493.9	1,404.1	2,474.1	842.1
Salem	5,125.0	2.0	35.0	53.7	161.7	806.4	3,681.1	385.2
Salt Lake City	6,127.4	3.0	40.6	62.8	244.8	850.4	4,524.1	401.7
San Diego	4,120.8	5.7	29.8	164.4	386.6	883.5	2,020.2	630.6
San Francisco	3,597.1	1.5	19.3	117.7	239.2	497.4	2,377.3	344.7
San Jose	3,899.7	1.1	27.0	86.0	260.1	563.7	2,696.9	265.0
Santa Rosa	3,582.5	5.0	30.9	52.5	314.7	874.3	2,120.8	184.3
Seattle	n/a	n/a	n/a	n/a	n/a	n/a	n/a	n/a
Tacoma	5,429.4	5.3	36.4	92.5	311.7	1,006.3	3,485.8	491.3
Tucson	4,974.4	9.0	30.1	86.2	257.0	820.4	3,189.1	582.6
U.S.	**5,078.9**	**7.4**	**36.1**	**202.4**	**388.2**	**943.0**	**2,975.9**	**525.9**

Note: Crime rate is the number of crimes per 100,000 population; n/a not available; (1) Defined as all areas within the MSA but located outside the central city
Source: FBI Uniform Crime Reports 1996

Crime Rate: Metro Area

MSA[1]	All Crimes	Violent Crimes				Property Crimes		
		Murder	Forcible Rape	Robbery	Aggrav. Assault	Burglary	Larceny -Theft	Motor Vehicle Theft
Colo. Spgs.	5,115.3	4.2	55.8	101.4	250.2	886.2	3,475.1	342.4
Denver	5,415.9	5.7	46.6	141.7	266.4	995.7	3,403.3	556.5
Eugene	6,898.0	3.5	40.3	132.4	236.5	1,260.5	4,743.9	481.0
Las Vegas	6,702.5	17.7	52.8	365.5	490.8	1,431.6	3,484.5	859.6
Los Angeles	5,442.4	15.1	32.7	497.5	732.7	940.9	2,247.9	975.6
Oakland	6,250.3	9.6	37.0	346.9	477.7	1,022.5	3,622.3	734.3
Phoenix	7,730.2	9.9	31.2	203.4	423.5	1,404.9	4,520.4	1,136.8
Portland	6,154.7	4.3	47.7	174.7	417.8	963.3	3,851.1	695.8
Pueblo	6,249.0	9.7	59.2	149.1	842.0	1,190.3	3,723.8	274.9
Riverside	5,560.6	10.1	33.2	245.0	526.3	1,385.4	2,510.1	850.5
Salem	6,572.7	3.5	51.4	93.7	132.8	905.9	4,910.6	474.9
Salt Lake City	7,037.6	4.2	47.0	101.5	268.9	970.4	5,070.3	575.4
San Diego	4,623.8	6.2	30.5	204.8	468.5	819.3	2,323.0	771.5
San Francisco	5,381.6	5.8	28.5	397.0	370.1	699.4	3,176.9	703.9
San Jose	4,020.3	3.0	34.4	110.3	414.3	564.9	2,532.2	361.2
Santa Rosa	4,220.7	4.1	41.6	78.4	323.5	846.1	2,694.1	232.9
Seattle	n/a	n/a	n/a	n/a	n/a	n/a	n/a	n/a
Tacoma	6,917.9	6.8	46.7	185.7	499.9	1,214.3	4,188.0	776.5
Tucson	7,853.6	9.4	47.7	197.0	555.0	1,177.0	4,874.2	993.2
U.S.	**5,078.9**	**7.4**	**36.1**	**202.4**	**388.2**	**943.0**	**2,975.9**	**525.9**

Note: Crime rate is the number of crimes per 100,000 population; n/a not available;
(1) Metropolitan Statistical Area - see Appendix A for areas included
Source: FBI Uniform Crime Reports 1996

Temperature & Precipitation: Yearly Averages and Extremes

City	Extreme Low (°F)	Average Low (°F)	Average Temp. (°F)	Average High (°F)	Extreme High (°F)	Average Precip. (in.)	Average Snow (in.)
Colo. Spgs.	-24	36	49	62	99	17.0	48
Denver	-25	37	51	64	103	15.5	63
Eugene	-12	42	53	63	108	47.3	7
Las Vegas	8	53	67	80	116	4.0	1
Los Angeles	27	55	63	70	110	11.3	Tr
Oakland	27	52	59	66	106	17.6	Tr
Phoenix	17	59	72	86	122	7.3	Tr
Portland	-3	45	54	62	107	37.5	7
Pueblo	-28	37	53	69	108	11.6	32
Riverside	24	53	66	78	114	n/a	n/a
Salem	-12	41	52	63	108	40.2	7
Salt Lake City	-22	40	52	64	107	15.6	63
San Diego	29	57	64	71	111	9.5	Tr
San Francisco	24	49	57	65	106	19.3	Tr
San Jose	21	50	59	68	105	13.5	Tr
Santa Rosa	23	42	57	71	109	29.0	n/a
Seattle	0	44	52	59	99	38.4	13
Tacoma	0	44	52	59	99	38.4	13
Tucson	16	55	69	82	117	11.6	2

Note: Tr = Trace
Source: National Climatic Data Center, International Station Meteorological Climate Summary, 3/95

Weather Conditions

City	Temperature			Daytime Sky			Precipitation		
	10°F & below	32°F & below	90°F & above	Clear	Partly cloudy	Cloudy	.01 inch or more precip.	1.0 inch or more snow/ice	Thunder-storms
Colo. Spgs.	21	161	18	108	157	100	98	33	49
Denver	24	155	33	99	177	89	90	38	39
Eugene	(a)	(b)	15	75	115	175	136	4	3
Las Vegas	< 1	37	134	185	132	48	27	2	13
Los Angeles	0	< 1	5	131	125	109	34	0	1
Oakland	0	< 1	3	99	168	98	59	0	6
Phoenix	0	10	167	186	125	54	37	< 1	23
Portland	(a)	37	11	67	116	182	152	4	7
Pueblo	(a)	(b)	64	118	160	87	70	24	39
Riverside	0	4	82	124	178	63	n/a	n/a	5
Salem	(a)	66	16	78	119	168	146	6	5
Salt Lake City	(a)	128	56	94	152	119	92	38	38
San Diego	0	< 1	4	115	126	124	40	0	5
San Francisco	0	6	4	136	130	99	63	< 1	5
San Jose	0	5	5	106	180	79	57	< 1	6
Santa Rosa	(a)	43	30	n/a	365	n/a	n/a	n/a	2
Seattle	(a)	38	3	57	121	187	157	8	8
Tacoma	(a)	38	3	57	121	187	157	8	8
Tucson	0	18	140	177	119	69	54	2	42

Note: Figures are average number of days per year; (a) Figures for 10 degrees and below are not available; (b) Figures for 32 degrees and below are not available
Source: National Climatic Data Center, International Station Meteorological Climate Summary, 3/95

Air Quality

MSA[1]	PSI>100[2] (days)	Ozone (ppm)	Carbon Monoxide (ppm)	Sulfur Dioxide (ppm)	Nitrogen Dioxide (ppm)	PM10 (ug/m3)	Lead (ug/m3)
Colo. Springs	n/a	0.08	5	n/a	n/a	76	0.01
Denver	1	0.11	7	0.024	0.033	96	0.05
Eugene	n/a	0.11	6	n/a	n/a	78	0.02
Las Vegas	13	0.10	10	n/a	0.027	328	n/a
Los Angeles	89	0.20	15	0.011	0.045	109	0.06
Oakland	11	0.14	4	0.011	0.022	45	0.02
Phoenix	10	0.12	10	0.020	0.032	130	0.05
Portland	4	0.13	7	n/a	n/a	70	0.11
Pueblo	n/a	n/a	n/a	n/a	n/a	49	n/a
Riverside	94	0.22	7	0.005	0.038	155	0.04
Salem	n/a	0.12	7	n/a	n/a	n/a	n/a
Salt Lake City	6	0.12	7	0.021	0.026	157	0.03
San Diego	4	0.13	6	0.017	0.022	92	0.02
San Francisco	0	0.10	5	0.007	0.022	59	0.01
San Jose	2	0.12	6	n/a	0.025	68	0.01
Santa Rosa	n/a	0.09	3	n/a	0.014	39	n/a
Seattle	1	0.12	7	0.019	0.020	93	n/a
Tacoma	0	0.10	6	0.028	n/a	74	n/a
Tucson	0	0.09	5	0.004	0.019	81	0.05
NAAQS[3]	-	**0.12**	**9**	**0.140**	**0.053**	**150**	**1.50**

Note: (1) Metropolitan Statistical Area - see Appendix A for areas included; (2) Number of days the Pollutant Standards Index (PSI) exceeded 100 in 1996. A PSI value greater than 100 indicates that air quality would be in the unhealthful range on that day; (3) National Ambient Air Quality Standard; ppm = parts per million; ug/m^3 = micrograms per cubic meter; n/a not available
Source: EPA, National Air Quality and Emissions Trends Report, 1996

Water Quality

City	Tap Water
Colo. Springs	Supplied from watersheds on Pikes Peak and Continental Divide. It's pure, filtered, fluoridated
Denver	Alkaline, 53% of supply hard, 47% soft; West Slope, fluoridated; East Slope, not fluoridated
Eugene	Neutral, very soft
Las Vegas	Alkaline, hard
Los Angeles	Los Angeles tap water hardness ranges from 4.2-15.1 gpg. The alkalinity also varies, ranging from 5.4-8.6 gpg. The Owens River Aqueduct accounts for approximately 70% of the water supply and is slightly alkaline and moderately soft with 4.2 gpg total hardness
Oakland	Alkaline, soft and fluoridated
Phoenix	Alkaline, approximately 11 grains of hardness per gallon and fluoridated
Portland	Neutral, very soft and not fluoridated
Pueblo	Alkaline, hard and naturally fluoridated
Riverside	Alkaline, medium hard and naturally fluoridated
Salem	Soft mountain water
Salt Lake City	Alkaline, hard and fluoridated
San Diego	Hard and not fluoridated
San Francisco	Alkaline, very soft and fluoridated
San Jose	Alkaline, very hard and not fluoridated
Santa Rosa	Alkaline, hard and not fluoridated
Seattle	Alkaline, very soft
Tacoma	Neutral, very soft mountain river water; stand-by aquifer well supply, relatively hard, not fluoridated
Tucson	Alkaline and very hard from South Side Reservoir No. 1 and alkaline, soft and not fluoridated from North Side Reservoir No. 3

Source: Editor & Publisher Market Guide 1998

Appendix A

Metropolitan Statistical Areas

Colorado Springs, CO
Includes El Paso County

Denver, CO
Includes Adams, Arapahoe, Denver, Douglas, and Jefferson Counties

Eugene-Springfield, OR
Includes Lane County

Las Vegas, NV-AZ
Includes Clark and Nye Counties, NV; Mohave County, AZ (as of 6/30/93)

Includes Clark County
(prior to 6/30/93)

Los Angeles-Long Beach, CA
Includes Los Angeles County

Oakland, CA
Includes Alameda and Contra Costa Counties

Phoenix-Mesa, AZ
Includes Maricopa and Pinal Counties (as of 6/30/93)

Includes Maricopa County
(prior to 6/30/93)

Portland-Vancouver, OR-WA
Includes Clackamas, Columbia, Multnomah, Washington, and Yamhill Counties, OR; Clark County, WA (as of 6/30/93)

Includes Clackamas, Multnomah, Washington, and Yamhill Counties (prior to 6/30/93)

Pueblo, CO
Includes Pueblo County

Riverside-San Bernadino, CA
Includes Riverside and San Bernadino Counties

Salem, OR
Includes Marion and Polk Counties

Salt Lake City-Ogden, UT
Includes Davis, Salt Lake, and Weber Counties

San Diego, CA
Includes San Diego County

San Francisco, CA
Includes Marin, San Francisco and San Mateo Counties

San Jose, CA
Includes Santa Clara County

Santa Rosa, CA
Includes Sonoma County

Seattle-Bellevue-Everett, WA
Includes Island, King and Snohomish Counties (as of 6/30/93)

Includes King and Snohomish Counties (prior to 6/30/93)

Tacoma, WA
Includes Pierce County

Tucson, AZ
Includes Pima County

Chambers of Commerce and Economic Development Organizations

Colorado Springs

Greater Colorado Springs
Chamber of Commerce
2 North Cascade Avenue, Suite 110
Colorado Springs, CO 80903
Phone: (719) 635-1551
Fax: (719) 635-1571

Greater Colorado Springs
Economic Development Corporation
90 S. Cascade Avenue #1050
Colorado Springs, CO 80903
Phone: (719) 471-8183
Fax: (719) 471-9733

Denver

Denver Metro
Chamber of Commerce
1445 Market St.
Denver, CO 80202-1729
Phone: (303) 534-8500
Fax: (303) 534-3200

Downtown Denver Partnership
511 Sixteenth St. #200
Denver, CO 80202-4250
Phone: (303) 534-6161
Fax: (303) 534-2803

Eugene

Eugene Area
Chamber of Commerce
1401 Williamette St.
PO Box 1107
Eugene, OR 97440
Phone: (541) 484-1314
Fax: (541) 484-4942

Las Vegas

Las Vegas Chamber of Commerce
711 E. Desert Inn Rd.
Las Vegas, NV 89109-2797
Phone: (702) 735-1616
Fax: (702) 735-2011

Las Vegas Office of
Business Development
400 E. Stewart Ave.
Las Vegas, NV 89101
Phone: (702) 229-6551
Fax: (702) 385-3128

Los Angeles

Economic Development Corp.
of Los Angeles
515 S. Flower Street, #32F1
Los Angeles, CA 90071
Phone: (213) 622-4300
Fax: (213) 622-7100

Los Angeles Area
Chamber of Commerce
P.O. Box 3696
350 S. Bixel Street
Los Angeles, CA 90051-1696
Phone: (213) 580-7500
Fax: (213) 580-7511

Oakland

City of Oakland
Economic Devel. & Employ.
1333 Broadway #900
Oakland, CA 94612
Phone: (510) 238-3015
Fax: (510) 238-3691

Oakland Metropolitan
Chamber of Commerce
475 14th Street
Oakland, CA 94612_1903
Phone: (510) 874-4800
Fax: (510) 839-8817

Phoenix

City of Phoenix Community and
Economic Development Dept.
200 W. Washington
City Hall
Phoenix, AZ 85003
Phone: (602) 262-5040
Fax: (602) 494-5097

Greater Phoenix Economic Council
2 N. Central Ave.
Phoenix, AZ 85004

Phoenix Chamber of Commerce
201 N. Central Ave. #2700
Phoenix, AZ 85073
Phone: (602) 254-5521
Fax: (602) 495-8913

Portland

Portland Metro
Chamber of Commerce
221 N.W. Second Avenue
Portland, OR 97209-3999
Phone: (503) 228-9411
Fax: (503) 228-5126

Pueblo

City of Pueblo
Dept. of Planning & Devel.
P.O. Box 1427
211 E. D Street
Pueblo, CO 81002

Pueblo Chamber of Commerce
302 N. Santa Fe Ave.
P.O. Box 697
Pueblo, CO 81002
Phone: (719) 542-1704
Fax: (719) 542-1624

Riverside

Greater Riverside
Chamber of Commerce
3685 Main St., Suite 350
Riverside, CA 92501
Phone: (909) 683-7100
Fax: (909) 683-2670

Salem

Salem Area
Chamber of Commerce
1110 Commercial St., NE
Salem, OR 97301-1020
Phone: (503) 581-1466
Fax: (503) 581-0972

Salem Econ. Dev. Corp.
350 Commercial St., NE
Salem, OR 97301
Phone: (503) 588-6225
Fax: (503) 588-6240

Salt Lake City

Economic Development
Corporation of Utah
215 S. State St. #850
Salt Lake City, UT 84111

Salt Lake Area
Chamber of Commerce
175 E. 400 South, Suite 600
Salt Lake City, UT 84111
Phone: (801) 364-3631
Fax: (801) 328-5005

San Diego

Greater San Diego
Chamber of Commerce
402 West Broadway, Suite 1000
San Diego, CA 92101-3585
Phone: (619) 232-0124
Fax: (619) 234-0571

San Diego Economic Devel. Corp.
701 B St. #1850
San Diego, CA 92101
Phone: (619) 234-8484
Fax: (619) 234-1935

San Francisco

San Francisco
Chamber of Commerce
465 California St. #900
San Francisco, CA 94104
Phone: (415) 392-4520
Fax: (415) 392-0485

San Jose

Office of Economic Development
50 W. San Fernando Ave. #900
San Jose, CA 95113
Phone: (408) 277-5880
Fax: (408) 277-3615

San Jose Metropolitan
Chamber of Commerce
180 S. Market St.
San Jose, CA 95113
Phone: (408) 291-5252
Fax: (408) 286-5019

Santa Rosa

Santa Rosa
Chamber of Commerce
637 First St.
Santa Rosa, CA 95404
Phone: (707) 545-1414
Fax: (707) 545-6914

Seattle

Greater Seattle
Chamber of Commerce
1301 5th Ave. #2400
Seattle, WA 98101-2603
Phone: (206) 389-7200
Fax: (206) 389-7288

Tacoma

Tacoma/Pierce County
Chamber of Commerce
950 Pacific Ave. #300
PO Box 1933
Tacoma, WA 98401-1933
Phone: (206) 627-2175
Fax: (206) 597-7305

Tucson

Tucson Metropolitan
Chamber of Commerce
P.O. Box 991
Tucson, AZ 85702
Phone: (520) 792-2250
Fax: (520) 882-5704

Appendix C

State Departments of Labor and Employment

Arizona

Arizona Dept. of Economic Security
P.O. Box 6123
Phoenix, AZ 85005-6123

California

State of California
Employment Development Dept.
P.O. Box 826880
Sacramento, CA 94280-0001

Colorado

Colorado Dept. of Labor
Labor Market Information
1515 Arapahoe St.
Denver, CO 80202

Nevada

Nevada Employment
Security Department
500 E. Third Street
Carson City, NV 89713-0001

Oregon

Oregon Employment Department
875 Union Street, NE
Salem, OR 97311

Utah

Utah Dept. of Workforce Services
Labor Market Information Division
140 East 300 South
P.O. Box 45249
Salt Lake City, UT 84145-0249

Washington

Washington Employment
Security Department
P.O. Box 9046
Olympia, WA 98507-9046